NORTHERN
DESTINY

A History of Canada

John S. Moir M.A. PH.D.
Robert E. Saunders M.A. M.ED.

J. M. DENT & SONS (CANADA) LIMITED

NORTHERN
DESTINY

A History of Canada

ISBN 0-460-93647-6

Maps / Ross Bennington

*Title page photographs – Top left: Detail from
a map entitled "Partie de la Nouvelle France"
published in 1685. Left centre: Spillway crest of
the Gardiner Dam, under construction as part of the
South Saskatchewan River Project (1960's).
Right: Aerial view of Ottawa, Canada's capital
city, looking towards the Parliament Buildings.*

ACKNOWLEDGMENTS

Source Material

The authors and publisher wish to acknowledge with thanks permission to reproduce
the copyright material listed below.

Barnes & Noble, Inc.: excerpt from W. L. Grant, ed., *Voyages of Samuel de Champlain, 1604-1618*, published by Barnes & Noble, Inc.
Canadian Broadcasting Corporation: excerpts from *The Way of the Indian* © by
the Canadian Broadcasting Corporation 1963, Toronto. This volume is a transcript
of a series of radio programmes.

Les Editions de l'Homme Limitée: excerpt from *Egalité ou Indépendance* by Daniel Johnson, published by Les Editions de l'Homme. [In *Northern Destiny* the excerpt appears in translation.]

The Financial Post: the translation "What Daniel Johnson Really Believes about Quebec" (from *Egalité ou Indépendance* published by Les Editions de l'Homme), from the 11 June 1966 issue of The Financial Post.

A. F. Flucke: excerpt from "Whither the Eskimo?", from *North* for January-February 1963, published by the Department of Indian Affairs and Northern Development.

Indian-Eskimo Association of Canada: excerpt from E. R. McEwen, *Community Development Services for Canadian Indian and Métis Communities* and E. R. McEwen, "Rights of Canada's First Citizens – The Indian and Eskimo".

The Macmillan Company of Canada Limited: excerpt from *The French Canadians 1760-1967, Volume I* by Mason Wade, by permission of the Macmillan Company of Canada Limited.

Rev. A. M. Nicholson: extract from the diary of the Rev. A. M. Nicholson.

Abraham Okpik: excerpt from "What does it mean to be an Eskimo?", from *North* for March-April 1962, published by the Department of Indian Affairs and Northern Development.

Ontario Department of Public Records and Archives: extract from the Bureau of Archives *Report* for 1916.

Penguin Books Ltd.: excerpt from *The Vinland Sagas: The Norse Discovery of America*, translated by Magnus Magnusson and Hermann Palsson, published by Penguin Books Ltd.

The Queen's Printer, Ottawa: excerpts from H. P. Biggar, ed., *The Voyages of Jacques Cartier*; A. G. Doughty, ed., *The Elgin-Grey Papers, 1846-1852*; A. Shortt and A. G. Doughty, eds., *Documents Relating to the Constitutional History of Canada*, 1759-1791; *The Northcliffe Collection*. Reproduced with the permission of the Queen's Printer, Ottawa, Canada.

The Ryerson Press: excerpts from J. S. Woodsworth, *My Neighbour: A Study of City Conditions*, by permission of The Ryerson Press.

Saturday Night: excerpt from John T. Schmidt, "Lo, The Poor Irresponsible, Lazy Indian".

The Toronto Public Library: excerpts from C. R. Sanderson, ed., *The Arthur Papers*.

Toronto Star Syndicate: article from the *Toronto Daily Star* for 3 January 1933 and excerpt from Val Sears, "Now Canada really knows price of foreign capital" (16 February 1968); reprinted with permission *Toronto Daily Star*.

U.S. News and World Report: selections from "The Case for a 'Free Quebec': Interview with a Leader in the Separatist Movement", U.S. News and World Report, 15 January 1968. From a copyrighted interview.

The use of the following material is acknowledged.

The excerpts from the Diary of Benjamin Marston: reprinted by courtesy of the Harriet Irving Library, University of New Brunswick, who supplied text of the original material.

The excerpts from *Word from New France: the selected letters of Marie de l'Incarnation*, translated and edited by Joyce Marshall: published by Oxford University Press.

Photographs

The authors and publisher would like to thank all those who have helped to provide photographs for *Northern Destiny*.

The cover art is from the painting "Prophecy" by John Meredith in The National Gallery of Canada, Ottawa; reproduced by permission of The Isaacs Gallery, Toronto, from a transparency courtesy of The National Gallery.

Aberdeen University Press: 319 (right).
Fred Adams: 318 (left), 359 (right), 375.
Archives de la Société de Jésus du Canada français: 87.
Archives du Séminaire de Québec: 261.
Archives of Saskatchewan: 416, 417.
Henry Birks Collection of Canadian Silver: 69 (left), 72 (centre, top right, bottom right).
British Columbia Government: 482.
British Museum: 82-3, 148, 168.
Buffalo and Erie County Historical Society: 224 (bottom right).
Canada Starch Company Limited: 270 (bottom).
Canada Steamship Lines: 224 (bottom left).
Canadian Broadcasting Corporation: 430.
Canadian National Railways: 268 (top), 269.
Canadian Pacific Railway: xiv (bottom), 307 (bottom right), 320 (bottom).
Chubb-Mosler and Taylor Safes Limited: 270 (top).
W. L. Clements Library, University of Michigan: 126-7.
Confederation Art Gallery and Museum, Charlottetown: 289 (top).
Craswell Studios: 289 (bottom).
Cunard Line: 244.
Department of External Affairs: 527 (top).
Department of Indian Affairs and Northern Development: 18 (bottom), 19, 476, 488, 493.
Department of National Defence: 374, 522, 527 (bottom), 530 (lower right).
Department of National Health and Welfare: 9.
Ford Motor Company of Canada Limited: 386 (right), 407 (upper right).
General Motors of Canada Limited: 359 (bottom left), 407 (lower right).
Geological Survey of Canada: 307 (bottom left), 358, 364.
Glenbow Foundation: 422.
The Hakluyt Society and Cambridge University Press: 27 (from *The Cabot Voyages and Bristol Discovery Under Henry VII*, ed. J. A. Williamson).
Hudson's Bay Company: 150, 156 (left), 264 (bottom).
Imperial Oil Limited: 312 (top right), 475.
Imperial War Museum: 382, 384, 464 (right).
Institut national des civilisations: 70, 261.
International Nickel Company of Canada: 6 (bottom), 10.
Iron Ore Company of Canada: 472.

Koehring-Waterous Limited: 385, 388, 410, 441.

Library of Congress: 24 (right), 114 (top).

McCord Museum, McGill University: 213, 265, 284.

McGill University's Department of Rare Books and Special Collections: 39, 85, 106, 117, 124, 125 (bottom).

Manitoba Archives: 264 (top), 335 (bottom left), 338, 342, 354, 397 (bottom left, bottom right), 415, 421.

Memorial University, Newfoundland: 132.

Metropolitan Toronto Library Board: 54 (right), 158, 219 (right), 220, 227 (left), 275.

Miller Services: 502 (top), 511.

Molson Archives: 134 (left), 203 (left), 268 (bottom).

Montreal Municipal Tourist Bureau: 487.

National Capital Commission, Ottawa: iii.

National Film Board: 20 (top), 467, 474 (top), 479, 480, 481, 505, 506-7.

The National Gallery of Canada, Ottawa: 69 (right), 72 (left), 205, 216, 411, 474 (bottom), 483, 484, 485.

National Geographic: 24 (left) © 1964 National Geographic Society.

National Maritime Museum, Greenwich: 25 (right, top centre, bottom centre), 286 (bottom).

National Museum of Canada: 17, 18 (top), 20 (bottom left, bottom right), 546.

New Brunswick Museum: 114 (bottom), 139 (top), 167, 174, 191 (right), 194, 227 (right), 228, 272, 288.

New Brunswick Travel Bureau: xiv (centre).

New York Public Library: 25 (left), 30.

Notman Archives, McCord Museum, McGill University: 316 (bottom), 317, 343, 344 (bottom), 345, 366, 368 (centre right, bottom), 369 (right), 376, 399, 401, 404, 408.

Nova Scotia Archives: 108, 239.

Nova Scotia Film Bureau: 42 (bottom left).

Nova Scotia Information Service: 107 (right).

Office du Film du Québec: 6 (top), 8, 71, 75 (right).

Office of the Premier, St. John's, Newfoundland: 500, 501.

Ontario Archives: 156 (right), 164, 170, 191 (left), 193 (lower right), 203 (upper right), 258, 259, 271, 282, 285, 294 (right), 312 (bottom), 318 (right), 319 (left), 320 (top right), 330 (top right), 335 (bottom right), 337, 340, 341 (bottom left, bottom right), 352, 353, 356, 359 (upper), 363, 369 (lower left), 407 (left), 428.

Ontario Department of Tourism and Information: 51, 486 (top).

Prairie Farm Rehabilitation Administration: ii (centre).

Provincial Archives, Victoria, British Columbia: 315, 335 (upper), 344 (top), 403.

Public Archives of Canada: 38, 42 (top, bottom right), 48-9, 54 (left), 60, 63, 66, 67, 68, 73, 76, 90, 92, 93, 105, 107 (bottom left), 109, 112, 116, 118, 126, 129, 131, 133, 134 (right), 139 (bottom), 151, 152, 157 (right), 165, 171, 172, 176, 181, 190, 193 (left, upper right), 195, 196, 200 (right), 202, 203 (lower right), 215, 217, 223, 236, 237, 241, 242, 243, 246, 250, 274, 283, 286 (top), 291, 292, 294 (left), 297, 305, 307 (top), 309, 311, 312 (top left), 316 (top), 320 (top left), 330 (top left, bottom), 336, 341 (top), 362, 378, 380 (right), 381, 383, 386 (left), 413, 419, 420, 424, 425, 426, 431, 437, 438, 446, 448, 449, 451, 455, 457, 458, 460, 462, 463, 464 (left), 523.

Québec Service de Ciné-Photographie: 7, 75 (left).
Royal Canadian Air Force: 380 (left).
The Royal Library, Copenhagen: 32.
Royal Ontario Museum, Toronto: ii (top), 14, 15, 43, 52, 89, 94, 107 (upper left), 125 (top), 157 (left), 160, 179, 200 (left), 219 (left), 224 (top).
Roy Peterson, *Vancouver Sun*: 510, 513, 529.
St. Lawrence Parks Commission: 201, 221.
Saskatchewan Government: xiv (top), 4.
The Stratford Shakespearean Festival, Stratford, Ontario, Canada: 486 – bottom left, photograph by Robert C. Ragsdale Limited; bottom right, photograph by Douglas Spillane.
The Toucan Press: 47, 48.
Trans-Canada Pipelines: 504.
Traquair Collection: 62.
United Church Archives: 368 (top, centre left), 369 (top left), 397 (top).
United Nations: 468, 524, 526, 528, 530 (left, upper right).
Universitetets Oldsaksamling, Oslo: 21 (left).
University of Heidelberg: 21 (right).
University of Minnesota: James Ford Bell Library: 28.
University of Toronto Library Photography: 41.
Windsor Star: 444, 502 (bottom).
Xavier College Archives: 360.
Yale University Library, 96.
Yale University Press: (Copyright © 1965 by Yale University).

Wherever possible, the sources of quoted material and photographs have been traced and acknowledgment given. Apology is made for any inadvertent errors or omissions.

PREFACE

"History," said Thomas Carlyle, "is the essence of innumerable biographies." History tries to explain the present in terms of the past, and its main ingredient is people. What have men done, said, and thought in all our yesterdays, and how have their actions, words, and ideas shaped our world of today? Every person who hopes to understand himself and his own age must begin by examining his roots in history. It is only too true that history can be perverted, can be turned into propaganda for the selfish purposes of an individual, a nation, or a race, but the wise man will always be on his guard, challenging the interpretations that historians put upon particular historical events and developments. He will ask questions, he will demand proofs, he will use his own critical judgment, he will seek the truth through the discipline of history. Yet he will never find complete truth, because history must always be the incomplete record of man's past achievements and past failures as written down and explained by other men whose judgment is as fallible as his own. Each generation will reread the past in the light of its own experiences and will often arrive at quite different conclusions from those reached by previous generations. There can never be absolutes in history; nevertheless modern man must continue his search for that elusive truth if he is to wrestle intelligently with the heritage of the past and gain a more enlightened future.

As students of history and particularly of Canadian history we have written this book to share with others our knowledge of and conclusions about Canada's past, hoping to show how that past has formed Canada and Canadians into the complex and sometimes contradictory image that they present to the world today. The First Canadians – the Indians and Eskimos – continue their contributions to Canadian life. Settlement of Canada by Europeans, originally the French and British but more recently peoples from all parts of their continent, as well as Asians and Africans, has made twentieth-century Canadians shareholders in a rich cultural legacy many times older than Canada herself. And beyond the gifts of the people lie the bountiful resources of land, forest, and water which make Canada the envy of so many less fortunate countries and which have moulded so many features of Canadian history. The forces of men and of nature, interacting on the stage of time, are the elements from which has been and will continue to be shaped a northern destiny for Canada and Canadians.

J.S.M.
R.E.S.

CONTENTS

Readers should note that book titles marked with a black star
have been published in paperback.

The diversity of the Canadian scene. Top: Aerial view of Hunt Falls, northern Saskatchewan, to show terrain typical of the Canadian Shield. Centre: Gently rolling hills of the upper St. John River Valley. Bottom: Rugged scene from the Kicking Horse River Valley near Field, British Columbia.

I

Canada – The Land and the People

The Resources of the Land

Canada is a land of paradoxes and contrasts. Occupying the northern half of the North American continent it is the world's second-largest country – only the Union of Soviet Socialist Republics is larger. Yet, with twenty million people, less than 1 per cent of the world's population, Canada is one of the smaller nations. From the Atlantic to the Pacific Ocean the land spreads out for 3,000 miles, and from Pelee Island in Lake Erie – its southernmost spot on the same latitude as Madrid and northern Japan – to Alert, Canada's military outpost on Ellesmere Island near the North Pole, is almost another 3,000 miles. At Alert the temperature seldom rises above freezing even in summer, but in southern British Columbia cactus is a native plant.

The huge size of Canada's territory is not in itself an advantage, because there are vast areas in which settlement is discouraged by severe climate, poor soil, or mountainous surface. In addition, natural barriers divide the land into distinctive regions. The Maritime region is separated from the St. Lawrence Valley Lowlands by the Appalachian Mountains. The next barrier westward, the Canadian Shield, covering almost one-half of the country's surface, curves in an arc around Hudson Bay from Labrador to Keewatin District and extends as far south as the St. Lawrence, separating the fertile prairies from the St. Lawrence Lowlands. This forest-clad Shield is composed of hard Pre-Cambrian rocks, the oldest on the earth's surface. Ages ago the Shield was a range of high mountains, but the grinding ice caps of the Glacial Age reduced the high peaks to mere rounded stumps, interlaced with thousands of small, clear lakes. West of the Shield the rolling open prairies slope gradually upwards for hundreds of miles to meet the greatest of Canada's natural barriers, the Rocky Mountains. The Rockies are made up of parallel ranges running in a general north-south direction and separated by broad valleys and plateaus, where such mighty rivers as the Fraser and Columbia begin their trek to the sea. The most westerly range, the Coastal Mountains, form Canada's Pacific Ocean frontier – a deeply indented shore clothed in tow-

1

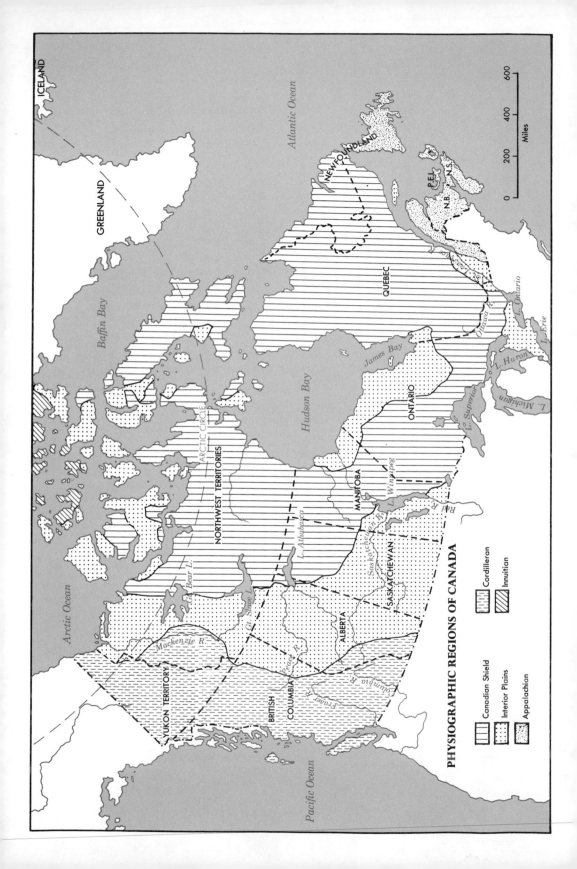

PHYSIOGRAPHIC REGIONS OF CANADA

Canadian Shield
Interior Plains
Appalachian
Cordilleran
Innuitian

Miles
0   200   400   600

ICELAND

GREENLAND

Baffin Bay

Arctic Ocean

Atlantic Ocean

ARCTIC CIRCLE

NORTHWEST TERRITORIES

Hudson Bay

James Bay

QUEBEC

NEWFOUNDLAND

P.E.I.
N.B.
N.S.

ONTARIO

L. Superior
L. Huron
L. Michigan
L. Erie
Ontario
Ottawa R.

MANITOBA
Winnipeg
Red R.
L. Athabasca
Saskatchewan R.

SASKATCHEWAN

ALBERTA

Gt. Bear L.
Gt. Slave L.
Peace R.
Mackenzie R.

YUKON TERRITORY

BRITISH COLUMBIA
Fraser R.
Columbia R.

Pacific Ocean

ering forests and reminiscent of Norway's fjords. North of the prairies and west of the Shield a broad band of forest stretches as far as the Rockies, but farther north, where the long winter limits plant growth, the forest gradually gives way to grasses and stunted scrubby bushes, and, in the most northerly areas, to Arctic tundra.

Thus nature has divided Canada into major regions – the Maritimes, the Shield, the St. Lawrence Valley Lowlands, the prairies, the neighbouring Arctic territories, and finally the Rocky Mountains and the Pacific coast region. But there are other barriers than landforms. The climate barrier of long, cold, winter months restricts outdoor activities throughout Canada, but in the vast Arctic areas, where temperatures as low as 70 degrees below zero have been recorded and precipitation is much lower than in the south, farming is virtually impossible and settlement is limited to scattered mining centres. Not surprisingly, nine of every ten Canadians live within 100 miles of the American border.

Nature has created topographic and climatic hurdles to Canada's development but she has also endowed the country with rich and varied natural resources. Ever since John Cabot discovered the vast fishing grounds off the Atlantic coast in 1497, Canada's fisheries have had an important place in her economy. Over 150 species of fish and shellfish are caught in Canadian waters. The most important catches from the Atlantic are lobsters, cod, scallops, and haddock, and, from the Pacific, salmon, halibut, and herring. The smaller Great Lakes fisheries yield whitefish, smelt, and trout.

The second Canadian resource to attract Europeans was furs, but with the decline of the fur trade after 1800 the forests provided the wood and wood products that today make up Canada's fifth most valuable export. The stands of timber – nearly one and three-quarter million square miles – form such a vast source of lumber and of pulpwood that Canada is the world's leading exporter of lumber and produces over half the newsprint of the western world. The clearing of the forests has, in turn, been the necessary prelude to farming in all regions but the prairies.

From the days of French colonial settlement until the First World War, Canada was primarily an agricultural nation. The industrial revolution in Europe created a huge market for farm products, especially wheat and other grains and later for cheese and fruit. At first the grain came from the St. Lawrence Lowlands; with the opening of the Canadian west around 1900, the prairies became a granary for the world. Today millions of tons of the world's best wheat are grown in the prairie provinces to feed people in every quarter of the globe. Dairy products come mostly from Quebec and Ontario, animal products from western ranches, and fruits from the Niagara region and the Okanagan Valley of British Columbia. New

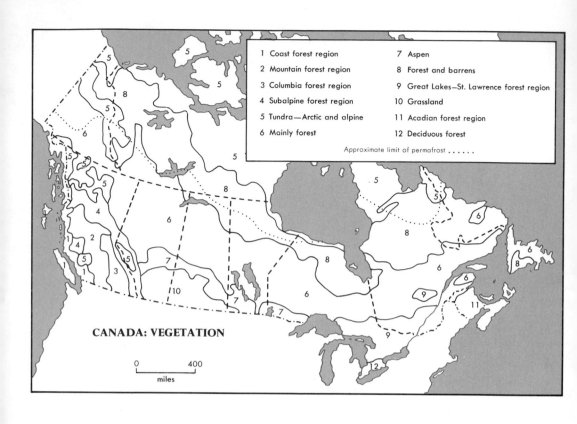

CANADA: VEGETATION

1 Coast forest region
2 Mountain forest region
3 Columbia forest region
4 Subalpine forest region
5 Tundra—Arctic and alpine
6 Mainly forest

7 Aspen
8 Forest and barrens
9 Great Lakes—St. Lawrence forest region
10 Grassland
11 Acadian forest region
12 Deciduous forest

Approximate limit of permafrost ......

0   400
miles

*A swathed grain field, fifteen miles west of Moose Jaw, Saskatchewan.
This prairie scene is characteristic of central Canada, and shows how
man has used to best advantage a climate and terrain ideally suited to
grain growing.*

Brunswick and the "garden province" of Prince Edward Island are re-nowned for their potatoes, while southern Ontario grows large quantities of vegetables and enough tobacco to supply Canada's needs.

Canada is also remarkable for the variety and quantity of her mineral resources. The Shield, a rich storehouse of gold, silver, iron, uranium, nickel, copper, and other minerals, is the source of 75 per cent of Canada's mineral production. Iron is also mined in New Brunswick and Newfound-land, and gold, zinc, and lead in British Columbia. Other mining op-erations include potash in Saskatchewan, talc in Ontario, asbestos in Quebec, and base metals in Nova Scotia. The oil fields of Alberta and Manitoba provide natural gas as a by-product. Canada leads the world in the production of nickel, zinc, and asbestos, and is second in uranium, cobalt, gold, and sulphur. Although coal, iron, and gold have been mined in Canada since early in her history, only since the beginning of this century has she begun to exploit her mineral resources, and their full ex-tent is still unknown.

Twentieth-century Canada is one of the world's leading industrialized nations. Canadian factories produce automobiles, food products, elec-tronic equipment, clothing, construction materials, paper and wood prod-ucts, iron, steel, and a host of other finished goods. Small as her population is, Canada is so far advanced in technology that her standard of living is

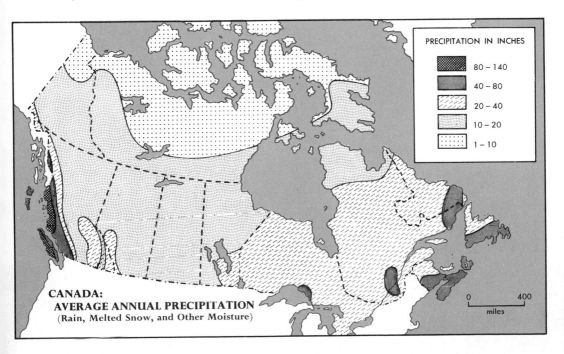

PRECIPITATION IN INCHES

80 – 140
40 – 80
20 – 40
10 – 20
1 – 10

CANADA:
AVERAGE ANNUAL PRECIPITATION
(Rain, Melted Snow, and Other Moisture)

0   400
miles

The city of Quebec from the air.

second only to that of the United States. Today Canada is in the unusual but fortunate position of being able to help in the development of countries much older and more populous than herself.

Modern industry needs raw materials, labour, capital, and energy – and of these the most important is energy. In the last half century oil, natural gas, and electricity have largely replaced wood and coal as fuel for Canada's homes and factories, and today Canada is the world's second-largest per capita consumer of energy. The main sources of hydro-electric power in eastern Canada are the rivers of the Shield, the Niagara and St. Lawrence rivers, and in western Canada the Peace, Columbia, and Kemano rivers. Only a third of Canada's hydro-energy has been developed, but already a new source of power – nuclear energy – has appeared which promises in time to be even more important than water power for Canada's development. Since the explosion of the first atomic bomb in the Second World War, Canada has played a leading role in harnessing nuclear energy for peaceful uses. Using uranium as fuel in atomic reactors, she has shown

The International Nickel Company's nickel complex at Thompson, Manitoba.

that thermal-electric power can be produced in such plants at low cost. In the nuclear age Canada is pioneering in a development whose importance for the future is beyond imagination.

The Canadian People

People in other countries may still think of Canada as a romantic "outdoor" land of farmers, cowboys, and Mounties driving dogsleds, but today about three-quarters of all Canadians are city dwellers. Despite, or perhaps because of, Canada's great distances, settlement is concentrated in several large pockets. Two-thirds of the people live in Ontario and Quebec, but only one-tenth in the four Maritime provinces. One in every three Canadians lives in the St. Lawrence Lowlands, Canada's smallest geographic region but the economic heartland of the country. One-fifth of the total population resides in either Montreal or Toronto and only one worker in every nine in the Canadian labour force is in agriculture. Rural life itself has been virtually urbanized by modern transportation and communication, so that most Canadian farmers enjoy a way of life very similar to that of city dwellers.

Canada's population is a tapestry woven of many racial, ethnic, and linguistic threads. The First Canadians – the Indians and Eskimos – together amount to less than a quarter million. The two so-called "founding races", the French and British, once comprised the rest of the population, but immigration has reduced their proportion to three-quarters of the total. Today one Canadian in twenty is of German extraction, while people from the Ukraine, Italy, the Netherlands, Scandinavia, and Poland each number several hundred thousands. In addition, Jewish, Asian, and Russian people each total over one hundred thousand.

Agriculture on the Montreal Plain.

A farm in Arthabaska County, Quebec.

In the twenty years after the end of the Second World War nearly three million immigrants from all parts of the world came to Canada. Over a quarter made Ontario their home, and a very high proportion found work in manufacturing. Their contribution to the Canadian mosaic is reflected in cultural activities such as music, ballet, drama, and the graphic arts, in sports, and even in Canadian eating habits. Yet Canada's population growth in fact owes little to immigration. The increase in population has been almost entirely the result of a high birth rate and low death rate. Almost as many people have left Canada in the last century as have settled here, and unfortunately for the country's growth the Canadians who emigrated were too often her skilled workers or from her professional class.

The Challenge and the Response

How has Canada the land influenced the growth of Canada the nation? The barriers created by nature have forced that development into certain fixed courses, but these courses could not predetermine all aspects of human growth in Canada. Europeans explored and settled Canada by way of her two natural entrances, the St. Lawrence and Hudson Bay. The Shield and later the Rockies blocked Canada's westward expansion for a time, just as the severe climate has delayed development of the north. But although these obstacles have been largely reduced by human determination and ingenuity, Canada's huge size remains a constant factor in every aspect of Canadian life.

Throughout her history Canada has been constantly pulled in two directions by geography and tradition. Her ties with Europe, in combination with the St. Lawrence–Great Lakes route that stretches half way across the country, have produced an east-west axis for development. At the same time the common geography and common challenges of the North American continent have inevitably drawn her into a north-south pattern of growth connected to the United States.

Because the Atlantic Ocean and the St. Lawrence River provided the first access to Canada by sea, European influences have always been important in Canada's growth. But also important have been the influences from Canada's southern neighbour, the United States. Since the geographical barriers run north and south, from east to west the only barrier between Canada and the neighbouring United States is really their man-made boundary, an artificial line that divides a natural geographic unity. It has been Canada's peculiar problem to try to balance these conflicting cultural, economic, and political influences to her own advantage. Thus she has drawn on two separate but related traditions – the one European, the other North American – and the result is a blending so intertwined as to defy separation.

Because so much of both the Canadian and American ways of life stem from a common inheritance – traditions such as political democracy, the rule of law, and the people themselves – it is difficult to define the differences between the two countries. It can be argued that many features of Canadian life are not so much imports from the United States as similar responses to the North American continental environment. In this sense both Canada and the United States have faced the same or similar challenges – the same natural barriers and vast distances – and their responses to these challenges have often been similar. Canada's pattern of settlement, of railway building, of technological growth, give Canada the appearance of being simply a northern extension of the United States. This appearance is, however, misleading, for in both obvious and hidden ways Canada differs from her American neighbour. Canada's vast distances decreed that her governments would share in building canals and railways,

To ensure that foods on the Canadian market are fit for human consumption, samples are collected daily and subjected to scientific examination by staffs of the Food and Drug Directorate's regional and district offices across Canada. Federal legislation dating back to 1875 has given the Food and Drug Directorate the responsibility for preventing hazards to health through foods and drugs.

The electron microprobe is one of the many sophisticated research tools used by Canadian industry to help in scientific discovery. With it, areas as small as one micron square (forty millionths of an inch) can be accurately located and the chemical constituents determined.

in the growth of air transportation, and in establishing communications systems such as radio and television. Rugged individualism and private enterprise were essential to Canada's national growth – but they were not enough. Canadians saw no contradiction in having their governments share in nation building. The opening of resource areas, continuous scientific research, programmes of conservation and development – all have been the joint efforts of the Canadian people and of their governments.

Canada has coped with the political problems of being a transcontinental nation by the same technique as the United States – by federalized government – but has consciously rejected such American political forms as republicanism or the congressional system. Instead, Canada has adapted the British practice of parliamentary and responsible government to a federal form to meet the challenges posed by her great size. Living next to a large and powerful nation, and sharing many of the same geographic features, the same type of industrial organization, and the same language, Canadians have been forced to develop their own nationalism to prove they are not Americans. Yet their sense of identity is largely negative – Canada is not American and Canada is not British. Canadians find their sense of national identity difficult to define, yet perhaps this difficulty may prove to be a blessing if it saves Canada from the type of chauvinistic, aggressive, and totalitarian nationalism that has plunged so many countries into disastrous wars.

Within Canada, there exists another basic challenge – two national heritages, French and British, sometimes incorrectly described as a conflict of "races" or of two languages. Most Canadians in fact share the same western European cultural tradition, and "English" is simply the name of a language, a language spoken by many people from other countries than England. The "French fact" is a part of Canadian history, as is the "English fact", but Canadians of other national origins cannot easily be fitted into such a simple dualistic pattern. The Canadian nation is a patchwork or mosaic composed of many peoples, but the Canadian habit of encouraging all groups to take pride in their own non-Canadian backgrounds has inevitably limited the growth of a uniform Canadianism. Immigrants to the United States enter the American "melting pot" and soon become Americanized. Immigrants to Canada are never fully "Canadianized", simply because Canada believes her unity lies in her very diversity. This is Canada's unique response to the basic challenge posed by the multinational origins of her people.

FURTHER READING

Pleva, E. G., ed. *The Canadian Oxford School Atlas* (Toronto: Oxford University Press, 1957). Essential for the study of the physical features of Canada.

Kerr, D. G. G., ed. *A Historical Atlas of Canada* (Toronto: Nelson, 1960). The most useful of the several historical atlases available.

Putnam, D. F. and Putnam, R., *Canada: A Regional Analysis* (Toronto: Dent, 1970).

Currie, A. W., *Economic Geography of Canada* (Toronto: Macmillan, 1945).

Canada Year Book (Ottawa: Queen's Printer). An annual publication containing the most recent information on Canada and special topical articles.

Canadian Annual Review (Toronto: University of Toronto Press). A yearly survey of current events and developments in Canada.

Innis, D. Q., *Canada: A Geographic Study* (Toronto: McGraw Hill, 1966).

Warkentin, John, ed. *Canada: A Geographical Interpretation* (Toronto: Methuen, 1968).

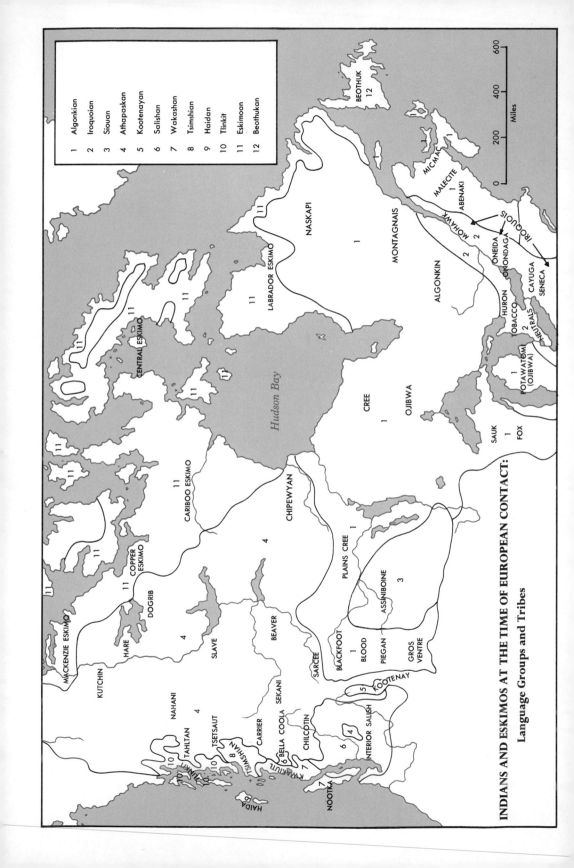

INDIANS AND ESKIMOS AT THE TIME OF EUROPEAN CONTACT:
Language Groups and Tribes

Key to language groups:

1. Algonkian
2. Iroquoian
3. Siouan
4. Athapaskan
5. Kootenayan
6. Salishan
7. Wakashan
8. Tsimshian
9. Haidan
10. Tlinkit
11. Eskimoan
12. Beothukan

0   200   400   600
Miles

BEOTHUK 12

MICMAC 1

MALECITE 1

ABENAKI 1

MOHAWK

IROQUOIS

ONEIDA

ONONDAGA

CAYUGA

SENECA

HURON

TOBACCO

NEUTRALS

POTAWATOMI (OJIBWA) 1

SAUK 1

FOX

NASKAPI 1

MONTAGNAIS

LABRADOR ESKIMO 11

ALGONKIN 1

CREE 1

OJIBWA 1

Hudson Bay

CENTRAL ESKIMO 11

CARIBOO ESKIMO 11

COPPER ESKIMO 11

MACKENZIE ESKIMO 11

CHIPEWYAN 4

PLAINS CREE 1

ASSINIBOINE 3

BLACKFOOT 1

BLOOD

PIEGAN

GROS VENTRE

KOOTENAY 5

DOGRIB

HARE

KUTCHIN

SLAVE

BEAVER

SARCEE

NAHANI

TAHLTAN

TSETSAUT

SEKANI

CARRIER

BELLA COOLA 6

CHILCOTIN

INTERIOR SALISH 6

TLINKIT 10

TSIMSHIAN 8

KWAKIUTL 7

NOOTKA 7

HAIDA 9

4

4

4

2

The First Canadians

The World of the Indians and Eskimos

When Europeans discovered the American hemisphere, they encountered a copper-skinned people whom they mistook for the inhabitants of the subcontinent which they were seeking. These natives of America had no general name for themselves, therefore the name "Indian" continues to be used even though modern scientists have tried to distinguish them from East Indians by using the invented title, Amerind.

The Indians that Columbus and later explorers met were still in a late Stone Age culture, technologically centuries behind Europeans. A few tribes used primitive tools of native copper that had been pounded into shape with stones, but they had no knowledge of the science of metallurgy. They had not discovered the wheel, that simple but essential tool which had been known in Asia and Europe for several thousand years. Part of the explanation of the Indians' slow cultural development lies in their physical isolation from Old World civilizations. Perhaps as much as thirty thousand years ago their ancestors had begun to move from Asia to America, probably across the fifty-mile land bridge now lying beneath Bering Strait. The Indians spread eastward and southward over the American hemisphere until they reached the Atlantic Ocean and the southern tip of South America. No others followed to bring the knowledge accumulated later by the civilizations of Asia, and no Indians returned to Asia with news of the new world they had found. Thousands of years passed before the American continent was rediscovered, this time from Europe instead of from Asia.

After the Indians, the racially related Eskimos entered North America by the same route from Asia in smaller numbers, but they turned eastward from Alaska, following the shores of the Arctic Ocean until the leading group reached Labrador. Perhaps the earlier arrivals, the Indians, prevented the Eskimos from moving southward into the richer prairie and forest lands. Whatever the cause, the Eskimos remained in the most northerly area of the Americas, where under the most severe climatic conditions the Eskimo culture gradually evolved, based on hunting and fishing and using bone and skin for tools because of the scarcity of wood. As late as 1900 some Eskimo groups were still living entirely in a Stone Age culture.

The American Indians of the prehistoric age can be divided into three main cultures. The most advanced were the city builders – the Incas in the Andes Mountains of South America, the Mayas in the tropical jungles of Central America, and the Aztecs of the high plateau land of Mexico – all of whom had sophisticated systems of government and social relations, and some knowledge of astronomy. The second culture group were the village dwellers of the eastern United States and Canada, and of the north Pacific coast region. Their villages of several hundred people were centres of small farms where crops such as corn, beans, squash, and tobacco were raised with the aid of hand tools. This simple pattern of agricultural life was varied by seasonal hunting expeditions or on the Pacific coast by fishing, especially for salmon. Hunting provided meat for their diet and skins for clothing. In the northern forests and on the wide prairies the third group, the hunters, lived a nomadic life, always on the move in search of better hunting grounds. Most of the Indians of Canada belonged to the hunting group, but in the St. Lawrence Valley and Lower Great Lakes region and along the coast of British Columbia, village communities of farmer-hunters were already well established when the Europeans arrived. The Canadian Indians at that time probably numbered about two hundred thousand, somewhat fewer than at present.

The early explorers in Canada still expected to find the real India or China or Japan – the famous lands of silks, jewels, and spices – but each tribe that they met in their westward journey was just as primitive as

Oil painting by the American artist George Catlin (1796-1872) entitled "Buffalo Hunting with Bow, Arrow, and Spear".

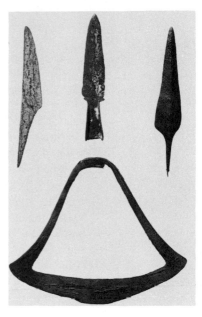

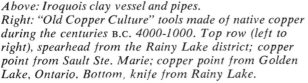

Above: Iroquois clay vessel and pipes.
Right: "Old Copper Culture" tools made of native copper during the centuries B.C. 4000-1000. Top row (left to right), spearhead from the Rainy Lake district; copper point from Sault Ste. Marie; copper point from Golden Lake, Ontario. Bottom, knife from Rainy Lake.

those already encountered. Except in British Columbia, where large split-log houses were built, the Indians' homes were no more than rough shelters of skin or bark, smoky, noisy, and dirty because several families lived and cooked in each lodge along with their only domesticated animal, half-wild dogs. The fish and animal flesh being dried over the open fires attracted flies through the small open doors into the dark, windowless huts. Eye diseases and early blindness were common among the eastern Indians, especially the women, because of the constant irritation from the trapped smoke.

The Indians hunted, fished, and worked with crude tools of stone, bone, or wood, and cooked their food in rough clay or bark vessels. Some tribes grew maize (Indian corn) which was pounded into a meal and boiled into a coarse mush called sagamité, occasionally enriched by the addition of fish or meat. This basic diet was supplemented by wild fruits and berries. Indians usually ate two meals a day, but when food was scarce, as it often was, they might go for days without eating. Tribal warfare was common. Adult captives might be tortured to death with terrible cruelty or occasionally kept alive as slaves, but children taken by a war party were frequently adopted as members of the tribe. In peace or war the life of the Indians was so hard and so dangerous that few lived to an old age.

All Indians were very fond of their children and seldom disciplined them. The education of Indian children consisted mostly of playing games in imitation of their parents – the boys practising hunting, fishing, and fighting, the girls sharing the housekeeping chores with their mothers. The tribal elders instructed the children in tribal traditions. Since they had no written language, the Indians recorded only the most important events

with signs painted on skins or carved on sticks. Most tribal history
was passed from generation to generation by word of mouth. Daily life
was filled with religious practices to appease the many unfriendly spirits
that the Indians thought lived in animals, trees, rocks, the wind, and the
water. Most Indians believed in one supreme spirit, Manitou, and in an
after-life in a vague spirit world. Bodies of the dead were generally put in
a high tree or covered with stones to save them from wild animals. Some
tribes held a great "Feast of the Dead" every few years, when all the bones
were collected and buried in a large common grave.

Next to the chiefs (sachems), the most important person in any tribe or
village was the medicine man (shaman) who with his spells, potions,
powders, and magic dances, could ensure good hunting, drive evil spirits
from the sick, bring rain, or curse an enemy. Boys became warriors and
full members of the clan and of the larger group, the tribe, by passing
rigorous initiation tests. As warriors they then had a voice at the meetings
around the council fire, although in some tribes – the Iroquois, for example – the women made the final decisions in such matters as war and
peace. The greatest virtue for an Indian was courage – his greatest weakness was a passion for gambling that might cost him all his possessions,
his family, and even his own freedom. Fearless in battle, unflinching under
horrible tortures, uncomplaining amid the greatest discomforts of cold,
heat, or hunger, the North American Indian reminded Europeans of the
warlike Spartans of ancient Greece.

Self-reliant and individualistic, the Indian was trained to survive
whether the enemy was a severe climate, wild animals, or a human foe.
From the war-party raids he brought back the scalps of his enemy as proof
of his strength. In the tribal council he could become renowned for eloquent oratory, which the Indians so much admired. A brave warrior captured in battle was given the privilege of death by slow torture at the
stake – to let him show his courage. Such a death was, however, too
honourable for a coward, who was forced to live out his life as a slave of
the village women.

Contact with the Europeans

It was the teeming fisheries of the Grand Banks and the Gulf of St.
Lawrence that first brought Europeans into contact with the Canadian
Indians. These fishermen soon discovered that the Indians had a com-
modity much more valuable than fish, namely the furs so prized in
Europe for making felt hats and trimming expensive robes. With the de-
velopment of the fur trade there began a regular contact between Old and
New World cultures. Europeans wanted the Indians' furs, and the Indians

for their part wanted the cloth and metal trade goods – shirts, blankets, knives, axes, pots, needles, and guns – and the liquor ("fire water") that the Indians could not produce themselves. The trade and the relationship thus founded formed the basis of Canada's life for almost two centuries and involved the Indians in the wars of the rival European nations.

As the demand for furs grew, this trade moved steadily across the continent until by 1800 it had reached the Rockies and the Arctic Circle. In this expansion Europeans relied on the native population not only to produce the furs, but also to provide knowledge of the land and of ways to survive in the land. Although by European standards the Indians were living a primitive life, they had developed certain tools and techniques that the Europeans in America soon adopted, such as the light but durable birchbark canoes used by traders to carry furs and goods over river highways and around impassable rapids, and the snowshoe for winter travel. The Indians showed Europeans how to travel "light" by using dried foods like pemmican – dried buffalo meat, shredded and mixed with fat, which would keep for months. Europeans adopted such articles of Indian clothing as moccasins and buckskin shirts that suited the needs of the traveller. Later generations of Canadians have taken up Indian games – lacrosse, which is officially Canada's national sport, and competitions with snow snakes, the long sticks that are thrown down ice tracks.

Unfortunately, the Indians received from the Europeans more than just the manufactured goods that they wanted so much. They contracted diseases unknown before in their civilization and against which they had little resistance. A smallpox epidemic, for instance, drastically reduced the Huron population in the early 1600's. Unable to understand the cause of these disasters, the Indians often blamed them on the supposed "bad magic" of missionaries. Another scourge that Europeans inflicted on the native population was liquor, usually brandy or rum, used in the fur trade by both French and English merchants. Physically, Indians were no more susceptible to the effects of strong drink than were Europeans, but be-

Corn cultivation among the Huron Indians. Huronia has been described as the granary of most of the Algonquins, and many of the northern Algonquin people exchanged their furs for Huron corn.

An Eskimo settlement in Duke of York's Archipelago, Coronation Gulf, 1913-16. The snow huts have windows of ice, and the owners' poles and harpoons are stuck into the walls. One of the sleds has been raised on snow blocks.

cause they believed that drunkenness was a kind of religious experience, they often pooled their small amounts of liquor so that one person at least would have enough to become literally "roaring drunk". The drunken Indian would run amuck, killing indiscriminately, but such murders were not considered a crime by the Indians, who naively blamed everything on the "evil spirit" that had entered the killer. Missionaries, responsible traders, and many Indian leaders protested against the selling of liquor, but the practice was so much a part of the fur trade that all attempts to stamp it out failed. Other effects of the liquor traffic could be seen in the ravages of disease among the native people. The Indians also learned to distrust the Europeans, who used liquor to cheat them out of their furs and lands.

Against this black record of liquor and dishonesty must be seen the heroic self-sacrifice of Christian missionaries, living amidst squalid and even dangerous conditions, trying to raise the moral and physical standards of the Indians at the same time that traders were giving too many examples of the worst aspects of European civilization. The self-sacrificing work of missionaries in teaching and healing among the native tribes is one of the most inspiring and romantic chapters in Canada's history. Over the space of three centuries, most of the First Canadians – Indians and Eskimos – have accepted Christianity, although a small number have held to their ancient religious beliefs.

New housing erected by members of the Eskimo housing co-operative at Apex Hill, near Frobisher Bay, in the Northwest Territories.

The First Canadians have posed a serious problem for Europeans since the first meeting. Should they be protected from European influences by being segregated, or should they be integrated into a European-style technological society? Churches, governments, educators, and even the Indians themselves have never agreed on the treatment of the native population. The Indians' greatest difficulty is the knowledge gap – the lack of adequate education – and its consequence, the lack of economic opportunity. On the reservations, the Indians are protected in their way of life by the government, but they are also treated as children in law and fact. Most reservations were established during the nineteenth century to make the Indians into farmers, yet many reservations are too small and too poor to provide a satisfactory life for the residents, especially since farming has become so highly specialized and expensive.

The recent trend in dealing with the Indian question is to encourage the Indians to leave the reservations, to find jobs "outside", and to become full members of the Canadian community. But few Indians have enough training for skilled work, and find themselves working at the poorest paying jobs, living in depressed city areas, cut off from their cultural roots and their own people on the reservations, and rejected by other Canadians. The problems of the First Canadians in this age of computers and space travel are many and will probably take many years to solve.

Despite all these handicaps, some Indians and Eskimos have succeeded in our modern society, and have become well known individually in the professions or collectively, as for example the reservation cattle ranchers in the west or the Caughnawaga high riggers from Montreal. In spite of the shortcomings in Canada's treatment of the Indians, there were never any Indian wars like those in the United States. Canada has, in fact, been a refuge for some American tribes fleeing from the American pioneer philosophy, "the only good Indian is a dead Indian". In the long course of Canada's development, the First Canadians have played an important role. In the days of the fur trade, the Indian hunters made that trade possible. In the days of exploration, Indian guides led Europeans across the continent. In the imperial wars between France and Britain, in the

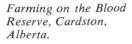

Farming on the Blood Reserve, Cardston, Alberta.

A highrigger from the Six Nations Caughnawaga Reserve working on the Burlington Bridge in Ontario, the first skyway built in Canada, completed in 1958 at a cost of $19 million.

American Revolution, in the War of 1812, and again in two world wars, Canadian Indians fought and died as valiantly as their European comrades. To Canada's modern economy and through the preservation of their cultural heritage of music, dances, handicrafts, and skills, the First Canadians will make a significant contribution in Canada's future.

FURTHER READING

Jenness, Diamond, *The Indians of Canada,* 4th ed. (Ottawa: Queen's Printer, 1958). The standard introduction to Canada's native population.

Jenness, Eileen, *The Indian Tribes of Canada* (Toronto: Ryerson, 1966)★. A summary of the larger study by Diamond Jenness.

Tooker, Elisabeth, *An Ethnography of the Huron Indians, 1615-1649* (Huronia Historical Development Council, 1967)★. A detailed study of Huron culture at time of contact with the French.

Left: Coiled basketwork made by the Indians of Hamilton Inlet, Labrador.
Right: Eskimo carving of a man carrying a walrus.

3

Discovering a Continent

Vinland the Good

In 1492 Christopher Columbus opened the door to a new historical age when he reached the New World, but his achievement was really the rediscovery of a hemisphere long occupied by Indians and Eskimos, and definitely known to some Europeans 500 years before Columbus. Certain passages in ancient Chinese manuscripts suggest that Chinese merchants reached the Pacific coast of America. Such visits are a historical probability, but like most claims of pre-Columbian discoveries of America, the evidence is too vague to permit us to accept or reject the stories with any assurance. The fable-filled *Voyage of St. Brendan*, written in the tenth or eleventh century, recounts how Irish monks and settlers, fleeing from Viking raids on Iceland and Greenland around 860, reached what might have been the Gulf of St. Lawrence. Still another legend relates that a Welsh prince, Madoc, took a large band of his followers to America in the twelfth century. But the only pre-Columbian discovery of America of which there is any certainty concerns the Vikings. Around the year 800, for reasons still obscure, bands of Vikings, sometimes as traders and some-

Below: This Viking ship, known as the "Oseberg ship", was found preserved in sand on the Norwegian coast.
Right: A portrayal of St. Brendan and a group of monks, from a medieval manuscript in the University of Heidelberg.

Volens deo post longum iter ab insula Gronlanda per meridiem ad reliquas congerminas partes occidentalis oceani maris iter fecientes ad occidentem glaciei tipicas et leiphus erissonus socij certam oceani uberrimam videlicet huyusu invenerunt quam britanim insulam appellarunt. homines Gronlande vicinorumque finium eam Sedes apostolice episcopus ierarnus in hoc terra spaciosa vero et opulentissima in ultimo anno post nri Pascali accessit in nomine dei omnipotentis longo tempore mansit estiuo et brumali postea versus Gronlandiam redit ad orientem hiemale deinde humillima obediencia superiori...

Groenlandia

Isolanda Ibernica

Vinlanda Insula
a Byarno repa
et leipho socijs

Mare Oceanum

Islanda insula

Ibernia

Zinglia terra insula

Magne
Insule
Beati Brandani
Branziliae
dicte

Desiderate
insule

Mare Oceanum

Beate isule
fortune

Rep
franc

hispanorum rep

aben

Bela

Re
Hia

magni

times as robbers, began to strike out from Scandinavia to east, south, and west, crossing Russia to Constantinople, conquering Normandy, ravaging from Britain to Spain and southern Italy. Other Vikings reached Iceland about 870, travelled on to establish two colonies in Greenland around 980, and finally about 1000 discovered the shores of America, where they built one or more short-lived settlements.

The most important records of these Viking exploits are two epic story-poems, the Saga of the Greenlanders, first written down about 1127, and Erik's Saga, a revision of the Greenland story using additional information. Despite many obscurities in the texts, these sagas do describe historic people who did make the voyages across the northern rim of the Atlantic Ocean and who did try to build a Viking colony in North America. The Saga of the Greenlanders tells how Bjarni Herjolfsson, sailing for Greenland about 985, lost his way and sighted an unknown land to the west. Some fifteen years later, Leif, son of Erik the Red who had started the Greenland colony, followed Bjarni's directions and found the same coast, which he named Helluland. Leif's Helluland was probably Baffin Island, and Markland was probably on the Labrador coast. But the saga's details about Vinland are so vague that writers have placed it as far apart as Virginia and Lake Ontario, although most authorities think that Vinland was on the New England shore. In 1961 a Norwegian explorer, Helge Ingstad, excavated the site of seven houses and a forge at L'Anse aux Meadows on the northern tip of Newfoundland, which are almost certainly ruins of a Norse settlement, but probably not of Leif's Vinland. No indisputable remains of Vinland, that first European settlement in the New World, have yet been discovered.

The Vinland Map, detail. Discovered in 1957, it has now been established that the map was drawn about 1440, probably by a monk in Basel, Switzerland, from an earlier original that has been lost. It is the earliest known map that shows any part of the Americas, and is the only surviving medieval example based on Norse cartography. In effect, the map proves that the Vikings explored the North American coast and gathered enough information to draw a representation of the Gulf of St. Lawrence and the Atlantic provinces.
The paragraph in Latin at the top left reads in part: "By God's will, after a long voyage from the island of Greenland to the south towards the most distant remaining parts of the western ocean sea, sailing southward amidst the ice, the companions Bjarni and Leif Eiriksson discovered a new land, extremely fertile and even having vines, the which island they named Vinland . . . ." The shorter paragraph below it reads: "Island of Vinland, discovered by Bjarni and Leif in company."

Above: The site of what is believed to be a Norse house, built about 1000 A.D. at L'Anse aux Meadows. Right: A medieval German representation of Tyrkir discovering grapes in Vinland. Some modern scholars believe that the "grapes" were grasses.

Leif's brother, Thorvald, visited Vinland about 1003 and was killed by natives whom the Norsemen called "Skraelings", meaning wretches. About 1010 Thorfinn Karlsefni took a colonizing group "with all kinds of livestock" to Vinland, because Vinland had three important resourees lacking in both Greenland and Iceland – timber, grapes, and wild grain. Thorfinn's group left about 1013 after battles with the Skraelings, but Leif's sister, Freydis, came the next year with some seventy settlers. Quarrels developed in the tiny settlement, and Freydis was blamed when half the people were massacred by her personal followers. This tragedy and attacks by the Skraelings seem to have ended the Vinland venture. Yet the discovery at L'Anse aux Meadows strongly suggests that other Norse settlements existed in America and that Norsemen still went to those shores for timber after Vinland was deserted.

The Skraeling attacks may be one reason why the Greenlanders abandoned their settlements in North America, but the Greenland colonies themselves disappeared during the centuries that followed. The adventurous Vikings had come, had seen, but had not conquered America. The discovery they made remains only a romantic prelude to Canada's history. The stories of Leif, of Freydis, of Thorfinn and his son Snorri, the first white child born in America, lay buried for centuries in the medieval sagas. But perhaps the memory of Vinland was not entirely forgotten. In the late Middle Ages, Iceland, where the Saga of the Greenlanders originated, traded with Bristol, England, and Bristol traded with Portugal. The memory of Vinland may have lingered in the European ports visited by Christopher Columbus and Giovanni Caboto.

In Search of Cipangu

Not until men began to explore outer space in the 1950's was there a geographical discovery of such far-reaching importance as Columbus' rediscovery of America. Every aspect of western European life was affected – geographical knowledge, economics, the relations between nations, and even Christian theology. The New World contained new peoples, new plants, and new animals that fascinated Europeans, who had hitherto believed that their world, centred on the Mediterranean Sea, comprised the whole world.

Even without Columbus, America would still have been discovered in a few years by someone else, since the Europeans were beginning to extend their influence far beyond the confines of Europe. For centuries caravans from the East had carried spices, silks, gems, and other luxury goods to western Europe. Towards the end of the Middle Ages, however, warlike Turks captured the trade routes in Asia Minor. In a bid to outflank the Turks, Portuguese sailors began to explore the sea route around Africa. In 1487 Bartholomew Diaz reached the Cape of Good Hope, and ten years later Vasco da Gama arrived in India. Western Europe had at last made direct contact with the fabled wealth of the Orient.

Behind these Portuguese explorations lay the initiative of Prince Henry the Navigator, whose navigation school had made sailing into a science. With maps that were more accurate, the magnetic compass, and stronger and larger ships, Europeans were better equipped to discover new worlds. Equally important to the expansion of Europe were such inventions as

Left: A ship, probably similar to the "Santa Maria" (of which no authentic illustrations exist) that appeared in the illustrated edition of a letter from Columbus printed in Basel, 1493.

Astrolabes and cross-staves were used to determine latitude. Centre top: Mariner's astrolabe, 1585. Centre bottom: A sixteenth-century Italian compass. Right: A sixteenth-century navigator sighting the sun with a cross-staff. From the scale on the staff he could read off the angle of the sun's inclination.

gunpowder, which made Europeans more powerful than other peoples, the printing press, which spread news of scientific and geographical discoveries, and above all the spirit of enquiry engendered by the Renaissance. Yet these were only some of the forces that made the overseas expansion of Europe possible. In the political sphere kings had finally broken the power of the feudal nobles, and with the aid of centralized administration were creating nation states in which the "new monarchy" directed national development. Supporting such "new monarchs" as Henry VII of England and Ferdinand II and Isabella of Spain was the new class of wealthy merchants who linked their own ambitions with those of their powerful rulers and accepted the new ethic of profits for profits' sake. By pooling their fortunes in chartered companies, by improved book-keeping and banking methods, these merchants provided the financial means to reach and exploit the riches of new lands. Thus, science, philosophy, government, economics, and above all a spirit of daring combined to herald the modern age.

In 1492, the year that King Ferdinand completed his political unification of Spain, he and Queen Isabella provided the Genoese navigator, Columbus, with three ships for an attempt to reach the Orient by sailing west across the Atlantic. Columbus, like many educated men and experienced travellers, believed the ancient Greek theory that the earth was round – their mistake lay in accepting faulty estimates of the world's circumference. In 1474 Toscanelli, a friend of Columbus, had produced a world map that telescoped distances so that Japan (Marco Polo's Cipangu) would be in Mexico! Columbus may have used this map but, given the imperfect state of geographical knowledge in that age, it is understandable why he believed that he had reached the spice islands of the East Indies when he sighted San Salvador on 12 October 1492. His report of lands rich in "many spices, and great mines of gold and of other metals" convinced the king and queen that they should finance another trip by Columbus. Before his death in 1506 he had made four voyages to his "indies" and had explored the coast of Central America, but he had not brought home the promised riches of the Orient. By then he knew that he had not reached the Indies, but that he had discovered "another world" of unknown dimensions.

Other nations of Europe, envious of Spain's prestige, now began to send their own expeditions westward. For several years Bristol merchants had annually despatched ships in search of the fabled "island of Brasylle". At some date before 1490, another Italian navigator, Giovanni Caboto (John Cabot), appeared in Bristol. Like Columbus, he was sure that he could reach the East more quickly and cheaply by sailing west, but he proposed to steer farther north than Columbus had. Henry VII gave

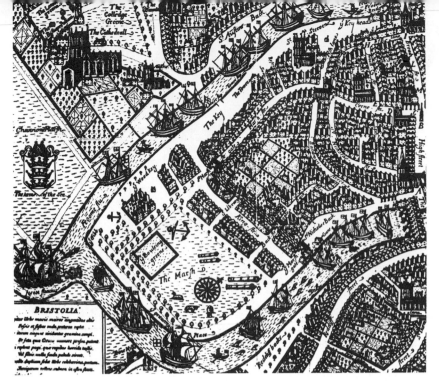

The port of Bristol: detail of a plan drawn in 1671, showing the quays and mercantile area at the junction of the Avon and Frome rivers. The Custom House stood on the Marsh, and the plan marks the streets (mentioned in a rental book of 1498-9) where John Cabot and the Bristol merchants had their houses.

Cabot permission to go exploring, the Bristol merchants paid his costs, and Cabot left Bristol with eighteen men on a small ship, the *Mathew*, at the beginning of May, 1497. On 24 June they sighted the coast of Canada. The place of Cabot's arrival has been claimed for Newfoundland, Cape Breton Island, and Labrador, but wherever his first landfall may have been, Cabot certainly saw Cape Breton Island before he returned to England in August, believing he had found the route to Japan. Henry VII, grateful for the honour given to England but never generous with money, gave Cabot £10 (worth about $1,000 today), a life annuity of £20, and a promise of help for another expedition. In 1498 he did provide Cabot with two ships and 300 men, and the Bristol merchants added three more ships to the expedition. Cabot's course on this second voyage is unknown, but because he failed to discover Japan, King Henry and the Bristol merchants lost interest in any further trips.

Nevertheless, John Cabot's voyages had three positive results. In 1497 he had announced the discovery of the great fisheries of the Grand Banks, although there is some evidence that English, French, and Portuguese fishermen had already been visiting them years before Columbus' epoch-making journey. The second result consists of two maps showing part of

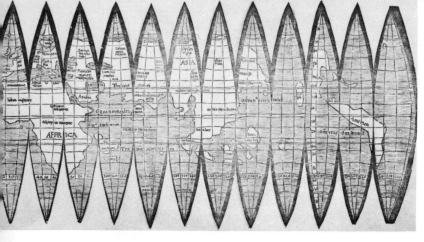

The map on which the name "America" first appeared was drawn by Martin Waldseemüller in 1507. It is printed on the bulge of Brazil, at the far right.

the North American coastline. Both maps, one by Juan de la Cosa, one of Columbus' pilots, the other anonymous, were drawn about 1500 – almost certainly from Cabot's surveys. The coastline may represent part of Newfoundland, or of Nova Scotia and the northeastern United States. The third result – England's claim to northern North America based on Cabot's discovery – later became the cause of international controversy.

The Mariner from St. Malo

One immediate result of Columbus' voyage had been the grant to Spain in 1493 by Pope Alexander VI of all pagan lands beyond a line 100 leagues west of the Azores. For reasons unknown this line was moved by the Treaty of Tordesillas in 1494 to 370 leagues west of the Azores, giving Portugal exclusive rights to all new lands east of the line. Despite this Treaty other nations had entered the exploration race in the north Atlantic, and the English discoveries by Cabot seemed to infringe Portugal's Tordesillas monopoly and challenge her interest in the fisheries. In 1500, on the order of King Manuel of Portugal, Gaspar Corte-Real visited Greenland, and the next year skirted the coasts of Labrador and Newfoundland. In 1502 Amerigo Vespucci, who had explored the coast of South America and perhaps of North America for Portugal, announced that these new lands were in fact a hitherto unknown continent, and Gerard Waldseemüller, a Dutch geographer, in his famous world map of 1507, named the new continent America, "because Americus discovered it".

Europeans were now aware of the New World's fisheries and hoped that its other resources might include precious metals and gems. But explorers still tried to reach the Orient through or around the land barrier of America. This search for a northwest passage was supposedly begun in 1509 by John Cabot's son, Sebastian, but no further searches for a northern route were made in the next half century. Spain, England, and Portugal had each been active during this first decade of exploration, but although French fishermen had been visiting Newfoundland at least since

1504, France did not join in the westward race until after Francis I, who came to the throne in 1515, had consolidated royal power by war, diplomacy, and government reforms. Having established the "new monarchy" in France, Francis was free to seek a foothold in the New World for his country, and on his orders the Italian Giovanni da Verrazzano explored the North American coast from Carolina to Nova Scotia in 1524.

From the days of Cabot to Verrazzano the exploration of the northern Atlantic area was confined to the coastline. In 1534, however, another chapter in Canada's history was opened when Francis I sent Jacques Cartier "to discover certain islands and countries where it is said one ought to find great quantity of gold and other rich things". On 20 April 1534 Cartier sailed from St. Malo, France, with two ships. After reaching Cape Bonavista, Newfoundland, he chanced on the Strait of Belle Isle and crossed the Gulf of St. Lawrence to Prince Edward Island. From here Cartier turned north and at Gaspé Harbour on 24 July he laid claim to the territory by erecting a tall cross bearing the French arms and the inscription "Long Live the King of France". Unaware that he was in the wide mouth of the St. Lawrence, Cartier reached the north shore of the river, turned eastward again and passed by Anticosti Island on his way home through the same strait. Jacques Cartier had discovered and explored the Gulf of St. Lawrence. He had missed the river itself, but he carried back to France two Indian captives who did know the river and who were to guide his next trip.

Encouraged by the success of this first voyage, King Francis gave Cartier money to continue his explorations in 1535. This time Cartier

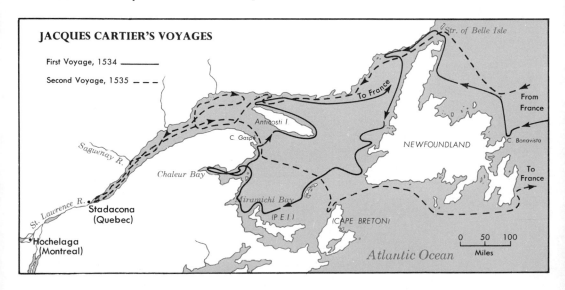

JACQUES CARTIER'S VOYAGES

First Voyage, 1534 ———
Second Voyage, 1535 – – –

followed the north shore of the St. Lawrence which, his two Indian captives said, led to the Kingdom of Saguenay and to Canada. He believed that Saguenay and Canada were large countries, but his guides were referring to the Saguenay River, and "kanata" was an Indian word for village. Soon the ships did pass the great cleft-rock mouth of the Saguenay, and near "kebec", literally the place where the waters narrow, Cartier encountered Donnacona, "the Lord of Canada". From here the explorer prepared to take his smallest vessel up the river in search of a village called Hochelaga, but for the first time the Indians became unfriendly because Donnacona did not want the Europeans to reach the tribes of the interior. Cartier, however, could not be dissuaded from his purpose, and soon his party were pushing up the river, marvelling at the wealth of fish, game, and wild fruit. On 2 October they approached the palisaded village of Hochelaga at the site of Montreal, and got a friendly reception from the inhabitants. The next day Cartier climbed the towering hill behind the village and named it "mont Royal". From its summit he could see the Ottawa River where, the local Indians indicated, silver and gold could be found. Two days later the excited sailors started back for Quebec.

As the season was now late, Cartier had to winter in a makeshift fort at Quebec. Here scurvy broke out among the sailors: their limbs became swollen and discoloured and their teeth fell out. About twenty-five men

A plan of Hochelaga, the walled Iroquois village where Montreal now stands, from a volume describing Columbus' voyages to the New World published in Italy by Giovanni Ramusio (1485-1557).

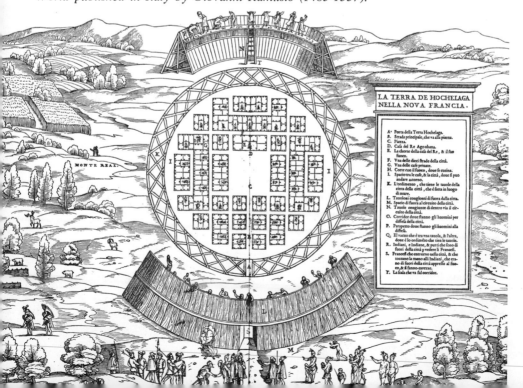

died, and only three of the more than 100 survivors were well enough to care for the sick. Fearing an attack by Donnacona's Indians, Cartier had both sick and healthy men hammer inside the ships to give the impression that all hands were well and busy. The danger of attack was reduced when Cartier learned to make an Indian remedy from hemlock bark, which cured the whole party in one week. About mid-April 1536, as the ice in the St. Lawrence broke up, Cartier prepared to leave Quebec. Before sailing, however, he captured "the Lord of Canada" and carried him back to France where he learned French and became a Christian, and where he later died.

On his second voyage Cartier had discovered a water route into the interior of North America. That route, the St. Lawrence River, later proved not to be the long-sought passage to the East, but its discovery was the start of the first post-Viking attempt at European colonization in Canada. The king determined on another voyage in search of Canada's wealth, but nothing was accomplished, because of war with Spain, until Cartier returned with five ships and two years' supplies in 1541. This time he built a fort at Cap Rouge, a few miles above Quebec, and began to collect what he thought to be gold, iron, and diamonds. Later, when all his finds proved worthless, the jibe "as false as a Canadian diamond" became a common saying.

Cartier was to have been accompanied in 1541 by Jean François de la Rocque, Sieur de Roberval, who was bringing 200 colonists at his own expense. Instead, Roberval did not set sail until 1542, after collecting "colonists" from French prisons and behaving for some months like a pirate. At St. John's, Newfoundland, Roberval met Cartier, who was going home. Cartier had left Cap Rouge because of Indian hostility, but he encouraged Roberval to carry on with the colonizing venture by describing the great attractions of the St. Lawrence. Roberval's four ships landed the settlers, "cows, oxen and sheep", "horses, and workmen to build houses" at Cap Rouge. During the next winter, however, scurvy killed about a quarter of the colonists.

The fate of Roberval's colony is unknown. Early in 1543 Roberval received more supplies from France and explored the St. Lawrence as far as the Lachine Rapids, but he returned to France in the same year and the settlers may have gone with him. Roberval had lost a fortune on his short-lived settlement and he had lost all interest in colonizing Canada. War between France and Spain had begun again in 1542, and for the next half century France was torn by wars, by religious strife, and by dynastic quarrels. Cartier's explorations and Roberval's colony inspired no imitators, and three generations passed before France's interest in the New World was rekindled.

This Icelandic map dated 1579 shows Leif's three landfalls: "Helleland" or Helluland (meaning Slabland), "Markland" (Forest Land), and "Winlandie" or Vinland. "Skraellings", the Viking name for the Indians, is apparent in the label "Skralinge Land".

HISTORY FROM THE SOURCES

The Records of Discovery

Historians have reached very different conclusions about the location of Leif's Vinland. Here is the account of Leif's voyage of discovery from the Saga of the Greenlanders. What information does it give about the geography, topography, and resources of Vinland that might help to identify the site of the Viking settlement?

    . . . The first landfall they made was the country that Bjarni had sighted last. They sailed right up to the shore and cast anchor, then lowered a boat and landed. There was no grass to be seen, and the hinterland was covered with great glaciers, and between glaciers and shore the land was like one great slab of rock. It seemed to them a worthless country.

    Then Leif said, 'Now we have done better than Bjarni where this country is concerned – we at least have set foot on it. I shall give this country a name and call it *Helluland*.'

    They returned to their ship and put to sea, and sighted a second land. Once again they sailed right up to it and cast anchor, lowered a boat and went ashore. This country was flat and wooded, with white sandy beaches wherever they went; and the land sloped gently down to the sea.

Leif said, 'This country shall be named after its natural resources: it shall be called *Markland*.'

They hurried back to their ship as quickly as possible and sailed away to sea in a north-east wind for two days until they sighted land again. . . . There were extensive shallows there and at low tide their ship was left high and dry, with the sea almost out of sight. But they were so impatient to land that they could not bear to wait for the rising tide to float the ship; they ran ashore to a place where a river flowed out of a lake. . . .

There was no lack of salmon in the river or the lake, bigger salmon than they had ever seen. The country seemed to them so kind that no winter fodder would be needed for livestock: there was never any frost all winter and the grass hardly withered at all.

In this country, night and day were of more even length than in either Greenland or Iceland: on the shortest day of the year, the sun was already up by 9 a.m., and did not set until after 3 p.m.

When they had finished building their houses, Leif said to his companions, 'Now I want to divide our company into two parties and have the country explored; half of the company are to remain here at the houses while the other half go exploring – but they must not go so far that they cannot return the same evening, and they are not to become separated.'

. . . One evening news came that someone was missing: it was Tyrkir the Southerner. . . . Leif rebuked his men severely, and got ready to make a search with twelve men.

They had gone only a short distance from the houses when Tyrkir came walking towards them, and they gave him a warm welcome. . . . [Tyrkir said,] 'I have some news. I found vines and grapes.'

'Is that true, foster-father?' asked Leif.

'Of course it is true,' he replied. 'Where I was born there were plenty of vines and grapes.'

They slept for the rest of the night, and next morning Leif said to his men, 'Now we have two tasks on our hands. On alternate days we must gather grapes and cut vines, and then fell trees, to make a cargo for my ship.'

This was done. It is said that the tow-boat was filled with grapes. They took on a full cargo of timber; and in the spring they made ready to leave and sailed away. Leif named the country after its natural qualities and called it Vinland.

The Vinland Sagas: The Norse Discovery of America,
trans. with intro. by Magnus Magnusson and Hermann Palsson
(London, 1965)★, pp. 55-8.

In August 1497 Raimondo di Soncino, the Duke of Milan's ambassador at London, reported to the Duke the news of Cabot's discovery. This subsequent letter, written in December, gives further details of the discovery.

Perhaps amidst so many occupations of your Excellency it will not be unwelcome to learn how his majesty here has acquired a portion of Asia without a stroke of his sword. In this kingdom there is a lower class Venetian named Master Zoanne Caboto, of a fine mind, very expert in navigation, who, seeing that the most serene kings, first of Portugal, then of Spain have occupied unknown islands, meditated the achievement of a similar acquisition for his majesty aforesaid, and having obtained royal grants securing to himself the profitable control of whatever he should discover, since the sovereignty was reserved to the crown, with a small ship and eighteen persons he committed himself to fortune and set out from Bristol, a western port of this kingdom, and having passed Ireland, which is still further to the west and then shaped a northerly course, he began to navigate to the eastern parts, leaving (during several days) the North star to the right; and having wandered about considerably, at length he fell in with *terra firma*, where he set up the royal standard, and having taken possession for this king and collected several tokens, he came back again. The said Master Zoanne, being a foreigner and a poor man, would not be believed if the crew, who are nearly all English and from Bristol, did not testify that what he says is true. This Master Zoanne has a drawing of the world on a map and also on a solid globe, which he has made, and shows the point he reached, and going towards the east, he has passed considerably the country of the Tanais. And they say that the land is excellent and [the air] temperate, and they think that Brazil wood and silks grow there; and they affirm that the sea is covered with fish which are caught not merely with nets but with baskets, a stone being attached to make the basket sink in the water, and this I heard the said Master Zoanne relate. And said Englishmen, his companions, say that they will fetch so many fish that this kingdom will have no more need of Iceland, from which country there comes a very great store of fish which are called stock-fish. But Master Zoanne has set his mind on something greater; for he expects to go from that place already occupied, constantly hugging the shore, further towards the east until he is opposite an island called by him Cipango, situated in the equinoctial region, where he thinks grow all the spices of the world and also the precious stones; and he says that once upon a time he was at Mecca, whither the spices are brought by caravan from distant countries, and those who brought them, on being asked where the said spices grow, answered that they did not know, but that other caravans come with this merchandise to their homes from distant countries, who again say that they are brought to them from other remote regions.

H. P. Biggar, ed., *The Precursors of Jacques Cartier,*
1497-1534 (Ottawa, 1911), pp. 19-21.

The site of Cabot's landing is unknown because no records of the voyages have survived. Jacques Cartier, however, wrote such full and precise accounts of his trips – accounts that are still in existence today – that there is no problem in identifying the places he visited. This passage describing his landing in Chaleur Bay gives his impressions of the natives and information that might interest France in this new land.

On Thursday the eighth of the said month [of July 1534] as the wind was favourable for getting under way with our ships, we fitted up our long-boats to go and explore this bay; and we ran up it that day some twenty-five leagues. The next day [Friday, July 10], at daybreak, we had fine weather and sailed on until about ten o'clock in the morning, at which hour we caught sight of the head of the bay, whereat we were grieved and displeased. At the head of this bay, beyond the low shore, were several very high mountains. And seeing there was no passage, we proceeded to turn back. While making our way along the [north] shore, we caught sight of the Indians on the side of a lagoon and low beach, who were making many fires that smoked. We rowed over to the spot, and finding there was an entrance from the sea into the lagoon, we placed our long-boats on one side of the entrance. The savages came over in one of their canoes and brought us some strips of cooked seal, which they placed on bits of wood and then withdrew, making signs to us that they were making us a present of them. We sent two men on shore with hatchets, knives, beads and other wares, at which the Indians showed great pleasure. And at once they came over in a crowd in their canoes to the side where we were, bringing furs and whatever else they possessed, in order to obtain some of our wares. They numbered, both men, women and children, more than 300 persons. Some of their women, who did not come over, danced and sang, standing in the water up to their knees. The other women, who had come over to the side where we were, advanced freely towards us and rubbed our arms with their hands. Then they joined their hands together and raised them to heaven, exhibiting many signs of joy. And so much at ease did the savages feel in our presence, that at length we bartered with them, hand to hand, for everything they possessed, so that nothing was left to them but their naked bodies; for they offered us everything they owned, which was, all told, of little value. We perceived that they are people who would be easy to convert, who go from place to place maintaining themselves and catching fish in the fishing-season for food. Their country is more temperate than Spain and the finest it is possible to see, and as level as the surface of a pond. There is not the smallest plot of ground bare of wood, and even on sandy soil, but is full of wild wheat, that has an ear like barley and the grain like oats, as well as of pease, as thick as if they had been sown and hoed; of white and red currant-bushes, of straw-berries, of raspberries, of white and red roses and of other plants of a strong, pleasant odour. Likewise there are many fine meadows with useful herbs, and a pond where there are many salmon. I am more than ever of opinion that these people would be easy to convert to our holy faith. . . . We named this bay, Chaleur bay [i.e. the bay of Heat].

H. P. Biggar, ed., *The Voyages of Jacques Cartier*
(Ottawa, 1924), pp. 54-7.

FURTHER READING

Parry, J. H., *Europe and a Wider World, 1415-1715* (London: Hutchinson University Library, 1949). Excellent brief discussion of European overseas expansion.

Oleson, T. J., *Early Voyages and Northern Approaches, 1000-1632* (Toronto: McClelland & Stewart, 1963). Most recent scholarly account of early explorations.

Oleson, T. J., *The Norsemen in America* (Canadian Historical Association Booklet No. 14, 1963)★. Summary account of Norse discovery of America.

Mowat, Farley, *West Viking* (Toronto: McClelland & Stewart, 1965). An imaginative study of evidence relating to Vinland.

Magnusson, Magnus and Palsson, Hermann (trans.), *The Vinland Sagas* (London: Penguin, 1965)★. A critical edition of the basic documents referring to the Vinland discovery.

Ingstad, Helge, "Vinland Ruins Prove Vikings Found the New World", *National Geographic*, November 1964.

Morison, S. E., *Christopher Columbus, Mariner* (New York: Mentor, 1956)★. An excitingly written biography.

Leacock, Stephen, *The Mariner of St. Malo* (Chronicles of Canada Series, reprinted by the University of Toronto Press, 1964). A highly readable biography of Jacques Cartier.

Brebner, J. B., *The Explorers of North America, 1492-1806* (New York: Doubleday, 1955)★. A brief but authoritative account of the march of discovery. Chapters 7, 8, and 9 refer to the early period of Canadian history.

Innis, H. A., *The Cod Fisheries* (Toronto: University of Toronto Press, 1954). The opening chapters examine the role of cod fisheries in early Canadian history.

4

The Foundations of New France

The Revival of Colonization

In the years following Roberval's attempt to establish a colony at Quebec, the interest of the western European states was largely diverted from the New World by recurrent civil and international wars. In the course of those wars the Spanish empire in America was harassed by Sir Francis Drake and the English "sea dogs", but in the northern part of the hemisphere the only activity was that of explorers still searching for the northwest passage. Martin Frobisher discovered Frobisher Bay and entered Hudson Strait during the course of three voyages made from England during the 1570's. In the next decade John Davis followed Frobisher's lead, but on none of his three explorations did he penetrate the Strait. Sir Humphrey Gilbert hoped to found an English colony to rival Spain's dis-

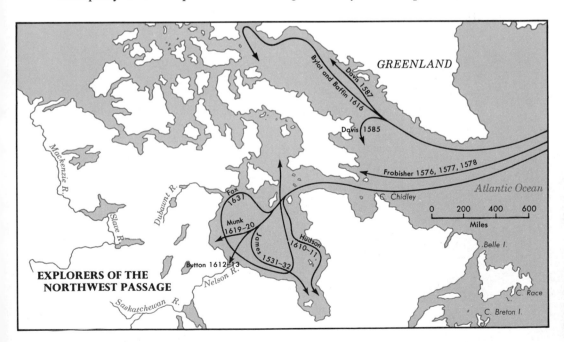

EXPLORERS OF THE
NORTHWEST PASSAGE

coveries, but his only achievement was to claim Newfoundland in 1583, prior to being lost at sea on the way home. Working for the Dutch East India Company, Henry Hudson explored the Hudson River in 1609 as far as the site of Albany. In the next year he did discover the passage through Hudson Strait to Hudson and James bays, where he wintered in 1610-11 before he was set adrift by his mutinous crew on the homeward journey.

Farther south Sir Walter Raleigh explored the North Carolina coast in 1584 and founded a settlement on Roanoke Island in the following year. Threatened by the Indians and Spaniards, this colony was abandoned, and two later English settlements in the same area in 1586 and 1587 mysteriously disappeared. The turn of the century, however, saw a rash of new settlement attempts along the Atlantic seaboard – at Jamestown, Virginia, in 1606; in Maine, 1607; and at Plymouth, Massachusetts, in 1620, by the *Mayflower* pilgrims. At the same time France showed renewed interest in the New World because the accession of Henry IV, a Protestant turned Roman Catholic, put an end to a generation of religious strife.

Although there had been no further attempts to colonize Canada, fishermen visited Newfoundland and the St. Lawrence River annually. Gilbert met thirty-six ships in St. John's harbour in 1579, and it was known that England, France, and Spain each had some 150 ships engaged in the fisheries. Fishermen from these countries took home furs purchased from the Indians, but no exact date can be fixed for the beginning of the fur trade. Furs were used in Europe for trimming expensive garments, but the most valuable fur was the beaver pelts that provided the raw material for the fine and expensive felt used in the hats worn by gentlemen. A beaver skin bought from the Indians for two biscuits or two knives returned a handsome profit when sold in France.

The shift of the economic pattern from fishing to a separate trade in furs introduced the chartered trading company. European monarchs generously granted monopoly privileges to their court favourites or sold them

Jens Munk's representation of his winter on Hudson Bay, 1619-20. Munk, probably a Dane, commanded two vessels sent by Christian IV of Denmark to discover the North-West Passage. The expedition of sixty-five men landed at the site of present-day Churchill in September 1619, where they wintered. At first all went well, but after Christmas scurvy struck, and by the following spring only Munk and two others remained alive. In the smaller ship the three sailed for Norway in July, reaching there in September.

As part of the ornamental scroll or design (called the cartouche) surrounding the title of his map, an early cartographer would often engrave a pictorial description relating to the map. In the cartouche on his map of Newfoundland and New France published in 1662, John Blaeu (pronounced Blow) the Dutch cartographer (1596-1673) depicted the seamen with their equipment and the fish that, next to furs, were the most important interests in North America to seventeenth-century Europeans.

to ambitious merchants. Rival kings chartered companies to exploit the same regions, but in practice anyone else's "rights" were ignored, since the only recognized international law was the law of superior strength. The merchants were left to deal with rivals by their own means. Still, to support their country's claims, kings usually required the companies to colonize as well as to trade. It was financially unrewarding to settle people in America – as Roberval had learned to his sorrow – so, whenever possible, chartered companies avoided their legal obligation to colonize.

After a futile attempt by the Marquis de Roche to found a settlement on desolate Sable Island off Nova Scotia, the next French venture into Canada was organized by Pierre Chauvin, a Huguenot (Protestant) fishing merchant. Chauvin was granted a monopoly of the fur trade on the St. Lawrence, and in 1600, with François Gravé du Pont (also called Pont-Gravé and Du Pont-Gravé) and Pierre du Gua, Sieur de Monts, established a post at Tadoussac, the main point of contact with the Indians on the river. This settlement failed and was abandoned in 1601. When other French merchants complained about Chauvin's monopoly, the King ordered Aymar de Chastes, governor of Dieppe, to draw up regulations for the trade. In 1603 de Chastes organized a fact-finding expedition, led by Gravé du Pont and with de Chastes' friend, Captain Samuel Champlain, as cartographer.

Champlain, a native of the port of Brouages, had already visited the Spanish empire in America before his journey to the St. Lawrence in 1603. At Tadoussac he met the Algonquins, who had long been engaged in a war with the Iroquois Five Nations who lived south of Lake Ontario. The French government had decided to support the Algonquins in that war because they controlled the fish and furs of the St. Lawrence Valley. This alliance inevitably shaped the course of French expansion in North America for the next century and a half, because the Iroquois allied themselves to France's enemies.

Champlain's exploratory trip carried him to Montreal, with short excursions up the Saguenay and Richelieu rivers. From the Indians there he learned of the lake and river route from the Richelieu that supposedly led to Florida. From the same source he also heard of the Great Lakes, Niagara Falls, and copper mines to the west. Champlain was now convinced that the South Sea was only a thousand miles beyond Montreal and that the soil, minerals, and furs of Canada made French colonization of that intervening land highly desirable.

While Champlain was in Canada, de Chastes died and Henry IV gave a ten-year monopoly of the fur trade to the Sieur de Monts, who promised to explore and settle the land and to Christianize the Indians. De Monts employed experienced sailors, including Champlain, and recruited 120 skilled workers for his colony, but no farmers. The St. Lawrence, however, was not the site of these renewed settlement attempts. Instead, de Monts decided to settle on the Atlantic coast and, after exploring the Bay of Fundy in search of a rumoured copper mine, he formed a colony on an island in the St. Croix River. Champlain continued the exploration along the coast of Maine before returning to the island. During the following winter nearly half the colonists died of scurvy, and by 1605 de Monts decided to move the settlement. The party reached Cape Cod, but after trouble with the numerous Indians they returned to Nova Scotia's sheltered Annapolis Basin and built Port Royal.

During the mild winter of 1605-06, Champlain completed charts of his explorations. Jean de Biencourt, Sieur de Poutrincourt, who had been granted land at Port Royal, arrived in 1606 with more settlers, including

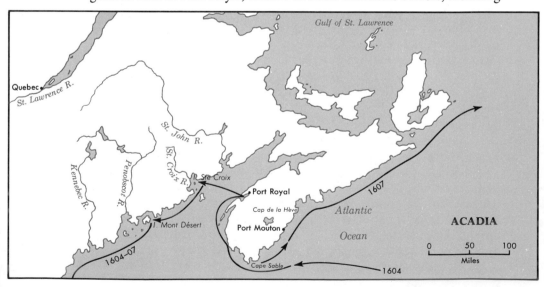

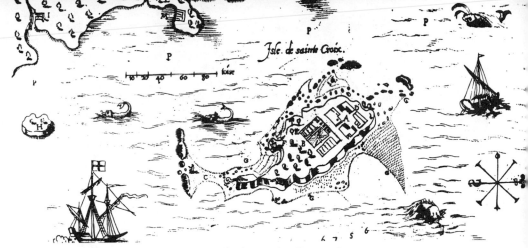

An early map showing Isle Ste. Croix. The letter A indicates the habitation; B, the garden; C, the little island on which the cannon were mounted; G, rocks; I (on the mainland) the place where the Sieur de Monts built a water mill.

Louis Hébert, the druggist who became Canada's first farmer, and Marc Lescarbot, a lawyer who wrote the first history of Canada. To break the monotony of life in the small settlement, Champlain established the Order of Good Cheer, which gave banquets and entertainment. In 1607 news reached the colony that de Monts' monopoly had been cancelled. To mark the colonists' departure for home, Lescarbot composed a poem, "Farewell to New France". Later, in 1610, Poutrincourt resettled his land, and the Jesuit missionary Biard baptized the local Indian chief and all his family. The conversion of these Indians to Christianity had been one of Champlain's ambitions during his years in Acadia.

Champlain's future, however, was to be in the St. Lawrence Valley, the land he had first admired. When de Monts managed to have his monopoly renewed for one year, he returned to North America in 1608 with Champlain as his lieutenant and founded a new settlement at Quebec. De Monts was interested only in the profitable fur trade – Champlain dreamed of colonizing a new France. The two ideals, profit and settlement, seemed doomed to defeat each other.

The Father of New France

At the new post of Quebec, Champlain and his twenty-three men began a permanent settlement by building a wooden house called the "Habitation". By the spring of 1609 only eight had survived the dread scurvy, but de Monts decided to maintain the settlement. Two threats had therefore to be removed: the competition from unlicensed European traders; and the Iroquois tribes, whose war against the friendly Algonquins endangered both Quebec and the trade. To meet these threats Champlain proposed to obtain the furs closer to their source, and to aid all enemies

A Logemens des artifans.
B Plate forme où eftoit le ca-
   non.
C Le magafin.
D Logement du fieur de Pont-
   graué & Champlain.
E La forge.

F Paliffade de pieux.
G Le four.
H La cuifine.
O Petite maifonnette où l'on
   retiroit les vtanfiles de nos
   barques ; que depuis le
   fieur de Poitrincourt fit

rebaftir, & y logea le fieur
Boulay quand le fieur du
Pont s'en reuint en France.
P (1) La porte de l'abitation.
Q (2) Le cemetiere.
R (3) La riuiere.

(1) Cette lettre manque dans le dessin ; mais la porte est bien reconnaissable tant par sa figure que par l'avenue qui y aboutit. — (2) K, dans le dessin. — (3) L, dans le dessin.

The "Abitasion du Port Royal", from the "Oeuvres de
Champlain . . ." edited by the abbé Laverdière in 1870.
The two-line explanation reads as follows: (1) This
letter is missing in the drawing; but the door is as
recognizable by its appearance as by the passageway
that leads to it. – (2) K, in the drawing. –
(3) L, in the sketch.

The rebuilt Port Royal Habitation
is an exact replica in detail and size
of the original buildings.

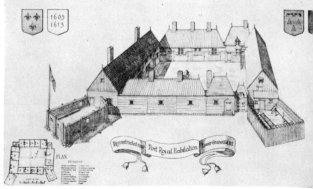

Plan for the reconstruction in 1939 of the Port Royal
Habitation at Lower Granville, a short distance from the
original site.

of the allied Five Nations of the Iroquois. In the summer of 1609 he met emissaries of another Iroquoian tribe, the Hurons, who also sought his help against the Iroquois confederacy.

The Hurons, living between the Great Lakes and the Ottawa River, controlled the two main fur trade routes from the interior. From their profitable position of middlemen between the French and the more westerly tribes, they were rapidly building a lucrative trading empire. But the Iroquois now coveted this position of their relatives the Hurons, and revived their traditional war against them with even greater ferocity. To protect the French interests Champlain was forced to use French power against the Iroquois. In 1609 he and two other Frenchmen joined a Huron war party on the Richelieu River and journeyed with them to Ticonderoga, where Champlain easily defeated the Iroquois with his arquebus. This action was the final French commitment to an alliance with the Hurons, who now invited Champlain to visit their territories. In addition to cementing relations with the Hurons, Champlain had, in the course of this journey to Ticonderoga, discovered Lake Champlain.

Although de Monts' monopoly had now lapsed and the fur trade was open to all, de Monts still sent Champlain back to Quebec in 1610. Again Champlain's "thunder tubes" helped to defeat the Iroquois on the Richelieu River, and after the cannibal victory feast Champlain persuaded his allies to take his young assistant, Etienne Brûlé, back to Huronia. But the free trade in furs of 1610 proved a disaster to everyone, and the problems of de Monts, a Huguenot, were compounded by the assassination of Henry IV. The new King of France was the boy Louis XIII – the real ruler was his mother, Marie de Medici, an enemy of all Huguenots. For

The defeat of the Iroquois at Lake Champlain, from Champlain's "Les Voyages de la Nouvelle France", published in 1632. Champlain stands alone between the two bands of warriors.

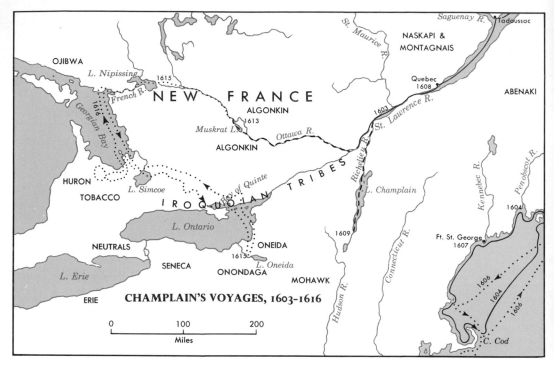

Saguenay R. Tadoussac
NASKAPI &
MONTAGNAIS
OJIBWA
St. Maurice R.
L. Nipissing 1615
French R.
NEW FRANCE
Quebec
1608
ABENAKI
Georgian Bay
ALGONKIN
1613
Muskrat L.
Ottawa R.
1603
St. Lawrence R.
ALGONKIN
Kennebec R.
Penobscot R.
HURON
TOBACCO
L. Simcoe
Bay of Quinte
IROQUOIAN TRIBES
Richelieu R.
L. Champlain
1604
IROQUOIAN
L. Ontario
1609
Ft. St. George
1607
NEUTRALS
ONEIDA
Connecticut R.
SENECA
1615
L. Oneida
L. Erie
ONONDAGA
MOHAWK
1606
ERIE
CHAMPLAIN'S VOYAGES, 1603-1616
Hudson R.
1604
1606
0   100   200
Miles
C. Cod

the moment, however, there was no change in French policy, and in 1611 Champlain was once more at his Habitation.

Champlain's Indian alliances and the work of his "young men" as interpreters were an advantage in the fur trade, but de Monts' company was not prospering against the strong competition. Champlain's solution was a combine of all traders to share the cost of the Habitation and to keep out any newcomers. Champlain was put in charge of the trade but he did not go to Quebec in 1612. Meanwhile, Nicolas de Vignau, one of the "young men", claimed that he had reached the northern sea by way of the Ottawa River and had seen evidence of a European settlement. Fired with dreams of greater trade and a route to the Orient, Champlain reached New France in 1613 and immediately went up the Ottawa River 100 miles beyond the site of Canada's future capital before Vignau admitted under Indian pressure that he had lied about his trip. Champlain's hopes were crushed and his summer wasted, but it is possible that Vignau had discovered the remains of Henry Hudson's expedition.

Back in France Champlain published an account of his voyages and planned two new ventures – a trip to Huronia and the great inland seas, and a mission to Christianize the Indians. For the missionary project he recruited four Recollet friars, but quarrels in the traders' combine kept them and Champlain from New France until 1615. In that year Champlain followed one of the missionaries west to Huronia only to discover that

Dutch traders at New York were encouraging the Iroquois to attack the French fur routes. With a handful of Frenchmen Champlain joined a Huron war party that followed the Trent River system south into Iroquoia – the Finger Lakes region of New York state. Their raid was a failure. French arquebuses were indecisive in close battle and the Hurons retired, forcing Champlain to spend the winter with them amongst the Tobacco (Petun) Indians south of Huronia.

When he reached France in 1616 Champlain found Canadian affairs enmeshed in court intrigue, with no attention being paid to colonizing New France. He tried vainly to awaken royal interest with reminders of the route to the Orient, and when he returned to New France in 1618 he found the colony stagnating. Merchants, greedy for profit, were ignoring their obligation to people New France because, in their opinion, colonizing would cost money, colonists would not help the fur trade, and Indians who turned to farming would be lost to trapping. And Huguenot traders were unwilling to promote Roman Catholic missions.

Champlain spent the winter in Paris, trying to gain support for New France, and when he returned to Quebec in 1620 drastic changes of policy were afoot. The combine's mismanagement was too obvious to be ignored any longer, and King Louis transferred the monopoly to Emery de Caen. Better times seemed at hand: the King sent direct financial aid, the Iroquois sued for peace, and more Recollet missionaries were arriving in Huronia. And the boundaries of the colony were being pushed westward – Brûlé had travelled as far as Lake Superior. Reassured by all these developments, Champlain spent the next four years in the colony.

New forces destined to alter the future of New France were now at work. In Europe the Recollets, finding their resources inadequate for the vast mission field, invited the rich and influential Society of Jesus to join them in New France. In 1625 Charles I, the new King of England, married Henrietta Maria, King Louis' sister, and even this remote event was to have disastrous results for New France, for England and France went to war over the non-payment of the Queen's dowry. When Champlain returned to Quebec in 1626, he found that de Caen had neglected the buildings and abused the settlers. To add to his troubles, the Montagnais Indians treacherously broke a peace signed in 1624 with the Iroquois, who now threatened the little settlement at Quebec. In June 1628 Champlain learned that some French traitors had guided six English ships to Tadoussac and that the enemy fleet was now approaching Quebec.

On 10 June a message from the English fleet informed Champlain that England and France were at war and that King Charles had commissioned a group of London merchants to seize Acadia and Quebec. The English leader was David Kirke, oldest of five sons of Gervase Kirke, an English-

Englands Honour re[v]ived.

By the valiant exploytes of Captaine *Kirke*, and his adherents, who with three
Ships, *viz.* the *Abigaile* Admirall, the *Charitie* vice Admirall, and the *Elizabeth* the
reare Admirall: did many admirable exploytes; as is exactly showne in the iusuing story.
To the Tune of King *Henries* going to *Bulloyne*.

Brave Souldiers of this island,
That fight by Sea, or by Land,
Attention give unto this gallant newes:
Which commeth to revive our hearts
Lately dul'd; to feele the smarts,
Of those true Christians whom our foes misuse.

Three Ships that lancht fo[r]th lately,
(Vessels tall and stately,)
Under the command of brave Captaine *Kirke*.
Hath had such auspitious chance,
Against our vaunting foes of France,
That all true English may applaude this worke.

Upon the second day of *May*,
One the coast of *Canaday*,
Our English vessels safely did arive;
And tooke a Ship of *Biskany*
Which did in the Harbour lie,
That by the trade of Fishing sought to thrive.

A Frenchman in her company,
They surprised valiantly,
And after that a vessel call'd the *Post*:
Our Englishmen in fight subdude,
Thus their good fortunes they persude,
And vext their Enemies on their owne coast.

I cannot tell you truely,
What past twixt then and *July*,
But in that month upon the thirteenth day:
Foure mighty and tall French Ships of Warre,
Came supposing us to scarre,
And so they did the cleane contrary way.

Sure never any mortall wight,
Beheld a fiercer Sea-fight,
Then was betweene those foure French Ships and ours:
They for full ten howers space,
Strove for Victory apace,
On either side the Sea men shewde their powers.

At la[st] (by Heavens assistance,)
After this long resistance,
Our English over came the French in fight:
And like brave Conquerors did surprise,
Both Ships and goods, in warlike wise,
Thus did they coole the Frenchmens courage quite.

And yet the (Lord be thanked,)
In all this bloody banquet,
Wherein so many Frenchmen were struke dead:
Not any one oth' English side,
In the furious Battell dyde,
This is a thing that may be Chronicled.

Neither was any of our men,
In the Skirmish wounded then,
But onely one who was a Trumpeter:
And he as I doe understand,
Was with a Bullet shot ith' hand,
Gods power then let's before our owne preferre.

For had not he us aided,
I needes must be perswaded,
We had not beene so merveilously saved:
As not one Englishman to dye,
In gaining such a Victory,
That may for after ages be ingraved.

*The ballad "Englands Honour revived" was first printed as
one of two poetical news sheets published in 1628, entitled
"News From Canada, 1628". The news sheets, consisting
of two ballads, form the earliest known separate publication
in English relating to Canada. A facsimile of one of the
ballads appears on the opposite page; a more legible copy of
the words is given above.*

...glands Honour rescued.

By the valiant exployts of Captaine *Kirke* and his adherents, who with three
Ships, *viz. the Abigale* Admirall, the *Charitie* vice Admirall, and the *Elizabeth* the
reare Admirall : did many admirable exploytes ; as is exactly showne in the insuing story.

To the Tune of King *Henries* going to *Bulloyne.*

BRaue Souldiers of this Iland,
That fight by Sea, or by Land,
  Attention giue vnto this gallant newes :
Which commeth to reuiue our hearts
Lately dul'd ; to feele the smart,
  Of those true Christian with our foes misuse.

Three Ships that lancht it absolutely,
(Vessels tall and statel ,)
  Vnder the command of braue Captaine *Kirke.*
Hath had such auspitions change,
Against our vaunting foes of France,
  That all true English may applaude this worke.

Vpon the second day of *May,*
One the coast of *Canaday,*
  Our English vessels safely did ariue ;
And tooke a Ship of *Biskay,*
Which did in the Harbour lie,
  That by the trade of Fishing sought to thrine.

A Frenchman in her company,
They surprised valiantly,
  And after that a vessell call'd the *Poss* :
Our Englishmen in sight subdue,
Thus their good fortunes they pursude,
  And vext their Enemies on their owne coast.

I cannot tell you truely,
What past twixt then and *July,*
  But in that month vpon the thirteenth day :
Foure mighty and tall French Ships of warre,
Came supposing vs to scarre,
  And so they did the cleane contrary way.

Sure neuer any mortall wight,
Beheld a fiercer Sea-fight,   (ours :
Then was betweene those foure French Ships and
They for full ten howers space,
Stroue for Victory apace,
  On either side the Sea men shewde their powers.

At last (by Heauens assistance,)
After this long resistance,
  Our English ouer came the French in sight :
And like braue Conquerers did surprise,
Both Ships and goods, in warlike wise,
  Thus did they coole the Frenchmen courage quite.

And yet the (Lord be thanked,)
In all this bloody banquet,
  Wherein so many Frenchmen were struke dead :
Not any one oth' English side,
In the furious Battell dyde,
  This is a thing that may be Chronicled.

Neither was any of our men,
In the Skirmish wounded then,
  But onely one who was a Trumpeter :
And be as I doe vnderstand,
Was with a Bullet shot ith' hand,
  Gods power then let's before our owne preferre.

For had not he vs aided,
I needes must be perswaded,
  We had not beene so merueilously saued :
As not one Englishman to dye,
In gaining such a Victory,
  That may for afuer ages be ingraued.

born merchant from Dieppe whom Champlain may have known. To Kirke's demand for the surrender of Quebec, Champlain gave a firm refusal. Kirke and his fleet left the St. Lawrence at once – privateering would be more profitable than fighting Champlain, and in any case one winter without aid from France would make Quebec an easy prize.

Kirke had barely departed when French sailors brought heartening news that the powerful Cardinal Richelieu had formed the Company of New France (also called the Company of One Hundred Associates) and that it had received a perpetual monopoly of the fur trade. The Company would send out 200 settlers per year and support three priests, and Protestants would be banished from the colony. Kirke, however, met the Company's fleet off the Gaspé and captured three ships in a fourteen-hour battle. Neither settlers nor supplies reached Quebec, and the colony was left to depend on its own resources for the coming winter. By the spring of 1629 starvation was threatening when David Kirke and his brothers reappeared. Champlain now had no choice but to surrender. On 20 July Louis Kirke hoisted the flag of England over Champlain's fort and fired a salute from the fort's guns. Champlain, his garrison, the missionaries, and all but five French families were carried off to England and later to France. When the Kirkes' ships bringing Champlain to London

Champlain's map of New France, published in 1632. It is based on his earlier map of 1616 but gives more details. The later map is in effect a pictorial summary of Champlain's explorations and cartographic knowledge of New France.

met the French relief force in the St. Lawrence, that force also surrendered. Quebec and the fur trade were firmly in the hands of the brothers
from Dieppe.

Neither Champlain nor the Kirkes could know that the war between
their countries had already ended, making the English seizure of Quebec
illegal. But Quebec was a valuable prize at the peace negotiations. The
Kirkes wanted compensation for their expenses, and King Charles wanted
the rest of his wife's dowry. When a treaty was finally signed in 1632,
Charles of England got the dowry and Louis of France got Quebec. The
Kirkes got nothing, but King Charles showed his gratitude by making
David Kirke governor of Newfoundland.

Once more the lily flag flew over Quebec, but life would never be the
same there after the first English conquest. Its buildings were ruined and
the Indians debauched. Brûlé had been killed by the Hurons, and Cardinal
Richelieu had given the Jesuits a religious monopoly in the colony by
barring the return of the Recollets. Almost from its founding the Company of One Hundred Associates was in financial trouble. Despite the
Company's losses at the hands of the Kirkes, Richelieu demanded that the
Company pay its debts. De Caen, who had regained the fur monopoly,
tried to recoup his losses by ignoring settlement, and Lauzon, the Com-

pany's intendant (manager) dishonestly acquired large estates in the colony
for his family. But despite these problems the colony was progressing.
Quebec's defences were rebuilt with stone, and a new post was opened at
Trois-Rivières. Champlain returned in 1633 and threw his full energy into
rebuilding the settlement. More Jesuits than ever went up to Huronia. In
Quebec, the Jesuits opened a boys' school, Ursuline nuns arrived to
teach the girls, and a hospital was built. A small but steady trickle of new
settlers began to arrive, many of them bringing livestock with them. The
Indian alliances were renewed and strengthened. Even the work of westward exploration was taken up again in 1634, when Jean Nicolet went to
Wisconsin – carrying an embroidered robe in case he met some Oriental
king.

In the midst of all these activities the colony of New France was entering the most crucial period of its history. The next quarter century would
be a time of severe testing. Perhaps it was an omen foreshadowing the
future problems of colonization, the fur trade, Indian relations, and
missions that Champlain died one-and-a-half years after returning to
Quebec. The indomitable explorer, faithful employee of the trading companies, and loyal subject of his king, the Father of New France died on
Christmas Day 1635. He was buried in the small chapel he had built in
gratitude for the recovery of the colony from England. French and
Hurons alike mourned his passing, and one Jesuit lamented the man "who
had done and suffered so much for New France, for the welfare of which
he seemed to have sacrificed all his means, yea, even his life".

Shadows Over Huronia

The Jesuit *Relations* (annual reports from each of the Jesuit provinces)
attracted much public attention in France to the prospects of the colony.
One direct result was the founding of Ville Marie (now Montreal) by a
company of religious men and women led by an experienced soldier,
Maisonneuve, with support from the Sulpician priests. As New France
developed from a fur trading outpost into a settled colony, the Jesuits
enforced a strict morality among the settlers, opposed the use of brandy
in the fur trade, began a college in Quebec, and sent missionaries to many
Indian tribes. In Huronia itself they built near Midland, Ontario, a combined farm, hospital, mill, smithy, and religious centre called Ste. Marie,
from which the priests went out to work in dozens of surrounding Huron
villages.

The very real threat of an Indian war still loomed on the horizon. Tribal
wars were common, but a new danger appeared when the rival Indian
tribes began to acquire firearms. Despite a Dutch prohibition of such

The reconstructed settlement of Ste. Marie, near Midland, Ontario.

sales, the Iroquois had obtained some arms from traders in the vicinity of Albany. Champlain had always opposed the sale of firearms to Indians unless they became Christians, but New France was such a good source of weapons that in 1641 the Iroquois threatened to destroy Trois-Rivières unless they were given French arms. Montmagny, the governor, drove the enemy away, but Champlain's peace of 1624 was certainly ended when the Iroquois struck at the Ottawa River fur trade route in 1641-2.

At this moment the small party that was to found Montreal arrived from France, but could not be dissuaded from their purpose by the Iroquois threat. A few short weeks after they had established Ville Marie, the Jesuit Isaac Jogues and two lay companions were captured on the Ottawa. Jogues later escaped to France with Dutch help, only to return to Canada and to a martyr's death. Iroquois attacks increased in frequency: in 1642 came the plunder of Fort Richelieu, which was being built at Sorel to prevent the Iroquois from using the Hudson River route as a warpath; in 1643 three Montreal settlers were murdered; Quebec suffered hit-and-run raids. The physical damage was slight, but the economic results were disastrous. The fur trade routes, the lifeline of New France, were cut for two years, and without the furs New France seemed doomed.

In answer to the settlers' pleas for help, 100 French soldiers were sent to New France. Small as this number was, peace returned for a time. Yet only a crushing defeat of the Iroquois could ensure the colony's future, and France refused to send more troops or to arm the Hurons because she was constantly at war in Europe. Facing bankruptcy, the Company lost its influence at court, as did the Jesuits when Richelieu died in 1642. As one solution for both the Company and the Jesuits, the fur monopoly was rented to a company formed by leading families in New France, the Company of Habitants. The next step was a peace reached with the Iroquois in 1645. For one year the fur trade worked fairly smoothly

A composite engraving from "Historiae Canadensis", published in Paris in 1664, showing the deaths of Father Isaac Jogues (left foreground) in October 1647 and Father Brébeuf and Father Lalemant (centre) in March 1649.

under the new conditions, then the Iroquois renewed the war by attacking the Hurons and murdering two French peace envoys. These attacks on the French and their Indian allies completely disrupted the fur trade operation during 1647.

The Hurons, however, were marked for total destruction. In the spring of 1649 large Iroquois raiding parties surprised and destroyed four villages in the heart of Huronia, and martyred two Jesuits, Brébeuf and Lalemant, with unspeakable tortures. The panic-stricken Hurons destroyed their own villages and fled to neighbouring tribes. The Jesuits burned Ste. Marie and followed their "children" in flight, but not before two more missionaries had died as martyrs. By 1650 Huronia was no more. The Hurons were scattered in small bands from Detroit to Quebec; their lands lay vacant for the next century and a half; the great Jesuit mission had disappeared forever; the Five Nations were undisputed masters of the interior fur trade.

The Dawn of a New Era

Unable to cope with the Iroquois raids, and unsupported from France, D'Ailleboust, the governor of Canada, sought an alliance with the New England colonies. The English settlers, however, feared that an alliance would invite attacks on them. So the guerrilla war continued, with attacks in 1651 on Montreal, Trois-Rivières, and Quebec. Five hundred warriors besieged Trois-Rivières in 1653. "No one is safe from the fury of the Iroquois," reported one nun, as the Ursulines considered leaving Canada. The very existence of New France was threatened, as much economically as militarily, for the value of the fur trade had been halved. Then suddenly the prospects of New France brightened once more. Jealousy among the Five Nations led each of the member tribes to make separate peace treaties with the French, and more than 100 male settlers arrived from France.

Peace and new settlers were not enough, however, to solve the colony's economic crisis. In 1653 not one pelt had been brought to Montreal, and although the trade revived in 1654, the Company of Habitants could not meet its obligations. The governor grabbed a large share of the fur trade profits for himself, the cost of living in New France jumped by 50 per cent, and France's Indian allies were still being attacked. On the credit side the colony was growing slowly as a few skilled workmen came each year, batches of girls arrived as brides for the bachelors, and new farms were laid out along the banks of the St. Lawrence.

By 1657 the One Hundred Associates were trying to escape the tangled affairs of New France by permitting the election to the colonial government of four local representatives to act as advisers only. This experiment soon ended, but another decision of 1657 permanently changed the course of New France's development. Several times the appointment of a bishop for New France had been suggested, but the actual choice had been partly delayed by the rivalry between the Jesuits and the Sulpicians. The Sulpician candidate, Father Gabriel de Queylus, was ultimately rejected by the young king, Louis XIV, in favour of François de Laval, whose sympathies lay with the Jesuits.

Before Laval arrived at Quebec in 1659, as apostolic vicar (missionary bishop) of Canada, the Jesuit-Sulpician clash broke out in public on both sides of the Atlantic. Queylus challenged the right of Jesuits to act as parish priests, and the Archbishop of Rouen tried to block Laval's consecration by claiming jurisdiction over the church in all French territories of the New World. The Jesuits looked on New France as one vast mission; the Sulpicians, as secular clergy, viewed it as an extension of Old France that needed parochial institutions to make it French. Two such strong-willed men as Queylus and Laval only intensified these pressures. Laval, however, had the full support of King Louis, and in 1661 Queylus was ordered out of the colony by the King himself. Soon Laval was quarrelling with the governor. In an age when social status was all-important, and when the business of church and state was intertwined, Laval demanded precedence over the governor, d'Argenson.

D'Argenson, however, had other worries than the prestige-conscious bishop. Having defeated several rival tribes, the Iroquois now saw no reason to maintain peace with the French, and in 1660 launched a 900-man army against Montreal. Unaware of the size of the enemy force on the Ottawa River, Dollard des Ormeaux, with sixteen other Montrealers and some forty Indians, set out in May to ambush the Iroquois at the Long Sault near present-day Hawkesbury. Instead, Dollard and his companions found themselves surrounded by hundreds of enemy warriors. For eight days they held off the attacking hordes, but in the end the surviving five Frenchmen were captured and killed. Montreal was warned of its danger by a few Hurons who escaped. It prepared for an attack, and the

Iroquois, having lost the advantage of surprise, abandoned their invasion of the colony. The trade routes were open, and sixty canoes brought 100 tons of furs to Montreal.

No one doubted that the Iroquois would return – and they did, in 1662, the bloodiest year in New France's struggle for survival. From Montreal to Tadoussac the war parties raided, killing sixty-eight men of the colony's less than 2,000 population. Then the tide of fortune changed again. Half the Iroquois tribes offered peace, but the decisive influence was a small-pox epidemic that decimated their numbers.

New France seemed to stagger from Iroquois war to Iroquois war, from financial crisis to financial crisis. D'Argenson, Davagour (the new governor), and Pierre Boucher, a leading settler, had each appealed in person to the young King Louis XIV to save New France from the Indian enemy outside and the unscrupulous operations by the Company of Habitants inside. Louis had assumed personal control of France's government in 1661 at the age of eighteen, with the intention of making France great. Beside him stood Jean-Baptiste Colbert, the economic genius who intended to make France rich. Both men agreed that Canada could contribute to France's prestige and France's wealth: the colony must therefore not be abandoned – it should and would receive the support too long denied it. The first step must be to end the inefficient system of company rule by making Canada a French province under direct royal control. The second step would be to provide enough soldiers to protect the colony. The third was to be the intensive colonization of Canada and the development of her economy.

In March 1663 Louis XIV announced that he had taken over control from the One Hundred Associates, and on 18 September royal government of the colony by an appointed Sovereign Council became effective. The golden age of New France was dawning.

Indians from Champlain's "Les Voyages de la Nouvelle France" (1632). Left: Pounding corn. Right: Algonquin warrior.

HISTORY FROM THE SOURCES

Champlain's Indian Alliances – Did They Cause
the Iroquois Wars?

*What was the origin of the famous war between the Hurons and their
relatives, the Five Nations' confederacy of the Iroquois? Was Champlain's alliance with the Hurons the real cause of the Iroquois' hatred
of the French? Cadwallader Colden, a scholar and scientist who became
lieutenant-governor of New York in 1761 and was regarded in his day
as the best-informed man on the affairs of the British colonies, wrote
his history of the Five Nations to explain the role of the Iroquois in
the French-English struggle for North America.*

The French settled at Canada in the Year 1603, six Years before
the Dutch possessed themselves of New-Netherlands, now called
New-York, and found the Five Nations at War with the Adirondacks, which, they tell us, was occasioned in the following Manner. . . . it once happened, that the Game failed the Adirondacks,
which made them desire some of the young Men of the Five Nations
to assist them in Hunting. These young Men soon became much
more expert in Hunting, and able to endure Fatigues, than the
Adirondacks expected or desired; in short, they became jealous of
them, and, one Night, murdered all the young Men they had with
them. The Five Nations complained to the Chiefs of the Adirondacks, of the Inhumanity of this Action; but they contented themselves with blaming the Murderers, and ordered them to make some
small Presents to the Relations of the murdered Persons, without
being apprehensive of the Resentment of the Five Nations; for they
looked upon them, as Men not capable of taking any great Revenge.

This however provoked the Five Nations to that Degree, that they
soon resolved, by some Means, to be revenged; and the Adirondacks
being informed of their Designs, thought to prevent them, by reducing them with Force to their Obedience.

The Five Nations then lived near where Mont Real now stands;
they defended themselves at first but faintly against the vigorous
Attacks of the Adirondacks, and were forced to leave their own
Country, and fly to the Banks of the Lakes where they live now. As
they were hitherto Losers by the War, it obliged them to apply
themselves to the Exercise of Arms, in which they became daily
more and more expert.

Cadwallader Colden, *The History of the Five Indian Nations
of Canada,* 2 v. (Toronto, 1903?), Vol. I, pp. 2-3.

Champlain's fateful trip to Ticonderoga with a Huron war party in 1609 was a result of the alliance he had just made with the enemies of the Iroquois. Does this account, written by Champlain about the forming of the alliance, explain anything about his own motives? Note the Indian's remark that Champlain and Gravé du Pont had agreed to an alliance in 1608. Why would the French have made such a promise?

We made a reconnoissance, and found that they were tribes of savages, called Ochateguins and Algonquins, on their way to Quebec, to assist us in exploring the territory of the Iroquois, with whom they are in deadly hostility, sparing nothing belonging to their enemies.

*   *   *   *   *

The next day, the two chiefs came to see me, when they remained some time without saying a word, meditating and smoking all the while. After due reflection, they began to harangue in a loud voice all their companions who were on the bank of the river, with their arms in their hands, and listening very attentively to what their chiefs said to them, which was as follows: that nearly ten moons ago, according to their mode of reckoning, the son of Yroquet had seen me, and that I had given him a good reception, and declared that Pont Gravé and I desired to assist them against their enemies, with whom they had for a long time been at warfare, on account of many cruel acts committed by them against their tribe, under color of friendship; that, having ever since longed for vengeance, they had solicited all the savages, whom I saw on the bank of the river, to come and make an alliance with us, and that their never having seen Christians also impelled them to come and visit us; that I should do with them and their companions as I wished; that they had no children with them, but men versed in war and full of courage, acquainted with the country and rivers in the land of the Iroquois; that now they entreated me to return to our settlement, that they might see our houses, and that, after three days, we should all together come back to engage in the war; that, as a token of firm friendship and joy, I should have muskets and arquebuses fired, at which they would be greatly pleased. This I did, when they uttered great cries of astonishment, especially those who had never heard nor seen the like.

After hearing them, I replied that, if they desired, I should be very glad to return to our settlement, to gratify them still more; and that they might conclude that I had no other purpose than to engage in the war, since we carried with us nothing but arms, and not merchandise for barter, as they had been given to understand; and that my only desire was to fulfil what I had promised them. . . .

W. L. Grant, ed., *Voyages of Samuel de Champlain, 1604-1618*
(New York, 1907; reprinted 1959), pp. 151-2.

When Quebec and Canada were restored to France in 1632 by the Kirke brothers, Champlain hastened to renew his Indian alliances the following year, promising to build a post at Trois-Rivières and to promote the settlement of the Indians in villages by encouraging French-Indian marriages. Father Paul Le Jeune, superior of the Jesuit missions in New France, recorded the following speeches of Champlain and the Indian leader at the renewal of their alliance. What light does this account throw on the motives of each party regarding the alliance?

On the 24th of May, eighteen canoes of Savages having descended to Kebec, sieur de Champlain, suspecting that they might go on to the English, who had three vessels at Tadoussac and a bark far up the river, went into the Cabins of these Savages, and made to them a very suitable address . . . He said to them . . . that the French had always loved and defended them, that he had assisted them in person in their wars; that he had greatly cherished the Father of the Captain to whom he was talking, who was killed at his side in a battle where he himself was wounded by an arrow; that he was a man of his word, and that, notwithstanding the discomforts of the sea voyage, he had returned to see them again, as if they were his brothers; as they had expressed a wish that a French settlement should be made in their country, to defend them against the incursions of their enemies, he contemplated granting this desire, and it would already have been granted but for the obstacles created by the English; he was, moreover, then engaged in repairing the ruins that these wicked guests had left behind them; that he would not fail to satisfy them all as soon as he attended to the more urgent affairs; that the Fathers (speaking of us), would remain among them and would instruct them as well as their children. Yet, notwithstanding the great obligations that they [the Savages] were under to the French, they had descended the river with the intention of going to see the thieves who came to pillage the French. He said they should consider well what they were doing; that these robbers were only birds of passage, while the French would remain in the country as it belonged to them.

* * * * *

[The Indian "Captain" begins his reply by referring to the proposed post at Trois-Rivières.]

"When thou shalt come up there with us thou wilt find a land better than this; thou wilt make, to begin with, a house like this to live in" (he indicated a little space with his hand); "that is to say, thou wilt make a fortress. Then thou wilt make another house like that," designating a large space, "and then we shall no longer be dogs who sleep outside, we shall go into that house." He meant to say an enclosed village. "Then we shall no longer be suspected of going to see those who do not love you. Thou wilt sow wheat; we shall do as thou dost, and we shall no longer go to seek our living in the woods; we shall no longer be wanderers and vagabonds.

"It was sieur de Caën, who believed that I had sent Beavers to the foreigners; I sent to those quarters a few Moose skins, not in trade, but to cut off the arms of our enemies. Thou knowest that the Hiroquois have long arms; if I had not cut them, we should have been taken by them long ago. I send presents to tribes who are their neighbours, to the end that they should not unite with them; it is not to offend the French, but to preserve ourselves.

"Thou sayest that we wish to go to the English; I will tell my men that they should not go there. I promise thee that neither I myself, nor they who have any sense, will do that; but if there is some young man who jumps over there without being seen, I shall not know what to do; thou knowest well that youth cannot be restrained. I shall forbid every one from going there. . . . Thou canst do everything, place thy boats in the way and capture the Beavers of those who attempt to go.

"Thou sayest that the Fathers will live among us, and will teach us. This good fortune will be for our children; we, who are already old, shall die ignorant. This blessing will not come as soon as we should like to have it.

". . . We do not want to go to the English; their Captain wanted to make an alliance with me and take me for his brother, and I did not desire it; I withdrew, saying that he was too great a Captain. I bethought myself well of a word that thou hadst said to us, that thou wouldst return; therefore I always awaited thee. Thou hast been truthful, thou wilt still be so in coming to see us in our country. I have but one fear; it is that in the association of the French with our people, some one may be killed, then we would be lost . . ."

This is about the answer of this Savage, who astonished our French people. They told me . . . that he won the hearts of all who looked at him, though they did not understand him.

The conclusion was that sieur de Champlain said to them: "When that great house shall be built, then our young men will marry your daughters, and we shall be one people." They began to laugh, answering: "Thou always sayest something cheering to rejoice us. If that should happen, we would be very happy."

R. G. Thwaites, ed., *The Jesuit Relations and Allied Documents,*
72 v. (Cleveland, 1896-1901), Vol. V, pp. 203, 205,
207, 209, 211.

FURTHER READING

Lanctot, Gustave, *A History of Canada*, Vol. 1 (Toronto: Clarke, Irwin, 1963). A thorough study of New France by a noted Canadian historian, covering the period to 1663.

Kinietz, W. Vernon, *The Indians of the Western Great Lakes, 1615-1760* (Ann Arbor: University of Michigan Press, 1965)★. A comprehensive description of the Indian tribes and their ways of life.

Bishop, Morris, *Champlain: The Life of Fortitude* (Toronto: McClelland & Stewart, 1963)★. The most reliable and readable of several biographies of Champlain.

Cranston, J. H., *Etienne Brulé, Immortal Scoundrel* (Toronto: Ryerson, 1949). A popular biography of this controversial figure.

Walsh, H. H., *The Church in the French Era*, Vol. 1 of "A History of the Christian Church in Canada" (Toronto: Ryerson, 1966). A modern and definitive work on the religious life of New France.

Mealing, S. R., ed. *The Jesuit Relations and Allied Documents* (Toronto: McCelland & Stewart, 1963)★. A selection from one of the most important sources for the history of New France.

F. X. Talbot, *Saint Among the Hurons* (New York: Doubleday, 1956)★. A highly readable biography of the Jesuit martyr, Jean de Brébeuf.

Ragueneau, Paul, *Shadows Over Huronia* (The Martyrs' Shrine, Midland, 1965?)★. Account of the end of the Huron mission, drawn from the letters of Father Ragueneau, superior of the Jesuits in Canada from 1650-3.

Innis, H. A., *The Fur Trade in Canada* (Toronto: University of Toronto Press, 1964)★. A revised edition of the 1930 classic, which devotes one chapter to the fur trade before the British Conquest.

Hunt, George T., *The Wars of the Iroquois: A Study in Intertribal Trade Relations* (Madison: University of Wisconsin Press, 1967)★. A definitive study of the important role played by the fur trade as a cause of Indian and European warfare in colonial America.

5
Royal New France

The New Constitution

The decision of Louis XIV to assume personal direction of his kingdom was one aspect of his scheme to make France once more the powerful state she had been before the long wars of religion sapped her strength at home and abroad. In his campaign to re-establish the glory of France, Louis had the power and Jean-Baptiste Colbert had the plan. Colbert, a middle-aged business man, was typical of the dynamic new class of lay experts who were replacing churchmen as the civil servants of the nations of western Europe. The task of Colbert, the efficiency expert, was to impose order on the chaotic finances and outmoded administration of a potentially strong country too long torn by intrigues and rebellions, and crippled by the self-interest of privileged aristocratic classes who paid no taxes and by wasteful institutions such as the numerous honorary government posts. The first road to French power, and hence to French glory, lay through increased trade. This expansion would be achieved by making the French economy self-sufficient through selling as much as possible to other nations while buying in return only absolute necessities. The second road lay through aggressive expansion – by war or negotiation – both inside and outside Europe. When Louis turned into this second road, he set

The city of Quebec in 1722, from La Potherie's "Histoire de L'Amérique Septentrionale" (1722) published in Paris.

France on her way to the loss of her empire and eventual revolution at home.

Louis' decision to assume direct royal control over New France had grown out of the pleas of the settlers for protection and the obvious failure of the chartered companies to promote settlement. Colbert's plans for New France were based on information provided by Bishop Laval and Pierre Boucher, the governor of Trois-Rivières who had come to Canada as a domestic servant. Boucher emphasized New France's need for immediate military and financial assistance from the Crown and more settlers from France if the colony was to survive and if its resources were to be used for the greater glory of France. His appeal struck a respondent chord with Louis and Colbert – New France, they decided, must be saved and expanded. The changes which they proceeded to make shaped the colony's development for the next century. Details became altered in the course of those hundred years, but the essential institutions remained intact because they served their purpose well and because the pace of change was slower in that pre-industrial age than it is today.

The first step in establishing royal New France in 1663 was the proclamation of a new constitution modelled on the provincial governments of Old France. A governor, the bishop, five councillors selected by them, and an attorney general made up the Sovereign Council, which exercised only such powers as were delegated to it by the authority of the Crown. Two years later an intendant was added to this body. The powers and duties of the Council included ratifying the king's decrees, sitting as an appeal court and, under royal supervision, regulating most aspects of life in the colony. The connecting link between the absolutist king and his various colonies was the minister of marine, who received from the governors reports that served as a basis for policy-making by the king and his advisers. In his own name the king sent general directions to the colonial officials, while the minister added instructions in detail. Day-to-day operations were carried on by civil servants, but Louis XIV, especially during the early years of his reign, took a personal interest in colonial affairs and personally decided on questions of great importance, such as Indian relations.

One unavoidable problem in governing Canada was the long period, sometimes as much as a year, required to obtain decisions from the distant mother country. Frequently an official in the colony had to take immediate action on his own initiative, a procedure recognized and accepted in France, subject to review, and if necessary repudiated by the king and his councillors. Fortunately such issues seldom arose in the history of New France, since the scope of government activity was much more limited and uncomplicated in the colonial period.

The most important member of government in New France was the governor, who was the representative of the Crown, and responsible for defence, Indian affairs, and relations with neighbouring English colonies, but also for the general conduct of all other officials. Next in importance to the governor was the intendant, whose duties in a French province or colony were actually much wider than the governor's. The main function of the intendant was to plan, promote, and supervise every aspect of the economic growth of the colony, in close co-operation with the minister. The governor was commander of all troops, but it was the intendant's job to arrange for feeding, clothing, arming, transporting, and housing the soldiers, and for building and maintaining fortifications. Although the slight overlapping of their powers occasionally caused conflict if both the governor and intendant were strong-willed and ambitious, this division of labour generally worked well and was especially effective in emergencies such as war.

The third important personage in the colony was the bishop, who had both religious and civil duties. As the senior churchman, the bishop was responsible to Rome for the work of the church, but as a member of Council he was also part of the royal government. Although bishops were appointed by the pope, traditionally the kings of France nominated them and received an oath of allegiance from them, thus creating the strong possibility of a conflict of loyalty in this church-state relation. Those who supported the pope's claim to sole authority over the church were known as ultramontanes; defenders of the ecclesiastical jurisdiction of the French monarchy were called Gallicans. At first Bishop Laval was allowed virtually a free hand in selecting the Sovereign Council, but when he clashed

The Saint-Gabriel farmhouse is on land purchased by Mother Bourgeoys of the Black Nunnery (or Convent of the Congregation of Notre-Dame) which she founded in 1659. The original wooden farmhouse on the site was destroyed by fire, but in 1698 it was replaced by this stone house which still stands. The side wings were added in 1726 and 1728.

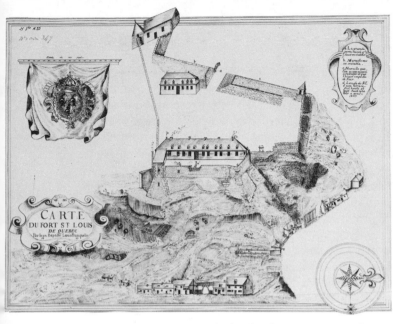

Plan of Fort St. Louis, residence of the governors of New France, drawn by Jean Baptiste Louis Franquelin in 1683. Franquelin, a French geographer, visited New France several times towards the end of the seventeenth century, and prepared many of the early maps and plans of the colony.

with the governor over seniority in the government he was relieved of that power in 1665. This event marked the beginning of the decline of church influence in the government of New France — henceforth Laval and his successors were progressively excluded from civil affairs as the governors and intendants obeyed Louis' order to control the church in the interests of Gallicanism.

A second shift in power within the Council developed as its chairman, the intendant, gradually assumed more authority than the governor who was Council's president. In 1703 the governing body was renamed the Superior Council and its membership increased to twelve. Council's contacts with the colonists were through the local captains of militia, the prominent and respected people in each parish appointed by order of Louis XIV in 1669 to command the militia, to communicate government decrees to the populace, to oversee the *corvée* (statutory labour) on roads and bridges, and to be the eyes, ears, and voice of the governor and intendant.

Like the councillors, the captains of militia were chosen because of their knowledge of the colony's conditions, but for a brief time New France did have a kind of popular representative called syndics. As early as 1647 the king had authorized the election of two syndics each from Quebec, Trois-Rivières, and Montreal. These syndics could speak in council but had no vote. No syndics were elected after 1674, and instead the intendants occasionally called assemblies of the residents to get their opinions on questions affecting their interests. The syndics and irregular assemblies were the nearest approach to representative government that Canada knew before the British Conquest, but it must be remembered that the government of the colony was modelled on the common European practices of that day when the idea of democracy was not popular.

Most monarchs had a very real sense of their responsibility as "father" of their subjects, and royal policies for New France were probably genuinely intended to promote the welfare of the colonists, who freely acknowledged the benefits they received from the paternalism and protection of the mother country. Only occasionally did the colonists find fault with government policies, and then they displayed a remarkable degree of independence and initiative.

Although the problems of Canada had at last attracted the attention of the French government, Acadia continued to be largely ignored after 1663, just as it had been since the collapse of Poutrincourt's first settlement and mission in 1613 when ships from Virginia destroyed the tiny settlements at Penobscot, Maine, and at Port Royal. Port Royal barely survived as a fur-trading post under Poutrincourt's son, Charles de Biencourt, and his lieutenant, Charles Latour, who claimed Port Royal seigneury for himself when Biencourt died in 1624. From 1629 to 1632 Port Royal was occupied by 100 Scottish settlers sent out by David Kirke's associate, Sir William Alexander, Earl of Stirling, to whom King James I had granted Acadia under the name of Nova Scotia. When Acadia was restored to France, along with Canada, Cardinal Richelieu organized a trading company for the area and made his cousin, Isaac de Razilly, governor. Latour resented this intrusion into what he considered his private domain, and his feud with Razilly's successor, the Sieur d'Aulnay, climaxed in 1645 when d'Aulnay captured Latour's fort on the St. John River and hanged most of Latour's men.

After d'Aulnay died, Latour reappeared in Acadia and aided the English and New England forces that occupied the territory from 1654-67, when it was returned to France by the Treaty of Breda. Foreseeing this development, Colbert had ordered the French settlers not to leave Acadia, and when the first census of the area was taken in 1671, 320 settlers were reported. Forty years later Acadia's population had risen to 1,500 as a result of immigration and a high birth rate. A number of seigneuries, most of them bordering on the Bay of Fundy, had been created in those intervening years. After Port Royal the main areas of settlement were around Minas Basin and Beaubassin (Cumberland Basin), but in each settlement the life of the Acadians depended on a largely self-sufficient agricultural economy, with fishing as a part-time occupation. As a mission of the diocese of Quebec, Acadia received a trickle of priests who served as spiritual and political guides, as teachers, and as judges of local disputes in the scattered communities. But the region remained so relatively isolated from both France and Canada that in the space of two or three generations after the Treaty of Breda a distinctive culture and an awareness of their own separate identity had appeared among the people called Acadians.

Seigneurs and Habitants

The St. Lawrence – the "River of Canada" – was the "main street" of New France, joining the small colony to the mother country across the Atlantic and to the fur empire on the west. Along the fertile lowlands that fringe its waters developed the agricultural society which characterized French-Canadian life for over two centuries. The basic pattern of life was moulded within the framework of the seigneurial system, a form of land tenure based on European manorialism, but not, as is sometimes suggested, feudalism, which involved the granting of land to knights in return for military service. The seigneurial system produced a cohesive society of seigneurs (lords of the manors), and habitants (the seigneurs' tenants), through a system of reciprocal obligations well suited to the frontier need for communal help and protection. Some seigneuries already existed in 1663, but 300 more were granted before 1750.

Then as now, all land belonged ultimately to the Crown, which granted large tracts to prominent citizens or corporations, such as religious orders, on payment of one-fifth of the value of the land and on condition that the

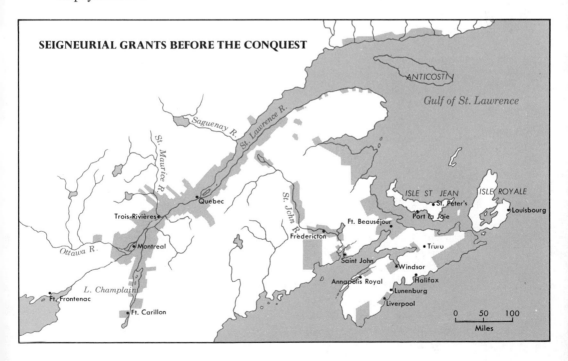

SEIGNEURIAL GRANTS BEFORE THE CONQUEST

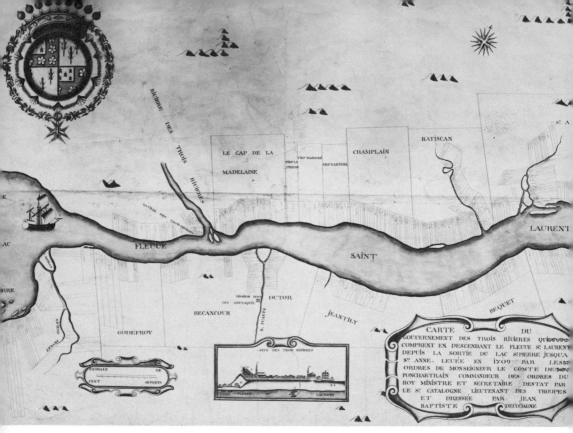

Strip farms under seigneurial tenure in the area of Trois-Rivières,
drawn in 1709 for Jérome de Pontchartrain, the Minister of Marine.

seigneurs found settlers for the land and provided them with a community
mill and bake oven, protection from enemies, justice in minor disputes,
and leadership in such projects as building a parish church. Failure on the
part of the seigneur to fulfil any of these obligations could lead to the
confiscation of his seigneury to the Crown. For their part the habitants
were obliged in return to make certain small payments to the seigneur.
The *cens et rentes* were nominal rents paid for the use of the land; *lods et
ventes* were a token payment on the transfer of lands from one tenant to
another; the *corvée* ordinarily amounted to three days per year of free
labour on the seigneur's own farm, usually at harvest time. In addition
each habitant paid to the seigneur one-fortieth of the flour ground at the
seigneurial mill (which the seigneur had built at his own expense) and a
small portion of fish caught, game killed, and wood cut on the seigneur's
property. All adult male settlers, seigneurs and habitants alike, were responsible for service in the militia, for a *corvée* on the king's roads and
bridges, and for payment of the tithe to the parish church.

Within each seigneury the individual farms of the habitants were
normally long strips of land, fronting on a river if possible. Such an ar-

rangement provided for easy communication, and the narrow farms also meant that the houses were close together for defence. This pattern of land holding gave the banks of the St. Lawrence the appearance of one long and continuous village, marked at intervals with the shiny tin spires of churches or the large imposing stone homes of the seigneurs. Every family lived close to its neighbours, close to the water, along the road that paralleled the shore. Both socially and geographically the seigneurial system was ideal in providing protection against Indian raids, neighbourly help with the heavier chores of farming, recreational activities such as the ever-popular country dances, and above all a sense of belonging to a community whose smallness of numbers was more than offset by its close-knit relationships. Significantly, when the government tried to alter this familiar pattern by creating centralized villages, the habitants resisted this change from their traditional pattern of river front strip farms.

Unlike the nobility of Old France, most of the seigneurs in Canada were neither powerful nor wealthy, and by 1763 most were former habitants who by hard work had saved enough to buy the privilege of a seigneury. They lived, ate, and dressed like their own habitants. The seigneurs' families did not attend the gilded court of Versailles – they were usually occupied in the same necessary manual labour in the fields as the habitants. Except for the public recognition of their social rank in such customs as occupying the best pew in church, there was little distinction between the average seigneurs and their tenants. The society of New France may have been a closed one, in the sense that economic opportunities were few and hence there was little motivation to break through the existing social strata, but life in New France was nonetheless incomparably better for the habitants than the marginal existence of their counterparts, the peasants of Old France. In Canada seigneurial rents were low,

Left: "French habitants or countrymen" from John Lambert's "Travels through Canada and the United States of North America in the years 1806, 1807 and 1808".
Below: Card money of New France. Actual playing cards, cut up, were first issued in 1685 and remained in use as currency until they were replaced by paper money called "ordonnances".

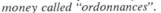

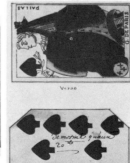

the food was good and, except for the Indian menace, the future secure. The net result was a farming community whose members were happy, sturdy, and self-reliant, and yet inclined to be easy-going, at times quarrelsome, and occasionally even defiant of the rules of state and church. The popular fondness, noted by visitors, for hunting, dancing, gambling, and drinking, and for engaging in law suits almost as a recreation, was proof that Canada had given her settlers both leisure time and unique (if human) traits unknown in the class-conscious and privilege-ridden societies of Europe.

The Institutions of the Faith

Next to the close ties of family, which were so strong in French Canada, the most important social cement was the Roman Catholic religion. From 1627 to the British Conquest no non-Catholic could legally enter the colony, although a few Huguenot merchants seem to have settled in Quebec despite the complaints of the bishops. Laval had come to Canada orginally as a missionary bishop, but in 1674 he was appointed bishop of Quebec with full control over religion for the whole French empire in North America. Conscious of the scattered nature of the settlements, he tried to organize his diocese as a vast mission, only to encounter opposition from the royal government in the person of Governor Frontenac, who demanded that the church be modelled on the rigid parish system so long established in Europe. To assist him in governing the church, Laval created a cathedral chapter at Quebec in 1684. Subsequently the diocese was divided into several "governments", each ruled by a grand vicar as the bishop's agent. Such an elaborate organization was needed because the successive bishops were frequently absent from the colony. Laval and his equally strong-willed successor, Saint-Vallier, spent only forty of their sixty-seven episcopal years in Canada. The third bishop never visited his

Trois-Rivières in 1685.

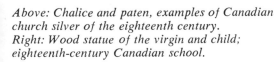

*Above: Chalice and paten, examples of Canadian
church silver of the eighteenth century.
Right: Wood statue of the virgin and child;
eighteenth-century Canadian school.*

diocese, a lack of interest symptomatic of the general decline of religious fervour in the eighteenth century.

As early as 1659 Laval had begun to organize the clergy and in 1663 he established his Seminary of Quebec, not only to educate young men for the priesthood but to serve as a retreat house, hospital, and place of retirement for all priests. In competition with the Quebec Seminary and sometimes at odds with the bishop was the Montreal Seminary operated by the Sulpicians, who became seigneurs of the whole island of Montreal in 1663 and who managed the several churches of that city as a single parish. Most of the senior churchmen, including the Sulpicians and the Jesuits, who still operated missions and the College of Quebec (the forerunner of Laval University), were Frenchmen from Old France. Most of the parish curés and the popular Recollet friars (who returned to New France in 1670) were, however, Canadian born, which created certain tensions within the church.

Of the several orders of nuns and brothers undertaking specialized religious work in New France, the Ursulines operated girls' schools in Quebec and Trois-Rivières, the Sisters of the Congregation taught boys and girls at various centres in the colony, two other groups of nuns maintained hospitals at Montreal and Quebec, and the Grey Nuns, organized by Marie D'Youville in 1737 for charitable work among Montreal's poor, took over the hospital for the aged and insane in that city. The custom of entrusting works of mercy and charity to various communities of the church formed the basis of one of the most enduring aspects of French-Canadian life.

The real heart of the religious life of the colony lay, however, in the parochial churches. A parish might include several seigneuries and

Left: Steeple built in 1696 and placed in its present position on the commemorative chapel at Sainte-Anne-de-Beaupré, Quebec, in 1878.
Above: Eighteenth-century Canadian steeplecock from a church near Montreal.

churches. Each parish was legally incorporated as part of the system of local government, but that system differed markedly from the parent model in France. For one thing every curé was removable – he had no permanent claim to his parish – because Bishop Laval had foreseen the need for flexibility in his huge diocese. For another, each parish was governed by a *fabrique* or corporation of three popularly elected church wardens, who controlled the physical and financial aspects of parish life and were responsible for establishing a free school in connection with the local church.

The beautiful historic churches, designed by local architects and ornamented in wood after the baroque style by generations of craftsmen, did not appear in any great numbers until the eighteenth century, when designers such as the Abbé Conefroy and master carvers like the Levasseur family began their artistic work. When Bishop Saint-Vallier made a pastoral tour in 1685, he found only four stone churches – the rest were wooden, in bad repair, and usually lacked even the essential furnishings for religious services. Nevertheless, from a very early date the individual curé held a position of great respect in the hearts of the habitants. To him they turned for advice on everything from family relations to farming practices. The curé was usually a Canadian, often born in that very parish,

A wing of Laval's Seminary in Quebec, built in 1678.

one of the people and yet a man educated beyond the level of any parishioners except doctors or lawyers.

The French Canadian was intensely devout, yet the church had constantly to fight against the inroads of very crude superstitions. The habitant faithfully attended church, and observed the holy days and fast days which, to the concern even of the church itself, filled almost half the calendar. But still the church and the curé found it necessary to condemn the too prevalent vices of excessive self-indulgence, extravagances of dress, vain displays of wealth, and an ingrained habit of challenging authority. When Bishop Laval attempted to double the tithe – previously one-twenty-sixth of the produce of the land – he met such determined grass-roots resistance that he was forced to accept the prevailing French-Canadian custom. Royal grants of land, such as the island of Montreal, and donations by pious individuals put the church in control of more than 25 per cent of the seigneurial territories, yet until the Conquest the church remained so short of funds that the royal government was forced to make substantial annual cash grants to the cause of religion in New France.

Like charitable works, education was the responsibility of the church, but because the schools depended on private initiative and funds no systematic organization or curriculum ever came into being. When farm chores and family interest permitted, children attended the parish school – if one existed. Reading, writing, the catechism, and good manners were the subjects taught at the elementary level. The only institution of higher education was the Jesuit college, where annually some 150 boys began a

In the old church at Rivière Ouelle, a Quebec parish founded in 1685, hangs a work painted in obedience to a vow – an example of "ex voto" art. The parish is the birthplace of the Rev. H. R. Casgrain, the nineteenth-century priest and historian, who in January 1860 wrote the story of the painting, a story which he explains he heard as a child from his mother.

In the days of seventeenth-century New France, a young officer, accompanied by his father, one soldier, and an Indian guide, set out one winter from Abenaki country to carry despatches to the governor. On the journey their guide was attacked and killed by an Iroquois, who in turn was killed by the officer. But without their guide the three men were stranded. Soon the two older ones died, although not before the young man's father had extracted a promise from his son that he would give a painting to the nearest church should he be saved. At the young man's prayers, the Virgin Mary appeared to him; the light from the vision attracted a passing missionary and some companions, and the young soldier was rescued. The painting expresses his gratitude for the miracle.

three-year course in the classical languages, rhetoric, and philosophy –
all subjects inherited from the medieval universities.

No printing press ever operated in New France, public libraries were
unknown and, to forestall the corrupting influence of free thinkers such as
Voltaire and the Encyclopedists, who ridiculed many practices of the
church, the church studiously censored all books entering the colony. The
power of religion was everywhere in New France, controlling or trying to
control everything from public behaviour to business relations. If this
authoritarianism stamped French Canadians with a submissive attitude
towards religion, it did at the same time contribute much to that social
cohesion and sense of identity which preserved the French-Canadian
outlook in the face of foreign conquest. The parish church, not the seigneury, was the real centre, visible and spiritual, of life in royal New
France.

Life in the Royal Colony

When New France became a royal colony in 1663, its population was
just over 3,000. A century later, at the Conquest, it had an estimated
70,000 settlers, but the neighbouring English colonies then contained a
million and a half people. During its first decades of royal government the
colony's population increased rapidly, thanks to the massive immigration
of several thousand Frenchmen. The new arrivals included a large proportion of craftsmen, many military recruits (such as the Carignan-Salières
regiment which settled along the Richelieu when disbanded), perhaps as
many as 3,500 *filles du roi* ("King's daughters"), who were eligible girls
sent from France as prospective brides for colonists, and finally a sprin-
kling of convicts banished to the colony. More immigrants came from
the Paris area than from any other part of France, but the dialect most
commonly spoken in French Canada was that of Normandy.

By 1700, when the population numbered 15,000, immigration had almost ceased; thereafter the increase was due almost entirely to a fantastically high birth rate of fifty-five per thousand, encouraged by government

*Left: Seventeenth-century Canadian wood table. Centre:
Silver tableware made in Quebec at the beginning of the
eighteenth century. Top right: Canadian silver dishes made
before 1750 and said to have been owned by Jacques Viger,
first mayor of Montreal, 1833-6. Bottom right: Thimble cup
(eighteenth century) made in Quebec.*

The French priest, Father Sébastien Rasles, was sent to Canada as a missionary in 1689. Put in charge of the Abenaki mission in Maine, he attempted to advise his flock in their political negotiations with the English in the thirteen colonies. He became the hated enemy of the English, and was killed in an Abenaki village by the New England militia in 1724.

subsidies and tax exemptions on early marriages and on families with ten or more children, and by fining parents of sons unwed over the age of twenty and of unmarried daughters over sixteen. In 1681 exactly half the population was under sixteen years of age. But if New France's birth rate was among the highest in the world, its death rate was also high—especially among infants, who were decimated by epidemics of childhood diseases for which contemporary medicine had no preventatives or cures. It is calculated that one of every four children died before its first birthday.

The bulk of New France's population consisted of self-sufficient farmers, who could build their own houses, mend their own shoes or harness, grow their own food, and spin and weave cloth for their own clothes. Skilled craftsmen were scarce and well paid – a carpenter received more than a Superior Councillor. The census of 1681 showed only fifty-six carpenters, thirty masons, four weavers, seven bakers, and thirty-four tailors among 372 tradesmen in a population of 10,000. The growth of industry was further retarded by the mother country's restrictions on any manufactures that would compete with French products. New France's role in the French empire was to produce raw materials – and furs were the only natural product for which there was a steady demand in France. Yet even the fur trade involved only a limited number of Canadians as traders, because the primary producers were the Indians.

Thus the major occupation in New France continued to be agriculture. Since bread was the staple food, wheat was the largest crop and peas next – few other grains were cultivated. Cattle were not raised extensively because available fodder was used for the several horses kept by each family as a mark of social prestige. Since pigs could live partly on garbage, they were the commonest farm animal. Fruits could be grown in Canada, as Louis Hébert (the first farmer) had shown in Champlain's time, but the habitant relied more on his vegetable garden to supplement the standard diet of bread and salted meats. Large quantities of fish, especially eels, were caught and preserved – the salt required for this was one of the colony's few imports. Conversely, New France had few exports except furs. Since Old France was agriculturally self-sufficient, the habitant had no incentive to grow more than he needed, and a crop failure meant that food had to be imported from the mother country. The agricultural revolution which introduced such scientific techniques as deep ploughing, crop rotation, the use of fertilizers, and selective breeding of livestock was still far in the future, so that by modern standards farming in New France followed inefficient and wasteful practices, such as the disposal of manure by heaping it on the river ice in winter.

In contrast to the simple life in the farming regions, city life in New France was almost as sophisticated as in Old France. Trois-Rivières remained little more than a village, but Quebec and Montreal grew to rival many European centres in the grandeur of their buildings and the complexity of their social organization. The presence of the church and of government offices accounted for such large and imposing structures as the governors' palaces, the convents, the cathedral church at Quebec, and the seminaries in the two cities. In Montreal substantial warehouses stored the furs and trade goods that formed the basis of New France's main commerce. Wealthy merchants in each city built attractive stone homes, surrounded by gardens and orchards. Government and military officers gave social tone to the balls and parties at Quebec, but Montreal, the commercial centre, was more noted for the wild orgies of drunken traders and Indians whenever the fur brigades arrived from the west. If the upper classes lived in a degree of comfort and artificial splendour in the two cities, a class of destitute people – the poor, the aged, and the orphans – could be found living in squalid quarters. The populations of Quebec and Montreal were about equal in 1666 – 550 people each – but a century later Quebec, the cultural and political centre of the colony, had 8,000 inhabitants while Montreal, the commercial hub, had less than 4,500. By the time of the Conquest one of every four Canadians was an urban resident.

In the market place, where townsman and farmer met to trade, the government's paternalistic control of the details of everyday life became apparent. The price, the quality, and the measurements of commodities such as bread, leather, flax, lumber, and firewood were strictly regulated by government decree and enforced by a host of minor officials. The government stipulated the number of butchers, innkeepers, or fur traders who might do business. Everywhere the citizen turned he was confronted by the royal authority which regulated the economic life of New France. Infractions of the civil law were tried in the seigneurial courts; more serious cases were tried in the lower courts, from which an appeal could be taken to the Superior Council presided over by the intendant. Other courts of New France were the *Officialité*, a church court controlled by

Left: Farmhouse of Julien Gendreau, built at the end of the eighteenth century, on the Ile d'Orléans. Above: Old farm typical of the Ile d'Orléans. The central chimney indicates that the house was probably built at two different periods. Across the St. Lawrence River is the basilica of Sainte-Anne-de-Beaupré.

the bishop, and the admiralty court instituted in 1717 to hear all cases affecting navigation. In criminal charges the accused was considered guilty until he could prove his innocence; he was immediately imprisoned and the use of torture, including the breaking of his limbs on the "wheel", usually extracted the desired confession. Conviction was followed by cruel punishments common to all European codes of justice in that age – hanging or strangling for such crimes as theft at night, or flogging and branding for lesser crimes.

The institutions of law, government, and religion in New France were imported from Old France with only minor adaptations, but the economic and social life of the colony was quite different from that of the mother country. The privileges which distinguished the upper classes in France were almost entirely lacking – the only social mark of a Canadian seigneur was his right to wear a sword. The economic development of the colony stood in even sharper contrast. The variations in agriculture imposed by the climate were understandable, but the failure of New France to sustain any strong manufacturing industry left the colony weakened by its over-dependence on furs and farming as a means of livelihood.

New France's lack of manufacturing industries was not solely the result of France's mercantilism (the prohibition of colonial production competitive with home industry), for Jean Talon, the first and "Great Intendant" appointed in 1665, had, with royal approval, tried to encourage manufacturing in the colony. Talon's experiments with subsidized brewing, shipbuilding, iron casting, lumbering, and the growing of flax and hemp failed because of high production costs, lack of markets, because cheaper goods were obtainable from the Dutch and English, and above all for lack of technical knowledge and business acumen on the part of the Canadians. Even the spasmodic attempts to develop trade with the French West Indies proved unsuccessful because New England could better supply the islands' needs and would buy their molasses in exchange. Shipbuilding did revive after 1730, thanks to government encouragement, but the industry was never as important to New France as it became to

Iron smelting, at the St. Maurice Forges north of Trois-Rivières, was the first heavy industry established in Canada. Despite discovery of iron deposits as early as 1670, the French government refused to allow the establishment of the industry. However in 1729 a private developer built a furnace, and the forges were in operation intermittently until 1883.

New England. The foundries of St. Maurice, near Trois-Rivières, managed to operate long after the Conquest, yet their history was marked by repeated bankruptcies of the various lessees. Other manufacturing concerns (for example, those that produced tar, bricks, stockings, and fabrics) operated briefly after 1700, but the rich resources of fish and timber were never effectively exploited in New France. In the eighteenth century, at the very time when these enterprises were beginning (or being revived after Talon's lack of success) the colony's economy was stunted by France's return to a stricter policy of encouraging the consumption of French-made goods in New France and of restricting the production of competing products in the colony. Thus the manufacture of canvas and felt hats in Canada was forbidden, and the establishment of other industries was discouraged. In its closing years the colony of New France was still dependent on its two basic enterprises, furs and farming, after a long and disappointing attempt to broaden the base of its economy and thereby close the developmental gap between itself and its English neighbours.

HISTORY FROM THE SOURCES

La Nation Canadienne – What Was Its Character?

The French Canadians' awareness of their own identity as French-speaking North Americans is rooted in their historical and geographic separation from France and in France's colonial policies. The mother country was 2,000 miles distant from New France and the Canadian winter sealed off communications for almost half the year. Further, the French-Canadian population had grown almost entirely from natural increase – it is estimated that only 10,000 French immigrants came to New France between 1608 and 1763. Not surprisingly most French Canadians had come to look upon Canada as their real homeland long before the British Conquest. *This feeling was shared by all but the upper ranks of the civil service and clergy, who were recruited directly from France. Understandably too, French Canadians had also begun to show traits of character and habits of mind quite different from those of contemporary Frenchmen.*

Pierre Charlevoix, a Jesuit historian, taught in Quebec between 1705 and 1709 and was sent by the French government in 1720 on a journey from Quebec to New Orleans.

I have already said, that they reckon no more than seven thousand souls at Quebec; yet you find in it a small number of the best company, where nothing is wanting that can possibly contribute to form an agreeable society. . . . Enough, in my opinion, to enable all sorts of persons whatever to pass their time very agreeably.

They accordingly do so, every one contributing all in his power to make life agreeable and chearful [*sic*]. They play at cards, or go abroad on partics of pleasure in the summer-time in calashes or canoes, in winter, in sledges upon the snow, or on skaits upon the ice. Hunting is a great exercise amongst them, and there are a number of gentlemen who have no other way of providing handsomely for their subsistence. The current news consists of very few articles, and those of Europe arrive all at once, though they supply matter of discourse for great part of the year. They reason like politicians on what is past, and form conjectures on what is likely to happen; the sciences and fine arts have also their part, so that the conversation never flags for want of matter. The Canadians, that is to say, the Creoles of Canada draw in with their native breath an air of freedom, which renders them very agreeable in the commerce of life, and no where in the world is our language spoken in greater purity. There is not even the smallest foreign accent remarked in their pronunciation.

You meet with no rich men in this country, and it is really great pity, every one endeavouring to put as good a face on it as possible, and nobody scarce thinking of laying up wealth. They make good cheer, provided they are also able to be at the expence of fine cloaths; if not, they retrench in the article of the table to be able to appear well dressed. And indeed, we must allow, that drcss becomes our Creolians extremely well. They are all here of very advantageous stature, and both sexes have the finest complexion in the world; a gay and sprightly behaviour, with great sweetness and politeness of manners are common to all of them; and the least rusticity, either in language or behaviour, is utterly unknown even in the remotest and most distant parts.

The case is very different as I am informed with respect to our English neighbours, and to judge of the two colonies by the way of life, behaviour, and speech of the inhabitants, nobody would hesitate to say that ours were the most flourishing. In New-England and the other provinces of the continent of America, subject to the British empire, there prevails an opulence which they are utterly at a loss how to use; and in New France, a poverty hid by an air of being in easy circumstances, which seems not at all studied. Trade, and the cultivation of their plantations strengthen the first, whereas the second is supported by the industry of its inhabitants, and the taste of the nation diffuses over it something infinitely pleasing. The English planter amasses wealth, and never makes any superfluous expence; the French inhabitant again enjoys what he has acquired, and often makes a parade of what he is not possessed of. That labours for his posterity; this again leaves his offspring involved in the same necessities he was in himself at his first setting out, and to extricate themselves as they can. The English Americans are averse to war, because they have a great deal to lose; they take no care to manage the Indians from a belief that they stand in no need of them. The French youth, for very different reasons, abominate the thoughts of peace, and live well with the natives, whose esteem they easily gain in time of war, and their friendship at all times.

Thus it appears . . . that every one here is possessed of the necessaries of life; but there is little paid to the King; the inhabitant is not acquainted with taxes; bread is cheap; fish and flesh are not dear; but wine, stuffs, and all French commodities are very expensive. Gentlemen, and those officers who have nothing but their pay, and are besides encumbered with families, have the greatest reason to complain. The women have a great deal of spirit and good nature, are extremely agreeable, and excellent breeders; and these good qualities are for the most part all the fortune they bring their husbands; but God has blessed the marriages in this country in the same manner he formerly blessed those of the Patriarchs. In order to support such numerous families, they ought likewise to lead the lives of Patriarchs, but the time for this is past. There are a greater number of noblesse in New France than in all the other colonies put together.

*   *   *   *   *

After all, it is a little their own fault if they are ever exposed to want; the land is good almost everywhere, and agriculture does not in the least derogate from their quality. How many gentlemen throughout all our provinces would envy the lot of the simple inhabitants of Canada, did they but know it? And can those who languish here in a shameful indigence, be excused for refusing to embrace a profession, which the corruption of manners and the most salutary maxims has alone degraded from its ancient dignity? There is not in the world a more wholesome climate than this; no particular distemper is epidemical here, the fields and woods are full of simples of a wonderful efficacy, and the trees distill balms of an excellent quality. These advantages ought at least to engage those whose birth providence has cast in this country to remain in it; but inconstancy, aversion to a regular and assiduous labour, and a spirit of independence, have ever carried a great many young people out of it, and prevented the colony from being peopled.

These . . . are the defects with which the French Canadians are, with the greatest justice, reproached. The same may likewise be said of the Indians. One would imagine that the air they breathe in this immense continent contributes to it; but the example and frequent intercourse with its natural inhabitants are more than sufficient to constitute this character. Our Creoles are likewise accused of great avidity in amassing, and indeed they do things with this view, which could hardly be believed if they were not seen. The journeys they undertake; the fatigues they undergo; the dangers to which they expose themselves, and the efforts they make, surpass all imagination. There are however few less interested, who dissipate with greater facility what has cost them so much pains to acquire, or who testify less regret at having lost it. Thus there is some room to imagine that they commonly undertake such painful and dangerous journeys out of a taste they have contracted for them. They love to breathe a free air, they are early accustomed to a wandering life; it has charms for them, which make them forget past dangers and fatigues, and they place their glory in encountering them often. They have a great deal of wit, especially the fair sex, in whom it is brilliant and easy; they are, besides, constant and resolute, fertile in resources, courageous, and capable of managing the greatest affairs. You, . . . are acquainted with more than one of this character, and have often declared your surprise at it to me. I can assure you such are frequent in this country, and are to be found in all ranks and conditions of life.

I know not whether I ought to reckon amongst the defects of our Canadians the good opinion they entertain of themselves. It is at least certain that it inspires them with a confidence, which leads them to undertake and execute what would appear impossible to many others. It must however be confessed they have excellent qualities. There is not a province in the kingdom where the people have a finer complexion, a more advantageous stature, or a body better proportioned. The strength of their constitution is not always answerable, and if the Canadians live to any age, they soon look old and decrepid. This is not entirely their own fault; it is likewise that of their parents, who are not sufficiently watchful over their children to prevent their ruining their health at a time of life, when if it

suffers it is seldom or never recovered. Their agility and address are
unequalled; the most expert Indians themselves are not better marks-
men, or manage their canoes in the most dangerous *rapids* with
greater skill.

Many are of opinion that they are unfit for the sciences, which
require any great degree of application, and a continued study. I am
not able to say whether this prejudice is well founded, for as yet we
have seen no Canadian who has endeavoured to remove it, which is
perhaps owing to the dissipation in which they are brought up. But
nobody can deny them an excellent genius for mechanics; they have
hardly any occasion for the assistance of a master in order to excel
in this science; and some are every day to be met with who have
succeeded in all trades, without ever having served an apprentice-
ship.

P. F. X. de Charlevoix, *Journal of a Voyage to North America,*
2 v. (London, 1761; reprinted Ann Arbor, 1966), Vol. I,
pp. 111-14, 263-6.

*Gilles Hocquart, intendant of New France from 1731 to 1748, is the
supposed author of a report dated 1737 describing French-Canadian life.*

The colony of New France may comprise about 40,000 people of
all ages and both sexes, about 10,000 of whom are capable of bearing arms.

Canadians are naturally large, well-built, and have a vigorous
temperament. As the learning of a trade is not controlled by master
craftsmen, and because since the beginning of the colony skilled
craftsmen were rare, each generation of Canadians has had to become self-reliant. The peasants handle an axe very skilfully; they
themselves make most of their own tools and utensils, and build their
own houses and barns. Some are weavers who make a coarse linen
cloth and a material they call drugget, which they use to clothe
themselves and their families.

They love being honoured and flattered, pride themselves on their
bravery, and are very sensitive to criticism and the slightest punishment; they are mercenary, vindictive, readily get drunk, use brandy
to excess, and are considered to be untruthful.

This description fits a large number of the Canadians, particularly
the country people. Those in the towns have fewer faults. All are
very devout; one sees few scoundrels; they are fickle, and have too
good an opinion of themselves – traits which prevent them from
succeeding as they should in the arts, agriculture, or commerce.
Added to this is the laziness encouraged by the length and harsh-

ness of the winter. Canadians love hunting, travelling by water, and exploring, and lack the rustic and unpolished manners of our French peasants. They are usually quite docile when their honour is appealed to, and when governed with justice, but they are by nature insubordinate.

Public Archives of Canada, Archives des Colonies, Série
C 11 A, M.G. 1/3, Vol. 7, pp. 40-1 (translation).

FURTHER READING

Lanctot, Gustave, *A History of Canada*, Vols. 2 and 3 (Toronto: Clarke, Irwin, 1964, 1965). Covers the period from 1663 to the British Conquest.

Eccles, W. J., *Canada Under Louis XIV* (Toronto: McClelland & Stewart, 1964). A scholarly study of the years 1663 to 1701.

Eccles, W. J., *Canadian Society During the French Regime* (Montreal: Harvest House, 1968)★. A stimulating account of life and institutions in New France.

Eccles, W. J., *Frontenac, The Courtier Governor* (Toronto: McClelland & Stewart, 1965)★. A critical and controversial biography of the "Fighting Governor".

Walsh, H. H., *The Church in the French Era* (Toronto: Ryerson, 1966). Chapters 8 to 11 cover the religious history of New France's last century.

Scott, H. A., *Bishop Laval* (Toronto: Oxford University Press, 1926). Uncritical biography but the only one readily available in English.

Trudel, Marcel, *The Seigneurial Regime* (Canadian Historical Association Booklet No. 6, 1956)★. Brief but definitive study.

Frégault, Guy, *Canadian Society in the French Regime* (Canadian Historical Association Booklet No. 3, 1954)★.

Eccles, W. J., *The Government of New France* (Canadian Historical Association Booklet No. 18, 1965)★. A short general description of the government of the royal province.

Wrong, G. M., *The Rise and Fall of New France*, 2 vols. (Toronto: Macmillan, 1929). A highly readable survey of the whole history of New France.

Glazebrook, G. P. de T., *A History of Transportation in Canada*, 2 vols. (Toronto: McClelland & Stewart, 1964)★. First Chapter of Vol. 1 deals with New France.

Trudel, Marcel, *Introduction to New France* (Toronto: Holt, Rinehart, 1968).

6

The Westward Expansion of New France

The Iroquois, Furs, and Brandy

New France's growth as a thriving agricultural community centred on the lower St. Lawrence Valley can never be adequately understood as an isolated development. It must always be viewed against the background of the colony's relationships to the exploration of the interior of the continent, to the Indian tribes and the fur trade, and to the power of England in North America, all of which became of primary importance to New France in the century after 1663. The granting of a new constitution to New France and the implementation of new policies to promote economic and population growth were, however, not enough to ensure the survival of the royal colony. The Iroquois Confederacy, which had already destroyed Huronia and threatened the life of New France for a generation, had to be crushed to remove both the menace of attack and the Iroquois blockade of the fur trade routes to the west. It was for this purpose – the destruction of the Iroquois menace – that the Sieur Prouville de Tracy was appointed lieutenant-general of North and South America and was

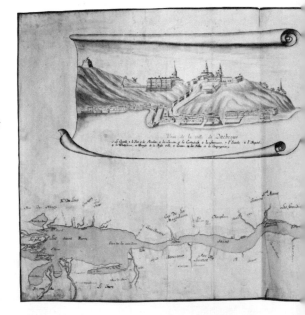

Map of the St. Lawrence River drawn by an unknown artist in 1700-1750. It is inset with views of Quebec (top left) and Trois-Rivières (top right).

sent to New France in 1665 along with more than 1,200 regular soldiers from five French regiments. Soon after his arrival Tracy built five forts along the Richelieu River, which was the Iroquois war route to New France, and in January 1666 he permitted the new governor, Courcelle, to lead an expedition of some 500 men into the Iroquois territory. The impetuous Courcelle achieved no victory by his winter campaign, but the Iroquois now realized that they were no longer safe from French attacks. In August 1666, for the first time, all five Iroquois nations sent representatives to a peace parley at Quebec.

The Mohawk and Oneida nations refused to accept any binding treaty, perhaps expecting that the English, who had seized Manhattan in 1664 and renamed it New York, would help them against the French. Urged on by Talon, Tracy sent 1,200 men, half of them regular soldiers, south to attack the Mohawks. The expedition destroyed Mohawk villages, but never met the enemy in battle and returned without attempting to attack the Oneidas. When these two tribes still did not offer peace, Tracy threatened them with another invasion in 1667. Lacking support from their sister nations and the English, they accepted Tracy's peace, which lasted for eighteen years. For the first time France and the confederacy were at peace and Jesuit missionaries were free to work in the Iroquois lands.

The end of the Iroquois menace permitted a rapid expansion of the fur trade on which New France's economy depended so heavily. Two important developments in the trade had occurred in 1665 – the West India Company had been granted a monopoly and coureurs de bois had begun to purchase furs directly from the Indians instead of acting merely

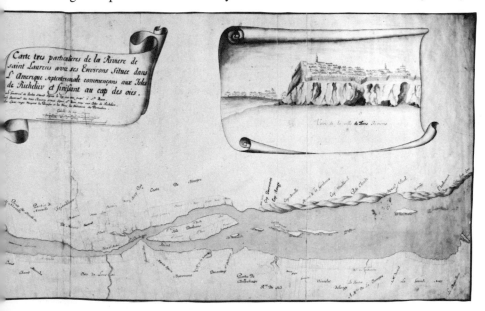

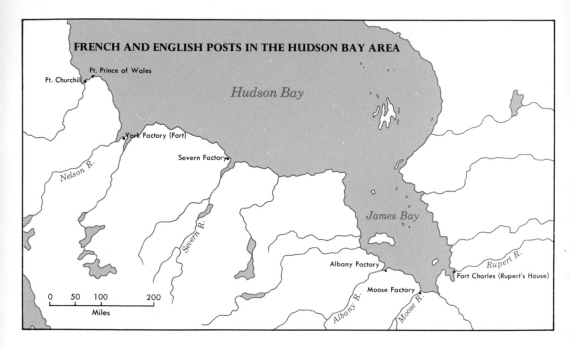

FRENCH AND ENGLISH POSTS IN THE HUDSON BAY AREA

Ft. Prince of Wales

Ft. Churchill

Hudson Bay

York Factory (Fort)

Severn Factory

Nelson R.

Severn R.

James Bay

Albany Factory

Rupert R.

Fort Charles (Rupert's House)

Moose Factory

0   50   100   200

Miles

Albany R.

Moose R.

as agents in the fur trade. The West India Company paid 36,000 livres annually (a livre was worth about 20 cents, and was a half-day's wages for a labourer) towards the colony's expenses, but to recoup some of its own costs the company insisted on exclusive control over all trade to and from the colony. French merchants, the habitants, and Talon protested so loudly against this aspect of the monopoly that Colbert insisted on freer terms. Continued complaints against the company's policies in Canada and in other French colonies finally led to the cancellation of its charter in 1674.

The activities of the coureurs de bois among the Indians very quickly led to a major dispute about the use of brandy in the fur trade. As early as 1660 Bishop Laval threatened to excommunicate anyone who sold brandy to the Indians, and in 1661 two traders had been executed for selling it. But in spite of royal prohibitions in 1663 and 1665 the brandy trade was allowed to go on because of the profits it earned. By 1668 drunk and disorderly Indians had become so common that the prohibition was renewed by the Sovereign Council in February. But in November the same body unaccountably reversed its stand on the use of brandy, permitting it to be sold to Indians in the settlements, perhaps hoping that in visiting the settlements the Indians would become more "civilized". Only the bishop and one other member of Council protested against this decision, which Talon had promoted despite his earlier opposition to brandy and despite the fact that his term as intendant was just ending. The immediate effect of this ruling was a rush of habitants, soldiers, and others to become fur traders, a rush so great that Council decreed in 1669 that nobody was to travel beyond the settlements without a royal licence. No amount of government restrictions or church denunciations, however, seemed capable of offsetting the attractions that the fur trade offered to adventurous and unscrupulous individuals, and for years the brandy trade remained a source of dispute in New France.

Westward the Course of Empire

Jean Talon is remembered primarily for his work in developing the economic life of New France. He intended a stable colony on the banks of the St. Lawrence to be the base of a mighty French empire in North America, which would control the still undiscovered land route to the Orient. Talon's dream of empire had been blocked until 1668 by the Iroquois domination of the routes to the west, but even in his first term as intendant, from 1665-8, he had prepared the way for the next step in France's exploration and conquest of the continent. Pierre Esprit Radisson and his brother-in-law, Médard Chouart, Sieur des Groseilliers, two typical coureurs de bois, had already reached lakes Michigan, Superior, and possibly Winnipeg in the late 1650's, and Sault Ste. Marie was already the advance post for the fur trade before Talon sent Jean Péré in 1668 to investigate the Lake Superior copper mines. Meanwhile two Sulpicians (Dollier de Casson and Bréhant de Galinée) and Robert Cavelier, Sieur de la Salle, who were respectively seeking souls and furs, were exploring the lower Great Lakes, which the Iroquois had kept closed for half a century.

Thus, missionaries and traders were again working together in this second phase of French expansion, but Talon, Colbert, and even King Louis promoted Gallicanism in New France by involving the Sulpicians

Fold-out engraving from Louis Hennepin's "Voyage curieux du R. P. Louis Hennepin, missionnaire recollet, & notaire apostolique", published in 1704. Father Hennepin (1640-1701) the missionary, explorer, and writer, came to Canada from what is now Belgium. He joined La Salle's expedition in search of the Mississippi (though his claim to have descended the river before La Salle was proved false), and explored as far west as Leech Lake in present-day Minnesota. Hennepin is popularly credited as being the first white man to see Niagara Falls, although in fact Brûlé was probably the first.

and Recollets in the work of exploration to balance the power of the ultramontane Jesuits. La Salle himself had abandoned training as a Jesuit and through his brother, a Sulpician in Montreal, had obtained in 1666 a seigneury jokingly called La Chine because of his passion to find the route to Asia. Talon, who had been reappointed intendant of New France in 1669, returned in 1670 and sent La Salle west again to find the Ohio River, which La Salle believed would flow into the Gulf of California, but La Salle was unsuccessful, and during his two-year absence western exploration was carried on by others. Missions and trading posts had been established at Sault Ste. Marie, on Green Bay, Michilimackinac Island, Fox River, and at Chequamegon, but it was from Sault Ste. Marie that the next great venture began.

While La Salle was still absent, Talon sent the Sieur de Saint Lousson to Sault Ste. Marie in 1671 to claim the western lands for the French Crown. The next year Talon and the new governor, Louis de Buade, Comte de Frontenac, sent Louis Jolliet and the Jesuit Pierre Marquette to find the Mississippi River, which was reported to be "the opening to Mexico". Their epic trip of 1673 down the Mississippi to the mouth of the Arkansas River convinced them that the Mississippi did not flow to the Pacific Ocean, but they discovered the shorter Chicago–Illinois River

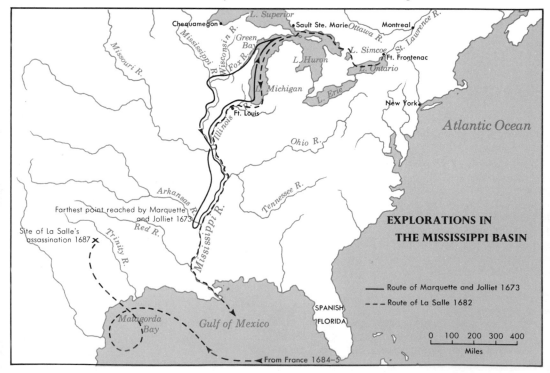

EXPLORATIONS IN
THE MISSISSIPPI BASIN

——— Route of Marquette and Jolliet 1673
– – – Route of La Salle 1682

0   100 200 300 400
Miles

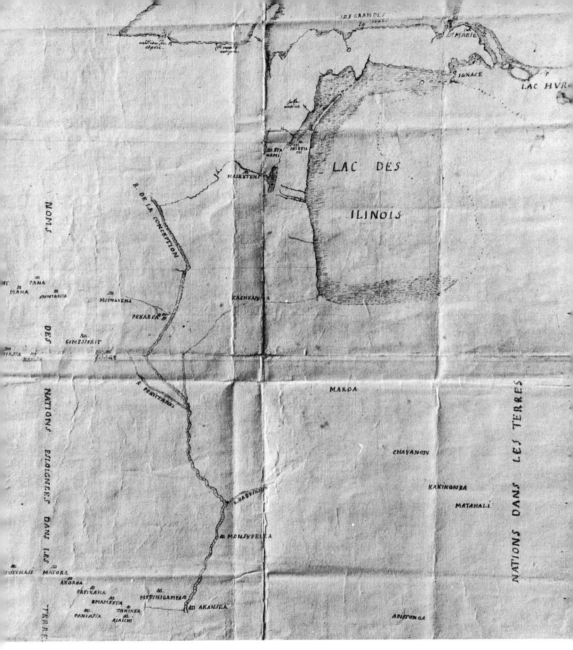

LES GRANDES EAUX

ST. MARIE

ST. IGNACE

LAC HVR

NOMS

R. DE LA CONCEPTION

LES STA GAMI

MASKVTENS

LES POTTERA NIS

LAC DES

ILINOIS

PANA

DES

MOINGVENA

KACHKASKIA

PEEAREA

SEMESSRIT

NATIONS

R. PEKITANOUI

MAROA

CHAYANON

ELLOIGNEES

KAKINONBA

MATAHALI

DANS

R. HABVKIGOU

NATIONS DANS LES TERRES

LES

M. MONSVPELEA

TERRE.

MATORA

AKOROA

PAPIKAHA

METCHIGAMEA

AKANSEA

ARISTONGA

EMAMSETA

TANINNA

PANIASSA

AIAICHI

In 1681 a map showing the discoveries made by the Jesuits in 1672 and by Marquette in 1673 was published in Paris and attributed to Marquette himself. Careful study has shown that Marquette did not draw that map, that it was more likely prepared by Father Dablon, superior of the Jesuit missions in New France from 1671 to 1680, and friend of Louis Jolliet. Marquette's own map, shown here, covers a larger area but shows only the regions that Marquette knew at first hand from his own travels. Dablon may have based his map on Marquette's and added information gained from Jolliet.

portage on their return trip. Jolliet's report delivered in 1674 filled the new governor with enthusiasm to be an empire builder, but the French king's new preoccupation with wars of grandeur in Europe determined that the empire of fur in the heart of North America would belong more to Count Frontenac than to King Louis.

During his first year as governor, Frontenac had discovered in the fur trade the means of reducing the heavy debts he had amassed as a soldier and courtier. Despite objections from the Montreal fur merchants, the governor invited the Iroquois tribes to reaffirm the peace at Cataraqui, the site of present-day Kingston, where he built a fortified trading post. Intent on making his fortune, Frontenac went himself to Cataraqui to trade almost every year, while attempting (with only slight success) to keep the Iroquois from trading with the English at Albany and to eliminate the illegal operations of the coureurs de bois. His high-handed actions against certain fur merchants involved him in a row with the Sulpicians and the governor of Montreal that earned him the king's displeasure. His continuing involvement in the fur trade led to an order from Colbert that he end his connection with the trade, an order that he easily avoided.

Both the legal and the illegal fur trade still flourished, thanks to brandy, and the efforts of the church to curb its sale only caused Frontenac to reissue the permission granted in 1668. Bishop Laval appealed directly to the king, who warned the bishop not to meddle in state affairs, but the professors of the Sorbonne decided that the brandy trade was a moral question in which the bishop had sole authority. When the dispute continued, Louis ordered Frontenac to consult the leading inhabitants. Twenty of them, not including the bishop, met in the so-called "Brandy Parliament" of 1678 and decided that the brandy trade was a necessary evil to keep the Indians away from English rum. Louis, however, decreed in 1679 that brandy could be sold only in the French settlements, and this compromise, as Laval admitted in 1682, did reduce the abuses of the trade.

The brandy dispute was only a by-product of the fur trade and, during the dispute, the work of exploration continued apace. When Radisson and Groseilliers arrived at Montreal in 1660 with 60 canoe-loads of furs, they were arrested and fined, and their furs confiscated for illegal trading. After vain protests in France against this treatment, both men sailed to Hudson Bay in an English trading expedition financed by Prince Rupert, cousin of Charles II. The large profit reaped in 1670 led Charles that same year to grant a charter to the Hudson's Bay Company which included a monopoly of trade in the Hudson Bay watershed. This English incursion from the north quickly drew off furs from the French posts on Lake Superior, and caused Talon to send the Sieur de Saint Simon and the Jesuit Albanel on an epoch-making trip in 1672 up the Saguenay and

The murder of La Salle, from Louis Hennepin's "A New Discovery of a Vast Country in America", first published at Utrecht in 1697. Duhaut, the principal conspirator in the murder of La Salle, blamed the explorer for the death of his younger brother, who became lost while La Salle was searching for the Mississippi. After shooting La Salle, Duhaut left his body to be devoured by wild animals. Father Charlevoix, the historian (1682-1761), wrote of La Salle: "Such is the fate of those men whom a mixture of great defects and great virtues lifts above the common sphere."

along the Rupert River to James Bay to claim the region for King Louis. For the next twenty years, however, the Hudson's Bay Company continued to trade in its chosen domain, unchallenged by the French.

In the Great Lakes region the years immediately following Jolliet's discovery of the Mississippi saw intensive efforts by La Salle to build a fur trade empire through exploration. In 1675 La Salle obtained the seigneury of Fort Cataraqui which, when rebuilt and renamed Fort Frontenac, served as a base for operations as well as a barrier to English and Iroquois intrusion into the area. After La Salle finally got permission to pursue his western explorations, he began to construct a chain of forts at the mouth of the Niagara River, and on the Miami and the Illinois rivers. His scheme to build a fleet of ships for the upper lakes trade collapsed, however, after his first vessel, *Le Griffon*, disappeared on her maiden voyage in 1679. Despite this and other financial setbacks La Salle began his long-planned trip to explore the length of the Mississippi in December 1681, and by the following April he had reached its mouth at the Gulf of Mexico and had claimed the whole Mississippi watershed for France. Hoping to build a base near the Spanish silver mines of New Mexico, La Salle got the king's support for a settlement in Louisiana, as he named the region. His expedition of 1684-85 landed far west of the Mississippi, however, and some of the rebellious settlers murdered him in March 1687. With Louisiana added to the St. Lawrence Basin and the Hudson Bay region, Louis of France possessed about half the North American continent, yet as a result of his European ambitions, French power was not equal to controlling or retaining such a vast empire.

New France Under Attack

In the same year that La Salle reached the Gulf, his partner, protector, and friend Frontenac was dismissed as governor of New France because

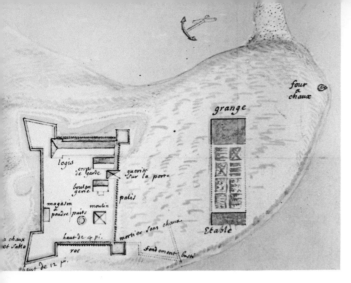

Plan of the fort at Cataraqui (Fort Frontenac) dated 13 November 1685. A small part of one bastion of the fort has been discovered beneath the parade square of the modern National Defence College and has been left bare so that visitors may see the stonework of La Salle's famous trading post.

of his quarrels with the Sovereign Council and the clergy and his blatant disregard of royal policies for the colony's economic well-being. One year earlier the Iroquois had challenged French interests in the west by attacking the Illinois tribe, and in 1682 they openly broke the long peace by ambushing France's Indian allies along the Ottawa fur trade route. Throughout 1683 and 1684 the Iroquois robbed French traders with impunity as the new governor, the Sieur de la Barre, first hesitated to precipitate war and then, having organized a war party, was forced to accept a humiliating peace after his men fell ill at Fort Frontenac in 1684. This diplomatic defeat weakened the French position among the western tribes, and in 1685 La Barre was replaced by the Marquis de Denonville. The job of this newest governor was to crush the Iroquois, protect France's Indian allies, and oppose any attempts by the English, who were arming the Iroquois, to extend their influence in Indian affairs.

Increased competition from English traders and English encouragement to native war had weakened France's hold on even her traditional friends, and by 1686 Denonville was strengthening the defences of New France to meet an inevitable attack. To forestall any English expansion on Hudson Bay he sent Pierre Chevalier de Troyes overland with a party that captured three of the company's posts – Moose Factory, Rupert House, and Albany – in a matter of five weeks. The only remaining English post was Fort Bourbon on the Nelson River, which had been seized from Canadian traders by Radisson in 1684. At several points in the west English traders were seized and robbed by the French in 1686, although no state of war existed between their nations. To climax his campaign against the enemies of New France, Denonville in 1687 attacked and dispersed the Senecas, strongest of the Iroquois tribes.

Denonville's preventative war united rather than discouraged the Iroquois. Onondagas and Mohawks attacked isolated settlements and even raided Montreal Island. In 1688 some reinforcements arrived from

France, but not nearly enough to stem the tide of Iroquois attacks. During that summer the Mohawks raided along the length of the Richelieu, and the French abandoned Fort Niagara and the post at Detroit. New France was on the defensive and its prospects darkened more when, in the wake of England's Glorious Revolution that removed James II, the new king William III declared war on France in May 1689. England and the Iroquois would now fight side by side against France in the New World, but not until August was the attack on New France renewed. Then, in a surprise night raid against Lachine, the Iroquois killed sixty-six settlers, most of them with barbaric cruelty. Denonville panicked in the face of these Indian tactics and ordered Fort Frontenac destroyed, thus leaving the west entirely open to English and Iroquois control.

In the midst of these calamities word reached New France that Frontenac, the fighting governor, was on his way back to the colony for a second term in office. His return in October 1689 brought new hope and purpose to the Canadians. Frontenac would fight fire with fire, and early in 1690 he despatched three separate raiding parties against Schenectady, Salmon Falls (north of Boston), and Casco, Maine. The destruction wrought by these raiders put the English settlements in a state of alarm, but Frontenac's real aim – peace with the Iroquois – was rejected by the Confederacy. Largely by diplomacy Frontenac restored the confidence of the western Indian allies, who now brought a rich cargo of furs to Montreal and reaffirmed their alliance against the Iroquois by joining Frontenac himself in a war dance.

While the allies were still in Montreal, word arrived of the approach of an English raiding party. This group did some damage at nearby La Prairie, but the larger force, of which this was only the advance guard, never appeared because its ranks of English and Iroquois had been reduced by smallpox. The English had planned a two-pronged attack on

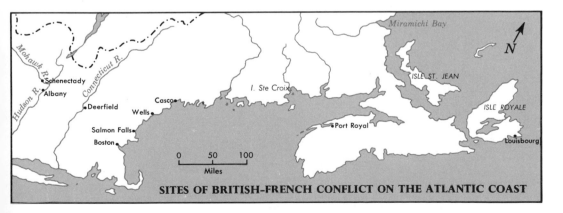

SITES OF BRITISH-FRENCH CONFLICT ON THE ATLANTIC COAST

The title of this map reads: "Plan of Quebec in New France, besieged by the English on 16 October 1690 until the 22nd of that month, when they were obliged to return home, after having been well beaten. By M. le Comte de Frontenac, Governor-general of the country".

the heart of New France. This first prong had failed to reach its objective, but the second, a seaborne invasion by 2,300 men on thirty-four ships, commanded by Sir William Phips, anchored at Quebec in mid-October and demanded Frontenac's surrender. The fighting governor's dauntless reply has become a legend of Canadian history: "The mouths of my cannon and my muskets will answer your general." Several attempts by the English to attack the city failed disastrously and one week later, as Phips sailed back to Boston having lost 600 men, Quebeckers rejoiced amid religious services and fireworks. Acadia, however, had been seized by Phips on his way to Quebec, and was only reconquered with the help of the Abenakis in 1692.

Frontenac was eager to carry the war to Massachusetts itself, but New France lacked the resources for such a venture and Old France had suffered too serious a reverse at the battle of the Boyne in Ireland to spare any troops for colonial wars. Although the other Iroquois tribes were preparing for another attack against New France, the Mohawks sued for peace after Phips' defeat. Iroquois and English raids against the Montreal

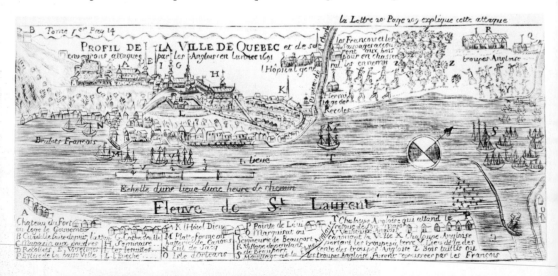

region during the summers of 1691 and 1692 ended in failure, and the western Indians honoured their alliance with the French by harrying Iroquois villages. To forestall any Iroquois attacks, in the winter of 1693 Frontenac sent a party against the Mohawks with such success that both Iroquois and English hesitated to attempt a second invasion. The English, in fact, were having difficulty in maintaining the alliance with the Iroquois, who were trying to negotiate a peace with Frontenac. The west was firmly under French control, the fur trade was flourishing, and supplies and some reinforcements were arriving from France.

The rest of 1693 and 1694 passed without serious molestation from the Iroquois, and in 1695 Frontenac rebuilt Fort Frontenac with stronger defences. At last, in the summer of 1696, the governor felt strong enough to attack the Iroquois in their own lands. A seven-week campaign smashed the Onondaga and Oneida tribes and ensured French domination of the whole Great Lakes Basin. Two years earlier Pierre le Moyne d'Iberville, New France's most famous soldier, had sailed from Canada to Hudson Bay and captured Fort Bourbon, which the English had renamed Fort Nelson. One of eleven famous brothers, d'Iberville's life was filled with adventure from the time he joined de Troyes' overland attack on the Hudson's Bay Company posts in 1686. For two years he had been in charge of the three captured posts, and in 1688 he seized two English ships in the Bay. In 1690 he led the raid against Schenectady; in 1695 he destroyed a New England post in Acadia, and the next year he captured every English settlement in Newfoundland except Bonavista and Carbonear. While d'Iberville was busy in Newfoundland, however, the Hudson's Bay Company regained Fort Nelson and with it control of Hudson Bay. This seesaw battle in the north continued in 1697 when d'Iberville's ship, the *Pélican,* overwhelmed three English ships in a major sea battle

D'Iberville's ship, "Pélican", wrecked off the mouth of the Nelson River. From La Potherie's "Histoire de L'Amérique Septentrionale" (1722).

(p.92) Phips' attack on Quebec according to M. le Baron de Lahontan's "Nouveaux Voyages" published in 1715.

off Fort Nelson. The French thus gained undisputed mastery of the Bay just one week before King William's War was ended by the Treaty of Ryswick in September 1697.

The Contraction of New France

The Treaty of Ryswick virtually restored the North American situation to what it had been ten years earlier. France kept all the posts on Hudson Bay except Fort Albany, but she returned Newfoundland to Great Britain, keeping only her tiny settlement of Placentia and her fishing rights along the coast. Acadia, the forgotten colony, was once more French territory as a result of the treaty. Although the war between the European powers had ended, the French and the western tribes continued their attacks on the Iroquois during 1698 until the Confederacy offered to negotiate a general peace. Frontenac, however, did not live to see this humbling of his old enemies. He died at Quebec in December of that year and the final treaty was arranged by Louis de Callières, the governor of Montreal, who succeeded him.

This important peace treaty embracing all the Iroquois and western tribes was not signed until the summer of 1701, yet by that time the expansionist policies of Frontenac and La Salle had already been put in motion once more. In 1700 d'Iberville, by command of King Louis, had founded New Orleans in order to block the expansion of the English into the Mississippi region, and in 1701 Lamothe-Cadillac built a new settlement at the strategic site of Detroit to rival the older post at Michilimackinac. Unfortunately the fur trade had been in difficulty for some time, because the European market was glutted with French furs. King Louis had saved the trade temporarily by a personal purchase of the huge surplus of pelts, but even a reorganization of the trade under a new monopoly failed to solve the basic problem of over-production, and it was not until

Louis Hennepin at Niagara Falls, said to have been drawn by Hennepin himself in 1678. The cascade at the right is caused by Table Rock, which fell into the Niagara gorge in 1850. From Hennepin's "A New Discovery of a Vast Country in America" (1699).

about 1715 that supply and demand were again balanced in the fur trade. By that date the whole situation of New France had been changed drastically as a result of the War of the Spanish Succession (sometimes called Queen Anne's War), which began in 1702.

The Treaty of Ryswick had proved to be more of an armistice than a peace. The fundamental conflict of French and British imperial aims in North America had not been resolved by King William's War or by the treaty of 1697. The English seaboard colonies were expanding westward as their populations grew, but the French possessions, stretching in a wide arc from the mouth of the St. Lawrence to the mouth of the Mississippi, barred their advance in every direction, while closer to hand was the potential threat of Acadia to New England. Raids such as the one on Salmon Falls by France's allies, the Abenakis, had not been forgotten, and if in the past France had ignored Acadia's strategic location as a base for attacking New England's seaborne commerce, there was no assurance that this neglect would continue. The outcome of this conflict of two European empires in North America would certainly be affected by Indian relations, as King William's War had shown, but ultimately it would depend on the amount of power, especially naval power, that Britain and France could spare from their European commitments for use in the New World.

Callières died in 1703 and his successor, Philippe Rigaud de Vaudreuil, anticipated that the most serious English threat in the renewed war would come from Boston. His first step was to neutralize the Iroquois by giving them presents and refraining from attacking them; his second step was to keep the English on the defensive, which he achieved by savage French-Indian raids on Wells, Maine, in 1703, and Deerfield, Massachusetts, in 1704. The New Englanders retaliated by attacking the Abenakis and two small Acadian settlements, but mindful of the strategic uselessness of such guerrilla tactics, they suggested in 1705 that New France and New England should remain neutral while their mother countries were at war. After discussions had continued for a year without any evidence of progress, the French and the missionaries encouraged the Abenakis to renew their harassment of New England, despite the fact that France declared she could send to Acadia "neither men, nor munitions, nor compensation to settlers . . . nor gifts for the Indians. . . ."

While the west was disturbed by Indian tribal intrigues and New York and Canada maintained an undeclared peace, the New Englanders responded to these newest raids from Acadia by launching a combined British-colonial seaborne attack on their tormentors at Port Royal. Their capture of the port in 1710 neutralized Acadia and encouraged another expedition against Quebec in 1711. Eighty-four ships carrying 10,000 men commanded by Sir Hovenden Walker entered the St. Lawrence, but near

Panel entitled "The Cataract of Niagara", from a map drawn by the Dutch geographer Herman Moll and published in London in 1715. A description below the panel reads: "A View of ye Industry of ye Beavers of Canada in making Dams to stop ye Course of a Rivulet, in order to form a great Lake, about which they build their Habitations. To Effect this, they fell large Trees with their Teeth, in such a manner as to make them come Cross ye Rivulet, to lay ye foundation of ye Dam; they make Mortar, work up, and finish ye whole with great order and wonderfull Dexterity. The Beavers have two Doors to their Lodges, one to the water and the other to the Land side. According to ye French accounts."

Anticosti Island a severe storm wrecked eight ships, drowned 700 men, and the expedition had to be abandoned. Quebec had been saved once more from invasion, and the next spring Detroit was also rescued when an Iroquois attempt to regain mastery of the fur trade ended in heavy losses at the hands of the French. A combination of good luck, French courage, and tribal jealousies had preserved New France, except for its Atlantic outpost, Acadia, but the conclusion of the War of the Spanish Succession by the Treaty of Utrecht brought greater and unexpected losses of territory to the royal colony.

Louis XIV's insatiable ambitions had started this disastrous war which left France near bankruptcy. He therefore had little choice but to accept the peace terms laid down by the coalition of European powers which had halted his search for glory. In North America France surrendered to Britain all claims to Acadia and to the Hudson Bay Basin, and all claims in Newfoundland except the right to fish and to dry fish on stipulated sections of the coast. Only the islands of Saint Jean (Prince Edward) and Isle Royale (Cape Breton) remained to France in the Atlantic region – New England's influence had triumphed at the conference table where her armed forces had failed in the St. Lawrence. Thus, the French menace to the English seaboard colonies had been removed and the great St. Lawrence–Mississippi arc of the fur trade was now under pressure from two sides: the Atlantic colonies on the east and the Hudson's Bay Company on the north. Any future French expansion in North America would be channelled westward by these pressures.

The Treaty of Utrecht marked a turning point in the long-term prospects for the French empire in North America, but if the treaty brought the loss of much territory in contrast to the strong position New France had held after the Treaty of Ryswick, there were at least two consolations. The vast areas ceded to Britain were really peripheral to the fortunes of the settlement on the St. Lawrence – Acadia contained only some 1,500 souls, Placentia in Newfoundland less than 700, and France's stake in Hudson Bay was literally a handful of isolated trading posts. Even more important for New France, the Treaty of Utrecht ushered in thirty years of peace during which the royal colony enjoyed solid growth based on its own natural and human resources.

HISTORY FROM THE SOURCES

New France and the Fur Trade

How important was the fur trade in the development of New France? Did the prosperity and the very existence of the colony really depend on furs, or did the trade in fact hamper and twist New France's growth? The following documents illustrate some of the conflicting opinions regarding the importance of the fur trade to New France. What changes in the colony may explain the difference between the attitudes expressed in the 1650's and those of a later generation?

The voluminous writings of Marie de l'Incarnation, who founded the Ursuline convent at Quebec in 1639, provide many glimpses of the colony in its early days. The following comments are from the news-filled letters she sent to her son, who was only twelve years old when his mother became a nun.

[1650]

. . . I see, moreover, that the troubles of this country will hold many things in suspense. For there are three things one must consider in the present state of affairs. The first, that neither we nor all

Canada can subsist two years longer without help. The second, that
if this help is lacking, we must, in the opinion of the more judicious,
either die or return to France. I believe, however, that if the enemy
has a war with the Neutral nation and the Andastoué [Susquehan-
nahs], this will be a diversion of arms that will enable us to subsist
a little longer. But if he continues in his conquests and victories,
there will be nothing for the French to do here. It will not be possible
to carry on trade. If there is no trade, no more ships will come here.
If ships no longer come, we shall lack all things necessary for life,
such as cloth, linens, and the greater part of our food, including the
bacon and flour that the garrison and religious houses cannot do
without. It is not that people do not work hard and that food is not
produced, but the country does not yet provide what it needs to
maintain itself. The third thing that retards our affairs is that if trade
fails because of continuation of the war, the Savages, who stop here
only to trade, will scatter in the woods.

[1652]

As for commerce, the trade from the south shore is almost destroyed, but that from the north is more abundant than ever. If the
merchandise were always brought promptly and in good time from
France, so that tardiness did not cause the beavers to be sent elsewhere, the merchants would be rich. But fundamentally, as long as
the habitants amuse themselves at this trade, they do not advance
their affairs as much as if they worked to clear the land and engaged
in traffic in fish, perch and porpoise oils, and other like commodities, in which trade is being introduced.

[1660]

A few months ago the Outaouak [Ottawas] came with a great
number of canoes laden with beaver, which relieves our merchants
of their former losses and suits most of the habitants, for without
commerce the country is worthless as regards temporal matters. It
can exist without France as far as food is concerned but depends
upon it entirely for clothing, tools, wine, brandy, and an infinity of
small commodities, and all these things are brought to us only
through trade. . . .

*Word from New France: the selected letters of Marie de
l'Incarnation,* trans. and ed. by Joyce Marshall. (Toronto,
1967) pp. 184-5, 208, 254.

The Relation of 1653, compiled from the reports written by the Jesuit missionaries, records the same opinions as those of Marie de l'Incarnation.

Never were there more Beavers in our lakes and rivers, but never have there been fewer seen in the warehouses of the country. Before the devastation of the Hurons, a hundred canoes used to come to trade, all laden with Beaver-skins; the Algonquins brought them from all directions; and each year we had two or three hundred thousand livres' worth. That was a fine revenue with which to satisfy all the people, and defray the heavy expenses of the country.

The Iroquois war dried up all these springs. The Beavers are left in peace and in the place of their repose; the Huron fleets no longer come down to trade; the Algonquins are depopulated; and the more distant Nations are withdrawing still farther, fearing the fire of the Iroquois. For a year, the warehouse of Montreal has not bought a single Beaver-skin from the Savages. At Three Rivers, the little revenue that has accrued has been used to fortify the place, the enemy being expected there. In the Quebec warehouse there is nothing but poverty; and so every one has cause to be dissatisfied, there being no means to supply payment to those to whom it is due, or even to defray a part of the most necessary expenses of the country.

R. G. Thwaites, ed., The Jesuit Relations and Allied Documents,
72 v. (Cleveland, 1896-1901), Vol. XL, p. 211.

The Marquis de Denonville, governor of New France from 1685 to 1689, was highly critical of the effects of the fur trade on the colony.

It seems to me, Monseigneur, that the place from which it is necessary for us to give an account of the disorders that are taking place is not only the woods, but the settlements. These disorders do not stem only from the youth of the country but from the freedom which parents and governors have given to the young people in letting them spend time in the woods on the pretext of hunting or trading. This, Monseigneur, has reached such an excess that from the time children are able to carry a gun, fathers cannot restrain them and dare not anger them. Imagine, then, the evils which can arise from such a way of living. In the families of those who are (or would like to be) gentlemen, these irregularities are much greater, either because of laziness or vanity; they have no other resources of subsistence but the woods, for not being used to handling a plough, pickaxe, or hatchet, their only tool being the gun, they must spend their lives in the woods where they have no priests to embarrass them, nor fathers, nor governors to constrain them.

*   *   *   *   *

... A fashion of dressing nude like the savages, not only on carnival days but on all days of feasting and debauchery, has been treated with leniency and as a joke. All these practices tend only to attract the young people to the manner of life of the savages, and to associate with them and be forever libertines like them. I cannot tell you, Monseigneur, the attraction that all young people have for this life of the savage, which is to do nothing, follow every whim and be removed from all control.

For a long time it has been considered a very good practice to visit the savages in our settlements in order to accustom these people to live like us and become instructed in our religion. I perceive, Monseigneur, that just the opposite has taken place, for instead of becoming accustomed to our laws, I assure you that they have given to us everything they have that is most wicked and have taken for themselves only that which is bad and vicious in us.

Denonville to the Minister, 13 November 1685

Public Archives of Canada, Archives des Colonies, Série
C 11 A, M.G. 1/3, Vol. 7, pp. 44-5 (translation).

By 1702, when the Jesuit Etienne de Carheil wrote the following letter to Governor de Callières, the fur trade seemed to be threatening the very existence of the Indian missions which the trade had fostered in Champlain's day.

At MICHILIMAKINA,
the 30th of august, 1702.

MONSEIGNEUR,

... It was only necessary to have seen all That is to be seen every day at Montreal, and That you yourself have only too often seen, to enable you to carry back to france enough to give Information to his majesty, and to constrain him to succor our missions. These are reduced to such an extremity that we can no longer maintain them against an infinite multitude of evil acts – acts of brutality and violence; of injustice and impiety; of lewd and shameless conduct; of contempt and insults. To such acts the infamous and baleful trade in brandy gives rise everywhere, among all the nations up here, – where it is carried on by going from village to village, and by roving over the lakes with a prodigious quantity of brandy in barrels, without any restraint. Had his majesty but once seen What passes, both here and at montreal, during the whole time while This wretched traffic goes on, I am sure that he would not for a moment hesitate, at the very first sight of it, to forbid it forever under the severest penalties.

In our despair there is no other step to take than to leave our missions and abandon them to the brandy traders, so that they may establish therein the domain of their trade, of drunkenness, and of immorality.

If his majesty desire to save our missions and to support the Establishment of Religion, as we have no Doubt he does, we beg him most humbly to Believe What is most true, namely: that there is no other means of doing so than to abolish completely the two Infamous sorts of Commerce which have brought the missions to the brink of destruction, and which will not long delay in destroying these if they be not abolished as soon as possible by his orders, and be prevented from ever being restored. The first is the Commerce in brandy; the second is the Commerce of the savage women with the french. Both are carried on in an equally public manner, without our being able to remedy the evil, because we are not supported by the Commandants.

In whatever light we may consider the Commerce carried on, as regards either the Common interest of Canada, or the advancement of Christianity, It would be Infinitely more advantageous for both if the savages themselves went down annually for that purpose to montreal, than it would be to send the french here to trade, in the way in which they come every Year. I do not Consider it necessary to give the Reasons, so Manifest are they. For It is evident that the latter method serves but to depopulate the country of all its young men; to reduce the number of people in the houses; to deprive wives of their husbands, fathers and mothers of the aid of their children, and sisters of that of their brothers; to expose Those who undertake such journeys to a thousand dangers for both their Bodies and their souls. It also causes them to incur very many expenses, partly necessary, partly Useless, and partly Criminal; it accustoms them not to work, but to lose all taste for work, and to live in Continual idleness; it renders them incapable of learning any trade, and thereby makes them Useless to themselves, to the families, and to the entire country, through having made themselves unfit for the occupations that are most Common and most useful to man. But It is not only for these Reasons, which affect this Life, – it is still more on account of Those which concern the soul, that This Sending of the french among the savages must appear Infinitely harmful to them. It Takes them away from all the holy places; it separates them from all Ecclesiastical and religious persons; It abandons them to a total deprivation of all Instruction, both public and private, of all devotional Exercises, and, finally, of all the spiritual aids to Christianity. It sends them into savage countries and into Impassable places, – through a thousand dangers, both on land and on water, – to carry on in a low, servile, and shameful manner a Commerce that could be carried on much more advantageously at montreal, where the people would have a much larger share in it (as in justice they should) than they have, and than they will have so long as it is carried on here.

* * * * *

So long as all the young men devote themselves to no other occupation than That of Coming here for Beaver, There can be no hope that the Colony will Ever become flourishing; it will always be poor, for it will always lose thereby What would most enrich it, – I mean the labor of all the young men.

Thwaites, ed., *The Jesuit Relations* . . . Vol. LXV,
pp. 189, 191, 193, 195, 219, 221, 223.

FURTHER READING

Nute, Grace Lee, *Caesars of the Wilderness* (New York: Appleton-Century-Crofts, 1943). An account of the colourful careers of Radisson and Groseilliers.

Rich, E. E., *The Hudson's Bay Company*, Vol. 1 (Toronto: McClelland & Stewart, 1960). The authoritative history of this famous fur-trading company.

Parkman, Francis, *La Salle and the Discovery of the Great West* (Boston: Little, Brown, 1897). Though dated in some respects by more recent research, Parkman's volumes are still notable for their literary style.

MacKay, Douglas, *The Honourable Company* (Toronto: McClelland & Stewart, 1966)★. A popularly written and reliable account of the Hudson's Bay Company.

Chapais, Thomas, *The Great Intendant* (Chronicles of Canada Series, reprinted by the University of Toronto Press, 1964). A short and readable biography of Talon.

7

Contest for a Continent

The Thirty Years' Peace

The last half century of the history of New France is divided into two unequal parts – unequal in length and contrasting sharply in the nature of the events that occurred. After almost thirty years of intermittent warfare, the Treaty of Utrecht began a period of thirty years of peace, during which New France consolidated its settled agricultural society along the lower St. Lawrence and its hold on the interior of the continent. This period of growth was followed by two major wars – the War of the Austrian Succession (also known as King George's War) from 1744-8, and the French and Indian War that began in North America in 1754, two years before the Seven Years' War of which it formed one operational theatre. The half century of contrasting growth and violence ended with the accession of Canada to the British Crown.

Canada, the St. Lawrence Valley section of New France, had only 18,000 inhabitants in 1713, but by 1763 the population had risen to about 75,000. This growth was almost entirely due to natural increase, since France took little interest in colonizing her largest North American colony. Although the mother country contained some twenty million people, only some 4,000 settlers came to Canada in the forty-year period 1714-58. Of this number 1,600 were disbanded soldiers, following the practice first established in 1668 when members of the Carignan-Salières regiment settled along the Richelieu; another 1,500 were indentured servants, and the third-largest group comprised 700 convicted salt smugglers. The population growth, therefore, came not from immigration but from a high birth rate, which doubled the number of colonists every twenty years. But still New France's population lagged behind that of the French West Indies, an area which proved much more attractive to immigrants, and behind the record of the English North American colonies, whose population jumped from 350,000 to 1,500,000 in the first half of the eighteenth century.

During this period new seigneuries were granted in Canada inland from the original river-front seigneuries which by now blanketed the shore of the lower St. Lawrence to well below Quebec. The pattern of Canadian agriculture did not change appreciably, but production of wheat and flax more than doubled. Large quantities of tobacco were grown, but most of that crop was consumed locally. During the thirty years' peace shipbuilding revived in Canada and a royal shipyard established at Quebec in 1731 launched several warships and merchantmen. The St. Maurice forges and three tar plants produced products for export, and an expanding lumber trade thrived on naval contracts. But these industries and several smaller manufacturing concerns remained relatively unimportant in the economic life of a colony whose imports always exceeded its exports, and whose total trade was only one-twentieth that of the French West Indies. The annual cost to France of keeping New France as a colony reached nearly a million livres (about $40 million by modern values) in 1746, and under the administration of the dishonest intendant, François Bigot, it soared to thirty million livres in 1759. Yet the French government abandoned various plans for direct taxation of the Canadians because of the colony's poverty.

While French society was thus entrenching itself in the settled parts of New France after the Treaty of Utrecht, exploration and the fur trade received a new impetus during the thirty years' peace. In 1690 and again in 1691-2 the Hudson's Bay Company had sent a twenty-year-old employee, Henry Kelsey, inland from Fort Nelson to encourage the Indians to come to the Bay posts. Kelsey seems to have reached the Saskatchewan River near The Pas, but the Hudson's Bay Company was content to let the Indians come down to its factories and undertook no further explorations

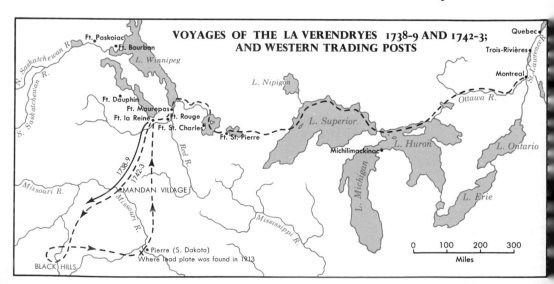

VOYAGES OF THE LA VERENDRYES 1738-9 AND 1742-3; AND WESTERN TRADING POSTS

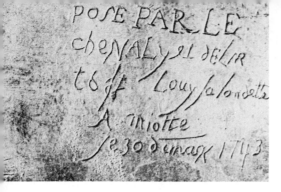

Lead plate (obverse at left) buried in 1743 by Pierre de la Vérendrye, found in 1913 at Pierre, South Dakota. The inscription reads: "Posé par le chevaly et de lar to St. Louy la Londette A Miotte le 30 de Mars 1743". It may be translated: "Deposited by the Chevalier and de la Vérendrye [La Vérendrye's son, François] witnesses – St. Louy de Londette A. Miotte, the 30th March 1743". The tablet, about eight inches wide, was probably made in Quebec.

until after the conquest of Canada. Excluded from Hudson Bay by the terms of the treaty, Canadian traders began to extend their operations throughout the west and northwest, and to intercept the Indians before they started the long river journey down to the Bay. Daniel Greysolon, Sieur Dulhut, had reached the Sioux country (west of Lake Superior) in 1680, but tribal warfare in that area between the Sioux, the Foxes, and the Illinois discouraged trading, and for two generations the French concentrated their interests on the Quebec–New Orleans route. Only when the supply of furs declined after 1713 did they again turn to the northwest route through Lake of the Woods, which Dulhut had explored in 1689 in his search for the western sea.

The new push westward began in 1730 when Pierre Gaultier de Varennes, Sieur de la Vérendrye, a soldier turned fur trader, got a trading monopoly in the Lake Winnipeg region and, with the aid of several sons and relatives, began to build a string of posts eventually reaching from Rainy Lake to the Assiniboine River. Credulously accepting Indian stories about a "River of the West" which emptied into the Pacific through a warm land with walled towns, white men, mines, cocoa, and "snakes of a prodigious size", La Vérendrye went southwest in 1738 into the country of the Mandans, only to discover that the fabled river was the Missouri. In 1742-3 two of his sons reached the Black Hills in South Dakota. For several years afterwards he was in financial difficulty and official disfavour and, in 1749, on his way to explore the Saskatchewan River as a possible route to the Pacific, La Vérendrye died. His achievement in finding a way around the troublesome Sioux, out of the difficult Shield country into the open prairies, had no imitators. With La Vérendrye's death French exploration of the interior came to an end and it was left to a Hudson's Bay Company man, Anthony Henday, in 1754-5, to be the first to explore the Saskatchewan River and the Canadian prairies.

The inscription on the reverse of the lead plate carries the Latin words: "Anno XXVI Regni Ludovici — XV — Prorege — Illustrissimo Domino —Domino Marchione — De Beauharnois M — D — CC — XXXXI — Petrus Gaultier De Laverendrie Posuit . . . ." In translation: "In the 26th year of the reign of Louis XV Pierre Gaulthier de la Vérendrye acting on behalf of the Marquis de Beauharnois deposited [this plate] in 1741 in the name of our most illustrious sovereign —the King".

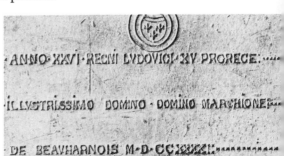

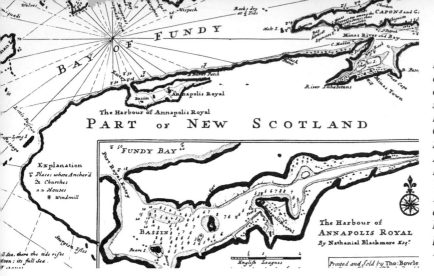

Detail from a map entitled "A Description of the Bay of Fundy showing ye Coast, Islands, Harbours, Creeks, Coves, Rocks, Sholes, Soundings &c. observed By Nat. Blackmore in ye Years 1711 and 1712". The map appeared in Herman Moll's "Atlas Minor", published probably in 1732.

Acadia Under British Rule

Article XIV of the Treaty of Utrecht allowed the Acadians one year to leave the lost province, but if they chose to remain they became British subjects, free to enjoy the Roman Catholic religion. Few left, and Acadia became the British colony of Nova Scotia, inhabited by some 3-4,000 Frenchmen employed in farming and fishing, about 1,000 settled Indians, and two small garrisons – one at the capital, Port Royal (renamed Annapolis), the other at the fishing station of Canso. Although the Indians were numerically insignificant, their hostility towards the English, which was encouraged by annual presents from the French government, was a constant threat to the peace of the colony.

The Acadians accepted the change of sovereignty easily, until an attempt by the authorities in 1713 to extract the oath of loyalty to the British Crown opened a new and ultimately tragic chapter of Acadian history. The Acadians refused the oath on the grounds that it conflicted with their duty to their religion and the French king, and threatened to move en masse to French-owned Isle Royale (Cape Breton) if the oath was insisted on. For two years the English authorities hesitated for fear of losing the colonists, but when the oath was again demanded in 1717 the Acadians countered with a proposed oath which would allow them to remain neutral in any future conflict between France and Britain.

The Lords of Trade and Plantations, the British government's advisers on all colonial matters, would accept no alternative oath and suggested the possibility of deporting any Acadians who still refused the unconditional oath. Governor Lawrence Armstrong did allow the Acadians to take their "neutrality" oath in 1726, without reporting to the Lords of Trade that the unacceptable clause had been included. When his deception was discovered, the British government, with the full approval of the French government, insisted on the unconditional oath. In 1729 Armstrong's successor did extract the desired oath, but only because he had given his word to the Acadians that their neutrality would be respected.

Here the matter of Acadian neutrality rested for a generation until it was reawakened by the armed contest between France and Britain for control of the whole continent. Missionary priests from Quebec were still regularly admitted to Nova Scotia to serve the religious needs of the Acadians and the Indians, but a few were expelled for acting as French agents to stir up resistance against the English. While insisting on an un-qualified oath, the British government had not been entirely deaf to the expressed fears of successive governors that the oath might cause Britain to lose these peaceable, useful, and, for the moment, irreplaceable settlers. For their part the Acadians had pleaded, and would plead again, that any oath of loyalty to Britain would bring down on their heads the savage revenge of the local Indians.

A more threatening development for the future of the Acadians was France's decision to convert Louisbourg, the capital of Isle Royale where several hundred refugees from Placentia had settled, into a major fortified seaport to protect the entrance to the St. Lawrence. Beginning in 1719 France spent three and a half million livres (four times the annual budget of New France) in the next quarter century on the harbour and fortress at Louisbourg. The port became a fulcrum in France's trade with Canada and the French West Indies, and by 1740, when Isle Royale's population had reached 4,000 and Canada's was 40,000, the island's trade was two-thirds as great as that of Canada, although it had only one-tenth the popu-lation. But a sea fortress of such strength was more than a protection for the St. Lawrence – it was also a threat to the safety and maritime economy of New England, and the proximity of the Acadians constituted a poten-tial fifth column to the neighbouring colonists should war break out.

The War of the Austrian Succession, which began in 1744 and involved France and Britain on opposite sides, was the signal for Louisbourg

Left: Louis XV medal struck in 1720 to commemorate the founding of the fortress of Louisbourg in that year. "Ludovigo-burgum fundatum et Munitum" (Louisbourg founded and fortified). Bottom left: The front of the barracks, facing the town; from an undated plan in the Bibliothèque Nationale, Paris. Bottom right: The reconstructed fortress of Louisbourg.

privateers to attack New England's commerce and the opportunity for New England to attack the French base. Governor William Shirley of Massachusetts won the support of New Hampshire, Rhode Island, and Connecticut for a colonial fleet of over 100 ships and an army of 8,500 to attack the great fortress. After a seven-week siege by this colonial expedition and a Royal Navy squadron, the French bastion surrendered in June 1745 to this vastly superior force. Old England and New England rejoiced at the victory, which assured British control over the North Atlantic.

Victorious in the land war in Europe, France hastened to redress this defeat in North America. Seven thousand men, with 800 cannon, set sail to recapture Louisbourg in 1746, only to return home in November decimated by disease and storms, without having sighted the fortress. What France could not regain by force of arms, however, she acquired with ease at the conference table in 1748. After winning striking victories in the Netherlands and India, Louis XV surrendered all his gains in return for Louisbourg at the Treaty of Aix-la-Chapelle. If Frenchmen were angered by this betrayal of France's interests, New Englanders were furious at the loss of Louisbourg, whose restoration to France left them once more under the constant menace of attack from that stronghold which the French began to rebuild as the "Gibraltar of the Atlantic".

While planning the capture of Louisbourg, Governor Shirley had not overlooked the potential danger to New England from the Acadians and their Indian neighbours. His suggestion that the Acadians be removed to New England and be replaced by British settlers was rejected; instead Britain concentrated on an alternative scheme for building on Chebucto Bay a naval base to balance the threat from Louisbourg. This new base, Halifax, was founded in 1749 with several thousand French- and German-speaking Protestant refugees from Europe's wars who had settled there and around Lunenburg. From this position of strength a new governor of Nova Scotia, Edward Cornwallis, demanded that the Acadians take the

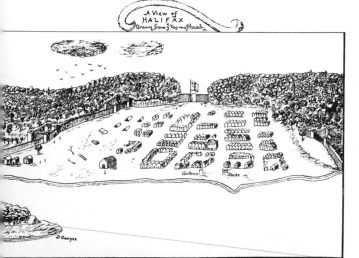

A contemporary drawing entitled "A View of Halifax Drawn from ye Top masthead", and "Published according to Act of Parliament January 25 1750 . . ." The only structures on the mainland that the artist has identified with labels are the Gallows and the Stocks.

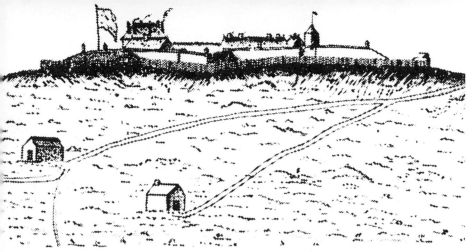

Fort Beauséjour in 1755.

oath of allegiance to King George. Once more the Acadians pleaded their neutrality, and threatened to emigrate. France, eager for such a migration to Isle Royale or Isle St. Jean or to the disputed Chignecto Isthmus, was employing the notorious Abbé Jean-Louis Le Loutre to foment Indian attacks on the English and to pay a bounty of 100 livres for each English scalp. During 1749 and 1750 the Chignecto area was the scene of recurrent clashes between Le Loutre's Indians and the English.

The Indian attacks diminished in 1751 and 1752, and the British government discouraged the governor from demanding the oath from the Acadians as long as they remained peaceful. But in 1755 the growing likelihood of war in the Ohio Valley caused Governor Shirley of Massachusetts and Colonel Lawrence, Administrator of Nova Scotia, to send a large fleet against Fort Beauséjour, which was defended by Le Loutre, his Indians, and 240 Acadians. Le Loutre escaped capture, but the presence of the Acadians there and the subsequent capture of Fort St. John, the last French defensive position in the area, both encouraged and enabled Lawrence to seek a final solution to the Acadian question. The Acadians still offered to take any oath that would not bind them to fight against France, but Lawrence and his Council were preparing to deport all Acadians who would not swear unqualified allegiance to the British Crown.

During the summer and autumn of 1755 about 7,000 Acadians were transported from the Bay of Fundy area to eight English seaboard colonies, and their vacant farms destroyed. Some Acadians escaped to Quebec and Isle St. Jean after hiding in the woods. The deportations continued in 1756 and 1757, and after the British capture of Louisbourg in 1758 Acadian refugees on Isle St. Jean were also removed. In the space of seven years 11,000 of the 15,000 Acadians in the Maritime region were deported, without evoking any protest from France who considered them British subjects, and without arousing any interest in Europe where the wholesale displacement and even destruction of population was a common feature of wars. Even the expelled Acadians and their descendants accepted what they called "the great disturbance" as a hazard of war and the price of their neutrality. The greatest sympathy shown for their misfortunes came from some of the colonies where the exiles were discharged.

Confrontation in the Ohio Valley

Upon the outbreak of King George's War, the Marquis de Beauharnois, governor since 1726, strengthened Quebec's defences and built Fort St. Frédéric on Lake Champlain as an added protection on the Richelieu route. Early in 1746 he sent a 700-man force against Annapolis to support the anticipated French fleet coming to retake Louisbourg. When the relief force failed to arrive, the Canadians abandoned their siege of Annapolis and contented themselves with the destruction of Grand Pré early in 1747. The loss of Louisbourg and its continued occupation by the English forces meant that Canada herself was now threatened with invasion, and Beauharnois resorted to Frontenac's tactic of preventative raids to keep the English colonies in a state of alarm. Savage raids by Canadians and Indians that brought burning and scalping to many New England frontier settlements in 1746 achieved their immediate purpose and also kept all the Iroquois tribes except the Mohawks neutral. Early in 1746, after Mohawk raiders had done minor damage as far north as Montreal, Beauharnois and his Indian allies formally reopened the Indian wars after two generations of official peace.

Throughout 1747 and 1748 the French held the initiative and advantage as they made repeated forays into New England and New York, to which the English colonies were unable to reply because Britain could spare no force from the conflict in Europe. Beauharnois had at his own request been officially relieved of the post of governor, but his successor, La Jonquière, while on duty with the navy, was captured by the English in 1747, and did not reach New France for two years. The Marquis de La Galissonière, a temporary replacement as governor, was prepared to continue the campaign of guerrilla raids – "It is our only means of ridding ourselves of fear," he said – but the Treaty of Aix-la-Chapelle ended King George's War early in 1748. The treaty did not define Canada's boundaries with Nova Scotia or with the western parts of the English colonies bordering the Ohio Valley. The determination of the boundaries was left to a proposed joint British-French commission, but in fact ownership of both areas – and especially of the Ohio Valley – remained in dispute and was a cause of the next war in North America.

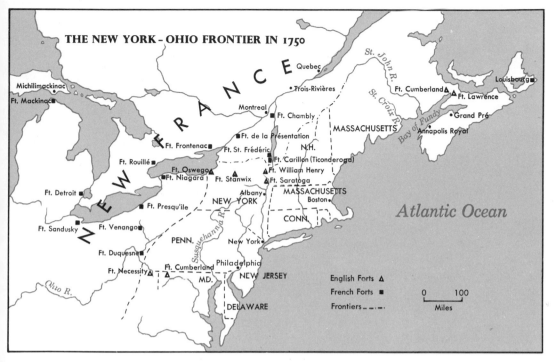

THE NEW YORK - OHIO FRONTIER IN 1750

NEW FRANCE

Michilimackinac
Ft. Mackinac
Quebec
Trois-Rivières
St. John R.
Ft. Cumberland
Ft. Lawrence
Louisbourg
Montreal
Ft. Chambly
St. Croix R.
Bay of Fundy
Grand Pré
MASSACHUSETTS
Annapolis Royal
Ft. Frontenac
Ft. de la Présentation
Ft. St. Frédéric
N.H.
Ft. Rouillé
Ft. Carillon (Ticonderoga)
Ft. Oswego
Ft. Niagara
Ft. Stanwix
Ft. William Henry
Ft. Saratoga
Ft. Detroit
Albany
MASSACHUSETTS
Ft. Presqu'ile
NEW YORK
Boston
Atlantic Ocean
Ft. Sandusky
Ft. Venango
CONN.
Susquehanna R.
PENN.
New York
Ft. Duquesne
Ohio R.
Ft. Necessity
Ft. Cumberland
Philadelphia
MD.
NEW JERSEY
English Forts △
French Forts ■
Frontiers _._._
0   100
Miles
DELAWARE

For several years individual traders from the English colonies had been making their way west over the Allegheny Mountains into the French-held Mississippi Basin. These frontiersmen posed no serious threat to French sovereignty in the region; the real menace came from the expanding population of the English colonies that followed close behind, pushing back the frontier as relentlessly as a marching army. The seaboard settlements could no longer contain the land-hungry masses, who looked with covetous eyes towards the fertile, undeveloped, trans-Allegheny empire of France. The first formal challenge from the English came in 1749 with the chartering of the Virginia Company to colonize France's Ohio Valley. To halt this intrusion, and incidentally to curb the activities of traders from New York and New England in the lower Great Lakes area, La Galissonière despatched in 1749 a strong force under Céloron de Blainville, who claimed the lands officially for France, built Fort La Présentation (now Ogdensburg) on the St. Lawrence, and Fort Rouillé (Toronto) on Lake Ontario. This policy of containment was pushed further after 1752 by the new governor, the Marquis Duquesne de Menneville, who began the construction of a chain of forts from Presqu'ile on Lake Erie to Venango at the junction of the Allegheny River and French Creek.

The governor of Virginia officially protested against the French action in what he claimed was English territory, but the last link in the iron chain of forts in the Ohio Valley was forged in 1754 when French soldiers drove some Virginia troops from crude defences they had just erected where the Allegheny and Monongahela rivers join to form the Ohio. The French proceeded to build Fort Duquesne there, but a second body of Virginia militia, under a young officer named George Washington, was already en route to recapture the strategic site when they learned of the approach of a Canadian force sent to intercept them. Washington and his men joined with a friendly Indian band and together they surprised and killed the French ensign, Jumonville, and some of his party. Duquesne called Jumonville's death "murder" – the young officer was merely coming to warn Washington off French territory. Washington's explanation was that Jumonville had shadowed him for two days without attempting to communicate his message. Nevertheless, Frenchmen had been killed in time of peace, on lands explored and claimed by France, and that volley from Virginia muskets was the opening blow of a new war in North America, known as the French and Indian War, while there was still peace between France and Britain for another two years.

Anticipating some French reprisal for the killing of Jumonville, Washington hastened to build a makeshift defence work called, appropriately, Fort Necessity. Five weeks after Jumonville had been ambushed, 500 colonial soldiers at Fort Necessity were attacked by 800 French and Indians. After losing eighty men in a one-sided battle, Washington surrendered the same day, supposedly to avoid a massacre at the hands of the Indians. This defeat and the subsequent destruction of Fort Necessity cleared the interlopers from the Ohio Valley. But of equal immediate importance was the decision of the western Indian tribes to return to the side of their old allies, the French, and the decision of the Iroquois Confederacy to remain neutral if and when the war, which now seemed inevitable, broke out between Britain and France.

Fort Duquesne's relationship to the Ohio Valley and the western Indian tribes required that the British make a stronger effort to seize that crucial position, and the year following Washington's defeat General Edward

George Washington served as an aide to General Braddock in the British expedition against Fort Duquesne in 1755. This lithograph by Junius B. Stearns (1810-85) shows the young Washington as soldier riding past the mortally wounded Braddock.

Braddock, the newly arrived British commander-in-chief, led a force of 1,400 regular and 450 colonial troops towards the fort. At the Monongahela River, about eight miles from its objective, the column was ambushed by 900 French and Indians. The British force was decimated and Braddock himself mortally wounded by the attackers, who remained hidden in the dense forest while firing on the closely packed column of red-coated troops. This disastrous "Battle of the Wilderness" proved to be the last serious encounter between French and British in the Ohio Valley, even though war was officially declared one year later. The British were more successful on the Champlain-Richelieu route, where colonial troops building Fort William Henry at Lake George repulsed a large French and Indian force sent to destroy this advance post. Such was the military situation in 1756 when the war officially began in Europe.

The Fall of New France

The outbreak of the Seven Years' War in Europe in June 1756 found France, Austria, and Russia allied against Prussia and Britain. Attacked by the three greatest powers on the European continent Frederick the Great of Prussia fought a brilliant defensive war, aided by the inability of his enemies to mount any co-ordinated offensive. Britain's role in that war theatre was largely confined to money subsidies to Frederick, and small and unsuccessful campaigns in King George II's German territory of Hanover. The real areas of conflict between France and Britain were in India and North America, and on the high seas where naval power could ensure ultimate victory in their colonial land battles.

In North America France was militarily better prepared for war than Britain. The brilliant soldier, Louis Joseph, Marquis de Montcalm-Gozon, arrived in New France as commander-in-chief in the spring of 1756, along with two crack regiments of regular troops to support the large and determined Canadian militia force. The defences of Louisbourg and Quebec were prepared for war, and Canada was now linked to Louisiana by the chain of forts recently built in the Ohio region. But New France suffered from several major handicaps. Its population of 60,000 was only one-fortieth the population of the English colonies; its defence system was stretched dangerously thin over the thousands of miles between the Gulf of St. Lawrence and the Gulf of Mexico; and its economic resources had been seriously undermined by François Bigot who, as intendant since 1748, was the leader of a clique called *La Grande Société* that systematically manipulated prices, profiteered in government contracts, and monopolized the trade in basic commodities to the colonists' loss and their own gain.

Detail from a plan dated 1758 showing land and sea operations during the siege of Louisbourg in that year.

The greatest potential strength of the British in North America lay in the material and human resources of the colonies – if they could be organized for a war effort – and the marked though not overwhelming superiority of the Royal Navy. Despite their much larger population the English colonies were not formidable in war because strong parochial loyalties prevented any effective co-operation between them, even when they faced the common threat of renewed French-Indian attacks. Typical of this disunity was their unanimous rejection of a "Plan of Union" proposed by Benjamin Franklin at the intercolonial Albany Congress in 1754. But at least the expulsion of the Acadians had strengthened Britain's position by ensuring that Louisbourg would receive no aid from any insurgent force in Nova Scotia.

As soon as the undeclared French and Indian War became officially the Seven Years' War with the opening of European hostilities, Montcalm captured three small English forts at the mouth of the Oswego River, thus ensuring uninterrupted communications between Montreal and the west while discouraging a projected British attack on Fort St. Frédéric and confirming the neutrality of all the Iroquois tribes except the staunchly pro-British Mohawks. Montcalm followed this important victory by the capture of Fort William Henry on Lake George in the summer of 1757. The surrender of the fort was unfortunately the occasion for the massacre

A contemporary view of the siege of Louisbourg, 1758: "Britain's Glory, or the Reduction of Cape Breton, by the Gallant Admiral Boscawen & General Amherst". The Town, with the Grand Battery of the Town, is in the background; the Island Battery is at the extreme left, the Lighthouse Battery at the right.

of some of the garrison by France's Indian allies, an incident used by the British to justify reprisals in subsequent years.

These British defeats in North America as well as serious reverses in Europe finally forced George II to accept his political opponent, William Pitt, as virtual prime minister in 1757. An excellent administrator, Pitt began to replace incompetent commanders with abler but less-known men of his own choice. But British defeats and disappointments continued during 1757 and into 1758. In the summer of 1757 a projected attack on Louisbourg from Halifax was abandoned when it was learned that a French fleet had reached the great fortress safely, and British ships sent to blockade the harbour were destroyed by an autumn hurricane. The next summer a huge force of 12,000 men under General James Abercromby renewed the advance towards Montreal along the Champlain–Richelieu route, only to suffer 1,600 casualties in futile charges against an impenetrable breastwork of felled trees outside Fort Carillon. Abercromby's disaster was, however, balanced by the recapture of Oswego and the destruction of Fort Frontenac, and by French abandonment of Fort Duquesne, which seriously weakened Canada's contact with the Ohio and Mississippi regions. The French also suffered a serious defeat in the east, where a force of 9,000 British regulars supported by forty warships captured Louisbourg after a six-week siege.

The year 1758 thus witnessed a turn in the fortunes of war in favour of Britain – 1759 would go down in British history as "the year of victories". The fall of Louisbourg gave Britain control of Isle Royale and Isle St. Jean and opened the way for an attack on Quebec itself. Pitt planned to capitalize on these gains in 1759 by mounting a three-pronged offensive to end French power in North America. The first attack would complete the separation of the St. Lawrence from the west by capturing Fort Niagara; the second would be directed against Montreal by the well-travelled road from Lake Champlain; the third prong would be a combined army-navy operation to reduce Quebec.

In July Fort Niagara fell to the British, and the French destroyed Fort Carillon and Fort St. Frédéric when faced by a larger invasion force. By this time the third prong under General James Wolfe had reached Quebec and was shelling the city from Lévis on the opposite shore. As the summer wore on, however, Wolfe was unable to force a major battle with Montcalm in spite of the terrible damage inflicted on Quebec city by British siege guns. A British landing on the north shore east of Quebec had been easily repulsed by Montcalm, and as autumn approached – when the siege would have to be lifted – Wolfe was no closer to conquering Quebec than he had been two months earlier. Then on 10 September Wolfe discovered a poorly guarded path up the precipitous cliff west of the city, and

The taking of Quebec, 13 September 1759, after the sketch by Captain Hervey Smyth, aide-de-camp to General Wolfe. The print shows a composite picture: it depicts the British fleet sailing up the St. Lawrence, Wolfe and his men scrambling up the narrow path, and the battle on the Plains of Abraham, all taking place at the same time.

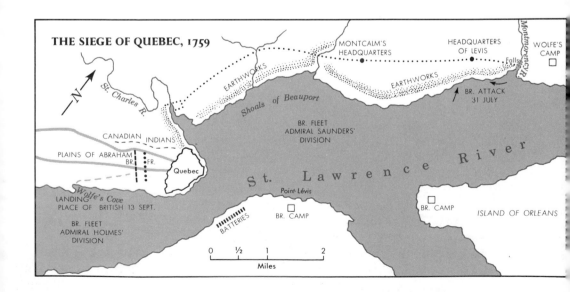

THE SIEGE OF QUEBEC, 1759

N

St. Charles R.

EARTHWORKS

MONTCALM'S HEADQUARTERS

EARTHWORKS

HEADQUARTERS OF LEVIS

Falls

Montmorency R.

WOLFE'S CAMP

Shoals of Beauport

BR. ATTACK 31 JULY

CANADIAN INDIANS

BR. FLEET ADMIRAL SAUNDERS' DIVISION

PLAINS OF ABRAHAM

BR. FR.

Quebec

St. Lawrence River

Wolfe's Cove

LANDING PLACE OF BRITISH 13 SEPT.

BR. FLEET ADMIRAL HOLMES' DIVISION

Point Lévis

BATTERIES

BR. CAMP

BR. CAMP

ISLAND OF ORLEANS

0   ½   1   2

Miles

on the morning of the 13th Montcalm faced 4,000 British infantry drawn up on the Plains of Abraham. Montcalm decided to give battle outside the city walls on the field which Wolfe had chosen, and in the short fierce struggle that ensued the French were swept from the field even as Montcalm and Wolfe lay mortally wounded. Five days later Quebec surrendered. Thus the British had captured the fortified gateway of New France, but all the colony upriver from Quebec was still in French hands.

While the soldiers of the British occupation force and the citizens of Quebec suffered from food shortages and cold during the winter of 1759-60, Montcalm's successor, Field Marshal Lévis, prepared a counterattack from Montreal to liberate the city. On 28 April Wolfe's successor in command, General James Murray, repeated Montcalm's error by marching out of Quebec – to meet Lévis at nearby Ste. Foy. This time it was the British who retreated in defeat to the safety of the walled city, and the French who waited for its surrender. Eleven days later, as Lévis watched for the arrival of a French fleet to force Murray's capitulation, the first ship of a British fleet sailed into harbour. Lévis had no choice but to retreat to Montreal.

In the early summer the French relief fleet, Lévis' last hope for help, was intercepted and destroyed in Chaleur Bay by the British. By September 1760 Murray's army was at the eastern gates of Montreal and his fleet was sailing up the river; a second army had advanced down the Richelieu to a position west of Montreal; a third and even larger force under General Amherst had arrived from Oswego and was encamped on the slopes of Mount Royal above the city. Encircled by 17,000 British soldiers, colonial militia, and Indians, with all hope of help from France gone, Governor Vaudreuil surrendered Montreal on 8 September 1760, just one year after Wolfe's victory at Quebec. The last French stronghold in North America thus fell to the British, the western posts were capitulating without a struggle, and the story of New France was at an end, just a century and a half after Champlain's first efforts at colonization.

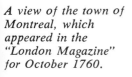

A view of the town of Montreal, which appeared in the "London Magazine" for October 1760.

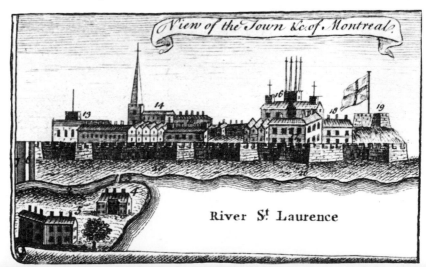

The expatriation of the Acadians, from an engraving.

HISTORY FROM THE SOURCES

The Expulsion of the Acadians – A Strategic Necessity?

Although such a move had been discussed before, the sudden expulsion of the Acadians from the old province of Nova Scotia in 1755 and their dispersal among the other British seaboard colonies to the south was planned and executed in Nova Scotia – the governments in Britain and in the other colonies were informed of the project only after it had been carried out. What factors caused the government of Nova Scotia to decide on the expulsion at this time? Was the action justified by the events of the Seven Years' War in North America?

On 28 July 1755 Jonathan Belcher, chief justice of Nova Scotia, presented to the Council of the colony a long, documented argument for the expulsion of the Acadians.

> The Question now depending before the Governor and Council as to the Residence or removal of the French Inhabitants from the Province of Nova Scotia, is of the highest moment to the Honour of the Crown and the Settlement of the Colony, and as such a juncture as the present may never occur for considering this question to any effect, I esteem it my duty to offer my reasons against receiving any of the French Inhabitants take the oaths and for their not being permitted to remain in the Province.
>
> 1. By their conduct from the Treaty of Utrecht to this day they have appeared in no other light than that of Rebels to His Majesty, whose Subjects they became by virtue of the Cession of the Province and the Inhabitants of it under that Treaty.
>
> 2. That it will be contrary to the Letter and Spirit of His Majesty's Instruction to Governor Cornwallis & in my humble apprehension would incur the displeasure of the Crown and the Parliament.

3. That it will defeat the intent of the Expedition to *Beau Séjour*.

4. That it will put a total stop to the Progress of the Settlement and disappoint the expectations from the vast Expence of Great Britain in the Province.

5. That when they return to their Perfidy and Treacheries as they unquestionably will, and with more rancour than before, on the removal of the Fleet and Troops, the Province will be in no condition to drive them out of their Possessions.

They have constantly since the Settlement obstinately refused to take the Oath of Allegiance, and have induced many of our Foreign Settlers to desert over to the French, and have always supplied the French Troops who have intruded upon this Province with Provisions, giving them a constant intelligence of all the Motions of the English, and have thereby forced the English to live in Garrison Towns, and they were unable to cultivate and improve lands at any distance, which has been the Principal cause of the great expense to the British Nation, and a means of more than half the Inhabitants who came here with an intent to settle, quitting the Province and settling in other Plantations, where they might get their Bread without resigning their lives.

From such a Series of Facts for more than 40 years, it was evident that the French Inhabitants are so far from being disposed to become good Subjects that they are more and more discovering their inveterate enmity to the English and their affection to the French, of which we have recent Instances in their Insolence to Captain Murrey hiding the best of their Arms and surrendering only their useless musquets, and in their present absolute refusal to take the Oaths of Allegiance.

Placide Gaudet, "Acadian Genealogy and Notes", House of Commons Sessional Paper No. 18, 5-6 Edward VII (1905), Appendix C, p. 63.

The same day that the Council heard Belcher's argument it decided to carry out the expulsion. Governor Charles Lawrence wrote to Colonel Monckton, the officer who had captured Fort Beauséjour at Chignecto, explaining the reasons for this decision and outlining the steps to be taken.

The Deputy's of the French Inhabitants of the Districts of Annapolis Mines and Piziquid have been called before the Council, and have refused to take the Oath of Allegiance to His Majesty; and have also declared this to be the Sentiments of the whole People; Whereupon the Council advised and it is accordingly determined that they shall be removed out of the Country, as soon as possible. And as to those about the Isthmus, all of whom were in arms and therefore entitled to no favour from the Government, It is determined to begin with them first; And for this purpose, orders are given for a sufficient number of Transports to be sent up the Bay with all possible dispatch for taking them on board; by whom you will receive particular Instructions as to the manner of their being disposed of, the places of their destination and every other thing necessary for that purpose.

In the mean time it will be proper to keep this measure as secret as possible, as well to prevent their attempting to Escape as to carry off their Cattle &ca: and the better to Effect this you will endeavour to fall upon some stratagem to get the Men, both young & old especially the Heads of Families into your power & detain them till the Transports shall arrive so as that they may be ready to be Shipped off: for when this is done; it is not much to be feared that the Women & Children will attempt to go away and carry off the Cattle: But least they should, it will not only be very proper to secure all their Shalops Boats Canoes and every other vessel you can lay your hands upon; But also to send out party's to all Suspected Roads & places from time to time that they may be thereby intercepted.

As their whole Stock of Cattle and Corn is forfeited to the Crown by their Rebellion, and must be secured and applied towards a Reimbursement of the Expence the Government will be at in Transporting them out of the Country; care must be had that nobody make any Bargain for the purchasing of them under any colour or pretence whatsoever, if they do, the sale will be void; for the Inhabitants have now (since the order of Council) no property in them, nor will they be allowed to carry away the least thing, but their ready Money & Household Furniture.

HALIFAX 8th August 1755.

DEAR SIR,

Last night a Vessel arrived from New York, by which we have it confirmed that General Braddock was attacked by the French on the 9th of July about nine miles from Fort Duquesne; that his Army was defeated . . . use your utmost Endeavours to prevent as much as possible this bad news reaching the Ears of the French Inhabitants.

The Transports for taking off the Inhabitants will be with you soon, as they are almost ready to sail from hence; and by them you shall hear further, and have particular Instructions as to the manner of shipping them, and the Places of their destination. I am hopeful in the mean time, that you will have accomplished the directions you had in my last with regard to the Inhabitants: as there may be a deal of difficulty in securing them, you will, to prevent this as much as possible, destroy all the Villages on the north & north west sides of the Isthmus that ly at any distance from the Fort of Beausejour; and use every other method to distress as much as can be, those who may attempt to conceal themselves in the Woods; but I would have all care taken to save the Stock and the Harvest upon the Ground which can be gather'd in with any safety to the Men, and prevent as much as possible the French fugitives and Indians from carrying off or destroying the Cattle.

The Northcliffe Collection (Ottawa, 1926), pp. 81, 83-4.

On 18 October 1755 the Marquis de Vaudreuil, governor of Canada, reported to the Minister of Marine and Colonies the beginning of the Acadian expulsion and explained the countermeasures he had taken.

Several reasons, Sir, have caused me to keep M. Boishébert [a captain of French troops] at the St. John River.
1. As long as I occupy that river and keep a detachment there, I retain Acadia for the King, and the English will not be able to say that they have forced the French to abandon it.
2. I will be sure of the loyalty of the Acadians and Indians, who, without the detachment, would feel abandoned and perhaps would give themselves up to the English.
3. M. de Boishébert will draw in all the Acadians from both near and far; he will try to reunite them with their families and form them into a corps. Thus reunited, the Acadians will be obliged for their own safety to repulse the enemy if they appear.
4. He will also busy himself with gathering the Indians together and forming them into an equally strong corps, he will correspond with M. Manach, the missionary at Miramichi, and if circumstances are favourable, will add the Indians of that mission to his own, to oppose the advance of the enemy.
5. He will be in a position to have informers all the time at Beauséjour and Halifax and to take prisoners who can tell him of the position and strength of the English.
6. He will be able to form parties of Acadians and Indians to harass the enemy at Beauséjour constantly and to prevent the enemy from cutting firewood.

Placide Gaudet, "Acadian Genealogy and Notes", House of Commons Sessional Paper No. 18, 5-6 Edward VII (1905), Appendix H, p. 177 (translation).

*In July 1756 five Acadians from Annapolis Royal who had escaped to
the St. John River wrote to their former curé, now in France, describing
the expulsion and their own adventures.*

We dare to hope, sir, that, sensible to our sufferings, you would be
good enough to send us news of yourself and to tell the King of
France of our loyalty. For, in truth, sir, I don't doubt that you have
seen some proofs of that loyalty. Poverty, exile, and all the unhappi-
ness of the world (even sin itself) aren't capable of making us
change our feelings; we were born French and we want to die French.

> H. R. Casgrain, "Les Acadiens après leurs dispersion", Royal
> Society of Canada, *Proceedings*, 1887, Vol. V, 21 (translation).

*To a special session of the Assembly of Pennsylvania in 1756, Jean-
Baptiste Galerm, an exiled Acadian, explained the tragic dilemma and
fate of the Acadians in connection with their request for compensation
for their losses.*

About seven years ago, at the time of the founding of Halifax, a
band of one hundred and fifty Indians came into our area, carried
off several of us from our homes and wanted to force us, by threats of
beatings, to join them to surprise and kill the English who were
busy building forts in different parts of the country; but on our firm
refusal, they left us after maltreating us and slaughtering our cattle,
etc. I myself took six weeks to recover completely from the beating
I received then. We could cite innumerable examples of the bad
treatment and losses we have suffered at the hands of the French
savages, because of our unbending attachment to our oath of loyalty.
Yet despite this strictly observed loyalty we were not able to prevent
the terrible calamity that descended on us, and which is owing, we
think, mainly to the unhappy situation and to the conduct of
several of our people who were settled at Chignecto, at the head of
the Bay of Fundy, where the French built a fort about four years
ago. Those of our people who were settled in the area, after having
seen several of their settlements burned by the French, finding themselves too distant from Halifax and from Annapolis Royal to hope
for help from the English, were obliged, we believe, more by force
and by fear than by inclination, to join the French and help them. . . .
. . . we were summoned to appear before the governor and council
at Halifax, where we were requested to take an unconditional oath
of loyalty; to this we could not consent because, in view of the situation of the government at that moment, we were afraid we would be
required to bear arms; but we were as agreeable as ever to swear the

oath of loyalty and give strong assurances that we would continue to be peaceful and faithful to His Britannic Majesty, with this one reservation. But in the present state of affairs, that not being considered satisfactory, we were made prisoners and our property, movable and immovable, was confiscated for the benefit of the King; and soon after, with nearly all our families, we were put on ships and carried to these English colonies. . . . Let me add that, notwithstanding the suspicions and fears with which many regard us, in the belief that we are a dangerous people ready to break our oaths without scruple, time will show that such is not our character. No, the deplorable situation in which we find ourselves is clear proof that it is a false charge . . .

> Placide Gaudet, "Acadian Genealogy and Notes", House of Commons Sessional Paper No. 18, 5-6 Edward VII (1905), Appendix H, pp. 25-6 (translation).

FURTHER READING

MacNutt, W. S., *The Atlantic Provinces* (Toronto: McClelland & Stewart, 1965). The only recent scholarly study on the Maritimes; its first two chapters describe the history of Nova Scotia to the Seven Years' War.

Parkman, Francis, *A Half-Century of Conflict* (Boston: Little, Brown, 1910). Colourful narrative of the French-English wars in North America.

Parkman, Francis, *Montcalm and Wolfe* (Boston: Little, Brown, 1910). The classic account of the Seven Years' War on the North American continent.

Stacey, C. P., *Quebec, 1759* (Toronto: Macmillan, 1959). Definitive study of the capture of Quebec.

Doughty, A. G., *The Acadian Exiles* (Chronicles of Canada Series, reprinted by the University of Toronto Press, 1964). Popularly written and not yet superseded despite new research in the field.

Wood, W., *The Great Fortress* (Chronicles of Canada Series, reprinted by the University of Toronto Press, 1964). A readable history of Louisbourg.

Willson, Beckles, *Life and Letters of James Wolfe* (London: Heinemann, 1909). The standard and most complete biography.

8

The Northern Colonies

The New Colony of Quebec

The Conquest of New France brought all the eastern part of North America under British rule and opened a new and hopeful era for the British empire. Freed from the French threat that had hung over them since the 1690's, the thirteen colonies and the British and American merchants now began to enjoy the full profits of the fur trade. On the Grand Banks and on the inshore fisheries of Nova Scotia and Newfoundland, fishermen from New England and from the West Country of England now outnumbered those from any other country. In this apparently unified, British, and prosperous North America only one immediate problem remained: how could the French-speaking Roman Catholic population of the newly acquired colony of Canada be fitted into an English-speaking and Protestant empire?

Under the capitulation terms, the inhabitants of Quebec had been granted certain concessions: free exercise of their religion was permitted; militiamen were to be given back their arms for hunting; and there were to be no deportations similar to the expulsion of the Acadians, although anyone wishing to return to France could do so. After the surrender the British occupation troops paid the Canadians for all their supplies rather than requisitioning them. But despite the good relations established after the Conquest, some of the habitants remained sullen and ill-disposed towards the British.

"A View of the Orphans' or Ursuline Nunnery, drawn on the spot"
(1759) by Richard Short, the purser of a British warship whose "Twelve
views of the principal buildings in Quebec" was published in 1761.

Montreal in 1760, from the watercolour by Thomas Patten (active 1760-2).

The economy of the former French colony had been disrupted by the war and the Conquest. Large numbers of farms along the south shore had been destroyed in the campaigns of 1759 and 1760. French money was now worthless in New France, and debts owed from France were uncollectable. The fur trade, the only source of exchange to pay for imports, was being rebuilt with British capital, and the French Canadians were excluded from senior positions in business. French-born civil servants and entrepreneurs departed, to be replaced by British; there were no leaders left for the French-Canadian people. The only wealth remaining in the colony was the land, the labour to work it, and its resources of fur and fish. Impoverished, barred from the higher levels in government and business, the Canadians were submerged by small British groups who controlled the political and economic life of the colony.

The church alone survived as an institution of New France, but it became the willing servant of the conquerors. In 1762 a requiem mass for the Protestant George II was sung in Quebec. The British government was prepared to continue the liberal religious policy begun in 1760. A bishop, Jean Olivier Briand, was consecrated in 1766 to ordain future clergy, and he co-operated readily with the British governors. But to placate the Canadians was not the only purpose of this liberal policy; the British set out to cut the church off from France's influence by refusing entry of French priests to Canada. The aim was to create a church in Canada which, although Roman Catholic, would be Canadian in person-

"A View of the Intendant's Palace", by Richard Short.

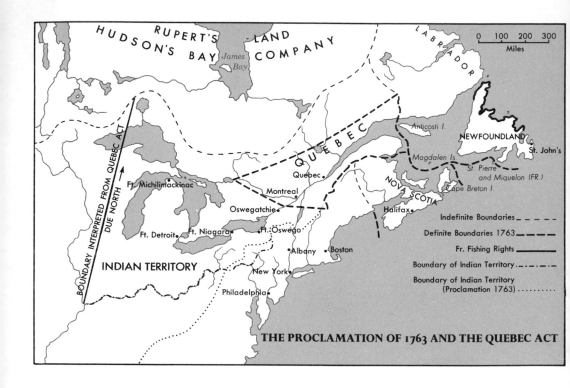

THE PROCLAMATION OF 1763 AND THE QUEBEC ACT

Indefinite Boundaries _ _ _ _
Definite Boundaries 1763 _ _ _ _ _
Fr. Fishing Rights _____
Boundary of Indian Territory _.._.._.-
Boundary of Indian Territory
(Proclamation 1763) ....

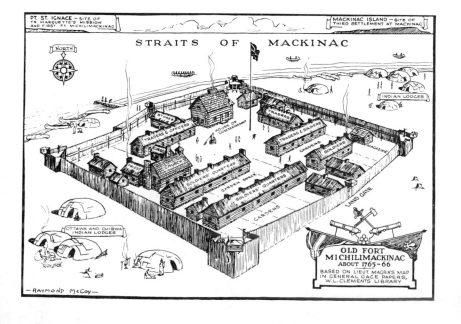

PT. ST. IGNACE – SITE OF
FR MARQUETTE'S MISSION
AND FIRST FT. MICHILIMACKINAC

MACKINAC ISLAND – SITE OF
THIRD SETTLEMENT AT MACKINAC

STRAITS OF MACKINAC

NORTH

INDIAN LODGES

OTTAWA AND OJIBWA
INDIAN LODGES

– RAYMOND McCOY –

OLD FORT
MICHILIMACKINAC
ABOUT 1765-66
BASED ON LIEUT MAGRA'S MAP
IN GENERAL GAGE PAPERS,
W.L. CLEMENTS LIBRARY

Sketch of the F
at Michilimackin
a The Commanding Offic
b Inhabitants Houses
by the Officers
c Provision Store
f Houses occupied by t
English Traders Hou
h Chaple and priests h
i a Well
k A Magazine
L Stables
m A Wharf
N a Garden
o Plat Forms in the Ba
on each of which are
a Run of Cannon Sig
pounders, besides a se
Iron cannon a b
Wall
p Turrets of Wood a
the Bastions, to secure
adjacent Grounds
The Pickets of the Fo
new lined, and the o
Land Curtains and
in good Order
English Traders
Scale Cot
Perk Lag.
Go

Scale Ten Fathoms t
Inch

nel and loyal to Britain, but by the 1770's some Canadians had come to suspect the church of trying to sway their loyalties, and mistrusted it.

Besides the problem of integrating people of French language and Roman Catholic religion into an English and Protestant empire, the government also had trouble in establishing its authority in the west. The Indian tribes who had traded with the French were organizing a war against the new rulers. Urging them on were French half-breeds and French traders still operating up the Mississippi from New Orleans. An Ottawa chief, Pontiac, was foremost among the Indians in organizing attacks on the British garrisons in the west and his name has been given to the uprising of the Indian coalition that extended from the Senecas of New York to the Ojibways of Sault Ste. Marie. The rebellion erupted in the spring of 1763 with a flurry of ambushes on the western posts. Fort after fort in the west fell until only Detroit held out. But the rising failed, because there was no co-ordinated plan. The posts were soon recovered by the British one by one, and the defeat of the Indian allies at Bushy Run, near the present city of Pittsburgh, destroyed the coalition. But Pontiac had shown how tenuous was Britain's hold outside the settled areas.

Even before Pontiac's rebellion the British government had been aware that a new policy for governing Quebec and administering the Indian lands had to be devised. By the Royal Proclamation of 7 October 1763 colonial boundaries were redrawn so that the Indian territory to the west of a line along the Appalachian watershed was closed to settlement, and Quebec was reduced to the St. Lawrence Valley. By excluding settlers from the Indian lands, the government hoped that diplomacy, gifts, and continued participation in the fur trade would pacify the western tribes. Only official Indian agents, soldiers, and licensed traders were supposed

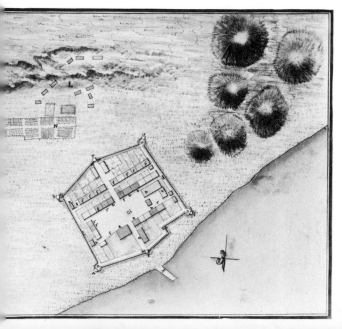

(p.126) An imaginary drawing of Fort Mackinac (near the present-day Mackinac City) about three years after the Indian massacre of the English inhabitants, based on Lt. Magra's map (pp.126-7) and descriptions of the fur trader Alexander Henry. Lt. Magra was a British soldier who served for some years in North America. His "Sketch of the Fort at Michilimackinac" is a hand-coloured manuscript that scholars have dated 1766. The designs that appear within the fort are really cartographic conventions for showing hills.

Henry escaped the massacre at Mackinac during Pontiac's rebellion because a friendly French Canadian hid him under a pile of furs in an attic.

to enter the west. As well, the proclamation provided that Quebec was to have an Assembly and English laws. By establishing familiar institutions in the new colony and by blocking westward settlement, the British government hoped to divert settlers northwards from New England to add to the handful of English-speaking businessmen in Quebec. Such a population movement, if large enough, might conceivably swamp and absorb the French-speaking community.

This policy for anglicizing Quebec failed. A few Scottish and American merchants came to work in the fur trade or supply the army, but English-speaking settlers were not prepared to live in a French-speaking community. Those few merchants who did come soon played dominant roles in Canadian society because of their wealth and position. The first governor, General Murray, disliked this group because of its constant complaints against trade regulations. This genial but military governor became increasingly sympathetic to the position of the submissive French and the few seigneurs whom he knew. He therefore delayed calling an Assembly that would necessarily be dominated by the tiny English minority, because English law barred Roman Catholics from holding office. Nor was he willing to carry out the next phase of Proclamation policy by introducing English civil law, which was entirely foreign to the new subjects. The imperial policy of integrating Quebec into the American empire was simply not put into effect in Canada.

Complaints against Murray's inaction by the Canadian merchants and their influential friends in London resulted in his recall in 1766. His successor, Guy Carleton, was another army officer and veteran of the Seven Years' War. Originally suspicious of the French, he too came to like them at a time when the growing discontent and disorders in the thirteen colonies made him increasingly distrustful of representative government and of the merchants who were demanding an elected Assembly. Carleton saw the Canadians as compliant and potentially loyal subjects of George III. Thus the overwhelming numbers of Canadians, together with the attitude of the governors, led to the abandonment of the 1763 policy for Quebec, but in the west the Indian menace ended as diplomacy and gifts did their work. By 1768 the British government realized that a new policy was necessary for Quebec which, as Carleton foresaw, would probably be French for all time. As uncertainty about the future swept the colony, the governor himself went to England in 1770 and remained there for four years to advise the government on colonial affairs.

The new policy was embodied in the Quebec Act of 1774, which aimed to please the supposed leaders of French-Canadian society – the clergy, the seigneurs, and the merchants. The continued existence of seigneurial tenure, in doubt after the Proclamation of 1763, had already been con-

This cartoon, intended to arouse anti-British feeling in the colonies, depicts Roman Catholic bishops dancing around a copy of the Quebec Act. Three British cabinet ministers look on; from left to right, Lord Bute, the Scottish favourite of young King George III, Lord North, prime minister and author of the Quebec Act, and an unknown minister.

firmed in 1771. Under the Quebec Act, Roman Catholics were guaranteed freedom of worship, and the church was given the right to hold property and could collect tithes. English criminal law, more lenient than the Roman law of France, was introduced, but French civil law was to remain. Instead of an elected Assembly, the appointed Council in which Roman Catholics might sit was given legislative power. The territory of the province was vastly enlarged so that it extended eastward along the north shore of the Gulf of St. Lawrence, westward to embrace the lands north of the Ohio River to the Mississippi, and northward to the watershed between the Great Lakes and Hudson Bay. All the best and most accessible fur country east of the Mississippi was therefore given to Quebec; although this acquisition pleased the Montreal merchants, it angered the colonists to the south by strengthening the barrier to westward settlement. Neither the merchants nor the American colonists were pleased by the Act's repudiation of the elected Assemblies. While the seigneurs and clergy might be pleased, the habitants, faced with the prospect of revived tithes and seigneurial obligations, were less than happy. Yet for all its defects, the Quebec Act recognized the special problem of Quebec, of the French within an English empire, and by granting protection to their language and religion it became the Magna Carta of cultural liberty to the Canadians.

The Atlantic Colonies

While the proclamation line drawn in 1763 failed to force settlement from New England northward into Quebec, it did lead to the migration of a small but steady stream of people from Massachusetts to Nova Scotia. As early as 1756 the immigrants had begun to come north to take over the lands left vacant by the Acadians, but these New Englanders were only a part of the movement into Nova Scotia. German farmers had been settled near Halifax by the British government in 1753 to strengthen the Protestant element in the province, although shortly after their arrival most of them moved to Lunenburg. Many Irish Roman Catholics came to Halifax and the villages around the coast to find greater religious freedom and a better life. After the Seven Years' War the diversity in both origin and religion of the province's population increased. Some Yorkshiremen from England settled on the north shore of Cumberland County. Scottish immigration began as Highlanders arrived, driven off their lands which were being cleared for sheep runs. The first shipload, a group of Presbyterians, arrived at Pictou in 1770. Other Scots, many of them Roman Catholics, went to Cape Breton. Of the more than 16,000 people in Nova Scotia in 1774, the majority were New Englanders, mostly Congregationalists, who, under the influence of the "Great Awakening" (the religious revival which swept the American frontier in the 1750's), became Baptists. Most of the Yorkshiremen were converted to Methodism shortly after their arrival. In this way the settlement of Nova Scotia created a society of many backgrounds and religious persuasions – a pluralistic society.

Halifax, capital of the province and a major British naval base, was the most English part of the province despite the large number of Irish Roman Catholics who had settled there. Government and dockyard officials and army and navy officers dominated the society of the town. The English merchants who supplied the garrison and naval station did a brisk business and became wealthy. Anglicanism was the official religion and the preference of the townsfolk. Indeed, Halifax seemed to be an English island in a very diverse sea. This separation of the capital from the rest of the province was the basic fact of political life: Halifax merchants and officials controlled the government but neglected the interests of the rest of the colony, thereby creating constant friction between the "old" and the "new" Englanders in the province.

Nova Scotia's first elected Assembly had been called in 1758, but as time went on even this body fell under the domination of Halifax. It was a long journey from many of the settlements to Halifax, and several remote ridings therefore elected merchants or lawyers in the capital to represent them. Through the Assembly and the Council, whose members were drawn from the same groups, the Halifax oligarchy dominated the province. When the New Englanders attempted to establish their own local governments (town meetings to elect local officials), the governor and his Council took fright. No grass roots democracy would develop in Nova Scotia if they could prevent it. As the New Englanders wished, the province was divided into townships and counties, but Justices of the Peace appointed by the governor controlled each county. The local landowners might nominate candidates for town clerk, constables, fence viewers, and poundkeepers, but the J.P.'s selected these officials. This form of local government, much modified from the democratic form the New Englanders had originally requested, ensured Halifax's control even of

"Charlotte-Town on the Island of St. Johns 1778", from a contemporary watercolour.

local affairs. The result could only be further friction between the settlements and Halifax.

Included in the province in 1763 was the island of St. John, later renamed Prince Edward Island in honour of George III's fourth son. Great interest in this island had been aroused in England by reports of fertile land there, but after an abortive effort by the British government to set up a proprietary colony on the island, in 1767 it was divided into sixty-seven lots of 20,000 acres each, most of them granted to British friends of the government. The island was separated from Nova Scotia in 1769, following petitions from these new owners. At the time there were only 271 inhabitants, most of them Acadians, but in the following year 120 Scottish families arrived to take up land. Although many settlers objected to renting land from an absentee landlord, the high quality of the soil attracted them, but even so a large number of those who came moved on to Nova Scotia, where free land was available to be granted. By 1774 the island had some 2,000 farmers and fishermen. Such a small population was inade-

Probably the earliest printed map (1775) showing the division of St. John's Island into lots by Captain Holland's survey of 1764-5.

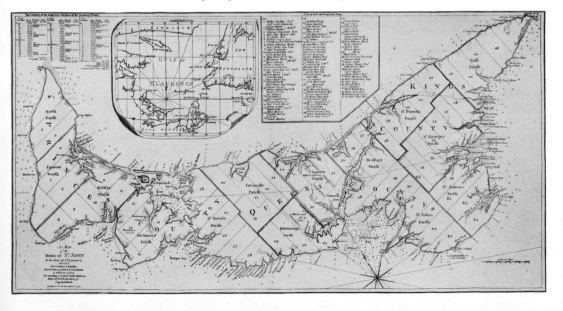

quate to finance a separate government, and the administrative officials were not even paid. The absentee owners, given land on condition that they encourage settlement, made no effort to send people out to the island, nor did they pay taxes to support the local government. Growth therefore was slow.

In Newfoundland the situation was different. From the time the island came under British rule in 1713, settlement had been discouraged, since the government regarded the island as a ship moored off the coast of North America for the convenience mainly of English fishermen. The Grand Banks were to be a "nursery" for English seamen. Sailors might land to get water or wood or to dry their fish, but officially there were to be no settlements, since in theory all the fishermen returned to England every year. Indeed, there was little to attract colonists, for good soil was scarce. Yet settlements developed as bases for the fisheries, although according to official policy these settlers were squatters and could own no land. The British government, in fact, tried to discourage settlers and keep them out. In 1751 the permanent population was about 4,500, but during the war it rose to 16,000 and remained at that level for the next twenty years. No formal government was set up on the island, although the current "fishing admiral" (the captain who arrived first each year) administered rough and ready justice, enforcing the agreed rules of the fisheries among the ships' captains and their men.

Most of the permanent settlers in Newfoundland were English, but a third were Irish, and in the town of St. John's the Irish outnumbered the English. Religious strife became normal as Roman Catholic and Protestant quarrelled on every pretext. Newfoundland was a lawless community from which the British government preferred to avert its eyes. When in 1775 parliament did legislate policy for the island, the new law

Cook's map of Newfoundland, 1775, from his original drawn five years earlier. James Cook, the British navigator and naval officer, took part in the naval operations at Louisbourg in 1758 and Quebec in 1759. Before his better-known voyages of discovery to western North America, his accurate and meticulous surveys of the St. Lawrence River and Halifax harbour, and later the coasts of Newfoundland and Labrador, proved his excellence as a cartographer.

"A View of the Town" (St. John's, Newfoundland), from the logbook of H.M.S. "Pegasus", 1786.

merely restated the old view of the island's status: shipowners in England were given bounties for fish and fined for leaving seamen behind. At the same time American colonists were barred from landing on the shores and therefore from fishing around the island, though the French had been allowed landing rights on the west coast since the treaty of 1763. From the New Englanders' point of view this law, Palliser's Act, was the maritime version of the Quebec Act because it limited their opportunities for economic expansion.

When the American Revolution began in 1774, the northern colonies on the Atlantic seaboard were still only sparsely settled. The people of the outlying communities around the shores of Nova Scotia and Newfoundland, and the few Acadians – most of whom had returned after the 1763 peace settlement and were living along the shore south of Gaspé in what is now New Brunswick – could communicate with each other only by sea. The mixture of Irish, English, Scots, Germans, Acadians, and New Englanders, with their differing religious beliefs, created a diverse society. The colonists, dependent on fishing and their small garden plots, did not exchange goods with one another: indeed they were competitors – trying to sell the same products in the same markets. And overshadowing the whole region were ships of the British navy, giving wealth and even life to Halifax and offering protection to all the outlying communities.

Revolution in the Thirteen Colonies

Between 1763 and 1774 serious troubles had developed in the thirteen colonies south of Nova Scotia. Some of these troubles could be traced to the recent acquisition of Canada from the French and to the policy of 1763. Following Pontiac's uprising not only had the land west of the proclamation line been closed to settlement, but forts had been built to prevent further Indian troubles. The British government, unprepared to accept the full cost of these garrisons after the long and expensive war, proposed that the colonies pay for them, at least in part. A series of efforts to impose taxes on the colonists without their consent led to rioting in many cities and towns so serious that the government could not hire tax collectors. It withdrew some of the taxes, and for a time used coercion to collect the remaining ones; but even these were abandoned and by 1774 only a symbolic tax, a tariff on tea, remained. After the Boston Tea Party and other similar incidents elsewhere, the government decided to make an example of Massachusetts. By four separate Acts, the colony was placed under martial law, its Assembly and constitution were suspended, and the port of Boston was closed. Then Canadian problems intruded again. On top of these "Intolerable Acts", as the American colonists called them, came the Quebec Act, a measure which looked to the Americans like a further repressive act because of its repudiation of representative government and its transfer of lands between the Ohio and Mississippi rivers to Quebec. The Massachusetts men prepared themselves to resist British authority. Now that the French threat had disappeared, the colonists no longer needed Britain for their security. When the British forces in Massachusetts tried to seize an arms cache at Lexington near Boston, the colonists rebelled. For Nova Scotia and Quebec the choice was either to join the revolution or try to survive in North America separate from the booming thirteen colonies.

The Continental Congress of the thirteen colonies invited Canada and Nova Scotia to join the Revolution and in early 1775 sent agents north to persuade the colonists in Quebec to co-operate. Then, in June 1775, a

Left: *An early revolutionary money bill, designed to promote the move towards the establishment of American liberty in the British colonies.*
Below: *Benedict Arnold leading his men north to Quebec to join Montgomery's forces. The engraving is entitled "Arnold's march through the wilderness".*

double invasion began with a thrust north along the Lake Champlain-
Richelieu River route to seize Montreal and another aimed at Quebec from
New England along the Chaudière River Valley. The province of Quebec
was unprepared: its garrisons had been sent to reinforce Boston. Instead
of aiding the British in gratitude for the Quebec Act, the habitants were
resentful and passive; when called on by their seigneurs and priests to
fight, they refused to respond. After a spirited defence south of Montreal,
Carleton abandoned the city and retired to Quebec. The Americans under
General Montgomery occupied Montreal and marched on to Quebec,
where they joined the other army led by Benedict Arnold. Both armies
laid siege to Quebec, but their attempt to carry the city by storm on New
Year's Eve failed, and Montgomery was killed. The siege continued until
May 1776, when British ships arrived with troops and supplies; then the
Americans began a slow retreat back to Montreal and continued southward from there. Carleton's forces, now reinforced, set off in desultory
pursuit, for the governor seemed unwilling to press the invaders too hard
because peace and compromise between the British and Americans might
still be possible.

   Obviously, if the Americans had found popular Canadian support in
1776, even the arrival of a British fleet would not have defeated the

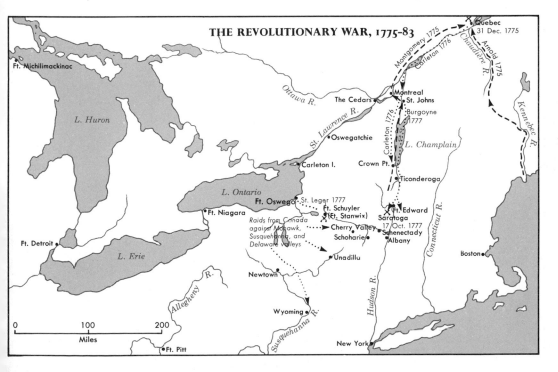

THE REVOLUTIONARY WAR, 1775-83

Americans – but this support was lacking. The Americans had sent a commission of three, among them Benjamin Franklin, the famous writer and scientist, to Montreal in an attempt to persuade the Canadians to join the revolution. The reception was civil but cool; because their livelihood in the fur trade depended on Britain, only a few American merchants supported the rebel cause. Most habitants felt no loyalty to Britain, but they were unwilling to accept the Americans. A few were friendly; some 150 left with the Americans. Yet while most of the French Canadians still traditionally disliked the Yankees and now distrusted their paper money, many of them were influenced by ideas from the south. After the events of 1776 there would always be a "patriot" movement in French Canada, a movement that espoused democracy as a protection for its language and culture.

In Nova Scotia, as might be expected because of the large number of recent New England settlers, there was considerable sympathy for the rebels. In 1776 a local effort to organize a rising in Cumberland County failed in an attempt to seize Fort Cumberland. Support for the revolutionary cause in the south shore ports dissipated when American privateers captured ships from those ports. Some Nova Scotians soon discovered that rich profits were to be had by privateering against the rebels and, after 1777, against their French and Spanish allies. But most Nova Scotians

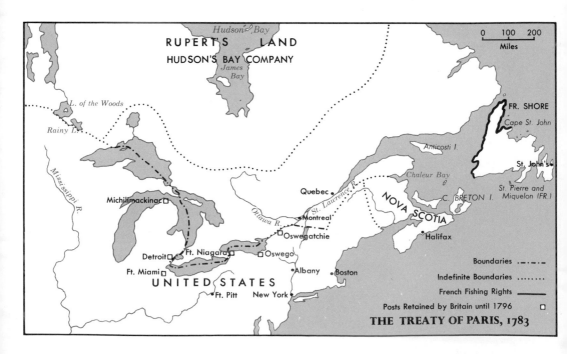

THE TREATY OF PARIS, 1783

preferred neutrality. Potential rebels remained quiet because of the over-whelming British sea power and their remoteness from the centres of dis-content. Moreover, Nova Scotians did not have the same grievances as the other colonies. Arbitrary British actions in Massachusetts were far away, and the western land issue was irrelevant. The mercantile system, restrictive as it might be to New England shipowners and merchants, was a protection to Nova Scotia. That province remained loyal by default.

In the thirteen colonies large British field forces were compelled to sur-render at Saratoga in 1777 and again at Yorktown in 1781, so that by 1782 British control in the rebellious colonies had been reduced to the city of New York. Although the British also controlled all the lands west of the Ohio River, they gave up hope of retaining their colonies and began negotiations with the colonies to reach a settlement. Benjamin Franklin, one of the American negotiators, suggested that to retain the goodwill of the new United States, Britain give up all this territory plus Quebec. In the Treaty of Paris, agreed on in 1783, the British ceded only the lands south of the Great Lakes to their former colonies and recognized their in-dependence. The United States therefore extended from the Atlantic to the Mississippi and from the Great Lakes and St. Croix River to Spanish Florida.

The Coming of the Loyalists

Many Americans in the thirteen colonies had remained loyal to Britain throughout the war. Particularly in the central colonies and in the western settlements in the south, large minorities were opposed to the revolution. By 1781 many Loyalist regiments had been raised to fight the rebels, but after 1783 these men and their families found it almost impossible to remain in their old homes in the new nation. They met persecution and charges of treason; their homes were broken into and pillaged by mobs; their very lives were in danger. But the laws of the land gave them no pro-tection, and neither the British nor the weak national government in the United States could protect them.

In order to put pressure on the Americans to protect Loyalist rights and property – and, incidentally, to placate the Quebec merchants – the British refused to turn over the western posts south of the Great Lakes which had been given to the Americans under the treaty. This refusal did not help the Loyalists, who were often terrorized by their revolutionary neighbours. Some of them had begun to leave the country during the revo-lution, and by 1781 the trickle had swollen to a stream. The better-off brought chests of clothing, linens, and silver, and much of their furniture with them by ship to Nova Scotia. But many poorer farmers from the in-

terior piled their few possessions on sledges and hauled them northward
on foot, while others carried their goods in ox-drawn carts. Some 100,000
Loyalists, possibly more, abandoned their homes. One-third of them went
to Britain, others went to the British West Indies, and a few even to Spanish Florida. The largest number migrated north to Nova Scotia and the
province of Quebec – in the spring and autumn of 1783 British ships carried some 30,000 north from New York to Nova Scotia. Others had already come; more followed by land.

The British government recognized that its obligation to the Loyalists
did not end in helping them to leave the United States. It provided them
with land, provisions for the first year of settlement, and tools to clear
and farm the land; it also promised to compensate them for their losses.
Most of these Loyalists were from the educated and wealthy class of the
eastern seaboard towns. Unaccustomed to pioneering, they were set ashore
on the frontier of the colony to fend for themselves as best they could.
Some Loyalists drifted back to the United States or went to Britain. But
the majority remained in their new homes – in the towns around the coast
of Nova Scotia, along the north shore of the Bay of Fundy, and in the St.
John River Valley. The original population was swamped by the Loyalists,
who now imposed their values and ideals on the province and, at first,
reinforced the Halifax oligarchy. But it did not take the Loyalists long to

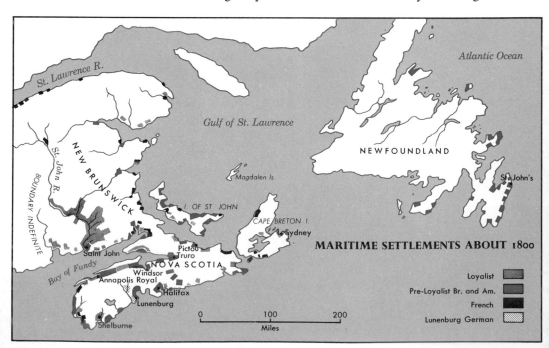

The founding of Sydney, Cape Breton Island, in 1785. The frame house on the hilltop (right centre) is that of Lt.-Gov. Des Barres; below it is anchored the brig "Maria", a Treasury Department ship making an official visit at the time.

tire of the remoteness of the capital and its society. The settlers in the St. John Valley and on the Fundy shore, whose distance from the capital prevented them from exerting influence and obtaining office, demanded the establishment of a separate government, and therefore New Brunswick and Cape Breton Island were created in 1784. The Loyalists thus transformed Nova Scotia from an outpost of New England into a truly British colony.

The United Empire Loyalist migration to Quebec was much smaller, numbering only about 6,000 people. Most were members of Loyalist regiments or frontier farmers who had made their way overland to seek new homes. From Vermont, New Hampshire, and northern New York they travelled up the Richelieu River to Sorel. Many went through the Mohawk Valley and crossed into Quebec at points along the St. Lawrence River. Butler's Rangers formed the nucleus of a settlement at Niagara, around which gathered more settlers from the interior of New York and Pennsylvania. These settlers were better fitted for pioneering than many who had gone to Nova Scotia, but there were few educated men or potential leaders among them. The hardships of making homes and farms were as great, however, and the first winters were cruel. After several years of coaxing crops from the soil between the stumps on the half-cleared land, there was a general crop failure in 1788. A number of settlers went back

"Encampment of Loyalists at Johnstown [Cornwall], A New Settlement, on the Banks of St. Laurence [sic] in Canada, taken June 6th 1784", from a watercolour by James Peachey (active 1781-93).

to the United States, but many of these returned to Quebec because they were attracted by the free land. There was much coming and going as Loyalists travelled back to settle affairs in their old homes, but after the "hungry year" of 1789 the settlements began to thrive. More people, many of them Mennonites or other religious minorities seeking secure religious freedom, as well as Americans disenchanted by the early years of independence, came to the province to settle the free land in the late 1780's. In fact, the whole migration into the western areas of Quebec was almost an extension of the American westward expansion after the revolution.

These English-speaking settlers were alien to the old French community of the province. Moreover, they wanted their familiar laws and governmental institutions. Once more, after dallying for several years, the British government bowed to the Loyalists' demands and in 1790 carved a new province out of the old one: with the exception of a triangular group of seigneuries at the confluence of the Ottawa and the St. Lawrence, the area west of the Ottawa River was separated from the rest. This new western province, at the upper end of the St. Lawrence, was named Upper Canada; the older province became Lower Canada. In 1791 the so-called "Constitutional Act" (an amendment to the Quebec Act) continued the rights given to Canadians under the Quebec Act and established a representative government in each province. Once again the Loyalist settlement led to the creation of a new political unit, the future province of Ontario. Significantly, Ontario's motto is *Ut incepit fidelis, sic permanet* (Loyal she began, loyal she remains), while amongst the Maritime Provinces it is New Brunswick that is called the "Loyalist Province".

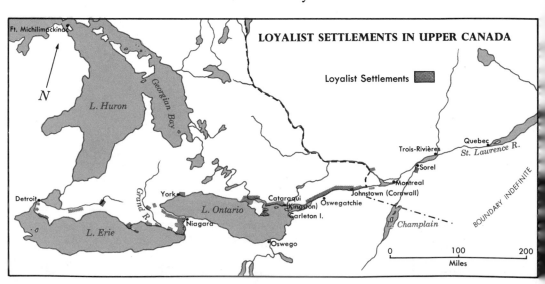

LOYALIST SETTLEMENTS IN UPPER CANADA

The coming of the Loyalists signalled a new beginning for the northern colonies, for these people began the task of rebuilding Britain's shattered American empire. Indeed, the future Canada was born in the American Revolution, for the Loyalists were the first substantial group of English-speaking immigrants to be added to the Canadian population. The distinctive society of Canada with her two languages and founding peoples and her diverse mosaic of national backgrounds and religious beliefs was emerging. These British North Americans were determined to preserve their distinctive heritage of political beliefs and institutions in the face of the republican experiment launched in the United States: it was to remain British that they had migrated.

HISTORY FROM THE SOURCES

The Conquest – What Did It Mean to the
French-Canadian People?

In 1760 when the French governor, the Marquis de Vaudreuil, surrendered to the English, some 65,000 French Canadians came under English rule. Would these people be able to survive as a group within a Protestant, English-speaking empire? Or would they be forced to assimilate themselves into this empire? What effect on the future of the French Canadians did the Conquest and its immediate aftermath have? Answers are hard to find, mainly because evidence from the French-Canadian side is lacking for the three decades after the Conquest.

The protection to the French Canadians, laid down in the Articles from the Capitulation of Montreal (8 September 1760), were confirmed in the Treaty of Paris, 1763, which ended the Seven Years' War.

ARTICLE XXI

The British General shall also provide ships for carrying to France the officers . . . having commissions or brevets from his most Christian Majesty, for them, their families, servants and equipages, and they shall likewise be victualled at the expence of his Britannic Majesty. They shall, however, be at liberty to stay in the colony . . .

ARTICLE XXVII

The free exercise of the Catholic, Apostolic, and Roman Religion, shall subsist entire . . . These people shall be obliged, by the English Government, to pay their Priests the tithes, and all the taxes they were used to pay under the Government of his most Christian Majesty.

ARTICLE XXXVI

If by the treaty of Peace, Canada remains to his Britannic Majesty, all the French, Canadians, Acadians, Merchants and other persons who chuse to retire to France, shall have leave to do so from the British General . . .

ARTICLE XXXVII

The Lords of Manors, the Military and Civil officers, the Canadians as well in the Towns as in the country, the French settled, or trading, in the whole extent of the colony of Canada, and all other persons whatsoever, shall preserve the entire peaceable property and possession of the goods, noble and ignoble, moveable and immoveable, merchandizes, furs and other effects, even their ships . . .

ARTICLE XLII

The French and Canadians shall continue to be governed according to the custom of Paris, and the Laws and usages established for this country, and they shall not be subject to any other imposts than those which were established under the French Dominions.

ARTICLE XLVI

The inhabitants and Merchants shall enjoy all the privileges of trade, under the same favours and conditions granted to the subjects of his Britannic Majesty . . .

A. Shortt and A. G. Doughty, eds., *Documents Relating to the Constitutional History of Canada, 1759-1791* (Ottawa, 1918), Pt. I, pp. 29-34.

The following proclamation from General Amherst in 1760 set the tone for future co-operation between conqueror and conquered.

Be it known, that we have constituted and appointed Mr. Gage, Brigadier of the King's armies, Governor of the town of Montreal and of its dependencies; and that in like manner we have appointed Mr. Burton, Colonel of His Majesty's troops, Governor of Three Rivers and its dependencies.

That in order to settle amicably as far as possible all differences which may arise amongst the inhabitants, the said governors are charged to authorise the officer of militia commanding in each parish or district, to hear all complaints, and if they are of such a nature that he can settle them, he shall do so with all due justice and equity; if he cannot decide at once, he must send the parties before the officer commanding the troops in his district, who shall in like manner be authorised to decide between them, if the case is not sufficiently serious to require its being brought before the Governor himself, who in this, as in every other case, shall administer justice where it is due.

That the troops, in the towns as well as in their cantonments, are provided for by the King in kind, and that it is expressly ordered that they shall pay for all that they buy from the inhabitants in ready money and specie.

As it is specially enjoined on the troops to live with the habitants in harmony and good fellowship, we likewise recommend the habitant to receive and treat the troops as brothers and fellow-citizens. It is further enjoined upon them to hearken to and obey all that is commanded them . . . and so long as the said habitants shall obey and conform to the said orders, they shall enjoy the same privileges as the ancient subjects of the King, and they may rely on our protection.

Shortt and Doughty, eds., *Documents* . . . , Pt. I, pp. 40-1.

This excerpt, which is part of a letter from the Earl of Egremont, the secretary of state, to Governor Murray, gives some indication of the British government's attitude to the church.

. . . His Majesty thinks it very material, that you should be apprized, that He has received Intelligence, which give some reason to suspect, that the French may be disposed to avail Themselves of the Liberty of the Catholick Religion granted to the Inhabitants of Canada, in order to keep up their Connection with France, and, by means of the Priests, to preserve such an Influence over the Canadians, as may induce them to join, whenever Opportunity should offer, in any attempts to recover that Country; It therefore becomes

of the utmost Consequence to watch the Priests very narrowly . . .
For tho' the King has, in the 4th Article of the Definitive Treaty,
agreed to grant the Liberty of the Catholick Religion to the Inhab-
itants of Canada . . . Yet the Condition, expressed in the same Article, must always be remembered, vizt: *As far as the Laws of Great*
Britain permit, which Laws prohibit absolutely all Popish Hierarchy
in any of the Dominions belonging to the Crown of Great Britain,
and can only admit of a Toleration of the Exercise of that Religion.

Egremont to Murray, 13 August 1763
Shortt and Doughty, eds., *Documents* . . . , Pt. I, p. 169.

Governor Murray did not implement any of the constitutional pro-
visions of the Proclamation of 1763. In so refusing he alienated the
small group of English merchants in Quebec.

Little, very little, will content the New Subjects but nothing will
satisfy the Licentious Fanaticks Trading here, but the expulsion of
the Canadians who are perhaps the bravest and the best race upon
the Globe, a Race, who cou'd they be indulged with a few priveledges
wch the Laws of England deny to Roman Catholicks at home, wou'd
soon get the better of every National Antipathy to their Conquerors
and become the most faithful and most useful set of Men in this
American Empire.

. . . I am confident too my Royal Master will not blame the
unanimous opinion of his Council here for the Ordonnance establishing the Courts of Justice, as nothing less cou'd be done to prevent
great numbers from emigrating directly, and certain I am, unless
the Canadians are admitted on Jurys, and are allowed Judges and
Lawyers who understand their Language his Majesty will lose the
greatest part of this Valuable people.

Murray to the Lords of Trade, 29 October 1764
Shortt and Doughty, eds., *Documents* . . . , Pt. I, p. 231.

The Board of Trade repeated the demands of these merchants in a
memorandum to the king.

Two great and important Considerations do yet however remain
to be submitted to Your Majesty; Viz^t

First, – The Propriety of calling a General Assembly, consisting of the Governor, the Council, and a House of Representatives, of which third Estate the situation and Circumstances of the Colony have not hitherto been thought to admit.

Secondly, – The repeated Complaints made by many of Your Majesty's Subjects there, and by the Principal Merchants trading to that Colony here, of Oppression and Misconduct in Your Majesty's Governor.

Upon the first of these Propositions, the only Objection to which, as we conceive, must arise out of the Present State of the Province, the Bulk of the Inhabitants of which being Roman Catholicks cannot, under the Regulations of your Majesty's Commission, be admitted as Representatives in such an Assembly . . .

As to what regards the Complaints exhibited against Your Majesty's Governor, they relate to such a Variety of Circumstances and Facts . . . and do refer themselves so much to the General State of Publick Measures there . . . that it will be most advisable, as well in regard to the Publick Interest, as in Justice to all Parties, that the said Complaints should be transmitted to Your Majesty's Governor, with Directions to return to this Kingdom . . .

> Board of Trade to the King, 2 September 1765
> Shortt and Doughty, eds., *Documents* . . . , Pt. I, p. 247.

The following passage from a mandement (an order from a bishop to his flock) dated 4 June 1763 reveals the attitude of the Roman Catholic church towards the Conquest. This mandement was issued by the senior vicar-general, Jean Olivier Briand, who administered the Canadian church after the death of Bishop Pontbriand in 1760.

The surrender of Quebec left you at the mercy of a victorious army. At first, you were undoubtedly alarmed, frightened, and dismayed. . . . Show me the vexations, the distortions, the plunders, that ordinarily follow in the wake of victory. Did not those noble victors, once they became our masters, appear to forget that they had been our enemies, in order to concern themselves solely with our needs and with ways of satisfying them? Surely, you have not forgotten the good actions of His Excellency, the illustrious and charitable General Murray, and the alms he gave to help the poor subsist! You have not forgotten his wise and generous measures to prevent famine in his government!

The apostle Paul, in many places, speaks of it as an indispensable obligation. By betraying the trust of your legitimate sovereign you would not only incur his wrath, lose his protection, and forfeit all the privileges he has been good enough to grant you, but you would also be guilty in the eyes of God. Twice guilty, since you would expose yourselves to being deprived of the right granted at the peace treaty to practise our holy religion, the only true faith. Consider carefully, then, dear brethren, how important it is for you to be loyal and submissive and how nothing can dispense you from a perfect obedience . . .

Mandements, lettres pastorales et circulaires des Evêques de Québec (Quebec, 1888), Vol. II, pp. 168-70 (translation).

Hugh Finlay, deputy postmaster-general of British North America from 1774 until 1799, wrote to Sir Evan Nepean in the secretary of state's office in England about British policy towards the Canadians. The Act he refers to is the Quebec Act.

. . . The Old Canadians are those we conquer'd in 1760 and their descendants, the new Canadians are composed of emigrants from England, Scotland, Ireland, and the Colonies now the United States: by the Act of the 14th of his present Majesty they are converted into Canadians, and Canadians they must ever remain. This doctrine is pleasing to the Noblesse or gentry of the Country, who will not easily get rid of French prejudices; – but to cherish a predilection for every thing that is french, is not, in my opinion, the most likely means to make Englishmen of the Canadians. . . .

Unless the Canadians can be brought to perceive that it is their int[e]rest to be attached to Great Britain, they will lean towards that Government which they may erroneously have conceived best calculated to promote their welfare; we ought not to forget their lukewarmness in 1775 – the better sort of the people in general, and the Clergy, behaved well, but we had little or no assistance from the peasantry, and all this arose from the insinuations of the Colonists, touching the supposed intention of the King and Parliament in passing the Quebec bill: it seems at present the wish of those who prefer french Law, and french Customs, to inculcate, that *if we introduce the English Commercial Law, the Estates and property of the Canadians will be annihilated* . . .

Finlay to Nepean, Quebec, 13 February 1787
Shortt and Doughty, eds., *Documents* . . . , Pt. II, p. 844.

FURTHER READING

Nish, Cameron, *The French Canadians 1759-1766* (Toronto: Copp Clark, 1967). A collection of short readings.

Brunet, M., *French Canada and the Early Decades of British Rule* (Canadian Historical Association Booklet No. 13, 1963)★. A nationalist and controversial view based on thin evidence.

Craig, Gerald M., *Upper Canada 1784-1841: The Formative Years* (Toronto: McClelland & Stewart, 1963). An excellent account of the early settlement of Upper Canada.

MacNutt, W. S., *The Atlantic Provinces: The Emergence of Colonial Society, 1712-1857* (Toronto: McClelland & Stewart, 1965).

Burt, A. L., *Guy Carleton; Lord Dorchester* (Canadian Historical Association Booklet No. 5, 1955)★.

Neatby, Hilda, *Quebec, The Revolutionary Age, 1760-1791* (Toronto: McClelland & Stewart, 1968).

Rawlyk, G. A., *Revolution Rejected* (Toronto: Prentice Hall, 1968). A book of primary and secondary readings on the reasons why British North Americans refused to join the American Revolution.

Upton, L. F. S., *The United Empire Loyalists: Men and Myths* (Toronto: Copp Clark, 1967).

Wade, Mason, *The French Canadians 1760-1967*, 2 vols. (Toronto: Macmillan, 1968)★. The authoritative history in English of the French-Canadian people since the Conquest.

Lanctot, Gustave, *Quebec and the American Revolution* (Toronto: Clarke, Irwin, 1967).

Burt, A. L., *The Old Province of Quebec*, 2 vols. (Toronto: McClelland & Stewart, 1968)★. An older account which minimizes the shock of conquest.

9

The River Versus the Bay

The Revival of the Fur Trade

After the French had surrendered in 1760, the fur trade, which had been interrupted by the war, was eagerly resumed, but most of the traders were now English or Scots, or Americans. They had arrived with the conquering army or come from the colonies to the south and brought their own experience of the fur business plus the capital needed to buy trade goods. The French-Canadian voyageurs still played their part by contributing their knowledge of trade routes and their experience in dealing with the Indians. With this joint enterprise of British capital and Canadian know-how the trade was quickly re-established south of the Great Lakes and Michilimackinac. As the traders pushed westward to rebuild the old French fur empire in the interior, Pontiac's uprising halted them only temporarily, and by the end of the 1760's they had advanced west of Lake Superior towards Lake Winnipeg.

The traders could have extended their routes and opened up territory even more rapidly had it not been for a series of difficulties they encountered. Western Indians frustrated their early efforts in the Lake Winnipeg area simply by seizing the trade goods; after 1771, however, these Indians were won over with gifts to the idea of trading. Also, beyond the lakehead it was difficult to carry enough supplies in canoes to last the whole winter: one trader, Joseph Frobisher, managed to survive a winter only by chewing

The city of Quebec in 1760, drawn by Hervey Smyth, "Aid du Camp to the late General Wolfe".

the beaver pelts he had bought. But these risks of inland trading were compensated for by enormous profits, since furs from the northwest were of higher quality than those from south of the Great Lakes.

As the traders advanced farther into the northwest in great numbers the rising cost of buying furs began to reduce profits, and the competition compelled the traders to co-operate more closely with one another. As early as 1775, four traders on the Saskatchewan pooled their stocks of trade goods and divided up the skins at the end of the season. The success of this joint venture foreshadowed the future consolidation of the trade; another factor leading towards it was the increasing competition from the Hudson's Bay Company. Efficient direction since the Treaty of Utrecht had brought consistent profits and increasing capital reserves to the company's operations, which had been little affected by the Seven Years' War. Its northern posts, Fort York at the mouth of the Nelson River and Fort Prince of Wales at the Churchill, had been particularly profitable because their hinterland had not as yet been penetrated by the Canadian-based traders, but the other two posts, Fort Albany at the mouth of the Albany River and Moose Factory at the confluence of the Abitibi and Moose rivers, had to pay higher prices to draw the Indians away from the "Pedlars from Quebec", as the company's men called their rivals. All these forts depended for their existence on the willingness of the Indians to bring their furs down the long rivers to the Bay.

Before the 1770's the company made no attempt to establish inland posts, because the cost and difficulties of maintaining them would have been enormous. Since large canoes were unknown in the north, it was impossible for the white traders to carry inland both trade goods and food. But with the European wares, the Crees and Assiniboines bought the furs from the hunting tribes and carried them down to the Bay, supporting themselves by hunting and fishing on the way. This conservative trading policy worked well until the competitive activities of the "Pedlars from Quebec" began to reduce the number of furs reaching the Hudson's Bay Company's northern posts. The company reacted quickly to this competition: several expeditions were despatched to buy furs from the Indians, and in 1774 a permanent post, Cumberland House, was built on Cumberland Lake near the Saskatchewan River to intercept some of the fur trade along the river.

The man chosen to found Cumberland House was Samuel Hearne, an Englishman who had joined the company in 1766 after serving as an officer in the Royal Navy. An experienced navigator, valuable as a map maker and explorer, Hearne was sent inland in 1771-72 to search for copper mines whose ore could provide a profitable ballast for ships returning to England with their light cargoes of furs. With the help of

Fort Prince of Wales, drawn by Samuel Hearne in 1777.

Indians, Hearne journeyed some 1,200 miles overland from Fort Prince of Wales to the Coppermine River and the Arctic Ocean, an exploration which revealed how desolate was the land. "My discoveries are not likely to prove of any material advantage," he wrote in his journal. Nevertheless, his work saved his successors from unprofitable expeditions into the sub-arctic. Being the only senior officer with experience of inland travel, Hearne was a natural choice to build the first post inland. The next year he became governor of Fort Prince of Wales and, except for a short imprisonment in France after the fort was captured in 1782, remained in command there until 1787 when he retired and returned to England.

This first inland post itself created numerous difficulties. There was the problem of transporting food and trade goods on the 800-mile trip – tobacco went bad, and iron kettles, another attractive trade item, proved to be uneconomically heavy to carry inland. Because the salaries paid the men were low even with bonuses for venturing inland, the results were low morale, a lack of incentive to expand the trade, and desertions of experienced men to the competitors from Montreal. Yet despite these difficulties the company's trade grew, and Cumberland House was a great success.

The success of the Hudson's Bay Company and the competition from its men in the interior forced the Montreal traders to join together in buying furs. The year after the informal agreement of 1775, eight of the mercantile houses of Montreal joined together to form the North West Company, each member holding two shares in the syndicate. The number of shares was increased periodically as more traders joined the company. At first this agreement was for one year only and was renewed annually, but after 1780 the annual arrangements gave way to longer ones. This kind of syndicate, in which trade goods and costs were pooled, furs were bought and marketed co-operatively, and the profits distributed annually, was imitated by other Montreal groups. Although the larger North West Company was better able to finance and organize the purchase, distribution, and transportation of trade goods to the traders in the west than any small group, a determined and well-financed competitor could not be beaten easily. Hence strong rivals were often invited to join the syndicate, and the number of shares was increased to accommodate them. As long as there was new territory to be opened up to the fur trade, the former competitors who joined the syndicate could be sent to rich fur-bearing areas farther west.

During the 1780's one Montreal firm, McTavish, Frobisher and Company, rose to pre-eminence in the trade. Simon McTavish, a Scots immigrant to New York at thirteen years of age, had been apprenticed to the fur trade and later built a business that he operated out of Albany. After the Conquest he moved north to Montreal, became one of the original partners in the North West Company, and by 1787 controlled four of the company's twenty shares. In that year he formed a partnership with Joseph Frobisher and with others as juniors, which gave the new firm of McTavish, Frobisher and Company majority control of the syndicate. After 1790 this firm handled all the business of the North West Company in Montreal and in London. Simon McTavish thus became the wealthiest and most powerful of the *bourgeois*, as the businessmen of the Montreal fur trade were called.

While the trade in the northwest flourished, the trade south of the Great Lakes dwindled. Traders in the southerly area first encountered troubles during the American Revolution. At that time the government of Quebec decided to permit only government vessels on the Great Lakes. Government goods received priority in shipping, there were not enough ships to keep the trading posts supplied, and the traders complained that

Voyageurs running the rapids on the Mattawa River.

A "canot du maître" – the type used to transport goods from Montreal to the northwest – painted in 1840 by Mrs. M. M. Chaplin.

these ships left trade goods behind on the government docks to be ruined by weather or stolen. After the Revolution, the traders held on to their posts in the face of growing American competition, but Jay's Treaty compelled them to hand these over to the United States in 1796 and forced the British government to withdraw its garrisons from adjacent forts.

Exploration to the Far West

The consolidation in the northwest fur business and the contraction of the trade in the southwest forced the traders ever westward and northward in search of furs. Peter Pond, an ex-soldier from New England, had opened the Athabasca country in the 1780's. From Indians of that region he had heard of a great river to the northwest, a river which he felt might flow to the Pacific. The reports fired the imagination of a young Scot, Alexander Mackenzie, who had entered the trade in 1778 and become a partner in the North West Company in 1787. In the spring of 1789 he set out from Fort Chipewyan by canoe with a party of voyageurs to find the supposed route to the Pacific. The party reached Great Slave Lake while it was still frozen, and had to wait for the ice to break up before they could paddle west into the great river. The course of the river shortly turned northward, but Mackenzie continued to follow it until he reached the "Frozen Ocean" at the mouth of the river that now bears his name. He had proved that the Mackenzie River was no route to the Pacific.

But Mackenzie was still driven by his desire to reach the Pacific. After building an advance post at the junction of the Smoky and the Peace rivers, he again set out westward in May 1793, with seven voyageurs and two Indians carrying a ton and a half of supplies, trade goods, and surveying instruments, all in a *canot du nord* – a canoe about eighteen feet long that could carry one-and-a-half tons with a crew of four or five men. The party followed the Peace River upstream to the Parsnip and portaged over the watershed to the Fraser River. Finding the Fraser too swift to navigate, they left supplies in caches, stored the canoe, and then, guided by local Indians, marched overland to the Pacific. After taking observations of latitude and longitude near Echo Harbour, Mackenzie wrote on a rock with a mixture of vermilion and melted grease the following memorial: "Alexander Mackenzie from Canada, by land, the twenty-second of July, one thousand seven hundred and ninety-three" – he and his men had been the first to cross the northern part of the American continent. Thirty-three days later they were back at their post at the Smoky and the Peace. Mackenzie's journal, published in 1801, told the English-speaking world of the significant accomplishment for which he was knighted that same year.

In the following year Mackenzie decided to leave the North West Company evidently because of the promotion of William McGillivray, Simon McTavish's nephew, and to join the New North West Company, a competitor of the original group. Some of the companies driven out of the United States by Jay's Treaty had obtained backing from British banks to form this new syndicate, commonly called the XY Company from the initials stencilled on its bales of trade goods. Upon Mackenzie's joining, it was renamed "Sir Alexander Mackenzie and Company". With good credit, experienced traders in the west, and the prestige of Mackenzie, the XY Company was a formidable competitor for the older syndicate, and for two years the two companies fought each other for control of the trade. Rum flowed freely as each tried to buy more furs than the other. Then in 1804 Simon McTavish died, and William McGillivray, his successor as senior partner, arranged a further amalgamation to end the struggle. One-quarter of the shares of the enlarged North West Company were given to the partners of the XY Company. Although Mackenzie was to receive a share of the profits, he was barred from any voice in the affairs of this newest organization, and the quarrel between Mackenzie and McGillivray was never resolved.

The amalgamation of the two companies forced a further expansion of the trading area to provide for all the "wintering partners" – those traders who remained year-round in the west to deal directly with the Indians. Moreover, the continuing rivalry with the Hudson's Bay Company, which had also been extending its inland operations westward, required the opening up of new fur territory beyond existing hunting lands. The North West Company chose another Scot, Simon Fraser, to open the Peace River and Rocky Mountain area. He shared Mackenzie's dream – to find an easy route to the Pacific – though he hoped to reach it by first finding the headwaters of the Columbia River, whose mouth had been discovered in the 1790's. Fraser began to build posts in 1805 along the upper valley of the river that now bears his name, but he did not attempt the journey until 1808, when he led a large party in four canoes down the river. Where the rapids became too dangerous, the party abandoned their canoes and struggled on foot along the precipitous banks until they again reached navigable water. They obtained dugouts from Indians and had almost reached the Strait of Georgia when some hostile Indians stopped them. Fraser took a rapid observation of latitude and concluded that this river was too far north to be the Columbia. Bitterly disappointed he returned home, where he could report only the discovery of a turbulent river and his failure to find a navigable route to the Pacific.

In the years immediately following Fraser's unsuccessful journey, the headwaters of the Columbia River were discovered by David Thompson, a brilliant surveyor and cartographer who had left the Hudson's Bay Company to join the Nor'Westers. He mapped the Kootenay region carefully in 1810 and the following year went down the Columbia River to its mouth, where, to his great surprise, he found Fort Astoria, built by John Jacob Astor's American Fur Company. Astor had made a fortune in the fur trade of the American west after the Canadian traders were forced out in 1796, and had then decided to use the mouth of the Columbia as a base for developing the fur trade in the mountains and for exporting these furs to China. When war came in 1812, Astor sold his fort to the North West Company, and the Oregon territory (what is now the state of Oregon and southern British Columbia) passed into British hands.

In the same year Thompson left the west never to return. His fame rests upon his extraordinarily accurate surveying work and his famous map of the west drawn for the North West Company post at Fort William. Thompson was typical of the new breed of explorers – those with formal training in surveying and cartography – who appeared in the early years

Fort Astoria as it was in 1813, from "Narrative of a Voyage to the Northwest Coast of America in the years 1811 [-1814]", by Gabriel Franchère, published in 1854.

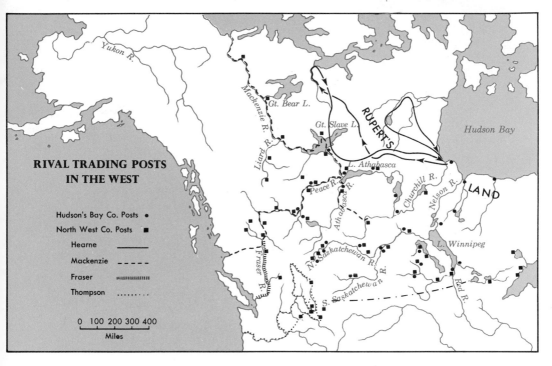

RIVAL TRADING POSTS
IN THE WEST

Hudson's Bay Co. Posts •
North West Co. Posts ■
Hearne ————
Mackenzie - - - - -
Fraser ıııııııııııı
Thompson ·········

0 100 200 300 400
Miles

of the century. He had been trained in surveying by Philip Turnor, who
was brought out by the Hudson's Bay Company in 1778. While the general outlines of transportation routes were known at the time, accurate
maps were needed by the traders, and it was Turnor who drew up reliable
maps of the area between Hudson Bay and Great Slave Lake. Another of
his pupils, Peter Fidler, surveyed a large part of what is now southern
Alberta and Saskatchewan. The results of Turnor's and of Fidler's work
were incorporated into Thompson's celebrated map. Drawn to a scale of
about one inch to fifteen miles, this remarkable map has, in recent years,
served as the base map for some of the areas outside those covered by the
Dominion Lands Survey.

Hudson's Bay Versus North West

By 1811 the relentless competition between the Hudson's Bay Company
and the Nor'Westers had spread over the whole northern part of the
continent. How to organize and manage the fur trade efficiently on a transcontinental scale was the main problem for both companies. Until the
1790's neither company was able to carry large quantities of goods into
the heart of the continent, because each lacked big canoes to handle inland
transportation. After 1795, however, that transportation problem was
solved for the Hudson's Bay Company – at least on the larger rivers and

Left: York boat in northern Manitoba, 1913.
Above: York boat of the Hudson's Bay
Company at Moose Factory, c. 1910.

Lake Winnipeg – by the development of the York boat, a keeled craft about forty feet long with a shallow draught. Portage roads complete with rollers for these boats were built at several places after 1800, and the company could then ship goods in bulk almost into the heart of the continent.

The Nor'Westers, on the other hand, still used canoes that gave them great mobility because they were easy to portage. Big canoes, the *canots du maître*, built only at Trois-Rivières and at St. Joseph's Island near Michilimackinac, carried freight goods from Montreal to the lakehead. Thirty-six feet long, six feet wide in the middle, and with a capacity of four tons, they were worked by a crew of eight or ten men who could travel the route at a steady six or seven miles per hour. But the food that had to be carried for the voyageurs reduced the paying cargo of the canoes – on long voyages more space was taken up by food than by trade goods. The voyageurs took with them light supplies such as dried peas, beans, salt pork, and pemmican. Pemmican, made of dried buffalo meat pounded into pieces the size of grain and mixed with fat, had a high food value, one pound being equivalent to five or six pounds of fresh meat. Except in hot weather it would keep for months.

As the trade expanded in the 1790's the Nor'Westers began to carry goods in ships on the Great Lakes and to make use either of the Niagara portage or the Toronto-Georgian Bay portage. Indeed, the company paid out £12,000, an enormous sum, to improve Yonge Street north from York for the route to Georgian Bay. In 1799 the Nor'Westers built a canal and locks at Sault Ste. Marie to handle small ships and *canots du maître,* In the west, they still used the *canots du nord,* because they were more versatile than the York boats, and enabled the Nor'Westers to penetrate regions accessible only by smaller rivers or by portages away from the great Saskatchewan waterway. But the longer range of the canoes used by the Nor'Westers was offset by the lower shipping costs of the Hudson's Bay Company.

For the Montreal-based group, however, the problem of how to keep the men who travelled the long routes supplied with enough food and trade

goods was linked with the lack of capital. Because of its practice of dividing profits each year, the syndicate had no capital reserves. Trade goods
had therefore to be bought on credit. Such goods sent out from England
in one season might not be sent up to Grand Portage – the depot was
moved to Fort William in 1804 – until the next spring, whereas the furs
bought by the traders would not be sent down to Montreal until the third
year. Thus an original capital investment would not yield any return for at
least three years, but meanwhile it would cost money in interest payments. Trade ultimately dependent on distant markets could mean tremendous profit or loss. The principal weakness of the North West
Company was its dependence on long-term credit to offset its lack of
capital reserves.

In contrast, the Hudson's Bay Company could use its reserve funds
instead of paying interest on borrowed money. But this considerable advantage was lost by the inflexibility of the English company's operations,
which did not permit its traders to deviate from the prices to be paid for
furs – prices that were laid down in the annual instructions from London.
The Nor'Westers, however, kept in closer touch with prices in London
and New York; long though the routes west were, their canoes could be
sent at almost any time carrying news of price movements so that the
wintering partners could adjust their buying prices. It was not unknown
for a winterer of the North West Company to know the prices at the most
recent Hudson's Bay Company sale in London before that company's
men had learned them. This flexibility, together with the partnerships held
by all the senior traders, which gave them a share of the profits and a
strong incentive to work, were the greatest competitive advantages of the
Nor'Westers. The low pay of the Hudson's Bay Company men led in the
1790's to poor morale and a number of desertions to the North West
Company. But after the absorption of the XY Company in 1804 limited
opportunities for promotion in the Canadian company, this trend was
reversed as experienced traders began to desert to the English group. At

*Below: Historic trade goods
recovered mainly by underwater
archaeology. Right: Canoe of Sir
George Simpson (the Governor-in-
Chief of Rupert's Land) at Fort
William, by William Armstrong
(1822-1914).*

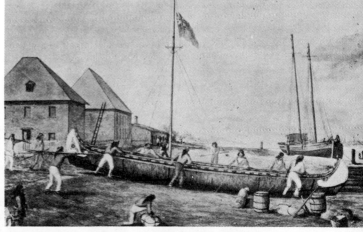

the same time profit-sharing incentives introduced by the Hudson's Bay Company improved employee morale. After 1804 the competitive advantages that had previously been relatively balanced between the two companies tipped increasingly in favour of the Hudson's Bay Company, especially because costs to the North West Company were soaring as traders drove farther west in search of furs.

Local competition between the companies became more fierce. And yet by 1811 fur prices had dropped heavily because of Napoleon's Continental System (a "paper" blockade of Britain and closure of the continent to British trade). These low fur prices hurt both groups and turned their competition into a struggle for mere survival. For the first time in a century, the Hudson's Bay Company paid no dividends to its shareholders in 1809, and none from then until 1815. Nevertheless the Hudson's Bay Company remained strong because of its large capital reserves, built up over a century of profitable operation, and because of its increasingly efficient methods, while the North West Company found it difficult to limit costs. The loose syndicate partnership made the enforcement of strict trading practices very difficult, particularly in the extension of credit to the Indians. Friction between the wintering partners and the Montreal *bourgeois* became more common. As the North West Company's trade routes grew longer, its finances more precarious, and its personnel relations more strained, the question was whether it could survive at all.

Charting the Pacific Coast

While the fur traders were pushing westward, another approach to the Pacific coastlands was made from the sea. The first European to sail into the north Pacific, Vitus Bering, was a Dane in Russian employ. He dis-

"Sea horses hunted by Captain Cook's expedition" from James Cook's "A Voyage to the Pacific Ocean . . . for making Discoveries in the Northern Hemisphere . . . in His Majesty's Ships the Resolution and Discovery, in the years 1776 [to] 1780", published in 1785. The "sea horses" were most probably walrus.

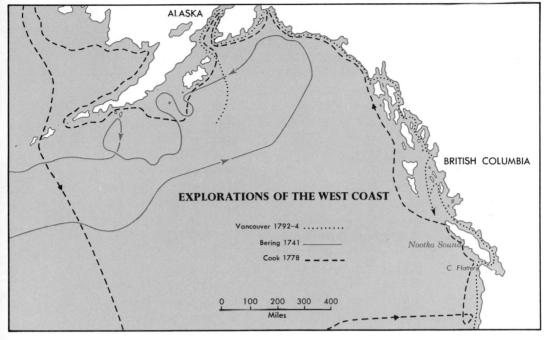

ALASKA

BRITISH COLUMBIA

EXPLORATIONS OF THE WEST COAST

Vancouver 1792–4 ....

Bering 1741 _____

Cook 1778 – – – –

Nootka Sound

C. Flattery

0   100   200   300   400

Miles

covered the strait between the continents and also the possibilities of the
fur trade in the Aleutian Islands. After Bering's death in 1741, Russian
traders came overland through Siberia to the Pacific and crossed to Alaska.
Russian interest in the west coast of North America prompted the Spanish
to send expeditions north to lay firm claim to the coast. In 1775, in his
thirty-six-foot vessel, the *Sonora*, Juan Francisco de la Bodega y Quadra
explored as far north as Alaska and claimed all the land south of 57°20′
for Spain.

Accurate mapping and active interest in the area by the Americans and
British developed only as a result of the news of Captain Cook's third
voyage. Cook, an experienced navigator and cartographer, had charted
much of the St. Lawrence River and Newfoundland coast in 1759-60 and
had subsequently made two voyages into the south Pacific. On his third
trip, after a leisurely cruise from England and a winter spent in the
Sandwich Islands (now Hawaii), Cook reached the coast of what is now
Oregon in March 1778. Shortly after making the landfall his ships were
driven out to sea again and he sailed north, missing the Strait of Juan de
Fuca, and sighting land again at Nootka Sound on Vancouver Island.
He continued northward, charting the coast and looking for a waterway
into the continent, but as winter approached, he decided to return to the
Sandwich Islands. There he was killed by natives in February 1779.

European interest in the Pacific was stirred by Cook's descriptions of
huge herds of sea otters, about which he wrote in his journal, posthumously

published in 1784. Sailors from the expedition told of selling the pelts for handsome prices in China on the return voyage. The demand for fur cloaks and trim spread to China, and in the late 1780's British and American seamen started sailing around Cape Horn to the Pacific, or eastward from Canton and Macao, to get sea otter. This rush for furs provoked the Spanish into building posts along the coast to protect their claims to it. They did not, however, occupy these posts continuously. The Spanish seizure of a British trader's fort at Nootka and of his ship led to an international incident between Britain and Spain in 1789, in which the Spaniards insisted that the seizure was justified because of the intrusion into their territory, but the British answered that the Spanish had no legal claim because they had not occupied the coast continuously. In 1790 the Spanish agreed to return the buildings and goods, and paid damages in compensation.

The British government had already been planning a second expedition to the west coast of America. This mission, under Captain George Vancouver, was in part a diplomatic one, for he was to receive officially the ship and post taken by the Spanish in 1789. But Vancouver's main task was to survey accurately the coast north from 30° – the peninsula of lower California – but not to "pursue any inlet or river further than it shall appear to be navigable by vessels of such burthen as might safely navigate the Pacific Ocean". These instructions may account for Vancouver's failure to explore the Columbia River, an omission which allowed the United States to claim the area later. His survey, made between 1791 and 1794, produced accurate charts of the coastline including, for the first time, a precise outline of Vancouver Island.

The transfer of property from Spain was a more difficult task than Vancouver's mapping job. Quadra still held the post at Nootka; he had received no instructions and was unwilling to hand it over to the English. In the course of their negotiations the two men came to like and respect

Friendly Cove, Nootka Sound, after a sketch made on the spot; from George Vancouver's "A Voyage of Discovery to the North Pacific Ocean . . .", published in 1798.

one another and to co-operate in the mapping work. Indeed Vancouver named the large island which now bears his name alone "Quadra and Vancouver Island". Once the inconclusive negotiation had come to an end, Vancouver's ships returned home after their long stay in Pacific waters, with charts as well as with plant specimens for George III's botanical garden at Kew Palace.

In the meantime, Spain had agreed in 1793 to withdraw her claims to the northern coast. The post at Nootka was abandoned and the Pacific coastline from the Columbia River to the Russian territory far to the north was now in British hands. Because the British were occupied with the war in Europe, the valuable sea-otter trade fell largely to the Americans, and ships of Boston merchants sailed from the sea-otter grounds to Canton with furs and returned to Boston loaded with teas, silks, and cottons. This very profitable trade flourished although the War of 1812 made sea communications risky. The sea-otter trade boomed along the British Columbia coast until the second quarter of the century, when the slaughter had taken such a toll that the operation was no longer profitable on a large scale. The North West Company and after 1821 the Hudson's Bay Company still continued to export other kinds of furs to Canton from Oregon for a number of years.

As for the disputed ownership of the Oregon territory, after the War of 1812 it was agreed that it was to be administered jointly by Britain and the United States. In the 1840's Britain's authority over the northern Pacific coast was challenged by the westward expansion of American settlement. The United States laid claim to the territory on the basis that the mouth of the Columbia River had been discovered by an American in the 1790's and that the first post in the area had been built by Astor. The conflicting claims resulted in an international crisis in 1844-5.

FURTHER READING

Campbell, Marjorie W., *The North West Company* (Toronto: Macmillan, 1957). A colourfully written history of the company and the people who operated it.
Easterbrook, W. T. and Aitken, H. J. G., *Canadian Economic History* (Toronto: Macmillan, 1956).

MacKay, Douglas, *The Honourable Company* (Toronto: McClelland & Stewart, 1966)★.

Rich, E. E., *The Fur Trade and the Northwest to 1857* (Toronto: McClelland & Stewart, 1968).

Campbell, Marjorie W., *McGillivray: Lord of the Northwest* (Toronto: Clarke, Irwin, 1962).

Brebner, J. B., *The Explorers of North America* (New York: Doubleday, 1955)★. A general account of continental exploration.

Warkentin, J., *The Western Interior of Canada: A Record of Geographical Discovery 1612-1917* (Toronto: McClelland & Stewart, 1964)★.

Innis, H. A., *The Fur Trade in Canada* (Toronto: University of Toronto Press, 1964)★. The basic economic study of the history of the fur trade.

Wallace, W. S., *The Pedlars from Quebec* (Toronto: Ryerson, 1954). A colourful and anecdotal series of accounts of the early traders in the northwest.

Thomson, D. W., *Men and Meridians*, Vol. 1 (Ottawa: Queen's Printer, 1966). A history of exploration and mapmaking before 1867.

Galbraith, J. S., *The Hudson's Bay Company as an Imperial Factor* (Berkeley: University of California Press, 1957).

10

The Foundations of British North America

The Emergence of Colonial Government

Despite the influx of United Empire Loyalists into the British American provinces, these colonies remained thinly populated. The west continued to be uninhabited except for Indians and fur traders; in Canada and the Atlantic colonies the handful of settled communities was small and most were of recent growth; French Canada was firmly established, as were a few areas in Nova Scotia. The majority of people were self-sufficient farmers still at the pioneer stage. The colonies were remote from each other; water routes provided the only communication between them. Their only link was a common loyalty to Britain.

The British government's view of its empire was not immediately changed by the revolution. According to this view a colony had to be subject to imperial control, and trade had to flow in directions which benefited the mother country. One of the lessons to be learned from the American Revolution was that tighter control over the colonies was needed. It was said that the trouble in the thirteen colonies had resulted from their enjoying too much freedom before 1763, and that the Assemblies had been allowed to do too much as they pleased. In the new empire, therefore, the executive levels of government representing the British government had to be kept strong, and the power of popularly elected Assemblies kept within strictly defined limits. This policy was, however, by no means oppressive, since Britain intended to preserve loyal colonies, not punish recalcitrant or rebellious ones, and the major irritant of the 1760's had been removed in 1777 when the British parliament agreed not to raise internal taxes without the colonists' consent. The provinces looked to Britain for the defence and protection of their trade and shipping and also for their markets. The Loyalists, moreover, stressed loyalty rather than liberty, and the traditional links with British life. In order to avoid any repetition of the bloodshed and turmoil they had experienced before coming north, most Loyalists supported the limitation of representative government.

Nova Scotia retained the form of government set up before the American Revolution. A governor, advised by an appointed executive council, was selected by the British government to govern the colony. This council also served in a legislative capacity, approving the bills sent up by the elected Assembly or recommending legislation for its consideration. The Assembly made the laws, represented the will of the people, and approved necessary taxation. The same form of government was adopted in New Brunswick and Prince Edward Island in 1784. When the province of Cape Breton was set up in that year, its population was considered too small for both an Assembly and a Council. Until 1820, therefore, when it was reunited with Nova Scotia, its Executive Council enjoyed legislative powers.

The Constitutional Act of 1791, which created the two provinces of Upper and Lower Canada, established the same form of government in each of them. Not only were the merchants' demands for an Assembly granted, but Roman Catholics were permitted to become members. Unlike the Maritimes, however, an additional check on each Assembly was introduced in the form of the appointed Legislative Council, which had to approve all legislation. The executive branch was similar to that in the Maritimes. The governor of Lower Canada was designated governor general of Canada and, after 1808, governor general of British North America. Although the lieutenant-governor in each province was responsible directly to the Colonial Office in Britain, the governor general was given nominal control over military affairs.

John Graves Simcoe, the first lieutenant-governor of Upper Canada, hoped to make his colonial government the "image and transcript", as he called it, of the British constitution. But there was a more democratic spirit in the colonies than in Britain. A large number of people enjoyed the right to vote, because the English forty-shilling freehold franchise had been introduced into the colonies, where it gave most farmers the franchise. There were many curbs on the Assemblies, however; for example, the separate Legislative Councils in the Canadas. The governors could

John Graves Simcoe was accompanied by his wife during his stay in Upper Canada as lieutenant-governor. Mrs. Simcoe kept a diary and notebook of her travels, sketching on the spot on birchbark. One of her birchbark sketches, drawn in 1796, shows Pointe aux Trembles on the St. Lawrence River shore of Montreal Island.

Dance in the Château St. Louis, by George Heriot. The Château, the governor's residence, stood on Dufferin Terrace in Quebec city until it was destroyed by fire in the 1830's. Heriot came to Canada in 1792; after serving in the army he was appointed post-master general of British North America.

reject bills or reserve them for consideration by the imperial authorities. And, even if a law were passed in the colonies, it might still be disallowed by Britain. All the revenues from land sales and customs duties levied by the British parliament – and these formed the largest part of the government's entire revenue – were at the disposal of the governors. Land taxes, licence fees, and further customs duties were the only sources controlled by the elected branches. Because the executive branch in each colony was financially independent, it was futile for the Assembly to attempt to legislate against the executive's wishes.

Besides this effort to limit popular government, Simcoe and those of like mind made an effort to create a conservative society (based on the eighteenth-century British ideal of property and privilege) by setting up a state church and a governing class to lead the people in showing loyalty to the government. While it proved impossible to create a colonial aristocracy in a society that lacked wealth, an attempt was made to establish Anglicanism as the state religion. An Anglican church had been established by law in Nova Scotia in 1758 and received financial support from the imperial government. The absence of an established church such as this and the influence of dissenting groups was commonly held to be one of the reasons for the revolution in the thirteen colonies. In the Canadas, the Constitutional Act of 1791 endowed the Anglican church with lands, called the Clergy Reserves. The income from these reserves was to be used to support what the Act called a "protestant clergy". In Lower Canada, however, the government moved gingerly for fear of offending the influential Catholic church; thus the Colonial Office remained carefully noncommittal over which denomination had the right to use the title "Bishop of Quebec". In spite of all the support given, it proved impossible in Nova Scotia and Upper Canada to create an effective established church because of the diverse religious composition of those provinces' populations. The colonial society was not growing according to plan – a conservative, Anglican, monarchical society was not emerging in British North America.

The colonies' troubles did not come singly: the Clergy Reserves, the privileges exercised by the Anglican church, and the restrictions on the powers of the Assemblies all caused problems. The difficulties were all the greater because small élite groups controlled the executive levels of government. Many of these officials were drawn from the educated and public-spirited few who had the wealth to be able to devote time to government, although some were office seekers who wanted the income and prestige. Loyalists, in particular, felt that they were entitled to positions in the colonial government and had a claim to the bounty of the imperial government. Before 1812, most members of the Assemblies accepted this type of leadership, their attitude prompted by loyalism. The colonial governments therefore worked tolerably well until the colonies became more mature communities and the people wanted a greater voice in governing their own affairs.

Social and Economic Growth in the Atlantic Provinces

The Loyalist migration gave the Atlantic provinces a sudden burst of growth but, after this spurt, settlements grew slowly and by the 1790's it had become obvious that the growth and prosperity of the early years was not continuing. This lag was caused by cuts in British expenditures on garrisons and in aid to the Loyalists, which meant that specie (coins) became so scarce that much of the trade between communities remote from the two main centres of Halifax and Saint John had to be carried on by barter. But, although trade was discouraged, self-sufficiency was encouraged. The lack of skilled labour also retarded some industries; for example, the forest industry in New Brunswick did not develop until after 1800 because there were no experienced lumbermen.

In 1790 instructions forbidding free land grants and requiring that Crown lands be sold were sent from Britain in the hope of obtaining more revenue for the provincial governments, a policy that lasted for seventeen years in the Atlantic provinces, but one that was never put into effect in the Canadas. The edict had little effect in Nova Scotia, where most of the good land was already occupied and where squatters had settled on what remained, but in New Brunswick land values plummeted, for settlement slowed almost to a stop. There was little immigration. Some Highland Scots continued to come, and many of those who went to Prince Edward Island were sponsored by the Earl of Selkirk, a wealthy philanthropic laird. Other Highlanders came to the north side of the isthmus and to Cape Breton – so many that Gaelic became and remains

Two engravings from eighteenth-
and nineteenth-century New
Brunswick.
Above: Timber booms on the St. John
River.
Right: Woodboats at the falls, Saint
John.

the everyday tongue of many people on the island. By the end of the
century there were some 80,000 inhabitants in the mainland colonies.
Another 16,000 lived in Newfoundland, but the island still had no formal
government because it had not developed to any great extent.

The small population and the primitive level of economic development
made it impossible for the Maritimes to replace New England as the chief
trading partner with the West Indies, and as early as 1786 Britain allowed
lumber to be imported into the Indies from the United States. Only the
better established and more fertile areas of Nova Scotia, such as the
Minas region, had beef and flour to sell. Nevertheless, the shipping industry flourished; fish was carried south to the West Indies and, because
American ships were prevented from using British harbours in the Carib-
bean, timber and foodstuffs were imported from the United States. The
war between Britain and France after 1792 ended this trade, because
French privateers operating out of American harbours and the West
Indies seized so many ships. United States' vessels began to smuggle goods
into the islands, and by Jay's Treaty in 1794 some of the West Indian ports
were opened to the Americans. Although Nova Scotia felt the loss of the
carrying trade, war supplies and convoys passing through Halifax light-

ened the economic blow. But New Brunswick was hurt seriously because the British navy would not provide convoy protection from Saint John or St. Andrews. The trade depression plus the land policy sent a tide of despair across the province, and by 1800 talk in the province was of opportunity in the Niagara area of Upper Canada: New Brunswick, it seemed, had no future.

In the long run, however, the war had a stimulating impact on the economy of the region. After 1801, and especially after the Continental System was imposed in 1806, Britain looked to North America to supply timber for ships and masts. Armies of lumbermen, many of them settlers who farmed in the summer, attacked New Brunswick's forests every winter. Huge rafts of squared timber were floated down the St. John River and the Miramichi, and loaded into specially built ships for transport to Britain. Local shipbuilding flourished and complemented the fishing and lumber industries as the British fleet gradually made the seas safe.

By 1815 the whole Maritime region was prospering. In New Brunswick the economy was built on lumbering, shipping, and shipbuilding. In Nova Scotia, although the best trees were gone, these industries, together with fishing and farming in the rich lands of Annapolis, the Minas region, and Chignecto, provided good livings for the people. In Prince Edward Island the farms flourished and there was some fishing and shipbuilding; markets both for the islanders' produce and for their ships existed in St. John's and Halifax. In Newfoundland the fisheries remained the basis of the economy. The patterns of life which had evolved in the region during these years endured until the coming of steam, iron ships, railways, and political union with the Canadas in 1867. The provinces emerged as communities primarily dependent on the sea – its fisheries and its commerce.

St. John's, Newfoundland, from a watercolour painted in 1798. The town shown here was built almost entirely of wood and was destroyed by fire in 1816-17.

Social and Economic Development in the Canadas

The two provinces of Upper and Lower Canada presented a sharp contrast to the Atlantic provinces in these years. Here growth was rapid. In 1791 the Canadas' population was 180,000 of whom only 14,000 lived in the upper province. By 1812 this figure had grown to 420,000 with some 90,000 in Upper Canada. Much of the increase in Lower Canada was caused by an extraordinarily high birth rate, for only about 10,000 immigrants, mostly from the United States, had come to join the few Loyalists in the Eastern Townships. In Upper Canada the immigrants, again mostly Americans who were flooding west from the seaboard states, accounted for most of the increase, though there were some group settlements such as the Highland Scots brought out to Baldoon, near Lake St. Clair, by Lord Selkirk.

Though Lower Canada remained predominantly Roman Catholic, Upper Canada developed as a religious mosaic, even as Nova Scotia had. Anglicanism and Presbyterianism flourished, mainly in the few towns that had grown up before 1812, but because these two denominations were unable to attract enough mission-minded clergy to work outside the towns, they were unable to reach the frontiersmen. Other protestant denominations, particularly the Methodists and Baptists, were more effective in rural areas. Adding to this religious pluralism in Upper Canada, Roman Catholic Scots settled in the eastern districts and a few Mennonites and Quakers came north from the United States.

In Upper Canada settlement was encouraged by generous land grants. Loyalists and their children were able to obtain free land, but any immigrant could receive 200 acres in return for taking the oath of allegiance to George III and paying registration and survey fees. So many Americans took advantage of these terms that Upper Canada began to resemble an American community, but the government of the province did not object to the large number of immigrants from the south, and continued to encourage them to settle in Upper Canada. By 1812, settlement was almost continuous along the St. Lawrence River and the north shore of Lake Ontario, and many areas along Lake Erie had also been settled. Nine-tenths of the population were estimated to be Americans.

Energetic leadership for the fledgling province was given by John Graves Simcoe, who had been commander of the Queen's Rangers (a Loyalist regiment) during the American Revolution. Simcoe believed strongly in the superiority of British government, and considered that the oath of allegiance, free land grants, and good government that provided British justice and liberty would create a loyal and prosperous population. Many immigrants from the thirteen colonies had been born subjects of

Mrs. Simcoe's watercolour sketch of the Mohawk village at Grand River, 1793.

George III and, in Simcoe's opinion, would return easily to that allegiance, since they had not yet had enough time to feel loyalty for the newly emerged United States.

The oath of allegiance and the free land grants were successful in bringing in settlers, and Simcoe began to put his ideas on good government into practice. He organized districts for local government in the province, and in 1792 pushed through the legislature a law to abolish slavery. Although he attempted to make the Anglican church the established church and to bolster it with government-supported schools and a university, these projects were never accomplished. During his administration, roads were built and plans laid for a provincial capital, London, at the forks of the Thames River. York, now Toronto, was established in 1793 as a military and naval base because of its excellent and defensible harbour; it served as the temporary capital, and after 1796 became the permanent seat of government. By the time Simcoe left in 1796, the colony was well established and developing more rapidly than any other part of British North America in these years.

During the same period of time, Lower Canada, the hub of the North American empire, had also advanced economically. Montreal, with a population of 30,000, was the most important city in British North America. Here lived the wealthy fur merchants and the importers and forwarders of goods destined for Upper Canada. Quebec city was the main centre for lumber merchants and their businesses – large-scale enterprises that required considerable capital and organization. The potential commerce with the interior, which involved buying wheat and furs for sale in Britain and selling British goods to Upper Canada and the American west, seemed enormous. The merchants had become enchanted by the

Mrs. Simcoe's sketch of Point à Bodet (today it is Rivière Baudette), 1792.

dream of a commercial empire around the Great Lakes and centred on Montreal, and demanded navigational improvements along the St. Lawrence. These entrepreneurs dominated the government by serving in the councils and used their positions to further their aims, but they ran into opposition from those members of the Assembly who represented French-Canadian rural interests.

The first Assembly, elected in 1792, had a majority of French-Canadian members, but there was no evidence of any anti-British feeling. In the mid-1790's, while Britain was involved in war with revolutionary France, there were a few in the province who responded to the ideas of liberty, equality, and fraternity, and agents from the United States and France encouraged the discontented, calling on them to emulate their brothers in France and the United States by rebelling. Although the clergy responded by denouncing such liberal ideas, there were riots in 1794 against a militia act and in 1796 against a law reviving the *corvée*. These, while not anti-British, were seen as such by the governor and the English merchants, and several of the trouble makers were arrested. Suspicious of the Canadians, the English-speaking minority entrenched themselves in the councils, where they influenced the governors to depend on them. Open conflict between French and English flared over taxation. Funds were needed for jails, court houses, and public works such as canals and locks on the St. Lawrence. The Assembly wanted customs duties, the councils preferred land taxes. Although the struggle was between differing economic interests, by 1805 overtones of racial conflict were clearly apparent.

In order to publicize the French-Canadian majority's position, Pierre Bédard, a lawyer and member of the Assembly, together with some associates, established a newspaper, *Le Canadien. Le Canadien* defended the rights of the Assembly and criticized the English-speaking oligarchy for monopolizing official positions and for distributing generous land grants amongst themselves and their friends. Although Bédard and his colleagues were apt students of British constitutional doctrines, their goal was not liberal constitutional government as such, but the use of parliamentary

Left: A cariole, by Mrs. M. M. Chaplin. Below: A Canadian cariole, from John Lambert's "Travels Through Lower Canada and the United States . . .", published in 1810.

The 85-foot-long wooden paddle steamer "Accommodation", the first steamboat in Canada. Built by John Molson at Montreal and launched in 1809, she plied between Montreal and Quebec. The journey took 66 hours (including the time spent anchored at night); the actual time under way was 36 hours. Her engines were made at the St. Maurice Iron Works at Trois-Rivières. During the War of 1812 she carried British troops up the St. Lawrence from Quebec.

institutions to preserve their language and culture against the anglicizing minority. They accused this minority of constantly trying to weaken the place of the French language and the influence of the Roman Catholic faith through such instruments as the proposed Royal Institution of Learning, a system of free parish schools under Anglican control.

The racial conflict reached its height when a new governor, Sir James Craig, an authoritarian soldier, decided in 1810 to dissolve the Assembly in the hope of obtaining a legislature more likely to do his bidding. He then seized the presses of *Le Canadien* and imprisoned Bédard and his partners without laying charges. In the following elections most of the sitting representatives, including Bédard, were returned. Craig then recommended that the constitution of the province be suspended. The British government responded to the crisis by appointing a new governor, Sir George Prevost, a French-Swiss by birth. Determined to conciliate the French Canadians, Prevost appointed a few leading Canadians to the Executive Council and some, Bédard amongst them, to the bench. The people responded warmly to Prevost and his policies, and his success in the next few years well demonstrated that the French Canadians were not disloyal – that they sought only to preserve their culture and way of life, free from English domination. That their loyalty was beyond question was proved in the war with the United States between 1812 and 1815, when they remained conspicuously loyal to their Canadian heritage.

The Second Challenge from the South

After the revolution the British North American provinces found themselves dwarfed by their neighbour the United States. The new nation, with a population of over 3,000,000 in 1783, grew rapidly until by the mid-1790's settlements had spread over the Appalachians into the Ohio Valley and south into Kentucky and Tennessee. Progress and prosperity were everywhere visible, too visible for the more slowly developing British colonies, where growth was less spectacular and the discontented eagerly pointed to the success of the republican experiment. Relations between the United States and Britain were uneasy during the years after the revolution. British North America was vulnerable to American attack not only because of its small population and the scattered development of its settlements, but because by accident of geography it provided its southern neighbour with an ever-present opportunity to attack Britain through her colonies. The survival of these colonies depended on Britain and in the long run on the settlement of Anglo-American problems. Such security had been provided by Jay's Treaty in 1794, which settled a wide range of issues from British occupation of the "old Northwest" to American access to British West Indian ports. But security was only part of the requirement for survival; more vital was the settlement of the land and the development of the economy. Until the tasks of nation building were completed, the possibility of annexation to the United States would always be present.

By 1811 relations between Britain and the United States had again reached a dangerous impasse. After new continental boundaries had been drawn in 1783, the British had retained the western posts. Aware that no provision had been made for Indian lands and that the Indians disliked the new boundaries, Britain planned to create an Indian buffer state between her colonies and the United States in the Ohio and Illinois country – a scheme prevented by the westward expansion of American settlement. The American government sent a series of military expeditions into the territory, and these finally defeated the Indians decisively at Fallen Timbers in 1794. By Jay's Treaty, signed in the same year, the British promised to turn over the posts still in their hands, thereby recognizing the failure of their western policy. Nevertheless, as long as British traders could legally enter the west and as long as the Indians traded with them, the suspicion that the British were encouraging the Indians to resist American expansion would remain. After 1805 the Shawnee chief Tecumseh and his brother, the Prophet, began to organize a new Indian confederacy to prevent American settlement in the "old Northwest". Their success in delaying western expansion alarmed the government, which sent a punitive expedition in 1811 that defeated the Indians at Tippecanoe and burned their villages and crops. From then on, the Indians had only Britain to depend on, and western Americans felt that they would never achieve security from the Indian menace until Canada was conquered and

British influence removed. Undoubtedly, the good land of the upper province and the weakly defended boundary also encouraged them.

The major issue between the countries, however, was maritime rights. The British blockade of Europe during the wars with Napoleonic France harmed American trade. The British stopped American ships on the high seas, searched them for war supplies that might be on their way to France, and seized real and suspected deserters from their own navy who were serving with the Americans. They even impressed American seamen into their navy. The high-handed exercise of this right of search, as the British called it, caused numerous incidents: a fight in 1807 between the British frigate *Leopard* and the U.S.S. *Chesapeake* almost precipitated war. President Jefferson persuaded Congress to pass an embargo on trade with Britain and France that went into effect in 1808. Two years later, the embargo was dropped in a humiliating surrender to Britain: if either Britain or France gave up her right of search, the president could authorize trade between that country and the United States. Many more American ships than British were engaged in the carrying trade, and because the embargo had the effect of confining American vessels to their home ports, it hurt American sea commerce more than British. But still George III's government did nothing to improve diplomatic relations with the United States. Following the congressional elections in 1810, westerners elected to the new congress, who were concerned about the Indian problem, began to demand war with Britain. British unwillingness to negotiate the maritime rights issue gave these "War Hawks" the opportunity to push the United States into a war which New England did not want. With preparations for hostilities already under way, President Madison reluctantly

*H.M.S. "Shannon" leading her prize, the American frigate "Chesapeake",
into Halifax harbour, 1813.*

signed the declaration of war on 18 June 1812, even while his ambassador in Britain was striving for a settlement.

The Atlantic provinces were kept safe from invasion by the defending British navy. The small United States navy did well in a series of duels between frigates until H.M.S. *Shannon* defeated the U.S.S. *Chesapeake* off Boston in 1813, but the superior strength of the British navy really counted. The blockade and privateering strangled American shipping, and shipowners from Halifax, Lunenburg, Shelburne, and Saint John profited greatly from both measures. Indeed, the work of supplying the British fleet, the revival of trade with the West Indies, and the privateering combined to bring boom times to the Maritimes region.

The Americans, ten times more numerous than the British colonists, could easily have conquered Upper Canada if they had had more co-operation from reluctant state governments, better co-ordination of their campaign operations, and if they had decided to attack the St. Lawrence River line of communications. Instead the Americans were preoccupied with land campaigns in western Upper Canada. Farms and mills, the fruits of two decades of labour, were destroyed by American raiders in the Niagara peninsula and in the southwest. Newark (now Niagara-on-the-Lake) and York, the major towns west of Kingston, were captured by the Americans and partly destroyed. Although a few farmers prospered by selling foodstuffs to the army, the cost of war to Upper Canada was high.

The credit for saving Upper Canada in 1812 belongs largely to Major General Isaac Brock, the civil administrator and senior military officer. He had served there since 1802 and knew the country well. A capable and energetic officer with a dashing and attractive personality, Brock inspired the defenders and quieted the defeatists. The Americans wrongly assumed that their compatriots who had settled in Upper Canada would support any invasion and that there was enough disaffection in Lower Canada for the British to have difficulties there. Brock realized that quick and decisive action would stifle any discontent. Accordingly, a small force of soldiers and North West Company men seized Michilimackinac and other western posts in the summer of 1812. Most of the Indians, influenced by these British successes, joined the war against the Americans. In August an attempted invasion from Detroit fizzled out when Brock acted decisively in the face of much larger American forces and compelled the rather timid American general, William Hull, to retreat to American soil and then to surrender his army and the fort. In October a second effort to invade through Niagara, supposedly co-ordinated with Hull's, failed at Queenston. Unhappily Brock was killed in the battle, but his dazzling series of strokes had galvanized the Upper Canadians into loyalty. Of the waverers, many now saw that the United States was not going to win

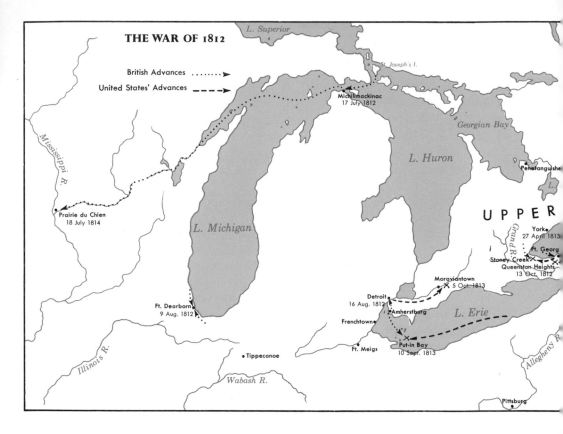

THE WAR OF 1812

British Advances .... →
United States' Advances -- -- →

L. Superior

St. Joseph's I.

Michilimackinac
17 July 1812

Georgian Bay

L. Huron

Penetangushe

L.

Mississippi R.

UPPER

Grand R.

York
27 April 1813

Ft. Georg
Stoney Creek ×
Queenston Heights
13 Oct. 1812

Prairie du Chien
18 July 1814

L. Michigan

Moraviantown
× 5 Oct. 1813

Detroit
16 Aug. 1812

Amherstburg

Ft. Dearborn
9 Aug. 1812

Frenchtown

L. Erie

Illinois R.

• Tippecanoe

Ft. Meigs

Put-in Bay
10 Sept. 1813

Allegheny R.

Wabash R.

Pittsburg

*The battle of Queenston Heights, 13 October 1812, from a drawing by
Major Dennis, engraved in London in 1836. In the original the colours
of the uniforms of the two armies were reversed – the British are shown
in blue, the Americans in red – and the date of the battle is given
incorrectly as 1813.*

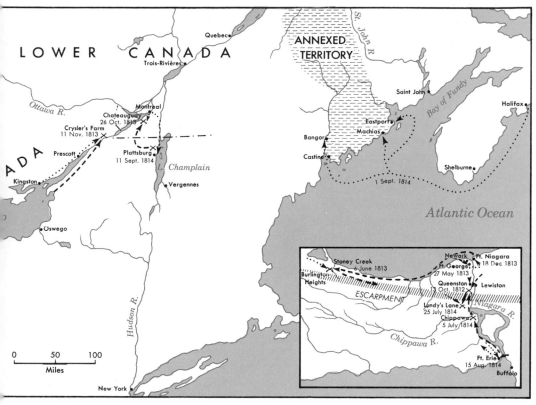

easily, and they remained quiet; a few joined the American forces; an unknown number left their homes and went to live in the United States, but Upper Canada was safer for their leaving.

Stalemate

Brock's victories at Detroit and Niagara had depended on his ability to move his small forces by water, and the victories around the upper Great Lakes had similarly depended on free movement on the lakes. Control of the lakes was crucial, therefore both sides began to build ships with furious haste to win the vital mastery. During the spring and summer of 1813, the Americans gained the upper hand on Lake Ontario. This temporary control of the lake had three consequences. First, in April the Americans captured York, destroyed a ship on the stocks, burned the public buildings, and, most serious for the British and Canadians, captured guns and supplies intended for ships being built at Amherstburg. Second, in May the same fleet landed 3,000 troops just west of Fort George, at the mouth of the Niagara River, forcing the British regulars and militia to retreat from that rundown and antique bastion; then in June and July the Americans occupied the rest of the Niagara Peninsula. Third, the ships being built for the British to maintain themselves on the upper lakes did not get the cannon they needed, and when Captain Robert Barclay was forced into battle against the Americans under Commodore Oliver Hazard Perry, all the British ships were either captured or destroyed. This battle on Lake Erie, often called the Battle of Put-in Bay, cost Britain control on the upper lakes, and British forces withdrew from Amherstburg because they could no longer be supplied. The soldiers and Indians retreated up the Thames Valley, closely pursued by American troops. Already demoralized, the British forces were defeated at Moraviantown and reduced to a rabble. More serious, the great Indian chief Tecumseh was killed in the battle and, without his leadership, his Indian confederacy collapsed. Although the Americans did not follow up their victory, the British withdrew from the western area of the province, leaving it a no-man's land roamed by American marauders until the end of the war.

Even before the events on Lake Erie, the tide of war had begun to turn. The British had withdrawn from the Niagara Peninsula to field fortifications at Burlington, with the Americans following slowly. In a daring night attack organized by Colonel John Harvey, the British defeated the invaders at Stoney Creek and halted their advance. Shortly afterwards, Indians with some British regulars (who had been warned by Laura Secord of an American plan to attack a British outpost) defeated another American force at Beaver Dams. While the British made no immediate effort to reoccupy the peninsula, the Americans made no more advances from the frontier. In the autumn of that year, the Americans suffered two more defeats when they launched a badly organized campaign against the St. Lawrence lifeline. One army was defeated at Crysler's Farm as it marched along the St. Lawrence River against Montreal. Another group, moving north from Lake Champlain, was repulsed at Chateauguay by Canadian militia. On the Niagara frontier the Americans were forced out of Fort George in December; they burned Newark as they retreated. A week later, 600 British regulars stormed the American Fort Niagara and by early January had raided and burned every American village along the Niagara River as far south as Buffalo. This series of victories ensured the safety of Upper Canada; except for the action at Chateauguay, Lower Canada had been spared the horrors of war.

The end of the wars in Europe in 1814 freed British regulars to take part in an invasion of the United States, which the British hoped would force the Americans to make peace. Events frustrated this hope. In early July an American army crossed the Niagara River, compelled Fort Erie to surrender, and then marched north, defeating a slightly smaller British

force of regulars and militia near Chippawa. Co-operation from the
American fleet on Lake Ontario would once again have forced a British
retreat from the Niagara frontier, but the American Commodore Chauncey hesitated to leave his base at Sackett's Harbour because he feared that
the British squadron under Commodore Sir James Yeo would attack the
base in his absence. The result of Chauncey's hesitation was that following a bitter fight at Lundy's Lane on 25 July – a battle fought into the night
hours and in which nearly a third of the two armies were casualties – the
Americans withdrew to Fort Erie. After a costly attempt to storm the fort,
the British retired. The stalemate continued throughout the autumn until
in November the Americans finally retreated, blowing up Fort Erie behind
them.   .

Elsewhere failure marked British campaigns. The great projected invasion of New York state collapsed following the destruction of the small
British fleet at Plattsburg on Lake Champlain in September. Prevost, an
excellent politician but a defence-minded soldier, pulled back his overwhelmingly large army because he was afraid of heavy casualties. In late
August British soldiers disembarked from the blockading fleet and captured Washington, burning its public buildings because they could find
no one able to negotiate a ransom for the city. The British then turned their
attention to Baltimore, but once they realized that the well-defended city
could not be taken except at heavy cost in lives, they retreated. An effort
late in 1814 to capture New Orleans ended in a costly defeat east of the
city in January 1815, two weeks after an agreement to make peace had
been signed. During the year it became clear at last to both sides that each
was able to repel invasion by the other, but that neither was strong enough
or willing enough to mount a successful invasion.

Negotiations for peace were carried on throughout the war. The willingness of each side to come to terms with the other depended on how well
the fighting was going at the moment. Serious discussions began in August
1814 as the British saw clearly that victory would not be possible without

*"Upper Canada Preserved" medal, issued by
the Loyal and Patriotic Society of Upper
Canada during the War of 1812. The
presence of the British lion prevents the
American eagle from seizing the Canadian
beaver.*

a major effort. Weary of the war, and advised by the Duke of Wellington that even he could not obtain much success in America without more soldiers and naval control of the Great Lakes, the British government agreed in the Treaty of Ghent to a cessation of hostilities, and the armistice took effect in February. The treaty itself was a return to the status quo – neither side had lost, neither side had won.

Outstanding issues between the two countries were to be settled by joint commissions. In 1818 it was agreed that the boundary between New Brunswick and Maine was to be the St. Croix River. Painstaking historical research determined its true course, but no agreement on the inland boundary between Maine and New Brunswick was reached until 1842. Great Britain and the United States also agreed that in the far west the forty-ninth parallel should serve as the boundary from Lake of the Woods to the Rockies, and that Oregon should be governed jointly for the present. The Americans were also given restricted fishing rights around the shores of the Atlantic Provinces. As well, the possibility of a naval race by each country on the Great Lakes was ended in 1818 by the Rush-Bagot Agreement, which provided that neither side would have armed ships on the Great Lakes bigger than necessary for policing the boundary waters. The issues which had supposedly started the war, maritime rights and Indian relations, were ignored.

In the British colonies the effects of the war were considerable. Heavy expenditures by the army put money, if only in the form of army bills of

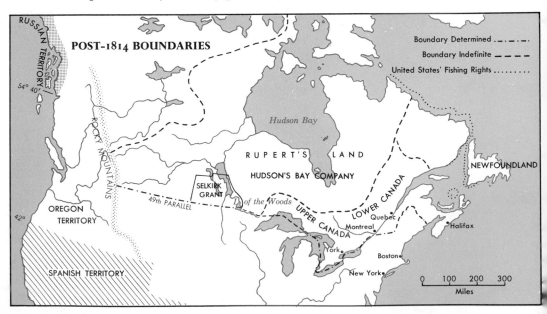

exchange, into the farmers' pockets. In those areas untouched by the fighting, prosperity had never been greater. But in the areas where the war had been fought, especially the Niagara region, the damage was considerable. After the war, the British government was very slow to compensate the victims, a tardiness that provoked much anger and resentment. But more important, the nation-making myth that the Canadian people had defended themselves successfully against American aggression took hold. According to this myth, the victory had been won by the brave militia protecting their homes; in fact, the decisive element had been the presence of British regulars. To the British, the war had demonstrated that with a determined effort the United States could have conquered Canada. To the United States it had shown that British sea power was too formidable to be challenged by a small navy. Neither nation forgot those lessons.

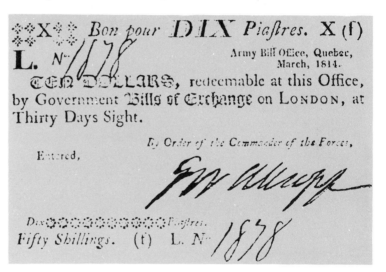

An army bill of exchange, dated March 1814. A piastre was the equivalent of one dollar. The word came into Canadian usage soon after the Conquest and is still popular in French-Canadian speech.

HISTORY FROM THE SOURCES

The Loyalists – What Was Their Tradition?

"*The story of a nation's heroes is the fountain from which it draws the wine of its later life. There is no inspiration that quickens the* ambition of youth, stimulates public service and deepens love of country like the memory of great men who have gone." Arthur Meighen, speaking in 1925, was really saying that nations need myths to give them a sense of cultural identity and purpose. British North America, distinct from the old thirteen colonies, came into existence with the immigration of the United Empire Loyalists to Quebec and Nova Scotia. Their migration and settlement became legendary in the society of nineteenth-century Canada. Within a generation these British North Americans had to fight to defend themselves against the very country which they had left and rejected. Thus the War of 1812 became a part of the legend. Descendants of the Loyalists and of those who had fought against the United States dominated the governments and the societies of the colonies until the 1840's. In founding English Canada what kind of values about government and society did Loyalists bring with them? Were these beliefs reflected accurately in the outpouring of patriotism later in the century?

The Duke de la Rochefoucault-Liancourt, a refugee from revolutionary France, toured North America in the late eighteenth century and subsequently published his impressions.

> . . . the American loyalists, who have actually suffered by the war, still harbour enmity and hatred against their native land and countrymen. These sentiments however are daily decreasing, and are not shared by the far greater number of emigrants, who arrive from the United States, Nova Scotia, and New Brunswick. There are malcontents in this country; but their number is small. Several new settlers, who migrate into this province from the United States, falsely profess an attachment to the British Monarch, and curse the government of the Union, for the mere purpose of thus wheedling themselves into the possession of lands. The high price of provision, the prohibition of a commercial intercourse, and the protracted delivery of the deeds by which the property of granted lands is conveyed to the occupiers, form, indeed, grounds of much discontent; but this is by no means of a nature to cause uneasiness to the government, which seems even to doubt its existence, though, in case of a war with the United States, it might render its situation extremely critical.

> W. R. Riddell, ed., *La Rochefoucault-Liancourt's Travels in Canada, 1785* (Thirteenth Report of the Bureau of Archives for the Province of Ontario, 1916. Toronto, 1917), p. 58.

Benjamin Marston was a Loyalist who became deputy surveyor-general in New Brunswick for a short time in the 1780's before leaving for Britain in search of a government position. He wrote the following commentary on the attitudes of his fellow-Loyalists in Nova Scotia.

Thursday 8 [Port Rosaway. May, 1783] – The Multitude object to the place which the Captains and Chief men had chosen for the Situation of their Town, because, say They 'tis a rough uneven piece of Land, so they propose to mend the matter by choosing 3 men from every Company to do the matter over again, That is to commit to a meer [sic] mob of 60 what a few Judicious men found very difficult to transact with a lesser mob of 20 – so this day has been spent in much controversial nonsense. This curs'd Republican, Town-meeting Spirit has been the ruin of us already – & unless check'd by some Stricter form of Government, will overset the prospect which now presents of retrieving our affairs. Mankind are often Slaves and oftentimes they have too much Liberty. . . .

Friday 16 . . . real authority can never be supported without some degree of real superiority . . .

Saturday 17 Arrived a Vessell from N. York also one from Halifax . . .

Saturday 24 . . . ashore all day appointing People to their Lotts. Some grumble, some are pleased. They are upon the whole a collection of Characters very unfit for the business they have undertaken – Barbers, Taylors, Shoemakers and all Mechanics bred and used to live in great Towns . . . Nothing so easy as to bear hardships in a good house by a good fireside with Clothes provisions &c.

Monday 26 – all the morning Locating as usual about Noon broke out a most furious fire among the dry Stuff in the Streets . . .

Wednesday 4 [June] – no Business today – 'tis the King's *birthday*. But any dissipation – any neglect of Business ought not to be in ye least countenanced at present in this place . . . a Ball tonight – all our Tent over but myself . . .

Monday 9 – Today lay'd out a half block for a few Elect ones . . . Company to dine with us . . . Sir Guy C – Commissions have made many men here *Gentlemen* & of course their wives & daughters *Ladies* whom neither Nature nor Education intended for that Rank . . . Propriety of Conduct – Chastity, & Decency of manners – seem to be no part of an H – Education . . .

Monday 26 [July] – a Great Riot today. The disbanded Soldiers have risen against the free Negroes to drive them out of Town because they labour Cheaper than they (the Soldiers) will . . .

The Diary of Benjamin Marston, in the
Harriet Irving Library, the University of New Brunswick.

In January 1784 the Loyalists who were going to settle at Kingston petitioned Governor Haldimand for tools, clothing, and farm animals, and for their constitutional rights as British subjects. What kind of government did these Loyalists want?

And in as much as the said Associated Companies have for years past Nobly Contended for the support of that Constitution or Form of Government, under which they long have Enjoyed Happiness, & for which they have at least sacrifised their All. Tis Therefore their Earnest Wish and desire that His Excellency for their Better Government & Good order when they arrive at the Place destined for their Settlement would be pleased to Establish among them a Form of Government As nearly similar to that which they Enjoyed in the Province of New York in the year of 1763 As the Remote situation of their new settlement from the seat of Government here will at Present Admitt of.

> Petition of the Associated Loyalists to his Excellency
> Lieutenant General Frederick Haldimand, Governor
> and Commander in Chief &C &C.
> Public Archives of Canada, *Haldimand MSS, B 215*, p. 132.

Robert Baldwin Sullivan, a moderate Conservative and member of the Executive Council of Upper Canada, wrote a memorandum about the province for the new governor, Sir George Arthur, in 1838 that illustrates the vitality of the Loyalist legend in the 1830's.

1. The opening this Province as a place of refuge for the Loyalists who joined the Royal Standard during the war of the American revolution and the assigning them lands as a free grant, was not only an act of Bounty but of Justice, indeed were it not for the possession of this Colony, it is difficult to say in what manner England could have provided for those who had fought for her and become exiles from their homes and property from feelings of unshaken loyalty, and it is hard to say how long this Province would have remained a mere hunting ground were it not that these exiles took up their abode in it and prepared the way for European Emigration. And although it is true that the promise of lands to the children of the U E. loyalists has in some measure impeded the settlement, of the Province from the fact that few of them when the time came for their procuring their respective grants were in a situation which made the attainment of wild land at a distance from the frontier an object of importance and therefore the rights which they held were sold to specu-

lators at almost nominal prices, and the lands remain in a wild state. Yet this is an objection of little importance when taken in connection with the whole measure which was on the one hand an important relief to the Government and on the other of incalculable benefit to the Colony. . . .

The first settlers in the Province, that is to say The U E. Loyalists although through danger suffering and deprivation, they adhered to the British Crown, yet had still many points of similarity in habits and education with the Americans who revolted. And this similarity of manners when the revolutionary war was at an end made the amalgamation of the American citizen with his more loyal countrymen & his descendents an operation of great facility, and to this admixture and the want of proper means of education, may be attributed in some measure the adherence of some of the descendents of the U E. Loyalists to republican principles and even to rebellion.

C. R. Sanderson, ed., *The Arthur Papers* (Toronto, 1957),
Vol. I, pp. 145, 154.

Popular interest in Upper Canadian history began in the 1850's. Canadian history and geography were taught in the schools and the epic of the Loyalists held a prominent place in the courses. William Canniff's history was one of the most popular books that dealt with this theme.

. . . In no country upon the face of the Globe, and at no period in the history of any country, has appeared a higher or purer order of patriotism, than is written upon the pages of the history of British America. British connection is to mostly every son of the land dearer even than life itself. At least it has been so in respect to those of whom we write, the U. E. Loyalists. Co-equal with the love they have to the British Crown, is the hearty aversion they bear to Republicanism. . . . The U. E. Loyalists have been as a barrier of rock against which the waves of Republicanism have dashed in vain. It has been the refugee-settlers and their descendants, who prevented the Province from being engulfed in its dark waters. In 1812, in '37, and at all times, their loyalty has never wavered. . . .

William Canniff, *A History of the Settlement of Upper Canada*
(Toronto, 1869), pp. 633-4.

In 1884, on the occasion of the centennial of the United Empire
Loyalists' settlement in Upper Canada, a celebration of the event was
held in Niagara. Among the speakers were Lieutenant-Governor Robinson
of Ontario, who was a son of one of the leaders of the Family Compact,
and the Anglican bishop of Niagara.

LIEUTENANT-GOVERNOR ROBINSON was called upon as the first
speaker. He thanked the chairman and the audience for their kind
reception of him. This was the third time he had been called upon
to greet the descendants of the U. E. Loyalists gathered together to
celebrate the deeds of their ancestors. At Adolphustown, on the
shores of the beautiful Bay of Quinté, thousands had gathered to do
honour to the noble dead, and but a few weeks ago he had had the
pleasure of meeting representatives of the U. E. Loyalists from all
parts of the Province, at Government House. The spot where they
now stood was historic ground. Here in this old town of Niagara the
first Parliament of Canada assembled, and they then passed the jury
law, and an act declaring that from that time there should be no
slavery in Upper Canada. Those were great and good laws, and the
fact that they were so early passed was a just cause of pride to
Canadians. . . . He dwelt upon the heroism of the men of the Revolutionary War, and of the war of 1812, as an incentive to the people
to cultivate the same spirit. He eulogized the Indians, representatives
of whom he saw present. If above our heads floated the British flag
to-day, they had to thank the Six Nation [s] Indians in large measure
for it. Some undertook to sneer at the feeling of loyalty, of which
they were proud. . . . The current literature of England showed that
the fact was being recognized that the colonies were almost of as
much value to the empire as was the empire to the colonies. If this
feeling was carried to its final outcome the result would be largely
due to the bravery and loyalty of the United Empire Loyalists, who
have saved to the British Crown this finest unoccupied part of the
world.

The Venerable BISHOP OF NIAGARA next spoke. . . . Many of the
settlers, who had fought valiantly in the revolutionary war as young
men, fought again as men well advanced in years under Generals
Brock and Riall and under Colonels Harvey and Bishopp, and other
noble soldiers, who led them to victory, when this peaceful Province
was invaded in 1812 by a body of men who thought that they had
only to show themselves on our shores to pluck this glorious Colony
from the British Crown. But they were mistaken – they found that
those who had endured hardships in the revolutionary war, were
ready to endure the same in defence of their wives and children and
their new homes in the wilderness. After doing their best to conquer
Canada, the invaders were glad, in 1815, to sue for an inglorious

peace, without having secured an acre of our soil! The Bishop said, that he was thankful to have been spared by a gracious God to have seen that day. He was an old man – had thankfully watched the growth of this country for nearly seventy years.

The United Empire Loyalists' Centennial, 1884,
(Toronto, 1885), pp. 81-90.

FURTHER READING

Burt, A. L., *The United States, Great Britain and British North America from the Revolution to the Establishment of Peace After the War of 1812* (Toronto: Ryerson, 1966)★. The authoritative account, first published in 1940.

Craig, Gerald M., *Upper Canada 1784-1841: The Formative Years* (Toronto: McClelland & Stewart, 1963).

MacNutt, W. S., *The Atlantic Provinces: The Emergence of Colonial Society, 1712-1857* (Toronto: McClelland & Stewart, 1965).

Creighton, D. G., *The Empire of the St. Lawrence* (Toronto: Macmillan, 1956). The classic account of the dream of commercial empire.

Hitsman, J. M., *The Incredible War of 1812* (Toronto: University of Toronto Press, 1965)★. The best survey of the war in Upper Canada.

Manning, H. T., *The Revolt of Lower Canada 1800-1835* (Toronto: Macmillan, 1962). A political history of these years.

Wade, Mason, *The French Canadians 1760-1967*, 2 vols. (Toronto: Macmillan, 1968)★.

Coles, H. L., *The War of 1812* (Chicago: University of Chicago Press, 1965). A balanced American history of the war.

Innis, M. Q., ed. *Mrs. Simcoe's Diary* (Toronto: Macmillan, 1967). An abridged but fascinating version of the day-to-day life of the wife of Upper Canada's founding governor.

MacNutt, W. S., *New Brunswick: A History 1784-1867* (Toronto: Macmillan, 1963).

Clark, A. H., *Three Centuries and the Island* (Toronto: University of Toronto Press, 1959).

11

From Mercantilism to Free Trade

The End of the Fur Trade

After 1811 the rivalry between the Hudson's Bay Company and the North West Company had become a fight to the death. Both companies were having serious financial difficulties, and therefore in that year the Montreal firm proposed a division of territories in the northwest. Such an arrangement was, however, unacceptable to the older company because it meant renouncing its claim to part of its vast lands, and so the destructive competition for furs continued in that region.

The largest shareholder of the North West Company, McTavish, McGillivrays and Company, had previously begun to broaden its operations in an effort to survive by joining with another Canadian group, Forsyth, Richardson and Company. The two companies formed a single new enterprise, the South West Fur Company, which re-entered the trade south of the Great Lakes in partnership with John Jacob Astor. The South West Fur Company's trade continued and expanded during the War of 1812, but when British traders were excluded from the United States after the war, the Canadians sold their interest to Astor at a loss in 1817. At this point Forsyth, Richardson and Company began to seek some new form of business other than furs, but McTavish, McGillivrays concentrated their efforts once more on the northwest in a do-or-die struggle with the Hudson's Bay Company for mastery of the fur trade.

While the fruitless negotiations between the two large companies had been going on, the Earl of Selkirk, who had brought settlers from Scotland to Prince Edward Island and Upper Canada, had been buying shares in the English firm. He persuaded the directors to grant him a tract of land, 116,000 square miles in extent, lying in the watershed of the Red River at the south end of Lake Winnipeg and across the series of waterways which were the communication route for the Nor'Westers. Here Selkirk hoped to settle more Highlanders. From this area came the indispensable pemmican supplies for the North West Company's canoe brigades, and the Hudson's Bay Company made the grant because it wanted to develop its own supply of foodstuffs in the interior and to damage its Canadian rival. The colonization project was bound to embitter the struggle for control of the fur trade.

The first of Selkirk's settlers arrived at the Red River in August 1812. Lack of livestock and tools caused great hardship during the first two winters, and the people barely survived on the available buffalo meat and potatoes. Expecting more settlers to arrive in 1814, the governor of the struggling colony banned the export of food from Selkirk's territory, which was called Assiniboia, and seized pemmican supplies belonging to the North West Company. The Nor'Westers saw this action as a step to ruin their trade, and at their annual meeting at Fort William in 1815 decided that the colony had to be destroyed. Efforts to turn the Crees and Assiniboine Indians against the settlers failed, but the buffalo-hunting Métis were only too willing to help. The settlers were twice driven from their homes and many left for Upper Canada. In 1816 a gang of Métis attacked and killed the governor and twenty-one settlers at Seven Oaks. Selkirk, who had come to Canada on his way to visit his colony, immediately set off with a hundred mercenary soldiers and in August seized Fort William and its contents of supplies and furs valued at £100,000. Some of his troops, which he sent on to the Red River colony, saved the settlement from complete extinction. But Selkirk's actions at Fort William involved him in a series of legal actions which dragged on for years, broke his health, ruined his fortune, and caused his early death.

The loss of Fort William hurt the North West Company seriously, for neither the furs nor the trade goods could be replaced at short notice nor

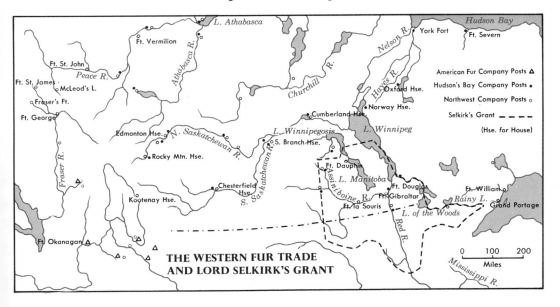

THE WESTERN FUR TRADE AND LORD SELKIRK'S GRANT

Colonists on the Red River, one of the earliest-known interior scenes (c.1822) from the Winnipeg area, by the Swiss painter Peter Rindisbacher, who as a teenager emigrated with his family to the Red River colony in 1821. At left: A Swiss colonist's wife; at centre: her husband and two children, and a colonist from Scotland; at right: a German colonist (seated), and a colonist from French Canada.

without additional loans. Tighter control of costs was essential during the following years at a time when the English company was paying high prices for furs in order to defeat its rival. The Hudson's Bay Company was able to offer iron goods that the Indians wanted, but which the Nor'Westers could not transport economically. The wintering partners of the Canadian syndicate, who bore the brunt of this competition, saw that the future would bring only stronger competition and contraction of their business. In 1819 a group of winterers led by Dr. John McLaughlin requested the Hudson's Bay Company to supply them and to buy their furs. This action forced McTavish, McGillivrays and Company also to begin negotiations with the London company. If the Nor'Westers had not quarrelled amongst themselves, they would certainly have been able to work out a reasonable amalgamation with the Hudson's Bay Company, for the English firm was in serious financial straits. But the Hudson's Bay Company was able to play one group off against the other and to work out an advantageous agreement with the Montreal partners in March 1821.

By this agreement McTavish, McGillivrays was given a substantial minority holding in the reorganized Hudson's Bay Company, but control of the company remained with the London management. Most of the wintering partners were given employment as chief factors or chief traders and given shares. All goods and furs were henceforth to be shipped via the cheaper water route through the Bay. Thus the century-old struggle between the Bay and the River ended with the union of the two companies, an early example of the tendency to monopolies in the Canadian economy. Montreal's fur trade empire had collapsed at the stroke of a pen, and by 1825 most of the older fur trade companies were out of business. The surviving companies, such as Forsyth, Richardson, had already switched to new lines of business. McTavish, McGillivrays and Company had to sell its shares in the Hudson's Bay Company to pay off its creditors; William McGillivray's two daughters died in poverty. To business-minded Montrealers it seemed that their only means of earning

a living would be the forwarding business to Upper Canada and the
United States.

The New Staples

Fortunately for the Canadian economy, at the same time as the fur trade
of Montreal failed, new staples were being developed to replace it. For
the next century, Canada's major exports were to be timber and wheat.
The lumbering industry in North America began to develop before 1815,
during the wars in Europe, mainly because the British navy needed tall
pines for masts and oak for the hulls of its ships. When the Continental
System imposed by Napoleon cut off Britain's traditional sources of supply
from the countries around the Baltic, the government turned instead to its
American colonies, where the naval contracts gave impetus to the development of the timber industry. The price of lumber from North America
was higher in Britain than that from the Baltic, however, because of the
greater cost of transportation. After the wars the colonial timber firms persuaded the United Kingdom to set tariffs on foreign timber to protect their
interests; from 1821 to 1842 the duty on foreign lumber was 55 shillings
a load, but on colonial lumber merely a nominal sum. Begun as a stopgap,
the North American timber industry thrived under these preferential
duties.

The lumber business developed rather differently from the fur trade,
although certain problems were common to both industries. Unlike the
fur trade, there was no tendency towards monopoly control, mainly because smaller capital investment was needed. It was easy for a few farmers
or fishermen, with teams of horses or oxen, to go together into the woods
in winter. Red and white pine, and hardwoods such as oak and walnut,
were cut out of the forests. The timber was roughly squared with axes;

*Below: A sawmill on the Salmon River at Shannonville (near
Belleville), in 1830.*
*Right: Oxen hauling logs at a lumbermen's camp in the New
Brunswick woods, in the early 1800's.*

no sawing was done until it reached Britain. The square timber trade was enormously wasteful – one-third of the usable wood was cut away in squaring, and if the heart of the tree was rotten, the whole timber was discarded. The tools required for the trade were simple – axes, peavies, and saws. In early spring the loggers would float their timber in rafts down to the ports, where it was sold to the timber merchants of Saint John and Quebec, who acted as middlemen. Big firms did not enter the timber trade until capital was needed to build sawmills or timber slides on rivers. Even then, the small groups of part-time loggers could still continue working on contract to supply the sawmill owners.

Like the fur trade, however, the success of the lumbering business depended on a market over which the producers and merchants had little control. The construction industry has always been very undependable in its demands, and the nineteenth century was no exception. In those days, too, the supply of timber was variable: if a winter's snowfall were light, the lumbermen could not move their wood out of the bush. Commercial news travelled so slowly across the Atlantic that estimates of market requirements and changes in demand did not reach the Canadas in time to allow the supplier to adjust production. A heavy demand in one year might induce big shipments the next, when the market would be glutted. Because timber was a high-volume, low-value commodity, transportation costs were a large part of the final price. Ships had either to be specially constructed – a risky venture considering the variable market – or converted by making loading ports at bow and stern. Therefore most timber ships were old, converted tubs, good for little else. Shipowners managed to find return cargoes (for example, salt to the Atlantic provinces), but their only sure cargo was immigrants to the colonies. Given this type of accommodation, it is no wonder that conditions on immigrant ships were so bad.

Most of these immigrants who came to the New World hoped to make a new life as farmers. If they had a little capital with them, they might buy a partly developed farm not too far from settlement. If they were poor, carrying clothing and a few prized family possessions, they would have a harder time getting established. Until 1827 free land was available from the government, but it was on the forest frontier far from any major community. Many poor immigrants therefore headed for the larger towns – Montreal, Kingston, York, or Hamilton – to look for employment. Works projects like the Rideau and Welland canals were built largely by such labour. Having saved a small amount of capital, men and their families would then look for farm land on which to settle. Many, if they could not receive a grant or buy a piece of land, became squatters. With luck a family could build a rude log shanty for the first winter and clear a couple of acres of land. During the next year, with help from neighbours, a squared log house might be built. Only the few wealthy settlers could avoid the hardships of the early years by purchasing established farms.

Before communities developed, life on the frontier was primitive. For a man there was constant heavy work clearing land or trying to cultivate the virgin soil. The first crop would be potatoes for the family to live on; then, as more land was cleared, wheat could be planted. A woman led a lonely life tied to family and home, perhaps miles from the nearest neighbour. A man would at least have the opportunity to talk to others when he went to the nearest mill or store to buy supplies or to have wheat ground. Far from schools, most children learned only the skills of farming and housekeeping from their parents. Even if a schoolmaster were available, he might stay only a few months before moving on, time only for the children to learn how to do simple sums, to read a few words, and to write their names. The great social events of the frontier were bees, for house-raising and barn-raising, for harvesting, or for any other work requiring many hands, and the camp meetings, when itinerant preachers arrived in the township and everyone gathered for several days to hear them. But after these occasions the people returned to the routine of pioneer farming – the men to clear more land, make their own implements, or build a piece of rough furniture, the women to weave their own woollen or linen cloth, preserve their own food, or make soap and candles. Frontier families had to be self-sufficient.

The major cash crop from such frontier farms was wheat. As early as the 1770's, Montreal merchants had sent the occasional shipment of wheat to Britain, but the cost of shipping was very high. Britain had not yet entered the age of rapid industrialization and urbanization which was to

Below: "The Rideau Canal, Bytown", by William Henry Bartlett, published in 1842. Top right: "The first eight locks and the . . . Cut Stone Bridge", by William Clegg, dated 1832. Bottom right: The north entrance to the canal, 1845, by William Burrowes. This drawing differs from Bartlett's artistic engraving, but since it was Burrowes who drew the plan for the canal, his version is likely to be the more accurate.

Clearing the town plot, Stanley, New Brunswick, in 1834.

create a huge market for wheat after 1800, but by that date the United States was also emerging as a second, if smaller, market for Canadian wheat. The development of Upper Canada was, however, in the long run closely tied to the export of wheat. A settler's first cash income came from potash (used in Britain for bleaching textiles and manufacturing gunpowder) produced by burning the hardwood timber to clear his land. On the cleared land not used for raising fodder or garden crops he grew wheat, a second and continuing source of cash income. In the first years on his land the farmer simply scratched the topsoil with a hoe or harrow. Implements were few and scarce, and nearly all were homemade tools. The pioneer farmer might also have a wooden "loyalist" plough, and a harrow constructed with a triangle of heavy timbers and iron teeth, drawn usually by oxen, which were more numerous than draft horses. After a few years during which the crops were grown between the stumps, the stumps were sufficiently rotted to be pulled out or burned.

Flour mills were located on almost every fast stretch of stream. Farmers brought their wheat to the millers, who took a portion of the flour as their fee and often bought the rest, which they forwarded to Montreal. Combined milling and general mercantile businesses were common. These merchants obtained tea, spices, ironware, and metal goods, and pottery, china, and fine textiles from Montreal or York wholesalers. In turn, the wholesalers and forwarders bought the goods on credit in Britain or the United States. The whole economy rested on a chain of credit, stretching from the farmer to the British merchant houses and wheat buyers. Indeed, in remote areas of the provinces, cash sales were unusual. Only the farmer who carted his wheat to one of the numerous little ports along the shores

Stanley, New Brunswick, in August 1835. This watercolour, and the one at the top of the page, formed part of a collection entitled "Sketches in New Brunswick", which was intended as a description of the land in the tract purchased by the New Brunswick & Nova Scotia Land Company in 1833, and to illustrate its operation during the years 1834 and 1835.

"A view of the mill & tavern of Philemon Wright at the Chaudière Falls on the Ottawa River, Lower Canada, 1823", by Henry Duvernet, a British army officer who was employed on the Ottawa River canals.

of Lake Ontario or Lake Erie received cash, and his sale price was higher because he had absorbed some of the transportation cost.

The price that the farmer received for his wheat depended on a market in Britain. This market was protected by high tariffs, called the Corn Laws, on all imported wheat. In 1815 the British government altered the Corn Laws. All wheat was to enter Britain duty free when the British price rose to over 80 shillings per quarter (eight bushels), but colonial wheat could enter at a reduced rate when the price was over 67 shillings. This arrangement was modified several times and duties reimposed, but the principle of preferential colonial treatment had been established. The millers and wheat merchants also hoped to persuade the British government to permit free entry of United States' wheat to the Canadas for milling, so that it could be exported to the United Kingdom as Canadian flour. The dream of the commercial empire centred on Montreal and the St. Lawrence was reappearing in a new guise, this time as the channel for the North American wheat export business.

This goal conflicted, however, with the interests of Upper Canadian farmers, who saw imported American wheat as competition which would lower their incomes. Nevertheless, American wheat was admitted for milling and export as flour. When in the early 1830's prices in the Toronto area dropped to 32 to 38 cents a bushel – an acute hardship because these prices did not even cover costs – farmers demanded high tariffs to keep the American wheat out. The farmers' resentment against the commercial interests and the low prices was intensified by crop failures in 1835 and 1836. Both these developments had a great deal to do with the discontent which preceded the rebellion of 1837. Yet the low returns to farmers resulted in large part from the high costs of transportation down the St. Lawrence. Indeed many Canadian millers found it more profitable to ship via the Erie Canal which was opened through New York state in 1825.

The Commercial Empire and the Canals

Wheat and timber were available as the staples for a new St. Lawrence empire, but until canals had been constructed to take ships down to

"Block House, at Merricks-ville on the Rideau Canal, between Bytow[n] and Kingston, Upper Canada, finished March 1839", by H. F. Ainslie.

Montreal, the potential of this empire could never be realized. As early as the 1790's merchants in the Canadas had been aware of the need to improve the St. Lawrence waterway, and the limitations of the St. Lawrence system were further emphasized by competition from the Erie Canal. After the Erie Canal opened in 1825, the cost of moving goods to New York from Buffalo dropped 90 per cent. The canal also cut into Montreal's hinterland; previously Montreal had supplied storekeepers in the new western states, but once the canal was in operation New York became the entrepôt of the trade, and the only way to recapture the role of supplier and to develop the staples trade was to build canals that would improve Montreal's links with the Great Lakes.

After seeing how the lack of canals hampered transportation to Upper Canada during the war, the British government asked the Upper Canadian legislature to help pay for canal improvements. There was no response from the legislature, so in 1817 the Royal Engineers reconstructed the old canals built in the 1780's along the St. Lawrence immediately west of Montreal. Yet if there were another war with the United States, this St. Lawrence route would be too exposed. Therefore the British government decided to construct a canal from the Ottawa River through the Rideau Lakes to Kingston. Built under the supervision of Colonel John By, after whom Bytown (now Ottawa) was named, the Rideau Canal was a remarkable feat of engineering for its time. There were forty-seven locks in its 133-mile length, some of which had to be blasted out of the rock of the Canadian Shield. But in the end the cost rose to over £1,000,000 from

Jones Falls (some thirty miles north of Kingston) in 1827-30, by William Clegg.

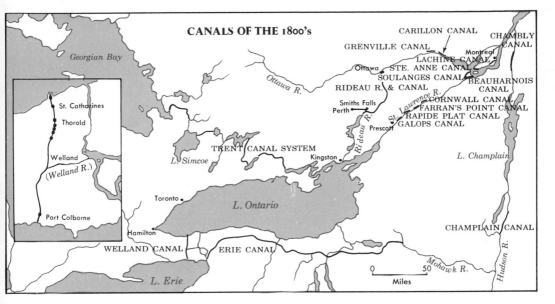

CANALS OF THE 1800's

Georgian Bay

St. Catharines
Thorold
Welland
(Welland R.)
Port Colborne

CARILLON CANAL
CHAMBLY CANAL
GRENVILLE CANAL
LACHINE CANAL
Montreal
Ottawa STE. ANNE CANAL
SOULANGES CANAL
BEAUHARNOIS CANAL
RIDEAU R. & CANAL
St. Lawrence R.
CORNWALL CANAL
Smiths Falls
FARRAN'S POINT CANAL
Perth
RAPIDE PLAT CANAL
Prescott GALOPS CANAL
Ottawa R.
Rideau R.

TRENT CANAL SYSTEM
L. Simcoe
Kingston
L. Champlain

Toronto
L. Ontario

Hamilton
CHAMPLAIN CANAL
WELLAND CANAL
ERIE CANAL

0   50
Mohawk R.
Hudson R.
Miles

L. Erie

the estimate of £169,000. The Rideau Canal was a magnificent engineering achievement, but it had limited commercial value because the locks were too small for most lake vessels to pass through, and the canal later became obsolete when new and larger locks were opened on the shorter St. Lawrence route.

The story of high costs, repeated on every future canal, probably deterred the British government from giving financial aid to other projects. A private company began to build a canal at Lachine, but because expenses rose the Lower Canadian government took over completion of the project. The cost so frightened the Assembly that no more canals were built in Lower Canada before 1840 except for the Chambly Canal on the Richelieu River. The Lachine Canal, completed in 1824, was only the first in a long series of necessary transportation projects begun privately and ending up in government hands after encountering financial troubles. In Upper Canada the Welland Canal, completed in 1829 as a necessary link between Lake Erie and Lake Ontario, followed the same pattern of financing. The promoters intended to build the canal and locks up the Niagara escarpment, in that way connecting the Twelve Mile Creek which flowed into Lake Ontario with the Welland River which flowed into the Niagara River. Above the Welland, however, the currents of the Niagara were too strong for ships to reach Fort Erie under their own power, and the water supply for the locks, even with an elaborate feeder canal from the Grand River, was insufficient to last a season. In 1830 the Welland Canal Company decided to extend the canal directly to Lake Erie, but even after this extension, traffic was light. Without canals on the St. Lawrence, shipping into Lake Ontario could serve only local ports. American shipowners preferred to carry goods to Buffalo and through the Erie Canal rather than use the Canadian canal, and revenues were insufficient to maintain the canal in good condition. In 1837, therefore, the Upper Canadian government assumed management of the work as the condition for paying to rebuild it, and in 1843 the government bought out the shareholders.

All hopes of building the facilities to make the St. Lawrence empire possible were frustrated for years by provincial politics. After 1824 the Lower Canadian Assembly was ostentatiously uninterested in canal projects. Without Lower Canadian co-operation in building canals the merchants' dream was impossible. The only solution was to weaken French-Canadian political influence by uniting the two provinces and then to carry canal-building schemes through the legislature. Such a union was proposed in 1822 after the Montreal merchants and their London associates had persuaded the British government that it would be advantageous to the colonies. When the imperial parliament learned that the French Canadians and most Upper Canadians strongly opposed the scheme, the bill was dropped. Nevertheless, to the merchants, political union remained a possible solution to the economic problem created by the divided control and opposing policies of the two Canadas towards development of the St. Lawrence waterway.

Growth and Immigration, 1815-1850

In the thirty-five years after the war with the United States all the British North American colonies grew and, for the most part, prospered. Until 1815, most immigrants had come from the United States; after 1815, there was a tremendous movement of English, Scots, and Irish into the province, although many more went to the United States. Some figures for population growth give an indication of the influx: between 1824 and 1850 the population of New Brunswick grew from some 74,000 to 194,-000, that of Nova Scotia from 104,000 to nearly 277,000. Newfoundland, with a population of 22,000 in 1815, increased almost fourfold by 1840; Prince Edward Island's population of 25,000 in 1822 had doubled by 1841. In 1825 there were 157,923 people in Upper Canada, in 1840 there were 432,159, and by 1850 791,000. Lower Canada's population also increased – from 479,288 in 1825 to 840,000 in 1850. Many of the immigrants, perhaps half, moved to the United States, but of those who remained the great majority settled in Upper Canada. In the mid-1830's cholera epidemics brought by disease-ridden immigrants weakened by the arduous voyage, together with the rebellions of 1837, slowed the tide, but in the decade after the rebellion the number of immigrants rose again, reaching 90,000 in 1847 as a wave of Irish came to escape the potato famine.

Most of the immigrants from Ireland and Scotland came to seek a new life, free from the overpopulation and land shortage, the poverty and harsh conditions of the new industrial towns. North America was prosperous, a land of promise where a man had the chance to be independent and to get ahead, and where he could own his own farm – a large one, too – not just a few acres. Private philanthropists such as Selkirk, and Peter Robinson (who founded Peterborough), helped many to come to new homes, and in the 1820's the British government also assisted emigrants. But not all immigrants were poor; many brought capital and skills with them and were able to establish or buy farms or to set up businesses in the towns.

Land companies also helped to promote development of the colonies. The Canada Company, which bought all the Crown reserves and the Huron Tract in Upper Canada, built roads, bridges, mills, schools, and even brick kilns for its settlers. The British American Company sold former Crown land in the eastern townships of Lower Canada but was not as successful as the Canada Company because the upper province was able to attract more immigrants. Colonel Thomas Talbot, who had originally come to Canada as Simcoe's secretary, acted as a settlement agent by persuading newcomers to settle in the area along the north shore of Lake Erie. The immigration of the 1820's and the consequent demand for land drove prices up, but the settler was likely to blame the land company and the speculator for his difficulty in finding a farm at a price he could afford. Nevertheless, with their advertising and their provision of essential services such as mills, stores, roads, and bridges, the land companies did

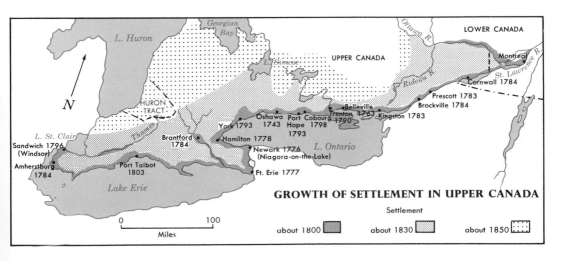

GROWTH OF SETTLEMENT IN UPPER CANADA

Settlement

about 1800   about 1830   about 1850

promote settlement in a way that could not have happened if the government had handled all sales.

As early as the 1820's a tendency to urbanization was evident in the colonies. Many small villages grew up around a mill, a tavern, and a general store, and Halifax, Saint John, St. John's, Quebec, Montreal, Kingston, York, and Hamilton, the only places of any size, acted like magnets in attracting new population. The towns formed the economic, civic, and cultural centres of provincial life. Some towns had small manufacturing industries such as furniture making, tanning, textiles, brewing, and distilling, but most functioned primarily as distributing centres. The most important large town in each province was the seat of its provincial government. For culture and entertainment the people looked to the towns. Each one, even the smallest, published a newspaper; the larger ones, York and Montreal among them, supported more papers than they do today. Every town had taverns – as many as one for each 200 inhabitants. Drinking provided cheap entertainment for hard-working settlers, and drunkenness and crimes of violence were common. Some of the large shops sold expensive imported goods: household articles, wines and brandies, books and newspapers. Since few people had much leisure time, there was little organized public entertainment. The garrison band might give concerts, travelling musical groups and theatrical companies (most of them American) might stay for a few days, and periodically there was a public hanging, but few other amusements were available and pioneers had to provide their own entertainment.

Public services – roads, water, and sewage disposal, for example – were virtually non-existent. Town sites had been surveyed, usually on a grid plan, and lots sold at the same time as the townships around them. But as towns grew beyond the planned grid, into the townships, they sprawled haphazardly across the countryside. Roads were unsurfaced tracks, although in some municipalities the magistrates did arrange to have the

Left: Hemlock swamps and corduroy road between York and Burlington in 1830, by James Cockburn, a British army officer who served in Canada from 1823-36. Below: Andrew's tavern, above Brockville, by J. J. Bigsby, from his "The shoe and canoe", published in 1850.

Upper Canada Village, which was created by bringing together selected houses, mills, churches, and furnishings, and arranging them so as to portray life in early Ontario. Top left: Kitchen of the Schoolmaster's House (1825). Top right: Man beating flax. Upper centre: Lighting equipment of the early 1800's. Lower centre: The doctor's "office", which was in his house (1846). Right centre: Kitchen scene. Bottom: The village's main street.

Looking eastwards along King Street, Toronto, in the 1830's.

main streets improved with gravel and have board walks laid. Neverthe-less, William Lyon Mackenzie in his newspaper could tell the tall story of a man walking along a street in York, Upper Canada's capital, who saw a hat in the road. Leaning over to pick it up, he found a man under it. "Pray sir, what can I do for you?" he asked. "Don't worry about me, sir," was the reply, "it's my horse under me that needs help!" Nor was there any public water supply beyond a well in the market square. Sewers did not exist: the citizens had to rely on natural ditches that drained off excess water. By the 1830's in York, there was concern about the quality of the water supply, but nothing was done for more than a decade. Pigs scavenged in the streets, performing the duties of garbage collectors. In some towns, voluntary boards of health were organized to administer hos-pitals or to advise the magistrates, but they had little influence. Despite many crimes of violence, there were no police forces; in only a few places did the magistrates employ constables. Catastrophes from fire were fre-quent, for the only fire protection was provided by volunteer fire com-panies.

The towns' problems were caused largely by uncontrolled growth and by the lack of municipal government institutions. Urban centres were gov-erned as part of the surrounding district by appointed Justices of the Peace, who were often unresponsive to the needs of the developing communities. Even when the justices were conscientious, they could make few improve-ments because their limited taxing powers produced only small financial resources. The annual town meetings of ratepayers had little authority except to appoint fence-viewers, poundkeepers, and similar minor offi-cials, with the result that what were strictly municipal problems fell under provincial jurisdiction. The lack of works and services was blamed on the provincial government. Only when the municipalities became incorpo-rated as cities – Saint John in 1785 (the first incorporated city in Can-ada), Montreal in 1832, Toronto in 1834, and Halifax in 1841 – could they organize services to grapple with their local problems. Yet despite all these disadvantages, people still came to the towns to work and to live, and the urban population grew at a more rapid rate than the rural population.

The Coming of Free Trade

British North America's economy had developed within the British imperial mercantile system, which gave colonial products preferential treatment in the form of prearranged prices or of tariff preferences in its markets. In the nineteenth century the economy of the Atlantic provinces was more varied than that of the other colonies: fish and timber were the main staples there and, together with the related shipbuilding and the carrying trades, were the important sources of income. Moreover, Atlantic provinces' shipping obtained some protection from the Navigation Acts, which limited foreign competition. But because those provinces could not supply the British West Indies completely with foodstuffs, they were unable to monopolize the islands' trade and American shipping was therefore admitted to West Indian ports. After 1815 Britain modified her tariffs to encourage the colonial economy. There was some cost to Britain in doing this, for the retention of tariffs, such as the Corn Laws, kept food and raw material prices high. By the late 1830's, however, British proponents of total free trade had organized the Anti-Corn Law League to publicize their claim that the Corn Laws raised the cost of living throughout Britain and their demand for a total repeal of the protective Corn Laws.

In 1842 Upper Canadian farmers petitioned the British government to allow their grain into Britain duty free, but repeated the request they had

Right: Preparing the ways for launching the steamer "Great Britain", then the largest vessel on Lake Ontario, at Prescott in 1830. Bottom left: Notice of freight rates published in 1825. Bottom right: The "Great Britain", from the watercolour by H. F. Ainslie, 1839.

Steam-Boat
NOTICE.

The Subscribers announce to the Public, that they have established the following Rates of Freight by their Steam-Boats, between the Ports of Quebec and Montreal, including the intermediate landing places, to commence on the 1st November.

UPWARDS.		DOWNWARDS.	
Pipes,	7s. 6d. each.	Pipes,	6s. 3d. each.
Puncheons,	6s. 3d. do.	Puncheons,	5s. do.
Hogsheads,	5s. do.	Hogsheads,	3s. 9d. do.
Barrels, according to size,	1s. 6d. a 2s do.	Ashes, p. Barrel, 1s. 8d.	do.
Bales, Cases, &c.	15s. p. ton admeasurement.	Pork, Beef, &c. p. do. 1s. 3d.	do.
		Flour, p. do. 10d.	do.
Iron,	15s. p. ton wt.	Apples, p. do. 7½d.	do.
Crates, according to size,	6s. 3d. a 7s. 6d. each.	Bales, Cases, &c. 10s. p. ton admeasurement.	
		Butter or Lard in Kegs, not exceeding 60 lbs. weight, 6d. each.	

The Prices for other Articles not enumerated above, to be regulated by the Masters of the Steam-Boats.

JOHN MOLSON & SONS, Agents
St. Lawrence Steam-Boat Company.

voiced since 1831 (and especially during the depression of 1836-7) for a heavy duty on American grain entering Canada. Canadian millers, however, objected to the proposed anti-American duties, while British farmers objected to any further reduction of the protection afforded by the Corn Laws. The imperial government compromised, changing the fixed colonial preference rate to a sliding scale very advantageous to Canadian farmers. When Canadian millers protested that they had been excluded from these benefits, a further compromise was made by Britain in her Canada Corn Act of 1843. By the new provision American grain milled in Canada was classed as "naturalized" Canadian flour, but only in return for the imposition by Canada of a Canadian duty of three shillings per quarter on American grain to protect Canadian farmers.

The Canada Corn Act was thus a boon to both the millers and the farmers of Canada. Existing grist mills were enlarged and the number of pairs of millstones increased from 584 in 1842 to 1,200 in 1848. Exports of wheat and flour from the St. Lawrence jumped from 1,194,000 bushels in 1843 to 3,883,000 in 1847. In vain the American Congress tried to recapture some of the lost trade of the Erie Canal by passing the Drawback Act of 1845, which allowed foreign goods destined for Canada to travel through the United States duty free.

This bubble of prosperity, however, burst unexpectedly and with serious results for the Canadian economy. In 1845 and in the following two years blight destroyed the potato crop that had provided the staple food of the Irish peasants. The famine and disease which followed killed an estimated 700,000 and forced countless numbers of poverty stricken and ill people to emigrate to North America. Faced with scenes of indescribable suffering in Ireland and pressured by the Anti-Corn Law League, Prime Minister Sir Robert Peel repealed the Corn Laws in 1846. This action, which permitted the duty-free entry of foreign grain to Britain, destroyed not only the protected position of British agriculture but also the recently achieved preferential position of Canadian grain and flour.

The repeal of the Corn Laws was a heavy blow to the Canadian economy and particularly to Canadian farmers and millers. The costly St. Lawrence canal system was nearly completed, new grain-growing land had been cleared, and large sums had been invested in milling equipment. But now the colonial preference in British markets was eliminated and Canadians would face stiff competition from American grain growers, whose trans-Atlantic shipping costs were only half those of the St. Lawrence route.

The production of Canada's second staple export, timber, which was concentrated largely in the Ottawa Valley, employed over 30,000 men. After 1842 colonial timber lost some of its tariff preference in Britain, and although the duty on foreign timber, mostly from the Baltic region, was still twenty-five times more than on Canadian, it travelled a shorter distance to Britain. Canada's timber trade suffered more from ill-regulated production than from competition, and this was the main reason that the volume of timber exports fell after 1845 and did not recover until 1851. Nevertheless free trade in grain was matched in 1846 by the virtual elimination of the colonial timber preference, thus striking a second blow at the Canadian staples economy.

The fact that the colonies had been allowed a large measure of freedom to set their own tariffs when free trade was introduced could not offset the third blow to Canada – a world-wide depression that began in 1847. Canadian protests against Britain's free-trade policy were many and loud, but all in vain. Free trade, which measured each economic function by the yardstick of utility and tested it in the crucible of unrestricted competition, had replaced mercantilism as the commercial creed of Britain and her empire. Canadian agriculture, lumbering, and commerce would have to find their own salvation. One way of escape from depression lay in the diversification of Canadian farming, which had previously relied so heavily on grain production. Another way might be the reinvestment of Canadian capital in other types of industry and commerce. A third and increasingly attractive alternative was the possibility of gaining greater access to the American market which now contained twenty million consumers.

"The Ice Bridge at Longueuil", by Cornelius Krieghoff (1815-72). In 1837 Krieghoff came from Holland to New York; he later moved to Longueuil near Montreal, and then to Montreal itself. By 1853 he had settled in Quebec. He painted a large number of Canadian scenes, many of which were bought by army officers and taken to England.

HISTORY FROM THE SOURCES

Life on the Frontier

This collection of readings is intended to give the reader some impression of pioneer life in Upper Canada – or Nova Scotia or New Brunswick for that matter – without posing any historical problem.

The following selection is from a series of impressions written by William Lyon Mackenzie in 1831.

> . . . Immense tracts of wild land are to be met with in Albion, and the town is remarkably well-watered, with an abundance of rapids, mill sites, &c. The oak ridges, or Queenston Mountain continuation, run through to King. The largest cleared farm belongs to Mr. William Wilson, from York, in England, who has a comfortable frame-house, and 100 acres under good cultivation. The Heward family of York have a grist-mill, and Mr. George Bolton, an English settler, has another. There are several saw-mills, and the growing crop promises fair. On twelve acres of wheat land Mr. Wilson expects this year to reap thirty-five bushels an acre – this is a first crop. There is in some places wheat damaged with smut, but perhaps this is owing to bad management. There is no post-office in Albion, Caledon, Esquesing, Erin, Chinguacousy, Adjala, Mono, or Tecumseth, although the population is over 6,000, it may be over seven. On the night I stopped in Albion, Mr. W. Wilson, the English settler, in whose house I slept, had eight sheep and lambs devoured by the wolves; and, on the previous Saturday, three men, in the far-back township of Mono, were caught in the forest in a storm. They crept below a hollow log for shelter, on which a large tree fell, and crushed them to death. Accidents are not unfrequent in new and remote townships. In Melancthon, a distant township, four children, one of them a girl of sixteen, went into the woods in search of a calf, and have not since been heard of. They have doubtless perished with cold and hunger.

> W. L. Mackenzie, *Sketches of Canada and the United States*
> (London, 1833), pp. 237-8.

Catherine Parr Traill, who came to Canada from Britain in 1832 and was the youngest sister of the more famous Susanna Moodie, describes a typical frontier house in the Peterborough region about 1835.

> The shanty is a sort of primitive hut in Canadian architecture, and is nothing more than a shed built of logs, the chinks between the

round edges of the timbers being filled with mud, moss, and bits of wood; the roof is frequently composed of logs split and hollowed with the axe, and placed side by side, so that the edges rest on each other; the concave and convex surfaces being alternately uppermost, every other log forms a channel to carry off the rain and melting snow. The eaves of this building resemble the scolloped edges of a clamp shell; but, rude as this covering is, it effectually answers the purpose of keeping the interior dry; far more so than the roofs formed of bark or boards, through which the rain will find entrance. Sometimes the shanty has a window, sometimes only an open doorway, which admits the light and lets out the smoke. A rude chimney, which is often nothing better than an opening cut in one of the top logs above the hearth, a few boards fastened in a square form, serves as the vent for the smoke; the only precaution against the fire catching the log walls behind the hearth being a few large stones placed in a half circular form, or more commonly a bank of dry earth raised against the wall.

Catherine P. Traill, *The Backwoods of Canada*
(London, 1846), pp. 93-4.

Perhaps Mrs. Traill felt the isolation of the frontier more than did other settlers because of the comfortable style of life she had enjoyed in England, but no doubt every settler experienced periods of loneliness.

Nothing hardly but an ox-cart can travel along the roads, and even that with difficulty, occupying two days to perform the journey; and the worst of the matter is, that there are times when the most necessary articles of provisions are not to be procured at any price. You see, then, that a settler in the bush requires to hold himself pretty independent, not only of the luxuries and delicacies of the table, but not unfrequently even of the very necessaries.

One time no pork is to be procured; another time there is a scarcity of flour, owing to some accident that has happened to the mill, or for the want of proper supplies of wheat for grinding; or perhaps the weather and bad roads at the same time prevent a team coming up, or people from going down. Then you must have recourse to a neighbour, if you have the good fortune to be near one, or fare the best you can on potatoes. The potatoe is indeed a great blessing here; new settlers would otherwise be often greatly distressed, and the poor man and his family who are without resources, without the potatoe must starve.

Once our stock of tea was exhausted, and we were unable to procure more. In this dilemma milk would have been an excellent substitute, or coffee, if we had possessed it; but we had neither the one nor the other, so we agreed to try the Yankee tea – hemlock sprigs boiled. This proved, to my taste, a vile decoction; though I recognized some herb in the tea that was sold in London at five shillings a pound, which I am certain was nothing better than dried hemlock leaves reduced to a coarse powder.

Traill, *Backwoods* . . . , pp. 124-5.

Major Samuel Strickland, brother of Mrs. Traill and Mrs. Moodie, describes a bee – a co-operative and sociable way of coping with some of the chores that faced every settler on the frontier.

Soon after my arrival at Darlington, one of my neighbours residing on the lake-shore invited me to a mowing and cradling Bee. As I had never seen anything of the kind, I accepted the invitation. On my arrival at the farm on the appointed day, I found assembled about forty men and boys. A man with a pail of spring water with a wooden cup floating on the surface in one hand, and a bottle of whiskey and glass in the other, now approached the swarm, every one helping himself as he pleased. This man is the most important personage at the "Bee," and is known by the appellation of the "Grog-boss." On this occasion his office was anything but a sinecure. The heat of the weather, I suppose, had made our party very thirsty. There were thirty-five bees cutting hay, among whom I was a rather awkward volunteer, and ten cradlers employed in cutting rye.

At eleven o'clock, cakes and pailfuls of tea were served round. At one, we were summoned by the sound of a tin bugle to dinner, which we found laid out in the barn. Some long pine-boards resting on tressels served for a table, which almost groaned with the good things of this earth, in the shape of roast lamb and green peas, roast sucking-pig, shoulder of mutton, apple-sauce, and pies, puddings, and preserves in abundance, with plenty of beer and Canadian whiskey. Our bees proved so industrious, that before six o'clock all Mr. Burke's hay and rye were finished cutting. Supper was then served on the same scale of profusion, with the addition of tea. After supper a variety of games and gymnastics were introduced, various trials of strength, wrestling, running, jumping, putting the stone, throwing the hammer, etc.

About nine o'clock our party broke up, and returned to their respective homes, well pleased with their day's entertainment, leaving their host perfectly satisfied with their voluntary labour. One word about bees and their attendant frolic. I confess I do not like the system. I acknowledge, that in raising a log-house or barn it is absolutely necessary, especially in the Bush, but the general practice is bad. Some people can do nothing without a bee, and as the work has to be returned in the same manner, it causes a continual round of dissipation – if not of something worse. I have known several cases of manslaughter arising out of quarrels produced by intoxication at these every-day gatherings. As population increases, and labour becomes cheaper, of course there will be less occasion for them.

Major Samuel Strickland, *Twenty-Seven Years in Canada West*
(London, 1853), Vol. I, pp. 35-7.

Edward Allen Talbot, who settled with his father and brother in London township about 1818, describes the assimilation of the immigrant into the frontier community.

It is very remarkable, that although the present population of this fine Province is composed of emigrants from almost every European nation, and from every state of North America, there should be so little difference in their manners, customs, and habits of life. Germans, Hollanders, French, English, Scotch, and Irish, after a few years' residence in Canada, forget their national customs and peculiarities, and become, in almost every particular, entirely assimilated to the people of America.

These emigrants, having generally been of the lowest class of society in their respective countries, – and consequently mere cyphers except in their own immediate sphere, – as soon as they arrive in Canada, begin to assume an appearance of importance, and to be quite ashamed of their former unassuming manners and native customs. The most absurd notions of equality and independence take instant possession of their vestiginous and unreflecting minds. As they travel through the Province and mingle with its inhabitants, they hear the dialects and peculiarities of their respective nations derided and ridiculed, while those of America, both Republican and Monarchical, are invariably defended and extolled.

E. A. Talbot, *Five Years' Residence in the Canadas*
(London, 1824), Vol. II, pp. 9-10.

Some Negroes had come to Canada in the Loyalist migration, but the passing of the Fugitive Slave Act in the United States in 1850 led to the organization of the "underground railroad" which smuggled thousands of escaping slaves to Canada and freedom.

The number of coloured persons of African descent in Upper Canada was, in 1848, 5,400; 3,000 of whom were males. . . . These

people are usually employed in the towns as waiters in hotels, barbers, and generally in performing the most burdensome and lowest
descriptions of labour, such as cutting up and preparing wood for
fuel. They have, as labourers, usually great powers of endurance;
and when their dispositions have not been soured by ill usage, they
are most generally civil and attached servants. There are also some
educated coloured persons whose qualifications and general conduct have assisted much to remove those prejudices against the race
that exist less or more all over America. . . .

Generally speaking, this coloured portion of the population, both
in the country parts and in the towns and villages of Canada, live
apart from the white inhabitants. They are very usually to be found
collected together in the least valuable corners of the towns – their
houses and style of living most frequently denoting a scale of civilization greatly inferior to the mass of the population surrounding them;
among whom, it can scarcely be doubted, they too bitterly feel themselves to be merely "the hewers of wood and drawers of water."

J. B. Brown, *Views of Canada and the Colonies*
(Edinburgh, 1851), pp. 62-3.

*Robert Gourlay, "the banished Briton", discusses the place of education
in frontier life in his controversial report on the province of Upper
Canada.*

The first inhabitants, as was stated in the historical sketch, were
generally poor, in consequence of the revolution. They had also to
struggle with the labours and privations incident to new settlements.
As their habitations were sparse, it was difficult for them to unite in
sufficient numbers to form good schools; and they could neither
afford much expense for instructors, nor allow their children much
time for receiving instruction. From such inevitable causes, education was neglected among them, until the neglect almost became
habitual. The want of books, at the same time, relaxed their taste
for reading.

A sense of these disadvantages excited desires for surmounting
them, which have at length produced some corresponding exertion.
Books are procured in considerable numbers. In addition to those
with which particular persons and families are supplied, social libraries are introduced in various places; and subscribers at a small
expence thus enjoy the benefit of many more volumes than they
could individually afford to purchase.

A spirit of improvement is evidently spreading. The value of education, as well as the want of it, is felt. The practicability of obtaining

it is considered. Gentlemen of competent means appear to be sensible of the importance of giving their children academical learning, and ambitious to do it without sending them abroad for the purpose.

Robert Gourlay, *Statistical Account of Upper Canada*
(London, 1822), Vol. I, pp. 245-6.

The camp meeting was a popular religious gathering of the country people. From the extract below, do you think that Shirreff was an unbiased observer?

. . . The ground in the midst of the forest had been prepared for the occasion, having had the brush or underwood removed, and trees laid in parallel rows, by way of seats, for five or six hundred people. On entering a square, formed by tents, in which the people reside for four or five days together, I was disappointed at the smallness of the assemblage, which did not exceed three hundred souls. Many people were walking up and down, engaged in mirthful conversation, and five or six small groups were standing in different parts, singing hymns in a low tone. . . .

A little while after entering the square, five or six old men placed themselves in front of a rude platform erected for the preachers, and commenced singing in a loud strain, on hearing which the different small parties came and joined the old men. The singing lasted about ten minutes, when praying succeeded, and each individual pronounced a different prayer aloud. At this time a minister placed himself on the platform or pulpit, and in a stentorian voice, ejaculated an impassioned prayer, which, by degrees, excited the feelings of the people below him, and when they reached what he, perhaps, considered the proper key, he descended and joined them on his knees.

I was standing close beside the worshippers, on a trough used for collecting the juice of the maple in spring, leaning my back against a tree, and gazing on the extraordinary scene. Many individuals of both sexes were bellowing at the utmost pitch of their voice, and clapping their hands in seeming transport; others were whining supplicatory strains, and wringing their hands in despair. The comely young woman and her companion, formerly noticed, joined the group in a standing position in the first instance; they soon became bathed in tears, and ultimately joined in prayer in a state of high excitement. A very emaciated old woman, with dishevelled locks of silvery whiteness, shrieked so loud and piteously, that the minister's voice became unheard, and something like a thrill of uneasiness vibrated on my nerves. Such was the confusion and discord, that I was unable to collect two connecting sentences from the prayer of any individual. When the devotees had seemingly reached the highest pitch to which their feelings would strain, the lady with the gipsy bonnet stepped forward near to where I was standing, and commenced singing in the most soothing and melodious tone. She was joined by her sister and brother, and soon afterwards by all the sect. In this manner prayer and praise succeeded each other . . . .

Many bystanders were laughing at the exclamations and postures of the worshippers; others were reading newspapers, or carelessly engaged in conversation.

There was something so different in the impassioned supplications of the minister, whose aim seemed to be to rouse the feelings, without impressing the minds, of his audience – in the time, place, and manner of addressing the Supreme Being, so different to what I had been accustomed to in the Presbyterian worship of Scotland, that at first I could not believe the sect was addressing the same Deity. The earnest, excited, I may say hysterical, devotions of one party, the indifference and unrestrained scoffing of the other, gave rise to such conflicting emotions, that I arranged to meet my friend in half an hour, and retired from the multitude.

Patrick Shirreff, *A Tour through North America*
(Edinburgh, 1835), pp. 183-6.

FURTHER READING

On the fur trade, the readings for Chapter 9 should be consulted.

Easterbrook, W. T. and Aitken, H. J. G., *Canadian Economic History* (Toronto: Macmillan, 1956).

Glazebrook, G. P. de T., *A History of Transportation in Canada*, 2 vols. (Toronto: McClelland & Stewart, 1964)★.

Tucker, Gilbert, *The Canadian Commercial Revolution, 1845-1851* (Toronto: McClelland & Stewart, 1964)★.

Creighton, D. G., *The Empire of the St. Lawrence* (Toronto: Macmillan, 1956).

Fay, S. B., *Life and Labour in Newfoundland* (Toronto: University of Toronto Press, 1956).

Craig, Gerald M., *Upper Canada 1784-1841: The Formative Years* (Toronto: McClelland & Stewart, 1963).

MacNutt, W. S., *The Atlantic Provinces: The Emergence of Colonial Society, 1712-1857* (Toronto: McClelland & Stewart, 1965).

Glazebrook, G. P. de T., *Life in Ontario: A Social History* (Toronto: University of Toronto Press, 1968).

I2

Crisis in the Colonies

The Revival of Unrest in Lower Canada

In 1815 the basic issue of the pre-war years had not been resolved: an English-speaking minority still ruled a French-speaking majority. Memories of Sir James Craig and of the persecution of Bédard were still very much alive even though Prevost had done so much to conciliate the French. The English minority, who controlled the Legislative and Executive Councils, was called derisively the "Château Clique" by the people. It was a mixture of government officials, speculators in lands in the Eastern Townships, merchants, and a few French seigneurs. The *Patriote* party, led by a few seigneurs, both English and French, and by a group of lawyers, enjoyed the support of the majority of voters.

Conflict between the executive and the Assembly began over finances. When Governor Sir John Cope Sherbrooke asked for funds from the Assembly in 1817, he explained carefully to its leaders why he needed the money, and the grant was forthcoming. His successor, the Duke of Richmond, faced the same problem in the following year, but felt that he would lessen his authority if he dealt with the Assembly and therefore refused to

Saint James Street, Montreal, 1829-30, by the Irish painter
R. A. Sproule, who emigrated to Canada in the late 1820's.

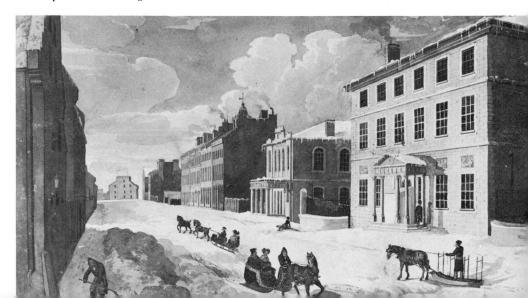

consult its leaders. The Assembly members saw that this issue gave them a chance to make their will prevail through control of the purse and refused to grant supplies. The result was a deadlock: neither side would give an inch to the other. This estrangement between the executive and the Assembly became even more marked after the futile attempt to unite the two provinces in 1822. The scheme to unite Upper and Lower Canada had been promoted by English merchants in Montreal as a means of enlarging the English-speaking community's influence and of building the St. Lawrence canals. Naturally enough the *Patriote* party saw the Union bill, introduced in the British parliament without the Lower Canadian legislature being consulted, as a new attempt by the English to subjugate them.

The French majority in the Assembly, whose belief in popular control of government went hand in hand with its concern to defend its culture, was not entirely an unreasonable opposition group. When the latest governor, Lord Dalhousie, was absent in England in 1825, the lieutenant-governor consulted the Assembly leaders and, with the help of Bishop Plessis, persuaded the Assembly to pass the necessary appropriations without conceding the principle of executive control over the administration. When Dalhousie returned to Canada, the impasse resumed. A large part of the government's problem was that it had no spokesman in the Assembly to explain its policies. Only a couple of English extremists, far more adamant in their views than the governor and his advisers, sat in the Assembly to defend the government, and the effect of their presence was to make co-operation between the executive in the Château St. Louis and the Assembly more difficult. Complete deadlock developed in 1827, when the governor dissolved the Assembly and called an election. Considerable pressure was exerted to elect some members favourable to the executive, but the returns again produced a house overwhelmingly opposed to the executive.

This opposition was spearheaded by the Speaker of the Assembly, Louis Joseph Papineau. The tall, handsome, and courtly Papineau was typical in many ways of a whole generation of educated French Canadians who found no outlet for their talents save in journalism and law and in a concern for the protection of their nationality. From the time that he was elected Speaker, Papineau was in effect the leader of the French-Canadian group in the Assembly. In his years of quarrelling with the executive he became attracted through reading and discussion to European and American democratic ideas. To Papineau, elective institutions like those in the United States seemed to be the panacea; an elected Legislative Council and executive would destroy English control and end the years of frustration. The seeming willingness of church leaders to co-operate with the

Louis Joseph Papineau addressing the representatives of the six counties at St. Charles. The reformers of the six counties of the Richelieu Valley had formed a political alliance and in October 1837 the largest of several anti-government rallies was held at St. Charles.

English made him increasingly anticlerical. Papineau, who found political compromise difficult, was unwilling to try to work with the English.

The clash over financial control of the government masked a host of other issues, the most serious being the growing discontent of the habitants. By 1820 the old seigneuries were so overpopulated that sons of the *censitaires* had to move away from their families to the freehold areas in the Eastern Townships, or to the New England states to seek work in the factories. Outmoded farming techniques and exhaustion of the land made this situation even worse. At the same time seigneurs were becoming interested in making profits from their holdings and were demanding the full obligations due to them. Looking for scapegoats on whom to blame his plight, the habitant pointed to businessmen, the government, immigrants – all of them English. The habitants' concern over immigration reflected their nationalism, but French-Canadian seigneurs were also to blame for the habitants' unrest because they played upon this fear of the English in order to gain political support.

While lumbering flourished, the agricultural economy of the colony was tending to stagnate. Surpluses of grain for export declined every year until in the 1830's it was necessary to import grain. As the habitants became poorer, they bought fewer goods, and with this decline of commerce in Lower Canada the merchants turned more to the lumber business and to trade with Upper Canada. These merchants wanted canals built along the St. Lawrence to save their business, but such a programme was impossible because the French-dominated Assembly was unwilling to increase land taxes to pay for improvements. Suspicious of the merchants who desired immigration, public works, and the expansion of commerce, the French-Canadian politicians were certain that the business class was trying to suppress the French-Canadian people, and they sought to make the merchants bear the burden of taxation through higher tariffs. In turn, the English merchants regarded the French Canadians as ignorant and obstructionist. All these problems seemed capable of being expressed as a simple conflict of nationalities, French versus English.

The *Patriote* victory in the 1827 elections ensured that the impasse between the executive and Assembly would continue. In the following

year a new government in Britain appointed a House of Commons committee to investigate the situation and make recommendations. The
committee heard evidence from both the colonial office and the Canadas.
On the key issue of public finances the committee recommended that
financial control be turned over to the Assembly on condition that the
Assembly vote a civil list (the salaries of government officials) for the
lifetime of the monarch. Their report also recommended that the personnel of the Executive and Legislative Councils be entirely separate – no
one should hold seats in both – and that judges should not sit in the
Councils. On the whole, this report was a victory for the Assembly's point
of view. To implement the committee's recommendations, control of
finances was handed over to the Assembly. The deadlock between elected
and appointed branches of the legislature seemed to have been broken.

After the initial success of this conciliatory policy a crisis arose in 1833,
when the Assembly refused to vote a permanent civil list in return for
control of the revenues. Papineau had now realized that the civil list made
the executive independent of the Assembly. In the following year, the civil
list was again rejected and, in addition, the Assembly under Papineau's
leadership passed the Ninety-Two Resolutions, a verbose recitation of
complaints against the provincial government. As Papineau's criticism of
the government became more violent and his proposed solutions more
radically democratic, moderate reformers like John Neilson, publisher
of the Quebec *Gazette*, and some *Patriotes* began to desert his cause. The
British government responded to this new crisis by sending out a new
governor, the Earl of Gosford, with a royal commission to investigate
on the spot the difficulties in Lower Canada. But Papineau and the radicals
made it clear that they would reject any and all recommendations of the
Gosford Commission. Therefore early in 1837 Lord John Russell, the

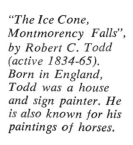

"The Ice Cone, Montmorency Falls", by Robert C. Todd (active 1834-65). Born in England, Todd was a house and sign painter. He is also known for his paintings of horses.

Colonel Wetherall advancing to capture St. Charles (25 November 1837), where the Rebellion of 1837 broke out in Lower Canada, and where the Confederation of the Six Counties was proclaimed. The rebels were scattered by Wetherall's column of British troops.

Colonial Secretary, introduced ten resolutions in the House of Commons, giving Gosford exceptional powers to end the financial deadlock in Lower Canada. The executive was authorized to use provincial revenues without the Assembly's approval and to legalize the collection of taxes not voted since 1833. Papineau and the radicals reacted bitterly against this arbitrary intervention by the imperial authorities.

This political crisis was intensified by the current economic situation. All classes felt the effects of the crop failure and the falling prices for timber. Radicals began talking openly of revolution, an idea implanted in Papineau and others by the 1830 revolutions in Europe. All the ingredients of rebellion seemed to be present: economic distress, crisis in government, and revolutionary leadership. The radicals organized L'Association des Fils de la Liberté to co-ordinate their activities. Papineau, by now swept along by other voices more extreme than his own, toured the province demanding action. Suddenly, in October, the Bishop of Montreal condemned the radicals and their programme. The less radical left the *Patriote* movement and, with their influence gone, the extremists became even more strident. In late November, when the government ordered the arrest of Papineau and others for sedition, the *Patriote* leaders fled into the country, hoping to organize forces to overthrow the government. But the habitants, influenced by their clergy and afraid of the government, did not rally to support the rebels and, after a couple of clashes between British troops and ill-armed habitants in the Montreal region, the uprising collapsed. Papineau and the other leaders escaped to the United States even before the fighting was over.

Upper Canada in Turmoil

In Upper Canada discontent also led to rebellion in 1837. But there the structure of government was probably less to blame; there was not the constant conflict between the elected Assembly and the appointed Councils

SCENES OF CONFLICT IN THE 1837 REBELLION AND PATRIOT WAR

that agitated Lower Canada. Anti-government majorities were elected to the Upper Canadian Assembly only in 1828 and 1834, but each held control just for two years because of strong reaction against them in the succeeding elections. The heritage of Loyalism and the conservatism of Upper Canadian society combined to give the government considerable public support. Nor were party lines as clear as in Lower Canada: many members of the Assembly were pro-government on some questions and against it on others. Politics tended to be more individualistic: most election issues were local rather than provincial. Above all, the issues of language and so-called "race" were absent in Upper Canada.

Government was directed by a small political elite, the "Family Compact", a nickname as misleading as "Château Clique" although it embodied a kind of half truth – that a small group of men dominated the appointed levels of government for nearly two decades. This oligarchy was drawn from the wealthier, better educated class in the province – a few businessmen, many lawyers, and a great many career administrators. Unlike Lower Canada, however, many influential people were critics of the government and provided leadership for the reform group.

The first signs of discontent in Upper Canada appeared after the War of 1812. With the ending of wartime demand for supplies and the circulation of army bills, prices and trade declined and at the same time the post-Napoleonic Wars depression made the situation worse. The British government was slow to pay for damages done in the war because it had hoped that sale of the lands confiscated from traitors would cover the loss claims. But because land values dropped and the amount of land to be sold off was less than anticipated, the problem dragged on for many years before even partial compensation was paid. Many people whose wealth was in land or who had speculated in land before the war also suffered from the decline in demand for land because of the lack of immigration from the United States.

This discontent was not voiced until 1817, when a group of members of the Legislative Council began to criticize the government. Although the governor prorogued the legislature to silence these critics, the issue would not die. In the autumn of 1817 Robert Gourlay, a Scot who had been associated with the radical movement in Britain and who was related through his wife to the two leading opponents of the government, immigrated to Upper Canada. A Don Quixote type, Gourlay was ready to fight government wrongdoing wherever he could find it, and he quickly persuaded himself that reforms were needed in Upper Canada. He published two manifestos criticizing the government and organized meetings throughout the province to petition the Prince Regent for remedies. The provincial government, worried lest Gourlay's meetings become the nucleus of an opposition movement, decided to suppress this troublesome Scot. The governor and Council persuaded the legislature in 1818 to pass a law prohibiting these meetings, and in December of that year Gourlay was charged with sedition under an act of 1804 which gave the courts the right to order him deported. In July 1819, after remaining in jail for six months, Gourlay was banished from Upper Canada. By that date the grievances of the post-war period began to lose their urgency as economic conditions improved, and the movement Gourlay had stirred disappeared with him. Yet in the heated political fights of the 1830's the reformers would hail Gourlay as a martyr for their cause.

The reform movement in Upper Canada was really born in the 1820's largely out of the alien and the church-state questions, the only two issues of province-wide interest. The alien question involved the right of American-born settlers to hold public office and to own property, which if denied would affect the majority of people in Upper Canada. The question arose when Barnabas Bidwell was elected to the Assembly in 1821. Bidwell, a former Congressman, had fled to Canada from Massachusetts

Left: Detail of J. P. Cockburn's watercolour of a picnic on Goat Island, Niagara Falls, on 27 October 1831. Below: A stagecoach operated by William Weller, whose coaches by 1837 ran daily between Kingston, Toronto, and Hamilton.

just before the war to escape charges of embezzling public funds. He took the oath of allegiance, settled in Bath, opened a school, and later practised law. An avowed republican, Bidwell became the leader of the anti-government group in his locality. Scandalized by the presence of such a man in the Assembly (even though he proved that he had repaid the missing funds), the government persuaded the Assembly to invalidate his election. The ruling clique pushed the matter further, however, by asking the British government whether aliens like Bidwell, who had previously taken the oath of allegiance to the United States, were entitled to civil rights in the province. Simultaneously a British court decided that civilians who had remained in the United States after 1783 had lost their rights as British subjects. The decision would probably never have been heard of in Upper Canada but for the enquiry, and when it was known, not even the most hardened anti-American and anti-democrat was pleased, since the bulk of the population (including many Loyalists) thereby lost its civil rights. Bills to re-confer these rights on American-born settlers were hotly rejected by the majority in the Assembly, who claimed that they wanted their rights confirmed, not conferred. The British government, confused by the storm against these bills, finally ordered late in 1827 that a provincial bill be passed. This confirmed the rights of anyone who had been resident in the province for more than seven years. But it was the colonial government that bore the odium of the two years' fumbling and whose intentions became suspect.

The other province-wide question concerned church and state relations. Most members of the "Family Compact" were Anglican; the leading spokesman for the oligarchy and persecutor of Gourlay was the Archdeacon of York, John Strachan. The Anglican church was by no means the largest Protestant denomination. Unable to attract many clergy from Britain, the Anglican communion enjoyed support only in towns where parishes had already been established and where there were full-time clergy. Outside the towns, the people were usually Methodists, though in areas of Irish and Scottish settlement Roman Catholicism and Presby-

Left: A winter's journey by sleigh in Upper Canada in the mid-nineteenth century. Below: T. H. Ware's sketch, drawn in 1844, showing a culvert on the Coldwater Road near Orillia.

Farm equipment used in the 1850's. (From a photograph taken in Upper Canada Village.)

terianism were predominant. In addition there were many other Protestant groups in various parts of Upper Canada. In a province where the majority of the population was not Anglican and where religious pluralism was strong, the relationship between the government and the Anglican church was unpopular.

This resentment was focused on Strachan, who had come to Upper Canada from Scotland in 1799 as a teacher, but soon after became the Anglican priest of Cornwall, where he opened a school. Through this excellent school passed John Beverley Robinson, Christopher Hagerman, John Macaulay, and many others who belonged to the "Family Compact" of the 1820's. Strachan moved to York in 1812 and in the next few years became a member of both the Legislative and the Executive Councils. The close friend and confidant of Lieutenant-Governor Sir Peregrine Maitland in the 1820's, he became a dominant influence in the government of the province. Though an able administrator, Strachan won many enemies by his Tory and high-Anglican views. After 1829, when a new governor arrived, his influence and that of the "Family Compact" waned, but he still remained the target for bitter attacks.

The church-state question entered politics mainly on two issues: the Clergy Reserves and education. The Clergy Reserves were land set aside under the Constitutional Act of 1791 to be rented for the support of "the Protestant Clergy" of the provincially established Church of England, but in the 1820's some Presbyterians began to claim state support for the Church of Scotland. A few Methodists also wanted a share of the income, but most Methodists and nearly all other Protestants opposed government aid to any particular church from public funds. Instead they advocated "voluntary" support of churches by their adherents, and argued that the Reserves should be used to provide public education for all citizens. The Reserves, amounting to approximately one-eighth of all the surveyed land, were also considered barriers to settlement. Above all, they were symbols of the privileged position of the Anglican church in the province – yet with so much unreserved land available, they attracted few tenants and produced very little income.

Anglican dominance in education also caused popular resentment. In the early years prosperous families had hired tutors or sent their children to private schools like Strachan's. In 1816, at the urging of Strachan, who was a vigorous advocate of public education, the government made money available to pay teachers for any elementary school which local communities wished to establish and a provincial board of education, appointed with Strachan as president, was established to distribute the funds and to select textbooks. Not surprisingly, the textbooks were English-made with a strong Anglican bias. Again at Strachan's urging, the British government in 1827 granted a charter for a provincial university – King's College, to be run by a council of professors (all of whom had to be Anglican) with Strachan as president. Led by the young Methodist preacher Egerton Ryerson, the public outcry against this Anglican-controlled institution was so great that the university did not open until the 1840's, when Anglican influence had been much reduced.

Other issues in Upper Canada either lacked province-wide appeal or general agreement as to remedies. There was anger over the heavy government subsidies to the Welland Canal Company in those areas which did not benefit directly from the canal's construction. Frontier farmers who wanted roads and bridges built were frustrated by the lack of municipal government to undertake such improvements. Often in debt, these same farmers blamed the government-controlled Bank of Upper Canada for the chronic shortage of loan money and the high interest rates. In some areas there was much discontent over land speculation, as many unimproved lots were kept off the market to allow their value to rise as the lots around them were settled. The government conscientiously tried to check this speculation by taxing uncleared land, but the collection of taxes was so difficult that speculators were undeterred. Some Reformers wanted control over provincial revenues so that they could control the executive: they resented the independence which the government enjoyed with the annual payments from the Canada Company for the lands it had bought.

The Reform majorities which controlled the Assembly in 1828-30 and again in 1834-6 were by no means united as a party, nor in agreement as to what they wanted, but constituted a spectrum of anti-government opinion. The moderates, led by Robert Baldwin, were concerned primarily with the problem of rule by a minority; to them the solution was simply to devise some constitutional means of making the executive responsive to the will of the elected Assembly. Some Reformers were concerned about church-state issues, others about economic problems. Marshall Spring Bidwell, son of Barnabas and an able lawyer with a small following in the Assembly, stood somewhere between the moderates and the radicals in his views. The more radical Reformers, led by the calculating physician and lawyer John Rolph and by the impulsive journalist William Lyon Mackenzie, attacked the government on a wide range of issues. Quick to contrast the backwardness of Upper Canada with the rapid expansion of the United States, they blamed the province's troubles on the colonial system of government. They claimed that a more democratic system, without privilege for any person or institution, would bring progress to Upper Canada.

The Reform victory in the 1834 election was in large part attributable to the repeated expulsion of William Lyon Mackenzie from the Tory-dominated Assembly between 1830 and 1834. But after the Reform victory the volatile little Scot was appointed chairman of a committee to gather and catalogue grievances, a task for which he was eminently fitted. The result was the *Seventh Report on Grievances*, which recorded all the misdeeds attributed to the government together with the testimony, relevant and otherwise, of numerous witnesses. In 1834 Mackenzie was elected mayor of the newly chartered City of Toronto, but he was ineffective in that position because of his involvement with partisan politics. He proved little more effective in the Assembly, where he never commanded the support of more than a handful of radicals. Increasingly irked at his failure to obtain power, Mackenzie turned towards the American idea of having all officials elected, and publicized his admiration of American methods and institutions in his newspaper, *The Colonial Advocate*.

The arrival in 1836 of a new lieutenant-governor, Sir Francis Bond Head, made the radicals' position even more difficult. After quarrelling

American-born Dr. Charles Duncombe settled in Upper Canada in 1820 near London. He soon became active in Reform politics and was elected to the Assembly for Oxford County in 1830, 1834, and 1836. He went to England in 1836, to lay charges against Sir F. B. Head for his conduct during the election of that year, but when he could get no support from the Colonial Office, he returned to Upper Canada just before Mackenzie's rebellion occurred. Duncombe reluctantly agreed to lead an uprising in the London area, but his tiny force, which met at the hamlet of Scotland, dispersed when news of Mackenzie's defeat at Montgomery's Tavern reached them. Duncombe fled to the United States where he remained until his death in 1875.

PROCLAMATION.
REWARD.

By Command of His Excellency the Lieutenant Governor.

A REWARD is hereby offered, of

Five Hundred Pounds,

To any one who will apprehend and deliver up to Justice,

CHARLES DUNCOMBE;

And a Reward of *Two Hundred and Fifty Pounds* to any one who will apprehend and deliver up to Justice, ELIAKIM MALCOLM; or FINLAY MALCOLM; or ROBERT ALWAY; and a Reward of *One Hundred Pounds*, to any one who will apprehend and deliver up to Justice, ———— ANDERSON, (said to be a Captain in the Rebel Forces); or JOSHUA DOAN.

All the above persons are known to have been traitorously in arms against their Sovereign; and to entitle the party apprehending either of them to the Reward, he must be delivered to the Civil Power, at Hamilton, Niagara, London, or Toronto.

GOD SAVE THE QUEEN.

16th December, 1837.

M STANTON Printer to the QUEEN'S Most Excellent Majesty

The attack and defeat of American sympathizers at Dickenson Landing, Upper Canada, from a coloured lithograph after the original by Coke Smyth.

with the Assembly and his Executive Council over his relationship to the Council, Head dissolved the Assembly and called an election. In a stormy campaign, Head himself went on the hustings to proclaim that the issue facing the electorate was whether they wished to remain a loyal part of the British empire or succumb to American republicanism. The Reformers, accused of republicanism because of the extreme statements of their radical adherents, were heavily defeated, their leaders rejected at the polls, and the Tories returned with an overwhelming majority in the election of 1836.

Mackenzie and his followers were angry over their failure to win public support. The depression which settled on the province in 1837 gave the radicals a sympathetic audience as Mackenzie and his followers began saying that the only hope for Upper Canada was to throw off its colonial status. Groups of farmers began to gather to practise musketry and to drill in support of the radical cause. In the area north of Toronto they met to hear Mackenzie speak of the need for a show of physical force and to prepare for revolutionary action if the *Patriotes* of Lower Canada rose. Mackenzie corresponded with the radical leaders to learn their plans. Head unwittingly encouraged Mackenzie's plans for "a brave stroke for liberty" by sending all the regular troops in the province to Montreal to help put down the rebellion which began there on 23 November.

Two pictorial accounts of the fate of Mackenzie's supply ship the "Caroline", set on fire by the British in December 1837. Left: The ship is swept over Niagara Falls – dramatic but inaccurate. Below: The ship burns upriver – less exciting but historically correct.

When news of the Lower Canadian rebellion reached Toronto, Mackenzie called his men to assemble early in December at Montgomery's Tavern, a few miles north of the city. From there they intended to capture the defenceless government without any bloodshed, but Mackenzie's mismanagement prevented any decisive move by the rebels. On 7 December loyal militiamen who had hastened to Toronto marched north against Mackenzie's small rabble. A few shots scattered the rebels, and Mackenzie fled through Niagara to the United States. Early in 1838 he proclaimed a Canadian republic on Navy Island in the Niagara River (two miles above the Falls) and attempted vainly to organize an invasion of the province with the aid of American sympathizers, but he soon left the island together with his new followers. Unlike Lower Canada, resistance to the rebellion in Upper Canada rose spontaneously and loyal militia units from outlying areas were still arriving in Toronto long after the fighting was over, or scouring the countryside trying to find traces of the rebels. The rebel cause collapsed dismally in the face of this overwhelming demonstration of loyalty to Britain and the provincial government.

Moderation and Harmony in the Atlantic Provinces

While there was some discontent in the Atlantic provinces during the quarter century after the War of 1812, reform movements were slower to develop there and were much less radical than those in the Canadas. The major causes of Canadian conflict were lacking in the Maritime region – there was neither a deep racial split as in Lower Canada, nor the profound anti-Americanism and Loyalism of Upper Canada. The reformers in the Atlantic provinces looked to Britain, not to the United States, for their models and inspiration, and the pro-government supporters never raised the cry of disloyalty against them. Other grievances were missing, too – there were no Clergy Reserves to excite greed, and the privileges enjoyed by the established Anglican church were less objectionable than in Upper Canada. Accordingly the Reform parties did not appear until the 1830's and were never as extreme in their views as those in the Canadas.

In Newfoundland there was no reform movement as such, nor was there any representative government until 1832. The rule of the naval admirals ended only in 1825 with the appointment of Sir Thomas Cochrane as governor, to rule with the aid of a Council in St. John's. Although Cochrane, a hard-working administrator, was popular, the islanders shortly began to demand an elected body to represent them. When the first elected Assembly met in 1833, religious quarrels between Protestant and Roman Catholic members broke out. Personal vendettas among the members were common, but genuine political parties were unknown. From this impossible situation Cochrane was recalled, yet his successors proved no more able to deal with the politics of the island. The British government undertook to pay the costs of government in 1834 and to allow the limited revenues from the island to be used by the Assembly. But the quarrelling local politicians, powerless to hinder the operations of the government and seemingly unable to govern themselves, so discredited the government of Newfoundland that in 1841 the British government appointed a House of Commons committee to examine the working of the island's constitution. In the following year the Assembly was reconstructed with its membership partly elected and partly appointed, a change that permitted political life to calm down while a shrewd governor, Sir John Harvey (of War of 1812 fame), ruled the island by collaborating with all factions. A fully elected Assembly was restored to Newfoundland in 1847.

The major problem in Prince Edward Island was the land question. Most of the land was owned by absentee landlords in England, who took little interest in their estates except to ensure collection of rents. That one-third of the land was held in freehold aggravated the remaining tenants, who resented paying rents, especially when squatters began to farm on vacant lands. The Assembly tried vainly to have undeveloped land revert to the Crown so that it could be re-granted or sold. Even the governor privately pressed for reversion, but the British government refused to take back the land. It correctly suspected that much of the clamour from the local government was made on behalf of speculators who wanted to buy the land cheaply. When the extremism of the group in the Assembly favouring reversion forced the Council to oppose its demands, the leaders did finally advocate the creation of an elected legislative council. Even then, the people's anger was not directed against the local governing élite, but against the absentee landlords. This concern with the land question tended therefore to divert the "reformers" from the major objective of the Canadian reformers (that of bringing the provincial governments more under the control of the inhabitants) and to sidetrack them towards the objective of bringing the province's lands under local control.

In New Brunswick, by contrast, a real quarrel developed between the elected Assembly and the appointed executive. The issue was not one of constitutional principle, but simply of who should control the revenues from the Crown lands rich with timber. At the centre of the storm was Thomas Baillie, Commissioner of Crown Lands, who did his best to ensure that the revenues from the Crown lands remained under executive control. The problem was not misuse of these funds, since the government used them to establish a college, to assist education, and to aid local agricultural and immigrant groups. Members of the Assembly simply wanted access to these funds so that they could be used for political patronage in the form of local improvement projects.

A change in the structure of the New Brunswick government in 1833 added fuel to the fire. The British government separated the functions of the Council: an Executive Council of five members was established, separate from the larger Legislative Council. The dominant figure in the new executive was Thomas Baillie. Many prominent old Loyalist families and timber merchants who had been left out of the executive now allied themselves with the anti-Baillie faction in the Assembly and joined in the battle for control of the timber revenues. Late in 1833 a delegation from the Assembly went to Britain and persuaded the imperial government to limit Baillie's authority over the disposal of lands. Yet only when the Assembly promised to provide a permanent civil list in 1837 did the British government hand over control of the timber revenues to that body. At that time the Colonial Secretary made a further major concession to colonial reform. The 1833 delegation had asked for an Executive Council more in harmony with the Assembly; in 1837 the new governor included two leaders from the Legislative Assembly in his Executive Council. Without conceding the principle of responsible government and without guaranteeing to continue this practice, the Colonial Secretary introduced into New Brunswick the answer to the demands of Canadian and Nova Scotia reformers – an executive more responsive to the wishes of the elected representatives of the people.

In Nova Scotia the basic political issue was rather similar to that in the Canadas – the domination of the provincial government by an élite

New Brunswick in the nineteenth century.
Right: Greenock Church, St. Andrews, New Brunswick. The church was built between 1817 and 1824. The oak tree in full leaf carved on the front was added by the builder: it was part of an heraldic device from his native town of Greenock, Scotland.
Below: A winter scene in Fredericton, 1836.

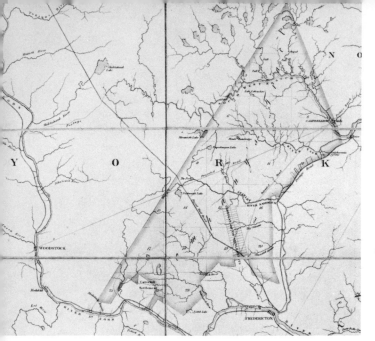

The title of this map reads: "New Brunswick and Nova Scotia Land Company. A Map of the Company's Tract of Land in the Province of New Brunswick. The tract of land containing 500,000 acres and upward purchased of H.M. Government, in fee simple and free and common soccage. Company's Office, London, 1834." The man chiefly responsible for setting up and organizing this land company was Thomas Baillie.

group. This oligarchy, known as the "Council of Twelve", was made up of the leading Halifax merchants, bankers, and government officials, and had run the province since the 1790's. Any wealthy man in high position was automatically a member of the élite group. Further, individuals who spoke out against the oligarchy were converted into its staunch supporters by the gift of posts in the government or appointments to the Council. While there was no strong opposition to the Halifax group in the province, there was a smouldering discontent over several issues. Anglican control of the university, the circulation of paper money of uncertain value by the Halifax Banking Company and other banks in the 1830's, and, the most crucial matter, the dominance of Halifax over the rest of the province – all these were minor causes of discontent. But because the ruling group in Halifax was more liberal than similar groups in the Canadas, it did not encounter significant opposition until the mid-1830's.

The event which suddenly created an anti-government party was the trial for libel of Joseph Howe, the editor and publisher of the *Nova Scotian*. Widely known throughout the province for his writing, Howe had published an anonymous article criticizing the local government of Halifax and, indirectly, the provincial government whose nominees were the magistrates – those who claimed to have been libelled. Although lawyer friends had advised him that he had little hope of being acquitted, Howe decided to undertake his own defence, and his skilful and powerful speeches to the jury won his case. Suddenly the political tensions of the previous twenty years burst into the open. After a speaking tour of the province, Howe returned to Halifax in triumph to win election to the Assembly in 1836.

Under Howe's leadership the Opposition in the legislature demanded that Nova Scotians enjoy the same political rights as Englishmen and that the Council should answer to the elected Assembly for its actions. Howe's Twelve Resolutions, passed by the Assembly in 1837, questioned the representative character of the Council, criticized its secret deliberations, and also contained a resolution aimed at disestablishing the Anglican church. Although Howe withdrew his Twelve Resolutions to show his moderation, they had some effect. The British government ordered that the Council be separated (as in New Brunswick and the Canadas) into two bodies: an Executive Council and a Legislative Council. To Howe's disgust, however, the Tories remained in control of both bodies. Only a little closer to his goal, Howe now had to wait for the British government to formulate a new colonial policy in response to the crisis in the Canadas.

None of the "reform" movements in the Atlantic provinces was as radical in its outlook as those in the Canadas. Issues tended to be narrowly parochial; those who were discontented were not as quick as their more westerly counterparts to blame the structure of government or look for extreme democratic solutions. Public opinion in the Atlantic provinces was therefore amazed by the rebellions in the Canadas – a form of political protest that they considered outrageous. Nevertheless, reformers such as Howe expected the Canadian troubles to benefit their own parties.

HISTORY FROM THE SOURCES

Rebellion Rejected?

The rebellions in the Canadas in 1837 failed in their immediate purpose. Why? What conclusions would you draw from the following evidence?

As evidence of growing unrest in Lower Canada reached the government of the upper province, Lieutenant-Governor Head decided to send all his available military forces to Montreal to help the government there maintain order. Sir John Colborne sent this reply after learning of Bond Head's decision. His opinion is no doubt based on his experience as governor of Upper Canada before Head.

. . . The alarm in this district is great, and rapidly increasing. In fact the counties between Longueuil and the upper part of the Richelieu are in a state of revolt. Many persons who have distinguished themselves for their loyalty, and as friends of order are menaced, and compelled to join the disaffected, or permit their property to be injured. I have received several applications for protection.

The grand point, and pivot, is Montreal. I am endeavouring to collect there such a force as will permit the apprehensive to sleep quietly, and to enable us to act with vigour when called upon by the Executive Government.

. . . You incur not the least risk, or responsibility in trusting to the good feeling of the Province of Upper Canada. You are fully warranted in making the arrangements which you have notified to me.

The diversion or demonstration which Mr. Mackenzie may make in Yonge Street, or *Alway* in the London District will do no good. . . .

Sir John Colborne to Sir Francis Bond Head, 6 November 1837
C. R. Sanderson, ed., *The Arthur Papers*
(Toronto, 1957), Vol. I, p. 19.

The Christian Guardian, *a religious newspaper published in Upper Canada by the Methodists, was the most widely read newspaper in the province during the 1830's.*

Canadians of every class! Canadian REFORMERS! are you prepared to shed the blood of your country-men? Can any thing Mackenzie can offer you compensate for the guilt you must incur if you enrol under his revolutionary banner, and *deluge your fruitful fields with blood*? For God's sake pause! Frown down the propagators of discord! Lift up your voices in prayer, and exert all your energies, to save your firesides and families from the untold horrors of civil war. The Royal Standard of Britain yet waves triumphantly, and invites the loyal and the good to unite in its defence, and still avail themselves of its PROTECTION against aggression.

The Christian Guardian, 6 December 1837

John Langton, *a gentleman of some means, had settled near Fenelon Falls in the Peterborough district, in 1833. Writing to a friend in Liverpool after the rebellion, he relates the reactions of the people to the rising.*

. . . I am convinced there are 99 constitutionalists to 1 Radical in the province. . . . the fact is that Mackenzie had never 500 men in arms in the Home District & those were of the lowest rabble with few exceptions & seemed more bent upon plunder than anything else. A few shots dispersed them and the projected rising in the London District never took place. . . . I am far from approving of the conduct of Sir Francis Head in allowing the insurgents to meet with arms & drill within 4 miles of the capital unmolested, but if he did allow it as a test of the loyalty of the province as he asserts certainly the result was most convincing. Not all the hopes of plunder even could draw 500 men to Mackenzie's Standard while almost every male inhabitant was in arms the moment the news of the insurrection reached them. Be it remembered there was not one single soldier in the province. Unfortunately Mackenzie escaped to the States where he was supplied with arms, ammunition, provisions and recruits in abundance. . . . With all this protection and assistance there were not 50 Canadians with Mackenzie on Navy Island. . . . There is some advantage in living in the wilderness – the news of the insurrection never reached us until 10 days after all was over tho' it took place less than 100 miles off, so we were saved a march to Toronto to show our loyalty.

> John Langton to Hugh Hornby, 20 February 1838
> Ontario Archives: *The Langton Collection*.

Robert Baldwin Sullivan, a cousin of Robert Baldwin and a member of the Upper Canadian Executive Council, wrote a lengthy report on the state of the province for the new lieutenant-governor, Sir George Arthur, in the summer of 1838.

Had the rebel leaders taken time to organize a really dangerous plan of insurrection there can be no doubt that it would have been discovered and the leaders would have been arrested and punished but the fact was that little was discovered because there was little to discover. [T]he state of affairs in lower canada and the vigilance of this Government hurried Mackenzie and his adherents into a premature rising the danger of which has been magnified to a considerable degree. It is true that great danger was apprehended at the time of the outbreak because sensible men were not prepared to ascribe absolute insanity to their enemies, but if the same opinion of the want of preparation and resources on the part of the rebels had been persisted in, which was entertained but the day before the rebellion[,] the rebels would have been justly and truly considered as an insignificant body of misguided men without numbers, plan, arms, munitions of war, design or resolution to fight. . . .

Memorandum from R. B. Sullivan to Sir George Arthur,
1 June 1838
Sanderson, ed., *Arthur Papers*, Vol. I, p. 170.

Bishop Signay, Roman Catholic bishop of Quebec, who normally made no comment on political questions, issued the following mandement in November 1837. Bishop Lartigue of Montreal supported his condemnation of rebellion.

"For a long time back, dear brethren, we hear of nothing but agitation, yea even of revolt, and this in a country which has hitherto been distinguished by its loyalty, its spirit of peace, its love for the religion of our fathers. On every side we see brothers rise up against their brothers, friends against their friends, citizens against their fellow-citizens, and discord from one extremity of this diocese to the other seems to have burst asunder the bonds of charity, which united the members of the same body, the children of the same Church, the children of that catholicity, which is a religion of unity. It is not then our intention to give an opinion, as a citizen, on any political question between the different branches of government, which is in the right and which in the wrong. This is one of those things which God has delivered to the consideration of seculars but the moral question, namely, what is the duty of a Catholic towards the civil power established and constituted in each State? This religious question falling within our jurisdiction and competency it is undoubtedly the province of your Bishop to give you all necessary instruction on that subject, and your province is to listen to him. Should then any wish to engage you in a revolt against the established government, under a pretext that you form a part of the Sovereign people, suffer not yourselves to be seduced. The too famous National Convention of France, though obliged to admit the principle of the Sovereignty of the people, because it was to this principle that it owed its existence, took good care to condemn popular insurrections, by inserting in the Declaration of Rights, which heads the Constitution of 1795, that the sovereignty resides not in a part, nor even in the majority of the people, but in the entire body of the citizens. Now who will dare to say that, in this country, the totality of our citizens desire the overthrow of the Government?"

Trans. in D. B. Read, *The Canadian Rebellion of 1837*
(Toronto, 1896), pp. 251-2.

Etienne Parent published the following exhortation in the widely read
Le Canadien shortly after the rising began in 1837.

If we emerge from our present plight without being crushed, let
it be an eternal lesson to those who have not been able to learn
from history, where it is written on every page, of the folly of agi-
tating people, of questioning the fundamental principles of the established social order, unless the oppression is directly felt by the
governed and there remain no alternatives other than hard and dis-
honorable slavery or armed resistance. The agitation which has been
aroused in this country has resulted in placing part of the population
in open opposition to the government. But who would now say that
the present government, with all its faults, is not preferable by far
to the state of affairs which exists today in the district of Montreal?
Would not the worst government be better than the anarchy which
now grips the upper part of the province, even if anarchy were to be
succeeded by a state of liberty; but no, it will be followed here as
elsewhere by military despotism. That is not all. After the sword of
the soldier has cut off the thousand heads of anarchy, then will come
the law, which will arm the government with repressive measures
that will necessarily retard the progress of the liberal cause . . . Thus
we shall perhaps soon see the government vested with extraordinary
powers which its creatures will certainly abuse. What will have
caused that? The fatal agitation which has been imprudently aroused
in this country, and which the leaders are no longer able to control.
Once again, let this be at least a lesson for the future, if Providence
reserves for us a future, which we must still hope.

Le Canadien, 22 November 1837
Quoted in Mason Wade, *The French Canadians 1760-1967,* 2 v.
(Toronto, 1968)★, Vol. I, p. 170.

Papineau, writing to his wife after the rebellion, was surprised at the
government's reaction to the agitation.

My hope was . . . to disappear and remain hidden in the homes
of some respectable farmers to let the storm pass whose duration and
violence I had not foreseen. We were in no way prepared to resist
the government. I believed there was danger of disturbances in the
town [i.e. by the English – ed. note] and in frightful persecutions by

the courts, I had not foreseen that the government would commence a civil war as little provoked as that which it has conducted with a brutal ferocity.

L. J. Papineau to his wife, 7 February 1838
Rapport de l'Archiviste de la Province de Québec pour 1953-1954 et 1954-1955 (Quebec, 1955), p. 398 (translation).

FURTHER READING

Craig, Gerald M., *Upper Canada 1784-1841: The Formative Years* (Toronto: McClelland & Stewart, 1963). A general history with the most recent survey of political events.

Manning, H. T., *The Revolt of French Canada 1800-1835* (Toronto: Macmillan, 1962).

MacNutt, W. S., *The Atlantic Provinces: The Emergence of Colonial Society, 1712-1857* (Toronto: McClelland & Stewart, 1965).

Dunham, Aileen, *Political Unrest in Upper Canada 1815-1836* (Toronto: McClelland & Stewart, 1963)★. An older account now reissued, but still a perceptive survey of the issues.

Kilbourn, William, *The Firebrand* (Toronto: Clarke, Irwin, 1956). A colourful and often critical biography of Mackenzie.

Ouellet, Fernand, *Louis Joseph Papineau: A Divided Soul* (Canadian Historical Association Booklet No. 11, 1963)★.

Beck, J. M., *Joseph Howe: Voice of Nova Scotia* (Toronto: McClelland & Stewart, 1964)★. A collection of Howe's writings and speeches together with a biographical introduction.

13

The Waning of the Old Colonialism

The Durham Report and After

The uprisings of 1837 were a serious shock to the British government, all too reminiscent of 1776. In a dramatic move the government appointed the Earl of Durham, noted for his connections with British radicals and for his leadership in the fight for the Reform bill of 1832 in Britain, as governor general of British North America and special commissioner to report on conditions and recommend remedies in the colonies.

Durham and two experts on colonial affairs, Edward Gibbon Wakefield and Charles Buller, who came to Canada with him in May 1838, were convinced that Britain's colonial empire should be saved; all disagreed with the feeling common in Britain that the colonies were a burden to the mother country and that their separation from her was inevitable. Buller, in particular, felt that further extension of self-government to the colonies would be necessary if they were to remain loyal to Britain. Wake-

Throughout 1838 Upper Canada was constantly upset by rumours of impending "Patriot" invasions and even of a second rebellion planned for 4 July. While most of these rumours proved to be groundless, several small-scale, widely scattered, and ineffective "Patriot" attacks did occur. The Canadian authorities had ample warning of most of the attacks because the "Patriots" openly bragged of their intentions and because British intelligence agents were planted in areas of "Patriot" activities. At the time when this reward was posted for Mackenzie he was indeed in New York city, but looking for support for his rebellious cause.

From the Lewiston Telegraph of Nov. 23.

We copy the following from a large half-sheet handbill which is in general circulation throughout the Province. It is useless for us to assure our royal neighbours that Mr. Mackenzie is in New York attending to his business.

ONE THOUSAND POUNDS REWARD!!

Information has been received by the Government, that WILLIAM LYON MACKENZIE, was yesterday afternoon seen within a few miles of this town, and is supposed to be lurking in some part of this District. Her Majesty's Loyal Subjects are reminded that the above reward will be paid for his apprehension; and they are called upon to make every exertion to take him, and deliver him to any Justice of the Peace, or to any Sheriff or Gaoler of the Province.

The following is the description of his person. A dark colored outer coat, large black Mustachios, a red Handkerchief round his neck and chin, and a dark colored cap. The Horse which he was last seen riding was a bay He may possibly change his dress, but his person is well known throughout the Province.   JOHN MACAULAY,
                                                            Private Secretary.

Government Office.   )
   November 18, 1838. }
R. Stanton, Printer, to the Queen's Most Excellent Majesty.

The Battle of the Windmill, November 1838, was the fiercest, longest, and bloodiest engagement of the "Patriot War". Some 200 "Patriots" held out for five days in a windmill (now a lighthouse) near Prescott. After about thirteen men on each side had been killed, the "Patriots" finally surrendered and 160 of them were taken prisoner.

field wanted to promote immigration to Canada from Britain as a means of relieving the poverty and overpopulation of the old country. Durham himself recognized that his report might become a blueprint for colonial policy not only in the Canadas but in the whole empire.

In Canada, Durham was faced with the task of pacifying the provinces as well as of investigating conditions. Abortive American invasions across the Detroit and Niagara rivers occurred in June 1838; nationalist anger lay barely submerged in Lower Canada. Durham acted quickly to create an atmosphere of conciliation and leniency. Treason charges were dropped against all except the leading rebels, most of whom had fled to the United States. Eight Lower Canadian rebels he exiled to Bermuda. Several rebels were transported from Upper Canada to Tasmania, and only two were executed in the province. However, when Durham's enemies in England attacked his recent action of exiling some other rebels to Bermuda, Durham resigned in a fit of pique after five months of investigations in Canada, including only eleven days in the upper province.

Soon after Durham left Canada on 1 November 1838, another short-lived uprising occurred in Lower Canada and invasions from the United States at Point Pelee and across the St. Lawrence River near Prescott were repelled. Yet these troubles were localized – there were no risings by sympathizers in other areas and the provinces remained outwardly quiet. Back in England, Durham finished and published his report by the end of January 1839. Avoiding the usual formal language of government reports, Durham produced an outspoken document that dealt scathingly with land and immigration policies and their failure to promote more rapid development. The report outlined the problems created by the lack of municipal government institutions and by the absence of budgeting from government expenditures. An appendix described the inadequacies of existing public educational institutions. But these important points were overshadowed by the three basic recommendations of the report: the need to reunite the

Canadas politically, to establish responsible government, and to differentiate clearly between local and imperial government responsibilities.

Durham believed strongly that the troubles in Lower Canada were due fundamentally to the racial conflict and that they could be solved only by assimilating the French Canadians into the English-speaking community. He viewed the absorption of the French Canadians by an English-dominated North America as inevitable because they were a people without a distinctive culture, "a people with no history and no literature", as he put it in a phrase which gave bitter offence. He pointed out that union of the two provinces would facilitate this assimilation and also make possible the construction of the St. Lawrence canals, thus opening the way for economic expansion which would attract British immigration.

Durham's second basic recommendation, the establishment of responsible government, had been suggested by Joseph Howe and, before him, by Robert Baldwin, the Upper Canadian moderate reformer. Baldwin favoured the adoption of the British cabinet system, in which the members of the executive held office only so long as they enjoyed the confidence of the majority in the elected legislature. Although this theory by no means commanded universal acceptance by British politicians, it was nevertheless acceptable to Durham and his British radical associates, who expected that its application to the colonial governments would put political power into the hands of the colonists themselves, allowing them to manage their own local affairs without interference from Britain. Durham was convinced that colonial self-government would not lead to the loss of the colonies but would instead strengthen their loyalty to the country which had trusted them by granting this right. Durham argued, however, that Britain should retain control of those powers that affected her own or the whole empire's interests. These were the constitutions of colonial governments, foreign relations and defence, imperial and foreign trade and immigration, and land policies in the colonies – all other areas could be left to the colonial governments.

Posting on the St. Lawrence, from a lithograph by Coke Smyth, who was drawing-master to Lord Durham's children during their stay in Canada, 1838-9.

Durham's report outraged Lower Canadian reformers by its proposal for union and by the anti-French tone of the sections dealing with their province. Upper Canadian reformers were ecstatic about it; the harsh criticisms directed at the Family Compact and the recommendation of responsible government seemed to justify the stand they had taken for so long. The Family Compact resented these criticisms; they believed that responsible government would mean the unchecked exercise of power by a party elected by the whim of the people. To bring French Canadians into the union, the Compact believed, would guarantee a solid bloc of hostile members in the legislature from that section of the new province. The more moderate Tories were inclined to like the economic possibilities of union, while at the same time agreeing with their conservative colleagues on responsible government. The debate over Durham's report raged for months.

In the autumn of 1839 the new governor, Charles Poulett Thomson, arrived in Canada to carry out the British government's policy. A brilliant administrator and former senior cabinet minister, Thomson intended to govern with the support of the elected legislature by producing popular policies and by dividing the opposition against him, but he had no intention of introducing responsible government as the term was understood in the colonies. A despatch from the Colonial Office in 1839 had freed Thomson's hand to replace the oligarchies in the councils; henceforth members of the Executive Council were to hold their positions at the pleasure of the Crown rather than during "good behaviour". Councillors could be retired as often as "sufficient motives of public policy" might require. The councillors were thus to become the servants of the governor, but only Joseph Howe realized that the despatch could also be used to establish responsible government simply by appointing new councillors chosen from the majority party in the Assembly. Thomson had no trouble putting his policies into effect in Lower Canada: the special Council appointed when the Lower Canadian constitution was suspended at the time of the rebellion approved the union measure. But in Upper Canada he had to use all his influence to win support for the union in the legislature. After hinting at an imperial guaranteed loan of £1.5 million, promising equal representation for each of the provinces in the new legislature, and holding out the hope, if not the certainty, that the capital would be located in Upper Canada, he persuaded the moderate Tories in the Assembly and Council to join the Reformers in passing the union bill.

Thomson's other great accomplishment in Upper Canada was a settlement of the Clergy Reserves question, by which one-half of the income was divided between the Anglicans and Presbyterians and the other half, when funds permitted, among all denominations. This skilful compro-

*The Tandem Club gathering in front of Dalhousie College on the Grand
Parade at Halifax for a sleigh ride.*

mise pleased the moderate majority, who were tired of quarrelling over the
Reserves. Thomson's success in these matters provided the necessary
Canadian support for the British parliament to proceed with the union
bill. He left Toronto in February by sleigh; thirty-six hours later he
reached Montreal, spending some weeks there on Lower Canadian business. Then he hurried to Nova Scotia. Howe, realizing that Lord John
Russell's despatch of October on the tenure of offices made responsible
government a real possibility, had carried a motion of no confidence
against the provincial executive. Lieutenant-Governor Sir Colin Campbell
had rejected the Assembly's motion, but Thomson broke this political
deadlock by having Campbell recalled. At the same time he sidetracked
Howe's pressure for responsible government by persuading Howe and
two other Reformers to join the Executive Council. After a quick visit to
New Brunswick, Thomson hastened back to Montreal to prepare for the
implementation of the union. Soon he received word that his many successes had earned his elevation to the English peerage as Lord Sydenham.

Everywhere moderate men rallied to the Sydenham system, which
promised an end to controversy and a beginning of measures to modernize
the colony's administration and to revive the economy. A new government
budgeting system was introduced and overhaul of the administrative system begun. Political reform in the shape of the reunion of the Canadas
had its own economic implications, for now, after fifty years of unsatisfactory division, the commercial empire of the St. Lawrence was again
reunited. The Montreal mercantile community and Upper Canadian
farmers stood to gain most by this development, since the customs
and transportation problems that had hampered economic growth of the
separated Canadas could now be dealt with by the united legislature.
Sydenham's imperial guaranteed loan of £1.5 million was earmarked
for the development of canals that would speed the two-way flow of
commerce on the St. Lawrence. This increased activity would, the gov-

ernor believed, divert men's attention from futile theorizing about responsible government to the useful and practical development of their colonies.

The Sydenham System

Sydenham's proclamation of the union of the two Canadas on 10 February
1841 stressed the advantages of the British connection, Victoria's desire
"to rule in the hearts of her subjects", and the challenge to Canadians "to
avail yourselves of the new era which now opens upon you". That new
era opened in March with a general election that was probably the most
violent in Canadian history. Several people were killed in riots, voters
were intimidated at many of the polls, and Sydenham allowed extensive
patronage, in the form of political jobs, to be used to influence the election results.

    Although Sydenham had acted as prime minister, party leader, and
campaign manager, the election results were not an unqualified triumph
for him. Of the 84 members of the first united parliament, only 24 were
"Sydenham men", but 29 others were moderate reformers who could be
counted on, with a little persuasion, to support his measures. The Upper
Canadian "Compact" had been reduced to a mere 7 representatives, and
Baldwin's "ultra reformers", as Sydenham called them, held only 5 seats.
English-speaking Canadians had heeded the governor's call for the rejection of extremes and the acceptance of patriotic, reasonable, middle-of-
the-road politicians. In Lower Canada the result was just the reverse.
Angered by this union that had been forced on them, French Canadians
elected a solid bloc of twenty followers of L. H. Lafontaine, the successor
to Papineau as spokesman of French-Canadian nationalism in Lower
Canada. These French members formed a hostile opposition that was the
only genuine political party in the Assembly.

    For over a year Francis Hincks, an Upper Canadian financier and
newspaper proprietor, had tried to promote an alliance of Lafontaine and
Baldwin by telling Lafontaine that the union could be used to preserve
French Canada and that the Upper Canadian reformers wanted to help.
He had told Baldwin that responsible government could only be won with
French-Canadian support. Lafontaine had suffered personal defeat in one
of the most violent local elections, but ironically his defeat produced a
new political alliance in parliament. Since Baldwin as a safety measure
had run in two constituencies and had been elected for both, he now offered one of them to Lafontaine; Baldwin himself resigned from Sydenham's government just before parliament opened, because the governor
refused to dismiss conservative councillors. Thus Hincks had the satisfaction of seeing his plan for a reform alliance succeed.

Lord Sydenham took up residence at Kingston, the new capital, in late spring, and began a round of sumptuous dinners and private conversations with all the moderate members of the new parliament. By the time parliament opened in July, he felt assured that his "system" of managing Canada by managing men would achieve "complete success". He tutored his ministers in the fine arts of parliamentary procedure and political manoeuvring. His legislative programme, including the setting up of municipal institutions in the form of district councils, an elementary school law for both provinces, and various public works projects, was enacted with only one exception – his plan for a central government bank was defeated by the colonial fear of paper money. Certain that, as he said, it would be "impossible for any Governor or any Parliament to prevent the Union Act working well", Lord Sydenham resigned as governor, but before he could return to England he was injured in a fall from his horse early in September 1841, and three weeks later he died of lockjaw.

In England the new Tory government of Sir Robert Peel, with Lord Stanley as colonial minister, appointed Sir Charles Bagot, the diplomat who had arranged the Rush-Bagot agreement, as the second governor of Canada. Sir Charles soon formed his own opinion of Sydenham's system: Sydenham, the political boss, had avoided facing the unpalatable fact that Lafontaine's French party existed; he had not reconciled the French Canadians to union – instead he had treated them, in Bagot's words, with "rudeness" and had "made enemies of them unnecessarily". Bagot could not see how it would be possible to perpetuate the Sydenham system while ignoring half the province's population. Sydenham's no-party government of moderates seemed doomed unless Lafontaine and his influence were included in the coalition. Lord Stanley, however, feared that such a move would destroy the main purpose of the union – to preserve the British connection by submerging French-Canadian power – and he called

Kingston, capital of the Union, 1841-4.

Timber rafts near the junction of the Ottawa and St. Lawrence rivers, by W. H. Bartlett (1842). These rafts, often loaded with other products such as pork and flour, were the most efficient means of conveying logs downriver from the inland forests to Quebec, where they were broken up and the timbers loaded aboard ship to be transported to the markets.

In spring, the cut and squared logs were formed into small rafts (cribs) to run the rapids, and once in calm water each crib put up a sail to help the oarsmen and the current to move it along. The men who worked the rafts lived in shanties on board during the trip.

on Bagot to prop up the government by adding dependable men from other parties.

Stanley's advice came too late. To avoid defeat in the new session of parliament, Sir Charles had already brought Lafontaine and Baldwin into his government in October 1842, but he made it clear that he did not intend to adopt Baldwin's version of responsible party government and that Baldwin was included in the government only because Lafontaine insisted. When Stanley learned of Bagot's "great measure" (the inclusion of Lafontaine in the government), he conceded that the move was inevitable. At least, as he explained to the imperial parliament, the government of Canada would continue "in accordance with the views and sense of the great bulk of the population . . . without entering into the abstract theories . . . of a responsible government. . . ."

How long Sir Charles Bagot could have avoided a clash with Lafontaine and Baldwin over their interpretation of responsible colonial government cannot be known, for Bagot died at Kingston in April 1843. His successor, Sir Charles Metcalfe, an experienced administrator who had served in India and Jamaica, arrived before Bagot's death. Like Bagot, he was anxious to do justice to the French Canadians and to remove their hostility towards the union. The French language was restored to official status, amnesty for rebels was introduced, and the seat of government was moved from Kingston to Montreal. Metcalfe advised the Colonial Office that the Baldwin-Lafontaine axis was an unholy alliance formed solely to grab power and reduce the Queen's representative to a "cypher". Bagot's council, he complained, pretended to be a cabinet and expected him to be "subservient to their wishes and party purposes". Metcalfe's ideal was to govern through "the good men of all parties".

Very soon after Metcalfe's arrival Baldwin began to demand complete control of government patronage, a claim that was the essence of his form of responsible government. Metcalfe's confrontation with Baldwin and

Lafontaine as to whether he would govern in the interests of the whole colony or only in the interests of their party did not occur until after parliament reconvened in the autumn. Baldwin and Lafontaine introduced legislation to outlaw the Orange Order, to secularize King's College at Toronto, and to democratize local government by removing the governor's control of district councils, but none of these controversial measures was the occasion for their final confrontation. The long expected crisis came in November, when Baldwin and Lafontaine demanded that the governor make no government appointments without their consent. Believing that public opinion was on his side, Metcalfe refused to surrender his responsibilities as governor, and therefore all the members of Council except Dominick Daly resigned.

Whatever public opinion may have been, Metcalfe discovered that most members of parliament agreed with the former ministers. With great difficulty he managed to find two men, William Henry Draper, a moderate Sydenham man (who had resigned from council to make way for Baldwin), and D. B. Viger, a former rebel of 1837, to join Daly as ministers. This three-man council ran the government until the autumn of 1844, when Metcalfe decided to seek public support for his interpretation of responsible government by calling an election. In the intervening months a variety of factors had swung public opinion in favour of the governor's interpretation of his powers. Numerous prominent people, such as Egerton Ryerson, had spoken or written in favour of the governor, and his opponents had seriously damaged their cause by dubbing Metcalfe "Old Square Toes" because of his conservatism, and "The Old Squaw" in reference to the discoloration of his skin by a painful cancer that was making him blind.

The election results of 1844 were rather indecisive since Lower Canada returned a majority of Lafontaine's party, but Upper Canada gave its votes to Lord Metcalfe, who now had 46 supporters in the 84-member parliament. Metcalfe's interpretation of responsibility had been approved by a slim margin, yet the government supporters included conservatives like Draper, no-party men, and even some remnants of the Family Compact. In the new parliament the government was led by honest but uninspired and uninspiring men, and on some crucial issues some ministers

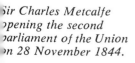

Sir Charles Metcalfe opening the second parliament of the Union on 28 November 1844.

voted with the Opposition. Given these conditions, little progressive legislation was passed. By the autumn of 1845 Metcalfe's health had declined
so far that he retired to England where he died less than a year later.

Sir Charles Metcalfe left Canadian affairs in a more uneasy state than
either of his predecessors. He admitted that the political situation was
highly unstable, but he could see no easy solution to the Canadian dilemma. Perhaps the only hope lay in separating Lafontaine from Baldwin,
thus creating a more natural alliance of French Canadians and English-
speaking conservatives.

The New Era in the Maritimes

To many Maritimers watching the events of July 1840 it seemed that a
new age was beginning. Governor General Thomson had arrived on his
grand tour of the region and changes followed in quick succession. The
political impasse created by Joseph Howe in Nova Scotia had been broken
when Lord Falkland replaced Lieutenant-Governor Sir Colin Campbell
and Howe was persuaded by Thomson to enter a coalition government
and work for "the well-understood wishes of the people". In New Brunswick Thomson found Lieutenant-Governor Sir John Harvey's model
system of ruling through what Thomson called "blarney" and a popular
Council corresponded to his own interpretation of responsible government, but he warned Harvey to adopt a firm policy in dealing with the
Maine lumbermen who were invading the rich Madawaska timberlands
in the bloodless Aroostook War.

While Thomson was still in Halifax, winning Howe's unstinting ap-
proval with the "magic wand" of his personality, Samuel Cunard, a native
Nova Scotian, epitomized this new age by inaugurating a fast trans-
Atlantic steamship service that promised to make Halifax the rival of
Boston and New York. Nova Scotia's diversified economy was finding in
Newfoundland a stable market for its exports of beef, poultry, vegetables,
and grain, and the General Mining Association of Sydney had ambitiously

The first Cunarder was a wooden paddle-wheel steamer, R.M.S.
"Britannia", which sailed from Liverpool (England) to Halifax and then
to Boston, in July 1840. The passage was completed in 14 days 8 hours,
at an average speed of 8½ knots.

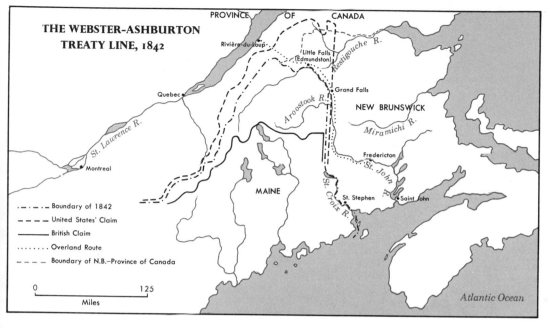

THE WEBSTER-ASHBURTON
TREATY LINE, 1842

PROVINCE OF CANADA

Rivière-du-Loup

Little Falls
(Edmundston)

Restigouche R.

Grand Falls

Quebec

Aroostook R.

NEW BRUNSWICK

Miramichi R.

St. Lawrence R.

Fredericton

Montreal

St. John R.

MAINE

St. Croix R.

St. Stephen

Saint John

.—..—..—.. Boundary of 1842

– – – – United States' Claim

———— British Claim

.... Overland Route

– – – – Boundary of N.B.–Province of Canada

0   125
|_____|
          Miles

Atlantic Ocean

invested £300,000 in Cape Breton's coal mines. New Brunswick's vast timber industry was expanding despite occasional recessions, and constituted the bulk of the province's exports that had risen 50 per cent in value during the preceding decade. Prince Edward Island's agricultural production had increased dramatically in the last generation and was beginning a healthy diversification. Newfoundland still drew its wealth from the sea, but fish, the staple product of past centuries, was now being challenged by the lucrative seal hunt. By North American standards the economic progress of the Atlantic colonies was still slow, but judged by the region's own past, the 1840's seemed bright with the promise of better days. "All is now peace and harmony," Governor General Thomson reported from the Maritimes, and he credited himself for this happy condition.

Certainly harmony had been restored to politics in Nova Scotia, where Howe, Uniacke, and Archibald – the three foremost Reformers – joined Falkland's council. Howe informed Sydenham that Falkland had won the trust of all Reformers by his friendliness. This trust still existed in 1841 when Howe visited the Canadian legislature at Kingston and confirmed Falkland's glowing accounts of Nova Scotian affairs. But slowly this mutual regard changed after Falkland began to show a preference for J. W. Johnston, the conservative Baptist whose support of government grants to church colleges angered Howe. At first Howe blamed Johnston for his own loss of popularity. Only after a general election in November 1843 did Howe turn openly against Falkland and resign from the gov-

Charlottetown, Prince Edward Island, from an original drawing of 1843. From left centre to right: St. Paul's Church, the Province House, and the Old Market Building (with cupola).

ernment when the lieutenant-governor appointed Johnston's brother-in-law to the Council.

The conflict was basically one of personalities, yet it masked Howe's ambition to create a genuine party government. Too late Howe realized that the Sydenham system of coalition was a postponement of, not a prelude to, responsible government. Too late he realized that his protest should have been made before he entered the recent election as a member of Lord Falkland's government. When Howe rejected Falkland's invitation to rejoin the coalition, Falkland announced that it would be "war to the knife" between them, and Howe replied in kind. In the public press and in the Assembly Howe poked vicious fun at the lieutenant-governor until, in February 1846, Falkland publicly accused two of Howe's friends of dishonesty. Howe's quick temper flared as he asserted that Falkland deserved to be horsewhipped. This ill-mannered outburst cost Howe the goodwill of many Nova Scotians, but in a matter of days the roles were reversed when Howe refuted the charge that he was "a place-hunting mendicant" by pointing out that he was a taxpayer whereas Lord Falkland, who had received £20,000 as governor, had never put a penny into the colony's treasury. With this single shot Falkland's political influence had been shattered and he shortly resigned from office.

Lord Falkland's successor was Sir John Harvey, hero of Stoney Creek in 1813, the governor of New Brunswick whom Sydenham had first praised as "a pearl" and then removed to Newfoundland in 1841 for failing to act firmly in the Aroostook War. In Nova Scotia Harvey courted Howe's friendship, although Howe feared that Harvey was trying to re-establish a coalition government. Howe did not know that Earl Grey, Colonial Minister in the new Whig government formed by Lord John Russell in the summer of 1846, had advised Harvey in March that "the direction of the internal policy of the colony should be entrusted to those who enjoy the confidence of the Provincial Parliament". Thus the principle of responsible government for the colonies, as formulated by Baldwin and promoted by Howe, was accepted by imperial statesmen who realized that the Sydenham system of coalitions could no longer forestall the rise of genuine political parties in the colonies.

Faced with party deadlock in his Assembly but unwilling in his own words to be identified "with any party", Harvey called an election in August 1847 in which the Reformers won a strong majority. Still the Conservative Council refused to surrender to the verdict of the voters until it was defeated in the new Assembly in January 1848. On 2 February the Reform cabinet was sworn into office – the first colonial ministry in the empire's history to be formed exclusively from a single majority party which explicitly acknowledged responsible government. The battle had been Howe's, but not the victory. Spokesman of Reform for more than a decade, Howe had never been acknowledged as the unquestioned leader of his party. His fits of anger, his tendency to deal in personalities, and the streak of vulgarity which coloured his conversation and private life had worked against his political success. It was James B. Uniacke, Howe's long-time friend, who became prime minister, while Joseph Howe accepted the lesser post of provincial secretary in this historic government.

Testing Responsible Government

Until a successor to the dying Metcalfe reached Canada, the temporary governor, Lord Cathcart, was content to leave the uneasy Canadian political situation undisturbed. One problem, the American claim to ownership of the Oregon territory, had been solved by Peel's government, which rejected the United States' claim to the Pacific coast as far north as 54°40', offering instead a treaty extending the prairie boundary of the 49th parallel to the Pacific Ocean. This proposal the American Congress accepted because of its current war with Mexico. Thus the new governor of Canada, Lord Elgin, at least could concentrate his attention on domestic issues after his arrival at the beginning of 1847.

Although only thirty-five years old, Elgin was already an experienced statesman. Elected to parliament as a Conservative in 1841, he had succeeded Metcalfe as governor of Jamaica in 1842 and now succeeded him as governor general of Canada. Elgin's second wife was the daughter of Lord Durham, and her uncle, Lord Grey, was Elgin's immediate superior as colonial secretary and also an intimate friend. Elgin announced to Canadians that he accepted completely Lord Durham's views on colonial government, and his first political move was an attempt to create a coalition between Draper's government and Lafontaine, an offer which Lafontaine ultimately rejected. Elgin was anxious to prove to French Canadians that he trusted them, but his experience with Lafontaine convinced him that the French Canadians did not understand the meaning of responsible

government and political compromise, that whenever they could not
have their own way they would, as he said, "revive the ancient cry of
nationality".

During Lord Elgin's first summer in Canada Draper resigned as government leader, to be succeeded by two old-line Tories of mediocre ability:
Henry Sherwood and Dominick Daly. Since it was impossible to form a
coalition government including the French Canadians, Elgin was forced
to persevere with the existing weak and divided government, at least until
an election. A much larger problem was the plight of thousands of destitute and disease-ridden Irish refugees. During 1847 and 1848, the years
of potato famine in Ireland, about 100,000 immigrants sailed in the
cramped holds of timber ships to British North America, but some 15,000
perished en route or in the immigrant hospital sheds of Grosse Isle near
Quebec. Canadians feared the newcomers and the plague they carried,
and many who sought to help the unfortunates died of the fever. Private
charity was insufficient to relieve their suffering, and the Canadian government had neither the means nor the organization to meet the needs of this
flood of misery. Protests to the British government against the practice of
dumping unwanted population into the colonies went unheeded. Apparently the only answer lay in Canada's gaining control over immigration,
even as she had recently gained control over her own tariffs.

Responsible government was only a minor issue in the election of
1847 – the Reformers were really complaining about government in-
effectiveness. The election result was a sweeping victory for the party of
Baldwin and Lafontaine in both sections of the united province. Grey ad-

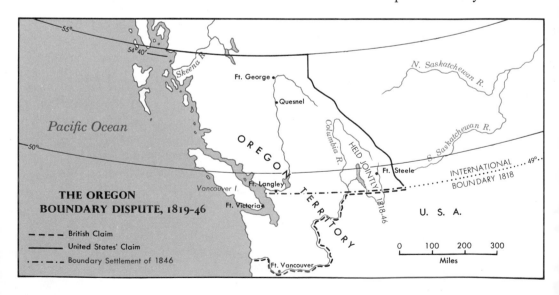

**THE OREGON
BOUNDARY DISPUTE, 1819–46**

– – – – British Claim
―――― United States' Claim
· – · – · – Boundary Settlement of 1846

vised Lord Elgin to accept a government from the majority party in the Assembly and to accept also that government's policies, "however unwise ... their measures may be", until he was sure that public opinion would no longer support those policies. When parliament met, the Sherwood-Daly ministry was easily defeated, and on 11 March Baldwin and Lafontaine formed Canada's first responsible government, based like Uniacke's on the principle of majority party rule.

The principle of responsible colonial government had been accepted by Harvey, by Elgin, and by the Colonial Office, but it was still untested in practice. Could a governor really treat all parties equally, regardless of which one was in power at any given moment? Would a governor (and the Colonial Office) bow to a cabinet's wishes if he disagreed with that cabinet's policies? The question remained unanswered in Canada during 1848 because the "Great Ministry" of Lafontaine and Baldwin was still planning its legislative programme. In 1849 responsible government was tested when the ministers introduced a bill to pay compensation for damages done in Lower Canada during the Rebellion of 1837.

This controversial bill was a belated measure of justice to Lower Canada, since Metcalfe had already settled Upper Canadian rebellion losses. But it was politically dangerous in that its loose wording allowed convicted rebels to claim payment for losses suffered because of their own treason. The conservative minority of the Assembly protested against "rewarding traitors", and public meetings of "loyal" Montrealers took up this cry. Nevertheless the bill passed easily in parliament on 9 March, and Lord Elgin then faced a fateful decision. He could disallow the bill, but that would nullify the principle of colonial responsibility for colonial affairs. He could reserve the bill for a decision by the imperial cabinet, but that would be evading his own responsibilities. He decided to give royal approval to the bill and risk the wrath of the "loyalists" who, incidentally, were almost exclusively English-speaking conservatives already frustrated by the loss of imperial tariff preferences. On 25 April, when he gave the royal assent, his worst fears were realized as a tumult of disapproval broke out in the parliamentary gallery and an egg-throwing mob chased his carriage back to his residence. Later that evening the rioters burst into the parliament and started a fire that destroyed the building. During the next few days mobs attacked other property, including the homes of Lafontaine and Hincks. Montreal's tiny police force could not restore order, but Elgin refused to use troops to quell the violence for fear of causing bloodshed. After four days the governor general again attended parliament, which was now sitting in the Montreal market building, to receive an address of loyalty. This time the mobs injured one of the governor's aides and nearly demolished his carriage with stones.

The burning of the Houses of Parliament in Montreal, from the 19 May 1849 issue of "The Illustrated London News".

After the rioting subsided, Montreal paid dearly for its rebellion, because the capital now moved alternately between Toronto and Quebec every two years. More important, however, was public acknowledgement that Elgin's reasonableness had preserved responsible government and had shown French Canadians the value of British justice and parliamentary practices. But Elgin was also aware that the Montreal riots had deeper causes than the Rebellion Losses bill. Since 1846 urban property values had fallen by 50 per cent and business was stagnating. Britain's free trade policies had raised genuine doubts about the political usefulness of belonging to an empire that offered no economic advantages. Although the Corn Laws had been repealed, the restrictive Navigation Acts, which were still in effect, were limiting the colonies' trade by preventing foreign ships, particularly American vessels, from carrying colonial goods to market and Lord Elgin advised that they should be repealed, "not for favour, but for justice". "You have no other course open to you if you intend to keep yr. colonies," Elgin wrote, to which Francis Hincks added that repeal "would remove every just cause of Complaint on the part of the Colonists". In 1849 Britain repealed the unpopular Acts.

After the riots in the spring of 1849, an annexation movement appeared in Montreal. In October a Manifesto was published discussing the advantages and inevitability of Canada's annexation to the United States. "Between the abandonment by England of her former system of protection to Colonial produce, and the refusal of the United States to trade with us on a footing of reciprocity," read the Manifesto, "Canada, to use the old proverb, is between the devil and the deep sea, and . . . we can see no way to get out of the scrape but by going to prosperity, since prosperity will not come to us." Lord Elgin reacted swiftly to this threat by firing every public official – and there were many – who had signed the Manifesto. By the summer of 1850 business had improved and Elgin reported, "Annexation is dead for the moment."

Like the Rebellion Losses bill riots, the annexation movement had been an impulsive, exasperated response to depression by a small number of

irritated Canadians, mostly English, Tory, Montreal merchants, but
Elgin knew that it could revive with another trade depression. He believed
that closer economic ties between Canada and the United States would
prevent annexation by making Canadians prosperous and therefore content with colonial status. "I cannot too often repeat it," he wrote to Grey
in 1849, "either this or annexation." Although the economic condition
of Canada and of the other British North American colonies continued
to improve, Elgin, with Grey's fullest co-operation, worked steadily but
quietly towards a reciprocity agreement with the United States until he
was able to convince American congressmen in 1854 that reciprocity in
natural products would benefit both countries. This Treaty, which held
forth such bright promises for prosperity, was Elgin's parting gift to
Canada when he retired after eight excitement-filled years.

HISTORY FROM THE SOURCES

The Meaning of Responsible Government

What did colonial Reformers mean when they talked about responsible government? Did the idea of responsible government have the same meaning for French-Canadian Reformers as it did for English Canadians?

In 1836 Robert Baldwin and the Upper Canadian Reformers had clashed with Lieutenant-Governor Sir Francis Bond Head over the implications of the cabinet system, which they sought to introduce in colonial government. At that time Baldwin provided a concise and classic statement of his understanding of responsible government in a letter to the colonial secretary.

> To conclude my Lord, I most earnestly recommend not only as *expedient*, but *necessary* for the preservation of the Connexion between this Country and Upper Canada: – First, That His Majesty's Imperial Government should at once adopt the final determination, that the Provincial Government as far as respects the internal Affairs of the Province, should be conducted by the Lieutenant Governor, with the Advice and Assistance of the Executive Council, acting as a Provincial Cabinet; – And that the same Principle on which His Majesty's Cabinet in [Great Britain] is composed, should be applied and acted upon in the formation, continuance in office and removal, of such local Provincial Cabinet: – Secondly that this Resolution of the Home Government should be inserted in the shape of a Specific Clause in the general Royal Instructions for the Government of the Province, and formally communicated to both houses of the Provincial Parliament; And Thirdly – That Sir Francis Head should be recalled, and a Successor appointed who shall have been practically acquainted with the working of the Machinery of a free Representative Government. –
>
> Robert Baldwin to Lord Glenelg, 13 July 1836
> Public Archives of Canada, Report for the Year 1923,
> Calendar of the Durham Papers (Ottawa, 1924), pp. 336-7.

Governor General Sir Charles Metcalfe inherited the results of Sir Charles Bagot's "great measure" – the presence of Lafontaine and Baldwin in a coalition Executive Council – but he soon became suspicious of the idea of responsible government as those two Reform leaders explained it. In May 1843 Metcalfe reported to Colonial Secretary Lord

Stanley the gist of a three-hour conversation between his private secretary and Lafontaine over the meaning of responsible government.

I learn that my attempts to conciliate all parties are criminal in the eyes of the Council, or at least of the most formidable member of it. I am required to give myself up entirely to the Council; to submit absolutely to their dictation; to have no judgment of my own; to bestow the patronage of the Government exclusively on their partisans; to proscribe their opponents; and to make some public and unequivocal declaration of my adhesion to those conditions – including the complete nullification of her Majesty's Government – a course which, under self-deception, he denominates Sir Charles Bagot's policy, although it is very certain that Sir Charles Bagot meant no such thing. Failing of submission to those stipulations, I am threatened with the resignation of Mr. Lafontaine for one, and both he and I are fully aware of the serious consequences likely to follow the execution of that menace, from the blindness with which the French-Canadian party follow their leader.

. . . I am disposed to hope that further reflection may cool his ardor, and that I may derive some advantage from the aid of time. I need hardly say, that although I see the necessity for caution, I have no intention of tearing up her Majesty's commission by submitting to the prescribed conditions. . . .

The sole question is, to describe it without disguise, whether the Governor shall be solely and completely a tool in the hands of the Council, or whether he shall have any exercise of his own judgment in the administration of the Government? Such a question has not come forward as a matter of discussion; but there is no doubt that the leader of the French party speaks the sentiments of others of his Council besides himself. . . .

J. W. Kaye, *The Life and Correspondence of Charles, Lord Metcalfe*, 2 v. (London, 1854), Vol. I, pp. 493-4.

After the indecisive election of 1844 William Henry Draper tried through the mediation of R. E. Caron to expand the Executive Council to include members of Lafontaine's French-Canadian Reform group, but Lafontaine rejected this offer and explained his interpretation of responsible government.

. . . I should observe at first that I infer from the tenor of your letter, although not stated in express terms, that you are of opinion that in the circumstances of the country the majority of each Province should govern respectively in the sense that we attach to that idea – that is to say, that Upper Canada should be represented in the Administration of the day by men possessing the confidence of the political party in that section of the province which has the majority in the House of Assembly, and that it should be the same for Lower Canada. Now, if this is your opinion it appears to me that it furnishes you with the means of offering to Mr. Draper "strong and irresistible" reasons in support of any advice given in harmony with this opinion. These reasons naturally present themselves without there being any occasion to offer them in detail. The present Administration, as far as regards U. C., is formed on this principle, but as regards L. C., its formation rests on an opposite principle. Why this distinction between the two sections of the Province? Is there not in this fact alone a manifestation of injustice, if not of oppression?

*   *   *   *   *

But it is said to you – We only wish to *join to us* some Canadians as French-Canadians. From that moment those who thus enter the Ministry enter it not in consequence of a constitutional right, not by the action of the opinion of their countrymen, but only by favour, by the good pleasure of a Governor. From that moment, as we learn by experience, they are without influence – they are no longer free agents; they are only instruments in the hands of the Governor, to do evil as to do good. If they have any capacity or talent they make them serve, sooner or later, to throw division among us.

*   *   *   *   *

. . . What French-Canadians should do above every thing is to remain united and to make themselves respected. They will thus make themselves respected in the Council, and will thence exercise the legitimate influence which is due to them, not when they are represented there only by the passive instruments of power, however numerous they may be, but when they shall be constitutionally represented there by a Lower Canadian Administration formed in harmony with principles which public opinion does not repudiate.

*   *   *   *   *

. . . I arrive, then, at a conclusion regarding which you cannot misunderstand me. It is that, as regards the Administration, Lower Canada should have what is granted to Upper Canada – nothing more, but also nothing less.

L. H. Lafontaine to R. E. Caron, 10 September 1845
Sir Francis Hincks, *Reminiscences of His Public Life*
(Montreal, 1884), pp. 150, 151, 152, 153.

In 1847 Baldwin and Lafontaine took advantage of the arrival in Canada of Lady Elgin, daughter of the late Earl of Durham, to put political pressure on the new governor general, Lord Elgin, by moving an amendment to the Address in reply to the Speech from the Throne. The amendment, which was defeated, credited Durham with recognizing the right of the colonies to have governors "responsible to the Provincial Parliament".

When reporting Lady Elgin's arrival the leading Reform newspaper, the Toronto Globe, made clear what English-Canadian Reformers expected of their new governor in terms of responsible government.

Many of our readers will, no doubt, be anxious to hear "what sort of a Governor Lord Elgin is likely to make" – but really the country has been so often deceived in Governors that it is dangerous to give an opinion on any of them until they have been tried.

. . . we are bound to confess that his conduct as yet has been strictly constitutional, as far as the public know – and as long as he does not exceed his constitutional duty, as long as he refrains from making himself a partizan in the cause of either of the great political divisions of the Province – though he should give his most strenuous legitimate support to the most extreme Tory government which was ever assembled – he shall be ever spoken of with respect by us.

Had Lord Elgin dismissed his ministers on his arrival, and called the Reform party to his aid, we could not have withheld our censure. But should the present Administration be broken down in Parliament – should they prove unequal to the task of grappling with the great commercial measures now urgently demanded by the country, or should they fail in carrying the ministerial measures, whatever they may hereafter prove to be, through the House, we shall expect his Excellency to come up to the constitutional mark, and to frown down all further trickery to enable the present men to keep their offices; the Reform party, consisting of three-fourths of the population of United Canada, will then expect his Lordship to give the helm of state into the hands of their leaders. We ask from Lord Elgin constitutional government – and that only – and we shall have it. We frankly, but respectfully, tell his Excellency, as the Reform Press did Sir Charles Metcalfe at the outset of his reign, that if he will let us fight out our own battles, he may live long and happily among us, with the respect of all parties – but if he should unfortunately assume the attitude of a partizan in our local disputes, and allow either party to use his name as a rallying cry – then we tell him plainly that his government will end in total failure.

Sir A. G. Doughty, ed., *The Elgin-Grey Papers, 1846-1852*, 4 v. (Ottawa, 1937), Vol. I, pp. 53-4.

Lord Elgin saw clearly the inherent differences between French and English Canadian Reformers which their common interest in responsible government obscured for a time.

> It is not so difficult to deal with the British opposition, because the individuals who compose that Party have at least some notion of fair play in carrying out the principles of Gov^t which they advocate. But with the French generally it is far otherwise. They adopt at second hand the political dogmas of the English liberals and assert them, whenever it is convenient to do so, with becoming force. But they are unwilling to admit – I might almost say they seem incapable of comprehending – that the principles of constitutional Gov^t must be applied against them as well as for them – and whenever there appears to be a chance of things taking this turn, they revive the ancient cry of nationality, and insist on their right to have a share in the administration, not because the Party with which they have chosen to connect themselves is in the ascendant, but because they represent a people of distinct origin – As the theories of Gov^t on which their claims to office respectively rest contradict each other, it is almost always possible for them when they are out of place to demonstrate on one or other hypothesis, that they are unconstitutionally treated.

> Elgin to Grey, 13 June 1847
> Doughty, ed., *The Elgin-Grey Papers* . . . , Vol. I, p. 52.

During the election campaign of 1847 Louis Joseph Papineau challenged Lafontaine's political leadership among French Canadians, and by doing so, as Lord Elgin commented, Papineau pointed up the ambiguity in Lafontaine's stand regarding responsible government: was responsible government for Lafontaine a genuine constitutional ideal or just a means of getting power to protect French-Canadian nationality?

> I cannot yet give You much information respecting the probable result of our Elections. I am inclined to think that the opposition will be the winners, by a small majority. Meanwhile considerable excitement has been produced by the appearance of a manifesto from the notorious L. J. Papineau who has been requested to represent two constituencies – This document is in a nolo episcopari strain – contains a pretty frank declaration of republicanism – expresses the writer's hatred of the British Gov^t – his distrust of Responsible Gov^t and concludes that the time is not yet come for his reappearance on the stage – Whether he will be elected or not is uncertain in the face of this quasi refusal – The French Liberals are a good deal

disconcerted by the tone of his address – on the one hand they do not like to proclaim that their sentiments are at variance with those of this redoutable chief who has still a hold on Canadian sympathies – on the other hand it is awkward to profess antimonarchical doctrines and a contempt for Responsible Gov^t at the time when the said Responsible Gov^t is likely to bring them into place – Besides it is doubtful whether Upper Canada liberalism may not be alienated by the assertion of such principles – I enclose the document that you may judge of its merit for yrself.

Elgin to Grey, 24 December 1847
Doughty, ed., *The Elgin-Grey Papers* . . . , Vol. I, p. 102.

FURTHER READING

Shortt, Adam, *Lord Sydenham* (Toronto: Oxford University Press, 1926). The only modern biography of Durham's successor.

Wilson, G. E., *The Life of Robert Baldwin* (Toronto: Ryerson, 1933). The only separate study of this important Canadian politician.

Longley, R. S., *Sir Francis Hincks* (Toronto: University of Toronto Press, 1943). The best biography of this important Reformer.

Kennedy, W. P. M., *Lord Elgin* (Toronto: Oxford University Press, 1926). Of several biographies of this important governor general, this gives the best appraisal.

Creighton, D. G., *John A. Macdonald:* Vol. I, *The Young Politician* (Toronto: Macmillan, 1952)★. A classic biography whose opening chapters describe Macdonald's rise to prominence.

Careless, J. M. S., *Brown of The Globe*, Vol. 1 (Toronto: Macmillan, 1959)★. A stimulating biography that describes Brown's role in Canadian politics in the 1840's.

Martin, Chester, *Empire and Commonwealth* (Oxford: Oxford University Press, 1929). Chapters 4 and 5 are detailed studies of the responsible government movement in Nova Scotia and Canada.

Masters, D. C., *The Reciprocity Treaty of 1854* (Toronto: McClelland & Stewart, 1963)★. A detailed study of Lord Elgin's solution to Canada's trade problem.

Careless, J. M. S., *The Union of the Canadas: The Growth of Canadian Institutions, 1841-1857* (Toronto: McClelland & Stewart, 1967). See particularly Chapters 8 to 12.

MacNutt, W. S., *The Atlantic Provinces: The Emergence of Colonial Society, 1712-1857* (Toronto: McClelland & Stewart, 1965). See particularly Chapter 10.

14

The 1850's — A Decisive Decade

The Great Ministry and Its Legacy

The Rebellion Losses bill is the best known of the 200 laws introduced by the Great Ministry of Baldwin and Lafontaine at the parliamentary session of 1849, but in fact it was one of the less important measures of the government's extensive reform programme. Baldwin revived his bill of 1843 to democratize the local administration of Canada West (as Upper Canada was now commonly called) by creating a system of popularly controlled municipal governments – villages, towns, cities, townships, and counties. This Municipal Corporations Act was supplemented in 1850 by an Assessment Act which laid down the modern principles for local taxation. Baldwin's plan to secularize King's College was also revived and the college endowment was given to the new provincial University of Toronto. The other colleges – Victoria and Queen's – did not, however, die of financial malnutrition as Baldwin hoped, because their churches supported them, and Bishop Strachan in 1852 founded Trinity College for the Anglicans, who had lost King's.

In this tide of reform there was one notable omission: the Great Ministry offered no plan to alter the Clergy Reserves. The Clergy Reserves question had been reopened in 1848 by the announcement that funds were now available to any churches not included in the 1840 settlement. Although a few churches did ask for a share, the cry for complete secularization of the Reserves was raised immediately. The failure of the Great Ministry to face this demand – a failure attributed to the fear of French

Canadians that other religious endowments might be abolished too – created a split in the Reform party before the end of 1849. A group of prominent Reformers from Canada West, comprised of a few pre-Rebellion radical reformers and of several younger men inspired by the liberal democratic reform movements in Britain and Europe, called for radical changes because they considered the government too conservative. Their platform included reduced government spending, the election of all public officials, separation of church and state, an elected Legislative Council, and honesty in government. These radicals, derisively nicknamed "Clear Grits" by George Brown, editor of the influential Toronto Reform paper, *The Globe*, challenged the conservatism of Baldwin. A similar though smaller group in Canada East, the *rouges,* confronted Lafontaine and the Roman Catholic church with demands for republican and secular institutions.

The Clear Grits won their first victory at a by-election in Canada West early in 1850. They now had the support of several newspapers and their programme for reform was winning the approval of many farmers, especially in the more recently settled areas west of Toronto. Clear Gritism was now a more serious menace to the government than the Conservative Opposition led by Sir Allan MacNab, which had not recovered from the disgrace of its own behaviour over the Rebellion Losses bill. Pro-govern-

The four sketches on pages 258-9 were drawn by Charles Davy Brown, who came to Canada from England in 1856 to learn farming near Galt, Ontario, on the farm of William Tye. Brown moved in 1858 to a farm of his own, which he called Nith Grove. These sketches, dated 1859-62, were probably drawn before he became well established there, for the scene on page 258 shows "a settler's cabin in a clearing", and the one to the right is labelled "interior of log house, our kitchen-dining room". The farmer at top right is using a scythe with a cradle attached.

ment newspapers, such as *The Globe*, accused the Grits of being American republicans; the Grits replied with references to "Mr. Reformer Tory Baldwin". Lord Elgin saw clearly the possible political results of this struggle: "If Clear Gritism absorbs all the hues of Upper Canadian liberalism, the French . . . will fall off from them and form an alliance with the Upper Canadian Tories."

The internal divisions of the Reform party in Canada West were multiplied early in 1851 after the returned rebel, William Lyon Mackenzie, defeated George Brown in a by-election. Brown was embittered because he had not been supported by Finance Minister Francis Hincks and the Reform party, which owed much of its success to his newspaper. There were, however, religious as well as political factors involved. Brown had accepted a challenge to comment on the so-called "papal aggression" – the re-establishment of the Roman Catholic hierarchy in Britain – and in the course of his comments had started a religious feud by criticizing also that church's interference in Canadian politics. Brown found himself attacked by the Clear Grits because he supported the government and by Roman Catholics because of his religious views, yet deserted by his party.

Brown's personal separation from the Reform party came soon after Robert Baldwin resigned as leader because his own followers from Canada West rejected his bill for court reform. The Great Ministry of Baldwin and Lafontaine was ended, and Francis Hincks assumed control of the western section of the party. Lafontaine soon followed Baldwin into retirement, and the cabinet was reconstructed with A. N. Morin as the leader of the Canada East Reformers.

When the Hincks-Morin government called a general election in December 1851, the government was returned with about the same number of seats as it had previously held – 18 in Canada West and 30 in Canada East – despite the Clear Grit agitation and George Brown's strong support for voluntarism (separation of church and state). Hopes that this parliament would deal with the Clergy Reserves question were dashed in 1852 when the new Conservative government in Britain refused to permit any change in the Clergy Reserves settlement of 1840. The main interest of the session of 1852 centred on the generous terms of Hincks' agreement with British contractors to build the Grand Trunk Railway in competition with the Great Lakes–St. Lawrence River transportation system.

When parliament met again early in 1853, certain government measures combined with other political factors to shake the government and the union to the roots. The Grits, George Brown, and John A. Macdonald (now emerging as the leader of younger, more moderate conservatives) attacked the ministry's religious policies, its new School Act which extended the provisions for separate Roman Catholic schools in Canada

The Gavazzi riots in Montreal (1853), from an unsigned contemporary watercolour believed to have been painted by James Duncan, who taught drawing and painting in the city from about 1830-78.

West, and its bill to increase the parliamentary representation in each section of the union from 42 to 65. The Canadian census of 1851 showed that the population of Canada West was now slightly larger than that of Canada East, so Brown used the representation bill to promote the idea of representation by population ("rep by pop"). This proposal was hailed in Canada West as a way of circumventing "French domination" – the recent school bill had been imposed on Canada West by the solid bloc of Canada East Reform – but to French Canadians "rep by pop" seemed a threat to assimilate them. The Union Act had imposed equal representation on Canada East in 1840 despite its larger population – why should the arrangement be abandoned now that the shoe was on the other foot?

Religious controversy between Catholics and Protestants had thus been joined to sectional and linguistic rivalries within a supposed union. Since its inception the union had operated more like a federation, with double-name ministries such as "Lafontaine-Baldwin" that acknowledged co-leaders from the two sections, dual administrative offices, and separate legal and educational systems. Upper and Lower Canada had not lost their identities in union: on the contrary, the existence of a single legislature had heightened their awareness of their differing ambitions in language, religion, politics, economics, and culture generally.

Further evidence of sectional conflict was provided by the Gavazzi riots in the summer of 1853. Alessandro Gavazzi, an Italian priest and national patriot, was touring North America to denounce the political policies of the papacy. His public address in Quebec city was the occasion for an attack by Roman Catholics in which his secretary was seriously wounded. Three days later Gavazzi's speech in Montreal was completed without serious incident, but as the Protestant audience left, troops posted to prevent rioting unaccountably fired into the crowd, killing ten people. Attacks on Protestant churches occurred in the next few days. When the tragedy was officially blamed on human error and no one was punished, Protestants were convinced that neither free speech nor justice existed in Canada East, while French Roman Catholics denounced their detractors as "fanatics". The Gavazzi troubles soon passed, but they had symbolized the conflict of two nations still warring in the bosom of a single state, and heralded the resurgence of the Orange Order as a political force in Canadian affairs.

Under the impact of these divisive issues the Hincks-Morin government began to crumble and Canadians began to talk of a realignment of parties, either a union of Protestants or a coalition of Upper Canadian Conservatives and French-Canadian Reformers. The revelation that Hincks had made a personal profit of £10,000 by manipulating railway bonds finally discredited the government. When parliament met in the summer of 1854, his government was easily defeated by the combined votes of enraged Clear Grits, jealous Conservatives, and disgruntled Morin moderates. An election followed immediately and the government lost more ground. In Canada East the change in party strength was slight, but in Canada West the splintered party lines were more confusing than ever. The new parliament convened in the early autumn of 1854 and rejected the government's candidate for Speaker, forcing the resignation of the whole ministry.

The Menace of Sectionalism

The defeat of the unprincipled Hincks-Morin government was the golden opportunity for which Macdonald had been planning for some time. Although the nominal leader of the English-speaking Conservatives was the aging Sir Allan MacNab, the effective leader was Macdonald. He had repeatedly insisted that his party was not the enemy of the French, that it had abandoned such old Tory principles as church establishment and imperial tariff preferences, and now stood prepared to promote "progressive conservative" policies by introducing necessary reforms. The French moderates accepted Macdonald's assertions and switched their support to the new political combination represented by the MacNab-Morin government.

The new government at once proceeded to keep its promises by introducing very un-Tory legislation – to nationalize the Clergy Reserves, abolish seigneurial tenure, and create an elected Legislative Council. These reforming Acts did much to allay sectional strife, and they also left the splinter parties politically weakened. A few Upper Canadian Tories still sat in opposition to the moderate government; the *rouges* remained a hopeless minority, increasingly under attack from the Roman Catholic church; George Brown and the Grits gradually drew closer together in their fight against what they considered to be the cynical expediency of Macdonald. A fourth splinter group, formed of old Baldwin Reformers and led by John Sandfield Macdonald, a Roman Catholic from Glengarry, had already emerged when Hincks ignored these former colleagues in an effort to hang onto office in 1853. Hincks became governor of the

Leeward Islands, and Morin left the government early in 1855 to become a judge, his place in the so-called Liberal-Conservative coalition being taken by E. P. Taché.

This transformation of the 1854 coalition into a strong party of moderates under new, dynamic leadership was completed in 1856 when Mac-Nab was pushed out of office by Macdonald and the younger men. The occasion for this manoeuvre, which created the Taché-John A. Macdonald administration, was the public outcry in Canada West at the government's failure to prosecute seven Irish Roman Catholics who had brutally murdered Robert Corrigan, a Protestant, at St. Sylvestre, south of Quebec. Upper Canadian Protestants had already been greatly angered when in 1855 the government forced a separate school act on Canada West by a majority of votes from Canada East. To protect their sectional interests some Upper Canadians began to demand an end to the union, but the furor slowly abated in 1856 and 1857 as public attention was diverted by the crisis in the Grand Trunk's finances and by the beginning of a major economic recession.

The menace of sectional conflict seemed to be waning. Discussions of "rep by pop", of separation of the Canadas, or even of a federation of the two parts were carried on in a desultory way. John Sandfield Macdonald was advocating Lafontaine's idea of governing by double majorities – any legislation affecting only Canada West or only Canada East must be supported by a majority of members from the section affected by the law – as a solution to the problem created by such bills as the recent Upper Canadian separate school law. For obvious reasons John A. Macdonald rejected both "rep by pop" and the double majority scheme. His position in parliament was, however, made less secure by the results of a general election late in 1857. The Clear Grits and Reformers won a majority of the seats in Canada West and the meeting of the new parliament next summer gave them a chance to show their strength on the seat of government question.

MR. BOWES AND HIS PETTICOATED FRIEND INTRODUCE THEIR CANDIDATE TO THE PEOPLE

The close connection between religion and politics in Canada during the 1850's is reflected in this cartoon comment on an 1857 by-election in Toronto. J. G. Bowes, the Conservative running-mate of Mayor Robinson, is attacked for his efforts to extend the privileges of Roman Catholic separate schools. He is depicted here as a "priest-ridden" donkey.

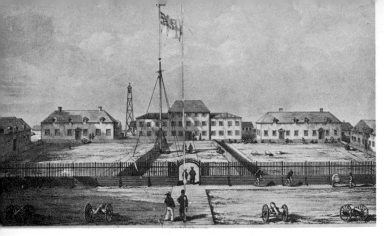

*Left: York Factory in 1853.
Below: The Hudson's Bay
Company's establishment at
Moose Factory in 1854.*

*In contrast to the growth of
urban communities and to the
importance of political life in
the Canadas, the trading settlements continued to be the only
means of communication
between the continent's
flourishing sections in east and
west and the comparatively
unsettled central areas.*

The moving of parliament between Quebec and Toronto every two
years had proved most inconvenient, but every large Canadian city was
convinced that it had the best claim to be the new capital. In desperation
the government had asked Queen Victoria to decide. Her choice, Ottawa,
was derided by its opponents as "a sub-Arctic lumber village" and "West-
minister in the Wilderness". When the Queen's choice was debated on
29 July a French-Canadian member moved its rejection and 63 members
voted with him, including several government supporters. Although the
government had a huge majority in Canada East and an overall majority
in the House, it had lost this division by 14 votes. The next day the government resigned, insisting that the seat of government question had been a
no-confidence vote. A week of political crisis followed.

The governor, Sir Edmund Head, a distant relative of Sir Francis Bond
Head, invited George Brown to form a government. Head considered the
Clear Grits' votes against Ottawa as an insult to the Queen and thought
it unlikely that Brown could get any support in Canada East after his
statements on papal aggression and separate schools. He warned Brown
that a general election was out of the question, but Brown managed to
form a coalition with the small *rouge* group, led by A. A. Dorion, and a
few independent Liberals. A provincial law required that newly appointed
ministers must resign their seats and stand for re-election, so no member
of the Brown-Dorion cabinet was in parliament when the Liberal-Conservatives easily defeated the government less than twelve hours after it
had been formed.

Montreal, Canada East, drawn in 1852 by Edwin Whitefield, an artist known for his accurate drawings of Canadian and American cities.

Brown and Dorion then asked the governor to hold a general election and when Head refused, the government resigned, having been in office for only two days. Brown was bitter at what he considered to be Head's partiality towards the Liberal-Conservatives, but worse was to come. On 6 August the jubilant Taché-Macdonald ministers were sworn into office once more, but to avoid having to seek re-election they assumed different ministries and then on 7 August resumed their original posts. A loop-hole in the law permitted such changes without a by-election, provided that the transfer was completed within one month. The "Double Shuffle", as Macdonald's stratagem was called, was perfectly legal, but it merely reinforced Brown's opinion that John A. was a thoroughly unscrupulous man.

Brown's two-day ministry and the Double Shuffle did produce two positive results. By combining with Dorion, Brown had "de-sectionalized" the Clear Grits and made future co-operation with the French possible. The second result was the inclusion in Macdonald's reconstituted cabinet of A. T. Galt, a promising young lawyer from the Eastern Townships of Canada East and spokesman for the English-speaking Protestants of that section. Just before the debate on the seat of government the Assembly discussed Galt's proposal for a federal union of all British North American colonies. The government had not supported Galt's proposal then, but now Galt accepted Macdonald's invitation to join a government that promised to work for British North American federation. Thus Macdonald committed his party to an idea that might prove useful or even necessary at some future date.

The Technological Revolution

By the mid-nineteenth century the industrial revolution with its related revolutions in transportation, communications, agriculture, and even the philosophy of government, had made Great Britain the wealthiest and most powerful nation in the world. In Britain this development had taken a hundred years, but in British North America the same changes occurred

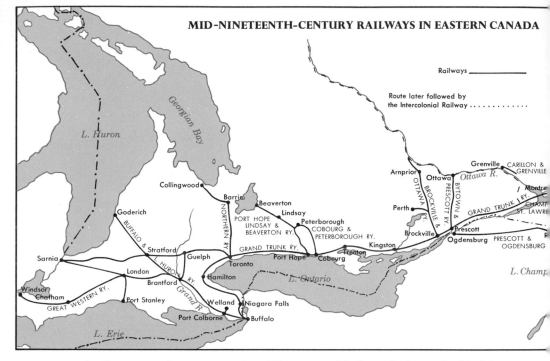

MID-NINETEENTH-CENTURY RAILWAYS IN EASTERN CANADA

Railways _____

Route later followed by
the Intercolonial Railway . . . .

in the space of one generation. The many-sided revolution coincided in
Canada with new ideas and ways of life inaugurated by the repeal of the
Corn Laws and the formation of the Great Ministry. In the Atlantic
provinces the technological revolution came more slowly and less painfully.

The first indication of the revolution appeared in 1847 with the introduction of Samuel Morse's electro-magnetic telegraph. That first telegraph line from Toronto to Hamilton was extended so rapidly that in less
than fifteen years 3,500 miles of wire traversed the province and connected it to Detroit, New York, and New Brunswick. Businessmen could
now send or receive orders in a matter of hours, and news from Europe
arrived in a matter of days instead of weeks. With more news and "commercial intelligence" to report to their readers, several Canadian newspapers now began to publish daily editions much larger in size than their
weekly editions. More newspaper columns were now devoted to advertising a wide variety of consumer goods, and readers got an added bonus in
the form of serialized novels by Dickens and other contemporary writers,
which were often pirated by ambitious editors anxious to increase circulation.

Steamship lines, such as Samuel Cunard's fast service from Liverpool
to Halifax, had speeded the trans-Atlantic crossing of goods and passengers since the end of the 1830's, but the age of the steam engine on wheels

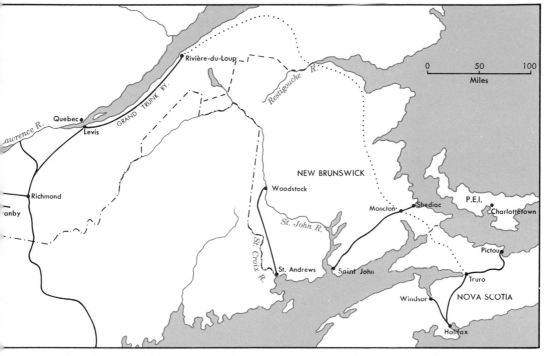

— the railway which revolutionized land travel – did not reach British North America until the 1850's. The railway mania which gripped the Canadas in the early 1850's was started with an Act of 1849 by which the government guaranteed part of the interest on capital required for railway building. British America's first railway, the sixteen-mile Champlain-St. Lawrence line, had been operating since 1836, but after the opening of the Northern, from Toronto to Georgian Bay, in 1853, a myriad of lines appeared rapidly in the Great Lakes–St. Lawrence region. These early railways were essentially portage lines linking an interior area to the St. Lawrence canal and river system. Twelve of the sixteen portage lines were in Canada West, and comprised 880 of the total 1,030 miles of track.

Entirely different in concept and purpose was the Grand Trunk Railway from Sarnia to Rivière du Loup, with a branch to Portland, Maine. The Grand Trunk was intended to be literally a trunk line replacing the Great Lakes–St. Lawrence water route by gathering all the portage or feeder lines into a single transportation system that could operate year round. The length of the Grand Trunk was 872 miles, making it by far the largest and most ambitious of the many railway schemes offered to Canada in the 1850's. The Grand Trunk had already received promises of aid from the Canadian government to build from Quebec to Hamilton, and in hopes that the imperial government would give a guaranteed loan for an extension from Quebec to Halifax, the Grand Trunk Railway was in-

A paper bank note printed for the Champlain & St. Lawrence Rail Road and dated 1837. After the bank panic of 1837, many private firms were empowered to issue currency on their own credit. The note shown here is interesting in that its value is given in Halifax currency (20 per cent less than sterling), the old French currency, and in Spanish dollars.

corporated in 1851. When the imperial government refused to help, British railway contractors undertook the construction and offered investors an 11½ per cent dividend.

The Grand Trunk scheme was too ambitious for a small colony and the beginning of the Crimean War brought a disastrous fall in Grand Trunk stock, which had been sold mostly in Britain. Anxious to save a railway deemed essential to Canada's growth, the provincial government granted the company $4.5 million in 1855. The next year the company was still in deep financial trouble, and in 1857 the terms of the government's aid were changed to a gift of $1.5 million, even though a world recession had just begun. When the Grand Trunk's deficit reached $3,000,000, the government took over the railway. British investors blamed the Canadian government for their own short-sightedness, and Canadian taxpayers blamed the corrupting influence of railway politics, but the Grand Trunk failed because it paid too high a price for branch lines, because construction costs had far outstripped estimates, and because it had not displaced the St. Lawrence water transport system. In 1862 only 6 per cent of the grain and 34 per cent of the flour reaching Montreal and 5 per cent of the grain and 10 per cent of the flour leaving there was carried by the Grand Trunk.

Financially Canada's first railway era was a disaster, especially since it coincided with the most serious depression to date, yet the railways did transform the life of the colonies in many positive ways. Three hundred bellowing and puffing engines transported politicians, farmers, salesmen, clergymen, craftsmen, and a host of others across the countryside at hitherto unimagined speeds. The produce of the farms reached the mark-

Canada's first railway train (1836), from a magic lantern slide in the McCord Museum of McGill University, Montreal. The Champlain-St. Lawrence was essentially a portage line to speed traffic around the canals.

ets in record time, and by the same means salesmen offered rural residents a bewildering variety of consumer goods – factory-made clothing, mass-produced furniture, labour-saving devices such as sewing machines and apple peelers, and sheer luxuries such as pianos for the farmhouse parlour. For better, and for worse, Canada entered into the age of the industrial revolution with the coming of the railways.

The steam engine was also creating the basis of a manufacturing industry in Canada. Steam turned the wheels and drove the machines in countless small factories making boots, shoes, glass, china, farm implements, boxes, stoves, sewing machines, and numerous other manufactured articles. The portability of steam engines also meant that milling and lumbering were no longer tied to areas where water power was available. Industry attracted population to the city from farms where new machines like the reaper-binder were reducing the farmers' need for manpower. Thus the first consequence of industrialization was urbanization – the growth of towns and cities with water and sewage systems, paved and lighted streets.

The 1850's saw the rise of urban industrial centres, particularly in Canada West but also in the Montreal area. Hamilton, Brantford, Kitchener, London, Galt, Ottawa, and many other towns now challenged Toronto's economic position. Partly as a result of the Irish immigration

Left: A wood token for a locomotive. Wood for use as locomotive fuel was bought by contract from wayside landowners and obtained for locomotives that needed it from woodpiles stacked alongside the tracks. Each engineer was supplied with tokens covering various amounts in cords; the supplier was paid with the number of tokens equivalent to the supply taken, which he remitted to the railway company for cash. Since the number of the locomotive appeared on each token, the railway company could check the fuel used by each locomotive and the efficiency of its engineer.
Below: the oldest-known photograph (December 1856) of a railway locomotive belonging to a Canadian system. The locomotive is one of the first used by the Grand Trunk Railway of Canada and is lettered Atlantic & St. Lawrence Rail Road, one of the companies incorporated into the Grand Trunk on its formation in 1853.

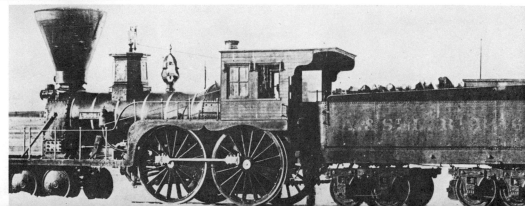

A woodcut showing the interior of the Taylor Company's original mid-nineteenth-century safe-manufacturing factory in Toronto.

the population of Canada West during the 1840's rose from 487,000 to 952,000; that of Canada East grew from 650,000 to 890,000. In the next decade the rate of expansion in the western section was again more rapid – the census of 1861 showed Canada West with 1,400,000 to Canada East's 1,100,000. Half of all immigrants were settling in Canada West, only 10 per cent in Canada East. The remaining 40 per cent soon left for the United States. By contrast with Canada the Atlantic provinces were receiving only a trickle of immigrants. This latest migration to British North America differed in quality as well as in quantity from earlier migrations. More immigrants were highly trained workers or professional men who brought their skills and capital from industrial Britain. They also brought advanced ideas, based on the experience of Britain's age of reform, that added to the ferment of Canadian political life.

Agriculture was also experiencing a technological revolution as field drainage, crop rotation, the use of fertilizers, and the employment of better and more sophisticated farm machinery became more common. Stable prices encouraged the farmers of Canada West to double their wheat production during the 1850's. Of greater significance was the trend to more diversified farming. The growing urban market for food increased the herds of pigs and cows in Canada West by 50 per cent, established the modern dairy and cheese industries, and promoted the cultivation of vegetable crops and the planting of fruit orchards. But as in so many other aspects Canada West outstripped Canada East in agriculture, owing to

The first starch factory in Canada, built by William Benson in Edwardsburg (now Cardinal) in 1858. Destroyed by fire in 1874, it is now the site of the Canada Starch Company Limited.

Dundas, Ontario, engraved by Hardy Gregory, an artist, lithographer, and lodge-banner maker. His view (1853) is taken from Cotton Mill Hill, at the south end of the main street, looking north.

better techniques, better herds, and better seed grain, which resulted in markedly higher production of oats, wheat, milk, cheese, and fruit.

Although Canada was entering the age of the industrial revolution, agriculture remained the backbone of the Canadian economy for many years and contributed the bulk of Canada's export trade. Small Canadian factories could not compete with British and American manufacturers in world markets, but those world markets did have an insatiable appetite for Canadian grain and lumber. In all but one year of the fifties Canada imported more than she exported, but her volume of exports was increasing and assuming a new pattern. Canadian sales to her traditional market, Great Britain, continued to rise, but exports to the United States rose at three times the rate to equal her exports to Britain. A slightly different pattern appeared in imports, for while Canada showed an $8,000,-000 annual surplus of trade in natural products with the United States (thanks to the Reciprocity Treaty), she still bought more from the United States than she sold to that country. Canada required her constant favourable trade balance with Britain to offset the deficit created by her increasing dependence on the United States.

Paradoxically these forward strides made in agriculture, industry, transportation, and communications coincided with the appearance of deep religious, racial, political, and cultural stresses that were making the future of the union precarious. Far from assimilating the French into an Anglo-Saxon pattern of life, the union was frustrating the aspirations and needs of the English-speaking population who now formed a majority of its population. Already in the fifties voices had been heard denouncing the union and calling for some new and drastically different constitutional arrangement.

Light and Shadows in the Atlantic Colonies

The achievement of responsible government in Nova Scotia in 1848 was duplicated in the other Atlantic provinces in succeeding years, but thanks to the changed attitude of the Colonial Office none of them experienced the kind of political warfare that had occurred in Nova Scotia. New Brunswick did not have anything like the division of parties that existed in Nova Scotia so that the introduction of responsible government was virtually unnoticed there. But in both provinces the Opposition refused for some time to acknowledge that government by the majority party constituted responsible government because they could not believe that a lieutenant-governor who had worked with one party as his government could treat the other party impartially if it became the governing party. Not until their Assemblies gained control over finances – 1857 in New Brunswick and 1860 in Nova Scotia – did the full range of responsible government become operative in those colonies. This slow development, by comparison with events in Canada, resulted in part from the absence of strong local government institutions to serve as nurseries for politicians, but particularly from the rudimentary state of party organization and operation as contrasted to the disciplined groups in Canada who did not hesitate to use every form of patronage for their own party's advantage.

Two sketches, from a group known as the St. Andrews Sketches, drawn by Lt. James Cumming Clarke in 1853-7 while he was serving in the army and holding the position of Town Adjutant in New Brunswick. Crudely drawn but lively, his sketches are interesting reminders of life in a small New Brunswick town in the mid-nineteenth century.
Right: A detachment hunting foxes. Below: A detachment pursuing deserters.

On Prince Edward Island responsible government was accepted in 1851, but within three years the practice was jeopardized by the political struggles of factions which were not parties and which did not appreciate the principles of the cabinet system. The Colonial Office granted responsible government to Newfoundland in 1855, but only with strong misgivings. The scattered and small (120,000) population, the economic power concentrated in the hands of the St. John's merchant community, the almost total lack of true political parties, but above all the three-sided denominational conflicts between Roman Catholics, Anglicans, and Methodists (virtually the only religious persuasions on the island) all combined to make the outcome of Newfoundland's venture into responsible government very uncertain. In the construction of cabinets, for instance, the first consideration had to be a balance of religious interests rather than party affiliation. Despite these local crosscurrents, however, Britain was anxious to see her oldest colony become self-reliant and self-governing, and to this end the imperial government agreed in 1857 to consult Newfoundland before making any changes regarding France's fishing rights around the island.

Compared to the violence and invective of Canadian politics in the 1850's, the political history of the Atlantic provinces in that period was calm to the point of being dull. The real dynamism lay in the economic development of the region, which was enjoying its golden age of prosperity. After the initial impact of British free trade policies, officials from New Brunswick and Prince Edward Island met with Nova Scotian officials at Halifax in 1849 to discuss their common trade problems. The heavy industrialization of New England in recent years had created at their very doorstep a large and attractive market for fish, farm products, and lumber. To gain access to this market, which was protected by high tariffs, the Maritime provinces held a strong lever in the form of the Atlantic fisheries. Since 1818 Americans had been barred from the inshore fishing areas, but those fisheries had not been extensively developed by the Maritimers themselves because the United States protected its own fishermen and substantially closed the American market to foreign fish through a system of bounties and prohibitive tariffs. If opening the inshore fisheries to American fishermen would open the large American market to fishermen of the colonies, that would be a fair exchange in the opinion of most Maritimers. To apply persuasive force to this lever, the British navy began to enforce rigidly the law excluding Americans from the inshore fisheries.

The reviving prosperity of the region, however, led the Maritimers to put a higher value on their fisheries, so that Lord Elgin was able in his successful negotiations of 1854 to exchange American access to the fisheries for reciprocity in lumber and agricultural products as well as

Between decks: the two-tiered double bunks on an emigrant ship in the 1850's.

fish – a better bargain than the Atlantic colonies could have hoped for a few years earlier. Two years after the Reciprocity Treaty came into force, New Brunswick's exports to the United States had nearly doubled in value, and half Nova Scotia's exports now went to that same market. The Reciprocity Treaty also provided for the free entry of Nova Scotia's coal into the United States, which now absorbed over 60 per cent of the province's production. Contemporary observers were unanimous in their opinion that the Reciprocity Treaty stimulated trade between the Atlantic provinces and the United States.

British free trade and reciprocity were both related, although indirectly, to the development of railways in Nova Scotia and New Brunswick. During the 1840's the possibility of building a line connecting the seaboard colonies to Canada and that province's market of 1.5 million people had been seriously considered and after the repeal of the Corn Laws Maritimers hoped that Britain would build this intercolonial railway to compensate for their loss of imperial tariff protection. In 1848 British surveyors actually mapped the future intercolonial route from Quebec to Halifax that followed the east coast of New Brunswick. Such a route not only offered Canada a year-round ice-free port, but it fulfilled a British defence requirement by avoiding the St. John Valley, a route that was considered a defence hazard because it was so close to the American border. A conference of delegates from New England, New York, Canada, Newfoundland, New Brunswick, and Nova Scotia met at Portland, Maine, in 1850 and laid plans for building the intercolonial with an extension to Portland, using money from both private and government sources. Joseph Howe immediately went to England to secure imperial support, but the British government refused to pay for the Intercolonial Railway and the colonies lacked the capital to undertake such a heavy expenditure on their own.

New England, however, was a nearer and larger market for the Maritimes than Canada, and American railroad operators expressed interest in Saint John and Halifax as terminals because they were closer to Europe than New York or Boston. Encouraged by this American interest and attracted by New England's market, the governments of the two colonies undertook the construction of several short lines which, they hoped, might some day become part of an intercolonial and New England railway. Nova Scotia built a line from Halifax to Truro (with a branch to Windsor) between 1854 and 1858, for a total of only 125 miles. By 1862 New Brunswick had completed a 90-mile railway from St. Andrews to Woodstock which had been started in 1844, and another line from Saint John to Shediac, a distance of 108 miles opened in 1860. None of these railways showed reasonable profits; all were essentially portage lines, and the American railroads had made no genuine attempt to build from Portland to connect with the Maritime railways. Disappointed by their failure to reach New England, the Maritimes' attention returned in the late 1850's to their original hope of an intercolonial railway that would link Canada with their seaports.

Blondin crossing the Niagara River on a tightrope, with his manager, Harry Colcord, on his back – a feat that took place on 17 August 1859. The great French acrobat, whose real name was Jean François Gravelet, astonished North America with his daring and successful tightrope exploits in 1859 and 1860: he walked across the Falls blindfolded; he rode across on a bicycle; he pushed a wheelbarrow across; he pushed a stove to the centre of the river, cooked a meal on it, and then lowered it to the waiting pleasure boat "Maid of the Mist" below him; he walked across on stilts. Billed as "the greatest wonder of the age", Blondin and his exploits encouraged a rash of stunts, none radically different from his or more daring, and none that had comparable public appeal. Blondin was the first and greatest performer over Niagara Falls.

HISTORY FROM THE SOURCES

The First Effects of the Industrial Revolution

The revolutions of the 1850's — in transportation, communications, commerce, and industry — had a visible impact on the British North American landscape, and especially on Canada West. The population of cities mushroomed, factories increased in numbers and size, agricultural production spurted ahead, and everyday life changed in countless ways. All these developments were accompanied by new ideas and followed by a wave of popular faith in the inevitability of Canada's future progress.

In the Preface to the large, multi-author volume, Eighty Years' Progress of British North America (Toronto, 1863), its editor, Henry Yule Hind, explorer and professor at Toronto's Trinity College, was optimistic.

> The rise of the United States, from a few feeble colonies to a high rank among nations, has never ceased to attract the attention of the world; and their career has been indeed so wonderful, that the quiet but equally rapid growth and development of the British North American provinces has received comparatively little notice. It will be seen from the following pages that they have at least kept pace with their powerful southern neighbors, and that, though laboring under some disadvantages, they have in eighty years increased tenfold, not only in population but in wealth; they have attained to a point of power that more than equals that of the united colonies when they separated from the mother country. They have, by means of canals, made their great rivers and remote inland seas accessible to the shipping of Europe; they have constructed a system of railroads far surpassing those of some of the European powers; they have established an educational system which is behind none in the old or new world; they have developed vast agricultural and inexhaustible mineral resources; they have done enough, in short, to indicate a magnificent future – enough to point to a progress which shall place the provinces, within the days of many now living, on a level with Great Britain herself, in population, in wealth, and in power. If in the next eighty years the provinces should prosper as they have in the eighty years that are past, which there seems no reason to doubt, a nation of forty millions will have arisen in the North.

> **H. Y. Hind, ed.,** *Eighty Years' Progress of British North America*
> (Toronto, 1863), pp. 3-4.

The unbridled enthusiasm about Canada's achievements and her "magnificent future" as a strong and wealthy transcontinental nation was epitomized by Toronto's Railway Festival to inaugurate the Toronto and Hamilton Railway in 1855. The workshop and the warehouse of the Northern Railway were converted by gas lights, flags, bunting, and a fountain with ducks into a ballroom and dining hall to accommodate some 4,000 people who danced until five in the morning with time out for a sumptuous supper that began at 1 a.m. Before these festivities started, the governor general, political leaders, and mayors of several Canadian and American cities attended a déjeuner where bumper toasts of champagne were drunk and appropriate speeches delivered to a convivial and appreciative audience. Toronto's Mayor Allan, who was chairman of the dinner, proposed the toast, "The opening of the Toronto and Hamilton Railway".

There are those sitting near me now who can recall the time when those who had occasion . . . to visit the upper end of Lake Ontario, had a weary day or two days' journey through mud and mire. . . . But see the change now – a comfortable morning's drive in a luxurious railway carriage brings the citizens of Hamilton and Toronto together in less than an hour and a half. (Cheers.) The increased prosperity and trade which that must bring to the two sister cities cannot but be productive of the greatest benefit to both. . . . [This railway] is the last link added to the great chain of railway communications which connects us with the Far West. – Nay more, though far removed from the ebb and flow of tide water, Toronto is now brought within 24 hours distance of the great seaport towns on the Atlantic. When you recollect what Toronto was a very few years ago, when I tell you that 60 years ago the first house was built, and that 23 years ago its population did not exceed 5,000, and that now it is upwards of 50,000 . . . I am sure you will respond heartily to the great toast of the day. . . .

In his toast, "Prosperity to the Railways of Canada and the United States", George Brown, newspaper owner, politician, and a "booster" of Canada's transcontinental destiny, compared Canada's recent progress to her depressed condition during the Annexation crisis.

. . . [In five or six years] we have built and have in operation 1250 miles of railway, and have 800 miles under contract. . . . And there is another great road which a great many of us yet hope to see under-

taken, and that is a road from Toronto to the Pacific. (Cheers.) . . .
We look upon this northern country as peculiarly our own. . . . In the
last five years not less than 80 million dollars have been invested on
rail roads. (Hear, hear.) The credit of the country has been raised,
the value of property has increased, and the produce of the country
has brought a higher price. We have been placed in communication
with markets that we never knew before, and if there is a country or
a city that have reason to be gratified that railroads are brought into
operation, it is Canada and the city of Toronto. (Cheers.)

The Globe, 21 December 1855

John Sheridan Hogan came to Canada from Ireland in 1827 as a boy of
twelve and worked as a printer, journalist, and editor until elected to
parliament for the Reform party in 1857. He disappeared in 1859 and
only a year and a half later was it discovered that he had been murdered
near Toronto by bandits. In 1855 Hogan's essay, Canada, won first prize
in competition for inclusion in the Canadian display at the great Paris
Exhibition.

The most striking effect of the rapid increase of population in
America is the rise and growth of towns and cities. . . . And to convey
an idea of the wealth that is created by population being thus suddenly centralised in a comparative wilderness, I have but to name the
fact, that within twenty years land was sold for a pound an acre in
many cities, towns and villages, in the western part of America,
where it is now purchased for twenty-five pounds a foot. There is not
an old inhabitant of Buffalo or of Chicago in the States, or of Toronto
or Hamilton in Canada, who cannot recount numerous instances
of property, now worth thousands, even tens of thousands of pounds,
being bought, twenty years ago, for a cow, or a horse, or a small
quantity of goods out of a shop, or a few weeks or months labour of
a mechanic. These things form the topics of fireside history in these
places. The poor refer to them as foundation for hope. The rich regard them as matters of congratulation. The speculator and the man
of enterprise learns from them how and where to found a town, and
to make a bold push for a fortune.
    In this singular and instructive feature of American progress, how
does Canada compare with the United States?
    The *"World's Progress,"* published by Putnam of New York, –
a reliable authority, – gives the population and increase of the prin-

cipal cities in the United States. Boston, between 1840 and 1850, increased forty-five per cent. Toronto, within the same period, increased *ninety-five* per cent. ...

Hamilton, a beautiful Canadian city at the head of Lake Ontario, and founded much more recently than Toronto, has also had almost unexampled prosperity. In 1836 its population was but 2846, in 1854 it was upwards of 20,000.

London, still farther west in Upper Canada, and a yet more recently founded city than Hamilton, being surveyed as a wilderness little more than twenty-five years ago, has now upwards of ten thousand inhabitants.

The City of Ottawa, recently called after the magnificent river of that name, and upon which it is situated, has now above 10,000 inhabitants, although, in 1830, it had but 140 houses, including mere sheds and shanties; and the property upon which it is built was purchased, not many years before, for *eighty pounds*.

*   *   *   *   *

... Agricultural machines and implements are extensively made in the Province; and Upper Canada stands almost unrivalled in the manufacture of cooking and ornamental stoves. Even in printing types, and stereotype plates, in philosophical and surgical instruments, and in piano-fortes and other musical instruments, she competes most creditably with other countries.

In cotton fabrics Canada has made but little progress, but in woollen goods and mixed fabrics she is a large producer, and of a quality so good as to have taken prizes at the New York and London Exhibitions.

In the manufacture of furs, and other articles for which her northern territory affords peculiar advantages, she is unrivalled; and the exquisite graining of her timber for cabinet work, especially that of the black walnut, has lately created a great demand for it in the European markets.

Passing over the less important manufactures, there remain the grist and saw mills of the Province, which minister to the first wants of the pioneer of the wilderness, and produce the staple exports of the colony. Of the latter, especially those on the river Ottawa and Saguenay, Canada has perhaps the largest in the world. The returns of the Census of 1851, though very imperfect, give 158 steam and 1473 mills worked by water-power, producing 772,612,770 feet of lumber per annum, exclusive of 4,590,000 planks. There were 1153 grist mills returned, of which 45 were steam power, employing a capital of over £1,000,000.

J. S. Hogan, *Canada* (Montreal, 1855), pp. 39-41, 58.

S. P. Day, a visitor to North America in the 1860's, wrote a two-volume work extolling the advantages of Canada over the United States as a future home for British emigrants.

Here is a country of immense extent, of unbounded material resources, marvellously fertile, teeming with natural advantages, and capable of maintaining in comfort millions of additional inhabitants. Rising and thriving cities, towns, villages, and hamlets are dotted over a vast extent of territory. Almost everywhere spring up churches, colleges, schools, and asylums of various kinds. The postal system is so far complete, seventeen hundred post-offices being in operation. The telegraph has been widely introduced, there being over four thousand miles of wires. Railways run through the country; steamboats ply on the lakes and rivers; majestic canals have been constructed; suitable systems of local and general government originated; statutory codes modified, decentrated, and consolidated; enlightened fiscal laws, in accordance with the European spirit of progress, put into operation; while every other adjunct and appliance of civilization has been brought into requisition and placed in harmonious combination.

In addition to all these advantages, excellent Macadamized and plank roads have been opened up by the Government, which are constantly being increased and extended . . . .

Canada may especially be regarded as a country of kindling energies, and "the land of hope" for the poor man. A country sixteen hundred miles long and two hundred and fifty miles broad, containing two hundred and forty millions of acres, possessing one thousand miles of coast, with a verdant, virgin soil, affords peculiar attractions for our redundant population. The climate, especially that of Canada West, is tolerably healthy, and will approximate in sanitariness to that of England, in proportion as the forests become cleared, and the swamps are drained. Land, as I have shown, can be obtained with facility, and at a trifling cost; taxation is nearly four-fifths less than in this country, while it is more equably and equitably divided; skilled and unskilled labour are highly remunerated; and the necessaries of life are abundant, and consequently cheap. Perfect political and religious freedom exist; life and property are secure; aliens can acquire and retain lands after three years' residence, while a freehold of the annual value of forty shillings affords an electoral qualification. No better field in the world than this for steady, unflagging labour; none where "industry, intelligence, and integrity" (the provincial motto), will raise a man to a respectable and independent position in society.

S. P. Day, *English America*, 2 v. (London, 1864),
Vol. II, pp. 330-1, 332-3.

FURTHER READING

The books listed in the FURTHER READING section for Chapter 13 should also be consulted.

Whitelaw, W. M., *The Maritimes and Canada Before Confederation* (Toronto: Oxford University Press, 1966)★. A useful general review of the background of Confederation.

Tucker, G. N., *The Canadian Commercial Revolution, 1846-1851* (Toronto: McClelland & Stewart, 1964)★. The old colonial system: the effects of its ending.

The Elgin-Grey Papers, 1846-1852, 4 parts (King's Printer, 1937)★. The most important documentary source on responsible government.

Beck, J. M., ed., *Joseph Howe: Voice of Nova Scotia* (Toronto: McClelland & Stewart, 1964)★. A selection of Howe's writings and speeches.

Cornell, P. G., *The Alignment of Political Groups in Canada, 1841-1867* (Toronto: University of Toronto Press, 1962). A scholarly study based on voting patterns in parliament.

Moir, J. S., *Church and State in Canada West* (Toronto: University of Toronto Press, 1959). A detailed study of religious issues in pre-Confederation politics.

Skelton, O. D., *The Life and Times of Alexander Tilloch Galt*, 2 vols. (Toronto: McClelland & Stewart, 1966)★. An abridged biography of this important finance minister and proponent of Confederation.

15

The Road to Confederation

The Forces of Unity

Galt's proposal for a confederation of the British North American colonies attracted little public attention in 1858, but various forces, some obvious and some hidden, were already working in the direction of colonial unity. With virtually all good farming land in the province of Canada already occupied, many residents and immigrants were looking towards the prairies as an area for future settlement. The Hudson's Bay Company's charter to rule Rupert's Land was due for renewal in 1858 and the Canadian government had sent Chief Justice William Henry Draper to London in 1856 to plead Canada's case for acquiring territorial rights in the west before the tide of American expansion occupied these empty lands as it had the Oregon region. At the same time the sectional conflict was increasing popular dissatisfaction and frustration in Canada West with the existing legislative union.

These two forces – the need for land in the west and the demand for some new constitutional arrangement – were both seriously discussed at the Reform Convention held at Toronto in 1859 to assess the defeat of the Clear Grit government the previous summer. George Brown had full support from the 600 delegates for his proposal to add the west to Canada, but when a minority demanded simple dissolution of the Union, he had a tough battle to pass his resolution favouring federation of the Canadas under a joint authority.

The Cartier-Macdonald government showed no interest in proposals for constitutional change, and even indicated privately that because its

This sketch of "The Settler's First Home" appeared in an 1862 issue of "The Canadian Illustrated News", accompanied by a letter. "Here I am," says the writer, "as busy as a beaver, cutting a tree into certain lengths for . . . making snake fences. The rapidity . . . with which an experienced chopper cuts them down would astonish you . . ."

During his visit to Canada in 1860 the Prince of Wales descended a timber-slide at Ottawa on a square-timber raft. The sketch, "drawn by our special artist" as its caption states, was published in "The Illustrated London News" for 20 October 1860.

French-Canadian supporters believed that acquisition of the west would create another English colony, it had no interest in territorial expansion. The government's attitude seemed to be justified by the lack of encouragement from the Colonial Office, which in 1858 hinted that confederation was merely a scheme of some Canadian politicians to escape the province's political strains and in 1860 refused to initiate any movement towards British North American federation. But Macdonald and Cartier could not escape the reality of growing political deadlock in their colony. The government had little positive legislation to offer parliament in 1860, and its public image was further damaged that summer during a tour of Canada by the Prince of Wales. The Prince's chaperon, the Duke of Newcastle, prevented the Prince from visiting Macdonald's home city, Kingston, because the Orangemen (who were outlawed in Britain) erected signs to display their loyalty.

In an attempt to regain lost prestige before the general election had to be called in 1861, Macdonald tried a new political venture – a speaking tour of Canada West – in the autumn of 1860. Before the election was held, however, two developments drew further attention to the idea of confederation: the latest Canadian census showed a population gap between the two sections of the province so wide that even Conservatives spoke of the justice of "rep by pop", while the outbreak of civil war in the American federation raised doubts about the very workability of any form of federal government. When the Canadian election took place that summer, the Conservatives' unofficial approval of "rep by pop" won increased strength for the government in Canada West but lost it many seats in Canada East where French Canadians viewed equal representation as the only safeguard of their political power. By re-emphasizing sectional differences the election of 1861 made Macdonald's position more difficult than ever.

The importance of the American Civil War for British North America became apparent late that year when an American federal warship stopped the British steamer *Trent* and seized two Confederate diplomats. The freedom of the seas had been violated and for a short time war between Britain and the United States seemed certain. Personal diplomatic intervention by Queen Victoria's consort, Prince Albert (his last important act

"River Front, Montreal", by John H. Walker, believed to have been painted in the late 1850's.

before his tragically early death) prevented an armed confrontation between the two nations, but the *Trent* affair forcibly reminded British North Americans that their own peaceful existence depended on cordial relations between Britain and the United States, as had been shown by the unfortunate War of 1812. Nevertheless colonial governments did have some responsibility for their own defence, and a defence commission set up in Canada recommended early in 1862 the creation of an active force of 50,000 men and a reserve force of the same size. A Militia bill to implement this report by calling out 30,000 men for two weeks' training at a cost of almost half a million dollars was defeated by seven votes from French-Canadian Conservatives who joined the Liberals in opposing the high cost of the militia scheme. The government resigned at once and a new cabinet was formed by John Sandfield Macdonald and L. V. Sicotte, both of whom accepted the so-called Double Majority principle as the solution to Canada's sectional troubles.

One result of the 1862 Militia bill episode was a growing conviction in Britain that colonies, especially in British North America, must be encouraged and perhaps even forced to relieve the British taxpayer of some of the heavy burden of colonial defence costs. A second result was the testing and final rejection of the impractical Double Majority theory as a political answer to the constitutional problem of the Union. John A. Macdonald predicted that the government would fall within a year: "Brown will fight them on Rep. by Pop. and split them in two. . . . defeated they will be, but not by our opposition. They will crumble to pieces before the end of the session from their own weakness." The failure of the Double Majority came in fact in 1863, when the J. S. Macdonald-Sicotte government passed another separate school act for Canada West only by the strength of Canada East votes in parliament. Soon afterwards the government was defeated by 5 votes on a no-confidence motion and another general election was called, the second in less than two years.

In this election the Conservatives in Canada East won new strength under Cartier, but in Canada West they lost even more seats than in 1861. The precarious balance of the political parties – Conservatives, Liberals, and Clear Grits – continued; the only change was that the Conservatives of Canada West were now publicly committed to supporting "rep by pop" and, by implication, a federation of Canada East and West. Shortly after the new parliament met early in 1864, the minority J. S. Macdonald-Sicotte government resigned and John A. Macdonald was faced with the almost impossible task of forming a new cabinet which he knew could not command a majority in the Legislative Assembly. Under the nominal leadership of the aged and respected Sir E. P. Taché, the Conservatives took office at the end of March, but on 14 June this government was defeated by a margin of 2 votes. Sectional deadlock had now destroyed three cabinets in less than three years. Another general election was unlikely to change the position of the parties. The old political system was obviously in ruins; some new arrangement to provide political stability, presumably by constitutional reform, was an absolute necessity for Canada.

A way out of this latest ministerial crisis and of the larger Canadian problem, sectionalism, was already being opened. A parliamentary committee headed by George Brown had just reported in favour of "a federative system, applied either to Canada alone, or to the whole British North American Provinces". Brown now offered to co-operate with any government that would use the crisis to settle the constitutional question; Macdonald, so long a defender of the union against his political enemy, Brown, now realized that change must come. In private conversation with Brown, Macdonald accepted the federal principle as the programme of a new coalition that would include Brown and two other Clear Grits. When this momentous announcement was made in the Assembly on 17 June, one diminutive French Canadian rushed across the floor and threw his arms around the neck of the towering George Brown. The constitutional log-jam had been broken: Canada West could yet achieve "rep by pop" with a federation that would protect the French minority position; by the same route Canada West could escape from the sectional deadlock that frus-

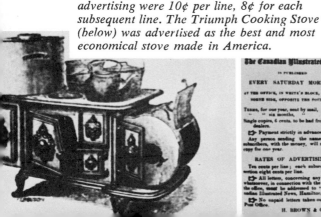

Advertisements from an 1862 issue of "The Canadian Illustrated News". Single copies of the periodical cost 6¢, an annual subscription (including mail charges) was $3. Rates of advertising were 10¢ per line, 8¢ for each subsequent line. The Triumph Cooking Stove (below) was advertised as the best and most economical stove made in America.

"The Great International Railway Suspension Bridge [over the Niagara River] connecting the New York Central and the Great Western of Canada Railways", from "The Illustrated London News" (1862).

trated its economic ambitions for expansion. A long and uncertain road lay ahead, but the first step had been taken by the formation of the Great Coalition in 1864.

The Project of Maritime Union

History and economic interests had combined to create in the Atlantic region four distinct colonies, each imbued with a strong, almost exclusive sense of provincial loyalty. Separately these colonies were tied by senti- ment, by trade, and by defence relations to Britain; Canada was a distant place, renowned for her bitter politics but otherwise a land virtually unknown to residents of the Atlantic colonies. Their one common interest with Canada – and this applied almost entirely to Nova Scotia and New Brunswick – was the project for an intercolonial railway. Such a railway would open the large Canadian market to the products of the Atlantic colonies and would provide at the same time a seaboard terminus for the Grand Trunk. But progress towards an intercolonial railway had been slight and the experience of dealing with the imperial government and Canada had been frustrating. The Canadian proposal of 1858 for an inter- colonial railway had been blocked by the refusal of imperial support, but the *Trent* affair brought a sudden change of heart in London. In April

The British steamship "Great Eastern", built entirely of iron in 1859 and at that time the largest ship afloat, from which the first successful Atlantic cable was laid in 1866. The cable stretched from Valencia in Ireland to Heart's Content, Newfoundland.

1862 the Duke of Newcastle wrote from the Colonial Office an encouraging reply to Nova Scotia's enquiry about the possibility of colonial union, colonial free trade, and an intercolonial railway. In September the colonial governors and statesmen met in Quebec for the first and only conference of its kind to discuss Newcastle's proposals for a stronger and more united British North America.

The Conference discussed union and free trade inconclusively, but all participants agreed that the essential railway link "in the chain of an unbroken highway through British territory from the Atlantic to the Pacific" would be built with the aid of an imperial guarantee. Canada was to pay five-sevenths of the cost; Nova Scotia and New Brunswick were to pay the remainder. But the Liberal government of J. S. Macdonald-Sicotte – the same government that had gained power by defeating the Militia bill – soon demanded an imperial subsidy for a projected mail route to the Red River as the price for Canada's participation in the Intercolonial Railway. The British, Nova Scotia, and New Brunswick governments bitterly charged Canada with double dealing, and Canada reacted by withdrawing entirely from the scheme. By the autumn of 1863 it appeared that the Intercolonial Railway project was dead – killed, in the opinion of Maritimers, by the petty politics of Canada.

In Nova Scotia Joseph Howe's government, formed in 1860, was defeated in 1863 at a general election and replaced by the Conservatives under the imaginative Dr. Charles Tupper, and in New Brunswick Lieutenant-Governor Gordon reported to the Colonial Office that he and his prime minister, Samuel Leonard Tilley, were convinced that a spirit favourable to Maritime colonial union now existed in that region. Yet at the same moment the prospects for a British North American federation were also reviving, thanks to events in the American Civil War. The victories of the northern armies at Gettysburg and Vicksburg made a total defeat of the South a real possibility, so that the British North American colonies were forced to consider their future defence relationship to a victorious North whose cause they admired but whose power and expansionism they feared.

The connection between defence and federation became increasingly obvious by 1864 as British North American opinion became strongly pro-southern out of fear of the North. At the same time Britain's cotton trade with the South was endangered by northern successes. Public reaction in the northern states to this unfriendliness led to demands for an end to the Reciprocity Treaty, from which British North America had profited handsomely thanks to the wartime need for food and lumber which British North America could so readily meet. The Intercolonial project assumed increasing importance as an imperial defence measure, and the return to power in Canada of the Conservatives under Taché and John A. Macdonald encouraged the Maritime colonies to hope that this new Canadian government would revive Canadian interest in the railway project so recently rejected by the more economy-minded Liberals.

By April 1864 the three Maritime provinces were agreed in principle that a meeting should be held that summer, possibly at Charlottetown, to discuss legislative union for their region. The inclusion of Newfoundland was neither suggested by them nor requested by Newfoundland. In due course delegates were appointed by each colony to meet at Charlottetown on 1 September to discuss Maritime union. Much of the initiative for the meeting had come from the governors of those colonies, but public opinion supported the idea wholeheartedly. Coupled with Maritime union was the hope of improving relations with Canada and perhaps of getting some final agreement on the Intercolonial Railway scheme. As a step in this direction the Saint John Board of Trade invited the Canadian parliament to send a delegation to their city in August. One hundred Canadians – politicians, newpapermen, and municipal officials – made the trip, which included visits to Fredericton and Halifax. By the time they returned to Canada, residents of New Brunswick and Nova Scotia were discussing a broader topic than Maritime union, namely a general federation of British North America.

Several weeks before the Canadian visit to the Maritimes, the possibility of expanding the scope of the Charlottetown Conference was being considered by the Maritime governors. In June, Brown had reluctantly accepted one of the three seats in the Great Coalition offered to the Liberals by John A. Macdonald on the understanding that a Canadian federation would be sought only after the more ambitious idea of a general British North American federation had been conclusively rejected. The proposed meeting at Charlottetown seemed a heaven-sent opportunity for the Canadians to promote the grander design. In July Governor Lord

The West Head lumber mill at Saint John, New Brunswick, 1850-60.

One of the earliest photographs in existence of Charlottetown in pre-Confederation years (probably the 1860's), showing the old Province House, the round Market Building, St. Paul's Church, and the local fire brigade (foreground).

Monck had asked the governors of the Maritime provinces whether a Canadian delegation could be received at Charlottetown and had been told that Canadians were welcome in an informal capacity. The conference had been called specifically to discuss Maritime union – its members had no authority to consider a general federation.

Despite the invitation to attend the Conference only as observers, the Great Coalition cabinet worked hard throughout the summer months to prepare a draft constitution for a federation of British America. By September the members were ready to make concrete proposals at Charlottetown. Macdonald, Brown, Cartier, and Galt, the leading planners, favoured a federation based on the traditions of monarchical and parliamentary authority, with a strong central government to prevent the rise of the "states' rights" controversy which had plunged the United States into its terrible Civil War. How the Maritime provinces would react to these principles remained to be seen, but already Conservative (*bleu*) French-Canadian newspapers were voicing opposition to the scheme because "Confederation means a league of independent states" and because, they said, French Canada must possess "full autonomy over its own social, civil, and religious institutions".

Conscious of these differences of attitude and uncertain how Maritimers would react to the Canadian proposals, Macdonald, Brown, Cartier, Galt, William McDougall the Clear Grit, Thomas Darcy McGee the Irish patriot turned Canadian nationalist, and two other cabinet members arrived from Quebec aboard the government steamer *Queen Victoria* amidst huge crowds attracted by a circus visiting the Island at the same time. As the Conference began its mixed round of parties and discussions on 1 September, the Canadian representatives were almost as

Delegates to the Confederation Conference in Charlottetown, 1864. John A. Macdonald is sitting on the steps.

numerous as the combined delegations from the three Maritime colonies. On 2 September, the first day of serious business, "Canada opened her batteries", so George Brown reported, with Macdonald and Cartier stating the arguments in favour of British North American federation. The next day Galt outlined the financial aspects of federation before the whole group adjourned to the *Queen Victoria* for a gay champagne party.

After a day of rest the presentation of the Canadian case for confederation continued on Monday, 5 September, with George Brown explaining how regional representation and "rep by pop" could be combined and balanced in a two-house legislature, and how power would be divided between the central and local governments of the confederation. The fourth day of the Conference was devoted to a question and answer session as the Maritimers sought clarification of obscure or difficult aspects of the Canadian scheme. Then the Canadians' work was finished, and the Maritime delegates spent the last day of their conference alone, discussing the merits of confederation as opposed to Maritime union. Maritime union had never been a popular project, and now the Canadians had overwhelmed it with their more ambitious plan for British America. The Maritime delegates were in unanimous agreement that "federation of all the Provinces [would be] highly desirable, if *the terms of union could be made satisfactory....*"

Thus the idea of a legislative union for the Maritimes was abandoned without serious examination at Charlottetown in favour of British North American federation, and the Conference adjourned to meet the next week in Halifax. The Halifax session was brief but momentous in its unanimous decision by Canadian and Maritime members to hold a new conference at Quebec on the official topic of a confederation of all British North America, including Newfoundland.

Disappointments and Dangers

The Charlottetown Conference had heard the principles and ideals of a British North American confederation outlined; the Quebec Conference that met on 10 October 1864 was to be the working session when the precise details would be established. At Quebec, delegates from all five eastern colonies (including Newfoundland) were caught up in a wave of optimistic nationalism. As one observer commented, "Never was there such an opportunity as now for the birth of a nation" – but the birth pangs were to last another three years.

The Canadian and Maritime delegations had differing interests in the confederation movement. For Canadians, and especially for George Brown, a sense of urgency hung over their deliberations. His province

While politicians talked of Union, most other people remained undisturbed by constitutional matters. A sketch drawn in 1863 shows a seal hunt in the Gulf of St. Lawrence.

could not go back to sectional deadlock – it must go forward to a confederation at best of all British North America, at worst of the two Canadas. The Maritimers saw confederation more as an escape from the blight of political parochialism which afflicted each of their home provinces. Confederation to them meant new and broader horizons, and the projected Intercolonial Railway summarized concisely their longing for greater challenge and greater opportunity. Since the Atlantic colonies would gain fewer material benefits from confederation, there would be less enthusiasm for the scheme in those colonies. Thus Tupper, Tilley, and the other delegates from that region were staking their political futures on the success of the confederation movement, more so than the Canadians for whom federation of the Canadas was at least an alternative.

The delegates at Quebec deliberated carefully for almost three weeks on resolutions that would form the draft of a new constitution for British North America. Their first difficulty was over representation in the upper house of the new federal parliament, for the entry of Newfoundland into the negotiations had upset the balance proposed at Charlottetown. After four days of hard bargaining Macdonald agreed to Tupper's motion that Newfoundland be given 4 Senate seats separate from the 24 assigned to the Maritime region. The next issue – representation for the Atlantic provinces in the 194-member House of Commons – left the delegates of Prince Edward Island deeply dissatisfied with the 5 seats to which its small population was entitled. The last major dispute concerned the division of powers between the central government and the provinces in the proposed federation. Some Maritimers strongly objected to the centralizing tendency of the resolutions, claiming that the result would be not a federation but a legislative union. In the end a majority of the Maritimers sided with Macdonald and Brown, the insistent advocates of a strong central government. Before the end of October agreement had been reached on the Seventy-Two Resolutions which would form the basis of confederation. It remained to be seen whether the average British North American would be as enthusiastic about the confederation scheme as the Fathers of Confederation who had met at Quebec.

The Quebec Conference had barely ended when opposition to confederation became evident in the Atlantic colonies and Canada East. The

Maritime delegations to Quebec had represented both their governments and opposition parties – Canada, of course, had a coalition government. Only Newfoundland's delegation did not contain bipartisan representation. With this kind of political support the prospects of achieving federation in the near future seemed bright, but the early publication of the Seventy-Two Resolutions in the colonial press provided a point of attack for an opposition to confederation that was more widespread and effective than the Fathers of the plan had anticipated. In Canada West a mere handful of Conservatives and John S. Macdonald Liberals attacked confederation as too expensive and too centralizing, and demanded that a general election be held to test public opinion. The opposition from Canada East was more serious, for the *rouges*, who were not part of the Great Coalition, as well as many *bleus* feared that the limited powers of the provinces in confederation would make the central government all-powerful in practice.

In the Atlantic provinces opposition to confederation appeared first in Prince Edward Island, where even the government was split by charges that the Quebec scheme was a sell-out of the Island's interests. As a result the confederates left the cabinet and the anti-confederates refused to take any official action on the Seventy-Two Resolutions. In New Brunswick, where a general election was due in 1865, Tilley's government found the election campaign turned into a referendum on confederation in which Lieutenant-Governor Gordon seemed to be siding with A. J. Smith, the leading opponent of the Intercolonial Railway and of confederation. The election involved in the broadest sense the political and economic future of New Brunswick, and Tilley failed to gain the expected support for confederation and the railway and all that they implied. The voting in early March proved disastrous for the confederation movement and for its New Brunswick proponents. Tilley, Gray, and Fisher, the three delegates at Quebec, lost their seats as 28 declared anti-confederates were elected in support of Smith.

Green Park, a house built in the 1860's at the head of Campbell Creek near Port Hill, Prince Edward Island, from an atlas published in 1880. The inset shows the owner's shipyard on the shores of Campbell Creek.

In Newfoundland and Nova Scotia the same expressions of local loyalty appeared soon after they arose in Prince Edward Island and New Brunswick. Many Nova Scotians objected to the federal principle, preferring the idea of a legislative union, and to the loss of provincial revenues that would result from the proposed higher tariffs under confederation. Between January and March 1865 Joseph Howe published his famous editorials against what he called the "Botheration Scheme" – editorials that did much to crystallize anti-confederate feeling in his province. Newfoundlanders felt even more intensely than Maritimers their isolation from Canada and their traditionally closer relations to Great Britain, so that there was less surprise when public opinion on the island showed itself hostile to confederation.

By early 1865 the bright promise of Quebec had dulled considerably and the results of the New Brunswick election seemed to doom confederation entirely, since the inclusion of that province was essential to the confederation scheme and to the Intercolonial Railway. Yet even while the resolutions were being hammered out at Quebec an event occurred that was ultimately to bring victory to the cause of confederation. On 19 October a handful of American Confederate soldiers raided St. Albans in Vermont, robbed the banks, and escaped into Canada. When brought to trial in Montreal they were released because the magistrate believed he had no jurisdiction in the case.

The St. Albans raid was only one in a series of incidents which provoked public anger in the northern states against Canada and Great Britain. Other infractions of Canadian neutrality had occurred, and the British-built Confederate ships *Florida* and *Alabama* had been destroying northern commerce. The American reaction to the St. Albans incident was an imminent threat of invasion of Canada by Union armies, and notice in March that the United States would cancel the Reciprocity Treaty of 1854 effective the next year. The threat of invasion was removed by the actions of President Lincoln early in 1865, but a new military danger arose from the Fenian Brotherhood, an Irish nationalist movement that found in the American traditions of manifest destiny and anti-British sentiment the excuse to punish Britain for what they called her "subjugation" of Ireland by attacking Canada. With the connivance of American authorities, motley Fenian "armies", reminiscent of the patriot groups of 1838, were formed in the border states.

British reaction to these results of the St. Albans raid appeared first in the form of strong government support for the confederation movement as a means of forcing the colonies to assume more responsibility for their own defence. When Canada and New Brunswick faced real threats of Fenian attacks in the spring of 1866, the British government took advan-

Left: In May 1870 the 400 Fenians who crossed into Quebec from New York state were repulsed at Trout River by British and Canadian troops. Above: Troops were stationed at a camp in the Niagara region to oppose Fenian raids.

tage of this situation and of the passing by the New Brunswick Assembly of a resolution favouring confederation to order Lieutenant-Governor Gordon to dismiss Smith's government and reinstate Tilley as premier. This action contravened the principle and practice of responsible government, but the massing of Fenian forces along New Brunswick's border one week later seemed to justify the imperial government's unusual measure. The expected Fenian invasion also provided the necessary incentive for the Nova Scotia legislature to accept Tupper's long delayed and vaguely worded motion in favour of colonial union.

By the summer of 1866 it was clear that the two island colonies were unlikely to join any confederation, yet there was still no agreement by the other colonies to the Seventy-Two Resolutions. The urgent need for action was reinforced by two Fenian invasions of Canada in the first week of June. One body entered Canada West at Fort Erie and defeated the Canadian militia at nearby Ridgeway before retiring to the United States; the second seized Pigeon Hill in the Eastern Townships south of Montreal but dispersed soon after plundering the neighbourhood. In New Brunswick the sequel to Gordon's political intervention was a provincial election in which Tilley and the pro-confederates won 33 of 41 seats, thanks in part to generous donations of money from the Canadian government. Yet this election victory and Tupper's resolution in Nova Scotia were small consolation for the loss of a whole year in achieving confederation.

In Canada George Brown resigned from the Great Coalition over personal differences with Macdonald, and in Britain the pro-confederation Liberal government of Lord John Russell was replaced by the Conservatives under Lord Derby, with Lord Carnarvon assuming the post of Colonial Secretary. Anxious to bring the confederation question to a head, New Brunswick and Nova Scotia sent delegations to London in the summer of 1866, where Lord Carnarvon assured them that the new government was equally anxious to promote confederation. But no Canadian delegation arrived, because the Canadian legislature was debating the Quebec Resolutions. This session, the last in the quarter-century history of the united parliament, ended early in August and almost at once a new Fenian scare caused Governor General Lord Monck to send an urgent plea over the newly opened trans-Atlantic cable for more British troops. At last in November Macdonald, Cartier, McDougall, Langevin, and Howland sailed to join Tilley, Tupper, and the other New Brunswick and Nova Scotia delegates in England.

Confederation Achieved

The delegates from Canada, Nova Scotia, and New Brunswick met in London's Westminster Palace Hotel at the beginning of December 1866 to put their confederation proposals in final form. Despite the fact that the Seventy-Two Resolutions had been adopted by Canada alone, they were used as the basis of the new federal constitution. Only two changes were made: provision for adding members to the federal upper house if it were deadlocked with the House of Commons, and provision for appeals to the federal government against any provincial law damaging to minority educational rights. When these London resolutions were in turn discussed with the Colonial Office, the title "Kingdom of Canada" was altered to "Dominion", partly to sidestep American anti-British feeling, and then the whole scheme was presented to the imperial parliament in February 1867. On 29 March the British North America Act became law, establishing the federal constitution of Canada with four provinces – New Brunswick, Nova Scotia, and Ontario and Quebec (the former colonies of Upper and Lower Canada). The structure planned at Quebec more than two years earlier had been so solidly built that even the personal intervention of that outspoken anti-confederate, Joseph Howe, at the Colonial Office had failed to change the basic principles of Canadian federation.

On 1 July 1867 the Dominion of Canada was born amid church services, pageantry, parades, picnics, peals of bells, and firework displays throughout its four provinces. In the Maritimes anti-confederation feeling showed itself briefly as a few houses were decorated with black crepe and the Halifax *Chronicle* printed a black-edged announcement:

> Died! Last night at twelve o'clock, the free and enlightened province of Nova Scotia.

But such gloomy expressions were the exception as the citizens of the new dominion, more than three million strong, joined from Sydney to Sault Ste. Marie in celebrating the birth of a new nation. Two days earlier the first

Shall we go to
Washington first, or
How(e)?

*In Nova Scotia Dr. Charles
Tupper had strongly advocated
Confederation and had led his
province into the Union – Joseph
Howe fiercely opposed the
measure and tried to get Nova
Scotia out of the Dominion even
after 1867. In this cartoon of
November 1868 Nova Scotia is
presented with a choice, but the
artist has clearly included his
own bias towards Ottawa.*

government of the new federation had been sworn into office with John A.
Macdonald, recently knighted by the Queen, as its first prime minister.

The preamble to the British North America Act describes the Canadian
constitution as "similar in principle to that of the United Kingdom". Loyal
to their British heritage, the Fathers of Confederation accepted much of
the unwritten constitutional customs of the mother country as their own.
In one respect, however, the Act departed from previous imperial practice: it created a federation. Because the British North America Act is a
statute of the imperial parliament, only that parliament has the right to
change its terms, and until 1949 the Judicial Committee of the Privy
Council was responsible for interpreting those terms. Except for the practice of responsible government and the right to set its own tariffs, the new
federation possessed in fact virtually the same power as the old colonies
had in 1840. Yet if Canada in 1867 was legally little more than a super-
colony, it was nevertheless understood in both Canada and Britain that the
full powers of a sovereign state – power to make war, peace, and treaties –
could be granted to Canada in the years to come. For the moment, however, Canada neither needed nor wanted these powers and responsibilities.

The new federal constitution provided for a Canadian parliament composed of the representative of the Crown, a Senate of regional (not provincial) members appointed for life, and a House of Commons (originally
with 181 members) elected on the principle of "rep by pop". Further,
since the cabinet or executive acting in the name of the Crown has only a
customary basis in British constitutional law, cabinet ministers were made
part of a larger and formal body called the Privy Council. The House of
Commons and the Privy Council were modelled on British practice,
whereas the Canadian Senate resembled its American namesake more
than it did the British House of Lords. Like the American Senate, the
Canadian one was intended to meet the problem of giving representation
to vast and diversified regions. Like its British model, much of Canada's

constitution remains unwritten or customary, but the written part – the British North America Act – has suffered from inflexibility because written constitutions become out-of-date and are usually difficult to change. The Fathers of Confederation did not and could not foresee the problems that would arise in federal-provincial relations over such matters as education, health, and the mass media of communications.

Unlike the American constitution, the British North America Act did not include a Bill of Rights or provision for election of judges or separation of legislative and executive power. In these matters the Act was traditionally British. In the adoption of the federal principle the Dominion of Canada did copy the American practice but with one important difference. The recent American civil war had emphasized the danger of giving too much power to the individual states, and it was the stated and well understood intention in 1867 that the provinces of the new dominion would be subordinate to the federal government. The provinces did not create confederation (Ontario and Quebec did not in fact exist before confederation) – confederation was an act of the imperial parliament and not a compact or agreement formed by independent states. The legislatures of the provinces were very like the old colonial Assemblies with their cabinets and responsible government, but now the federal government formed a new level of power between them and the mother country.

"Fathers of Confederation" by Robert Harris (1849-1919). The windows in the background were, in fact, all the same size, but the artist enlarged one of them to focus attention on the central figure. Painted in 1884 and reproduced many times, the original was destroyed in the fire that burned down the Parliament Buildings at Ottawa in 1916.

To ensure that the states' rights issue would not arise in Canada, Section 92 of the British North America Act spelled out precisely the powers of the provinces. Section 91 defined the powers of the central government and then went on to give it all unspecified powers under the "peace, order, and good government" clause. The federal government got all the powers needed by a national government to promote national interests – control of money, banking, trade, commerce, fishing, shipping, defence, criminal justice, and, most important, "the raising of money by any mode or system of taxation". The federal government could also appoint lieutenant-governors, disallow provincial laws, appoint senior judges, and create federal courts – all of these provisions further restricted provincial power. Only in one area that might have been considered a national concern – education – did Canadian experience dictate that provincial control be established. In 1867 the intentions of the Fathers of Confederation regarding the nature of Canadian federalism were quite clear.

HISTORY FROM THE SOURCES

Regional Views of Confederation, 1865

The confederation of British North America was an attempt to weld together colonies with different historic traditions, diverse economic interests, and strong local loyalties. At its birth Confederation was hailed by some as the beginning of "a new nationality" and the dawn of "our new destiny"; but others denounced it as "a mess of pottage" and "an outrage". Why did Newfoundland and Prince Edward Island remain outside the new federal union and why did strong opposition to Confederation appear in the other colonies? What issues and ideals motivated these regional reactions for and against Confederation?

Only in the province of Canada did the Quebec Resolutions receive a thorough scrutiny by a colonial parliament. The Canadian Confederation debates fill 1,032 double-columned pages. From this mass of material the most important statements by the most important Canadian "Fathers" – Macdonald, Brown, Cartier, and McGee – have been frequently reprinted, but the best defence of Confederation was made by Premier Sir Etienne Taché in the Legislative Council. "Let every man in Canada who has a doubt about Confederation read this unanswerable speech," commented the Quebec Morning Chronicle.

I stated that the province stood in a twofold danger – of being dragged violently into the American Union, and, in the next place, as we stood on an inclined plane of slipping down gradually, and without our being aware of it, into the vortex below. It seems to me that the thing was plain enough. . . .

. . . We are, in our present position, small, isolated bodies, and it may probably be with us, as in the physical world, where a large body attracts to itself the smaller bodies within the sphere of its influence. If we do not make those alliances with the Lower Provinces – if we do not open with them those communications, political, social, and commercial, which are essential for our own interest, we shall little by little lose some of those principles we now esteem so much; we shall lose little by little our attachment to the Mother Country and the interesting reminiscences which with many of us, now give intensity to that attachment; and we shall become – you may depend upon it hon. gentlemen – more democratised before we are aware of it. . . .

. . . An honorable gentleman has stated that I expressed myself to the effect that, if this Confederation did not take place, Canada could not become prosperous. I never said anything of the kind. I said expressly the contrary. Perhaps I may not precisely apprehend the meaning of the word "prosperous." But I said this, that Canada had within itself all the means to become populous, to become wealthy, to become a great people. But on the other hand I said that Canada and the other British American Provinces, without union, could not become a "powerful," as distinguished from a prosperous people. I said that we in Canada could not become a powerful people unless we had some maritime elements, unless we had the means, by having harbors and ports of our own open at all seasons, of communicating freely with all the nations of the world. . . .

The honorable Knight showed how responsible government protected the French Catholics in Lower Canada under Confederation, saying that if ever an act of flagrant injustice was to be attempted in the Federal Government, the whole of the Lower Canadians would join as one man, and by uniting with the minority against the Government – because honorable gentlemen must know that there always will be minorities – by means of thus strengthening the minority any Administration could be cleared out of their places in twenty-four hours. My honorable friend stated this, and he stated it justly; he said so, well aware of what he was saying. But the honorable gentleman from DeLormier comes forward and says: "Don't you recollect that at one time the Upper Canadians, with the minority from Lower Canada, united to impose upon Lower Canada their will?" I tell you, honorable gentlemen, that they never did harm to Lower Canada, and that they never could do harm to Lower Canada had they so chosen. And why? The French had the use of their own language conceded to them in order to bring them to support the Government, and much more would have been done to accomplish the same end.

Parliamentary Debates on the Subject of Confederation of the
British North American Provinces (Quebec, 1865),
pp. 342, 343, 345.

Joseph F. Perrault, a parti rouge member in the Canadian Assembly, voiced French Canada's fears of the Confederation scheme in the course of a five-hour speech, the second longest made during the Confederation debates.

. . . But will the object proposed be attained? Shall we be stronger under Confederation than we are now? Cannot the Governor General of the Provinces of British North America raise troops throughout the whole extent of the provinces placed under his jurisdiction? Is not the militia of all those provinces under his immediate command? We are told, Mr. Speaker, that Confederation will give us a more uniform military organization than that which we now possess. But there is nothing to prevent the formation of that organization under the present Constitution, and I have no hesitation in saying that under that Constitution the several provinces will defend themselves to better advantage than under Confederation. Is it not precisely by creating here a military power, hostile to the adjoining powerful republic, that we shall bring on war and its attendant calamities? . . .

. . . It was only through the heroic resistance and a happy combination of circumstances that we succeeded in obtaining the political rights which are secured to us by the present Constitution. The scheme of Confederation has no other object than to deprive us of the most precious of these rights, by substituting for them a political organization which is eminently hostile to us. The hostility of the scheme of Confederation being admitted I maintain that its adoption will entail the most disastrous consequences. To impose upon the French-Canadians this new Constitution, which they do not want, is to tempt their anger and to expose ourselves to deplorable collisions.

... I say further, that those who vote for the scheme of Confederation take the shortest way to lead us into annexation to the United States. I am not the first to express this opinion; several hon. members from Upper Canada have expressed it before me within the precincts of this House, and it is because those members from Upper Canada desire annexation to the United States that they vote in favor of the scheme of Confederation. The hon. members from the west, whose words are so loyal, will be the first to pass over to the enemy with arms and baggage, should an invading army ever appear on the frontier.

Parliamentary Debates on the Subject of Confederation of the
British North American Provinces (Quebec, 1865),
pp. 621, 626.

Joseph Howe was probably the most able and the most vocal anti-Confederationist in any of the British North American provinces. His famous "Botheration Letters", published anonymously as editorials in the Halifax Morning Chronicle during the winter of 1865, convinced many Maritimers that Confederation was merely a Canadian scheme which promised nothing but disadvantages and degradations to the other colonies. In an effort to influence British government policy, Howe wrote privately to his acquaintance, Foreign Secretary Lord John Russell (who had become Earl Russell in 1861), itemizing his objections to the Quebec Resolutions.

1. That, by adopting the principle of Representation by population, the Maritime Provinces will be forever swamped by the Canadians.
2. That, if the Canadas, always in trouble of some sort, and two or three times in open rebellion, should repeat such eccentricities, we should be compromised, and our connexion with the Mother Country endangered.
3. Because the plan of double Legislatures, tried in Scotland and Ireland and swept away, is cumberous and expensive, and cannot be carried out without raising our ad valorem duty, which is now only 10 percent to 20.
4. That, when we raise our duties to this point, for the benefit of 3,000,000 of Canadians, we burthen our trade with the Mother Country and with our British brethren in 50 other Colonies scattered all over the world.
5. That when the Tariff is thus raised but £250,000 currency will be left for defence, a sum utterly inadequate, for any such purpose

while nothing is gained by weakening the unity of command and control now possessed by Her Majesty's Government.

Howe to Russell, 19 January 1865
Joseph Howe Papers, Public Archives of Canada, M.G. 24,
B 29, Vol. 8, pp. 575-7.

Three of Prince Edward Island's seven delegates to the Quebec Conference publicly opposed the Confederation scheme soon after their return home. In their opinion Confederation offered no advantages, political or economic, to their island. The following resolution, passed at the last of several public meetings in Charlottetown, reflects the Island's sense of separation from its sister colonies and lists the reasons for the Island's ultimate rejection of Confederation in May 1866.

Resolved, That this meeting – having heard a very full and able discussion on the question of the proposed Confederation of the British North America Provinces – though of opinion that a Union might be consummated on principles and terms adapted to this Colony – dissimilar as it is to the neighboring Provinces from its insular position, the entire interruption of its navigation during five months of the year, and other circumstances, such as the granting away of its lands in large tracts to non-residents by the Crown, yet decidedly object to the details of the scheme agreed upon by the Quebec Conference, especially those in reference to finance and representation, as most injurious, unjust, and illiberal to a people so situated and confidently relies that the said details will by no means receive the sanction of the Legislature or Government of this Island.

The Islander (Charlottetown), 17 February 1865

To Ambrose Shea, Newfoundland's leading delegate at the Quebec Conference, Confederation seemed to be the opportunity to break through the typical pettiness of colonial politics.

We do not apprehend any very serious difficulty in the passage of the Scheme in our Legislature, but it is not wise to be over Confident and we shall endeavour to be ready for what may possibly arise. Some of our Mercantile Men fear a large amount of increased taxation and as this is a point on which it is easy to alarm the masses every where, I wish to be clear in meeting the objections that may be raised & hence the request I make for the returns I have named [?].

. . . With us in this Colony the question will break up our local parties and if even for no other reason I should hail its introduction on this account. In these small Provinces we have no really different interests to form legitimate causes of separation & grounds of party action & the disputes necessarily become sectarian & personal and engender a very low state of public feeling. . . .

* * * * *

This Confederation business costs me the Enjoyment of a Winter in Cuba . . .

A. Shea to A. T. Galt, 15 December 1864
Galt Papers, Public Archives of Canada, R.G. 19,
IV, A 1, Vol. 4, Pt. 1, No. 799.

FURTHER READING

Morton, W. L., *The Critical Years: The Union of British North America 1857-1873* (Toronto: McClelland & Stewart, 1964). The most recent scholarly study of the era of Confederation.

Creighton, D. G., *The Road to Confederation* (Toronto: Macmillan, 1964). A modern appraisal of the complex Confederation movement.

Waite, P. B., *The Life and Times of Confederation* (Toronto: University of Toronto Press, 1963)★. The Confederation movement as viewed by contemporary newspapers.

Winks, Robin, *Canada and the United States: The Civil War Years* (Baltimore: Johns Hopkins, 1960). The role of the United States in the Confederation movement.

Cornell, P. G., *The Great Coalition* (Canadian Historical Association Booklet No. 19, 1966)★. A brief analysis of the Brown-Macdonald government.

Waite, P. B., *The Charlottetown Conference* (Canadian Historical Association Booklet No. 15, 1963)★. A succinct reconstruction of the events of that famous meeting.

Whitelaw, W. M., *The Quebec Conference* (Canadian Historical Association Booklet No. 20, 1966)★. A short account of the meeting which formulated the 72 Resolutions.

Waite, P. B., ed. *The Confederation Debates* (Toronto: McClelland & Stewart, 1963)★. An abridgement of the debates of the Canadian parliament on the 72 Resolutions.

Beck, J. M., ed. *Joseph Howe: The Voice of Nova Scotia* (Toronto: McClelland & Stewart, 1964)★. Part 4 contains Howe's statements against Confederation.

Careless, J. M. S., *Brown of The Globe*, Vol. 2 (Toronto: Macmillan, 1963)★. Covers Brown's role in achieving Confederation.

Creighton, D. G., *John A. Macdonald:* Vol. I, *The Young Politician* (Toronto: Macmillan, 1952)★. Final chapters describe Macdonald's contribution to Confederation.

16

One Dominion

Canada's First Prime Minister

Because Macdonald had been the leading architect of Confederation, it was natural that he should be called upon to form the Dominion's first government. With careful attention to the interests of various regions, of French and English, of the different religious persuasions, and of the political groups that had joined to make Confederation possible, he chose a cabinet that included both Maritimers and central Canadians, Roman Catholics and Protestants, Conservatives and Reformers, and ten Fathers of Confederation. The first senators were also chosen according to all the varied interests within the new nation. When the first general election was held that autumn, Macdonald's coalition won no less than 100 of the 181 seats – the simple fact was that for the present, old party lines were blurred and no effective organized opposition existed within the new parliament.

The old Reform party of the Province of Canada had lost its leader when George Brown suffered defeat in that first election. Alexander Mackenzie and young Edward Blake, both from Ontario, now spoke for the Reformers – but their party could find little to criticize in the Confederation that they had helped to create. The only vital source of opposition was in Nova Scotia, where Joseph Howe was leading the "anti-Confederationists" in demanding repeal of the British North America Act. The "antis" had won every Nova Scotia seat in the recent election except that held by Dr. Tupper, and Howe was personally appealing to the imperial government for an end to Confederation. Sir John A. Macdonald (he had been knighted on Dominion Day along with Cartier, Galt, Tilley, Tupper, McDougall, and Howland) countered Howe's challenge by repeating his government's promise to complete the intercolonial railway that Maritimers wanted so badly. When Howe's plea for repeal was rejected by the imperial government in 1868, he demanded instead a more generous financial settlement for Nova Scotia within Confederation. Such "better terms" were something that Macdonald could and did arrange, by giving an annual subsidy to the province and by reducing its debt, although the "better terms" were not offered to the other three provinces. At the same time that this agreement destroyed the economic arguments of the "antis" in 1869, Macdonald completed his victory by persuading Howe himself to join the federal cabinet.

Sir John A. Macdonald's persuasive personality and dynamic policies dominated the first twenty-five years in the life of Confederation. The influence of the "old chieftain" – prime minister for all but five of those years – on Canada's development was so great that the whole period has been properly called "The Age of Macdonald". Better than any other man, "John A." (as he was affectionately known) understood Canadian hopes for building a new nation and he offered practical policies towards that goal. For all his faults and personal weaknesses, Macdonald could win political support because he understood Canada and his fellow Canadians.

When the citizens of Canada celebrated the birth of a new nationality on that first Dominion Day with parades, picnics, and pyrotechnics, Macdonald knew that the task of nation building was only beginning. Three British North American colonies had been merged by imperial statute into a "super colony" with four provinces – the Dominion of Canada – but the new dominion had barely started its evolution to independence. Macdonald, however, was not concerned with independence for Canada; he knew the political, economic, and military value of the British connection.

In 1867 Canada was far from complete in terms of territory. Prince Edward Island and Newfoundland had both rejected Confederation because of strong local loyalties; Rupert's Land and the Northwest were still the private preserve of the Hudson's Bay Company, and on the Pacific coast the two underpopulated colonies of Vancouver Island and British Columbia had just been united under a single government. It was Macdonald's self-appointed task to complete Confederation by joining these vast territories on the east, north, and west to the new Dominion, particularly the great Northwest, before American migration could occupy

A shipyard near Murray Harbour, in southwest Prince Edward Island, during the shipbuilding boom of the 1870's.

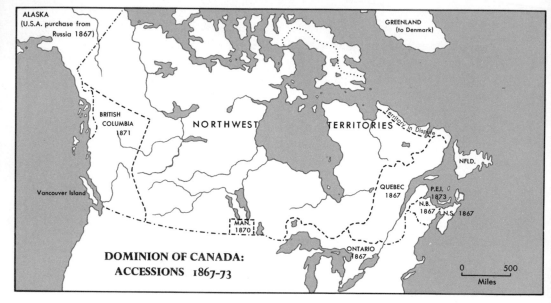

ALASKA
(U.S.A. purchase from
Russia 1867)

GREENLAND
(to Denmark)

BRITISH
COLUMBIA
1871

NORTHWEST

TERRITORIES

Territory in Dispute

NFLD.

Vancouver Island

QUEBEC
1867

P.E.I.
1873

N.B.
1867

N.S. 1867

MAN.
1870

ONTARIO
1867

DOMINION OF CANADA:
ACCESSIONS 1867-73

0   500
Miles

that area as it had the Oregon Territory. In seven short years that task
had been completed, except that Newfoundland did not join Confederation
until 1949. The area of the Dominion was expanded by the addition of
the Northwest in 1870, of British Columbia in 1871, and of Prince
Edward Island in 1873.

Confederation Reaches the Pacific

A decade before Confederation the Clear Grits had awakened Canadian
interest in the prairie lands by pointing to their economic potential, but
negotiations by the Province of Canada to buy the Northwest had stalled
before 1865. In December 1867 Macdonald's government revived the
purchase scheme, and in the following July the imperial parliament passed
the Rupert's Land Act permitting such a sale. Several months later
Canada and the Hudson's Bay Company arranged the final terms: the
company would keep its fur trade monopoly and posts, plus one-twentieth
of the fertile lands, and Canada would take possession of the Northwest
on 1 December 1869, after paying $1.5 million.

William McDougall, the former Clear Grit who had acted as Canada's
agent, was appointed first lieutenant-governor of the Northwest. Late
in October 1869, as he approached Pembina from Minnesota, a self-
appointed "National Committee of the Métis of the Red River" ordered
him to stay out of the Northwest. The committee's secretary was Louis
Riel, a Métis – one of mixed European and Indian blood. Some Métis
farmed in the Red River area, but all of them depended on buffalo hunting
for their very existence. Confederation threatened to open the west to

A woodcut entitled "Murder of Scott at Fort Garry". Riel made an example of Scott to intimidate those who opposed the Provincial Government. Nearly 200 people witnessed the execution. When the first volley by the firing squad failed to kill Scott, one of the squad finished the job with a pistol.

English-speaking settlers, who would drive away the buffalo and destroy the Métis' way of life. Neither the Hudson's Bay Company nor the Canadian government had informed the Métis of their plans, and the Métis were disturbed by the pro-Confederation activities of a small "Canadian" party led by Dr. Christian Schultz at the settlement and by the arrival of Canadian surveyors. The uncxplained movements of the surveyors seemed to challenge the "squatters' rights", the only title that 90 per cent of the Métis had to their lands.

The bearded and eloquent Louis Riel, just twenty-five years of age, a natural leader of the Métis, had been sent to Montreal by Bishop Taché, to train for the priesthood. Unsuited to the religious life because of emotional instability, he returned to the Red River with more education than his fellow Métis and with a burning ambition to defend their lands and way of life. Riel shortly after became president of the "National Committee". A Métis List of Rights was despatched to Ottawa, and a "Provisional Government" of Manitoba was created with Riel as president. Undoubtedly he had the support of the Métis and of many settlers on the Red River who shared his fear of the influence of the local "Canadian" party. Largely to intimidate that party, Riel seized several of its members and shot one, Thomas Scott, an Orangeman from Ontario, for supposed disorderly conduct and insubordination. Scott was reputed to be a troublesome person, but by killing him Riel had taken the law into his own hands as he admitted, "to make Canada respect us".

Below: A group of Métis at Maple Creek, Saskatchewan, in 1884. Right: Red River carts, 1889. These carts, built entirely of wood, were used in the Red River area to bring in meat from the buffalo hunt and to carry goods.

The execution of Scott provoked anything but respect for Riel's self-appointed government. The people of Ontario demanded revenge for this act, which Macdonald described as a "barbarous murder". The fact that Scott had been an English Protestant and that Riel was a French-speaking Roman Catholic revived the "racial" and religious hatreds that had cursed the old Province of Canada. Regardless of what Macdonald wanted to do in the name of justice, he was faced with the certainty that either Ontario or Quebec would be angered; therefore he delayed acting against the Métis as long as he could. But the fact remained that Manitoba was in revolt, despite a verbal promise of amnesty to the rebels, and so a mixed force of Canadian Militia and British regulars under Sir Garnet Wolseley struggled westward in the summer of 1870 through the forests and lakes of the Rainy Lake region to restore order. When the soldiers finally reached Fort Garry (the future site of Winnipeg) in the last week of August, Riel and his supporters had fled, putting an end to the Red River uprising of 1869-70. Most of the Métis "List of Rights" was written into the Manitoba Act of 1870: French and English were made official languages, local customs were to be protected, Indian treaties were promised, and subsidies were given to the new province. But the basic causes of the revolt remained unresolved and would again be a challenge to Macdonald and Canada.

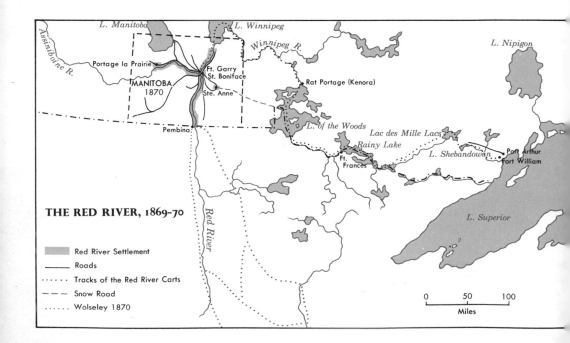

THE RED RIVER, 1869-70

Red River Settlement
Roads
Tracks of the Red River Carts
Snow Road
Wolseley 1870

0   50   100
Miles

Far to the west of Riel and the Red River, the settlers of British Columbia had watched the achievement of Confederation with mixed feelings. A minority were Americans who had arrived in the gold rushes of the late 1850's and who naturally hoped to see British Columbia annexed to the United States. In 1867 the United States bought Alaska from Russia, and the acquisition of the rest of the Pacific coast would, as American politicians intended, eventually bring all British North America into the American Union. Other people, mostly government and Hudson's Bay Company employees, wanted British Columbia to remain a Crown colony, but the largest group believed that the colony's only hope of remaining British lay in joining the Canadian Confederation.

In 1869 the Colonial Office sent Anthony Musgrave to British Columbia as governor to promote Confederation, and when the colony's legislature met in 1870 it passed a resolution in favour of union with Canada. There were, however, certain conditions attached to this offer: British Columbia must be linked to the east by a railway, and Canada must absorb the colony's heavy debt and provide capital for the development of its communications. Macdonald was anxious to complete Confederation from sea to sea, and if the demand for a transcontinental railway within ten years seemed unrealistic, that did not prevent the Canadian government from accepting the high price in order to obtain the Pacific coast and a sixth province for the Dominion. Despite protests from the Reform Opposition at Ottawa that these arrangements placed too heavy a burden on the young country, British Columbia entered Confederation on 20 July 1871.

The mere legal accession of the Northwest and British Columbia to Confederation was not enough – they must be physically and economically joined to their sister provinces if Canada were to grow into a strong nation. The railway linking east and west was an absolute necessity but, equally important, Canada required a blueprint for her economic development. Yet before such plans could mature, Canada needed a settlement of

The Wolseley expedition to the Red River in 1870 portaging below the Kakabeka Falls, eighteen miles west of Fort William. The engraving, from a drawing by William Armstrong (1823-1914), was published in "The Canadian Illustrated News" in October 1871.

Anglo-American differences to end those very tensions that had played so important a part in creating Confederation and thereby to ensure Canada's security in North America.

The Treaty of Washington and the Pacific Scandal

When the United States cancelled the Reciprocity Treaty in 1866, American fishermen lost the right to visit Canada's Atlantic coast fishing grounds, but Americans were in fact permitted to fish there until 1870 if licensed by the Canadian government. Macdonald hoped to use the fisheries as a bargaining point to renew reciprocity and to get compensation for the damages caused by the Fenian raiders who had invaded Fort Erie in 1866. The United States, however, was no longer interested in reciprocity and denied any responsibility for Fenian activities. But it was interested in the fisheries and even more in a negotiated settlement of its differences with Great Britain, such as the havoc wrought on Union shipping during the Civil War by the British-built *Alabama*. For its part W. E. Gladstone's government in Britain was anxious to restore friendly relations with the United States at any reasonable cost.

Under these circumstances the two great powers had no difficulty in agreeing to a joint commission to settle their problems. The appointment of Macdonald as one of the five British commissioners appeared at first sight to be an honour for Canada, but in fact he was thus placed in a potentially awkward position. As a British Commissioner he might have to support a settlement that damaged Canada's interests – and he was Canada's prime minister! When the commission met in Washington in the spring of 1871, Macdonald discovered that his British and American colleagues expected Canada to sell permanent fishing rights to the United States, although those fisheries were his best bargaining point for payment

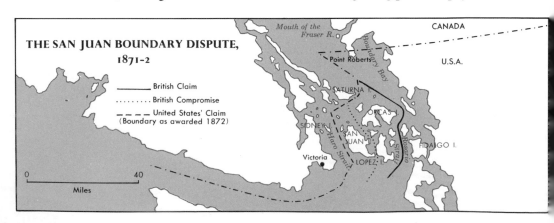

THE SAN JUAN BOUNDARY DISPUTE, 1871-2

——————— British Claim
· · · · · · · · British Compromise
— — — — United States' Claim
(Boundary as awarded 1872)

The British High
Commissioners (with their
secretary, back row at left)
meeting in Washington, 1871.
Sir John A. Macdonald,
standing with arms folded,
was resented by at least two
of his fellow commissioners
for being a colonial, and the
American commissioners
could not understand why
Macdonald was included in a
British Commission.

of Fenian damage claims and for reciprocity. The United States would go no further towards reciprocity than to offer free trade in salt, firewood, coal, and salted fish – an insulting offer that Macdonald flatly rejected.

Gladstone's government was so anxious to obtain a settlement that it next proposed to accept any arrangements if Canada's parliament would approve the parts affecting Canada's interests. Macdonald was now confronted with the dilemma of accepting the unacceptable as a commissioner, or of quitting the commission and leaving Canada without a voice in the settlement. A further American offer to include reciprocity in lumber was rejected by Macdonald and his cabinet. The final American offer, to buy fishery rights for ten years and permit free entry of Canadian fish into the United States market, was the best that Macdonald could get, and one that the British government considered entirely reasonable. To sweeten this unpleasant medicine the British government agreed to pay compensation for the Fenian depredations, since the United States had refused to discuss the issue.

By the terms of the treaty the United States bought access to the rich Canadian fisheries (the price to be settled by arbitration), and the disputed San Juan boundary was referred to arbitration. Canada got access to the inferior American fisheries and, in exchange for giving the Americans navigation rights on the St. Lawrence, obtained rights on Lake Michigan. Canada received fewer concessions than she had hoped for, and Macdonald knew only too well that the treaty would give the Opposition in parliament its first real opportunity to play on Canadian national pride. To weaken the Opposition attack, Macdonald avoided calling parliament for as long as possible. When parliament did meet in 1872, the government diverted some public attention from the treaty by passing a free homesteads bill (the Dominion Lands Act) for the west and an act legalizing trade union strikes. Also, the government had succeeded in winning Prince Edward Island to Confederation, thanks to a generous financial offer which solved that colony's heavy railway debts. As expected, the Opposition was bitter about the loss of the fisheries, but Macdonald's

Petrolia, Ontario, named in honour of the discovery of rock oil, was renowned as the first "oil capital" of Canada. Left: "The Oil Wells of Mr. John D. Noble at Petrolia", from "The Canadian Illustrated News" (1871). Above: Petrolia in 1874.

measures gained him enough popular support to win the general election that followed in 1872.

The Conservative government had weathered a major crisis over the Treaty of Washington, and with a margin of 6 seats in parliament could look forward to Macdonald's next step in nation building – the construction of the promised railway to the Pacific. Before the election of 1872 two rival groups had been formed in the hope of getting the valuable contract. Macdonald's friend, D. L. Macpherson, headed the Toronto-based Interoceanic Railway Company; Sir Hugh Allan, the Montreal shipping magnate, led the rival Canadian Pacific Railway Company that was backed by American capitalists. Macdonald preferred to have the railway built with Canadian money, but he knew that Allan was the more experienced businessman. Macdonald was vaguely disturbed to learn that Allan had given more than $150,000 to the Conservatives' election fund, including $85,000 to Sir George Cartier, on the understanding that Allan would be made president of the Canadian Pacific syndicate.

Conscious of his party's heavy commitment to Sir Hugh Allan, Macdonald managed to arrange a merger of the two companies soon after the election. In the meantime, however, incriminating documents had been stolen from Sir Hugh's office and turned over to the parliamentary Opposition. In April 1873, a Liberal (Reform) member charged in the House of Commons that the CPR had bribed the Macdonald government to get the railway contract. At first Macdonald was unconcerned by the charges, but as public skepticism increased, he decided to answer his accusers by

Sir John A. Macdonald and Lady Macdonald on the new CPR in the 1880's near Fort William.

appointing a Royal Commission to investigate. Even before the commission began its work, however, Sir George Cartier died and more incriminating documents concerning Allan's gift of election funds to Macdonald were released. Distrust of the Conservative government's honesty spread abroad and, as a result, Allan was unable to raise money in England, the main source for borrowing capital for his railway.

The commission's investigations showed that Sir John had personally acted quite properly in his relations with Sir Hugh Allan, but that the dead Cartier had foolishly damaged his party by his desperate promises to Sir Hugh regarding a railway charter. Macdonald believed that the Pacific Scandal was now closed and that his government had been saved from the worst consequences of Cartier's mistake. But he was wrong – in the parliamentary session that opened late in 1873 his own party members began to desert him one by one. As the government's majority dwindled on successive votes, Macdonald resolved not to wait for certain defeat. He would resign at once and let the Liberals try their hand at governing Canada.

The Liberal Interlude

The new Liberal government led by Alexander Mackenzie took office in November 1873 and immediately called a general election for January. The voters showed their dissatisfaction over the Pacific Scandal by giving the Liberals 133 seats to the Conservatives' 73. The faith of Canadians in Mackenzie's honesty was not misplaced, but events were soon to show that honesty alone could not solve Canada's problems. Even as the Liberal government was assuming office, the effects of a world-wide depression struck Canada. As prices fell and unemployment spread, it became obvious that the new government had no adequate policies to cope with the crisis. Perhaps Sir John and the Conservatives would have been no more successful than Mackenzie and the Liberals in attempting to solve a prob-

MISS CANADA'S SCHOOL

Miss Canada (to the boy at the head): "Now Alexander, be very careful, or I'll put you where John is!"

n this "Grip" magazine cartoon of 873 the new premier, Alexander Mackenzie, is warned that he will nd himself wearing a dunce's cap ke Macdonald if he gets into rapes like the Pacific Scandal. The members of parliament in the class" include Louis Riel (fifth om right).

lem whose causes lay outside Canada. But Sir John was no longer Prime
Minister, and so it was on Mackenzie and his ineffective government that
popular discontent centred.

Despite its large parliamentary majority the Liberal government was
not strong. Mackenzie lacked the firmness of a real leader. The Liberals
were largely an Ontario party, and with two exceptions the cabinet members seemed to deserve the nickname "Incapables" that the Opposition
gave them. Those exceptions were Sir Richard Cartwright, the energetic
Minister of Finance whose free-trade instincts seemed out of place in a
time of recession, and Edward Blake, whose legal abilities far overshadowed Mackenzie's modest talents. When Blake quit the cabinet early
in 1873, dissension within the Liberal party soon reached such heights
that Mackenzie invited him to return as co-leader. These internal troubles
were enough to sap the government's will, but the opposition of the
Roman Catholic church in Quebec to the Liberal party completed its
frustration.

Since the 1850's, when Pope Pius IX began his holy war against
materialism, anticlericalism, nationalism, and liberalism in Europe, a considerable part of the Quebec Roman Catholic clergy had increasingly
denounced the *parti rouge* – Quebec's branch of the Liberal party – as a
threat to religion. The Liberal party's denial of any hostility to religion
was rejected out of hand by the more extreme Ultramontanes (the pro-
papal group). Pope Pius's *Syllabus of Errors* of 1864 was the inspiration
for the "Catholic Programme" in which some of the Quebec bishops
called on Roman Catholics to support the Conservatives. Political pro-
nouncements and activities of parish priests at elections were approved
and defended by a pastoral letter of these bishops in 1875. The following year the full impact of Ultramontane-Conservative alliance was felt
by the Liberal government when it lost seats in Quebec by-elections.

The government's lack of effective leadership and its dependence for
support on its provincial party organizations became painfully evident
when it tried to find economic policies that would meet the differing regional needs of Canada in the midst of the deep depression. Traditionally
the Liberals stood for free trade and minimum governmental expenditure.
But Canadian manufacturers were clamouring for tariff protection, and
any reduction of public spending would only increase unemployment.
Anxious to save money and reduce the growing deficit in its budget,
Mackenzie's cabinet resolved to delay Macdonald's transcontinental railway project. British Columbia insisted that the railway had been part of
the terms of that province's entry into Confederation, but the Liberal
government refused to be bound by what it considered Macdonald's over-
generous nation-building commitments. Even the governor general's in-

sistence that Mackenzie fulfil the promise to British Columbia proved in the end to be fruitless. In place of a railway the government would provide $1.5 million each year for the construction of a carriage road westward and a railway from Nanaimo to Esquimalt. Mackenzie remained adamant that his piecemeal policy was the best that could be done in the face of the economic difficulties, but British Columbia rejected his plan and the Senate blocked the proposed Nanaimo-Esquimalt railway.

This abortive scheme to cut costs by delaying railway construction was not, however, as important as the Liberals' hope to get at the heart of Canada's economic problem by renewing the reciprocity treaty with the United States. Freer trade had always been part of the Liberals' creed, and now the depression added an element of urgency. Undeterred by Macdonald's failure to obtain reciprocity in 1870, the Mackenzie government sent George Brown, now a Liberal senator, to the American capital in search of the same elusive quarry. Their most cherished hopes seemed to come true when Brown returned with an American agreement to renew and even to expand the arrangements of 1854 in exchange for a Canadian promise to enlarge the country's canals and abandon claims to compensation for the fisheries. Unfortunately for the Liberals, and perhaps for Canada, the United States Senate rejected this treaty after it had been signed by the American administration.

The anticipation of reciprocity with the United States had heartened the Liberals, but it had also deeply upset Canadian manufacturers who would have faced strong American competition if the Treaty of Washington had in fact been ratified. Perhaps to allay these fears – and certainly against all its past professions of economic policy – the government determined in 1874 to increase the tariff rates that Macdonald had established. The Conservatives were overjoyed by this unexpected chance to accuse the embarrassed Liberals of inconsistency and desertion of their much touted free-trade principles. During the next three years the Mari-

A gold-mining claim on William's Creek in the Cariboo Mountains of British Columbia, during the 1860's.

British ships at Quebec loading square timber. The large timbers were winched into the hold through special portholes in the bow and stern by means of a donkey engine, which is the source of the popular Canadian folk-song "Donkey Riding".

time provinces protested against these higher tariffs, but manufacturers in Ontario and Quebec were encouraged to demand even more protection. Sensing a chance to win more votes in the heavily populated industrialized central provinces of Ontario and Quebec, Macdonald decided to make tariff protection a central plank in his Conservative platform, even though privately he sympathized with the ideal of free trade.

A general election was due in 1878 and Macdonald was determined to regain power even if his policies did offend the smaller provinces. In that election, the Conservatives attacked the government's record as timid and unimaginative. The years of Liberal rule had been years of economic depression, said the Conservatives, who promised to promote railways, industry, tariffs, and immigration, to restore the economy, and build a stronger Canada. The Liberals replied weakly by pointing to their thrift and honesty. Their years in office had not been entirely fruitless – the North West Mounted Police had been created, the Supreme Court of Canada established, the secret ballot introduced, and Royal Military College built at Kingston. In the constitutional field Blake had convinced the Colonial Office that the next governor general must be instructed not

Left: Timber coves near Quebec city, 1872. Opposite: Wheat stacks and a wagon load of grain (Manitoba, 1887).

These photographs, in addition to several others in this book, were taken by William Notman (1826-91) or members of his firm. Born in Scotland, Notman settled in Montreal in 1856 and started a photography business. The firm specialized in Canadian scenes and portraits, which now constitute an unrivalled pictorial record of that age.

to interfere in Canadian politics as Dufferin had done over British Columbia and the transcontinental railway. But these achievements were not enough to win the voters' support. The memory of the Pacific Scandal was more than offset by the appeal of Macdonald's imaginative programme. Even farmers were attracted by his National Policy, a term he had used as early as 1872 to describe protective tariffs. When the ballots were counted, Macdonald and the Conservatives had won 137 seats in parliament to the Liberals' 69, almost exactly reversing the results of 1873.

Nation-Building Renewed

Once back in power, Macdonald revived his nation-building policies which had been set aside during the six years of Liberal government. His first step was to implement the National Policy in the budget of 1879. General tariff rates were raised from 10 to 20 per cent, and rates on manufactured goods such as footwear, furniture, glass, and china went up to 30 per cent. Government subsidies for Cape Breton coal enabled Nova Scotian mines to compete against American coal imports and there was even a tariff on agricultural products, pleasing though of little value to the farmers.

The National Policy was frequently attacked in the 1880's as a scheme to help the very industrialists who gave money to the Conservative party, and as a scheme which put an unfair burden on farmers and consumers by raising their cost of living. Some protection for Canada's "infant industries" against American and British competition seemed necessary, but Canadian manufacturers still demanded tariff protection after they were well established. There was some truth in the accusations of the Liberal free traders that the National Policy penalized the working man and that the close connection which it fostered between industry and the Conservatives invited political corruption. On the other hand Canada's "infant industries" could not satisfy the needs of the home market, and the tariff

*Left: Inside a hardware store in St. John's,
Newfoundland, around 1888.
Above: Blacksmith's shop at Cobourg, Ontario,
1880.*

revenues from imports helped to pay for other projects such as the long-
awaited transcontinental railway.

How far the National Policy was responsible for the gradual improvement of the Canadian economy in the 1880's and how far it promoted
the industrialization of Canada is still debated by economic historians. Of
the National Policy's political success in winning votes there can, however, be no question. Before Macdonald's death in 1891 the National
Policy had been vital to Conservative victories in three general elections.
Macdonald's National Policy met the hopes of most Canadians so successfully that it was adopted virtually intact by the Liberal party after
they came to power in 1896.

The second major nation-building project undertaken by Macdonald in
the 1880's was the belated construction of a transcontinental railway to
join the Dominion from sea to sea. That railway had been promised to
British Columbia in 1871, had caused Macdonald's fall in the wake of the
Pacific Scandal, and had been postponed by the Liberals to save money.
The Liberal policy of piecemeal government construction of the railway
was at first continued by Macdonald, but by the 1880's a Pacific railway
was even more urgent a need than it had been a decade earlier. The railway could carry immigrants to develop the rich farm lands of the west,
and those settlers in turn would buy the manufactures of eastern Canada
with the income from grain exported to European markets via the same
railway. A transcontinental railway was now essential to tie together the
vast regions of Canada in one political and economic whole.

Macdonald had known from the outset that government assistance for
the railway would be a necessity because the cost of such a long railway –
longer than any in the world at that time – would be too great for private
enterprise alone. Early in 1880 the government began discussing terms
with members of a Montreal syndicate who were prepared – as the Grand
Trunk Railway was not – to accept Macdonald's insistence on the expensive all-Canadian route to the Pacific, following the rocky north shore

around Lake Superior rather than an easier route across American territory via Chicago. The leading figures of the Montreal group were Canadian-born James J. Hill, who had found fame and fortune as a railway-builder in the United States; George Stephen, a Scottish shepherd who had risen by hard work and determination to become president of the Bank of Montreal; and Stephen's cousin, Donald Smith, who had started as a Hudson's Bay Company clerk at the age of eighteen. Behind these men stood the financial resources of American, French, German, and Canadian interests – neither British capital nor government were interested in such a risky venture.

The charter granted in 1881 to the Canadian Pacific Railway Company gave the syndicate the existing 700 miles of track, a $25 million government subsidy, 25 million acres of good prairie lands (tax free for 25 years) in a chequerboard pattern 24 miles deep on both sides of the railway route, and full tax and tariff rebates on all materials and equipment for the railway. These terms were generous – too generous in the opinion of the Liberals and the rival Grand Trunk Railway – but still insufficient for the magnitude of such a construction scheme, as events soon proved. The company repeatedly found itself facing bankruptcy and forced to beg for further government support. The financing of Canada's first transcontinental railway became an achievement rivalling in drama the epic story of the line's actual construction.

Left: This poster, dated 1869, was displayed in Europe and eastern Canada.
Below: An advertisement for emigrants to Manitoba (early 1880's).

PUISSANCE DU CANADA.

V.   R.

EMIGRATION
POUR LA
PROVINCE D'ONTARIO.

Aux Capitalistes, Fermiers, Cultivateurs, Artisans, et Journaliers,

et toutes personnes désirant améliorer leur sort en émigrant dans un pays nouveau. On attire l'attention des émigrants sur les grands avantages offerts par la Province d'Ontario. Les rentiers peuvent facilement obtenir 8 pour cent sur des garanties de première classe.

LES FERMIERS AVEC UN PETIT CAPITAL

peuvent faire ici l'acquisition d'une ferme avec l'argent qu'il faudrait à la simple exploitation d'une petite ferme dans la Grande-Bretagne. Une bonne terre défrichée avec une maison, grange et dépendances peut s'obtenir dans de bonnes localités pour £4 à £10 Stg. par acre, et les cultivateurs peuvent aisément obtenir de l'ouvrage à des prix élevés.

Comme encouragement le Gouvernement offre aux émigrants

UN OCTROI GRATUIT DE TERRE
(SANS FRAIS AUCUN)

Tout chef de famille peut obtenir, à la condition de s'y établir, un octroi gratuit de deux cents acres de terre pour lui-même, et cent acres de plus pour chaque membre de sa famille, garçon ou fille, au-dessus de l'âge de 18 ans.

TOUTE PERSONNE ÂGÉE DE PLUS DE 18 ANS PEUT OBTENIR UN OCTROI GRATUIT DE 100 ACRES.

Ces octrois gratuits sont protégés par une loi qui les exempte de toute saisie pour aucune dette contractée avant l'émission de la patente, ainsi que durant l'espace de vingt (20) ans après. Ces terres sont facilement accessibles avec les anciens établissements et pourvues de communications postales régulières.

DES ÉTATS DES PRIX COURANTS DE LA MAIN-D'ŒUVRE,

et des terres défrichées à vendre seront tenus aux diverses agences d'immigration dans la Province, lesquelles sont chargées d'indiquer aux émigrants les endroits où ils peuvent facilement obtenir de l'emploi. Plusieurs nouvelles lignes de chemins de fer et autres travaux publics sont en voie de construction, où se peint d'être commencés, lesquels donneront de l'emploi à un nombre presque illimité de journaliers.

Les personnes désirant avoir des informations plus détaillées concernant la Province d'Ontario, sont priées de s'adresser personnellement, ou par lettre, aux agents d'Émigration Canadiens en Europe, savoir : WM. DIXON, 11 Adam Street, Adelphi, London, W.C.; J. G. MOYLAN, Dublin; CHARLES FOY, Belfast; DAVID SHAW, Glasgow; et E. HIMAYS, Agent Continental à Anvers; JOHN A. DONALDSON, Toronto; R. H. RAE, Hamilton; WM. J. WILLS, Ottawa; JAS. MACPHERSON, Kingston; I. STAFFORD, Québec; J. J. DALEY, Montréal; R. CLAT, Halifax, Nouvelle-Écosse; RODT. SHIVES, St. Jean, J. J. G. G. LAYTON, Miramichi, Nouveau-Brunswick.

On peut se procurer des ces messieurs des brochures, publiées sous l'autorité du Gouvernement d'Ontario, contenant toutes les informations quant aux sources grave et du coûte de la vie, etc., dans la Province.

JOHN CARLING,

DÉPARTEMENT D'IMMIGRATION,
Toronto, Octobre, 1869.

Commissaire d'Agricole et des Travaux Publics pour la Province d'Ontario.

MANITOBA.

ALLAN LINE.

3000 NAVVIES, or MEN USED TO FARM WORK, REQUIRED AT ONCE.

The Allan Steamship Co. has received information from SIR A. T. GALT, Minister for Canada in London, that Messrs. MANNING, McDONALD, McLAREN & Co., Contractors for a Section of the Canadian Pacific Railway, will give steady employment to the above-mentioned number of single men for about three years— Winter and Summer.

LOWEST RATE OF WAGES, One and a-Half Dollars per day.

For Special Labour a higher rate is paid.

Suitable shanty board provided at the rate of Three and a-Half Dollars per Week.

By arrangement between the Canadian Government and the Allan Line, the rate of Ocean Passage for these men—

LIVERPOOL TO QUEBEC

IS TO BE **£5,**

Payable by the Men themselves before Embarkation.

On arrival at Quebec, a Free Railway Pass will be given from there to Manitoba, on the men signing agreements to repay such advance from wages earned while in the employ of the Contractors.

Passage Tickets can be obtained from

ALLAN BROTHERS & CO.,
Alexandra Buildings, 19, James Street,
LIVERPOOL.

To supervise the building of the CPR the company employed two
Americans, William Van Horne as general manager, and Thomas G.
Shaughnessy as purchasing agent. Their monumental tasks were to obtain
materials and equipment, an army of men and horses and all the food
and supplies they would need, and to ensure that the construction moved
forward without delays. The laying of track began from both east and
west, with one team toiling up the Fraser Valley towards the forbidding
Rockies, another driving westward from Winnipeg across the rolling
grasslands of the prairies, and a third building through the granite Shield
country of Ontario. Van Horne had flamboyantly promised to build 500
miles of track on the prairies during 1882, the first working season. Using
5,000 men and 3,500 horses from sunrise to sunset, and sometimes also
at night with the aid of lamps, he achieved this fantastic goal. Relentlessly
the ribbon of steel was pushed forward, but behind the bustling construction camps the company was facing its first financial crisis by 1883.

The heavy cloud of depression had returned to dry up the supply of
money and settlers, the Winnipeg-based land boom in the west ended suddenly, the crops of the first settlers were destroyed by drought, and construction costs of the CPR soared beyond their estimates. Reluctantly the
government agreed to a $22.5 million government loan in exchange for
a mortgage on the rail line itself. "We are going to stand by the CPR,"
Macdonald told Governor General Lord Lorne; his government had no
choice but to support the undertaking of which it had been the main
promoter. But the sale of CPR shares still lagged in 1884, thanks in part

Less than five years after its
incorporation, the CPR completed it
Montreal-Vancouver railway with
the driving of the last spike at
Craigellachie in Eagle Pass, the
Rocky Mountains. The spike was
not a gold one, but an ordinary
spike, ". . . just as good," said Sir
William Van Horne, "as any of the
other iron spikes used to build the
railway." Through rail service bega
the following summer.

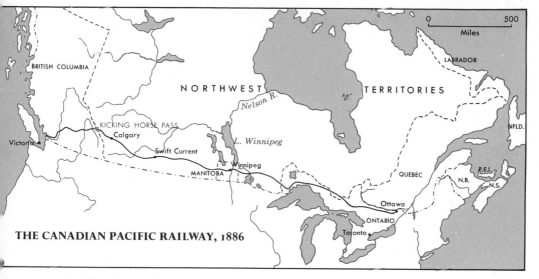

THE CANADIAN PACIFIC RAILWAY, 1886

to the Grand Trunk's propaganda about a "Canadian Pacific Bubble" and the public scare after the giant American railway, the Northern Pacific, went bankrupt in 1883. In the early weeks of 1885 Smith and Stephen pledged their own property to get another bank loan, but by April Van Horne had no money to pay his workers.

Suddenly the CPR's fortunes changed for the better, ironically because of events which threatened that very Canadian unity which the railway was supposed to ensure. Louis Riel had returned to the west to lead a final and futile Métis protest against the relentless advance of the age of steam and steel. The second Riel rebellion proved the value of the transcontinental railway, unfinished though it was, when thousands of volunteers were rushed westward in a matter of days to suppress Riel's uprising. The Canadian government provided another $5 million in cash, as part of a new and advantageous arrangement, and British investors rushed to purchase the last $3 million of CPR bonds when they were offered for sale. Canada and the CPR had both been saved by Riel.

On 7 November 1885, high in the interior plateau of British Columbia, at a way station called Craigellachie, Donald Smith drove the last spike in the steel of empire that linked the St. Lawrence to the Pacific and preserved Canada's western inheritance. The building of the CPR was a daring and imaginative undertaking conceived by Sir John A. Macdonald and carried to completion in the face of apparently insurmountable difficulties of time, space, geography, and economics which would have discouraged men of lesser determination than Macdonald, Stephen, Smith, Van Horne, and Shaughnessy.

HISTORY FROM THE SOURCES

Macdonald's Plans for Building the Canadian Nation

Although out of office for five years after the Pacific Scandal, Sir John A. Macdonald never lost sight of the greater ends for which Confederation had been conceived. Shortly before the general election of 1878 which restored the Conservatives to power, Sir John wrote to the British Chancellor of the Exchequer suggesting an extension of Lord Dufferin's term as governor general because of Dufferin's great interest in policies to build a stronger Canada.

> . . . I am satisfied that the time has come for the formation of a regular force – closely connected with the Imperial army and worked up to the same standard of training and discipline. Without this Canada will never add to the strength of the Empire, but must remain a source of anxiety and weakness.
>
> We must commence modestly, in order to carry the country with us – but a nucleus once formed, it could easily be expanded by degrees as necessity required. Now a new Governor would be powerless in advocating the adoption of such a Scheme. Lord D [Dufferin] who is not only popular in the ordinary sense of the word, but has acquired the confidence of Parliament and people would carry the country in its present warlike mood with him, if he took up the subject warmly and pressed it in his own winning way. The opportunity should not be lost – it may not occur again in our time.
>
> Again Lord D has made the subject of the construction, route and requirements of the Canadian Pacific Railway his especial study. Until this great work is completed our Dominion is little more than a "Geographical Expression." We have as much interest in B Columbia as in Australia, and no more. The Railway once finished we become one great united country with a large inter-provincial trade, and a common interest. Were the Railway in existence now the Imperial Government need have no anxiety about the military protection of Vancouver Island and its harbours from Russian attack – and the coal supply so necessary for the North Pacific Squadron would also easily be secured from attack.
>
> At present Canada has no means of sending a military force or munitions of war to B C and that burden must therefore be thrown on England.
>
> Lord D if he remains should be specially instructed to press the early completion of this work which he could do with an authority to which no newcomer could pretend.
>
> Lastly, it is of importance to Imperial interests that Newfoundland should be added to the Dominion. It would complete the great

scheme of British North American Confederation begun in 1867 –
it would relieve the Colonial office from the trouble and responsibility of the direct Government of the Island and it would throw
upon Canada the burthen of its defence. And that defence would
necessitate the creation of something like a Naval Force by our
Government.

But more than all, in any future negotiations with the United
States on the troublesome question of the Fisheries, the subject
could be dealt with as a whole.

Macdonald to Sir Stafford Northcote, 1 May 1878
Sir John A. Macdonald Papers, Public Archives of Canada,
M.G. 26, A 1 (a), Vol. 79, pp. 710-14.

*The aims and means of Macdonald's National Policy, which had helped
the Conservatives to win the recent election, were explained by Finance
Minister Sir Leonard Tilley in his budget speech of 1879.*

. . . Mr. Chairman, there has been, and very naturally so, a good
deal of interest and anxiety manifested on the part of the friends of
the National Policy, as it is called, in regard to its early introduction.
I can quite understand that, because believing as they do, and as a
majority of this House do, that that policy is calculated to bring
prosperity to the country, it was but natural that they should be
anxious for its introduction, and that not a day should be lost. And
it is satisfactory to know that, great and difficult as is the responsibility which rests upon me here, I trust that the proposition I am
about to submit will be sustained, not only by a majority of this
House, but by an overwhelming majority in the country. It was
natural, therefore, Mr. Chairman, that the friends of this policy
should be anxious for its introduction, and it was pleasing and satisfactory to see that even the Opposition vied with the friends of the
Government in their anxiety for its introduction.

*   *   *   *   *

. . . Lying as we do alongside that great country, we were looked
upon as a desirable market for their surplus products, and our
American neighbours, always competent to judge of their own interests and act wisely in regard to them, put forth every effort to obtain
access to our market. It is well known by the term slaughter-market
what they have been doing for the last four or five years in Canada;
that in order to find an outlet for their surplus manufactures, they
have been willing to send them into this country at any price that
would be a little below that of the Canadian manufacturer. It is

well known also that they have had their agents in every part of the Dominion seeking purchasers for their surplus, and that those agents have been enabled, under our existing laws, to enter those goods at a price much lower than they ought to have paid, which was their value in the place of purchase. It is well known, moreover, that the United States Government, in order to encourage special interests in the country, granted a bounty upon certain manufactures, and gave to them the exclusive market of the Dominion, and, under those circumstances, we have lost a very important trade, possessed previous to 1873, in addition to the loss of the West India trade, and by the repeal of the 10 per cent. duty on tea, we lost the direct tea trade, and all the advantages resulting from it, by its transfer from the Dominion to New York and Boston. Under all those circumstances, and with the high duty imposed by the United States on the agricultural products of the Dominion, by which we are, to a great extent, excluded from them, while the manufactures of that country are forced into our market, we could not expect prosperity or success in the Dominion, so long as that state of things continued. These are some of the difficulties which have led to our present state of affairs.

*   *   *   *   *

. . . I think this House will not object if, in the propositions before me, they touch more heavily the imports from foreign countries than from our Fatherland. I have this to say to our American friends: In 1865 they abrogated the Reciprocity Treaty, and from that day to the present a large portion of the imports from that country into the Dominion have been admitted free. We have hoped, but hoped in vain, that by the adoption of that policy we would lead our American friends to treat us in a more liberal spirit with regard to the same articles. Well, after having waited twelve years for the consideration of this subject, the Government requiring more revenue, have determined to ask this House to impose upon the products of the United States that have been free, such a duty as may seem consistent with our position. But the Government couple with the proposal, in order to shew that we approach this question with no unfriendly spirit, a resolution that will be laid on the table containing a proposition to this effect: That, as to articles named, which are the natural products of the country, including lumber, if the United States take off the duties in part or in whole, we are prepared to meet them with equal concessions. The Government believe in a reciprocity tariff, yet may discuss Free-trade or Protection, but the question of to-day is – Shall we have a reciprocity tariff, or a one-sided tariff?

*   *   *   *   *

. . . I may say, at the outset that, in considering this question of the tariff and protection to our industries, the Government considered how they could best discharge their duty to the Dominion; how they could best accomplish the object the country desired to see accomplished. We might obtain two million dollars by the imposition of duties upon certain articles, and appear to give protection, but in reality give none whatever. We might obtain a revenue from the increased duties, but not place it in such a position as to give real encouragement and protection to the industries they desire to protect. And, therefore, Sir, in arriving at the conclusions at which we have arrived, and which are to be submitted to the House, we submit them with the full conviction that they will be effective in their character and give ample protection to all who are seeking it, and who have a right to expect it.

Canada, Parliament, *Debates of the House of Commons*, 1879
(Ottawa), Vol. VI, pp. 410, 414, 415, 416.

When introducing the bill to charter the Canadian Pacific Railway, Sir Charles Tupper described the central role of the railway in promoting Macdonald's other nation-building policies.

. . . if, with a country which, according to a high American authority, embraces three-fourths of the remaining wheat zone on the American continent, if, with this advantage, and our other advantages, we hesitate in discharging our duty to the country, we should be unworthy of the position we occupy, either as statesmen or patriotic Canadians. No person can look abroad over the Dominion without feeling that the Great North-West Territory is the district to which we must look for our strength and development. Just as the older of the United States look to their Great North-West, with its rapidly increasing population, adding hundreds of thousands and millions to their strength, not only may we look for strength by reason of an additional Customs Revenue from the increased population of that Territory, but we must look upon that western country as a field for the manufacturing industries of the older and more settled parts of Canada. Every person acquainted with this country knows we have exhausted to some extent its bread-growing power, but under the National Policy that Canada has adopted, we must look forward not only to building up thriving centres of industries and enterprise all over this portion of the country, but to obtaining a market for those industries after they have been established; and I say where is there a greater market than that magnificent granary of the North-West, which, filled up with a thriving and prosperous

population, will make its demands upon Ontario, Quebec, Nova
Scotia and New Brunswick for these manufacturing products that
we, for many years, will be so well able to supply?

. . . At this moment the eyes of a large portion of the civilised
world are centered upon the Great North-West of Canada, and hundreds of thousands of people in every foreign country, as well as the
British Empire, are studying the question as to whether they shall
come with their capital and industry and build up Canada into a
great, prosperous and progressive country. Under these circumstances, hon. gentlemen opposite are unwise and unpatriotic in making this a battle ground of party. There was no necessity for it. I
recognise, to the fullest extent, the advantage of having two great
political parties grappling with each other, not on the low grounds
of personal or party ambition, but on a great national question on
which a broad line of demarcation can be made between them, and
regarding which they can do battle for great principles on which
they differ. We have such a question in the National Policy without
dragging in the Pacific Railway. If we are defeated on that issue,
hon. gentlemen opposite will take our places irrespective of the
policy of the Pacific Railway. Having that line of demarcation between us, let us, on the great national question of the Canadian
Pacific Railway, unite as a band of brothers, irrespective of old
parties, show not that we are Liberals or Conservatives, but that we
are Canadians, and that in every word that is uttered, whether we
sit on the Treasury Benches or on the Opposition side of the House,
we feel we owe it to Canada, to ourselves and to our children, to
do all that men can do to strengthen the hands of those who are
engaged in a great national enterprise, upon the success of which
the rapid progress and prosperity of our common country depends.

Canada, Parliament, *Debates of the House of Commons*, 1880
(Ottawa), Vol. IX, pp. 1424-5.

FURTHER READING

Creighton, D. G., *John A. Macdonald:* Vol. II, *The Old Chieftain* (Toronto: Macmillan, 1955)★. The second volume of a classic biography examines Macdonald as Canada's first prime minister.

Careless, J. M. S., *Brown of The Globe*, Vol. 2 (Toronto: Macmillan, 1963)★. Describes Brown's career after Confederation.

Thomson, D. C., *Alexander Mackenzie, Clear Grit* (Toronto: Macmillan, 1960). The only biography of Brown's successor and Canada's second prime minister.

Stanley, G. F. G., *Louis Riel* (Toronto: Ryerson, 1963). The definitive biography of the Métis leader.

Stanley, G. F. G., *The Birth of Western Canada: A History of the Rebellions* (Toronto: University of Toronto Press, 1963)★. The Canadian west during the first two decades of Confederation.

Gibbon, J. M., *Steel of Empire* (Toronto: McClelland & Stewart, 1935). A lively history of the CPR.

Morton, W. L., *Manitoba: A History*, 2nd ed. (Toronto: University of Toronto Press, 1967)★. One of the best of the provincial histories.

Farr, D. M. L., *Canada and the Colonial Office, 1867-1887* (Toronto: University of Toronto Press, 1955). Discusses early developments towards dominion status.

17

Old Tensions and New Strains

Riel's Rebellion

Riel's uprising on the banks of the South Saskatchewan River at the end of March 1885 had not come as a complete surprise to the Canadian government. Since the previous autumn Ottawa had been receiving reports that Riel had returned to the Canadian west at the urgent request of some Métis who believed their rights were being ignored by the government. After the Red River rebellion Riel had been officially a fugitive from the law, charged with the murder of Thomas Scott, but his whereabouts and activities had been well known to many people. In 1871 he had appeared at Red River, offering to lead the Métis against an anticipated Fenian invasion; the next year, at Bishop Taché's request, he had gone to the United States with funds secretly given by Macdonald's government. But in 1873 the restless Riel returned to Manitoba and was elected to the Canadian parliament for Provencher in a by-election, and re-elected in 1874 at the general election. Next he appeared suddenly in Ottawa, took the oath of office as a member of parliament, and disappeared immediately to avoid arrest. He was subsequently expelled from the House and sentenced *in absentia* to ten years' exile. When his unstable mind gave way Riel was secretly confined in Quebec asylums for two years. By 1878 he was in Montana, working as an interpreter and trader, obsessed with a sense of "mission" to establish a Métis state in the Canadian west, which was to be ruled by a North American pope.

It was in Montana that Riel's Métis friends found him in 1883 and told him that their staple of life, the buffalo, were disappearing in the face of white settlement, that they had sold their Manitoba lands to speculators, and that Macdonald's government had turned a deaf ear to their pleas for new lands. In the summer of 1884 Riel determined to return to the Canadian Northwest to lead his people in their struggle against the onward march of white settlement.

During the winter of 1884-5 Riel repeated the tactics which had been used at the Red River in 1870. He began by sending a petition to Ottawa demanding a railway to Hudson Bay, a provincial legislature for the

Northwest, better treatment for the Indians, and land grants to the Métis. Macdonald and the cabinet were aware that real or imaginary grievances were felt by Indians, Métis, and white settlers alike in the Saskatchewan region and Macdonald was ready to make large concessions to maintain peace. But Riel's hint to the government that he would desert his friends and his "mission" for $100,000 showed Macdonald the extent of the Métis leader's irresponsibility. While the government pondered Riel's attempt at blackmail, it also moved to meet the demands of the west by appointing a commission to examine Métis land claims. Realizing that his personal ambitions were thus being circumvented, Riel decided to repeat his old tactic of using force. He seized the tiny village of Batoche on 19 March and made its parish church the headquarters for a provisional government, on the pretext of preventing an attack by the North West Mounted Police, who, with the CPR, symbolized the new power of Canada in the west which had been lacking in 1870.

From Batoche Riel's lieutenant, Gabriel Dumont, attacked a force of Mounted Police and volunteers at Duck Lake. Crucifix in hand, Riel watched the struggle from a distance. Small roving bands of Indians now joined in the uprising by sacking Battleford and murdering isolated settlers, but these actions were unco-ordinated and disunited – only one thousand rebels took up arms. Most Indians followed the advice of the famous missionary Father Lacombe to remain peaceful, while most Métis and white settlers refused to support an uprising led by the half-mad religious fanatic.

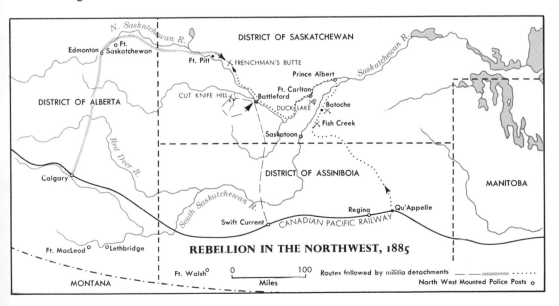

REBELLION IN THE NORTHWEST, 1885

Left: The capture of Batoche. Above: Officers of Canadian militia units posed for this photograph in Saskatchewan (1885) during the Northwest Rebellion.

The news of the Duck Lake encounter galvanized the government into action to prevent a general Indian uprising. "I want to show what the Canadian Militia can do," Militia Minister Adolphe Caron told the first detachments despatched westward from Ottawa to join a thousand militiamen assembling in Winnipeg. By 6 April one column was advancing on Batoche under General Middleton, while only days later two other forces moved north from Swift Current and Calgary in a pincer movement against the Indian bands of chiefs Poundmaker and Big Bear on the north branch of the Saskatchewan. Batoche was captured on 12 May and Riel surrendered three days later, while the Indian bands, after checking the militia at Cut Knife Hill, were soon scattered and defeated. By the beginning of July the Northwest Rebellion was over.

The immediate results of the "rebellion" were the destruction of Métis property, imprisonment of Métis leaders, the disarming of the Indians, and the confiscation of their government annuities to compensate the victims of violence. Henceforth the Métis disappeared as a society, being absorbed by the relentless tide of settlement, and the Indians were confined to their reservations. But the punishment of Riel was not so easily settled. His trial for treason began at Regina in July. He refused to plead insanity and was found guilty – with the recommendation of clemency for consideration before the sentence of death was carried out. This verdict reawakened in central Canada all the passions that had slumbered since Confederation. English-speaking Canadians remembered Riel as the murderer of Thomas Scott and demanded his death; French-speaking

Louis Riel (standing, centre right) addressing the jury in the Court House, Regina, during his trial in July 1885.

Canadians saw in Riel a symbol of French-Canadian nationalism and demanded leniency for a man whose heresy proved his insanity. Confronted with a choice which would inevitably alienate one group or the other, the government reviewed a medical commission's finding that Riel was unstable but sane, and then decided unanimously to order his execution.

The Challenge of Provincialism

Riel's death on the gallows at Regina on 16 November 1885 crystallized all the divisive forces that challenged Canadian unity and provided them with a rallying cry. Confederation had been conceived by its founders as consisting of a strong central government, with the provinces as distinctly subordinate authorities dealing only with localized matters. Yet in both the constitutional and financial relations of the Dominion and its provinces the deliberate intention to avoid the "states' rights" issue which had plunged the neighbouring republic into civil war were upset soon after Confederation by a series of political and judicial decisions.

As early as 1869 Joseph Howe had succeeded in winning "better terms" (a more advantageous financial settlement) for Nova Scotia despite the objections of Edward Blake that the federal government had no right to make special deals with only some provinces. When Manitoba and British Columbia entered Confederation, the financial settlement of 1867 was further distorted by the juggling of statistics, and when Prince Edward Island joined in 1873, the generous grants from the federal government nullified the original attempt at equality of treatment. The depression of the 1870's, compounded by the technical changes affecting the Maritime economy, struck a heavy blow at the smaller and less industrialized provinces – Ontario alone of all the provinces was able to produce balanced budgets in those difficult years. It was from Ontario, too, that the strongest arguments for the "compact" (provincial rights) theory of confederation came. Were the provinces subordinate to the central power of the federal government, as the Fathers of Confederation believed; or was the Dominion merely the creature of the provinces, as Edward Blake and Oliver Mowat (his successor as premier of Ontario in 1872) maintained?

Mowat, once a student in John A. Macdonald's Kingston law office, became the most outspoken advocate of "provincial rights" and hence the most dogged opponent of Macdonald's centralist interpretation of Confederation. As long as Mackenzie was prime minister and the Liberals were in power at Ottawa, a confrontation between Ontario and the federal government was avoided, but in 1879 Macdonald challenged Mowat over the issue of the Ontario-Manitoba boundary. The previous year a board of arbitration had awarded 144,000 square miles between Port

The provinces frequently used the anniversary of Dominion Day to protest against federal inroads into provincial rights. In this cartoon of 1879 from "Grip" magazine, Sir John A. receives a dusty answer from the provinces when he congratulates them on their anniversary. He is told: "Mind your own federal business, and permit us to manage our local affairs to suit ourselves, according to the terms of Union . . .!"

Arthur and Lake of the Woods to Ontario, thus closing off Manitoba from direct access to the Great Lakes and effectively making it a landlocked "postage stamp" province. Macdonald, to provoke Mowat rather than to aid Manitoba, denounced the boundary settlement as a worthless scrap of paper and enacted a statute which, with deliberate vagueness, stated that the two provinces shared a common but undefined boundary.

This manoeuvre was intended to compensate Manitoba for the federal retention of the province's natural resources under the Manitoba Act of 1870, and to penalize Ontario for its continued support of a Liberal government at Toronto. Mowat rejected Macdonald's action, and both provinces proceeded to hold elections and to grant timber rights in the disputed area. When this jurisdictional dispute threatened to end in violence, the matter was referred to the Judicial Committee of the Privy Council, which in 1884 determined in favour of Ontario and the original boundary settlement of 1878.

The Manitoba boundary case was only one of a series of constitutional issues referred to the Judicial Committee of the Privy Council, most of whose decisions went in favour of the principle of provincial rights. The most decisive case, *Hodge vs. the Queen* in 1883, contradicted the intentions of the Fathers of Confederation by granting powers to the provinces in addition to their exclusive jurisdiction under Section 92 of the British North America Act. During the next decade, successive decisions by the Judicial Committee broadened the scope of the provinces' operations, but without enlarging their taxing powers. Macdonald's attempts to maintain the federal residual powers granted by Section 91 had provoked many of these constitutional appeals, and his repeated disallowance of Manitoba railway acts which infringed the CPR charter's "monopoly clause" forced the Conservative government of John Norquay in Manitoba to oppose his policies.

It was the execution of Riel which, ironically, brought together all the forces advocating provincialism, including public opinion in Ontario and Quebec which held such opposing views on Riel. In Quebec the strongly racist *Parti Nationale*, formed by a coalition of anti-federal Liberals and Conservatives, had chosen the demagogic Honoré Mercier as its leader in 1883. It was Mercier who voiced Quebec's cry for revenge on the government which had "martyred" Riel and who, with an election platform of provincial rights, ousted the Conservative government of the province in 1886. Mercier challenged Macdonald and Macdonald's interpretation of Confederation in 1887 by calling an interprovincial conference to discuss federal-provincial relations. The conference was attended by the Liberal premiers of Nova Scotia, New Brunswick, and Ontario (Mowat acted as chairman), and by the Conservative, Norquay. The Conservative premiers of Prince Edward Island and British Columbia, however, refused to join in challenging the federal government.

Most of the resolutions passed by the Conference seemed to be inspired by Mowat, since they urged more provincial autonomy. The Maritime premiers were more interested in getting more money than in broadening their responsibilities, but the Conference's objects were frustrated by Macdonald's refusal to consider constitutional changes and by the provinces' inability to act without federal co-operation.

The Interprovincial Conference had given a false picture of provincial unity, as the Jesuit Estates controversy revealed in 1887. Rents from the property of the Society of Jesus, which amounted to some 900,000 acres in Quebec, had been used for education ever since the last of the Canadian Jesuits died in 1800. Although the Order returned to Canada in the 1840's it did not regain its lands, which were held in trust by the Crown. The Jesuits, the Quebec bishops, and even the Protestant schools, all of which had been receiving money from the Estates, laid claim to the

THE WOLF AND THE LAMB
or MIGHT MAKES RIGHT

The lamb (the premier of Ontario, Oliver Mowat) stands on a paper that reads "Provincial Rights: No Ottawa Domination".

The Mowat government was said to be hostile to the federal policy of Protection; but, as most of the electors were aware, the provinces had no control over Dominion monetary affairs. In a cartoon drawn shortly after the federal election of 1882, Mowat is shown presenting his argument – an argument regarded as useless except to impress ignorant voters.

Papa Mowat: "Adam, have you any idea what John Joseph is driving at?"

Adam: "Yes, I think he means that he would like you to give him separate high schools and colleges, as well as common schools."

The Old Lady [Public Opinion]: "Then he shall have them – at his own expense."

From certain remarks made by Archbishop John Joseph Lynch (the first Roman Catholic archbishop of Toronto) many people believed that the Roman Catholic church was on the point of requesting separate schools for higher grades than the grades already granted. The "Adam" of this November 1882 cartoon is the Honourable Adam Crooks, then Minister of Education for Ontario.

valuable properties, and Mercier determined to settle the complex dispute by a provincial Act. The Protestant schools were assured of $60,000, and the balance ($400,000) was to be divided between the Jesuits and the bishops by the papacy. It was this provision to employ the pope as arbitrator that revealed the depth of religious and provincial rivalries in Canada.

In Ontario, Protestants revived the old cry of "popish aggression" in Canadian affairs, and D'Alton McCarthy, Macdonald's heir apparent as Conservative leader, organized the Equal Rights Association to oppose political interference by the Roman Catholic church. McCarthy and the Orange Order demanded disallowance of Mercier's Jesuit Estates Act, but for once Macdonald refused to interfere with provincial rights. In the House of Commons the issue cut across party lines when eight Conservatives were joined by five Liberal members as the "Noble Thirteen" to vote in vain for disallowance.

McCarthy's frustration over the Jesuit Estates Act soon led to his strange alliance with the forces of provincialism in Manitoba. After a speaking tour of Ontario to arouse public opinion against French and Catholic domination of Canada, during the autumn of 1889 McCarthy visited the west, where the Liberal government responded to his appeals by abolishing the province's denominational school system. These schools – both Roman Catholic and Protestant – had evolved since Manitoba entered Confederation, but their support from provincial taxes was not legally protected by the Manitoba Act of 1870. In that score of years Manitoba had been populated largely by immigrants from Ontario – the French and Catholic population had not increased significantly – and the new Manitoba School Act was a copy of the unitary school system in Ontario but without its provision for separate schools. The new Manitoba

School Act of 1890 embodied English and Protestant political domination of the province, and even though many people thought that it was unjust to the French and Catholic schools, it was nonetheless solidly based on a legal technicality.

Although the federal government had the power to disallow the Manitoba school law, this action was not taken because a federal election was in the offing and because Macdonald considered that there had already been too much disallowance of Manitoba laws. One alternative to disallowance was to challenge the legality of the new secular school act in the courts, and this was the course followed by the defenders of denominational schools with the full support of the Roman Catholic church. After years of litigation in the courts of Manitoba and Canada, the Judicial Committee of the Privy Council determined in 1895 that the appeal was "well founded", but that redress must come from the Dominion parliament who could "legislate or not as they think fit". Thus the constitutional issue of the Manitoba schools was thrown back into the arena of party politics again in 1895.

In the five years since the passing of the Manitoba Schools Act much had happened, however, to complicate that vexed question: new faces had appeared on the political stage, and new problems beset the federal government. Hector Langevin, the last remaining contemporary of Sir John in federal politics, had been charged with complicity in the case of Thomas McGreevy, MP, who had accepted payoffs for the Conservative party from a company getting government contracts. McCarthy, after his

Left: An ox-team in 1874 on the Cariboo Road, the 400-mile-long wagon trail built in the 1860's along the Fraser Valley from Yale to Barkerville, British Columbia, during the gold rush.
Bottom left: Mennonites arriving at Winnipeg, 1876.
Bottom right: The steamer "Algoma" bringing immigrants to the site of present-day Killarney, Ontario.

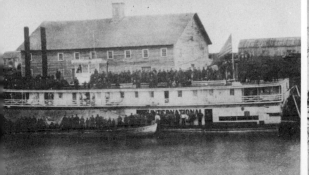

triumph over the Manitoba schools question, further strained French-English relations by advocating the abolition of the official use of the French language in that province. The question, said McCarthy, is "whether this country is to be English or French". The National Policy, now ten years old, and the completion of the CPR had not noticeably lightened the depression which hung over Canada, and the development of the Canadian west had been disappointingly slow. These difficulties were increased by the McKinley tariff, which was about to raise the protective American tariff to unprecedented heights. Once more Canadians were attracted by the Liberals' promotion of the idea of reciprocity with the United States – commercial union, as it was now popularly called. It was against this background of racial and religious tensions, weakness in his party and government, and unrelieved gloom in the business world, that Macdonald suddenly dissolved parliament on 2 February 1891.

Fortunately for Macdonald a ready-made election issue was presented to him when, by means still unknown, he got an advance copy of a pamphlet advocating commercial union written by the editor of the Liberal *Globe*, Edward Farrer, who had recently been conferring with American politicians. Macdonald eagerly accepted this challenge from the advocates of a continental destiny for Canada by replying with his traditional appeals to loyalty and Canadian nationalism within the British empire. For the electors Macdonald made the issue a simple and clear choice: the Conservatives and Canadian independence, or the Liberals and annexation. "As for myself," the Old Chieftain announced, "my course is clear. A British subject I was born – a British subject I will die. With my utmost effort, with my latest breath, will I oppose the 'veiled treason' which attempts by sordid means and mercenary proffers to lure our people from their allegiance."

The cry of "The Old Flag, the Old Man, and the Old Policy" carried the election for the Conservatives, but only by a slim margin. Quebec and Ontario returned about the same number of Liberals as Conservatives, and only the loyalty of the Maritimes and the west ensured a Conservative triumph. But even this was a pyrrhic victory, for Macdonald's all-out campaigning during the harsh winter months had so sapped his strength

This cartoon, headed "Laying Out the Grit Campaign" and showing the Liberals as American puppets, was a Tory campaign poster in the 1891 election. The Liberals were openly supporting "Commercial Union" (that is, reciprocity with the United States), which would have had the greatest effect in industrialized Ontario. The cartoonist is stressing Macdonald's claim that reciprocity would surely lead to annexation.

A stagecoach at Yarmouth, Nova Scotia, in the late nineteenth century. Regular stage-coach runs had been started in the Maritimes at the beginning of the nineteenth century between Halifax and Windsor, and by 1850 the routes extended from Halifax throughout the region.

that a series of strokes during the spring ended with his death on 6 June. The passing of "John A." marked a milestone in the life of the Dominion which he had done so much to create, and in which the quarter century after 1867 would forever be "The Age of Macdonald". For a strong Canada, independent of the United States, allied to Great Britain, and self-reliant in her balance of agriculture and industry, Macdonald had ultimately sacrificed himself. The first Father of Confederation would have smiled at the irony which saw him buried in an American-made casket copied from that of President Ulysses S. Grant, in an undistinguished plot owned by his brother-in-law, at Cataraqui.

The Eclipse of Conservatism

The death of Macdonald so soon after the election of 1891 left the government and the Conservative party without strong leadership. D'Alton McCarthy had committed political suicide by his attitude on the Jesuit Estates Act and his organization of the Equal Rights Association; he could never gain the support of French Canada, which was essential to the leader of a national party. For similar reasons, John Sparrow Thompson, Minister of Justice and the strongest contender to fill Macdonald's place, was also passed over for the time being. Thompson, a Nova Scotian Methodist, had been converted to Roman Catholicism, which cost him popular support among Orangemen. Langevin's political career had been destroyed by the McGreevy scandal. Virtually by default the positions of prime minister and leader of the Conservatives passed to seventy-year-old Sir J. J. C. Abbott, a man who had signed the Annexation Manifesto of 1849.

Abbott's life in politics had never indicated any more than mediocre talents, and as a senator he was unable to give personal direction to affairs in the centre ring, the House of Commons. He added to his problems by failing to recognize Joseph Adolphe Chapleau, leader of the Quebec *bleus* and a past master in the use of political patronage, as the natural successor to Langevin in the role of an English-speaking prime

minister's French-Canadian lieutenant. Chapleau left the cabinet to become lieutenant-governor of Quebec, and the Conservatives then had no
French Canadian to match the appeal and eloquence of Wilfrid Laurier,
the rising young orator who had been chosen leader of the Liberal party
in 1887.

Abbott's attitude to political life showed why he was at best a compromise as Conservative leader. "I hate politics," he had written, "I hate
notoriety, public meetings, public speeches, caucuses, and everything
I know of that is apparently the necessary incident of politics . . . ." Yet
it was not this attitude nor its consequences for his party but simply ill
health that forced his retirement before the end of 1892. For the second
time in eighteen months the Conservatives were leaderless. But in 1892
they did not hesitate to accept the best man available, J. S. Thompson,
and this time there was no public objection on religious grounds.

Thompson was almost immediately faced with the Manitoba schools
question. The Judicial Committee of the Privy Council had just determined that the Act of 1890 was valid, and Roman Catholics in Manitoba
now applied to the governor general in Council for remedial federal legislation as provided for in Section 93 of the British North America Act. The
government was uncertain whether Section 93 covered such action, and
applied to the Supreme Court of Canada for a ruling on this question of
jurisdiction. Obviously the Conservative government was reluctant to
use coercive powers against the province of Manitoba. Coercion would
certainly cost the government votes in Ontario, yet failure to remedy the
grievances of the Roman Catholics would just as certainly anger Quebec,
which had not forgotten or forgiven the government that executed Riel.
The government's problem was not solved but only further prolonged
when the Supreme Court decided in February 1894 that the government
lacked the necessary remedial power, and Roman Catholics of Manitoba
then appealed their case to the final authority, the Judicial Committee of
the Privy Council.

To a lesser degree Laurier and the Liberals were on the horns of the
same dilemma, despite their traditional sympathy for provincial auton-

*Kempthorne School, near Boissevain,
Manitoba, in the 1890's – a typical
rural school house on the prairie at the
time of the Manitoba schools question.
The school was built in 1893, but is no
longer in use owing to the consolidation
of school districts.*

omy. The Liberals, however, did not have to make such a decision – the government did – and so Laurier took refuge in references to "the sunny ways" of conciliation. Further, at the Liberal Convention in 1893 Mowat had charted an attractive course for the national party by asserting that Liberals would uphold the British connection and moderate protective tariffs. In the wake of this declared policy the Liberals in 1894 acknowledged the importance of the new industrialism by wooing support from big business interests at the very moment that Conservative Finance Minister George Foster upset the same group by lowering tariffs.

In the end Thompson never faced his moment of truth over the Manitoba schools question, for he died suddenly at Windsor Castle, where he was a guest of Queen Victoria, on 12 December 1894. Ironically this was the second day of the appeal before the Judicial Committee of the Privy Council. For the third time in as many years, the Conservatives were searching for a leader. The succession now passed to Sir Mackenzie Bowell, a former Grand Master of the Orange Order and Canada's last prime minister drawn from the Senate. Bowell, however, had fewer political talents than any of his predecessors and within his cabinet he soon faced a revolt caused by the Manitoba schools question.

Early in 1895 the Judicial Committee of the Privy Council delivered its famous verdict on the Manitoba schools question: the federal parliament had the power to remedy the complaint of the Roman Catholics. Bowell tried vainly to avoid the issue by seeking the prior approval of Greenway's Liberal government in Manitoba to federal legislation. No agreement was forthcoming, and Bowell's position with the Quebec *bleus* was further weakened when his French federal leader resigned in protest over the lack of a remedial bill. Seven other ministers showed their general lack of confidence in Bowell by resigning *en masse* in January 1896, thus precipitating a crisis in the cabinet and in the country. The day was saved for the Conservatives by Sir Charles Tupper, who returned from his post as High Commissioner in London to enter the cabinet. Six of the ministers who had just resigned rejoined Bowell's government on the understanding that Tupper would introduce the remedial school law and take over the prime ministership shortly.

The promised bill was brought into a parliament whose life was almost over, but a combination of the Liberals, the Quebec *bleus* (now led by Israël Tarte), and Orange Conservatives, filibustered until Tupper in desperation assumed office as prime minister and called a general election on the Manitoba schools question. In the election that question was certainly central but the Liberal low tariff policy adopted in 1893 was probably more important in the Maritime provinces, while Ontario was distracted by the campaign for total prohibition of the liquor trade. Few

Sir Wilfrid Laurier at an election rally in the park at Amherstburg, Ontario, in June 1896. The election took place on 23 June but Sir Charles Tupper and his government refused to resign until 8 July, when the governor general, Lord Aberdeen, indicated that he no longer had any confidence in them.

voters apparently believed that coercion of Manitoba was either feasible or likely, for Manitoba itself returned a majority of Conservatives. The decisive province, however, was Quebec, where the Roman Catholic church openly supported the cause of Conservatism and coercion, only to be defied by an electorate that preferred to vote for Wilfrid Laurier, a favourite son, rather than for Roman Catholic schools in Manitoba. Promising conciliation in place of coercion, "Barabbas" Laurier, as some priests called him, took 49 of Quebec's 65 seats, which gave him a clear majority of 30 in the House of Commons. The Liberal victory of 1896 marked the end of the long reign of Macdonald's Conservatives. It remained to be seen if the Laurier years would also mark the end of Macdonald's nation-building programmes such as the National Policy and federal domination over the provinces.

The Legacy of "John A."

The Canada which Macdonald left in 1891 had changed much since those exciting days of the 1860's. It had changed unbelievably from the primitive agricultural society that had greeted him as an immigrant boy seventy years earlier. Largely under Macdonald's inspiration and guidance Canada had expanded from four small provinces in 1867 to seven in 1891, bound together from sea to sea by the CPR's "steel of empire". The emerging industrialism of that mid-Victorian age, represented by farm implement factories, boot and clothing mills, and wood-working shops, had expanded slowly but surely under the aegis of Macdonald's National Policy to include the manufacture of a wide variety of consumer products: canned foods, tools, labour-saving machines like sewing machines and hand-powered washers, and glass and china.

The Maritime provinces had changed least in the past quarter-century. Prince Edward Island still depended exclusively on its sale of agricultural products, and lumbering still dominated New Brunswick's economy. In Nova Scotia lumbering, fishing, and agriculture were still important, but the burgeoning cities of central Canada created a demand for Cape Breton coal – 1.2 million tons were shipped to Quebec and Ontario in

The City Passenger Railway Company's sleigh in a snowstorm in Montreal, from "The Canadian Illustrated News" for March 1870. In late nineteenth-century winters these sleighs were substitutes for a winter street-car service.

1882 – and Great Britain provided a steady market for Nova Scotia's new apple-growing industry of the Annapolis Valley. Except for Montreal, where heavy industry had been well established before Confederation, Quebec still retained its essentially rural character. Its surplus population was emigrating, not to the Canadian west, but to the textile mills of New England. Some 132,000 people had left between 1881 and 1891 because no more farm land was available in the province, and as yet Quebec had only started to exploit its vast potential of mineral, timber, and hydro-electric resources.

Unlike Quebec, where industry was centred in a single city, manufacturing in Ontario was spread widely throughout the southern region. Toronto was already the industrial giant of the province, but in addition to the developing "little Ruhr" in the Grand River Valley, almost every town, village, and hamlet possessed some small factory that produced wood products or farm implements or tools or clothing. Until centralization of the industrial process drove these modest enterprises into oblivion, they formed an essential part of the local economy and, when they died, many small urban centres died with them.

Although Manitoba had begun economically as a western extension of the commercial empire of the St. Lawrence, and had been populated mainly as an extension of Ontario, it had developed a strong regional

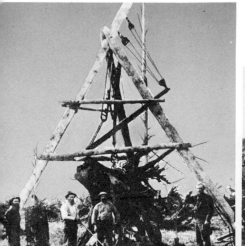

Two photographs from Ontario, taken around 1880. Left: A "stumper" being used to remove a large stump. Below: A chopping bee.

Left: Main Street, Winnipeg, looking north from Portage, in 1891.
Below: A sketch map of Winnipeg, 1884.

economic and political identity quite early. Dissatisfaction with federal disallowance of provincial railway charters and the related issue of high freight rates had caused some emigration to the Dakotas, but in the two decades since the Manitoba Act the population had risen from 25,000 to over 152,000, and the settlement of small bands of Scandinavians was a harbinger of the great wave of European immigrants soon to come. Winnipeg, with a population of 30,000 in 1892, served as the shopping centre and metropolis for the whole west during these years of land booms and recessions, bumper crops and droughts, and was now competing with Fort William for control of the grain trade. A grain blockage by the farmers in 1887 convinced Macdonald's government to end the CPR monopoly but not in time to save Norquay's Conservative administration from being replaced by the voters in 1888 with Thomas Greenway's Liberals.

In Canada's farthest west the completion of the CPR had made Vancouver – a city of only 5,000 – an international port, "the gateway to the Orient", the "Terminal City" for trans-Pacific mail and commerce and, after 1891, the home base for the luxury fleet of "flying Empresses" that plied between Canada, Japan, and India. The coal mines of Nanaimo now fuelled the ships of many nations but British Columbia's economy looked westward for markets rather than east to her sister provinces. As late as 1888 timber rights could still be leased for as little as one cent per

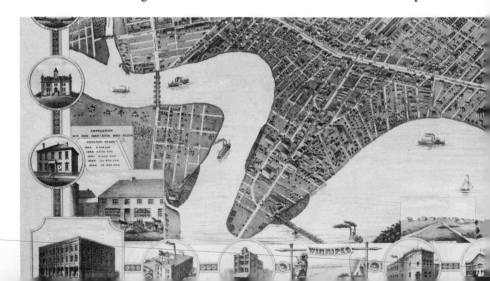

The Royal City Sawmills at New Westminster, British Columbia, in 1887.

acre, but large-scale lumbering and fishing operations had only just been started. Like Manitoba, British Columbia complained of the CPR's transportation monopoly, but in addition it objected to the railway's control of extensive mineral rights and its supposed influence in provincial politics.

Important as the new manufacturing industries in Canada were, farming still formed the backbone of the national economy and employed almost three-quarters of the work force. The growing urbanization in the eastern provinces increased the trend to mixed farming, which provided the variety of meat, dairy products, fruit, and vegetables consumed in the city. The staple grain trade still existed, but already the potential of the Canadian prairies as the "bread basket" of the world was beginning to be exploited. In 1872 the Grange movement (an American fraternal organization for farmers) had entered Canada, and soon individual Granges began to demand government action on high tariffs and high freight rates. By creating a group consciousness among farmers, the Grange prepared the way for the more militant Patrons of Industry. First organized from the United States in 1889, the Patrons could boast five years later of over 50,000 members – 5,000 in the prairies alone – and of an independent Canadian organization since 1891. Their main objective was lower tariffs, for which 40,000 of them petitioned in 1893, and to gain this objective they were prepared to enter party politics. Seventeen Patron candidates were successful in the Ontario election of 1893. Although the driving force of the Patrons waned rapidly, they had in their heyday given voice to the farmers' protest against the National Policy because it protected manufacturing at the expense of agriculture.

In contrast to the farmers' unions, there had been little organization of industrial labour by 1891. Most trade unions included only the small segment of highly skilled workers, and in a generation of low wages and high unemployment their membership grew slowly. The Canadian Labour

Vancouver, British Columbia, in the 1880's.

Union, organized in Ontario in 1873, had collapsed before the end of that decade. The arrival in 1881 of an American body, the Knights of Labour, marked a new departure, since the Knights included unskilled workers. The Knights were prominent in the creation of the federated Trades and Labour Congress in 1883, but like the Canadian Labour Union the Congress was essentially an Ontario manifestation until the mid-nineties. The fact that most Canadian unions were locals of parent American bodies created no difficulties – the slowness of trade union growth was due to the lack of industrialism outside the two central provinces and to the firm opposition to trade unionism by the Roman Catholic church in Quebec.

Except for Ontario, where Mowat's government was beginning to pass protective labour legislation, Canadian factory workers were largely at the mercy of the popular insistence on complete freedom of contract, and of employers who demanded long hours for low wages and showed little sense of social responsibility towards their employees or consumers. Child labour, union busting, and sweatshop conditions were seemingly justified by the high returns paid to stockholders – for example, one anti-labour, price-fixing combination allowed cotton-mill owners to pay a 32 per cent dividend!

Despite the long depression which had stunted but not stopped Canada's growth, life in the 1890's was for most people more comfortable than ever before. Large and comfortable brick homes dotted the settled countryside, huge mansions, gaudily decorated, embellished the cities,

Steam threshing in Manitoba, 1887.

Sir George Stephen's house in Montreal, 1884. Sir George was president of the CPR *from 1881-8.*

horse-drawn street cars provided transportation for the urban residents. In the average home family photographs decorated the parlour, where overstuffed horsehair furniture, upholstered in sombre hues of velvet plush, testified to the widely-shared affluence of society and the stability of family life. On winter evenings the viewing of stereopticon slides revealed a new dimension of life to the many who could not as yet afford the Grand Tour to Europe's capitals – in summer on the lantern-lit decks of pleasure cruisers ladies in bustle dresses danced with gentlemen in stiff celluloid collars and Prince Albert suits, to the lilting waltzes of Strauss.

Yet in the midst of pleasure and comfort there were causes for concern. The cities had their slums, where low incomes, alcoholism, and crime were awakening the social conscience of the well-to-do. Poverty was now accepted as an economic ill – and the cause of social evils – rather than the simple result of sinful human laziness. City-centre missions where food, clothes, comfort, and aid were dispensed to the less fortunate were widely supported by the churches. The temperance movement, which was synonymous with prohibition, was active and strong in all provinces to combat the supposed source of all social evils, the "liquor trade". Charitable and social organizations could count on the generosity of the wealthy for funds and organizational ability, and the same small group promoted such varied cultural activities as symphony orchestras, art galleries, choral groups, and educational foundations. A low rate of taxation and the admonitions of clergymen that wealth was a social trust encouraged such philanthropy. Macdonald's Canada had changed much in the quarter-century since Confederation, but even more drastic changes were in store for Macdonald's heirs.

HISTORY FROM THE SOURCES

Why Louis Riel Was Hanged

Louis Riel was tried for the crime of high treason and found guilty. But was he hanged for his part in the Northwest Rebellion or was his execution a judicial murder in revenge for his killing of Thomas Scott at Fort Garry fifteen years earlier? Was Riel the victim of his own violent ambitions or was he martyred by Orange influence as part of a plot to destroy the French-Canadian nation? Medical authorities said that Riel could distinguish between right and wrong, but the question remains whether or not his delusions and fantasies were proof of insanity.

Le Monde, a Conservative Montreal paper, defended the government's policies up to the moment of Riel's death, but then Le Monde joined French-Canadian Liberals in denouncing his execution.

> The hanging of Riel is a bloody concession made to Orange fanaticism; it is the explosion of a blind rage against the French-Canadian nationality. . . . If the English unite against us to crush us, let them know that we are not a nation of slaves who will allow those of our own people who battle heroically for the rectification of grievances to mount the scaffold. French Canadians too know how to unite, not to quench in blood a fierce hatred but to make their rights respected. . . . It's quite clear that the intention is to destroy the French Canadians; but the French-Canadian nationality is too strong and healthy a tree for fanaticism to blow it down.
>
> *Le Monde*, 17 November 1885 (translation)

The Toronto Daily Mail, a leading English Conservative newspaper, offered a long and reasoned editorial defending the course of justice in Riel's case.

> There has never been a doubt of his guilt; in fact he confessed it by his sanity. He has had a fair trial. . . . The crime of which he was convicted is the most heinous known to our code, and no extenuating circumstances were discoverable. Lastly, it was the Felon's second offence, the death penalty passed upon him on a previous occasion having been commuted to five years' banishment. . . . Unfortunately an uproar has been stirred up in Lower Canada by certain politicians who are prepared to sacrifice the interests of law, order, and stable government in the Dominion provided they can

embarrass the Federal Administration. The dishonesty of these persons is fairly established by the fact that whilst they are striving to make a martyr out of RIEL in the eyes of French Canadians, their political allies in Ontario have been loudest in calling for his blood.

[His defenders] allege in the first place, that Louis Riel was insane. But why did they not establish this at the trial? . . . It is worthy of note also that his friends never dreamt of impugning his standing as a rational being until he stood indicted for a capital offence. . . .

The principal ground, however, upon which the execution of this man has been opposed is the allegation that his was a political offence, and that nowadays political offences are not visited with the death penalty among civilized nations. . . . The dynamitard claims that his crime is a political one. When reminded that in the pursuit of his work of destruction he sometimes takes the life of innocent persons, his reply is that this is only an unavoidable incident of his warfare.

. . . from first to last, as the Catholic missionaries and his half-breed victims testified, his conduct was that of a selfish, cowardly, and unscrupulous adventurer, always ready to sacrifice the lives of others for the accomplishment of his own wild designs.

Daily Mail, 16 November 1886

When Riel's execution was debated by the House of Commons in its 1886 session, the rising young French-Canadian Liberal, Wilfrid Laurier, defended Riel's actions by comparing his rebellion to the struggles for freedom by European nations and blamed government policies for making Riel's rebellion necessary.

. . . I appeal, upon this occasion, as I did elsewhere, to every friend of liberty, to all those who, during twenty-five years past, have felt their hearts thrill whenever a struggle for freedom was going on in any corner of the world; . . . and when at last – at last – a section of our own countrymen rose in arms to claim rights long denied them, rights which were immediately acknowledged to be just, as soon as they were asked with bullets, are we to have no sympathy with them? Though, Mr. Speaker, these men were in the wrong; though the rebellion had to be put down; though it was the duty of the Canadian Government to assert its authority and vindicate the law, still, I ask any friend of liberty, if there is not a feeling rising in his heart, stronger than all reasoning to the contrary, that these men were excusable?

* * * * *

The contention laid down is that when the people of Canada are
to examine the action of the Government in executing Riel, the question whether or not the rebellion was provoked is not to be taken
into consideration. Was there ever a more unconstitutional, more
intolerable doctrine propounded? I say it is contrary to the true
doctrine, for if there is any occasion when the Government is bound
to search into the matter to see if provocation has been given for the
committal of an offence, which has involved the death penalty, it
is when the offence charged is purely a political one. . . . With the
Government all rebellions are alike, whether provoked or not, and
they have all to be treated in the same way. You are to look at all
rebellions as utterly bad. . . . I say, on the contrary, that this is one
of the grounds on which I arraign the Government. It was their duty
when they came to consider, whether the death sentence should be
carried out on Riel, to consider whether he had received provocation
for the deed which brought him into that situation; and having
failed to do so, the Government, on their own confession, stand
guilty of having failed in a duty, which is one of the most sacred
that ever can fall upon man.

> Canada, Parliament, *Debates of the House of Commons,*
> 1886 (Ottawa), Vol. XXI, pp. 179, 180.

*J. A. Chapleau, Secretary of State in Macdonald's government, had de-
fended Riel's lieutenant, Ambroise Lépine, at his trial in 1874 for partici-
pating in the Red River rebellion. Speaking in reply to Laurier in 1886,
Chapleau stressed the differences between the 1870 and 1885 rebellions.*

. . . Louis Riel, when he arrived in the North-West, commenced
his work, as the evidence which has been brought before the House
shows, by trying to captivate the sympathy of the people. He was
a master in that art. After having succeeded in that, what did he do?
When he saw that the people were not ready to accept all his views,
he began a political agitation. He did not address himself to the
Government, but went on with his agitation; and, when, as in one
instance, a venerable bishop, Bishop Grandin, had him at a meeting,
and said: "Perhaps this is not the course you should follow," immediately you see Louis Riel not only trying to captivate the sympathies
of the people and alienating from them the Government and the
officials, but even alienating those who, according to the words of the
great writer, whose authority I have cited, "are in the best position
to know the wants of the people and to advise the rulers of the coun-

try." He alienated them from his cause, he created a new religion, he was a renegade and an apostate. Then, Mr. Speaker, Riel did nothing of what is considered to be the necessary conditions in order to justify the rising of a nation. He is inexcusable, if he is judged according to the rules accepted by the Church. But there is another rule by which he, perhaps, wanted to be judged; that is the political rule which is this – the man who rises against the Government, if he succeeds, might be a hero; if he succumbs he is a traitor and he is executed. Riel has chosen what he wanted to have – not the rule of a justifiable rising, but the human political rule, to be applied to him; to be considered a hero if he succeeded, or a felon and a traitor if he failed, and to be acted upon as such; as he was treated and as the law acted upon him.

. . . It is useless for my hon. friends on the other side to try to make of this rising, as my hon. friend from Quebec East (Mr. Laurier) has been trying to make it, an insurrection that might be justified and excused. It is of no use for them to try to make of Riel a martyr, as my hon. friend from Maskinongé (Mr. Desaulniers) said he did, or a hero, as my hon. friends opposite have tried to prove him, or even an insane man, as some of my friends on this side have been disposed to think him, giving the benefit of any doubt they had, not to the law, but to that humane tenderness which exists for a man who is condemned to the gallows. No, Sir, history, in its impartiality, shall not decree him a hero. The *bonum commune*, the interest of the nation was not the motive of his actions. He had dreamed of being a Napoleon, but he was ready and willing to be the chief of a guerilla band, ruling by violence and terror over the region of his exploits, living on plunder and waiting for the accident of a fortunate encounter to secure a heavy ransom with the safety of his own life. Here is, in my opinion, and I speak with the sincerity of my heart and of my conscience, such is my opinion of Louis Riel's campaign, surrender and death: Riel was not an ordinary criminal, who, under the impulse of strong ruling passions, and for lucre, lust and revenge, committed murder, arson and pillage, with "malice aforethought." Riel has been an unscrupulous agitator, getting up a rebellion against the Sovereign for the sake of personal ambition and profit under the color of redressing public grievances.

Canada, Parliament, Debates of the House of Commons,
1886 (Ottawa), Vol. XXI, pp. 349, 354-5.

Chapleau, who was second only to Sir Hector Langevin in importance among French-Canadian Conservatives, had decided after much heart-

searching to support the execution of Riel for reasons he explained to Macdonald at that time.

I spent the greatest part of the night in preparing my memorandum in support of my disagreement in the Riel case. Just as I was sending it this morning, I hesitated, in face of the terrible responsibility of an agitation on such a question where national animosities would surely meet to fight their battle, and after a long meditation I have decided not to incur that great responsibility.

I believe in the guilt of the prisoner. His mental delusions would be the only extenuating point against the full application of the law in his case.

In the state of doubt in which I am with regard to that point, I prefer giving the benefit of the doubt to the law than to the deluded criminal.

We may be called to suffer, my Quebec colleagues and myself, I more than others, at the hands of our people, owing to the intense feeling which exists in our Province. (It is a further reason with me not to abandon my colleagues, as it would look like desertion at the hour of danger.)

However, I prefer the risk of personal loss to the national danger imminent with the perspective of a struggle in the field of race and religious prejudices. We will have to fight perhaps to fall. Well I prefer, after all, to fight and to fall in the old ship and for the old flag.

I would prefer, in this case, that the Minute of last evening's Council would record my assent to the decision of the Council.

J. A. Chapleau to Sir John A. Macdonald, confidential,
12 November 1885
Sir John A. Macdonald Papers, Public Archives of Canada,
M.G. 26, A 1 (b), Vol. 204, pp. 558-60.

FURTHER READING

In addition to the books cited for Chapter 16, see the following:

Brown, R. C., *Canada's National Policy, 1883-1900* (Princeton: Princeton University Press, 1964). Analyses Canadian economic nationalism as practised by Conservatives and Liberals.

Sissons, C. B., *Church and State in Canadian Education* (Toronto: Ryerson, 1959). Chapter 3 examines the Manitoba schools question.

18

The Laurier Years

The Liberals Take Office

Although the election returns of 1896 gave the Liberals a clear majority of thirty, Sir Charles Tupper refused to resign for six days. At last, on 11 July, Laurier was sworn into office and two days later he filled all the cabinet posts but one. The new government was composed of such outstanding politicians that it was promptly dubbed the "Ministry of All Talents". The important post of Public Works was filled by Israël Tarte, who had broken the long Conservative hold over Quebec. The aging Oliver Mowat resigned the Ontario premiership to become Minister of Justice and deal with the thorny Manitoba schools question. W. S. Fielding, Minister of Finance, and A. G. Blair, of Railways, were two experienced and capable men who would have to cope with the fate of Macdonald's nation-building policies, while Sir Richard Cartwright, the Liberal financial critic, was relegated to Trade and Commerce because of his recent involvement with the Commercial Union movement. The only empty portfolio was the important office of the Interior, which Laurier was reserving for Clifford Sifton, Minister of Education in Manitoba and the best informed man on the needs of western Canada, who remained waiting in the wings until the Manitoba schools question was settled.

The first issue confronting Laurier's new government was that vexed and long-drawn-out problem of Manitoba's separate schools. In the election campaign Laurier had promised that the province would not be forced by federal legislation to restore separate schools. Discussions towards a settlement were undertaken by Mowat and Tarte, with Sifton acting for Manitoba. Before the end of 1896 an agreement had been reached: denominational schools would not be part of the public system, and language rights for the French and other minorities would be restricted. The essence of the Manitoba School Act of 1890 had been preserved. This solution was widely accepted in the west and Sifton now assumed the post of Minister of the Interior. In the east, however, the settlement was the signal for an outburst of ultramontane condemnation of Laurier and Tarte as traitors to their race and their religion.

The first airplane at the Lakehead (1910) at its landing ground on Kelly's race track at the corner of Edward and Arthur Streets, Fort William.

Laurier had already vainly approached the papacy for support, but threatened by religious strife that could destroy Canadian confederation, he renewed his appeal, this time successfully. Cardinal Merry del Val, a young and energetic companion of the pope, spent several months in Canada interviewing all the parties involved before reporting his findings to the pope, who delivered his judgement in December 1897 through an encyclical letter. While upholding the traditional Catholic view of education and justifying the bishops' past opposition, the encyclical ended with a strong recommendation for compromise: "It is expedient and useful to make use of such concessions" as the Tarte-Sifton settlement contained. Only Archbishop Langevin of St. Boniface rejected this advice, and two meetings with Laurier did not reconcile him to the loss of denominational schools in Manitoba. But in the end conciliation triumphed over coercion; slowly the archbishop's holy war against state schools subsided, and the church-state question in Canadian education slumbered for another decade.

The west entered into two more of the government's central policies: tariff revision and the settlement of the prairies. In 1897 the Liberals' first budget proclaimed that Canada's tariff would now be directed towards raising revenue, not towards protection as in the days of Macdonald. But the change was largely in name – the element of protection was still there, thinly disguised. Decreased protection for manufactures was offset by government bounties to the Canadian iron and steel industry, for example. In 1896 Laurier had promised the western farmers free trade, but the additions to the free list were limited to fence wire, binder twine, cream separators, and a few similar items. True, tariff schedules were simplified and most specified (fixed) duties were changed to *ad valorem* (a proportion of estimated value). But the Liberal budget was certainly still far

In the north at the turn of the century (1902) the Eskimos were still pursuing their traditional way of life. The white ornaments in these men's lips are made of stone, kept in place by a "shoulder" carved into the stone.

from free trade: the only important innovation was a maximum and minimum rate, the latter a preferential rate from which only Great Britain could profit. The Liberal budget looked strangely like a protectionist Conservative budget. There was something there for everyone – farmer, factory worker, and industrialist – but not too much for anyone.

Although almost two decades had passed since Macdonald's National Policy had been introduced, and one since the CPR had been completed, by 1896 the Canadian west had not fulfilled its great agricultural promise and the Canadian east was still plodding slowly towards its goal of industrialization. The generation-long world depression of trade had been a factor in slowing down Canadian economic growth, and emigrants from Britain and continental Europe had bypassed Canada for the greater attractions of the United States and Australasia. The shortage of investment capital had been felt in all countries, but particularly in developing ones such as Canada. Manufacturing, still concentrated largely in Ontario and Quebec, had expanded very little because of small consumer demand, a shortage of capital, and strong competition from better established foreign manufacturers. Less than 20 per cent of the labour force was engaged in the manufacturing industries, and agriculture was still the country's largest source of employment. Prices of all commodities and the volume of exports had fallen 20 per cent during the 1870's and showed no marked recovery during the next fifteen years.

The mineral resources of the Shield were still not being exploited and the lumber industry suffered from cutbacks in building and railway construction in Britain and the United States. Paper manufacturing, based on the vast forests of the Shield, was similarly underdeveloped – only sixty-eight employees were reported by the industry in the census of 1881. Between 1872 and 1896 Canadian prices of iron and steel fell 58 per cent, grains and flour declined 45 per cent, and meat and dairy products dropped by 30 per cent. The Maritime provinces had begun to feel the economic pinch soon after Confederation, but British Columbia was probably the most seriously retarded province because of its heavy dependence on foreign markets for its primary products – lumber and fish.

Below: Steam threshing at Mount Pleasant (near Brantford), Ontario, in 1905.
Right: A barn-raising bee in Kincardine Township, Ontario, in 1910.

The only bright spot in this gloomy picture was the reduction of trans-Atlantic freight rates by 85 per cent; if Europe's market did revive, Canadian producers would be able to ship at a decided advantage.

Although the pace of Canada's development since 1867 had been slow, it had not been negligible. The country's population had grown from 3,689,000 in 1871 to 4,833,000 in 1891, despite the fact that over a million Canadians had emigrated to the United States. In 1871 the prairies had less than 75,000 inhabitants; by 1896 there were 325,000, about two-thirds of them in Manitoba. By strange good fortune the Liberals took office in the very year that dramatic economic improvements appeared throughout the world. The discovery of gold in South Africa in the late 1880's led to a sharp rise in the world's monetary resources. Prices and wages began to rise and an increased demand for Canadian grain was further stimulated by the roller milling technique that made finer flour and by the lower freight rates. World markets for lumber, pulpwood, and minerals were once more open to Canada, and the net result of all these changes was a boom in the nation's export trade.

Coincidental with these economic improvements came a flood of immigrants to fill the prairie wheat lands – "the last best west" – and to provide skilled workers for the blossoming industrial revolution in the central provinces. The exhaustion of free homestead land in the United States diverted a stream of settlers from the United States, Britain, and eastern Europe northward to Canada's untapped west in what was effectively the last great North American land rush. Once again Canada's west looked optimistically to its own long-promised development, and its most ardent advocate was Clifford Sifton, the energetic westerner who promoted a vigorous immigration policy with spectacular success. Convinced that publicity could attract the right type of settler to move into the vacant western lands, Sifton appointed immigration agents in many countries and advertised in newspapers and periodicals (1,700 of them in the United States), offering free lands and assisted passage. Handbills and pamphlets in several languages, public lectures, tours of the west by newspapermen and politicians, and even foreign tours by successful western settlers – all these and other means were used in the United States, Britain, and central and eastern Europe to promote public awareness of the prairies' potential.

Immigrants arriving at the CPR *station in Winnipeg, about 1912.*

The result of Sifton's campaign was a veritable tidal wave of immigration that rushed on until 1913, seven years after Sifton had resigned from Laurier's cabinet. Between 1896 and 1903 367,000 immigrants arrived and between 1904 and 1913 almost two and a half million more, making up two-thirds of Canada's 34 per cent population growth, an increase larger than any other major country in the world. Wheat acreage tripled in the fifteen years 1896-1911, and wheat production quadrupled in the same period. Good crops, such as that of 1901 when over fifty million bushels of wheat were harvested, put money into the hands of new settlers, who needed the clothes, tools, and food which eastern factories could produce. As new areas in the west were opened, new urban centres appeared there almost overnight. Winnipeg, with 30,000 inhabitants in 1892, had grown to 150,000 by 1911 to become Canada's Chicago, the gateway and emporium of the west. Thus the development of the west also promoted urbanization and industrialization in other parts of Canada.

New Provinces and New Problems

Flushed with the boom that was going on within its own borders and in its vaster hinterland, Manitoba demanded a westward extension of its boundaries to take in the 164,000 settlers in the districts called Assiniboia, Saskatchewan, and Alberta. The federal government, however, supported the request of those settlers for the establishment of new provinces. In

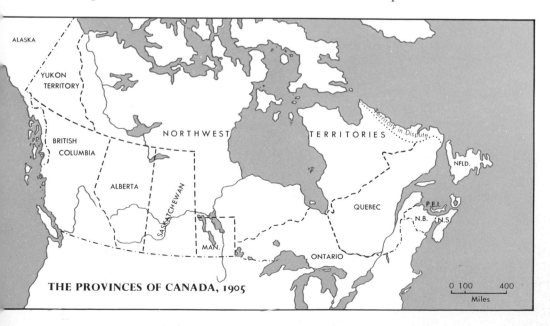

THE PROVINCES OF CANADA, 1905

1905 Saskatchewan and Alberta, Canada's eighth and ninth provinces, were created with full provincial status, but not before the problem of educational privileges had been raised again. When Laurier attempted to provide for separate schools in the provincial constitutions, F. W. Haultain, premier of the Northwest Territories, demanded complete provincial control over education. He was supported by public opinion in Manitoba and Ontario, and by Sifton who resigned from the cabinet on this issue. Laurier reluctantly accepted the secular school system for Alberta and Saskatchewan, with provision, however, for religious instruction during class hours. This latest conflict over church-state relations in education shook confidence in Laurier in the west, in Ontario, and in Quebec where Henri Bourassa, Laurier's rival for leadership of French-Canadian national feeling, had won popular support by his adamant defence of denominational schools.

Education was not the only western issue to trouble Laurier's government. In the 1890's the interests of prairie grain farmers had clashed with those of the railway and grain elevator owners. The farmers complained of high freight rates and criticized the economic power of the eastern financial institutions which lent them money and held mortgages on their farms; they also complained of the high prices of clothes, farm equipment, and other necessities, which they blamed on the tariff protection given to eastern manufactures. To meet these complaints Laurier was forced to move in several ways towards government regulation and even public ownership of essential services. Lower freight rates were imposed on the Canadian Northern Railway, and the opening of a new line to Port Arthur in 1902 forced the CPR to reduce its charge. The co-operative grain growers' associations, formed in the prairie provinces after 1902 to handle grain sales, had to be recognized by the government as the voice of the western farming community.

Other westerners, too, voiced discontent in the midst of prosperity. In Winnipeg, the commercial hub of the west and centre for industries related to food production and transportation, a militant trade union movement emerged. British socialist influences were particularly evident in

Left: House of stucco, wood, and thatch in Alberta, typical of many of the homes built by the Ukrainians who settled there at the end of the nineteenth and the beginning of the twentieth centuries.
Right: School children on the prairies, c. 1910.

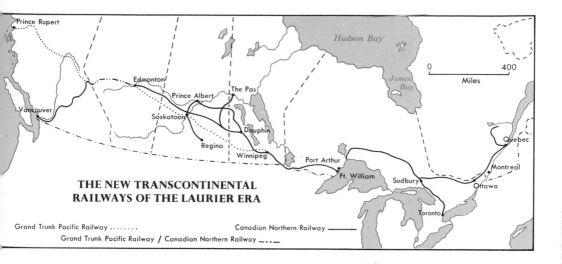

THE NEW TRANSCONTINENTAL
RAILWAYS OF THE LAURIER ERA

Grand Trunk Pacific Railway ....   Canadian Northern Railway ————
      Grand Trunk Pacific Railway / Canadian Northern Railway —.._—

Manitoba, where municipal socialism (public ownership of power and telephone systems and of street railways) set an example for urban development in other parts of Canada. American settlers in the Canadian west urged the adoption of democratic political party methods to make their elected representatives directly answerable to the voters, as was done in the neighbouring mid-western United States, and they joined the criticism of the eastern-based old political parties who supposedly favoured big business interests. Unlike the British and American settlers the large number of Scandinavians, Galicians, Ruthenians, Ukrainians, and other European immigrants in the west were not at first politically active, but they posed their own problem: how could they be made into "good Canadians" on the Protestant, Anglo-Saxon model that Ontario projected through Manitoba into the west? Assimilation was achieved in time by means of the educational systems which "anglicized" the second generation of immigrants.

The wheat boom in the west also created a transportation problem when the facilities of the CPR proved inadequate to handle the huge harvests. There was an obvious need and a public demand for increased railway freight services. As early as 1896 two enterprising railway contractors, William Mackenzie and Donald Mann, began to assemble a system of feeder lines, with financial support from the Manitoba government. By 1903 their railway, the Canadian Northern, extended from Port Arthur to Portage La Prairie and connected with the Northern Pacific in the United States, making it the third largest system in Canada. Soon the Canadian Northern acquired lines in the Maritimes, Quebec, and Ontario, and a westward extension to Edmonton. Only two stretches – through northern Ontario and across the Rockies to the Pacific – were needed to make the Canadian Northern into Canada's second transcontinental rail-

Construction work on the Grand Trunk Pacific Railway in western Alberta, 1910.

way. But the operations of Mackenzie and Mann were based on a shaky financial structure that left the company without reserves in any period of recession. To enable the Canadian Northern to become transcontinental, Laurier's government, with the approval of the Opposition, guaranteed $105 million Canadian Northern bonds between 1903 and 1914, and various provincial governments added another $130 million in guarantees.

Mackenzie and Mann's railway empire had been created despite strong CPR objections, but it soon had another envious competitor in the Grand Trunk. By exploiting public interest in the mining and lumbering of northern Quebec and Ontario and in the potential farm lands of the clay belt north of Lake Superior, the Grand Trunk got Laurier's promise that the federal government would build another line from the Maritimes to Winnipeg. This new line would be leased to the Grand Trunk's subsidiary, the Grand Trunk Pacific, whereas the Grand Trunk Pacific would build track from Winnipeg to the Pacific coast, with a government guarantee of interest on its bonds for seven years. In 1903, on the eve of this generous agreement with the Grand Trunk Pacific, A. G. Blair, Minister of Railways, resigned because he disapproved of Laurier's policies. "This is not a time for deliberation," commented Laurier, "it is a time for action. The flood-tide is upon us that leads on to fortune. . . ." Laurier was wrong. A decade later the flood-tide led to misfortune and bankruptcy for both the Canadian Northern and the Grand Trunk Pacific.

Although the most memorable feature of the Laurier years was the development of the Canadian west, Ontario and Quebec also shared in the great economic boom. The Shield, particularly in the areas of Lake St. Jean and north of Trois-Rivières, offered the ideal combination of hydro-electric power and vast stands of spruce which by the turn of the

The Crown Chartered Mine in Porcupine, Ontario, 1910. The first gold claim in the Porcupine area was staked in 1905, and the first mine went into operation two years later.

century were being exploited by large pulp mills, most of them owned by Americans but manned by French Canadians. In the late 1880's copper-nickel deposits had made Sudbury an important mining centre in Ontario, and in the next generation the discovery of silver at Cobalt and gold at Porcupine and Kirkland Lake opened another chapter of the hard-rock mining industry in the province. Gold from the Yukon and from British Columbia added to the remarkable increase in Canadian mineral production, which doubled its total value between 1900 and 1912.

The improvements in transportation and the shift in world consumption to products which Canada could supply meant that the country's export trade increased at an unprecedented rate during the first decade of the twentieth century, but still she had a large deficit in her international accounts almost every year. In part this deficit was a result of the rapid increase of foreign investment, especially by Britain and the United States, in Canada's burgeoning economy. Although investments in Canada by Canadians quadrupled in the first decade, domestic money supplies alone could not fill the heavy demands for new capital by a society rapidly becoming industrialized. Interest payments to foreign investors could only be met by greater Canadian productivity.

Protected by the moderate Liberal tariff and stimulated by the needs of Canada's rapidly enlarging population, manufacturing industries increased their production of a wide variety of goods. The building of new rail lines required vast amounts of iron and steel from Canadian mills. Clothing, food, and utensils were manufactured in ever-increasing quantities, and the introduction of electricity created a new way of domestic living based on labour-saving devices. Where life in Victorian Canada had been marked by hard work and bustling activity, the Edwardian age was

The automobile – symbol of the new prosperity in the early 1900's.
Left: A two-cylinder McLaughlin touring car at Bowmanville, Ontario, 1908.
Bottom left: The McLaughlin Carriage Company's factory at Gananoque, Ontario. Fire destroyed the Oshawa plant in 1899 and the operation was moved to temporary quarters until it was rebuilt. The company's production of cars began in 1907.
Bottom right: A steam car at St. John's, Newfoundland, 1903-4.

Two scenes from North Sydney, Nova Scotia, showing property of the Gowrie Mines in 1891. Left: The shipping piers. Right: The company's patent fuel factory.

one of comfort, stability, and leisure. The golden years before 1914 will always be remembered for social gentility, "Tiffany" lamps, striped blazers, and straw "boaters"; for gay dances on moonlight pleasure cruises, for the first experimental – and expensive – motor cars, for the exclusive clubs of the rich; for the grand city houses built by a generation of highly successful businessmen to display their huge fortunes and their unbridled optimism.

Not all Canadian regions shared in the new prosperity which the twentieth century seemed to have brought with it. Cities with well-lit streets and horse-drawn street railways attracted more and more people away from the conservative life on the family farm, where modern conveniences were slower to appear. But the Maritime provinces, particularly, were bypassed by the boom of the Laurier years. Between 1891 and 1911, when Canada's population grew from 4.8 to 7.2 million, Nova Scotia's population increased by only 42,000, New Brunswick's by a mere 30,000, and the population of Prince Edward Island declined by 16,000. Markets for the Maritimes' traditional products – fish and timber – were waning, and the development of hydro-electric power in the central provinces had started Nova Scotia's coal mines on the road to ruin. By almost every standard of measurement – economic, demographic, or even political – the Maritimes were becoming Canada's forgotten provinces.

Canada's Imperial Relations

In 1884 the Imperial Federation League had been founded in London to promote a federal union of Britain and her colonies – a union which would also be a unitary defence system and trading bloc. Soon Canadian League branches were formed by prominent people, mostly Conservatives. Three years later, on the occasion of Queen Victoria's golden jubilee, the British government called the first Colonial Conference, at which the Australasian colonies urged the idea of a defence union, in view of their isolated position in the Far East. British officials, however, were reluctant to discuss the League's programme, and Canada's representatives – two minor political figures – said that the British and American navies already provided Canada with adequate protection, and, they might have added, at no cost to the Canadian taxpayer.

Most aspects of imperial relations were discussed at the 1887 conference, but no concrete decisions were taken. A second and less important conference was held at Ottawa in 1894. A third conference, called in 1897, the Queen's sixtieth anniversary on the throne, was attended by the colonial prime ministers, including Laurier who was making his first trip abroad. The various aspects of imperial affairs were again discussed, but no decision regarding defence was recorded and the political relations between Britain and her self-governing colonies were dismissed as "generally satisfactory". Two years earlier Joseph Chamberlain had taken the post of Colonial Secretary with the avowed intention of promoting imperial unity, and had in a short time enlarged the importance of his office until he was second only to the prime minister. Laurier was content with Chamberlain's vague statement that joint responsibility for imperial policies would require joint control by all parts of the empire. "A colony, a nation – never before in the history of the world were these two words associated before" was Laurier's definition of the changing role of the colonies. But even this position was viewed by French Canadians as subservience to imperialism, and the outbreak of the Boer War just two years later created a political crisis in Canada that revealed the differing attitudes of French- and English-speaking Canadians towards the imperial connection.

In 1899, after several years of increasing tension, the Boer (farmer) republics of Transvaal and the Orange Free State declared war on Great Britain and her empire. Although British public opinion was divided over the "rightness" of the war, most English-speaking Canadians, especially in Ontario and British Columbia, demanded that Canada offer military aid to the mother country. By contrast, French Canadians viewed the war as British aggression against a linguistic minority similar to the Métis. Legally Canada had no commitment to share in any of Britain's wars, yet if Laurier refused Canadian aid he would turn pro-British Canadians against his government. On the other hand, Canadian participation in the war would increase French Canada's isolationism and fear of imperial centralizing tendencies. Laurier compromised, hoping to preserve Canadian unity: Canada would send a volunteer contingent, but Britain would maintain it in South Africa.

This compromise satisfied neither group of Canadians. For the French Canadians it meant Canadian involvement in a British war; for English Canadians the measure was so inadequate in meeting the demands of loyalty that almost 7,000 volunteered for service with the British army in South Africa. The fact that Canadians brought honour to their country by

In January 1900 "The Illustrated London News" (published in London, England) printed this photograph of the Canadian contingent marching up Adderley Street in Cape Town, South Africa, at the beginning of the Boer War.

their determination and valour in the Boer War merely intensified the memory of Laurier's fence-sitting on English-French issues.

In May 1902 the Boer War ended after 300,000 British soldiers finally harried 75,000 Boers into submission. Weeks later the colonial prime ministers gathered in London for the fourth Colonial Conference and the coronation of Edward VII. The recent war had fostered colonial nationalism rather than imperial unity. The colonies were now less interested in Chamberlain's plans for an Imperial Council, joint sharing of imperial defence costs, and imperial free trade. The conference's only concrete proposal was that Britain should abandon free trade, and when Joseph Chamberlain found no support in the British cabinet for the establishment of tariffs on foreign goods entering Britain nor for imperial preferences, he resigned in 1903.

The next conference – the first to be called an Imperial Conference – met in 1907, after a Liberal government had taken office in Britain. The only decisions reached by the prime ministers were that self-governing colonies would be called "dominions" and that a permanent secretariat should be set up for imperial conferences, which would in future be held every four years. After twenty years of conferences no progress had been made towards imperial federation, imperial free trade, or joint imperial defence. The simple fact was that the loosely knit empire was evolving into the alliance intuitively foreseen by Lord Durham – an association of self-governing nations, bound together only by a common loyalty to inherited institutions and traditions. Suddenly, however, the issue of imperial defence was reawakened in 1908 by the discovery that Germany was building a navy to challenge Britain's supremacy on the high seas.

To meet this challenge Britain embarked on a naval armaments race in 1909 and summoned the dominion prime ministers to an emergency imperial conference on defence. Abandoning its ideal of an integrated imperial navy, the British admiralty proposed that the dominions create navies for their own defence, a proposal to which only Australia responded immediately and positively. Laurier's government recalled that Canada was implicitly protected by the United States' Monroe Doctrine, which guaranteed the independence of nations in the western hemisphere

Contrasts in the north, photographed during an official tour of Hudson's Bay Company posts, c.1900-10. Left: An Indian mother and children. Right: The Commissioner's party.

against European interference. When the Canadian parliament met that autumn, however, the Conservative Opposition demanded some action. Robert Borden, a Nova Scotia lawyer who had become the Conservative leader in 1901, called on Canada to assume a fair share of the cost of her own defence. Since the Boer War the Liberal government had reorganized, enlarged, and re-equipped the Canadian militia through a drastically increased defence budget, but this present threat was a naval one. How much naval protection should Canada undertake, and in what form? Some Conservatives favoured a direct Canadian contribution to the Royal Navy; other Conservatives and most Liberals wanted a two-squadron Canadian navy, and it was this plan that Laurier finally offered to parliament early in 1910 in his Naval Service bill.

Laurier's bill proposed the creation over several years of a modest Canadian navy of eleven ships. The Opposition retorted that world developments did not justify such a leisurely pace of defence preparations – only a direct contribution to the imperial fleet would meet the gravity of the situation. Shrugging off Opposition taunts about his "tin-pot" naval programme, Laurier scoffed at the panic of his opponents. "If England is at war, we are at war," he admitted, but "if we do have a navy, that navy will not go to war unless the parliament of Canada chooses to send it there." That remark was directed at French Canadians, who condemned his naval bill as a surrender to imperialism of Canada's vaguely defined autonomy. The existence of a Canadian navy would, they believed, lead directly to participation in Britain's wars, without participation in the formulation of British foreign policy. Isolationist French Canadians in fact did not want Canadian participation in policy making; pro-imperialist

The rugged and undeveloped north in 1900-10. Below: Poling up the Abitibi River. Right: A settler's farm in northern Ontario, showing cleared and cultivated riverside land.

Canadians did not ask it. To the first group, the very existence of Laurier's navy would be a threat to Canada's assumed independence; to the second, his small "tin-pot" navy would demonstrate virtual disloyalty to Britain in her hour of need. Once again Laurier's desire for a compromise that would protect Canadian unity had the reverse effect of estranging the public opinion of both sections from Liberal policies.

The Pull of Continentalism

Just three days before Laurier faced the new parliament of 1896, a prospector in the Yukon territory filed claim to his gold strike on Rabbit Creek. When word of his find reached the outside world, the last great gold rush of modern times began and presented Canada with the first serious crisis in Canadian-American relations since the days of the Fenian raids. To reach the Klondike River gold fields thousands of prospectors entered the Yukon via the Lynn Canal or the more southerly Stikine River. Both routes crossed coastal lands of the Alaska panhandle, but the international boundary had been so vaguely described in the Anglo-Russian Treaty of 1825 as to defy definition. Since the American purchase of Alaska in 1867, no agreement had been reached between Canada and the United States on which range of mountain peaks should form the international border. A joint High Commission, established in 1896 to settle several issues between the two countries, failed to resolve the difficulty of the Alaska boundary, and two American draft treaties drawn up in 1901 were rejected by both Canada and the new and aggressive American president, Theodore Roosevelt. Finally, in December 1902, Laurier met Roosevelt and convinced him that the dispute should be settled by arbitration.

The tribunal of arbitration was to be composed of six "impartial jurists of repute", half appointed by Britain and half by the United States. The American members – Secretary of War Root and the senators Lodge and Turner – were far from impartial, since each had already denounced Canadian claims regarding the boundary. The British appointees – British

Dawson, in the Yukon, became the main centre for the Klondike gold rush in 1896-1900. Left: Dawson Gold Commissioner's office in 1898. Below: The main street in 1898.

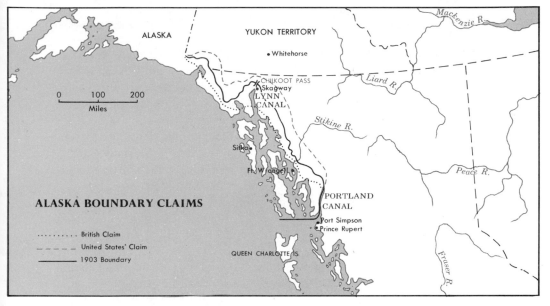

ALASKA BOUNDARY CLAIMS

.... British Claim

- - - - - United States' Claim

———————— 1903 Boundary

Chief Justice Lord Alverstone and two Canadians, Lieutenant-Governor Sir Louis Jetté of Quebec and an Ontario lawyer, A. B. Aylesworth – at least had not expressed their opinions on the case. The American and Canadian members took an uncompromising stand on their own country's territorial claims, and hence it was Lord Alverstone who held the deciding vote. He decided in favour of the American claims, thereby filling the Americans with self-righteous satisfaction and the Canadians with self-righteous indignation. Jetté and Aylesworth refused to sign the award, calling it "a grotesque travesty of justice"; Canadian newspapers commented bitterly: "Canada again offered as a sacrifice on the altar of Anglo-American friendship". Many knowledgeable Canadians admitted that the Americans had had a better – but not unquestionable – legal claim to the disputed areas of the Alaska panhandle. Popular opinion in Canada, however, continued for many years to believe that the Alaska boundary award had been a "sellout" of Canada's national interests, a half-truth that Borden and the Conservatives repeated for their own party advantage.

In the long run the result of the Alaska settlement was to remove the last major cause of friction between the two countries. Canadians continued to express their dissatisfaction with American policies, such as the prohibitively high Dingley tariff of 1897, but it was in economic relations that Laurier came close to establishing continental accord between the United States and Canada. The traditional Liberal enthusiasm for reciprocity and free trade (or at least lower tariff arrangements) with the United States had been publicly abandoned in Laurier's budget of 1897, and as late as 1907 he had warned: "There will be no more pilgrimages to

Washington. We are turning our hopes to the old motherland." Nevertheless, the proximity of the American market of ninety million consumers,
the increased capacity of the Canadian economy in the midst of the turn-
of-the-century boom, and the continued desire of western farmers for free
trade caused Laurier to try one more pilgrimage.

In the autumn of 1910 a thousand prairie farmers descended on Ottawa, demanding an end to price-fixing by eastern industrialists and a
beginning of North American reciprocity in farm products. Immediately
afterwards, President Taft gave the editor of the Toronto *Globe* a message
for Canadians: "I am profoundly convinced that these two countries,
touching each other for more than three thousand miles, have common
interests in trade. . . ." For Laurier, beset by dwindling popularity and
government scandals, this hint at reciprocity destroyed any lingering
loyalty to Macdonald's National Policy. By January 1911, Fielding and
William Paterson, Minister of Customs, had returned from Washington
with an agreement for free trade in the natural products of farm, forest,
fishery, and mine, and for drastically lowered duties on a number of manufactured articles. To avoid the fate of George Brown's Reciprocity Treaty
of 1874, this agreement would be passed simultaneously by parliament
and the American Congress so that only a simple majority vote would be
required.

The whole agreement looked like a Liberal dream come true, and
its approval by parliament seemed certain. Then Laurier made the fateful decision to delay parliamentary approval until the American Senate
had passed its bill. The Conservatives now gained time to marshal public

Bonsecours Market on Commissioner Street, Montreal, in 1900.

opinion in defence of the National Policy. Business interests, manufacturers, banks, and railways quickly joined the Conservative press in denouncing reciprocity as a threat to Canadian independence and imperial solidarity. Reciprocity would, they loudly insisted, be the antecedent to annexation, not the antidote, as Lord Elgin had said in 1854. Soon their voices were joined by those of leading papers of all political persuasions in industrialized central Canada, although the prairie and Maritime provinces looked favourably on the measure because it could alleviate their economic plight. After almost four weeks of emotion-charged debate in parliament, the session was adjourned to let Laurier attend the fifth Imperial Conference and the coronation of George V. When parliament reconvened in mid-July, the Opposition resumed its obstructionist tactics. Ten days later Laurier carried the debate to the voters by calling a general election for September.

Reciprocity was undoubtedly the central election issue, but the campaign was complicated by the recent school disputes in the prairie provinces, by the Naval Service dispute, and in Quebec by Bourassa's decision to align his *League Nationaliste*, founded in 1903 to enlarge French-Canadian rights, with Borden's pro-empire Conservatives, in opposition to Quebec's favourite son, Sir Wilfrid Laurier. An ill-timed remark by President Taft about exploiting Canadian resources was used by the Conservatives to emphasize the political dangers of reciprocity. Perhaps the most damaging blow to Laurier's hopes came from his former cabinet colleague, Clifford Sifton, who organized the "Revolt of the Eighteen", a public repudiation of reciprocity by eighteen prominent Toronto Liberals who were also leading figures in the Canadian business world. Deserted by friends in Ontario, opposed by his fellow French Canadians, the seventy-year-old Laurier fought a hard but defensive election battle, making as many as two public speeches per day. At Saint John he summarized his own peculiar position for the audience:

> I am branded in Quebec as a traitor to the French, and in
> Ontario as a traitor to the English. In Quebec I am branded
> as a Jingo, and in Ontario as a Separatist. In Quebec I
> am attacked as an Imperialist, and in Ontario as an anti-
> Imperialist. I am neither. I am a Canadian. . . . I have had
> before me . . . a policy of true Canadianism, of moderation,
> of conciliation. . . . I now appeal with confidence to the
> whole Canadian people to uphold me in this policy of
> sound Canadianism. . . .

Laurier's confidence was misplaced: conciliation, moderation, and sound Canadianism were not enough to win an election in 1911. When Canadians rejected the Liberal government, the age of Laurier was over.

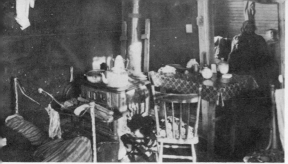

Living Conditions in Edwardian Canada: A Comparison.
Opposite page. Top: Slums in Winnipeg, 1912-13. Centre left: Slums in
Montreal, 1912-13. Centre right: Sherbrooke Street at McTavish,
Montreal, 1896, with Sir George Drummond's house at right. Bottom:
Inside Sir Hugh M. Allan's house, Montreal, 1903.
Above. Top left: Slums in Winnipeg, 1912-13. Lower left: Children in a
Toronto slum area, 1900. Right: Inside Sir George Stephen's house,
Montreal, 1884.

HISTORY FROM THE SOURCES

Poverty and Plenty – Urban Life in Edwardian Canada

The Laurier era witnessed not only the peopling of the prairies but
also the rapid industrialization and expansion of Canada's cities. Between 1891 and 1908 Montreal's population grew from 268,000 to
373,000, Toronto's from 181,000 to 314,000, Winnipeg's from 26,000
to 140,000, and Vancouver's from 14,000 to 93,700.

What problems did this growth of the cities create? J. S. Woodsworth, a Methodist minister and later founder of the CCF, was a
prominent spokesman for the Social Gospel – a widely held belief that
Christianity must concern itself as much with the betterment of human
living as with the salvation of souls. In his book My Neighbour: A Study
of City Conditions, A Plea for Social Service (1911) Woodsworth quotes

from reports of social workers such as *J. J. Kelso, who told the tenth Canadian Conference on Charities and Corrections about living conditions among the working class of Toronto.*

> . . . I pass up and down through the central district a great deal and have often been struck with the haphazard way in which people are allowed to live. Not long ago, I was going down one of these streets and I saw a crowd of Italians hurrying into a small building. It seemed as if the whole street was going in. I enquired of a little girl standing by, what was the matter, and she said: 'Those are only the men going to dinner!' The house would probably not have more than five rooms and there were at least 25 to 30 of these men living there. On another occasion I went through the foreign district after 11 o'clock at night with one of the City Officers, and in every room we went to there were at least four to six persons sleeping, and there were no less than three cottages or houses, one behind the other, in this same overcrowded condition. Often the better class of citizens do not know what is going on, so these wretched social conditions are allowed to grow until they become well-nigh intolerable. Many will tell you that we in Toronto are free from slums, but they are only shutting their eyes to evils that exist. Some of these vile hovels are old cottages built 60 years ago and not improved in any way since – floors sunk, walls out of shape, plaster off, windows broken, and yet these houses are bringing to their owners about four to six times the rent that was paid many years ago when they were in good order. Poor unfortunate people pay $8 and $10 a month for one or two rooms, with no closet, but only vile cesspools used by all alike. They are enough to infect the city, and our Health Department ought to order the pulling down of such places.

> J. S. Woodsworth, *My Neighbour: A Study of City Conditions,*
> *A Plea for Social Service* (Toronto, 1911), pp. 102-3.

Woodsworth cited a news item from the Winnipeg Telegram of 15 October 1909 to portray the problems of his own city.

> The health inspector rudely paid a midnight visit to the place at 47 Austin street the other night, the place being where Mrs. Chudek runs her boarding-house.

There he found thirty-two men living, where there should be seven, according to the laws of health. Scientists say that in a room where human beings live, there should be 400 cubic feet of air space to each man. In Mrs. Chudek's house it worked out at 91 cubic feet to each occupant, a fact which, not only being uncomfortable, was dangerous to the human health.

There were four rooms and each filled literally to the roof. The boarders were located in rooms as follows:–

One room, 13 ft. by 8 ft. by 8 ft., 6 occupants; should be 2.
One room, 12 ft. by 8 ft. by 8 ft., 6 occupants; should be 2.
One room, 13 ft. by 9 ft. by 8 ft., 8 occupants; should be 2.
One room, 13 ft. by 12 ft. by 7 ft., 12 occupants; should be 2½.

Figured out, this means there are thirty-two people where there should be seven, and each gets 91 cubic feet of air, instead of 400.

If these people had even kept the place decent at all, the case might not be quite so bad, but in the words of the health officer, it was 'filthy.' The bedclothes, chairs and everything in the rooms were covered with dirt.

In handling this case, the magistrate addressed the woman and said: 'People are supposed to live like human beings and not like hogs. In your house there was not space for a dog, let alone a man. Besides being overcrowded the place was abominably filthy and as a starter I'll fine you twenty dollars and costs.'

J. S. Woodsworth, *My Neighbour . . .* , pp. 219-20.

W. L. Mackenzie King, who investigated labour conditions in Canada for the Laurier government, described the drug problem among the Chinese community in British Columbia's cities, and how that problem affected other residents.

In the coast cities of Vancouver, Victoria and New Westminster, there are at least seven factories carrying on an extensive business in opium manufacture. It is estimated that the annual gross receipts of these combined concerns amounted, for the year 1907, to between $600,000 and $650,000. The crude opium is imported from India in coconut shells, it is 'manufactured' by a process of boiling into what is termed 'powdered' opium and subsequently into opium 'prepared for smoking.' The returns show that large amounts of crude opium have been imported annually, and that the value of the crude opium imported in the nine months of the fiscal year 1906-7 was greater than the value of the amount imported in the twelve months of the preceding year; the figures for these periods being $262,818, and $261,943, respectively.

The factories are owned and the entire work of manufacture is carried on by Chinese, between 70 and 100 persons being employed. One or two of the factories have been in existence for over twenty years, but the majority have been recently established. It is asserted by the owners of these establishments that all the opium manufactured is consumed in Canada, by Chinese and white people, but there are strong reasons for believing that much of what is produced at the present time is smuggled into China and the coast cities of the United States. However, the amount consumed in Canada, if known, would probably appal the ordinary citizen who is inclined to believe that the habit is confined to the Chinese, and by them indulged in only to a limited extent.

The Chinese with whom I conversed on the subject, assured me that almost as much opium was sold to white people as to Chinese, and that the habit of opium smoking was making headway, not only among white men and boys, but also among women and girls. I saw evidences of the truth of these statements in my round of visits through some of the opium dens of Vancouver.

Canada, Parliament, *Sessional Papers*, 42, Vol. 17,
No. 36 b, p. 7 (1908).

FURTHER READING

Schull, Joseph, *Laurier: The First Canadian* (Toronto: Macmillan, 1965). The most recent and comprehensive of several biographies.

Borden, Henry, ed. *Robert Laird Borden: His Memoirs*, 2 vols. (Toronto: McClelland & Stewart, 1969)★. Autobiography of Canada's wartime prime minister.

Penlington, Norman, *Canada and Imperialism, 1896-1899* (Toronto: University of Toronto Press, 1965). The background of Canadian involvement in the Boer War.

19

Canada Comes of Age

The Problems of Borden's Government

The 1911 election results were, in Borden's words, "a matter of amazement throughout the country". Seven of Laurier's cabinet ministers had been defeated, including Fielding and Paterson who had negotiated the reciprocity agreement. The standings in the House of Commons were almost exactly reversed from those of 1908 – the Liberals were now reduced to 87 seats, the Conservatives increased to 134. Laurier had lost 16 seats in Quebec and 24 in Ontario. "It is the province of Ontario which has defeated us," he lamented, ". . . it was not reciprocity that was turned down, but a Catholic premier."

After fifteen years in opposition the Conservatives faced a difficult task in forming a government. Borden chose such obviously strong figures as G. E. Foster and G. H. Perley. Reluctantly he included Colonel Sam Hughes despite "his erratic temperament and his vanity". F. D. Monk, the Quebec Nationaliste leader, had to be included, though he soon proved to be unco-operative and a source of conflict among the Quebec group. The other cabinet members were capable but not distinguished men, yet from its inception Borden's government suffered from two serious weaknesses. Too many ministers believed that they, not Robert Borden, had won the astounding electoral victory; too many were associated with big business interests, and four of them were millionaires. For several years Borden struggled to impose his leadership on these diverse interests and to create a more popular image for his government.

When the first session of the new parliament met later in 1911, the government avoided any reference to naval policy. Laurier derided the past differences of opinion between the Quebec members and the other ministers over his own Naval Service Act, but Borden refused to divulge his plans. Instead he introduced a bill to create a Tariff Commission which would plan a "scientific tariff" in line with Macdonald's National Policy. This bill was so drastically amended by the Liberal senators that Borden had to abandon the Tariff Commission. This display of power by a hostile Senate majority was but a forewarning of more serious future conflicts with the government. When two more bills suffered the same fate in the upper house, Foster accused Laurier of using his party's unassailable position in the Senate to "slaughter" government measures irresponsibly.

More serious consequences followed from this stalemate in the Canadian parliament when Borden did announce his naval policy a year later. After the first session closed in 1912, Borden and three other ministers had hastened to London to confer about Canada's role in the growing confrontation of naval power between Great Britain and Germany. Discussions with Winston Churchill, First Lord of the Admiralty, confirmed Borden's fears of the possibility of war, and convinced him that something more than Laurier's "tin-pot" navy was required from Canada. Yet at the same time he asserted publicly that Canadians would never be "merely silent partners" in any scheme for "imperial co-operation". On his return to Canada Borden prepared his Naval Aid bill. His plan was to have Canada contribute $35 million towards the building of three British warships of the Dreadnought class, ships which could at any future time become part of a Canadian unit in the Royal Navy. F. D. Monk resigned from the cabinet in opposition to this plan even before it was presented to parliament, and French-Canadian Conservatives were divided over Borden's proposal.

Introducing his bill to the House of Commons in December 1912, Borden pointed out that Canada had no facilities to build warships, nor did she really need to undertake what he called "the hazardous and costly experiment" of creating a separate Canadian Navy. Co-operation with the existing imperial defence organization would ensure the same objectives "upon just and self-respecting terms". When Borden finished speaking, members of the Commons and visitors rose amidst thunderous applause and sang "Rule Britannia" and "God Save the King". This show of enthusiasm merely masked the disunity now expressed by Laurier's demand for a two-squadron Canadian navy to protect the Atlantic and Pacific coasts. After a Christmas recess parliament resumed consideration of the

H.M.C.S. "Niobe" at Halifax in 1910. Two old British cruisers, "Niobe" and "Rainbow" (both launched in the 1890's) were the first ships purchased for the Canadian Navy, which was created in 1910. Bought for training purposes, they were turned over to Britain when the war began and were used for patrol duties.

Sealing ships at St. John's, Newfoundland, about 1912. The ship in the foreground is the "Neptune", considered one of the most modern in operation at the time.

bill. Exactly four months later, in the face of a Liberal filibuster, the bill was finally pushed through the Commons by the use of closure to end the tumultuous and disorderly debating, although five Quebec Conservatives voted with the Opposition. The next obstructive step by the Liberal Opposition was to use its majority in the Senate to "slaughter" the Naval Aid bill. Laurier demanded that the bill be rejected by the Liberal senators or he would resign as Liberal leader. Reluctantly several Liberal senators bowed to this demand for party unity at the expense of national security. The Naval Aid bill was lost. But the prolonged controversy over Canada's defence policy had again demonstrated how national issues could arouse different reactions from French- and English-speaking Canadians, regardless of party affiliation.

Even while the naval policy was being considered, two other issues created similar problems for Borden's government. In 1912 the District of Keewatin had been annexed to Manitoba without any provision being made for denominational schools. Neither the Roman Catholic church nor Monk and the Nationalistes had protested, but in a three-hour speech at Montreal, Henri Bourassa drove a deep racial wedge into the Conservative-Nationaliste alliance by attacking politicians and churchmen alike for betraying French Canadians. Archbishop Langevin then took up the Nationaliste cause with a call for united action by all Frenchmen in North America: "By guarding our religion . . . we guard our race."

At almost the same moment an even more serious controversy arose over Ontario's famous Regulation 17. This school Regulation, suggested by a Roman Catholic bishop, M. F. Fallon, limited the use of French as a language of instruction to the first two years in schools where it was already in use. The intention was to ensure adequate training in English for all students, since less than 10 per cent of the French-speaking teachers in Ontario's separate schools were professionally qualified and the result was inefficient and inadequate education for French-speaking pupils. The strongest opposition to Bishop Fallon and Regulation 17 came from the Ottawa Valley. The Ottawa city separate schools, with 8,000 pupils, were closed during part of 1914 in protest while the legality of Regulation 17 was argued through various courts. Even Pope Benedict XV's statement that Ontario Catholics needed "a thorough knowledge of English" could not pacify opposition whipped up in Quebec by Bourassa's charges of an Orange plot against French culture, by his threats of annexation to the United States, and by his criticism of English-speaking Canadians as materialistic, "loud", "intolerant", and "Yankee". For the moment Laurier seemed indifferent to those developments in Ontario schools and to the agitation in Quebec.

Thus, as menacing clouds of war gathered over Europe, Borden's government was beset by the old Canadian questions of race, religion, and relationship to Great Britain. But other and more practical problems were also appearing in the short years between the election of 1911 and the beginning of the First World War. The Canadian Northern Railway, built mainly with financial help arranged for by Laurier's government and whose promoters, Mackenzie and Mann, he had knighted in 1911, was saved from collapse by a $45 million guarantee from Borden's government. The Grand Trunk Railway was also in trouble, but not so deeply – it received only $16 million. Both railways had to be finished because Canada had invested so much in them, yet their troubled affairs had compromised both political parties, had burdened the Canadian taxpayer, and still gave no assurance of being any nearer to a solution.

Behind the immediate difficulties of the railways lay the even more threatening state of the Canadian economy. The Laurier boom years had

Alexander Graham Bell's hydroplane in the harbour at Baddeck, Nova Scotia, about 1912. Famous as the inventor of the telephone, Bell invented many other electrical devices (including a primitive "iron lung") and constantly experimented with air-borne machines.

given way to another world recession soon after the Conservatives took office. As prices fell on the international markets the total value of exports declined from $443 million in 1913 to $399 million in the following year. The tide of immigrants to Canada dropped from over 400,000 in 1913 to 150,000 in 1914, but by then most of the arable land in the west had been occupied. Farm labourers were still needed, but in manufacturing centres, and especially in Winnipeg, many newcomers could not find jobs. In 1912 and 1913 the provinces had renewed their demands for increased subsidies. The provincial revenues of Quebec and Ontario were proportionately greater than those of the Maritimes or prairie provinces which, along with British Columbia, had much heavier provincial debts than either Quebec or Ontario. Ironically the Canadian economy was rescued from further difficulties and boosted to unimagined heights of productivity and affluence by a great human tragedy, the First World War.

In Flanders Fields

In June 1914 Borden received the honour of a knighthood from the King. Sir Robert had just begun a short holiday at the end of July when telegrams from Britain warned him that war in Europe was likely and that the British empire would be involved if France were attacked. Hastening back to Ottawa the prime minister assured the British government on 1 August that "the Canadian people will be united in a common resolve to put forth every effort and to make every sacrifice necessary" to defend the empire. For the next three days the cabinet sat almost continuously, preparing emergency measures to meet the crises which war would create. At 8:55 p.m. on 4 August, the Cabinet received the fateful message – war had been declared. As part of the empire, Canada was automatically at war, but it remained to be decided what role she would play in the actual hostilities.

In 1914 Canada had a population of 7,700,000. She had a 350-man navy, a regular army of 3,000, and a volunteer militia of 64,000 – a numerically insignificant force by European standards and one deficient in training and equipment. With the outbreak of hostilities, flag-waving crowds in the streets of Montreal sang the Marseillaise and "Rule Britannia" while impassioned patriotic speeches were heard from Halifax to Vancouver. The government announced that Canada would send one division to the defence of France. A rush of volunteers came from all walks of life, especially from city dwellers and immigrants from Great Britain. But Colonel Sam Hughes as Minister of Militia created his own chaos by ignoring the detailed plans for mobilization – he bypassed the existing militia organization to form an entirely new army structure. Nevertheless, within the first month over 32,000 men were assembled at Valcartier, near Quebec, and despite Hughes' officious interference, the first division reached England in October where its training was completed in the mud of Salisbury Plain.

By February 1915, when the first Canadians reached the battle lines in Flanders, the war on the western front had settled into the pattern of trench fighting and artillery duels that characterized the conflict until the summer of 1918. On 22 April a green cloud of chlorine gas released by the Germans suffocated French troops in a two-mile sector of the Ypres line beside the Canadian position at St. Julien. This first gas attack in history left the Canadian flank exposed and the Canadians fought doggedly to close the gap. Two days later the Canadians received a direct gas attack. Their lines did not break but over 6,000 were dead, wounded, or missing when the fighting subsided after three days. Three weeks later the Canadians joined in the abortive attacks at Festubert and Givenchy, and lost over 3,000 more men. The summer of 1915 was relatively quiet for the Canadian First Division but in September and October, after the Second Division arrived to form the Canadian Corps, it supported the ineffective Artois offensive which cost the Allies 260,000 casualties against 150,000 for the Germans.

By now the war had become an endurance test for nations and for their armies facing each other across the killing-ground of "No-Man's Land" amid the filth of the trenches. The crash of heavy artillery and the staccato chatter of machine guns filled day and night, shattering the nerves even of experienced soldiers, but cold, wet, disease, and disillusionment in the trenches were as potent an enemy as the Germans. After minor battles fought during the ensuing winter, the Second Division lost 1,953 men in holding one mine crater at St. Eloi in April 1916. The summer was passed by the Corps (now strengthened by the Third Division) under steady attack in the Ypres Salient. At Mount Sorrel in the first two weeks of June the Canadians suffered 9,600 casualties – almost twice the

Lt.-Gen. Sir Julian Byng looking at some trench mortars captured by the Canadians at Vimy Ridge in 1917.

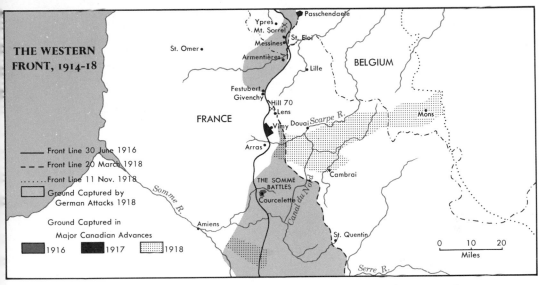

THE WESTERN
FRONT, 1914-18

———— Front Line 30 June 1916
– – – Front Line 20 March 1918
.... Front Line 11 Nov. 1918
☐ Ground Captured by
   German Attacks 1918

Ground Captured in
   Major Canadian Advances
■ 1916   ■ 1917   ▥ 1918

Map labels: Passchendaele, Ypres, Mt. Sorrel, St. Eloi, Messines, St. Omer, Armentières, BELGIUM, Lille, Festubert, Givenchy, Hill 70, Lens, Douai, Scarpe R., Mons, FRANCE, Vimy, Arras, Cambrai, Somme R., THE SOMME BATTLES, Courcelette, Canal du Nord, Amiens, St. Quentin, Serre R.

0   10   20
Miles

enemy's losses – in regaining 1,200 yards of shell-churned ground; in September the Canadians joined in the terrible battle of the Somme (where tanks were used for the first time) and after a full week of fighting captured the village of Courcelette at a cost of 7,230 men. The Fourth Division joined in the Somme offensive and by the end of that winter the Canadian losses accounted for 25,000 of the Allied total of almost 625,000.

Hardened by battle experience, the Canadian Corps was chosen to attack strategic Vimy Ridge in the spring of 1917 in a new Allied offensive. The capture of the Ridge on Easter Monday, 9 April, was planned and executed by General Sir Julian Byng with the utmost attention to detail. Behind a creeping barrage from more than 700 guns the Canadian Corps, four divisions strong, swept over its objective in a matter of hours to achieve a military victory of the first magnitude – "an Easter gift from Canada to France" the French called it – and at a cost of only 3,600 dead. The battle of Vimy Ridge inspired pride in Canada and in Canada's sons, and brought promotions for Byng and for Arthur Currie who became the first Canadian Commander of the Canadian Corps. But Vimy Ridge was the only victory of the Battle of Arras, and the loss of 200,000 Allied soldiers in the over-all offensive caused mutinies in the French army and disgrace for the French general who had planned it.

In April and May of 1917 Canadians participated in the inconclusive battles of the Scarpe, and in the Corps' hardest battle, Hill 70, in August. In mid-October the Corps was moved north to Flanders to the sadly familiar fields at Ypres for the most terrible contest to date – the battle of Passchendaele. Knee-deep mud and water covered a battlefield commanded by German concrete pillboxes, but through a morass of twisted

Left: A group of Canadian soldiers in the trenches.
Above: Canadians carrying trench mats across the mud
and swamp of the Passchendaele battlefield, after the
Allied victory of 1917.

metal and rotting bodies two Canadian divisions fought their way in six days against seven German divisions to a barren victory.

After Passchendaele the Corps returned to the area of Vimy, from where the final offensive was launched against the weary armies of an exhausted Germany on 8 August. In the "One Hundred Days" that followed, the Allied advance was measured in miles, not yards, and by 11 November, when Germany acknowledged defeat, the Canadian Corps was at the gates of Mons, the Belgian city where British troops had suffered their first reverse in 1914.

For Canada the cost of four dreadful years of war had been 60,661 dead, but many more of the 628,000 Canadians who enlisted would carry the physical and mental scars of battle for years to come. Over 80 per cent of the 150,000 Canadian battle casualties were suffered by the infantry. Although Canada's major military contribution had been that superb fighting machine, the Canadian Corps, another 8,800 men had enlisted with the Royal Canadian Navy, 134 Canadian naval vessels had patrolled the country's coasts against the submarine menace, and individual Canadians such as the air ace Billy Bishop had won enduring fame with the Royal Flying Corps in countless dogfights in the skies of Flanders. Canada had every reason to be proud of her war effort, and she emerged from the "ordeal by fire" with a heightened awareness of her capabilities. Canadian nationalism had been born in the midst of the slaughter of the First World War.

The Crisis of Conscription

Almost from the moment that the war began, Borden's government encountered increasing difficulties on two fronts – within the cabinet and in national unity. Militia Minister Sam Hughes naïvely appointed his friends as "special purchasing agents". These agents proceeded to supply the government with inferior, unsatisfactory, and unstandardized wagons, clothing, and arms. Hughes stubbornly defended the adoption of the Ross rifle

– an excellent target weapon but one that jammed or misfired in battle –
until Canadian soldiers forced a change by throwing away the Ross to
pick up the superior Lee-Enfields from dead British comrades. Serious
charges of favouritism in shell and fuse contracts were sustained by a
Royal Commission investigation in 1916, which proved that Hughes had
given shell contracts to friends and speculators who made millions in
profits from small investments.

Hughes' policies on recruitment and promotions in the Canadian Corps
also embarrassed the government. His appointment of a Protestant clergy-
man to recruit in Quebec was a blunder in public relations, and his wholesale promotions to officer rank left many officers without jobs at a time
when rank and file reinforcements were lacking. The First Contingent
had 400 surplus officers when it reached England. Hughes and his friend
Colonel J. W. Carson, his personal representative in London, created such
administrative chaos in the relations of the cabinet to the British War
Office that finally, in 1916, Borden appointed Sir George Perley resident
Overseas Minister in London and head of a new Overseas Military Council. When Hughes angrily criticized Perley and Borden, the prime minister
took the long-overdue action in November 1916 of dismissing him because
he had tried "to administer your Department as if it were a separate Government in itself". Thereafter the affairs of the Canadian Corps and of the
cabinet proceeded with more efficiency and harmony.

Borden had been partly responsible for these troubles, since he had
tolerated Sir Sam in his cabinet for five years, but he was almost
entirely responsible for the most serious wartime issue in Canada's
national life: the conscription crisis. At first there had been no shortage of
volunteers in Canada – almost 220,000 had enlisted by the end of 1915 –
and in January 1916 Sir Robert promised that Canada would put half a
million soldiers in the field. Considering the high rate of casualties on the
Western Front, however, his pledge would require another 300,000 re-

*Left: Robert Borden and Winston Churchill leaving the
Admiralty offices (London), 1912. Below: General Sir
Sam Hughes (centre, with field glasses) visits the front
in August 1916.*

Two Handley-Page heavy bombers on an aerodrome near Dunkirk, April 1918. Many Canadian crews flew these large aircraft which, with a bomb load of nearly 1800 pounds and a range of over 150 miles, were used for night raids.

cruits each year. Hughes believed that a force of this size was entirely feasible, but after March 1916 enlistments began to decline and the December monthly report showed only 5,000 recruits – one-sixth of the March figure and an actual decrease for the total strength of the Corps.

There were several reasons for the diminished enlistments. The initial patriotic enthusiasm for the war had worn off, and the main sources of recruits – the urban population and recent British immigrants – had been largely exhausted. The wartime demand for foodstuffs had encouraged an expansion in Canadian agriculture that absorbed more men, and the wartime growth of manufacturing industry required an increased supply of skilled workers. Since wars are won in factories and on farms as well as on battlefields, factory workers and farmers could point to the essential nature of their jobs. Yet all these demands, military and civilian, had to be met from a total population of less than eight million. In addition, there were psychological brakes on volunteer recruitment. The terrible wastage of life in the trenches was a sobering consideration. Some Canadians, seeing the fortunes made by profiteers, believed that private wealth should be conscripted for national service. Last, and probably least, recruiting had fallen off because of intensive anti-war propaganda that was especially, but not exclusively, heard in the province of Quebec.

In August 1914 the enthusiasm to defend France and Britain had swept Quebec like all other provinces, and the Roman Catholic church had supported Canadian participation as a duty of the faithful. Laurier greeted the decision to send Canadian soldiers by calling the war "a noble cause" – the struggle for freedom against oppression – and gave Canada's answer: "ready, aye, ready". The government failed to exploit this initial enthusiasm by creating French-speaking army units, and of the volunteers of the First Contingent less than 4 per cent were French Canadian. But an important element in cooling French-Canadian ardour was the nationalism of Henri Bourassa, who wrote in *Le Devoir* that this war was not Canada's war, that Britain had entered it from self-interest, dragging Canada with her, and therefore Canada should contribute to the war on her own terms. His increasing criticism of the government's war policies

won him the nickname "Von Bourassa". He countered by calling English
Ontarians "Prussians" for their support of Regulation 17.

By 1915 Bourassa had replaced Laurier in the affections of French
Canadians as his crusade against Regulation 17 became part of a campaign against greater Canadian contributions to the war. Recruiting meetings in Montreal became scenes of violence. The two themes – Regulation
17 and "England's war" – had become intertwined, raising passions on
each side to fever pitch. In vain did Laurier call the French-Canadian
attitude "deplorable" as he, too, pleaded in May 1916 for French-language
educational rights. Against this ominous background of growing national
disunity and racial confrontation, of drastically declining enlistments, Sir
Robert Borden took the first step towards conscription.

In October 1916 Borden appealed for volunteers and authorized a
national manpower census. The volunteers did not step forward, and the
registration of manpower was viewed by French Canadians and by farmers
of Ontario and the west as the prelude to conscription. Troops passing
through Quebec city were pelted with stones and rotten vegetables. In
April 1917, the month of Vimy Ridge, Canadian casualties were twice as
high as enlistments. On 18 May Borden reported to the House of Commons on his London visit of the previous month and announced the necessity of conscripting from 50,000 to 100,000 men to support "the battle
for Canadian liberty and autonomy . . . being fought today on the plains
of France and Belgium". One week later he asked Laurier to join a
Union government pledged to introduce conscription after a mandate had
been obtained at a general election. Sir Wilfrid Laurier declined the invitation and refused to support conscription.

Borden's Military Service Act was introduced in parliament on 11
June. Three weeks of debate broke the Liberal party in two as party

*This cartoon, entitled "Crumbling", appeared in
"The Canadian Liberal Monthly" for October
1916, and refers to the variety of scandals and
charges of mismanagement of the war effort
(mostly involving Sir Sam Hughes) and the
declining prestige of the Conservative party,
which had been turned out of office in two
provincial elections during 1916. The labels on
some of the crumbling turrets at the top of the
cartoon read: Poor Horses, Hay & Feed Scandal,
Shell Contracts, Ross Rifle, Binoculars, Fuse
Scandal.*

After the Russian Bolsheviks had made peace with Germany in March 1918, Canadians were sent to eastern and northern Russia to save Allied supplies from the Bolsheviks and to try to reopen an eastern front. This scene shows Canadian gunners with their 18-pounder field gun near Murmansk in 1919.

members from Ontario, the Maritimes, and most of the west supported conscription. Only two English-speaking members sided with Laurier but all French-Canadian Conservatives except four supported their leader. Laurier's proposal for a general election to test public opinion was rejected by both houses of parliament, and conscription became law at the beginning of August. The racial and religious war which Laurier and Roman Catholic church leaders had feared seemed near when the home of a leading English Montrealer was dynamited and a man was shot during one of many conscription riots in the city that summer.

Borden had decided to test conscription in a general election and, as a prelude, parliament passed the Military Voters Act enfranchising all British subjects in the Canadian forces, and the Wartime Elections Act which enfranchised female relatives of soldiers but disenfranchised conscientious objectors and all enemy aliens naturalized since 1902. These two Acts increased voting support for Borden's government and for conscription. The so-called "Khaki election" was held on 17 December but in the interval ten Liberals joined Borden in a Union government to prosecute the war. The election campaign showed clearly how the emotional issues of the war had divided "the two Canadas". Only three Unionists were elected in Quebec; elsewhere in Canada the Laurier Liberals won only 20 of 150 seats. Laurier himself was defeated in Ottawa by the only successful French-Canadian Unionist, but was returned with a huge majority in another riding. In the new parliament French-Canadian members sat in isolation from the members for the rest of Canada; in the cabinet French Canada was unrepresented. Talk of secession began to be heard in Quebec.

Although Ontario and western farmers resisted conscription by claiming exemption, public attention focused on Quebec's reaction. By the end of March only 30,000 Canadians had been called for service but 5,000 of these had become draft dodgers. At this date anticonscription riots in Quebec city wounded five soldiers, killed four civilians, and did heavy damage to property. Wider public opposition to conscription was voiced outside Quebec after exemptions for farmers' sons were cancelled in April, but Germany's last desperate offensive on the Marne in the summer of 1918 did much to sober Canadian feelings and to promote volunteer enlistments.

By the end of the war conscription had produced almost the 100,000 reinforcements that Borden had set as its goal. The total number of conscripts who actually went overseas was equal to two divisions, and about half of these reached the fighting front. More than 27,000 men, 40 per cent of them from Quebec, failed to report for military duty. On balance, conscription did fulfil its purpose of maintaining the Canadian Corps in the field until victory was won, but its price was racial antagonism that persisted for decades, a Liberal party temporarily shattered along linguistic lines, disillusionment for a heart-broken Laurier whose life ended just three months after the war, and Quebec's continuing rejection of the Conservatives – "the party of conscription" – for forty more years.

The Impact of War on the Home Front

The parliament created by the Khaki election to institute conscription also passed another measure of political and social significance in 1918. The limited federal voting privileges extended to women by the Wartime Elections Act of 1917 was enlarged in 1918 to give all women a vote in federal elections. The municipal franchise had been won by women about 1900, and in 1916 and 1917 the three prairie provinces, followed by Ontario and British Columbia, had given women the right to vote in recognition of their contribution to the national war effort. Borden's government insisted that the right be confirmed for Canada by a federal statute which only Laurier and his Quebec followers opposed. The right of women to be members of parliament was not passed into law until 1920. A second measure in 1918 established national prohibition by order-in-council. In the late Victorian era the Women's Christian Temperance Union had

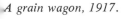
A grain wagon, 1917.

promoted the cause of teetotalism with great vigour and moderate success, but the goal of legalized prohibition was only achieved during the war, ironically thanks less to moral preachments than to the wartime need to conserve grain for food. Late in November 1917 the government had used its powers under the 1914 War Measures Act to prohibit distilling and limit brewing. Before 1917 all provinces but Quebec had stopped the sale of intoxicating liquors, but it required the federal order-in-council of 1918 to bring about national prohibition of both the manufacture and sale of such beverages.

Equally important as these developments were the economic changes promoted by Canada's participation in the war. One of the first needs in wartime is capital, and as Britain's financial resources became unavailable Canada turned from this traditional money market to seek new supplies of cash and credit at home and in the United States. The national debt rose sevenfold – an increase of $3 billion – and although $2.1 billion was raised in Canada as Victory Loans, large-scale United States investment became a permanent factor in Canada's economy. A federal income tax was instituted in 1918. The war also introduced unprecedented government control over producer and consumer alike, and in so doing went far towards preparing Canadians for increased government economic regulation even in peacetime.

For most sectors of the Canadian economy, which had been gripped by the serious recession of 1913-14, the outbreak of the war was an incentive to rapidly increased expansion. The value of base metal exports rose two-and-a-half times, wood pulp and newsprint more than seven-and-a-half times. The demand for wheat doubled the price and caused an 80 per cent expansion of wheat acreage. British orders for munitions and other war supplies created a manufacturing boom that brought Canada over $1 billion. Canadian steel capacity doubled during the war and was adequate for national needs until the Second World War. Over 65 million shells were produced and an estimated 60 per cent of the shrapnel fired in

Left: Women workers in a munitions factory in Verdun Quebec, during the First World War.
Below: An automobile assembly line in 1914.

France by the Allies was made in Canada. The war created a Canadian aircraft industry that produced 3,000 planes. Canadian shipyards launched 103 ships with a dead-weight total of 367,000 tons. About 300,000 workers were engaged on war contracts, and trade union membership rose from 166,000 to 374,000 during the war years. Thanks to the war, manufacturing production surpassed agriculture and other staples by 1919. The Canadian economy had matured in response to the Allies' demands for food, wood products, munitions, and other manufactured goods. Canada had proved that she had the natural, industrial, technological, and financial resources to support a major role in the war, and presumably in the peace that was to come.

The two transcontinental railways built in the Laurier era did not prosper as a result of the war. The Grand Trunk Pacific line was completed in September 1914, the Canadian Northern four months later. But much track work on each was still needed, and with the outbreak of war the cost of wages and material rose at the same time that capital investment from Britain stopped. Loans could be obtained in the United States, but interest rates were higher there. When both companies turned again to parliament for aid in 1916, it was apparent that some new policy was necessary. Once more the government came to their rescue but only temporarily, pending the report of an investigation by a royal commission.

That report, received in 1917, recommended that the Grand Trunk, Grand Trunk Pacific, Canadian Northern, and the Intercolonial and National Transcontinental be merged into a single system under private ownership, with the government guaranteeing payment of interest on existing securities to save private investment, public credit, and national interest. This course would have added a billion dollars to the national debt. The government, however, decided on even more drastic action: it would nationalize the Canadian Northern, the company nearest to bankruptcy. To the Opposition this plan seemed intended to rescue the Bank of Commerce, which had a lien on almost all common stock of the railway. The Canadian Northern became government property in September 1918, and $10.8 million was paid for its shares.

The Grand Trunk Pacific was saved for the moment by a further $7.5 million loan in 1917. During the next year the government decided that both the Grand Trunk and Grand Trunk Pacific would have to be acquired. As bankruptcy loomed for the Grand Trunk Pacific early in 1919, the government was forced to take over its lines, telegraphs, steamships, and hotels; six months later the Grand Trunk was also acquired. The settlement of the tangled finances of the Grand Trunk and its subsidiaries was not made until 1921, and two years later all the government-owned lines – a total of ten companies – were consolidated into the Canadian

National Railways. The only important rival of the CNR was the private enterprise Canadian Pacific by which Macdonald had first promoted Canadian economic unity. To save that same economic unity Macdonald's party was forced to solve the railway mess by nationalization.

Fire engine on skis, 1917. In the early years of the twentieth century the horse-drawn fire engines in use since the early 1800's were gradually being replaced by gasoline-driven engines. Though it has shafts for a horse, this engine could have been pulled by a horse or by motor power.

HISTORY FROM THE SOURCES

The Conscription Crisis – Where Is Canada's "Front Line"?

All the arguments in favour of conscription were underscored by one single question: where is the real "front line" of Canada's defences? Do Canadian interests end at her ocean shores, or do Canadians stand on guard for Canada by serving beyond their home and native land?

The debate on the conscription bill in the House of Commons in 1917 was long and serious, and more sad than bitter in its tone. Sir Robert Borden began the debate with a lengthy review of the war and of the statistics of enlistments and casualties.

> . . . The reinforcements now available will last for only a few months, the precise number of which, for military reasons, I am not at liberty to state. We all are proud that Canada has played a splen-

did and notable part in this war. The achievements of her troops have placed her in the very forefront of the nations, and the question before the House and the country to-day is this: Is Canada content to relax her efforts in the most critical period of a war which concerns her heritage, her status, and her liberty? I am confident that the answer of the House and the country will be the same, namely that Canada cannot and must not relax her effort.

* * * * *

It has been said of this Bill that it will induce disunion, discord, and strife, and that it will paralyze the nation's effort. I trust that this prophecy may prove unfounded. Why should strife be induced by the application of a principle which was adopted at the very inception of Confederation?

* * * * *

I am yet willing to consider, for ever since this war began I have had one constant aim and it was this: to throw the full power and effort of Canada into the scale of right, liberty and justice for the winning of this war, and to maintain the unity of the Canadian people in that effort.

But I cannot shrink, and I will not shrink, from the determination to support and sustain the Canadian troops now at the front. It is said that the consequences of this measure are to be dreaded. Why they should be dreaded I cannot understand, for it introduces no new principle.

Canada, Parliament, *Debates of the House of Commons*, 1917 (Ottawa), Vol. III, pp. 2187, 2195.

Sir Wilfrid Laurier supported Canada's participation in the war but warned of the dangers of imposing conscription without prior public discussion.

. . . The law of the land . . . declares that no man in Canada shall be subjected to compulsory military service except to repel invasion or for the defence of Canada.

* * * * *

The law of the land gives power to the Government to repel invasion – that is what I understand by "the defence of Canada".

* * * * *

. . . If the enlistment of French Canadians does not compare favourably with the enlistment of their compatriots speaking the English language, it is to be noted that the disparity between the enlistment of men who are Canadian-born and men who are British-born is also somewhat marked. What can be the cause of this disparity? The English-born are at the top of the list, the Canadian-born speaking the English language come next, and the Canadian-born of French origin are at the bottom of the list. It is suggested that enlistment has proceeded negatively in proportion to the length of time that the men have been in the country.

. . . Immigration has been constant from the British Isles, and the connection between the British settler and his motherland has been maintained. This is not the case as between the French Canadian and old France.

*   *   *   *   *

. . . When you have such a state of affairs you see how deep are the differences on this question. Can you say that it is wise, that it is good policy, that it is conductive to harmony, in the face of such a condition, to force upon the people compulsory service? It seems to me that the Government would have been better advised if, instead of proposing compulsory service, they had maintained the unity of all the elements that compose our population. . . . The solution of our present problem is to appeal to our people, to appeal to them to lay aside passion and prejudice and ask them to make a sacrifice of something that they hold dear upon the altar of our common country.

Canada, Parliament, *Debates of the House of Commons,*
1917 (Ottawa), Vol. III, pp. 2392, 2398, 2399, 2401.

J. A. M. Armstrong, Conservative member for North York, raised directly the question of Quebec's war effort.

Why is conscription necessary at this time? I do not wish to be offensive, and as far as possible I shall avoid any acrimonious remarks, but I believe in calling a spade a spade, and in justice to the rest of Canada, I must say that the reason why conscription faces us to-day is because French Canada has failed to do its duty.

*   *   *   *   *

. . . One of the saddest sights this country ever saw or ever will see was when the leader of the Opposition stood up in his place in this House and opposed this Bill. He, the acknowledged leader of

French Canada and the chief of a great party in this country, should have been reminded by that flag beneath whose broad folds he stood of all the privileges and liberties which his French compatriots enjoy, and which have been guaranteed by the nation for which that flag stands. It should have reminded him of the great men in days gone by who have lived and died for the nation it represents, and of the boys who at that very hour were fighting and bleeding and dying on the fields and in the trenches of France and Flanders for the liberties of which we boast so proudly in this House.

Canada, Parliament, *Debates of the House of Commons,*
1917 (Ottawa), Vol. III, pp. 2547, 2548.

H. Boulay, Conservative member for Rimouski, summarized the reasons for French Canada's opposition to conscription.

We are opposing conscription for different reasons which deserve consideration:

1. Because our traditions, our constitution, our status as a colony are opposed to it;

2. Because we have already sent overseas to help the Allies a sufficient number of men considering our population and our financial means;

3. Because the mandate which we received from the people in 1911 does not enable us to enact such a measure, especially without beforehand consulting the people;

4. Because we are not as fairly dealt with as we should be by the English speaking majority in this country, and because a feeling has been created by the Liberal party in 1896, and by ourselves in 1911, in opposition to the levying of troops of any kind. I may add that this measure is contrary to our traditions, because we have a responsible Government in this country. Our representative public men, whenever we were called upon to legislate on questions of war, a militia bill, or amendments thereto, have always expressed the view that Canada could not send her troops outside the country, except, and exclusively, for the purpose of its own defence.

Canada, Parliament, *Debates of the House of Commons,*
1917 (Ottawa), Vol. III, p. 2754.

*Outside parliament, Henri Bourassa, the leading French-Canadian Na-
tionaliste and rival of Laurier as spokesman for French Canada, urged
his compatriots to oppose conscription by every legitimate means.*

> French Canadians, don't forget that at this very moment, as at all
> turning points in our history, you are the defenders of order and the
> constitution, the guardians of the national tradition and of legitimate
> popular liberties. Sooner than you think, it will be demonstrated that
> by opposing the designs of foreign supporters of this war, you are
> the most faithful subjects of the King whose loss is being prepared at
> this moment in his own kingdom. Don't go reducing your role, so
> noble, so necessary, by childish and dangerous rash actions.

*   *   *   *   *

> Today and tomorrow, in the fullness of our prerogatives as free
> men but Christianly disciplined, let us take the necessary measures to
> affirm our rights and to protect the vital forces of the nation. Against
> the attempt of the government, unjustifiable at this hour, let us
> oppose, not verbose and sterile agitation, but strong and orderly
> action.

Henri Bourassa, La Conscription (Montreal, "Le Devoir",
1917), p. 8 (translation).

*The Canadian Annual Review, 1917, chronicled the growing violence
of language which led to the use of physical force in opposition to
conscription.*

> From the May 20th announcement of Conscription a new and
> violent phase developed. It commenced with a protest in Quebec on
> May 21 organized by Oscar Drouin, President of the Young Liberal
> Club, and a group of young men; with 10,000 people listening to
> heated speeches and cries of "down with Borden," statements such
> as that of Ald. E. Dussault that it was the duty of Canadians to
> defend Canada and nothing more, or of Oscar Drouin that he would
> fight even to death against Conscription. A Referendum or Election
> was the demand by resolution, an anti-Conscription League was
> formed and a series of meetings around Quebec organized. At Ste.
> Anne de Bellevue (May 20) a young man's meeting was addressed
> by Charles Query who declared that "Borden is taking your sons by
> force and sending them away to be killed" and by I. Vautrin, Presi-
> dent of the local Liberal Association. At Lafontaine Park, Montreal
> (May 23), 15,000 people heard T. Marsil describe Sir R. Borden as

"the tool of Downing Street" and Ubald Paquin, a young journalist, declare that: "Conscription is organized murder, systematically calculated and prepared in advance; it is the suicide of a nation; it is total oblivion in the mire of militarism and Imperialism; it is the sinister obliteration of a people and its personality." The air of the cities and centres became day by day more heated. A parade of protest in Montreal where numerous meetings were held nightly, resulted in small riots on May 24 and the smashing of the windows of *La Patrie*. One large meeting was told by L. N. Ricard that: "All we owe England is Christian forgiveness. Proportionally, Canada has done more for the War than England itself," while Mayor Martin stated that Sir R. Borden "would send our children to the slaughterhouse without a mandate from the people."

... One of the bitterest of the speakers of this period was Tancrède Marsil, a Nationalist-Conservative who had edited two short-lived and violent papers in Montreal and, in the intervals, made many vehement speeches and organized a Sons of Liberty League. At a meeting on June 12 he declared that "force called for force" and urged a general labour strike; at Hochelaga (June 15) he said that "in 1837 the people rose because it was a tribute of money that was exacted but to-day it is a tribute of blood" and added that it was necessary "to oppose violence with violence" against the work of fools. ... [and] at Chambly (July 22), gave vent to wilder utterances such as the assertion that to obtain soldiers "they have thrown workmen in the street to starve and replaced them by women and children, by 'blokes' and Chinese."

In August anti-draft meetings were held everywhere. At Lafontaine Park, Montreal (Aug. 8), Fernand Villeneuve, a very young man, gave this advice to the crowd: "If a recruiting officer comes to you do not be afraid to give him a threshing, and if you have anything to shoot with don't be afraid to use it." F. X. Moisan denounced the English as too cowardly to face the Germans and added: "If you are resolved to have justice and liberty, be resolved to sprinkle the soil of the Province of Quebec with your blood instead of reddening the soil of Flanders with it for the benefit of England." Ubald Paquin declared that the English had become more Boche than the Germans and that the Colonies were to England simply reservoirs from which to draw men: "He who enrols is a traitor to his race, and a coward, and should be afraid to walk the street in khaki, for all honest men will have the right to spit their contempt in his face." On the 9th Villeneuve let loose this language: "It is not out of fear that the French-Canadian is opposed to Conscription. It is out of love for our country and hatred for England."

Canadian Annual Review, 1917, pp. 493, 495.

FURTHER READING

In addition to the biographies of Laurier and Borden (see FURTHER READING for Chapter 18), see the following:

Nicholson, G. W. L., *The Canadian Expeditionary Force, 1914-1918* (Ottawa: Queen's Printer, 1962). The official military history of Canada during the First World War.

Swettenham, J. A., *To Seize the Victory* (Toronto: Ryerson, 1965). The military operations of the Canadian Corps and the political background to Canadian participation in the First World War.

Armstrong, E. H., *The Crisis of Quebec, 1914-1918* (New York: Columbia University Press, 1937). A critical study of the conscription crisis.

Goodspeed, D. J., *The Road Past Vimy* (Toronto: Macmillan, 1969).

20

Canada After the First World War

Post-War Change

With the First World War over, the returning soldiers marched down the main streets of their home towns, proud of their victory, their appearance extra neat, their exuberant bands extra loud. But the Canada to which these soldiers came back was different from the Canada they had left. In the crusade to defeat the enemy, class barriers had been weakened. Women who had done men's work during the war were not disposed to return too readily to domestic duties. Educational opportunity was widening, especially in the wealthier provinces, as fees for high school education were abolished, vocational and technical training were developed, and the school leaving age was raised. Finally, prohibition on the sale of alcoholic beverages, introduced in the provinces during the war as a patriotic gesture to save grain, was still in force except in British Columbia and Quebec, and remained so until 1925.

Most important, perhaps, post-war Canada was a discontented society. The war left the working class in the cities and towns embittered against the government, mainly because prices had risen faster than wages and because industry had slowed down as it returned to peacetime production. During 1917 there had been 160 strikes and lockouts; in 1918 the number had risen to 230; in 1919 to 326. Workers wanted to bargain collectively with their employers to obtain higher wages and shorter hours

A victory parade float, with the theme "Britain and her Dominions", moving through the streets of St. John's, Newfoundland, in 1919.

of work, but the owners and managers of businesses saw labour organizations as conspiracies to reduce profits. The moderate approach of the Trades and Labour Congress was too slow for many workers especially in the mining and lumber camps of northern Ontario and the west. The Marxist ideas of the International Workers of the World, the "Wobblies" (whose initials, said their detractors, stood for "I won't work") spread like a prairie fire. The IWW's platform argued:

> The working class and the employing class have nothing in common. There can be no peace so long as hunger and want are found among millions of working people and the few, who make up the employing class, have all the good things of life. . . . It is the historic mission of the working class to do away with capitalism.

According to the IWW, their goal could be achieved only if all the workers united in one movement. At Calgary in March 1919 the One Big Union, the OBU as everyone called it, was born. The average member of the OBU joined to get better wages and working conditions when the Congress seemed to be powerless. He was equally ignorant about the philosophies of Marxism and capitalism.

When the Calgary convention ended, its delegates returned home spoiling for battle against their employers. It was in this militant atmosphere that the Winnipeg General Strike occurred. On 1 May 2,000 metal trades workers struck, demanding eighty-five cents an hour and a forty-hour week. Moreover they wanted industry-wide negotiation, rather than negotiations in different plants by small groups of employees with their own employers – the only conditions for discussion to which employers would agree. On 13 May the Winnipeg Trades and Labour Council declared a general strike after more than fifty unions went out in sympathy with the metal workers. The city was paralyzed as postmen, streetcar drivers, milkmen, even the firemen, left their jobs. The policemen would also have struck, but at the Council's Strike Committee's urging, they remained on the job. After a few days the Committee allowed milk and bread deliveries to resume, but other workers refused to return to their jobs. Small sympathy strikes occurred in Toronto, Vancouver, Edmonton, and Calgary, but there were no riots, no demonstrations.

The rhetoric of the OBU leaders, however, frightened businessmen and the middle class: Russia's Bolshevik revolution seemed to have spread to Canada. The government, in a panic, rushed through parliament an amendment to the Criminal Code, empowering it to act against "unlawful organizations" with few safeguards for those charged. A citizens' anti-

Right and at foot of page: Scenes during the Winnipeg General Strike, 1919. Note the guns mounted on the Canadian Army Service Corps vehicles (right).

strike committee was set up in Winnipeg, and its own newspaper, *The Citizen,* publicized their views: ". . . the so-called general strike is, in reality, revolution – or a daring attempt to overthrow the present industrial and government system." Gradually owner-operated businesses in the city re-opened, and the newspapers put out abbreviated editions. Striking non-union workers, who had been without wages for three weeks, drifted back to work.

Meanwhile union strikers began to demonstrate through the streets of the city in almost gala processions. Then on 5 June the mayor banned processions, and four days later fired all but fifteen of the police force, replacing them with special constables and the Royal North West Mounted Police. On the following day there was a five-hour riot, and one week later, on 17 June, the Mounties arrested the strike leaders in a pre-dawn raid and charged them under the recent amendment to the Criminal Code. The arrests touched off further rioting – on 21 June ("Bloody Saturday") armed and mounted policemen charged a "silent parade", firing pistols and swinging baseball bats, after which soldiers with rifles and machine guns blocked off the main streets of downtown Winnipeg. In all the Winnipeg outbreaks, two men had died, thirty were injured, and ninety-one arrested. But already the strike was collapsing without its leaders, who were sentenced to short terms in prison. The whole episode made union men bitter: collective bargaining, hard to achieve before the general strike, was now far more difficult, and the recession of 1920-3 hurt the unions even more. Trade union membership began to fall and continued to decline through the rest of the decade.

The agricultural scene was also disturbed by new forces. Late in the war the national farmers' organization, the Canadian Council of Agriculture, had issued a statement of objectives, the "New National Policy", to challenge all the Liberal and Conservative national policies. It rang with a sense of injustice and called for reciprocity with the United States, free trade with Britain, lower tariffs, public ownership of railways and utilities, and higher taxes on business profits. After the war, anger with the government took positive form amongst the farmers. They complained that government freight rates raised costs to farmers, and that the 1917 promise not to conscript farmers' sons had been ignored by the Union government.

In Ontario the farmers' groups formed the United Farmers of Ontario which, together with some independents and labour representatives, won sufficient seats in the provincial election of 1919 to form a government. In the following session of Canada's parliament, several western members of the Union government and several Liberals decided to sit as farmers' representatives under the leadership of Thomas A. Crerar, a cabinet member who had resigned over the failure of the 1919 budget to reduce tariffs. Encouraged by these developments, United Farmers parties sprang up in all the prairie provinces, winning control of Alberta in 1921 and becoming the major opposition in the others. The farmers' dissatisfaction further increased following the collapse of agricultural prices in 1920. A national convention of farm groups and parties at Winnipeg established the National Progressive Party under the leadership of Crerar, adopted the Council of Agriculture's "New National Policy", and demanded government marketing agencies and the recall and referendum, American constitutional ideas that would give the ordinary voter a more direct voice in government. The recall was the means by which voters in a constituency could force an election at any time if they lost confidence in their representative, and the referendum made it possible for them to vote on legislation.

Besides this challenge from labour and organized farmers, the Conservative and Liberal parties had their own problems. During 1919, the Union government began to collapse as ex-Liberals rejoined their party or sat as farmer independents. Prime Minister Borden resigned in ill health. His successor, Arthur Meighen, was a brilliant debater and parliamentarian but an unsuccessful leader. Born and educated in Ontario, Meighen had practised law in Manitoba until elected to parliament in 1908. He became solicitor-general in 1913 and entered the cabinet as Secretary of State in 1915. His clear incisive intellect, his belief that a political leader must give leadership rather than ride the passing breeze of public fancy, his taste for literature, his hatred of woolly-mindedness – all these attri-

A field of wheat stooks at Standard, Alberta, in 1920.

butes made him contemptuous of most politicians of his generation. But
Meighen had already made enemies. He had piloted both the Wartime
Elections Act and the National Registration Act through the Commons
and, further, many traditional Conservative supporters, particularly Montreal financiers, opposed the public railway system, of which he had been
the chief advocate. As prime minister, Meighen presided over a government whose ranks were being thinned by defections, so that when by
1920 the Union government coalition had become at best a pretence,
Meighen dropped the term and called his government Conservative.
Faced with an impending election, the Conservatives were burdened with
an unpopular leader, the memory of unpopular wartime measures, and
widespread farm and labour resentment.

While the Liberal party might rejoice over the return to the fold of ex-
supporters of the Union government, they too had problems. As a result
of the conscription crisis, the Liberals had become a Quebec-based
French group with a rump of English-speaking supporters. When Sir
Wilfrid Laurier died in 1919, there seemed to be no successors with his
magnetic appeal to lead the party back to power. The only obvious choice,
Sir William Fielding, long-time finance minister under Laurier and the
leading member from the Maritimes, had alienated the Quebec wing over
conscription. Almost by default the mantle of leadership fell on William
Lyon Mackenzie King, one of the few prominent English-speaking Liberals who had sided with Laurier in that crisis of 1917.

Born to a daughter of William Lyon Mackenzie, King was never allowed to forget his rebel grandfather. A contemporary of Meighen's at
the University of Toronto, he had gone on to pursue graduate studies at
the University of Chicago and at Harvard. Having specialized in economics, political science, and sociology, King was academically the best
prepared of any politician of his time. His research on labour and industrial conditions caught the eye of Laurier, who persuaded him to join the
newly formed Department of Labour in 1900. King soon became deputy

minister of that department. In 1908 he entered politics, won an Ontario seat, and in the following year became Minister of Labour. Defeated in 1911, he did research for the party and then became a labour consultant in the United States. He gave this up in 1917 to try politics again, but was defeated in the "Khaki election" and had to remain as an adviser to Laurier for the next two years. A singularly astute politician, King proved to be the leader who established the Liberal domination of federal politics. Using the political strength of Quebec as his base, he set about to regain English-Canadian support for his party. To cope with Progressive inroads in traditionally Liberal areas, King's strategy was to divide the movement and to persuade its leaders to support him.

As might have been expected, Progressives and Liberals gained in the election of 1921, but the magnitude of the change was staggering to the Conservatives. The Liberals won 117 seats, the Progressives 65, Independents 3, and the Conservatives retained only 50. The election confirmed the sectional rifts of wartime, for over half the Liberal seats were in Quebec – the others were from the Maritimes or urban areas of Ontario. The Progressives swept the prairies and won many rural Ontario seats. There was no national party in Ottawa, and there was no majority party in the Commons. Unable to persuade either Crerar or E. C. Drury, the farmers' premier of Ontario, to enter his cabinet in a coalition, King decided to form a minority party government. From the Progressives' viewpoint, the alternative to King was Meighen; therefore they supported King.

King's record was unimpressive in domestic matters. Many of the Progressives became increasingly disenchanted with him as year after year no change was made in the tariff and no wheat marketing board was set up. The government produced only one major piece of legislation: the Industrial Combines Investigation Act of 1923, an attempt to control the growth of monopolies and combinations and to limit competition and profit in the public interest. This lack of action by the government was due largely to the protectionist groups within the Liberal party, which were unwilling to see Liberal policies move in a Progressive direction. But Liberals and Progressives could agree that Canada should avoid foreign entanglements, and that Britain should not interfere with Canada's foreign policies. King was, therefore, able to enlarge Canadian autonomy within the Commonwealth, and it was in this sphere that his government's achievements were apparent.

Economic Lights and Economic Shadows

The period of economic adjustment which followed the First World War was marked by recession in most national economies. The unrest of

Threshing with a gasoline tractor in Alberta, 1920.

Canadian farmers and industrial workers at the beginning of the 1920's was a reflection of the "little world depression". But in 1923 prosperity returned to the western world. In Canada unemployment began to decline, commodity prices rose on the world market, and the second period of great economic expansion in Canadian history began.

The wheat economy of the western provinces shared in the revival of trade. As prices climbed to reach a maximum of $1.68 a bushel at Fort William in 1924, land even as far north as the Peace River country was brought into cultivation and by 1928 wheat acreage was 40 per cent greater than in 1919. In 1927, however, the wheat yields declined, and because prices also had begun to slip, farm income dipped too – though not disastrously. The farmers attributed the continuing steady if somewhat reduced prices to the wheat pools, the co-operative marketing organizations which they themselves had set up when the government had failed to act in Laurier's time. In 1928, however, the total wheat crop broke all records and Canada sold half of all the internationally traded wheat.

As before 1914, the post-war boom was accompanied by expansion in other sectors of the economy. There was considerable immigration, over 100,000 people a year during the decade. Most immigrants chose to live in urban areas where they easily found work. A few settled on the land, but except for the Clay Belt of northern Ontario and the Peace River country, Canada's farming frontier had virtually closed by the beginning of the First World War. Although no more main railway lines were built (in fact, the Canadian National cut back its service where lines paralleled each other), many branch lines on the prairies and to new mining areas were constructed. As a result of farm pressure the government also completed the Hudson Bay Railway to Churchill, but the short navigation season prevented this port from becoming an alternative to either Vancouver or Montreal.

The greatest economic expansion of the decade occurred in the extractive industries. Before the war, natural gas had been found in the Turner Valley of Alberta. In 1920 oil was discovered at Norman Wells in the Northwest Territories, and two years later the oil wells started production. The application of new chemical refining processes made possible the exploitation of lower grade ore resources than in the days of crushers and heat methods. Prospectors rushed in to the Shield to find economically useful ore bodies. Daring bush pilots, willing to bring in supplies and even equipment for building mills and hoists, opened the north. The gold and copper workings at Rouyn, at Val d'Or, and Red Lake, the silver and lead mines at Keno Hill in the Yukon, the silver and radium mines at Great Bear Lake were all developed between 1920 and 1930. Canadian development in mining drew world attention as promoters sold stock to raise capital for developing everything from good mineral prospects to moose pasture. Most of Canada's mineral output was exported to the industrial markets of the United States. By 1929, Canada had also become the world's second producer, after the United States, of aluminum. As early as 1895 some aluminum had been produced at Niagara because hydro-electric power was readily available there, but the real expansion came with the construction of the huge Alcan plant and associated power installations at Arvida on the Saguenay River.

Cheap and available hydro-electricity made expansion of other industries possible too. Installed capacity in electrical power increased 300 per cent in the decade. By 1930, seven out of every ten homes had electricity, and Canadians were the largest per capita domestic users of electrical power in the world. Electricity for domestic use created a market for the newly devised household appliances – electric refrigerators, stoves, washing machines, irons, radios – and industry sprang up to meet the demand. But the real importance of this increase in the generation of electricity was its stimulus to other manufacturing industry. The pulp and paper industry, which required electricity for its processing, made giant strides. Modest annual rentals of forest areas and low stumpage dues to the provincial governments, plus cheap electricity, gave Canadian pulp and paper producers a tremendous price advantage in world markets. Other industries using the cheap power resource, but not exclusively dependent on it, grew too. Between 1918 and 1929, annual production of automobiles rose from 69,801 to 188,721, and that of commercial vehicles doubled. The quantity of gasoline refined rose six times, the production of tires nearly doubled. Iron and steel output doubled to fill the needs of manufacturing industries such as those producing automobiles and electrical appliances.

Slightly over half of Canada's manufacturing output came from Ontario, another 30 per cent came from Quebec, a concentration of industry in central Canada that attracted more and more people to the cities of the region. By 1931 just under one-third of Quebec's population lived in Montreal, just under one-fifth of Ontario's in Toronto. Whereas in 1921 slightly over one-half of Canada's people lived in rural communities, the census of 1931 showed that over one-half lived in urban areas. Manufacturing and service industries were now the major employers in Canada and urbanization grew hand in hand with industrialization.

British Columbia more than shared in Canada's economic development. With a labour force largely drawn from the prairies and from the east and with business talent and capital which had migrated west, the province boomed during the twenties. The lumbermen found markets in the United States, Australia, and Britain, the mines and smelters sold their metals in the United States, the fruit growers of the Okanagan began to sell their produce in eastern Canada and in Britain. Greater Vancouver thrived and expanded as prairie wheat flowed through its elevators; a stock exchange, banks, and insurance companies made the city a financial centre. Industries such as saw-milling, flour milling, brewing, food processing, and light engineering expanded rapidly to meet both local and export demand. This prosperity attracted thousands more to move to the west coast throughout the decade.

The Atlantic provinces region did not share in the growing prosperity evident in the rest of the country. Nova Scotia and Prince Edward Island showed a decline in population while New Brunswick's population growth was far smaller than that of other provinces, thus reflecting the slow tempo of the region's economy. Before 1914, transcontinental railway construction had given business to the steel mills of Sydney, but there was

British Columbia in the 1920's. Left: An apple-packing plant in the interior of the province. Below: A lumber export wharf on the Fraser River.

no sure market in the twenties. Employment in the fisheries rose slightly in New Brunswick, but dropped by a quarter in Nova Scotia. Although the pulp and paper industry created some employment in New Brunswick, both the amount of cultivated land and employment on farms decreased. For Maritimers, the twenties was a decade of frustration and growing unemployment.

Nor did all classes of Canadians prosper equally in the "roaring twenties". Not only were there regional economic problems, but the agriculture throughout the country began to encounter trouble. Wheat prices dropped slowly after 1924. Net income to farmers began to drop after 1926 as income failed to rise as fast as costs. In the year preceding the depression, farm income was nearly a third lower than in 1926. Only in central Canada and in British Columbia did the average person benefit from the boom; elsewhere he was left out.

Mackenzie King's Triumph

The great tasks of national policies – the settlement of the west, the construction of the transcontinental railways, the development of secondary industry encouraged by protective tariffs – all were completed or well under way by the mid-1920's. As wheat prices rose in the early 1920's, much of the farmers' anger against these policies dissipated. In Ontario, the United Farmers' government collapsed in discord in 1923 and was replaced by a Conservative government. On the federal scene withdrawal of financial support by one of the western co-operatives and the resignation of Crerar from the leadership of the Progressives further weakened the movement. Liberals and Conservatives both hoped to win a majority in the next election, yet neither party seemed to offer any new or constructive programmes. Except for Ernest Lapoine, French Canada's

Advertising by billboard in 1929. This advertisement appeared in Montreal.

leading representative, King's cabinet lacked men of political distinction. The Conservatives offered no attractive alternative – Meighen seemed satisfied to continue traditional Conservative policies and to attack the government at every opportunity for its lack of leadership.

The general election in the autumn of 1925 confirmed the country's political uneasiness. The Conservatives reversed the humiliation of 1921 by winning 116 out of the 245 seats, though only 4 of these were in Quebec. The Liberals were reduced to 101 members, and the majority of English-speaking ministers, including King himself, were defeated: they still seemed to be the party of French Canada. The number of Progressives dropped to 24, largely from the west, as the Conservatives picked up seats from them in Ontario and the Liberals won a few on the prairies. These 24, ironically, held the balance between the Liberals and Conservatives as had the 65 after 1921. King, who was returned in a by-election, managed to hold on to power with the support of the Progressives and Labour members, whom he bought with promises of tariff changes and an old age pension.

Soon, however, King's government was rocked by charges of corruption in the customs service involving the smuggling of liquor to the United States where prohibition was still in force. Despite protests from Washington the Canadian government had made no serious effort to stop the highly profitable but illegal trade in Canadian liquor which was carried in motor boats across the Detroit and Niagara rivers, in fast schooners sailing from Maritime ports, and in automobiles over back roads from Quebec and New Brunswick into neighbouring states. Ships loaded with liquor left Montreal supposedly for the West Indies, but just two days later they returned with empty holds. Goods, however, were also being smuggled across the border into Canada, and several Canadian companies who were being hurt by this illicit commerce were responsible for unearthing the customs scandal after they formed the Commercial Protective Association and hired a private detective to investigate their problem.

When this investigation indicated that the Chief Preventive Officer of Montreal was connected with the smuggling, the Association early in 1925 demanded that the prime minister and the Minister of Customs take action. King, however, ignored their charges for eight months, and the Minister of Customs retired to the Senate after being defeated in the 1925 election. In desperation the Association turned over its evidence to the Conservatives, who demanded a parliamentary investigation when parliament met early in 1926. Even Liberal members of parliament were shocked by the Association's revelations, and the government at last and reluctantly appointed an investigating committee. This committee examined the Association's evidence, and also heard stories implicating the new Minister of Customs in the smuggling racket. Aware that the scandal could be used to their party's political advantage, the Conservatives moved a parliamentary vote of censure against the government.

In a desperate attempt to avoid defeat at the hands of a united Conservative and Progressive Opposition, King asked Governor General Viscount Byng of Vimy to dissolve parliament before the censure vote could be passed. This Byng refused to do, so King and his cabinet resigned. The governor general then invited Meighen to form a government, and having secured the support of enough Progressives, Meighen took office with the announced purpose of calling an early election on the issue of Liberal corruption. Since Meighen's strength in the Commons was still uncertain, he avoided the legal requirement that ministers taking office more than thirty days after a general election must resign and seek re-election, by appointing a cabinet of *acting* ministers. Only Meighen actually resigned. This stratagem, reminiscent of the Double Shuffle of 1858, maintained the government's slight margin in the Commons, but two days after the new government was formed King attacked the cabinet as illegal because the acting ministers had not taken the oath of office. The Progressives were disturbed by this charge, and when the government tried to adjourn the debate it was defeated by one vote, a vote ironically cast in error. Meighen therefore had to ask Byng to dissolve parliament for an election.

King went out onto the hustings claiming that Canada was in the midst of a constitutional crisis. He called Byng's refusal to grant him a dissolution in the first place an attack on responsible government. He criticized the governor general for giving Meighen what he had been refused. Indeed, there was a constitutional issue. Did the governor general have the prerogative right to refuse to dissolve parliament although he had to accept his minister's advice on other matters? The consensus among constitutional experts is that Byng was legally right, although he would have been wiser politically to have granted King the dissolution. In the election of September 1926 the Liberals gained 15 seats; the Conservatives lost 25 although they won more votes than the Liberals. Progressives, United Farmers, Labour, and Independents won the other seats and once more held the balance. It was a narrow victory for the Liberals in which the constitutional issue, despite the emphasis given it by King, may not have been important. The Conservative tariff policy no doubt persuaded many Progressives to vote Liberal, and Meighen's unpopularity in Tory circles may have weakened the Conservative campaign. A slight shift in votes in Ontario and the unwillingness of Liberals and Progressives to fight each other for the same ridings in Manitoba made a difference of more than twenty seats. King returned triumphant to office.

Meighen, defeated in his own riding, resigned from the leadership of the Conservative party the following spring. King had destroyed his hated rival. Politics in Canada took on a calmer aspect, for R. B. Bennett, the new Tory leader, did not feel the same bitter animosity towards King that Meighen had felt. King carried out his promise: tariffs were lowered very slightly; the old age pension was introduced – a great triumph for J. S. Woodsworth, the Labour member from Winnipeg. Since constitutionally the federal government could not assume welfare responsibilities, the law provided that if a province established an old age pension the federal government would make a grant to that province equal to half the cost of the pensions. There was no other important legislation – politics did not seem important to Canadians, who were too busy trying to make money and to enjoy life as never before.

The Twenties Roar

The common impression of the "Roaring Twenties" is one of big long cars which needed to be refilled at every gasoline station, of New Orleans-style jazz, of bootlegging and gangsterism, and of a social revolution against "Victorianism". Today's movies and television encourage this colourful illusion. There were some of these picturesque elements in Canada, but the revolution, such as it was, proceeded modestly. The most obvious change was in the status of women. The war had brought a large number of women out of their homes to do work, voluntary or paid, for the patriotic cause. The franchise extension in 1919 recognized this change by extending the vote to women. Between 1921 and 1931 the

Below: 1924 Ford truck.
Top right: 1927 Model "T" Ford. This was the last year of production for the famous Model "T".
Bottom right: 1925 Cadillac.

An office in Montreal, 1924.

number of women employed rose by nearly 40 per cent, mostly in the clerical and personal service occupations – domestic service became less acceptable than it had been before 1914. Even if women did stay home and raise a family, they had fewer children – the birth rate in Canada dropped steadily from the beginning of the First World War until 1939 – and housework was made easier as a wider variety of canned foods and household appliances became available.

Symbol of this new era was the automobile: the number of cars tripled in the decade. Their speed was slow by today's standards – the usual speed limit was only 35 m.p.h., although the big straight eights could easily go twice that. To travel fifty miles without a punctured tire was quite an accomplishment on the washboard gravel highways. The pneumatic tires, unlike the old iron ones, ruined the macadamized surfaces because they sprayed the gravel out behind them, so that roads had to be rebuilt for fast auto traffic with asphalt, concrete, or "tarmac". Between 1921 and 1930 provincial expenditures on highways rose three and a half times, faster than any other item in the budget. With good roads around the big cities, the Sunday afternoon drive became a family recreation. Not many people could own a car, for even the 1926 Model T Ford selling at $385 was more than many farmers and industrial workers could afford. There were some Canadian-made cars such as the Brooks Steamer, only a few of which were made; the Overland, made in Toronto; and the McLaughlin, which had a Buick engine.

Just as the growing popularity of the automobile reduced distances, so too did the development of radio. Thousands fiddled with the "cat's whisker" of their crystal sets to hear through their earphones the earliest radio stations, in Toronto and Montreal. Crystal sets disappeared as the development of the vacuum tube and the speaker in the early twenties opened a new era in radio. By 1929 there were seventy-nine broadcasting companies, although most of them operated only a few hours during the day and again in the evening. Much of the programming was from United States' networks. The only nationwide network in Canada operated over telegraph lines by the CNR, whose programmes could even be heard through earphones on the trains. Nevertheless the sparse and dispersed population of Canada discouraged the rapid development of private radio. As late as 1930 only one out of five Canadian families had a radio receiver, and most of these lived in or near the bigger cities.

After the war evidences of the emergence of a distinctive Canadian culture could be seen in the wide popular interest aroused by such mass entertainment forms as spectator sports, movies, radio programmes, and phonograph records. It was perhaps more difficult to create a specifically Canadian literature, because so many of the important themes of literature are universal, though the subject matter can be national or even local. Canadians began to read in school books and in popular editions the work of their own poets such as Duncan Campbell Scott, Bliss Carman, and Sir Charles G. D. Roberts. Their lyrics describing the country all sounded a distinct Canadian note. Writing in French, Robert Choquette, Gonzalve Desaulniers, and Alfred Desrochers reflected the feelings and unrest of their province. Modern Canadian poetry in English dates from the publication of E. J. Pratt's *Newfoundland Verse* in 1923, his *The Witches' Brew* in 1925, and his two miniature epics in *The Titans* in 1926. Other poets, such as A. M. Klein, F. R. Scott, and Robert Finch, began to publish their work in periodicals. The best of Frederick Philip Grove's Canadian novels, among them *Over Prairie Trails,* were published in the twenties. But only two Canadian authors were widely read outside Canada: Stephen Leacock, whose stories and novels amused the whole English-speaking world in the twenties, and Mazo de la Roche, whose millions of devoted readers awaited each new *Jalna* novel. Canadian creativity was now beginning to bear comparison with that of the older world.

Canadian scientists began to make major contributions to knowledge during the twenties. In 1922 Frederick Banting, J. J. R. MacLeod, and Charles Best discovered insulin, an achievement that won a Nobel prize for Banting and MacLeod. Banting subsequently opened an institute to assist medical research in Canada, which by the late 1930's was working on the important field of aviation medicine. Dr. Wilder Penfield came from the U.S.A. to McGill University, where he planned and opened Canada's first university-owned hospital, the Montreal Neurological Institute. In fields other than medicine, Canada also made significant contributions. Sir Charles Saunders, a world authority on grains, developed many new strains of wheat at the Experimental Farm in Ottawa. Much of the basic

Left: A steam roller with attached steam hammer being used to break up the road surface.
Above: Two steam rollers smoothing the road surface.

work in nuclear physics which would lead to the development of nuclear power was done at McGill under the direction of Ernest Rutherford who was later awarded a Nobel prize. In applied science, Andrew G. L. McNaughton devised the Cathode Ray Directional Finder, keyed to radio signals, for aircraft navigation. But the major development of the inter-war years was the founding in 1923 of the National Research Council, directed first by Dr. Henry Marshall Tory and, after 1935, by McNaughton. Although grossly underfinanced, the NRC in the inter-war years laid the foundations for a successfully expanded research operation during the Second World War.

Perhaps no trend was more important to the revolution in Canadian life than the secularization of Canadian society which went hand in hand with its urbanization. As people became more mobile, moving from job to job and from city to city, they struck shallower roots in the community. The material progress that marked the decade, and the shocking slaughter and inhumanity of the war, created private doubts about traditionally accepted moral and religious values. The scientific view of the world and the nature of man, especially in terms of Sir Charles Darwin's commonly accepted theory that man is merely the highest evolved form in the chain of animal life, created popular doubts about the truth of traditional Christian beliefs. Religious observance had been an important part of every Canadian's life in the nineteenth century, but by the 1920's this was no longer so. One result of this secular spirit was the attempt of Canadian theological scholars after 1900 to restate Christian beliefs in terms that could be accepted by the whole community.

Another reaction to secularism was church union. Rural communities, especially in the west, found it difficult to support an indefinite number of churches which reflected denominational differences and appeared to prevent the growth of a community social life. A proposal to merge the Methodist, Presbyterian, and Congregational churches had led to the opening of negotiations in 1903. A basis of union was agreed on by 1908, but debate within the Presbyterian communion prevented agreement until after the war. Finally, the Presbyterians split on the issue, about one-third of their membership preferring to remain independent, while the majority of poorer rural and mission congregations joined the union with the Methodists and Congregationalists. Finally, in 1925, the United Church of Canada was born. The name is significant – it was to be a Canadian church.

In all these various ways Canadians were acquiring a sense of their own nationhood in the years after the First World War. Most English-speaking Canadians had thought of themselves as British subjects before 1914. Even in French Canada, where a sense of French cultural identity had long existed, Canadian nationalism could not be clearly distinguished before the war. But in the trenches of France and through the sacrifice of battle, an awareness of Canadianism had grown. Achievements in sports, in the creative arts, and in science built not only pride but also a recognition that something called a Canadian identity existed. Painting in particular helped Canadians to form an idealized image of their land. A

Left: "Forest Landscape (I)" by Emily Carr (1871-1945). [Oil on paper, 36" x 24"]
Below: "A September Gale, Georgian Bay" by Arthur Lismer (1885-1969), painted in 1921. [Oil on canvas, 48" x 64"] Lismer, Lawren Harris, A. Y. Jackson, F. H. Varley, Franklin Carmichael, J. E. H. MacDonald, and Franz Johnston – all painters of Canada's rugged northland – were the original members of the so-called Group of Seven (1920-33), a group of painters who through their art presented Canada as a land of wilderness and stark beauty.

nationality was being created and, except for the staunchest imperialist, Canadians approved of any moves that would give Canada greater independence. In 1929 it looked as if Laurier's prophecy was coming true: this was to be Canada's century.

FURTHER READING

Careless, J. M. S., and Brown, R. C., *The Canadians 1867-1967* (Toronto: Macmillan, 1967).

Easterbrook, W. T., and Aitken, H. J. G., *Canadian Economic History* (Toronto: Macmillan, 1956).

Allen, Ralph, *Ordeal by Fire* (Toronto: Doubleday, 1965). A colourful anecdotal approach to Canadian history between 1918 and 1945.

Hutchison, Bruce, *The Incredible Canadian* (Toronto: Longmans, Green 1952). The only good, short biography of King.

Graham, Roger, *Arthur Meighen*, 3 vols. (Toronto: Clarke, Irwin, 1960-65).

Dawson, R. M., *William Lyon Mackenzie King: A Political Biography 1874-1923* (Toronto: University of Toronto Press, 1958).

Neatby, H. B., *William Lyon Mackenzie King: The Lonely Heights 1924-1932* (Toronto: University of Toronto Press, 1963).

Morton, W. L., *The Progressive Party in Canada* (Toronto: University of Toronto Press, 1950).

McNaught, K. W., *A Prophet in Politics* (Toronto: University of Toronto Press, 1959). Biography of J. S. Woodsworth.

Masters, D. C., *The Winnipeg General Strike* (Toronto: University of Toronto Press, 1950).

Swettenham, J. A., *McNaughton:* Vol. 1. *1887-1939;* Vol. 2. *1939-1943;* Vol. 3, *1944-1966* (Toronto: Ryerson Press, 1968/9).

21

The Hungry Thirties

Vanishing Prosperity

The post-war boom years ended on 29 October 1929, the day that the New York stock market crashed. Share values tumbled, and with them the confidence that had buoyed the world economy. The next ten years were the worst years of depression Canada and the world have ever known. The causes of the depression lay mostly outside Canada. Post-war European economic recovery had been greatly speeded up by American investments and loans; many business undertakings outside the United States were largely dependent upon American assistance, and American money became one of the major international currencies used in world trade. In the United States itself prosperity seemed obvious – unprecedented investment on the stock exchanges pushed stock prices to unbelievably high levels. People who could not afford to pay for the stocks they wanted bought "on margin" – that is, they borrowed money, using the stocks they were buying as security. Then, for complex reasons, came the crash: stock prices fell drastically, wiping out fortunes and sucking in all the available cash of those who had bought on margin. The wealthy suffered heavy losses; the less wealthy had their savings entirely wiped out.

Stock market scene in the 1930's.

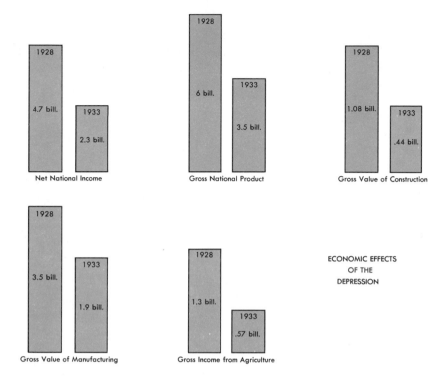

1928 4.7 bill. 1933 2.3 bill.

Net National Income

1928 6 bill. 1933 3.5 bill.

Gross National Product

1928 1.08 bill. 1933 .44 bill.

Gross Value of Construction

1928 3.5 bill. 1933 1.9 bill.

Gross Value of Manufacturing

1928 1.3 bill. 1933 .57 bill.

Gross Income from Agriculture

ECONOMIC EFFECTS
OF THE
DEPRESSION

Like the preceding boom, the crash affected all parts of the world. Americans who still had money curtailed their investment and spending; no more money went out of the country as loans. Foreign governments could no longer obtain American money to pay back wartime loans. Governments in Europe and Latin America imposed rigid currency and trade controls in 1930 and raised even higher the tariff walls which they had been building during the past decade. Many countries devalued their currencies in order to encourage exports and discourage imports: the same amount of foreign money could now buy more goods from a nation with devalued currency, but there were no buyers because individuals in all countries had cut back on personal spending. This falling demand for goods created world-wide unemployment and world-wide despair.

Canada was extremely vulnerable to fluctuations in the world economy. Thirty per cent of her national income came from exports, the majority of which were primary products. The lumbering and mining industries were hit very badly. The pulp and paper industry, having overexpanded its plant facilities in the 1920's, encountered major difficulties and many firms went bankrupt. Most seriously affected was farming, which had not shared in the boom of the years after 1926. Farm implement plants closed and farm prices, particularly for wheat, fell catastrophically. Part of the enormous 1928 wheat crop had been sold, and the substantial remainder had been held by the wheat pools until the following year in the hope of higher prices. When these prices did not materialize, the pools held back on sales of even the 1929 crop, but other countries such as Argentina and Australia sold at prevailing prices. When the Canadian pools were finally forced to sell, the markets were already glutted. The pools would have failed except for provincial government assistance. Prices dropped steadily in the next three years, to 54¢ a bushel for No. 1 Northern at Fort William in 1932 from the $1.60 of July 1929. To protect their own farmers, other countries raised their tariffs. Prices of other commodities such as fish, potatoes, apples, and dairy products also fell to a fraction of their 1928 levels and the total value of Canadian exports fell from the high of $1,363,788,000 reached in 1928 to $497,913,000 in 1932.

Canadian investors, like their American counterparts, had been infected with speculative fever. Their willingness to put money into mining, particularly, led to the promotion of worthless properties. Even money invested in "blue chip" stocks (shares of well-established industries) dwindled to a fraction of what it had once been worth. The combined value of the shares of thirty-five major companies lost five billion dollars in dropping from the 1929 highs to the 1931 lows. As the stock market fell, so did the rate of investment in productive facilities. As in the United States, there was a sudden and serious drop in investment and spending by those who still had money left after the crash. By 1933 capital investment in Canada was only one-quarter that in 1929.

The statistics overlook an important aspect of the depression: the unequal way in which various regions were affected. Generally speaking those areas dependent on one primary product suffered most. The prairie provinces were hit hardest. By 1932 for some farmers it was as profitable to burn their wheat for fuel as to sell it. To add to the misery the southern parts of Alberta and Saskatchewan were hit by severe drought. Rainfall had been light and uneven from 1929 until 1932, but in the following five years hot dry winds stripped even the topsoil from the land. Prairie farm income fell so low that thousands in despair abandoned the hard land and headed for the greener fields of Ontario, British Columbia, or the United

Drought in the 1930's in southern Alberta and Saskatchewan accentuated the effects of the depression. The once prosperous farms of the 20's became dusty and desolate wastes, the farm buildings standing in deserted sand dunes. Twenty-five per cent of Canada's farms suffered crop failures.

Unemployed men at Calgary, on their way to Ottawa in 1935 to protest against conditions in the relief camps, preparing to board freight cars.

States. According to the 1941 census some 214,000 people left the prairies during the decade.

The Atlantic region, though hard hit, did not experience the same shock as other areas of Canada. Personal income, which had been lower than in other regions, did not drop as severely as in other parts of the country. There was a larger number of self-sufficient families whose income came in part from fishing and farming, in part from forestry or from mills and small industries. Although laid off from employment, they still had their homes and the bare necessities of life. Nevertheless prices for products such as fish, lumber, potatoes, apples, and newsprint from the Atlantic region fell desperately low. Newfoundland, partly because its markets for both fish and newsprint were in Europe, felt the impact of the depression more slowly than the adjacent Canadian provinces, but when in 1931 the demands from these markets suddenly ceased, the effects were disastrous. Near bankruptcy, the government of the smallest dominion surrendered self-government. A commission appointed by the British government took over responsibility for administration and the island reverted to colonial status.

Ontario and Quebec suffered somewhat less than the Maritime provinces and the prairies. The industrial areas continued to produce and sell goods behind the protective tariff although output was curtailed. Unemployment was high in all industrial cities and those with jobs either worked short time or at very low wages. Some companies had to be reorganized to survive. In order to prevent collapse in the pulp and paper industry, the provincial governments began allocating orders to ensure that the businesses and the towns dependent on them survived. Farmers, most of

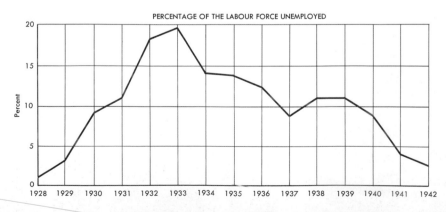

PERCENTAGE OF THE LABOUR FORCE UNEMPLOYED

whom practised mixed farming, saw their incomes drop, but they still produced and sold some produce. In contrast, because of Canada's near world monopoly, nickel-producing areas remained relatively prosperous. As the prices of goods dropped, the gold mining areas thrived. Thus, even within central Canada the effects were uneven.

A survey of the statistics and the regional effects of the depression shows the general dimensions of the problem, but it hardly reveals the depth of human misery. Not everyone could obtain welfare; just residents could apply. Every town had its soup kitchen to give out food to hungry transients. In cities men with families tried to maintain them by selling for a nickel apples that they bought for two cents each. Many single men worked on government projects such as highways and lived in work camps at the sites; others tried to survive in "jungles" of tin and tarpaper shanties. Many men "rode the rods" back and forth across the continent, restlessly seeking work which was not there. The frustration bred of despair occasionally led to violence, as in 1935 when a group of relief camp strikers, who had begun a march on Ottawa from British Columbia, clashed with police at Regina after their leaders had returned from the capital.

Unemployment in industries such as farming and manufacturing, the first to be affected by the collapse of the export trade, spread quickly to men employed in the transportation and handling of the products. Soon men in all Canadian industries were losing their jobs. One family in ten had to depend at some time on welfare relief provided by the municipal or provincial governments. In 1933-4 a Saskatchewan family of five received vouchers for a food allowance of $11 plus a 98-lb. bag of flour for one month. Families were not permitted to buy fruit or even certain vegetables; they saw their necessary possessions such as lamp chimneys, dishes, pots, and furniture break without hope of being able to replace or repair them. Potatoes, bread, sugar, a little meat, a few eggs, and weak tea, or coffee made with roasted wheat provided an inadequate diet. By 1937 doctors were commonly reporting malnutrition, especially among

When they reached Regina, about 2,000 of the western strikers were given food and shelter while their leaders continued the journey to see Prime Minister Bennett. On their return, after completely unsuccessful discussions in Ottawa, mass meetings in downtown Regina in which the city police intervened resulted in the Regina Riot of July 1935.

children. In Newfoundland in 1932 relief of \$1.60 for an adult and \$ .80 for a child per month was given. As someone said of relief, it was too little to live on, too much to die on. Wealthier Toronto gave vouchers for food including meat, milk, and vegetables for a family of two adults and three children worth about \$5.50 per week in the spring of 1934, but until the previous spring Torontonians needing help had had to queue up to obtain a dole of food or clothing. For every family on relief, four others had incomes barely above relief levels. To men wanting work it was demoralizing to live on relief week after week, and many of those with jobs had to forego the real necessities of life. By 1933 the cost of relief had exhausted the credit of most provinces to such an extent that provincial and municipal revenues were reduced to a trickle. Town after town defaulted on bonds; in many places municipal employees worked for weeks without wages. Doctors took fees in labour or in kind. In rural areas barter and exchange of services replaced money; school teachers were often paid in kind or boarded around the community. As even the national economy crumbled, the dominion government was helpless to act because it had no authority under the British North America Act to intervene in the field of social welfare. No one in Canada seemed able to reduce the severity of the depression.

The National Parties and the Depression

At the beginning of the depression, in 1930, the King government's response was to hope that it would go away. After first denying that any depression existed, the government did grant small sums of money to the western provinces for relief payments. As welfare costs rose and revenues declined, the provincial governments clamoured for assistance from the federal authorities. King answered that only the provinces could constitutionally provide direct relief and other social assistance and in a rare moment of indiscretion he stated that he would not give federal funds to any of the five provinces that had Conservative governments for "these alleged unemployment purposes". "I would not give them a five-cent piece," he added twice for emphasis. This expression of indifference to human misery returned to haunt him in the election that autumn.

The negative Liberal response to the economic crisis was a positive opportunity for the Conservatives. Leading the attack on the government was Richard Bedford Bennett, who had succeeded Meighen in 1927 as Conservative leader. A vigorous personality and a powerful speaker, Bennett had become wealthy through his law practice in Calgary. He had served in both Borden's and Meighen's cabinets and was the only Tory to hold onto his seat in Alberta throughout the twenties. He promised to use the Canadian tariff as a weapon to gain reciprocal trade arrangements with other countries. He advocated the creation of an imperial preference system of tariffs to encourage greater Commonwealth trade. What appealed to the people more than anything else was Bennett's promise to do something about the depression. The election reflected this mood of dissatisfaction. The "five-cent piece" speech was hurled at King by countless hecklers. The Conservatives won 137 seats, 25 of them in Quebec, the Liberals retained only 88, while the farmers' parties and independents were reduced to 20.

Once in office, however, the Bennett government proved to be a one-man show. After the frustrations of the previous decade there were few able Conservatives willing to chance their private careers for public office. Bennett's cabinet was therefore weak, and worse, it was divided between free enterprise traditionalists and those who had been influenced by the progressive currents in politics and who wanted the federal government to act to relieve the social problems. As the depression continued, these divisions became more bitter and Bennett became more authoritarian in his dealings with his ministers. The fortunes of the government – and of the Conservative party – were therefore tied to one man, the prime minister, and to his policy of national economic recovery within a framework of imperial preference.

Immediately after the election Bennett called a special session of parliament in which tariffs were raised by an average of 10 per cent. This action did help industry in central Canada but tariff protection did not increase exports. Instead many resource-producing areas, like the prairies, were forced to pay higher prices for many goods and enjoyed no benefits from increased sales of their products. Bennett appointed an agent to handle grain sales. He also attacked the railway problem, which had once again appeared because of the decrease in traffic. A royal commission appointed in 1931 recommended that the railways discontinue many unprofitable branch lines and pool their services in highly competitive

A relief project of the depression years at the RCAF *Station, Trenton, Ontario (1933). Below: Making cement blocks. Right: Digging operations for the administrative building.*

areas. Both measures, although unpopular with businessmen and in the areas affected, were put into effect.

In hopes of increasing exports Bennett persuaded the British and other Commonwealth governments to attend an Imperial Economic Conference at Ottawa in 1932 to discuss his scheme for preferential tariffs between Commonwealth members. Britain, who had adopted protective tariffs the previous year, and the other dominions came reluctantly, for no government – including Canada's – was willing to run the political risks of exposing its domestic industry to competition even from within the Commonwealth. After weeks of discussion the conference only narrowly avoided failure – by agreeing to preferences on specific commodities. Canada received concessions in the British market for her foodstuffs, lumber, and metals, and some British manufactures received preference in Canada in return. During the following years trade between Canada and the United Kingdom increased, but Bennett could not reconcile his contradictory Conservative policies of economic nationalism to protect Canadian industry and imperial trade preferences to encourage Commonwealth trade.

The depression reached its worst in Canada in 1932 and 1933. The government announced a major public works programme to create jobs and gave direct grants to the provinces to cover one-half of welfare costs. Special subsidies were also given to the prairie provinces. For a short time in 1933 unemployment reached a high of 22 per cent of the work force and the drain on the revenue resources of the nation to support the unemployed was enormous. As grants to the provinces increased it became clear that the federal government alone had the financial resources and the credit to cope with unemployment relief. Of the provinces only Ontario and British Columbia seemed able to handle the burden. British Columbia, hard hit by the loss of markets for its fish, minerals, lumber, and farm produce, went deep into debt as its premier, T. D. Pattullo, spent huge sums of money on welfare and public works to reduce social suffering. This unorthodox approach to the human problems of the depression made conditions more bearable in British Columbia, but other

Tractor making fill; a relief project at Princeton, British Columbia, 1933.

A "Bennett buggy", the horse-drawn vehicle used in many parts of the western provinces by those unable to afford gasoline for their old cars or replacements for their worn-out motors.

provinces, particularly the prairies and the Maritimes, could not provide the same standard of welfare.

Although the tariff policies of the Bennett government failed to solve the crisis of the depression, that government does deserve credit for two other nationalistic measures. The Bank of Canada was established in 1934 to manage the nation's monetary system, and in the previous year the Canadian Radio Broadcasting Commission was set up to create a national, distinctively Canadian, radio network to broadcast in English and French. At precisely this time, however, Bennett became enmeshed in attempts at economic changes that were to cause his political defeat in 1935. Some of his more radical ministers persuaded him in 1934 to investigate the retail trade. The Royal Commission on Price Spreads revealed that many companies were making enormous profits by underpaying employees and overcharging customers – in some Quebec textile mills, for instance, a worker earned only eight dollars for a seventy-two-hour week. Shaken by these revelations and convinced that Roosevelt's "New Deal" was solving United States' economic problems, Bennett decided to gamble that the Privy Council would permit the Canadian federal government to legislate in the social welfare field.

In January 1935 Bennett announced his programme in six radio broadcasts and then presented his "New Deal", as the legislation was quickly dubbed, to parliament. The programme was embodied in six Acts. The Trade and Industry Commission Act to provide government surveillance over prices, to eliminate unfair business practices and to strengthen anticombines laws, was based on evidence being presented to the Royal Commission on Price Spreads. The titles of the others are self-explanatory: The Minimum Wages Act, the Limitation of Hours of Work Act, the Unemployment Insurance Act, the Natural Products Marketing Act, and the Weekly Rest in Industrial Undertakings Act. In addition to the "New Deal" Acts the Prairie Farm Rehabilitation Act was passed to tackle the soil and water problems of the southern prairies and the Wheat Marketing Board was set up.

The Bennett "New Deal" rested on the assumption that the day of laissez-faire government was over and that the national government must

A destitute Saskatchewan family from an abandoned farm in the north returning to Saskatoon (June 1934).

intervene decisively in the economy. The programme seemed sweepingly radical in Canada and its constitutional implications were enormous, yet it was greeted with scepticism and treated as an election gimmick. The electorate could not believe the genuineness of Bennett's belated conversion to state intervention on behalf of the ordinary citizen and blamed him for failing to solve the depression. The programme even divided the Conservatives, some thinking that "R.B." had become a socialist, others that he had not done enough for the small businessman. The Liberals cried "King or Chaos", challenged the constitutionality of Bennett's "New Deal", and made vague promises about social reform and tariff reduction. The October 1935 election was a disaster for the Conservatives: they retained only 39 seats, mostly in Ontario, while the Liberals won 171. The other seats were won by a few Independents and by the new protest parties – the Co-operative Commonwealth Federation and the Social Credit party.

The Parties of Protest

The storm centre of the new wave of political protest against the old parties was western Canada, where the depression had hit hardest. The farmer protest of the 1920's had never entirely dissipated, although King and the Liberals had tried to absorb the movement. Moreover Independents in Quebec picked up a substantial vote in 1935, enough to elect 5 members. For all the Liberal sweep in the election, that party increased its share of the national popular vote by only 3 per cent. The Conservative losses were transferred largely to the "third" parties, which had increased their share of the vote to 22 per cent from 7 per cent in 1930. Quite evidently a large part of the electorate, especially in the western provinces, was still disillusioned with the working of the Canadian party system.

The first new party to appear was the Co-operative Commonwealth Federation, organized at a convention in Calgary in 1932. Its support came from the various farm organizations in the prairie provinces (who were concerned, as in the early 1920's, with the effects of national policies such as the high tariff), from middle-class intellectuals and others influenced by British socialism and the British Labour party, and from the ranks of the Progressive movement and the Independent Labour party. Together with a few labour leaders, these various elements joined to form a new party which would offer a substantial alternative policy to those of the Conservative and Liberal parties.

At a convention in Regina the following year the party drew up its programme: "We aim to replace the present capitalist system with its inherent injustice and inhumanity by a social order from which the domination and exploitation of one class by another will be eliminated, in which economic planning will supersede unregulated private enterprise and competition, and in which genuine democratic self-government, based upon economic equality, will be possible." While some supporters of the CCF had qualms about the socialism proclaimed in the Regina Manifesto, all could agree that greater government intervention in society was necessary to provide for the welfare of the people and to curb abuses by big business.

James Shaver Woodsworth, who had led the small labour group in parliament throughout the twenties, was elected leader of the party. A former Methodist minister, he had resigned from the ministry because the church seemed unconcerned about social problems and uninterested in the working class. Woodsworth believed that Christian principles could be applied to society only through some form of democratic socialism. He criticized Marxist Communism for its materialism and its revolutionary assumptions, but he also believed that in the capitalist system wealth was unfairly distributed and the wealthy had too much influence. During the Winnipeg General Strike in 1919 he had been arrested for publishing supposedly seditious statements – some of which were merely Biblical quotations. After the charges had been dropped Woodsworth was elected in 1921 member of parliament for Winnipeg Centre, for which he sat until his death in 1942.

After its initial success on the national level in 1935, the CCF made little progress. The party was accused of being a Communist front, and its leaders were branded as dangerous radicals. Unlike the British Labour party, the CCF received little support from labour. North American unions have never questioned the economic foundations and values of their society, but have contented themselves with increasing the workers' share of the wealth created. Social criticism and questioning of social values has been largely a middle-class intellectual pursuit. The Trades and Labour Congress took its lead from the American Federation of Labour, which avoided political alignment and concerned itself solely with problems of wages, hours, and working conditions.

Another western protest party was the Social Credit movement, which sprang up in Alberta. The party was led by William S. Aberhart, a high school principal who was president of the Calgary Prophetic Bible Institute, a fundamentalist Baptist organization. Gifted with immense energy and organizational ability, Aberhart had gained an enormous following as a radio evangelist throughout the province. In 1932, concerned about the hardships of depression, Aberhart began studying the Social Credit teachings of the Scottish engineer, Major C. H. Douglas. In order to maintain purchasing power and the value of goods, Douglas had written, government should pay "social dividends" to all citizens. Together with this economic theory went a criticism of banks and financiers for their restrictive control over the money supply. Douglas, while he would destroy the influence of these financiers, had no intention of destroying private ownership of farms and factories. He could see no purpose in political parties – parties merely fought over the methods of attaining the same goals: freedom and prosperity. The process of establishing individual freedom was a technical question for experts to solve – the average voter was not competent to choose among methods.

In depression-ridden Alberta, the Social Credit philosophy fell on politically fertile ground. The United Farmers of Alberta, which had held power since 1921, was now an ineffective organization, but rejection of the old party system had been drummed into the people for fifteen years. According to the UFA, industrial and financial interests – the traditional exploiters of farmers – controlled the old parties through providing campaign funds; the old parties would therefore continue to ignore the needs and the rights of the farmers. These criticisms had been offered by Henry Wise Wood, the political philosopher of the UFA who was passionately determined to make government more responsive to the will of the people.

These attitudes were consistent with Social Credit teaching. Indeed many UFA members were convinced Socred supporters long before the 1935 election. In the autumn of 1932 Aberhart had begun to mix the two

William S. Aberhart in the 1930's. Aberhart's interest in Social Credit dated from 1932, when a teacher friend introduced him to the theories of Major Douglas. "It struck me at that time," the friend later noted, "that Aberhart would be the man who could launch an educational programme on monetary reform. Anyone hearing him in those days would certainly agree that he could sway his audiences. One could not help but recognize his dynamic personality and gift of oratory."

The unemployed in the 1930's: hungry, listless, and resentful.

faiths, Social Credit and fundamentalist Christianity, in his broadcasts. "Bible Bill", as his critics called him, set up Social Credit study groups in the Bible Institute and encouraged their formation elsewhere. By 1934 strong pressures were building up within the movement for Social Credit to enter politics as a party. In December Aberhart announced that for the next election "reliable, honourable, bribe-proof businessmen who have definitely laid aside their party politic affiliations will be asked to represent Social Credit in every constituency"; then he organized a party on a province-wide basis. His election appeal boiled down to vituperation against the financiers and the promise of a $25 a month "social dividend". "Vote for Results" was his slogan. In the provincial election in 1935 Social Credit swept 56 of the 63 seats and then went on to win 17 seats in the 1935 national election, returning 15 members from Alberta and 2 from Saskatchewan.

Soon after he became premier, Aberhart found that Social Credit theory was easier to preach than to practise. His legislation to control banking, finance, and credit was rejected by the courts as beyond the authority of a provincial government. Some laws were even disallowed by the federal government. Even before Aberhart's death in 1943 the Social Credit movement in government had become a rather conventional, conservatively oriented group. The prosperity of the war years and the exploitation of Alberta's oil fields killed the demand for the implementation of Social Credit policies. The future attitudes of the party could be seen in the 1944 campaign of E. C. Manning, Aberhart's successor, to save Alberta from socialism.

The third political protest developed in Quebec, which had changed rapidly during the First World War and the twenties. Industrialization around Montreal, the mining, pulp and paper, and hydro development in outlying areas, and a scarcity of good farm land had drawn many Québecois into the towns. The 1921 census revealed that more than half

Quebec's people lived in urban areas, a disquieting fact to French-Canadian social theorists who idealized the religious farming family, and to a minority of nationalists who saw ownership and management of the province's natural resources passing into the hands of those who spoke English. The Liberal government of L. A. Taschereau, while proclaiming its concern for provincial and French-Canadian rights, was more willing than other provincial governments to alienate large portions of the public domain for mining, forestry, and electrical development by outsiders. Because the educational system of Quebec with its strong religious and classical emphasis did not produce engineers and managers, the English-speaking dominance of business was natural, but nevertheless resented.

During the depression years the average French Canadian paid more attention than before to the nationalists who blamed their situation on "foreign control" of the provincial economy. Criticism of the Liberal provincial government was widespread because of its failure to introduce welfare measures. The government's main response to industrial unemployment was to sponsor settlement of marginal farm lands. The resurgent nationalism and the demand for welfare led to a split in the provincial Liberal party which had controlled the province since 1897. The dissidents, headed by Paul Gouin, son of the longtime former premier Sir Lomer Gouin, became L'Action Libérale Nationale (ALN), a group which was favourably received by many people and which won the support of various nationalist groups. To fight the 1935 provincial election Gouin and Maurice Duplessis, leader of the province's Conservatives, formed a coalition called the "Union Nationale Duplessis-Gouin". Too late Taschereau promised to introduce old age pensions and other social measures and began an extensive public works programme of new roads, bridges, and public buildings. The election results were, however, a shock to Taschereau, as the Union Nationale won 42 of the 90 seats.

When the legislature met in 1936 Duplessis was the effective leader of the Opposition since Gouin had little parliamentary experience. The son of a judge and a lawyer by profession, Duplessis had entered the Legisla-

Maurice Duplessis at a gathering in the country in the 1930's. The Union Nationale depended on considerable support in the rural areas of Quebec, and the only parts of the party's original programme that were actually carried out were measures to help these rural areas. Credit to farmers at low interest rates was granted, agricultural schools were established, a minimum wage for forestry workers was set, roads were improved or built, and the government helped rural areas to build schools and hospitals.

tive Assembly in 1927 representing Trois-Rivières, which continued to choose him in every election until his death. He soon made his reputation as a hard-hitting debater and astute parliamentary tactician and was chosen leader of the Conservative party in 1933. He saw the alliance with the ALN as only a means of ousting the Taschereau government. Although a vigorous nationalist and defender of provincial rights, Duplessis was essentially a practical politician bent on making himself prime minister of the province. He forced a revival of the Public Accounts Committee and launched an enquiry into the workings of the Liberal administration which revealed a morass of corruption, of payoffs to ministers, of nepotism and of the squander of public funds. Taschereau resigned in disgrace and his successor, Adelard Godbout, called an election and rebuilt his cabinet with new, untainted men. This belated conversion to honest government did not save the Liberals. The Union Nationale increased its number of seats to 76. Thus began the Union Nationale's domination of Quebec politics, which lasted until Duplessis' death in 1959 except for the years 1939-44 when the Liberals had a majority. Duplessis ruled the province using methods reputedly learned from Taschereau. He too gave concessions to English-speaking big business, controlled trade unions closely, and used the provincial police to break strikes. His promise to nationalize hydro-electricity was forgotten. So was social reform except for measures to aid the rural areas of the province. "Le chef", as Duplessis' followers called him, held on to nationalist support, however, by posing as the guardian of Quebec's traditional cultural values and provincial rights.

Ontario also witnessed a change of government as dramatic as that in Quebec. The provincial Conservatives had been in power since 1923 and had become complacent. The prime minister, George S. Henry, gentleman farmer and president of a prosperous dairy company, was touted as "Honest George", a man who could "plow a straight furrow", but in the provincial election of 1934 he proved no match for the ebullient, forceful Mitchell Hepburn, Liberal leader since 1930 and a member of the federal parliament. Long before the election Hepburn had been criss-crossing the province regularly, denouncing the administration at Queen's Park. Attacking supposed government extravagance and promising social justice for all, he painted a picture of a government which had lost touch with the reality of the depression. "The little guy," Hepburn once remarked, "does not get enough of the good things of life, and anyway, it's good politics to give a hand to the majority." Almost single-handed this cynical crusader overturned the Tory government, raising the Liberal party's representation from 14 seats to 71 of the total of 90.

Once in office Hepburn sold off the ministers' limousines, reduced the number of civil servants, closed down the lieutenant-governor's residence,

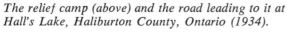
The relief camp (above) and the road leading to it at Hall's Lake, Haliburton County, Ontario (1934).

and cancelled many power contracts. But in spite of his promises the only social reform introduced by Hepburn was the old age pension. He did, however, lead a crusade against trade unions in Ontario. The Canadian Congress of Labour, aided by the American Congress of Industrial Organizations, had been organizing a number of companies as employment conditions improved in 1936 and 1937. The conflict between Hepburn and the CCL climaxed with a bitter strike over collective bargaining at the General Motors plant in Oshawa in 1937. Hepburn personally intervened in the negotiations and used the provincial police to break the strike.

Hepburn bitterly hated Mackenzie King and after 1937 he constantly and publicly attacked the policies of the Liberal government in Ottawa, especially King's failure to do anything about unemployment. When war came in 1939 he attacked King for not doing enough for the war effort, but when he suddenly resigned from office in 1942 he left a divided party behind him. Hepburn's successor as premier was forced to resign from office in the following year when a Liberal convention picked another man as leader. In 1943 the Liberals were swept out of office almost as dramatically as they had come in a decade earlier. The revitalized Conservatives under the handsome and forcefully eloquent George Drew gathered enough votes from disillusioned Liberals to form a minority government.

The protest movements of the thirties were successful at the provincial level but had little impact on national politics. Only in the Maritimes were there no political protest movements urging government to deal more effectively with the depression. Frustration over the failure of the economy, frustration over the inability of the federal government to act in the situation, and dislike of provincial governments grown too comfortable in long years of power were the essential ingredients of these protests. Surprising was the degree of social conservatism in the various movements; all of them, except the CCF, seemed interested only in preserving the existing social order. A few people joined extremist groups such as the

Communist party (which even elected some members to various levels of government), or the Fascist party in Quebec, but the majority wanted only a return to the good times of the twenties. The disquieting feature of these protests, however, was the emphasis placed by each, except the CCF, upon the leadership of one man. Canadians, it seemed, were looking for a Messiah to lead them out of the wilderness of depression. Yet each group was more than merely a passing protest, for each survived the return of prosperity to become a viable force in Canadian political life.

The Return of the Liberals

When the Liberals returned to office in 1935, King brought into his cabinet some first-rate administrative talent. Ernest Lapointe returned as Minister of Justice; J. G. Gardiner, former premier of Saskatchewan, entered the cabinet as Minister of Agriculture; C. D. Howe became Minister of Railways and Canals and Minister of Marine. The cabinet's membership was impressive but its performance was disappointing. More money was made available under the Prairie Farm Rehabilitation Act. In 1936 the Canadian Radio Broadcasting Commission, with only three stations, was reorganized as the Canadian Broadcasting Corporation and took over the old CNR network; in 1937 Trans-Canada Air Lines was organized. Some tariffs were lowered but despite these measures the depression continued. As King said, and as Bennett before him had argued, until world economic conditions improved, the Canadian economy would lag and people would suffer.

The burden of welfare payments and the financial dependence of the provinces upon federal grants in order to give relief to the unemployed raised the question of the relationship between province and federal government. By the 1930's the Judicial Committee of the Privy Council had restricted the authority of the federal government to those areas listed in section 91 of the British North America Act and in so doing had expanded the scope of provincial authority. Most economic and social problems were considered to touch upon "property and civil rights", an area reserved to the provinces. Although section 91 gave the dominion government the power to regulate trade and commerce, this authority had been restricted by judicial interpretation. This limitation on the powers of the federal government meant that the one level of government with the credit and the tax resources to deal with the depression was unable to do so. When King referred the Bennett "New Deal" legislation to the Judicial Committee, that body declared in 1937 that five of the Acts were *ultra vires* – that is, outside the authority of the federal government. Only the Natural Products Marketing Act was accepted as being *intra vires*.

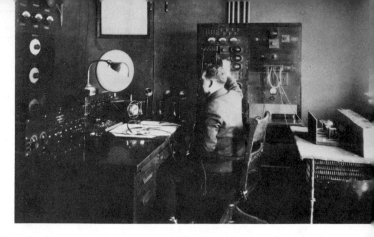

A compact operating room of station CNRO, *Ottawa, in the 1930's. Operated by the radio department of the Canadian National Railways, the station contains 500-watt equipment, transmitting panel, power panel, motor generator, and an elaborate speech input panel connecting* CNRO *with other radio stations in Montreal and Toronto.*

Shortly after this King appointed a royal commission under the chairmanship of Newton W. Rowell, Chief Justice of Ontario, to study dominion-provincial relations. After Rowell's death, Joseph Sirois, a Quebec lawyer, took over. Aided by a huge staff of experts the commission conducted research, heard submissions, and tried to find a solution to the constitutional and financial difficulty of Canadian federalism. The Rowell-Sirois Report – three volumes and eighteen supporting special studies – was published in 1940. Its recommendations were based on the assumptions that welfare services had to be made uniform across the country, that the existing division of powers in the federal system had to be retained as much as possible and, finally, that the central government had to have greater fiscal authority to counter depression cycles. Its basic recommendations were four in number. First, the dominion government should assume the debts of the provinces; in return, the provinces should withdraw from the fields of personal and corporate income taxes and succession duties, thus creating a more uniform taxation system for all Canada in these two major revenue areas. The commission then recommended that the existing grants to provinces, originally given under the BNA Act and since then increased from time to time, be abolished in favour of adjustment grants based on the need of the individual provinces that would allow each to provide a suitable standard of welfare services. Finally the commission report recommended that the dominion government assume responsibility for unemployment relief.

These wide-ranging proposals were discussed at a dominion-provincial conference in January 1941. Led by Mitch Hepburn, T. D. Pattullo, and W. S. Aberhart, the premiers refused to consider handing over any greater financial powers to the federal government because they did not want to be dependent on Ottawa for money to pay for services. King did not press this issue. As the depression had lifted and the war now engaged all Canada's energies, the problems examined by the Rowell-Sirois Report seemed less acute. Nevertheless the report had some results: the BNA Act was amended in 1940 to permit the Dominion to establish a system of unemployment insurance, and in 1942 the first of a series of tax-rental agreements to meet the financial needs of wartime was signed between the federal and provincial governments. The report had also reiterated the popular conviction, created by the experience of the depression, that government must assume more responsibility for the welfare and economic well-being of the people. The problem left unsolved was which level – provincial or dominion – should have primary responsibility for this welfare, a problem made more acute each passing year by increasing provincial expenditures for education, highways, health, and welfare. Perhaps the commission failed to recognize sufficiently that Canada is a federal state because of her history, her regionalism, and her language differences; it assumed instead that Canada is difficult to govern because she is a federal state.

By 1940, as the war entered its second year, unemployment in Canada was still at the 9 per cent level. Farm income, particularly on the prairies, was already rising with the demand for wheat, and mining areas began to revive as the demand for metals increased. But only in 1942 did unemployment drop to 3 per cent; the decisive impetus came after 1940 when Canadian manufacturing industries expanded to produce the hardware of war and when recruiting for the army absorbed the unemployed as Canada was called upon to make up for the great loss to the Allied cause occasioned by the fall of France.

During the 1930's, movies (comedies in particular) provided people with an escape from the harsh realities of the depression.

HISTORY FROM THE SOURCES

The Human Side of the Depression

The depression years will not mean much to a reader if he understands them only in terms of the statistics for unemployment, the gross national

product, or even per capita personal income. The real problem is how
did Canadians live during this catastrophe that many believed signalled
the end of the economy on which their society was based. The following
documents attempt to show how they did live.

The following statements are from interviews with Alberta farmers.

The winter of 1932 was grim and tough. Eggs were five cents a
dozen; hogs two cents a pound; cattle around five or six cents a
pound. There was great pressure put on by creditors to collect debts
for land and machinery. The situation grew desperate in 1933. Evic-
tions for non-payment of debts began to take place. I had to go out
north of ————— to give a family the bad news that they were to
be evicted immediately. On this farm a man and his wife, three or
four children, and a bed-ridden mother-in-law lived in an old shack.
I had to tell that middle-aged man and his fragile wife, "My instructions are to put you on the road allowance at once." Another time I
had to seize all a man's furniture. This man lived in a poor shack
on a farm with his wife and children. He owed money for the furniture which he had in his possession. I was ordered to take his furniture away from him. The furniture was removed.

*   *   *   *   *

. . . We began to feel that the situation was hopeless. Year after
year we farmed, and each year thought we'd have enough to provide
for our wife and family and it didn't come to pass. . . . Every week
when I went to the post office, I got a bunch of dunners (bills). I
took these home in my wagon six miles unopened and gave them to
my wife to open. She opened them because she had more pluck than
I had. I didn't have the courage to open them. I said to my wife,
"Open these and see what they are going to do next." But these
creditors didn't threaten me as much as they did my sick illiterate
neighbour who had five children and was depending for groceries on
the sale of eggs at four cents a dozen. That wife carried 24 dozen
eggs six miles, for which she received 96 cents in trade to buy groceries for a family of seven.

*   *   *   *   *

Conditions were very terrible at Magrath during the early thirties.
Wheat was 19 cents a bushel; the best pigs sold at two dollars each,
not two dollars a hundred but *each.* A number of farmers shipped
cattle to market, and were billed back for excess freight – the cattle
didn't pay the cost of freight charges. Hundreds of people in our area
were on relief. Mortgages and interest piled up to excessive rates. I
had a quarter section with 100 acres irrigated. Irrigation taxes on my
100 acres piled up to $9,000. What was the use of paying any kind

of taxes when you had $9,000 against a quarter section? Practically every farmer fell heavily into debt and was also heavily mortgaged.

Quoted in J. A. Irving, *The Social Credit Movement in Alberta* (Toronto, 1959), pp. 238-40.

This account is taken from the diary of a United Church minister, the Reverend A. M. Nicholson, who was stationed in northern Saskatchewan.

Saturday, March 30th. . . . J———— had hot cakes for us for breakfast with syrup he made with white sugar and water. He had a drink made from roasted wheat which he called "Bennett Coffee". We had dinner at K————'s. They had three fried eggs for four people and some potatoes, tea, bread and corn syrup. Relief allowances were always so low that food was very scarce at the end of the month they complained. We went to E———— T————'s for the night. I had known E———— when I taught school at Davidson 15 years before. Dry years drove him north. He has a small 2-roomed log house.

Sunday, March 31st. What poverty! Their tea kettle sprung a leak last Fall and the trouble with the relief system said F———— was it assumed that people never required a new lamp chimney, tea kettle or wash basin. For five years they had been seeing one utensil or implement after another wear out without being able to replace it. Mr. and Mrs. J———— P———— kept us for the night. J———— homesteaded near Strasburg about 30 years ago. He put up good buildings – later bought another quarter on which he paid $2,000 cash. Finally he lost the half because he could not meet his payments. Mrs. P———— in her early fifties is almost blind because she cannot get the necessary medical care for her eyes.

In most small towns cash was scarce.

Hanover, Jan. 3 – A system of barter is on the uptrend in Hanover. According to a census of businessmen not only farmers, but town citizens are daily exchanging produce of their own growth to merchants for necessities of life and paying accounts to professional men, the same way a prominent doctor attended a farmer's family and took a cow in payment.

The barber paid for Christmas turkey with shaves and haircuts; a young farmer gave the druggist a string of sausage for tubes of toothpaste and shaving cream; a newspaper agent took potatoes and half a pig in payment for subscriptions; a gent's furnisher outfitted a prospective groom and took his winter's wood supply in exchange; a dentist took chicken for pulling an aching tooth; a lawyer gave legal advice and had his car washed in payment; a ladies' wear merchant takes groceries in exchange for ladies' articles; a tailor receives his bread in payment on an overcoat and groceries for a suit of clothes; a butcher took his winter's supply of hay and oats in exchange for meat; a merchant in a neighbouring town took fire insurance from a local agent and pays the premium with groceries; a gent's furnisher has enough fowl promised on Christmas gifts to last him all winter; a blacksmith repaired runners on a cutter and took poultry in exchange; and a harness maker exchanged a set of harness for several cords of wood.

. . . a garage owner took half a beef and a load of shingles for repairing a couple of cars; a dry goods merchant takes eggs, butter, cream, fowl in exchange for various articles; a piano tuner took live chickens in payment but got the worst of a deal as some chicks died . . . during the summer many citizens exchanged garden produce for various articles.

Toronto Daily Star, 3 January 1933

A Royal Commission examined working conditions and wages.

Ample evidence was secured . . . to support the following summary conditions: –

(1) There are extreme variations in wage rates; ranging from less than 5 cents per hour in a Quebec country home-work contract shop, to 65 cents in a Toronto union factory. These variations are of two main types; variations between factory levels and, even more important, variations between provincial levels.

(2) There are therefore extreme and unfair differences in cost, "unfair" because they do not result from differences in efficiency of management. For example, the making of boys' pants cost 25 cents per dozen in a Quebec country home workshop, $1.50 in a union shop; men's suits of comparable quality varied in direct labour costs from $2.26 (Quebec country factory) to $4.71 (Toronto non-union). Differences resulting from efficiency are desirable and healthy. Differences that result from exploitation cannot continue to be tolerated. Humane consideration for labour's welfare, and economic consideration for the success of business enterprise alike condemn them. They produce intolerable conditions of employment

and life, and create intolerable industrial chaos. In the long run, they profit not even the exploiter.

(3) Wage rates and earnings are often exceedingly low. Quebec country home-workers probably cannot average 50 cents per day. Male pieceworkers in one large Montreal factory averaged 16 cents per hour, less than the minimum of 18 cents for inexperienced females. One man of ten years' experience worked 70 hours per week in a Montreal contract shop, to earn $7 at 10 cents per hour. One man of four years' experience earned $3 per week, or 5.5 cents per hour in a Quebec country factory. In one Montreal factory, all workers, men and women together, averaged 25 cents per hour. In 1932, out of 115 men in two thoroughly good Toronto union shops, 57 earned for the year less than $800; 88, less than $1,000; only 27 over $1,000; and only 2 over $1,600. . . .

(4) Hours of employment are often oppressively long. Thirteen hours a day, 60 hours a week, are not uncommon in rush periods. One man in a Toronto ladies' cloak contract shop, for nine consecutive weeks, worked over 16 hours per day; in this same shop, a woman often worked till midnight, 2 a.m. or 5 a.m. Eighteen, out of one group of 26 Toronto factories, reported frequent overtime. . . .

Report of the Royal Commission on Price Spreads
(Ottawa, 1937), pp. 110-11.

FURTHER READING

The books listed in the FURTHER READING section for Chapter 20 should also be consulted.

Report of the Royal Commission on Dominion-Provincial Relations (Ottawa: Queen's Printer, 1940), Vol. 1.

Fowke, V. C., *The National Policy and the Wheat Economy* (Toronto: University of Toronto Press, 1957).

Irving, J. A., *The Social Credit Movement in Alberta* (Toronto: University of Toronto Press, 1959).

Quinn, H. F., *The Union Nationale: A Study in Quebec Nationalism* (Toronto: University of Toronto Press, 1963).

McKenty, Neil, *Mitch Hepburn* (Toronto: McClelland & Stewart, 1968).

Zakuta, Leo, *A Protest Movement Becalmed* (Toronto: University of Toronto Press, 1964). An unconvincing account of the CCF, but the only one readily available now.

Laporte, Pierre, *The True Face of Duplessis* (Montreal: Harvest House, 1960).

22

Canadian External Relations

Canada's Commonwealth Relations

By 1914 Canada had enjoyed independence in domestic affairs for sixty years. Although in theory the British government had retained the power to disallow Canadian laws, in fact it had never used this power. In practice the only area of Canadian affairs in which the British government still exercised control was in the conduct of external relations. But even in this field Canada had some voice, for since 1859 she had determined her own tariff policies. The Canadian High Commissioner in London had negotiated formal and informal trade agreements with other countries although he was officially designated as a British representative. Since 1892, trade agents had been appointed in foreign countries, and in 1907 they were given official status as Canadian Trade Commissioners and also charged with handling immigration matters. Britain still controlled matters of international politics, however: Canada could sign no treaty by herself, could appoint no ambassadors nor declare war. Canada had a Department of External Affairs (established in 1909) over which the prime minister presided, but it was little more than a record office.

The Conservatives, led by Sir Robert Borden, had won office in 1911 on a platform combining Canadian nationalism and loyalty to Britain. A firm believer in the unity of the empire, Borden nevertheless had no intention of blindly following the British lead. But when war threatened in the summer of 1914, Borden's reaction was to offer Canadian support unquestioningly. He cabled London that Canada would "make every sacrifice necessary" if Britain became involved in the European war.

The first burst of loyalty and enthusiasm died down, however, as the members of the cabinet began to plan Canada's contribution to the war effort and looked to Britain for information on the actual conduct of the war. Adding to their confusion was the impact of the war on the Canadian economy. A depression had settled over the country during the previous winter, and the coming of war had hurt exports at a critical time. Many manufacturers hoped that the war would revive prosperity, for although imports from Europe would drop, war contracts would probably become

Sir Robert Borden (centre) at an Ottawa ceremony during the Victory Loan campaign in 1918.

available. But the government still faced increasing unemployment, which would only be partly relieved by army recruiting, but which might be solved by war contracts. For the next year the government begged and cajoled London, but obtained neither contracts nor information.

Resentment in Canada grew as the United States prospered by selling war materials to Britain. Instead of information about the war from London, the cabinet received requests for more manpower, requests which they did their best to fill. Then in 1915 Borden went to England to seek war orders and to obtain facts about the conduct of the war. In six weeks of talking he got neither. Finally he went to the Colonial Secretary, Canadian-born Bonar Law, and told him bluntly, "Unless I obtain this reasonable information which is due me as prime minister of Canada, I shall not advise my countrymen to put further effort into the winning of the war." This kind of talk brought an immediate British response: Borden met Lloyd George, the Minister of Munitions and after 1916 the prime minister. On Lloyd George's recommendation the Imperial Munitions Board was set up and quickly began placing large orders in Canada, but it was clear that strong words were necessary to remind British politicians not to take Canada for granted.

Borden's journey to England had yielded no significant intelligence about the war, therefore on his return the prime minister wrote to Sir George Perley, the High Commissioner in London:

> Is this war being waged by the United Kingdom alone, or
> is it a war waged by the whole empire? It can hardly be
> expected that we shall put 400,000 or 500,000 men in the
> field and willingly accept the position of having no more
> voice and receiving no more consideration than if we were
> toy automata.

Other dominion prime ministers felt the same frustration. After becoming prime minister, Lloyd George immediately acted to organize an

Imperial Conference for the following spring. This Imperial War Conference met as two bodies. The full Conference met on alternate days and
discussed constitutional matters. The Imperial War Cabinet, consisting of
senior British ministers concerned with the war effort, together with the
dominion premiers and representatives of India, met on the other days to
discuss the war. The Conference decided that consideration of constitutional changes should be left until after the war but Borden made an
important point in a resolution which he moved and which was accepted
that:

> any such readjustment, while thoroughly preserving all
> existing power of self-government and complete control of
> domestic affairs, should be based upon a full recognition of
> the dominions as autonomous nations of an Imperial Com-
> monwealth, should recognize their right to an adequate
> voice in foreign policy and foreign relations, and should
> provide effective arrangements for continuous consultation
> in all important matters of common Imperial concern. . . .

The Imperial War Cabinet was also worthwhile to Borden. In 1917 the
dominion prime ministers heard for the first time explanations of the
strategy of the war and the manpower and material requirements. When
the Conference and cabinet met again in 1918, the smaller body again
discussed the war effort and made plans for an even greater effort in 1919
and 1920. From Borden's point of view the Imperial War Cabinet was an
ideal means by which the dominions could have a voice in the empire's
foreign policy without sacrificing any of their autonomy.

Borden's ideal of a unified imperial foreign policy arrived at through
consultation with the dominions seemed to have been realized when, in the
autumn of 1918, the Imperial War Cabinet became in effect the British
empire delegation to the Paris Peace Conference. At that conference, the
basic decisions were made by the "big four": the United States' delegation
headed by President Wilson, the French led by Prime Minister Clemen-

*The Imperial War
Conference met in
London in 1917. In
the front row,
Canada's Prime
Minister Borden is
second from the left;
on his left is General
Smuts of South Africa
who is standing next
to Britain's Lloyd
George.*

ceau, the Italian by Prime Minister Orlando, and the British by Lloyd George. When any matter affecting a dominion arose, that dominion was represented on the panel. At Borden's insistence, the dominions (each of which had contributed as much as any small nation) were also admitted to full membership in the full sessions of the Peace Conference. Each dominion representative signed the peace treaty on behalf of his country but also as a part of the British empire delegation. The Covenant which set up the League of Nations was a part of that treaty; Canada, the other three dominions, and India all joined the League as independent members. While there was some objection that by seating these members of the empire Britain would have six votes, nevertheless when the first Assembly met in 1920 all were seated. Borden and other Canadian nationalists were overjoyed by this recognition of Canadian nationhood.

Imperial co-operation had been possible during the war when Britain and the dominions had had a common purpose – but could this co-operation and agreement continue in the post-war world? At the first conference of British and Commonwealth representatives after the war, in 1921, Prime Minister Arthur Meighen persuaded the British government not to renew its alliance with Japan because of American disquiet over the treaty. Apparently a dominion could influence British policy. The British government promised to supply the dominions with information on foreign affairs. Then the whole Conference went on to Washington as the British empire delegation to the naval disarmament conference. Initially, then, imperial consultation and co-operation seemed possible.

Yet even Canadian Conservatives had doubts about this possibility. Borden, while in London in 1918, had noted in his diary: "I am beginning to feel that in the end and perhaps sooner than later, Canada must assume full sovereignty. She can give better service to G.[reat] B.[ritain] and U.S. and the world in that way." Meighen, at the 1921 Conference, had argued that in an area where any dominion had a primary interest, it should have the determining voice in the empire's policy in that area. The logic of Meighen's position was bound to lead to complete autonomy (self-government) for Canada in her foreign policy, for he would not sacrifice his country's interests to a Commonwealth majority. Nevertheless, Meighen and other Conservatives still hoped to maintain the diplomatic unity of the empire and were quick to criticize Mackenzie King's policies after he became prime minister in 1921.

William Lyon Mackenzie King and his Liberal party were opposed to what they called the "centralized imperial control" of foreign policy; they felt that a common foreign policy for the whole empire was impossible. The imperial cabinet concept might well mean that Canada would be involved in problems – and committed to support Britain and the other dominions – in areas where Canada had no interest. King, an isolationist, believed that Britain would never really allow the dominions a voice in her foreign policy.

King had an opportunity to give a practical demonstration of his views in 1922, during the "Chanak Crisis". Under the 1920 peace treaty with Turkey, the Dardanelles were to have been neutralized and occupied by an international force. During war with Greece, the Turks repudiated this treaty and threatened to occupy the international zone along the strait. British troops, occupying the zone by themselves and with their headquarters at Chanak, might have had to fight to defend the area. The British government immediately asked for support from the dominions. The request was made known to the dominions and to the newspaper press almost simultaneously. King first heard of the request when a reporter asked what he intended to do about the British appeal. Angered that he had not been consulted in advance, the prime minister noted in his diary that he thought the British government was really trying "to test out centralization vs. autonomy". Arthur Meighen, now Conservative leader of the Opposition, stated that Canada should have said, "Ready, aye, ready" to Britain's appeal. King informed the British government that Canada would send no aid without a full discussion in her parliament (which was not in session at the time) and further information from the British about the crisis. Britain did not need to press her request again because the Turks made no attempt to occupy the disputed zone, and the crisis passed as quickly as it had arisen.

The "Chanak Crisis" showed clearly that Britain could not expect the dominions to follow her lead in foreign policy automatically. The Canadian government's reaction was the same as that of the Union of South Africa – only Australia and New Zealand had offered support. The ideal of diplomatic unity was not possible if there was not constant consultation in arriving at policies and if the separate members could not agree on what were the interests of the empire as a whole. In the following year, when Britain and the other great powers had worked out a new treaty with Turkey, King told the British government that Canada felt no obligation to support the settlement just because Britain had signed it. A foreign policy common to the empire as a whole was proving impossible to achieve.

To pursue his policy of no automatic commitments to any other nation, King had to make Canada independent in foreign affairs. He made his point in 1923 when he demanded that an agreement with the United States to regulate the halibut fishery in the Pacific be signed by the Canadian representative alone, without the usual additional signature of the British ambassador. The British government had no objection, but the American Senate, doubtful of Canada's authority, reluctantly ratified the treaty. At

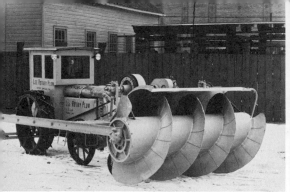

Canadian machinery of the 1920's.
Above: A snow plough attached to a tractor (1928).
Right: A portable steam boiler and engine used for
driving farm machinery.

the Imperial Conference that autumn King argued, with South African support, that each dominion should be free to pursue its own external policies where no empire interests were at stake; each should be able to establish foreign representation; each should be able to negotiate its own treaties with other nations. The Conference's final communiqué was more guarded:

> This Conference is a Conference of the several govern-
> ments of the Empire; its views and conclusions on Foreign
> Policy . . . are necessarily subject to the actions of the
> Governments and Parliaments of the various portions of
> the Empire and it trusts that the result of its deliberations
> will meet with their approval.

In 1925 King asked that a clause be inserted into the Locarno Treaties, which were signed by Britain, France, Belgium, Germany, and Italy to guarantee the eastern boundaries of France and Belgium, to exempt the dominions from the terms of the treaty unless each specifically accepted the obligations of that agreement. None did so.

The Chanak Crisis, the Halibut Treaty of 1923, the Imperial Conference of 1923, and the Locarno Treaties all demonstrated that the empire of 1919 had transformed itself into a Commonwealth of Nations in which the senior members were, in practice, self-governing. The Imperial Conference of 1926 formally recognized this new situation by a report of the whole conference on the nature of the Commonwealth. The Balfour Report, named after the former British prime minister who chaired the committee which drew up the preliminary draft, described the dominions as

> autonomous Communities within the British Empire, equal
> in status, in no way subordinate one to another in any
> aspect of their domestic or external affairs, though united
> by a common allegiance to the Crown, and freely associated
> as members of the British Commonwealth of Nations.

One other issue had yet to be clarified. After the King-Byng constitutional crisis of the same year, King was determined to narrow the governor general's prerogative powers as much as possible. He raised the problem at the conference and it was agreed that henceforth the governor general would represent only the Crown, not the British government. The relationship of the governor general with his ministers was to be the same as that of the British monarch with his ministers. This change in function of the governor general was further recognized when, in 1928, the British government appointed a high commissioner to Ottawa to represent the government of the day but not the Crown. King had already named Canada's first foreign representative, Vincent Massey, whom he appointed minister to Washington in 1927, and at the beginning of the Second World War Canada also had legations in France, Japan, Belgium, and the Netherlands in addition to high commissioners in the other Commonwealth countries.

Although Canada was now self-governing in practice, there were still several legal limitations on this independence. Some of these limitations were removed in 1931 when the British parliament passed the Statute of Westminster, giving legal definition to dominion status. The Statute declared that no British law would apply in any dominion except by that dominion's consent; it also repealed the Colonial Laws Validity Act, which had provided that British law overrode any colonial law; and it gave the dominions the power to pass extra-territorial laws – that is, laws applicable to Canadians outside Canada. But even after this Statute had been passed, other limitations remained. The Judicial Committee of the Privy Council was still the final court of appeal for civil and constitutional cases until the Supreme Court of Canada replaced it under an amendment to the British North America Act in 1949. But the British North America Act, which set up Canada's federal system, can still be amended only by the British parliament.

By the 1930's the empire had become a Commonwealth of autonomous nations. Canada had not been alone in bringing about this change; South Africa and Eire had supported every step leading in this direction. Nor had opinion in Canada been seriously divided on the demand for autonomy. Loyalty to Britain was still a powerful emotion, but all Canadians agreed that their country was no longer a colony.

Canada and Her Southern Neighbour

Canada's other partner in the North Atlantic Triangle, the United States, has always been of vital concern to Canadians. In the twentieth century, the United States, previously viewed as a threat to Canada's survival, has replaced Great Britain in the traditional role as Canada's major market, source of capital, and provider of military security. This new and powerful influence did not make Canada's relations with the United States any easier, however. "Manifest destiny" – the idea popular in the 1840's that the mighty United States should and would annex the entire North American continent – no longer worried Canadians. But Canada's position next door to a powerful state, a nation ten times her strength, has inevitably created some frictions between their respective domestic and foreign policies. Sharing a single continent, the two nations have a common concern over such matters as pollution of air and water, natural resources, and the development of shared water resources such as the Niagara River.

Potential friction over the use of international waterways has been avoided through the creation of the International Joint Commission. Before 1909, such problems as the damming of international rivers, the movement of log-booms on these rivers, and the use or the diversion of their waters had to be settled one by one by negotiation. After that year, however, the new IJC dealt with such problems. Three commissioners representing each country – the Canadians were originally appointed officially as representatives of the British government – are members of the commission, which has wide powers to investigate and settle any problem. Only when deadlocks occur, and these have been few, are the problems turned over to the respective governments for direct negotiation. The existence of the IJC means that problems are dealt with quietly and effectively.

After the First World War, the prospect of building the St. Lawrence Seaway frequently attracted attention as an international project, since the St. Lawrence River and the Great Lakes offered a magnificent natural route over 2,000 miles long, reaching into the heart of the continent. Before 1914 the United States had deepened the channels above Lake Erie to accommodate ships of 25-foot draft, and by 1932 the Canadian government had completed the rebuilding of the Welland Canal to the same depth. But the lower St. Lawrence canals between Ogdensburg, N.Y., and Montreal could handle only ships drawing under 14 feet. Considerable pressure from both the Canadian prairies and the American mid-west was placed on the two governments to deepen the St. Lawrence canals. But railway and east coast shipping interests opposed the project, as did a number of big cities in the east. Nor was the work economically feasible, it was thought, unless the hydro-electric potential of the river were harnessed at the same time. The IJC investigated the project and recommended engineering studies, but although such a construction project would have been a boon to the economy during the years of the depression, nothing was achieved until after the Second World War, when the power

RUNNER WITH GL
AWAITING SIGN

LOADED OUTBOARD
SPEED BOAT

*These photographs, published in the 1920's, show
rum-running across the Detroit River. Left:
Officials breaking open boxes in search of rum.
Above: A rum-runner at work.*

needs of Ontario and New York state made development necessary and
when the Canadian government was threatening to build its own St.
Lawrence canals.

One constant problem involving both Canada and the United States
was the smuggling across their common border. After the United States
had enacted the 1920 prohibition amendment to the constitution, the
smuggling of liquor from Canada to her southern neighbour began. The
Canadian government was unwilling to interfere with this trade, for the
distilling and export of liquor was legal – and profitable – in Canada. Only
in 1924, after it had become clear that the people involved in the rum-
running business might also be smuggling narcotics, did the Canadian
government agree with the United States to suppress smuggling. The whole
problem of liquor smuggling ceased after 1934 when the United States
repealed prohibition, and out of the 1924 agreement has come increasing
co-operation between all levels of police in the two countries.

The pattern of future economic relations between the two countries
was also established between the wars. Canada's dramatic rejection of
reciprocity in 1911 had hardly affected the growth of economic links between the two countries. Canadian imports from the United States had
doubled between 1900 and 1910 and rose another 80 per cent by 1914,
and during the war the United States replaced Britain as Canada's major
trading partner. Trade between Canada and the United States during the
years shown in the graphs on p. 445 had become vital to Canada. The
1937 figures reflect the diversion of trade to the Commonwealth that followed the 1932 Ottawa Trade Agreements. Although these figures are
merely percentages, they suggest a further problem for the Canadian
economy – Canada's unfavourable balance of trade with the United

States. The changing pattern of investment in Canadian industry from Britain and the United States again reflected Canada's growing ties with her southern neighbour.

The rapid development of resources and industry was made easier by the enormous inflow of American investment, but this trend increased Canada's dependence on the United States. Because many American-controlled companies operating in Canada preferred to process raw materials in the United States, American capital entering Canada was used mainly in the exploitation of natural resources needed by American manufacturing industry. Before the First World War the problem of United States' domination of the Canadian economy had been acute in some industries, particularly nickel mining and pulp and paper, but after the war both federal and provincial governments encouraged Canadian capital to develop paper making and mineral refining, also providing work for Canadians. A great deal of Canadian capital also went into building branch plant subsidiaries. Canadian tariff policy encouraged the expansion of industries such as automobile assembling by giving lower rates to

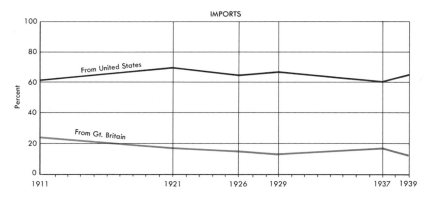

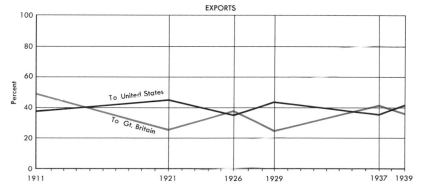

The long-term decline in the value of imports from Britain shows clearly in these graphs, as does the tendency for Canada to develop a surplus balance of payments in her trade with Britain.

Prime Minister W. L. Mackenzie King and the president of the United States, Franklin Delano Roosevelt, during Roosevelt's visit to Quebec city in 1936.

parts than to completed cars. As early as 1925 there were some 700 branch plants of American companies. Perhaps another 1,000 factories were controlled by American interests. The Ottawa Agreements of 1932 encouraged the establishment of even more branch plants to take advantage of the British and Commonwealth tariff preferences, but despite all Canadian efforts, some industries were still dominated by American capital; these included patent medicines, automobiles, petroleum, electrical goods, and rubber goods.

This growing dependence on American trade meant that Canada was also increasingly vulnerable to American tariff policy. Democrats in the United States have traditionally favoured relatively low tariffs, Republicans high protective ones. Thus in 1913 the Underwood Tariff, passed by the new Democratic Congress and administration of Woodrow Wilson, opened the American market to many Canadian raw materials. When, after the war, the Republicans won control of Congress, tariffs were raised to a level higher than ever before, a rise that accounts largely for the de-

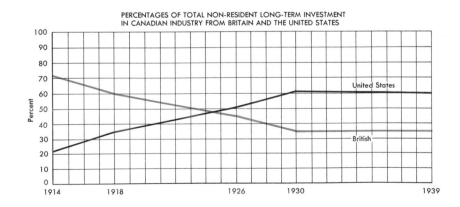

PERCENTAGES OF TOTAL NON-RESIDENT LONG-TERM INVESTMENT IN CANADIAN INDUSTRY FROM BRITAIN AND THE UNITED STATES

cline in value of Canadian exports to the United States (shown on p. 445) in the twenties. Canadian protests or requests for favoured status were to no avail. The last straw for many Canadians was, therefore, the higher United States' tariffs introduced in 1929 and 1930 to protect the American economy in the growing world depression. Prime Minister Bennett later remarked bitterly that he could do more for Canada if he could control United States' tariff policy than he could as prime minister. Canadian resentment against American tariff policy allowed Bennett to introduce higher tariffs in retaliation, and to promote a diversion of trade to the Commonwealth at the Ottawa Conference of 1932 in order to reduce Canadian dependence on the United States' market. Only when the Democrats returned to power with Franklin Delano Roosevelt as president did American trade policy change. Agreements between Canada and the United States in 1935 and 1938 lowered tariffs on a wide range of products covering about 80 per cent of Canadian exports to the United States. Once more Canada was able to sell in the large and profitable American market.

Despite Canada's close economic relations with the United States, it was not obvious in the 1930's that her security would depend largely upon her southern neighbour when the League of Nations became unable to maintain world peace. In 1938, in the midst of Italian, German, and Japanese aggression and sabre-rattling, Roosevelt while visiting Canada gave his assurance that "the people of the United States will not stand idly by if domination of Canadian soil is threatened by any other empires". The American government at least recognized that Canada was vital to United States' security. This pledge, treated cautiously by Prime Minister King but welcomed by Canadians at large, heralded close co-operation between the two countries in their mutual defence, a co-operation which began in 1940 before the United States had officially entered the war.

Canada and the World Crisis

Through the decades between the wars there was a lack of interest and understanding in Canada regarding countries outside the North Atlantic Triangle. In parliament there was virtually no discussion of foreign affairs, and any debates on the subject dealt with Canada's relationship to the Commonwealth or the League. Canadian newspapers reported foreign events, except in Britain or the United States, as if they were happening in places too remote to be of any concern to Canadians. In fact Canadians seemed agreed that the best way to treat the non-Commonwealth and non-American world was to ignore it.

Although Canada was a charter member of the League of Nations, Canadians had misgivings about those clauses in the League's Covenant

Canada's delegation to the League of Nations at Geneva, 1928. From left to right: Dr. O. D. Skelton (Under-Secretary of State for External Affairs); Philippe Roy (Minister to France); Senator Raoul Dandurand; W. L. Mackenzie King, Prime Minister and Secretary of State for External Affairs; Charles Dunning (Minister of Railways and Canals); Dr. W. A. Riddell (Canadian Advisory Officer in Geneva).

that required member nations to punish aggressors. They also constantly regretted the absence of the United States from the League, and worked quietly to encourage its membership. Canadians further mistrusted the League because it seemed to be essentially a European institution. Newton W. Rowell, Canada's first representative at Geneva, told the first Assembly:

> It was European policy, European statesmanship, European ambition, that drenched this world with blood. . . .
> Fifty thousand Canadians under the soil of France and Flanders is what Canada has paid for European statesmanship trying to settle European problems. I place responsibility on a few; I would not distribute it over many; but nevertheless it is European.

Some Canadians resented Rowell's nationalism, but Prime Minister Meighen reflected the opinion of most Canadians when he expressed to Rowell his "appreciation of the stand you took in stating to the Conference, as frankly as you did, the price the world has paid for the European diplomacy of the last hundred years". Canadians wanted to stay aloof from Europe's problems, as Senator Dandurand informed the League Assembly in 1924 when he said, "We live in a fire-proof house, far from inflammable materials. A vast ocean separates us from Europe."

Canada's retreat towards continental isolationism was tempered only by her membership in the League and in the Commonwealth. Prime Minister King uttered pious phrases about the League as a world force that would promote understanding, but he really distrusted it. The government accepted the presidency of the League in 1925 reluctantly, and primarily because of the position's prestige. Canada's acceptance of a non-permanent membership of the Council in the following two years was equally reluctant and undertaken only for the same reason.

With these attitudes Canadians were unprepared to meet the crisis of the 1930's. They did not recognize the world danger of Nazism in Germany or Fascism in Italy: these new forces seemed merely to be signs of the rebirth of old troubles in Europe, troubles to be avoided if possible. Having visited Hitler in 1937, Mackenzie King told a journalist that the Fuehrer was "a simple sort of peasant, not very intelligent and no serious danger to anyone . . . obsessed with the recovery of neighbouring territory inhabited by Germans. . . . When he had brought these territories into the Reich . . . he would be satisfied." No more complete and tragic misreading of world developments by Canadians and their leaders could be imagined, although they were not alone in the world in misjudging events and men in Germany and Italy.

World peace and collective security were shattered by Japan's attack on Manchuria in 1931, when all the great powers were preoccupied with the depression. Some countries even sympathized with Japan's ambitions. When Canada's representative at the League informed the Assembly that Canada was unwilling to spend a single dollar to maintain troops in the Far East, he was merely expressing a feeling common, if unspoken, in that body. The Assembly passed a resolution condemning Japanese aggression, but did not put any of the Charter's economic or military provisions into effect to restore peace.

The failure of the League to act against Japan encouraged further aggressions. In 1935 the Italian dictator, Mussolini, sent his army into a defenceless Ethiopia. The League Assembly condemned the Italians for aggression and imposed limited sanctions designed to prevent Italy from importing necessary war supplies. But these sanctions did not include oil, a basic requirement in modern warfare that Italy did not possess. After prolonged discussion of whether or not to include oil in the list of prohibited commodities, Canada's representative, Dr. W. A. Riddell, acted without instructions from Ottawa when he proposed that oil be included in the list. Riddell's action startled the world, particularly the government in Ottawa, and King's government repudiated its representative's initiative. In the spring of 1936, Mackenzie King probably spoke for Canada when he said of Riddell's action in the House: "Do honourable members

Prime Minister W. L. Mackenzie King and Dr. W. A. Riddell (Canadian Advisory Officer in Geneva) at the Geneva Conference of 1936.

think it is Canada's role at Geneva to attempt to regulate a European war?"

Thus, King consistently refused to commit Canada to any action on international issues. Not only was he conscious of Canada's position in the world as a small nation, he always claimed he was frightened that foreign affairs would divide Canadians again as in 1917, and that the only way to avoid such a split was to avoid positive stands on external problems. King also discouraged discussion of foreign affairs in parliament as much as possible. He seems to have been anxious to prevent the formation of any positive public opinion on external affairs that might destroy isolationism. Yet he was less than honest with the public about his policies. He told Hitler privately in 1937 that in the event of a war of aggression "nothing in the world will keep the people from being at the side of Britain". If many of King's followers in that year had known this, they would have revolted against his leadership. Anxious to avoid debate in Canada, unwilling to make any commitments, King nevertheless was personally prepared to follow the British lead in peace or war.

In Germany Hitler rearmed in defiance of the Versailles Treaty and began the relentless course that led to war. In 1936 he remilitarized the Rhineland; in March 1938 he annexed Austria; in September of the same year he won the acquiescence of prime ministers Chamberlain of Britain and Daladier of France to the dismemberment of Czechoslovakia. Most Canadians hoped with Mackenzie King that Hitler's territorial ambitions were now fulfilled, and King cabled Chamberlain: "The heart of Canada is rejoicing tonight at the success which has crowned your unremitting efforts for peace." Then in the following March came the shock of disillusionment, when Hitler occupied the rest of Czechoslovakia.

King's willingness to accept British leadership in foreign policy and his public stance of isolationism may have encouraged the British leaders in their appeasement of Hitler. "Dominion opinion was at the time overwhelmingly against a world war. This opposition was continually in our minds. Time after time we were reminded of it either by the High Commissioners in London or by . . . the Secretary of State for the Dominions," one former foreign secretary has written. On the other hand, while dominion policy did not influence Chamberlain's thinking, he certainly used it to stifle opposition to his appeasement views among some of his colleagues.

Canada watched these critical events passively, hoping to see world war avoided, but unwilling, indeed unable, to stop or control those events. She voiced with unaccustomed fervour her approval of British policies, while at the same time resisting all British efforts to improve the Commonwealth's defences. At the Imperial Conference of 1937 King applauded

*King George VI, flanked by Mackenzie King and (with arms folded)
Stanley Baldwin, Britain's prime minister, at the Imperial Conference
of 1937. With them are the prime ministers of New Zealand, Australia,
and the Union of South Africa. Particularly significant among the
conclusions drawn by the meeting was the admission that the dominions
(except New Zealand) no longer considered the authority of the League
of Nations to be binding – a conclusion induced by a loss of faith in
conciliation policies, and a desire to avoid involvement in any European
power struggle.*

Britain's attempts to keep peace but offered no assurance of Canadian
assistance in any collective Commonwealth preparations for war that were
initiated by Britain. Beginning in 1937, however, the Canadian government did increase its own budget for defence and began to reorganize its
armed forces, but these preparations for a new war proved less than adequate to meet the coming storm.

When war came in September 1939, King called parliament into an
emergency session to declare war officially. The declaration, made on 10
September, one week after hostilities began, was the deliberate act of an
independent nation – Canada was not automatically included in the
British declaration as she had been in 1914. There was little opposition to
the declaration except from some groups in Quebec who saw the war as
none of Canada's business. In parliament, J. S. Woodsworth, the pacifist
leader of the CCF, opposed the war, but his own party supported the
declaration. King told parliament:

> I have made it the supreme endeavour of my leadership
> of the government of this country to let no hasty or pre-
> mature threat or pronouncement create mistrust and
> divisions between the different elements that compose the
> population of our vast Dominion, so that, when the

moment of decision came, all should see the issue itself
that our national effort might be marked by unity of
purpose, of heart and endeavour.

Whether he had in fact achieved his goal remained to be seen.

FURTHER READING

Keenleyside, H. L., ed. *The Growth of Canadian Policies in External Affairs*
(Durham, N.C.: Duke University Press, 1960).

Glazebrook, G. P. de T., *A History of Canadian External Relations,* 2 vols.
(Toronto: McClelland & Stewart, 1965)★.

Keenleyside, H. L., and Brown, G. S., *Canada and the United States,* 2nd ed.
(New York: Knopf, 1952).

Craig, G. M., *The United States and Canada* (Cambridge, Mass.: Harvard
University Press, 1968).

Eastman, S. M., *Canada at Geneva* (Toronto: Ryerson, 1946)★.

Eayrs, James, *In Defence of Canada,* 2 vols. (Toronto: University of Toronto
Press, 1964-1965)★.

Dawson, R. M., *The Development of Dominion Status, 1900-1936* (London:
Oxford University Press, 1937).

23

The Second World War

The End of the Twenty-Year Armistice

On 1 September 1939 German armies slashed across the eastern boundaries of their country into Poland. Two days later both Great Britain and France declared war on Germany in support of Poland. That same day public opinion was shocked by the news that a German submarine, without warning, had sunk the British passenger liner *Athenia,* carrying 1400 passengers including nearly 500 Canadians, on her way from Liverpool to Montreal. Among the victims of this ruthless attack was a ten-year-old girl from Ontario.

Prime Minister King called parliament together in emergency session on 7 September to declare war officially. With only one dissenting vote, cast by J. S. Woodsworth, the formal declaration of war was passed:

> We do hereby Declare and Proclaim that a State of War
> with the German Reich exists and has existed in Our
> Dominion of Canada as and from the tenth day of
> September, 1939.

Canada, like her allies, was quite unprepared for the kind of war she faced. During the apathy of the 1920's and the retrenchment of the depression, the Canadian armed forces had declined in numbers, essential supplies, and morale. Canadians, after the 1914-18 war, were not prepared physically or psychologically for a new horror. The belief that Canada was a fire-proof house far from the combustible area of war, the feeling that there was not even a threat of war, had kept military expenditures to a minimum in the decade after the First World War. Then during the depression the armed forces' budget had been further cut to reach its lowest point of under $14 million spent in the 1933-4 fiscal year. A staff report in 1936 on the state of the armed forces revealed that the weapons of the army were all of First World War vintage, that they had no tanks, and that their transport was entirely inadequate. The Air Force had no aircraft of post-1921 design and the Navy had only four destroyers, two

of them so obsolete as to be worthless. The general staff had regularly
pointed out these shortcomings, but nothing had ever been done. These
revelations, together with the threatening international situation, persuaded the King government to begin a reorganization of the Canadian
armed forces.

To improve the efficiency of the armed forces, the Joint Staff Committee
of the heads of the three services recommended a five-year reorganization
that would cost $200 million. In the government's opinion, such an
expensive programme was not politically feasible, but the budget for the
armed forces was increased and by a programme of strict priorities a
number of necessary steps were taken. Defences on the Pacific coast were
strengthened; four British destroyers were bought so that the Navy now
had six – after scrapping the two old ones – and four minesweepers were
built; the RCAF obtained a number of training aircraft. It was a very modest
start towards meeting defence needs, nevertheless it was a start which
meant that Canada was better prepared for war than she had been in 1914.
However, as the official historian of the Canadian army has written, "the
preparations were utterly inadequate by comparison with the scale of the
coming emergency".

The original plans for mobilization and the war effort were tailored
more to meet political needs than the external menace. Beginning on 1
September two divisions with a total authorized strength of 60,000 men
had been mobilized, but after their complement was complete the Chiefs
of Staff were told that there was to be "no stimulation to recruiting at the
present time". The government assumed that Canada's contribution to
the war would be mainly economic – for foodstuffs and war materials
– while the need for Canadian manpower would be limited. This emphasis on materials rather than on men would prevent the spectre of
conscription rising to create a new political crisis. King did not want to
create a large army; he hoped instead to concentrate Canada's efforts on
the Air Force and Navy, which would require less manpower. Such a
limited war effort could be justified only if the war did not last long, and
most people anticipated a short and successful war.

During the winter of 1939-40 criticism of this timid policy grew. In
January 1940 Premier Mitchell Hepburn of Ontario pushed a resolution
through the legislature condemning the federal government's war policies
as inadequate; King's response was to dissolve parliament for an election
on the issue. In the so-called "phony war", before the successful Nazi invasions of Denmark, Norway, and France, King's policy won general support from the voters, who gave the Liberals 181 of the 245 seats – a strong
majority that gave King a position of power for the duration of the war.

King's critics were gagged. The Conservatives were routed and unable to provide any effective opposition in parliament.

The Allied disaster at Dunkirk in May and the fall of France a month later shocked all Canadians into the realization that the war would not be short. Suddenly Britain and the Commonwealth had to stand alone against Germany and Italy. All assumptions about a limited war effort had to be abandoned. But the government's "no-conscription" pledge remained – for overseas service. As a compromise, the government introduced in June 1940 conscription for home defence while recruiting drives were begun and more volunteer troops were sent overseas. Canada's four destroyers were sent across the Atlantic to join British forces. An RCAF fighter squadron was despatched to England in time to fight in the Battle of Britain later that summer. With British orders for equipment pouring into Canadian factories and the Canadian armed forces expanding, the country's economy began to take up the slack left by the depression. At last the Canadian government was fully committed to supporting the war against the Axis powers.

Canada at the War Fronts

After Dunkirk, Canada's armed forces enlarged dramatically. By June of 1944, 250,000 soldiers had been sent overseas, and some 730,000 men and women had joined the army. By the end of the war the RCAF had grown to 250,000 men and was rated the world's fourth largest. The RCN also expanded until it became the fourth largest among the Allies, comprising 1,000 ships and 100,000 men by 1945.

The Royal Canadian Navy was largely a small-ship force of corvettes, frigates, destroyers, and minesweepers: its battleground, the North Atlantic, where a grim, persistent war was fought over one of the roughest, coldest seas in the world; its enemy, the German submarines, trying to break the seaborne communications joining the United Kingdom to the factories and farms of North America. By the end of the war Canadian ships were escorting 80 per cent of the convoys crossing the Atlantic. Canadian sailors had destroyed or shared in the destruction of many sub-

Four-engined Lancaster aircraft, such as the one shown here, were flown during the Second World War by twelve RCAF squadrons based in Britain. In 1941, three twin-engined planes of the RCAF carried out the first Canadian bombing raid; by the end of the war 200 RCAF bombers loaded with 900 tons of bombs were being sent out on a single raid. Radar guided the bombers to their target, even when clouds obscured it.

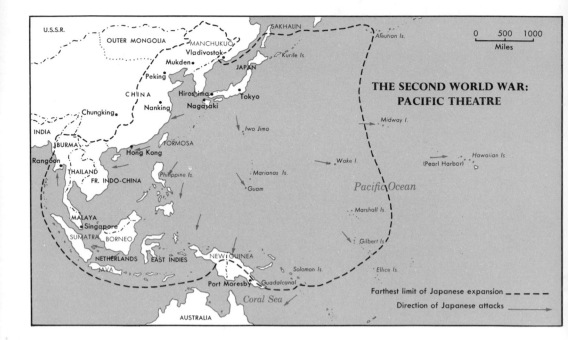

marines, had taken part in the landing operations at Dieppe and in the Mediterranean, and had made a considerable contribution to the D-Day invasion of France.

The Royal Canadian Air Force played an equally important role. Nearly one-third of its personnel were engaged in the British Commonwealth Air Training Plan which produced over 131,000 trained men for air crew duty. A large Home War Establishment guarded Canadian coastal waters, fought submarines in the Atlantic, and in 1942-3 took part in the operations against the Japanese in the Aleutian Islands. By war's end, forty-eight Canadian squadrons had been sent overseas and many Canadian airmen were also serving with RAF and Commonwealth squadrons. The strategic air offensive against Germany by Bomber Command took an appalling toll of lives as night attacks were carried out in the face of heavy concentrations of searchlights, flak, and night fighters. The vast majority of those shot down died; few of the casualties lived to be recorded as wounded or as prisoners of war. The RCAF suffered far more casualties in proportion to its strength than either of the other services.

The Canadian Army overseas grew from the single infantry division of almost 16,000 personnel sent in December 1939 to three divisions of infantry, two armoured divisions, and two armoured brigades. The first taste of battle for Canadian soldiers came in the hopeless defence of Hong Kong in December 1941, where two partially trained battalions of nearly 2,000 men had been sent direct from Canada. Those who survived the tragic battle lived out the war in wretched conditions in POW camps. After a long enforced wait, the army in Britain had its baptism of fire in the bloody assault on Dieppe on 19 August 1942. Five thousand Canadians and 1,000 British troops made up the striking force, which was withdrawn after ten hours of carnage costing 3,300 casualties. The raid was a tactical disaster, but it was of some value in planning later combined land, sea, and air operations. These costly actions at Hong Kong and Dieppe, followed as they were by long months of inactivity, provoked bitter comment in Canada about the apparent mismanagement and futility of Canada's military role.

Partly to silence these criticisms, the First Canadian Infantry Division was despatched in the summer of 1943 to join in the invasion of Sicily. Well trained but still inexperienced in battle, the division proved its mettle in the thirty-eight-day campaign over the mountainous island. For the ensuing campaign up the Italian peninsula, the Fifth Division joined the First to form the First Canadian Army Corps under the command of Lieutenant-General H. D. G. Crerar. For a brief moment victory in Italy seemed near, for Mussolini had been deposed in July, and on 8 September the new Italian government accepted unconditional surrender. But the Germans, prepared for this action, simply occupied the land and sent heavy reinforcements south to hold the country. The campaign turned into a costly, painfully slow advance over the rugged mountainous landscape and rough narrow winding roads where gains were measured in yards. At Christmas, the Canadians at Ortona found themselves in a fierce, hand-to-hand, house-to-house struggle won only at a high cost. During the winter of 1943-4 heavy rains flooded the many small rivers, turned the hillsides into greasy muck, and the roads into quagmires.

The beach at Dieppe where the main Canadian force landed in August 1942. (Photographed in 1944.)

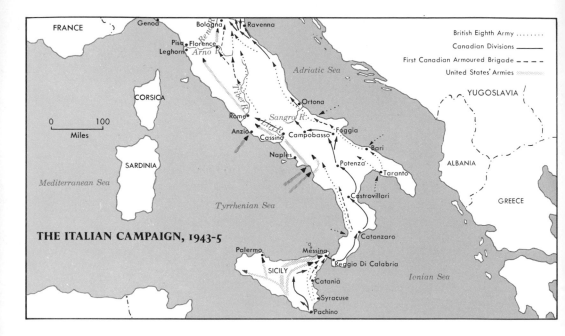

FRANCE

Genoa
Bologna
Ravenna
Pisa Florence
Leghorn *Arno R.*

Adriatic Sea

British Eighth Army ....
Canadian Divisions _____
First Canadian Armoured Brigade _ _ _ _
United States' Armies

CORSICA

YUGOSLAVIA

Ortona
Rome *Sangro R.*
Anzio
Cassino Campobasso Foggia
Naples Bari
Potenza
Taranto
Castrovillari

0   100
Miles

SARDINIA

ALBANIA

Mediterranean Sea

Tyrrhenian Sea

GREECE

THE ITALIAN CAMPAIGN, 1943-5

Catanzaro

Palermo
Messina
Reggio Di Calabria
SICILY
Catania
Ionian Sea
Syracuse
Pachino

The Germans remained behind their *Gustav Line* south of Rome until after the capture of Monte Cassino cracked it. Rome was liberated in June 1944, but even then the Germans retreated skilfully, contesting every mountain and river. Only in the summer of 1945 did the Allied forces break through into the Lombardy Plain, but by then the Canadian Corps had been secretly moved to northwestern Europe to join the First Canadian Army in the final attack on Nazi-held Europe. Meanwhile in the autumn of 1943, General Andrew McNaughton, who had commanded the Canadian Army in Britain from the beginning, was forced to resign because he had opposed separating the Canadian forces to send two divisions to Italy. His successor, General Crerar, commanded the First Canadian Army during the rest of the war, and was succeeded in Italy by Major-General E. L. M. Burns.

A mule train of the Second Canadian Infantry Brigade moving through the country-side near Campobasso, Italy, in October 1943. Note the carefully camouflaged vehicle in the right foreground.

More crucial than the Italian campaign was the invasion of France and the liberation of northwestern Europe. After months of preparation, the assault on the German west wall began on D-Day, 6 June 1944. After preliminary air and naval bombardment had softened up the German defences, the Third Infantry Division of 14,000 men landed in Normandy at H-Hour with the main invasion force. The Allied forces were able to secure their bridgehead by the end of the first week of fighting, and after hard combat the combined British-Canadian forces took Caen in July. In the interval Canadian Army headquarters had moved to France, and General Crerar took command of some twenty miles of front south of Caen.

A German counter-attack southwards in Normandy presented a great opportunity for the Allies. To cut their lines of retreat, American armoured forces were diverted northwards and the Canadian Army was ordered to drive south to Falaise and beyond to link up with the Americans. The Fourth Canadian Armoured Division and the First Polish Division almost closed the Falaise Gap; and with American support inflicted very heavy losses on the retreating German forces – 50,000 prisoners taken, and thousands of men killed or wounded, countless tanks, guns, and fighting vehicles destroyed – but the really decisive victory eluded their grasp.

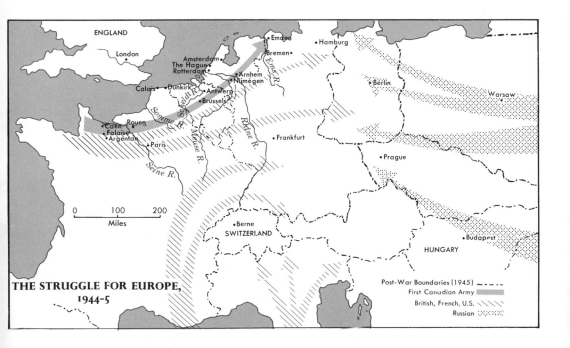

THE STRUGGLE FOR EUROPE, 1944-5

Post-War Boundaries (1945) ·—·—·
First Canadian Army
British, French, U.S. \\\\\
Russian

Canadian troops and equipment landing in Normandy, July 1944. The screen of captive balloons ("barrage balloons") at top left was intended to prevent enemy aircraft from bombing and strafing the operation.

The Allied victories in Normandy which had cost the Germans some 400,000 men, half of them prisoners, and enormous quantities of equipment, had broken the German resistance in western France. Turning north to follow the retreating enemy, the Canadians entered Rouen at the end of August and then drove north along the Channel coast, while the British seized Brussels and Antwerp in early September. The Americans had already liberated Paris late in July and were pushing on through Belgium towards the German border when they were stopped by fierce fighting on the lower Rhine.

The back of Germany's resistance was broken, however, with the failure of her Ardennes counter offensive in December 1944. This so-called "Battle of the Bulge" cost the Germans another 120,000 men, 500 tanks, and the last of their offensive aircraft. In a hard-fought winter campaign, Canadians cleared German forces from the Scheldt Estuary so that the large harbour of Antwerp could be opened. In March, when the weather improved, the British and Americans broke through into Germany while the Canadian Army advanced into the Netherlands and the North German Plain. Although lacking the equipment to resist effectively, the Germans fought fiercely as they retreated. By April their strength had been exhausted, and German soldiers surrendered so fast that they overflowed the temporary POW camps. In early May the northern Netherlands were liberated completely and the Canadian Army received the unconditional surrender of German forces facing it. On 8 May victory in Europe was proclaimed as the German armies surrendered.

The Economics and Politics of War

The war in Europe was over, but the victories had been bought at the cost of many lives. Though there had been 23,000 casualties in the Canadian Army, this number fell far below the loss exacted by the slaughter of 1915-18. But the nature of the two wars had been vastly different. The mobility of action in the Second World War and the absence of bitter attacks against well-entrenched positions both contributed to the lower casualty level. A higher proportion of soldiers was wounded in 1939-45, but better medical care ensured that far fewer died than in 1914-18. Canadian participation had been greater than in the First World War, for over a million men and women had joined the armed forces – nearly 10 per cent of the nation's people. Countless thousands of others worked in war industries or on the farms to produce the food to sustain the Allied cause. When the war came in 1939, depression still hung over Canada. Unemployment dropped slowly until the autumn of 1940 when after the fall of France the all-out war effort began and the demand for labour began to soar.

In the next five years the Canadian economy grew fantastically; the gross national product (the total value of all goods and services produced) more than doubled between 1939 and 1945. Yet though agricultural output increased 30 per cent between 1939 and 1945 the number of workers employed on farms decreased steadily as improved methods and mechanization increased the land's productivity. Canadian farms diversified their output to meet British needs; even the prairies turned increasingly from grain to the production of beef, pork, dairy products, flax, and oil seeds. Other primary industries expanded, too. The forests yielded more timber and more pulp and paper than ever before. Canadian mines supplied most of the Allies' demands for nickel, copper, lead, and zinc. The newly discovered uranium mine on Great Bear Lake, taken over by the government, produced the uranium for the Manhattan Project, the joint British-Canadian-American programme of atomic research that produced the first atomic bomb. This whole development brought new strength to the Canadian economy and enabled the country to adjust more easily to the conditions of the post-war world.

Secondary industry grew even more rapidly than primary industry. With foreign supplies of many manufactured articles no longer available, Canada was forced to produce a considerable range of items that she had previously imported – such as electronic equipment, optical glass, roller bearings, and diesel engines. Canadian shipyards launched over 1,000 naval and cargo vessels; aircraft plants turned out nearly 15,000 planes; auto plants built 700,000 trucks and 50,000 armoured fighting vehicles. Completely new industries grew up, producing synthetic rubber, petrochemicals, and plastics, and most of these war-born industries have made permanent contributions to the Canadian economy.

The government's management of the economy during wartime was extraordinarily successful. The war effort proved to be enormously costly, totalling $20 billion in the course of the six years. By 1945 the federal debt had risen to four times its pre-war level, yet Canada was more able than any other participant to finance her war effort out of direct taxation. In 1942, to utilize more effectively the tax resources of the nation, the federal and provincial governments entered a tax-rental agreement for five years whereby the provinces gave up their right to collect personal and corporate income tax. In return, the federal government paid increased subsidies to the provinces. The agreement enabled the federal government to introduce limited equalization payments, which gave the less wealthy provinces slightly higher per capita grants than the wealthier provinces. Tax rates were increased to pay for the war as far as possible on the basis of "pay as you go". In addition, the government was able to borrow vast amounts of money from Canadians through the sale of "Victory Bonds". This taxation, borrowing, and enforced savings through payroll deductions aided the government's effort to control inflation by restricting the amount of money available for the general public to spend. Thanks also to the efforts of the Wartime Prices and Trade Board, the prices of goods did not rise unduly – only 19 per cent during six years instead of 54 per cent as in 1914-18.

Compared to the difficulties of the British people, or to those of people in German-occupied countries, Canadian living standards were scarcely affected by the war. Some goods were in short supply or sometimes unobtainable, but these were mostly durable consumer goods such as automobiles and refrigerators. New tires could not be obtained; private cars could use only three gallons of gasoline a week; choice in clothing was restricted; meat, sugar, and butter were rationed; but no one did without necessities and indeed the general living standard was higher than ever before because more people were enjoying higher incomes and the government had committed itself to alleviating the worst poverty.

During the war years the government had produced several major items of social legislation. Following an amendment to the British North Ameri-

A convoy of ships destined for Europe assembled in Bedford Basin, Halifax, in 1941. In an attempt to prevent attacks by German submarines, merchantmen crossing the Atlantic were sent in convoys guarded by destroyers, corvettes, and aircraft carriers, and were frequently routed to the north of Iceland.

Bombing-up a Halifax four-engined RCAF *heavy bomber, August 1943. Like the Lancasters, these aircraft came into use in 1942 to replace the veteran twin-engined Wellingtons and Hampdens flown by the* RCAF *since the beginning of the war.*

ca Act in 1940 the government introduced Unemployment Insurance. In 1944 the Family Allowance Act was passed, establishing the so-called "baby bonus", a measure designed largely to put more wealth into the hands of people in the poorer agricultural areas of the nation. The National Housing Act, intended to provide low interest mortgages for housing with the government contributing part of the loan and guaranteeing the rest, was passed the same year. Like all Liberal policies, this social legislation was a collection of moderate measures but it satisfied most voters' desires for social welfare schemes.

Canada entered the war as united in patriotism as she had been in 1914. Considering the opposition to military expenditures and the feeling that the nation should keep clear of Europe's troubles, the degree of this unity is surprising – in fact it was an artificial unity created by Prime Minister King's policy of avoiding controversy in the 1930's, a policy that created the impression of general agreement. This unity was abruptly broken when Premier Duplessis called a provincial election for late October on the issue of possible war measures infringing on the autonomy of Quebec, an action that was almost a call for Canadian neutrality in the war. Led by Ernest Lapointe, King's Quebec lieutenant, the Quebec ministers in the federal cabinet campaigned through the province, threatening to resign from the cabinet if Duplessis were re-elected. They told the voters that Quebec's representatives in the cabinet constituted the barrier to conscription being introduced in the country and promised that the federal government would never introduce conscription for overseas service. The federal government's commitment to a moderate war effort won it support in Quebec: Duplessis was heavily defeated by the provincial Liberal party.

In the Second World War, as in the First, conscription turned out to be the only divisive issue in Canada. The National Resources Mobilization Act (NRMA) met the first criticisms of the government's programme, but in English-speaking Canada demands for unlimited conscription were increasingly heard. The attack on the United States by Japan in December 1941 raised to a fever pitch the agitation to repeal the section of the NRMA

Above: H.M.C.S. "Iroquois" laying a smoke screen off Halifax, June 1944. Right: Canadian tanks advancing during the Italian campaign.

that limited conscription to home defence service. King decided to appeal to the people in a plebiscite to release the government from its pledges against applying overseas conscription and announced his decision in January 1942.

The political rift between English and French Canadians over Canada's role in the war had been patched up in 1939, but now national unity was shaken by the prospect of conscription. French-speaking Canadians recalled that the 1939 "no-conscription" pledges had been addressed to them and felt that King was trying to escape his promises by the trick of a plebiscite in which the majority of voters would be English speaking. In the vote on the question, "Are you in favour of releasing the government from any obligation arising out of any past commitments restricting the methods of raising men for overseas service?" 64 per cent of the voters favoured giving the government a free hand. In Ontario, Manitoba, and British Columbia the "yes" vote was over 80 per cent; in Quebec 72 per cent voted "no". This result showed the cleavage of opinion. The government amended the NRMA but still did not send conscripts to Europe. A few conscripts were despatched with the Americans to reoccupy the Aleutian Islands, but this action could be explained away as a home defence measure.

The long-feared manpower crisis came only in the autumn of 1944. Losses in the heavy fighting in Normandy had been unexpectedly high and recruiting for general service in the previous year had failed to provide enough trained infantry replacements. Yet there were thousands of trained conscript infantry in Canada who refused to "go active" – the "zombies" as they were called, a term meaning the "living dead". After a quick visit to the fighting front, J. L. Ralston, Minister of Defence, recommended in October that these conscripts be sent overseas. King, unwilling to accept the political consequences of such a decision, accepted Ralston's resignation instead. General McNaughton, the new minister, tried vainly to use his personal prestige to find volunteers for overseas service. When the vast majority of "zombies" refused to volunteer for general service, the Chief of the General Staff and other senior officers expressed the view that the voluntary system could not meet the immediate need for reinforcements. King seems to have persuaded himself that a military revolt against his government was imminent – he had also convinced himself by this time that overseas conscription was politically necessary. To save the government, he ordered 16,000 conscripts sent overseas.

This time, however, the conscription issue turned out to be far less destructive of national unity than in 1917. The House of Commons gave King a vote of confidence, although thirty-four French-Canadian Liberals voted against him and one minister, C. G. Power, resigned. There was a wave of desertions from the NRMA forces. In the Quebec election of August 1944, Duplessis and the Union Nationale had returned to power on an anti-conscription platform; now the Quebec leader began sniping at King and his government. But the Bloc Populaire, the ultra-nationalist, anti-war party which ran a slate of candidates in the provincial election and again in the 1945 federal election, won little support from the Quebec voters. By administering the conscription medicine in two doses, King avoided a major crisis. For French Canada the crisis came in 1942 when the plebiscite was held, for English Canada it occurred in 1944 when King made the decision to send men overseas. The war in Europe ended six months after that decision; of 16,000 conscripts authorized to be sent, only 13,000 were actually despatched to Europe. Thus King managed to avoid a repetition of the bitter French-English split of 1917-18. But when he called a general election for 11 June 1945 his large wartime majority was nevertheless sharply reduced to a bare majority of 125 in the 245-seat House. The Progressive Conservatives, as they were now called, under their new leader John Bracken, won 67 seats, the CCF 28 seats, Social Credit 13, and others, including Bloc Populaire, 12. But with the support of the CCF, who thought the Liberals a lesser evil than the Conservatives, King carried on with no difficulty.

The Diplomacy of War

From 1939 until 1945 Canada's chief goal was to help win the war. Major decisions about strategy and on post-war planning were made by the great powers – the United States, Britain, and the Soviet Union – without consulting their smaller allies. King personally regretted Canada's minor role in the direction of the war, but he recognized that Canada was a relatively small nation, making a relatively small contribution, and did not protest. Instead he promoted the theory of the North Atlantic Triangle in which Canada was seen to be the hub of the American-British relationship, interpreting each to the other. He also believed that the influence of the one power would balance that of the other, so that Canadian independence would be maintained and Canada's role as mediator enhanced.

Above all, King wanted to avoid closer relations between Canada and the United Kingdom. He had no intention of allowing wartime co-operation to draw Canada back into the British orbit and thereby compromise Canadian independence. In 1940 he had dissuaded Prime Minister Chamberlain from calling a Commonwealth Prime Ministers' Conference. Later, when the Australian prime minister began to press for a revival of the Imperial War Cabinet, he and Churchill both discouraged the idea, although from quite different motives. Only with reluctance did King attend the Commonwealth Prime Ministers' Conference in 1944 and then he told the assembled premiers that in a time of stress such as this, they were better at home in their own countries. That same year, Lord Halifax, the British ambassador in Washington, speaking in Toronto, urged a common foreign policy for the Commonwealth in the post-war world. He argued that the giants – the United States, the Soviet Union, and China – would be the dominant forces in international affairs, and that the Commonwealth was a necessary balancing fourth power. Convinced that Halifax had unwittingly revealed a British plot to reassert influence over Canada, King used the occasion to lecture the House of Commons on the virtues of informal consultation and co-operation.

Always fearful that Britain might try to reassert her influence over Canada's destiny, King refused to allow either Commonwealth co-operation or the North Atlantic Triangle to entangle Canada in the affairs of the United Kingdom. However he was less wary of the United States, partly because of his close personal relationship with President Franklin Delano Roosevelt. From the beginning of the war the United States was gradually drawn into the hostilities and the alliance against the Axis powers. During the winter of 1939-40 both Canada and the United Kingdom bought quantities of American war materials. After Dunkirk the United States gave Britain fifty over-age destroyers in return for bases in the American hemisphere, such as Gander in Newfoundland. In August 1940, while the United States was still neutral, King and Roosevelt met at Ogdensburg, New York, to discuss continental defence and made an agreement to establish the Permanent Joint Board on Defence to co-ordinate and direct their co-operative effort. As trade between the two countries increased, Canada began to show a deficit in her balance of payments. Buying huge quantities of coal, steel, and iron, Canada could not earn the United States' dollars to pay for them even with tight exchange and import regulations. The prime minister and the president met again in April 1941 at Roosevelt's country estate, Hyde Park, and arranged to solve Canada's exchange difficulty by greater specialization of production. Henceforth,

Canada was to place orders for items like machine tools and airplane engines in the United States, and in return the United States would buy such goods as small arms and ammunition from Canada. This agreement allowed Canada to conserve United States' currency and led to further arrangements which integrated more closely the war production and the economies of the two countries. The entry of Japan into the war led to even closer co-operation as the United States constructed the Alaska Highway through Canada and built air bases and weather stations in western Canada. The requirements of continental defence and of the joint war effort drew the two nations together.

Despite her impressive war effort Canada, like the other small Allied powers who had helped to win the war, was not asked to any of the major conferences on war policy and post-war planning. King felt slighted when in August 1941 Churchill and Roosevelt met off Newfoundland for their first conference, without informing Ottawa. When those two leaders met again in 1943 and 1944 in Quebec city – King participated in some of the discussions in 1943 – he was quite pleased. As he recorded in his diary, "the important thing was to have the meeting held at Quebec". But Canada was invited to the Dumbarton Oaks Conference in Washington in 1944 where the plans for the United Nations were laid. Those plans ensured the dominance of the greater powers in the post-war world by making the United States, Britain, France, China, and the USSR permanent members of the Security Council, each with a veto power. Although privately sceptical about the feasibility of these plans, the King government raised no public objections and approved the powers given to the Council to enforce collective security. After the experience of the League, Canada was afraid not to give the United Nations adequate powers to maintain peace and equally afraid of allowing the great powers to dominate the organization. Out of this fear would be born in future years the concept of Canada as a middle power working with the world's other middle

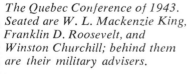

The Quebec Conference of 1943. Seated are W. L. Mackenzie King, Franklin D. Roosevelt, and Winston Churchill; behind them are their military advisers.

Prime Minister Mackenzie King signing the Charter of the United Nations on behalf of Canada in June 1945.

powers in the United Nations to create a power bloc, but for the present she joined forty-nine other nations at San Francisco in 1945 to found the United Nations.

The experience of the war years completely changed Canada's international outlook. One historian has spoken of the "revolution of 1940" in which Canada passed from her British century into her American century. Until 1940 the weight of British power and influence had been more than sufficient to balance American influence, but after the Ogdensburg Agreement Canadian security depended on the United States. Thus the two nations were tied almost indissolubly together. For Canada this meant the acceptance of American leadership in international relations, a leadership about which Canadians have always felt some reservations. The comforting theory of a North Atlantic Triangle has therefore lived on in Canada partly because Canada wants to believe that Britain is still a counterweight to the United States, partly because the theory seems to give Canada influence in both London and Washington.

FURTHER READING

Pickersgill, J. W., *The Mackenzie King Record, 1939-1944* (Toronto: University of Toronto Press, 1960).

Pickersgill, J. W. and Forster, D. F., *The Mackenzie King Record, 1944-1945* (Toronto: University of Toronto Press, 1968). The war years surveyed by King's secretary and quoting long extracts from King's diary.

Granatstein, J. L., *Conscription in the Second World War 1939-1945* (Toronto: Ryerson, 1969)★.

The Official History of the Canadian Army in the Second World War, 3 vols. (Ottawa: Queen's Printer, 1955-1960).

    1. Stacey, C. P., *Six Years of War: The Army in Canada, Britain and the Pacific*

    2. Nicholson, G. W. L., *The Canadians in Italy, 1943-1945*

    3. Stacey, C. P., *The Victory Campaign: The Operations in Northwest Europe, 1944-1945*

Snyder, L. L., *The War: A Concise History, 1939-1945* (New York: Dell Laurel Edition, 1964)★. An excellent general survey.

24

The Years of Affluence

The Foundations of Canadian Prosperity

By the time Canada emerged from the Second World War the prosperity and full employment of the war years made the depression seem remote. Nevertheless there was a sense of doubt and hesitancy in many politicians and businessmen – the war had brought good times economically, but so had the First World War and after that war had come the Great Depression. Would history repeat itself? For many Canadians, the problem of the post-war years was to find a secure and steady job as war industries began to lay off workers and convert to peacetime production. Many businessmen hesitated to invest in new enterprises. Yet the worst did not happen. Instead there were years of continued high employment as Canadians spent their accumulated savings from the war years to buy consumer goods, especially durable goods such as automobiles and household appliances.

The return from a wartime economy to peacetime conditions was accomplished with a minimum of dislocation, thanks largely to the positive role of government in creating and facilitating post-war adjustment policies. The Department of Veterans' Affairs did a far more effective job in returning the thousands of servicemen to civilian life than the government had done in 1919 and 1920. After 1945 returning veterans had first call on the jobs they had left when they enlisted. Thousands of ex-servicemen were enabled to further their education with fees and living allowances paid by the government. Others were helped by low interest loans to start businesses, build homes, or buy land. By allowing virtually a whole generation of Canadians to realize their occupational and professional abilities and by spreading over many months the veterans' return to the labour force, no sudden crises of unemployment or of ex-servicemen searching for jobs occurred. In addition, the Wartime Prices and Trade Board continued to exercise control over the nation's economy to avoid possible inflation, since the demand for goods would certainly have caused prices to rise rapidly. These economic regulations prevented inflation from eroding the value of wartime savings, but control of the economy, acceptable

in wartime, became increasingly unacceptable in peacetime. Complaints
from businessmen that the controls were hindering the growth of the
economy and from provincial governments worried about the continued
centralization of power forced the federal government to end its emergency powers over the economy. By 1949, however, when the last controls
were removed, the work of post-war adjustment was complete. The national economic picture since the war has been one of tremendous prosperity
and economic growth, which can be illustrated by the increase in Canada's
gross national product. Some of the increase shown in the graph is due to
inflation, but even when this is taken into account Canada has had since
1945 a rate of growth faster than that of most other countries. The average Canadian has shared in this growth: the average industrial wage rose
from $32 a week in 1945 to $107.50 in 1968 and real income more than
doubled. One index of prosperity is the annual sales of automobiles; sales
rose from 153,334 units in 1947 to 683,639 in 1966.

The generation of Canadians that has grown up since the war takes
prosperity for granted. But not all Canadians are well off; the Atlantic
provinces and many rural areas of Ontario, Quebec, and Manitoba suffer
from underemployment of manpower and from slow economic development. While there were brief recessions in 1953-4 and in 1957-61 during
which the national level of unemployment rose as high as 9 per cent of the
labour force, unemployment in parts of Quebec and the Maritimes was
16 to 18 per cent. But even in these areas conditions have been better
since 1945 than they were between the wars.

The basic strength of Canada's economy has continued to come from
her primary industries. Pulp and paper, other wood products, minerals,

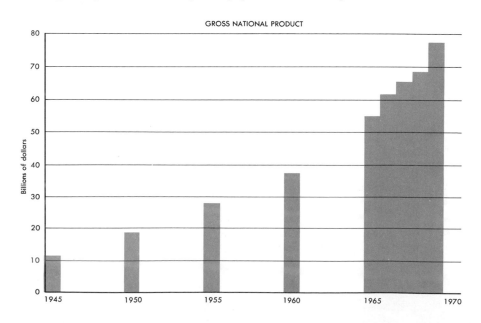

GROSS NATIONAL PRODUCT

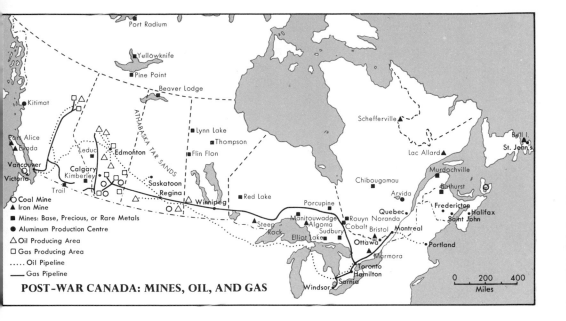

POST-WAR CANADA: MINES, OIL, AND GAS

Legend:
- ○ Coal Mine
- ▲ Iron Mine
- ■ Mines: Base, Precious, or Rare Metals
- ● Aluminum Production Centre
- △ Oil Producing Area
- □ Gas Producing Area
- ..... Oil Pipeline
- —— Gas Pipeline

and wheat have continued to be major sources of export income and to be the mainstay of the economy. By 1952 the value of wheat exports had risen to $450 million, but as European agriculture recovered in the mid-1950's wheat exports fell off, leaving a huge surplus in storage in elevators and on farms throughout the country. Only with the development after 1958 of new markets in the Communist bloc countries, particularly China and the Soviet Union, did those surpluses disappear. These were not stable markets, however, and in the late 1960's wheat surpluses again began to accumulate. Wheat still remains an important element in the Canadian economy, but forest products are now Canada's most important exports. Sawn lumber and plywood both go in large quantities to the United States, although the plywood industry has felt the impact of foreign competition in recent years. Pulp and paper head the list of Canadian exports. Canadian mills have a capacity nearly as large as that of the rest of the world, but in recent years over-capacity has appeared as markets in the United States have grown more slowly than production facilities. As a result, paper companies suffered shrinking profits in the late 1960's.

Oil and natural gas are now among the most valuable of Canada's resources. After years of exploration and drilling, discovery in 1947 of the Leduc field southwest of Edmonton started a spectacular oil boom in the west. Immense reserves of oil were mapped out in Alberta, Saskatchewan, and southwestern Manitoba, enough oil to last twenty years at present production levels. Pumping and refining plants were built and pipeline networks constructed to move the oil across the country. The Athabasca tar sands, the world's largest reserve of oil, are now being developed and methods to extract the oil have been invented. Exploration for new oil fields, even in the Arctic, continues. With the growth of the oil industry has come the exploitation of natural gas. In the early days the natural gas found when oil wells were drilled was allowed to go to waste or burn itself off. After the war this gas was increasingly used for heating to replace gas made from coal. In 1954 the Alberta government authorized companies to export natural gas from the province after local needs were met. By the end of the decade gas pipelines paralleled the oil lines across the country from the Pacific to the St. Lawrence Valley.

The oil and gas industries have been as important to the post-war Canadian economy as wheat and pulp in the earlier years of this century. Royalties on oil and gas production have enabled the governments of Alberta and Saskatchewan to reduce provincial debts and to provide many social services for their citizens. The petro-chemical industry that has grown up in the last twenty years is now one of Canada's major secondary industries. Before the war Canada imported 95 per cent of her petroleum requirements; she now produces enough to be self-sufficient and to make oil one of the country's ten leading exports.

Almost as important as the oil discoveries has been the development of large deposits of high-grade iron ore. After the war Canadian ore bodies were exploited to meet the growing demand from the United States. The pits at Steep Rock (west of the Lakehead), which were opened in 1938, send thousands of tons of ore to the smelters of the American mid-west. Huge iron deposits, long known but remote, in Quebec and Labrador are now being mined. A harbour to accommodate big ore carriers was constructed at Sept Iles on the St. Lawrence and a railway was built north to Knob Lake and Schefferville to open the area. The bulk of this production goes to American smelters in Ohio and Pennsylvania through the St. Lawrence Seaway. British Columbia can also look forward to a market in Japan for iron ore from its mines; the Canadian Pacific Railway has an-

Left: Labrador City, the centre of iron-mining operations some 300 miles north of Sept Iles, Quebec.
Below: A completely automated ore train carrying crude ore from the loading pockets to the crusher.

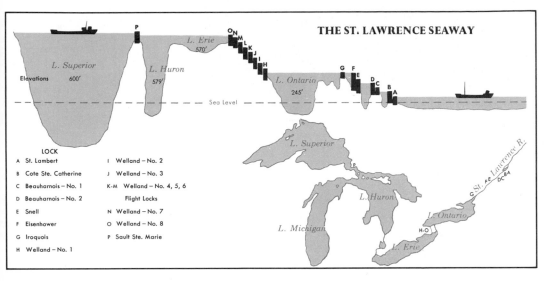

THE ST. LAWRENCE SEAWAY

L. Superior
Elevations 600'

L. Huron
579'

L. Erie
570'

Sea Level

L. Ontario
245'

LOCK		
A	St. Lambert	
B	Cote Ste. Catherine	
C	Beauharnois – No. 1	
D	Beauharnois – No. 2	
E	Snell	
F	Eisenhower	
G	Iroquois	
H	Welland – No. 1	
I	Welland – No. 2	
J	Welland – No. 3	
K-M	Welland – No. 4, 5, 6	
	Flight Locks	
N	Welland – No. 7	
O	Welland – No. 8	
P	Sault Ste. Marie	

L. Superior

L. Huron

L. Michigan

L. Ontario

L. Erie

St. Lawrence R.

nounced its intention of building a new rail line and harbour for the ore-carrying ships.

In the two decades since the war the value of mineral production in Canada has risen six times as the country expanded the production of minerals which she already produced in large quantities. Lynn Lake, opened in 1954, and Thompson, in 1960, both in Manitoba, are now major nickel producers. Murdochville in the Gaspé, Chibougamau in northern Quebec, and Manitouwadge in Ontario have joined Sudbury, Flin Flon, and Noranda as the leading copper producers. While British Columbia continued to supply more than half of Canada's lead and zinc, other mines were opened elsewhere, including Pine Point on Great Slave Lake. Extensive exploration has also revealed that Canada has rich resources of many minerals required for modern industry. One of the world's largest potash beds was opened in Saskatchewan. The exploration and mining of titanium, molybdenum, and bismuth, metals of the space age, began in the late 1950's. The most publicized mineral of the 1950's, however, was uranium. Developments at Beaverlodge in northern Saskatchewan and at Elliot Lake and Bancroft in Ontario found an enormous market in the United States, but the slow exploitation of nuclear power for peacetime uses brought the boom to an end by 1960. So much uranium oxide had been stockpiled that by 1965 production was almost at a standstill. The long-term prospects for Canadian uranium are good because, as these stockpiles dwindle and as the demand rises, particularly for the generation of electricity, the uranium mining industry will revive.

While the primary industries have been the chief support of the economy since the Second World War, the major cause of prosperity has been the growth of secondary industry. The construction industry alone con-

tributes nearly one-fifth of the total value of production, double its importance in the 1920's. Until 1939, manufacturing represented a little over 40 per cent of the value of production, but since 1945 it has represented nearly 55 per cent of the gross national product. Nearly half these manufacturing industries, however, process natural resources.

Much of Canada's economic development has been due to American investment, particularly in resource industries. A considerable part of Canadian industry is owned or controlled by Americans, a fact which causes much uneasiness among Canadian nationalists. Charges have been made that United States-owned plants exclude Canadians from management, that they fail to compete with their American parent companies in world markets, and that they are subject to American rather than to Canadian laws. The problem of American domination in the Canadian economy has been a political issue since the early 1960's, when groups in all the major political parties began to demand government controls over foreign investment. Yet these same critics fail to realize that the problem, except in the resource industries, has been created by the national policy of tariff protection followed by all Canadian governments, a policy designed to prevent the Canadian economy from becoming resource oriented

"Smelter Stacks, Copper Cliff", by Charles F. Comfort (b.1900), painted in 1936. [Oil on canvas, 40" x 50"]
The artist's impression of this industrial complex is portrayed as tall stacks belching thick smoke into the sky, the smelter standing in land that is a treeless waste as a result of air pollution from the smelter.

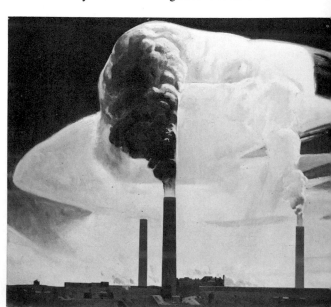

A bird's-eye view of the Imperial Oil refinery on the south bank of the South Saskatchewan River at Edmonton, Alberta. The white pillbox structures are the storage tanks. Opened in 1955, the refinery includes the first lubricating oil plant in western Canada.

and to encourage the development of manufacturing. The policy has encouraged the establishment of branch plants and subsidiaries.

There has been and is a close correlation between Canadian prosperity and the level of American consumption of Canadian products. The economies of both countries, at times of high United States' demand, complement each other very well. In return for raw materials and semi-processed commodities, Canadians may buy manufactured goods and such non-Canadian luxuries as oranges and winter vacations in Florida. American primary producers often worry about Canadian competition, however, and then press their government for protection. The result has been quotas on oil and natural gas imports from Canada, duties on copper and steel. At times of low United States' demand, it is imports that feel the pinch first, and this slackness reflects itself in the Canadian economy with layoffs in the resource industries and low prices for exports. At these times, too, the value of the Canadian dollar slips in comparison to that of the American dollar because Canadians are not able to earn enough foreign exchange to buy the goods and services Canada wants from the United States.

Closely allied to the economic relations of the two countries is the problem of sharing their resources. The boundary between Canada and the United States is not a natural frontier: fish swim through it, rivers traverse it, ore bodies no doubt lie under it, stands of timber straddle it. President Kennedy and Prime Minister Pearson in 1963 stated that it was "the desire of the two governments to co-operate in a rational use of the continent's resources" – oil, gas, electricity, timber, fish, strategic metals, and minerals. The sharing of water and electricity has raised basic questions about Canada's future. In the development of the Columbia River, the American negotiators urged the short-term advantages of the sale of hydro-electricity to the United States, and Premier Bennett, looking to the development of the Peace River, was inclined to favour sale to the Americans because his province's needs would be met. Canadian critics did not wish to see long-term commitments of power that might be needed for Canadian development. The original agreement of 1961 was therefore modified in 1964 to provide a better financial deal for Canada. Water as a resource in itself is also a problem, for as more United States' fresh–water sources are polluted, many Americans see Canada as a vast source of clean water. Should Canada sell her water like any other commodity? If so, she must determine her own long-term needs and what is a fair price for this valuable resource. In connection with Canada's ocean resources the government wants to extend Canadian territory from the traditional three-mile limit to twelve miles, and it has declared the Bay of Fundy to be Canadian waters. This doctrine has not been acceptable to American fishermen nor to their government.

Twenty Million Canadians

Related to Canada's economic growth is the tremendous increase in population that has occurred since the Second World War. The nation of about 12,000,000 people in 1945 grew to nearly 20,500,000 in 1968. Unlike earlier periods of growth, this post-war rise has been primarily the result of natural increase. In the 1950's Canada's birth rate was one of the world's highest, reaching a peak of 28 per thousand in 1957. Since then it has fallen off and in 1968 it was at its lowest level since the depression. Nevertheless the high proportion of young people in the population will mean continued rapid population growth for years to come.

Immigration has also contributed to this population growth. In the late 1940's immigration barriers were lowered and governments, both federal and provincial, established immigration programmes. Thousands of displaced persons, mostly from eastern Europe, came to Canada. Since 1948

Mid-twentieth-century life in the Northwest Territories. Left: An Eskimo construction worker learns to use a power tool. Bottom left: Eskimos at Frobisher Bay building a frame house. Bottom right: Boat building at Tuktoyaktuk.

over 2.5 million people have migrated to this country. An average of over 150,000 people came each year in the 1950's, 282,164 in 1957 alone, the highest level since 1913. Because of the continuing immigration of various racial groups from other countries, Canadian society is marked by a diversity of cultural, ethnic, linguistic, and racial backgrounds which have tended to forestall the development of conformity and uniformity in Canadian life. Over 150 nationalities have been combined in the Canadian mosaic to produce this rich diversity, although the English and French – the so-called charter groups – have been the dominant cultural influences that have set the standards and ambitions for all other divisions.

Non-charter groups, who now form some 27 per cent of the population, frequently settle in specific urban neighbourhoods where they can preserve much of the way of life brought from their homelands. When such groups also live at a lower economic level than other Canadians, their neighbourhoods become ghettos or ethnic islands which pose many social and educational problems. Immigrant groups have always formed their own social clubs where they can share and perpetuate their own national traditions, and while these associations add to Canada's cultural diversity, they may also delay the full sharing of their members in the varied political and social life of Canada. Such organizations may even continue in Canada the rivalries and animosities begun in the old world – the activities of the Orangemen in nineteenth-century Canadian life are a good example of this.

The continuation of ethnic self-awareness in Canada is reflected to some extent by the economic occupations of these groups. People of British and Jewish background are employed more often than others in higher income professions, whereas for reasons of education French and Italians are found in disproportionately large numbers in the lower income jobs. Since the Second World War the largest group of immigrants has come from the British Isles, the second-largest from Italy, and the third from Germany. About 10 per cent of all immigrants are from the United States. The skills of all immigrants have contributed enormously to Canada's economic growth; their tastes, national costume, folk songs and dances, and continuing interest in the foods and customs of their mother countries have made Canada a more diverse and colourful land since 1950.

Another Canadian cultural problem is posed by the 200,000 Indians, 80,000 Métis, and 12,000 Eskimos who make up 1 per cent of the population and are probably the most distressed of all Canadians. The historic system of Indian reservations and treaty rights has done much to preserve the Indian culture which Indians value highly, but for economic and educational reasons the Indians have remained on the lowest rung of Canada's ladder of affluence. The Métis, since they are not Indians, cannot share in

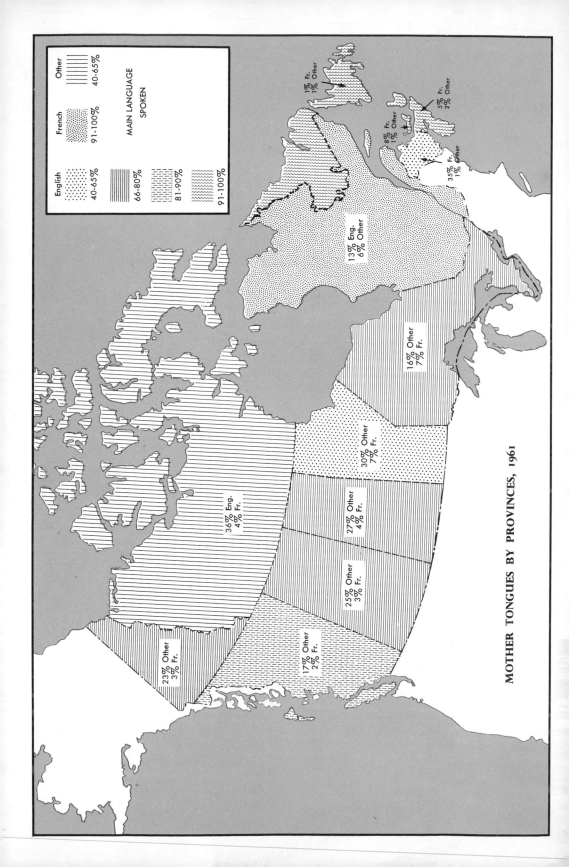

MAIN LANGUAGE SPOKEN

English	French	Other
40-65%	91-100%	40-65%
66-80%		
81-90%		
91-100%		

1% Fr.
1% Other

5% Fr.
2% Other

8% Fr.
1% Other

35% Fr.
1% Other

13% Eng.
6% Other

16% Other
7% Fr.

30% Other
7% Fr.

27% Other
4% Fr.

36% Eng.
4% Fr.

25% Other
3% Fr.

23% Other
3% Fr.

17% Other
2% Fr.

MOTHER TONGUES BY PROVINCES, 1961

such paternalistic benefits as the government offers the Indians, yet the Métis find themselves rejected in the white community which cannot fit them into the industrial economy because of their general lack of training. In contrast to the Indians the Eskimos have no treaty rights or reservations and because of their geographic isolation have only recently come into contact with modern Canadian society. Nevertheless many nomadic Eskimo hunters have been trained with little difficulty to fill important jobs in northern settlements.

Canada's population growth has been accompanied by a changing distribution of population across the country. There have been considerable changes in the regional population strengths in the last quarter-century. The proportion of Canadians living in the mainland Atlantic provinces has dropped over 2 per cent since the war. The prairies have also suffered a relative decline in population, a trend begun during the depression but accentuated since the war even though Alberta's population is growing at 4 per cent per year. On the other hand British Columbia, where the development of major resource projects has attracted many people, has increased its proportion of the total population by over 2 per cent. Ontario has grown more quickly than any of the other provinces – about one-third of all Canadians now live in that province. This regional shift in population also reflects a second change, the rapid growth of cities since 1945. The urban share of the population grew from 62 to 74 per cent between 1951 and 1966. The ten largest Canadian cities grew at a rate twice as fast as the rest of the country. Metropolitan Montreal, still the largest urban area in Canada, and metropolitan Toronto, the second largest, now contain about one-quarter of Canada's people.

These population shifts reflect the changing economy of the nation. People have moved from the rural areas into the cities not only because industrialization seemed to offer better economic opportunity, but also because changing technology has meant that less labour is needed on the farms and in the resource industries. Growth in industry has been largely concentrated in the Montreal-Toronto region and in the "Golden Horseshoe" of southern Ontario because of their larger market and closer prox-

The advances in technology and communications in the twentieth century have enabled an ever-increasing variety of mass-produced goods to be manufactured and distributed to large numbers of people in many parts of the world. In this clean and well-lighted modern shoe factory in Winnipeg these workers are checking quality and quantity at the cutting tables.

An aerial view showing part of Fogo Island in Notre Dame Bay, Newfoundland, a scene typical of the province's coastal districts. The town of Fogo itself is a fishing centre, where there are canning and cod-liver-oil plants. The name Fogo comes from the Portuguese word "fuego", meaning "fire"; the island and town were named after one of the Cape Verde Islands.

imity to the most flourishing section of the American market, the availability of cheap hydro-electric power, the large labour pool, and the concentration of transportation facilities. The relative decline in the population of the Maritime provinces reflects the failure of that outlying region to share in the industrialization that has occurred largely in central Canada and in the immigration of the post-war years. Saskatchewan and Manitoba have not attracted more population and remain relatively less industrialized because of their dependence on agriculture and the resource industries.

Although urbanization, the result of industrialization, produces a higher standard of material living than an agricultural society can achieve, urbanization in itself produces many complex physical and emotional problems for the modern city dweller. Large cities are being strangled by the volume of motor traffic and need expensive rapid transit systems to move their population within the city. The concentration of population in areas of high-rise apartments requires the provision of cultural and recreational facilities – theatres, art galleries, museums, as well as parks, playgrounds, swimming pools, and other areas for athletic activities – which are less necessary in rural regions. The same concentration of urban population creates problems of noise, of air and water pollution, and of garbage and sewage disposal. City residents, even in the most crowded conditions, find themselves alone, strangers to their neighbours in the next house or apartment, with no sense of belonging to a neighbourhood or community. One Canadian family in every four moves to a new home each year – a reason why the urban churches have lost much of their contact and influence with city populations.

As suburban sprawl – the extension of the city into the surrounding countryside – occurs, the core of the older city becomes gradually deserted, with many schools and churches no longer required. In this "flight to suburbia" old residential areas decay physically and socially, and urban planners are faced with the task of urban renewal, the restoration of depressed areas by rebuilding to meet the modern needs of modern industrialized society. In the meantime this blighting of the city's centre undoubtedly contributes to increased crime and violence and to the general unrest that afflicts today's city populations in Canada as well as in the United States and other countries.

The Search for a Canadian Identity

Parallel to the American influences on Canada's economy is the powerful influence of American culture which has disturbed many Canadians since the publication in 1951 of the Massey royal commission report (the Royal Commission on National Development in the Arts, Letters, and Sciences). Underlying this concern is the assumption that Canada is more than just a political entity – that a people worthy of the name nation should have their own distinctive and recognizable way of life. The United States, with its mass circulation magazines and newspapers, its radio and television, its popular music and popular books, is seen as a threat to the evolution of Canadian nationhood in the social sense because these American influences cross their common border so easily. Fears that Canada is becoming a cultural colony of the United States may well be a survival of the nineteenth-century view that United States' life was somehow debased and vulgar, inferior to that of Europe and of Britain in particular; but the fact remains that affluent Canadians want and can afford these commodities of culture even though they may cost Canada her chance of developing a distinctive Canadian way of life. The total educational experience of Canadians, which is not confined simply to the years of formal schooling, could promote a sense of pride in Canadianism without destroying the valuable cultural contribution of all the ethnic groups in the Canadian mosaic.

Today's great preoccupation in Canada with education is partly the cause and partly the result of affluence. A larger proportion of Canada's population than in any previous generation is now attending school and

The University of Alberta (foreground) and the city of Edmonton.

spending more years in the educational system. Continuing education is the key to advancement in this scientific and industrialized world and new emphasis is being placed on technical training, particularly at the post-secondary school level. In all fields of education new curricula are being devised and new courses of instruction are being introduced to meet the changing needs of modern society. For Canada the great boom in education has created many challenges, but also a major problem in the high cost of constructing and operating so many schools and universities.

Like Canadian education, the Canadian literary scene in recent decades has been marked by unprecedented growth in the quality and quantity of writing and by an eagerness to experiment with new forms and new styles. A new group of talented writers has appeared, which includes among many names of distinction such poets as Irving Layton and James Rainey, novelists such as Gabrielle Roy and Mordecai Richler, and playwrights such as Gratien Gélinas. Canadian scholarship has been well represented by many outstanding writers including Northrop Frye, Phyllis Grosskurth, and Donald Creighton, who have international reputations.

Since the war Canadian magazines have found it so difficult to compete with their mass-circulation American counterparts that many have ceased publication, but there has been a most promising development in the appearance of several high-quality literary periodicals such as *Tamarack Review,* which have joined the long list of older and well-established quarterlies published under the patronage of Canadian universities. In 1961 the O'Leary Commission, which was investigating the difficulties of Canada's periodical press, reported that three out of every four general-interest magazines purchased in Canada were of American origin. While Canadian newspapers have not faced the same problem of competition from the United States as the magazines, their important role in mass communications has been undermined in recent years by the "instant news" provided through television. The two main post-war developments in the Canadian newspaper field have been the reduction in the number of dailies serving major cities and the absorption of numerous small weeklies by the two newspaper empires operated by the Southams and Lord Thomson of Fleet – developments which may have restricted the independence and variety of Canadian newspapers.

Simon Fraser University, North Burnaby, British Columbia. Built on the top of Burnaby Mountain and with a beautiful outlook over the Fraser River and Vancouver harbour, the university was opened in 1965 and named in honour of the fur trader and explorer.

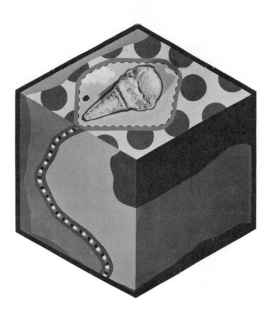

"The Ballad of a Wise and Curious Wizard" by Gary Lee-Nova (b.1943).
[Liquitex on canvas with illuminated plastic ice-cream cone, 60" x 69" — hexagonal]

Achievements in the visual arts are apparent not only within the traditional confines of the galleries but in the daily life of art students, both professional and amateur, and in the urban vistas of modern cities. Modern artists such as Guido Molinari, Greg Curnoe, Jack Chambers, and Marcel Barbeau offer works of originality and abstraction that please the eye and challenge the imagination. Among the sculptors are Les Levine, Michael Snow, Ulysse Comtois, and Iain Baxter (who could perhaps be more accurately termed a "multi-media visual informer"). The sculptors of today present their ideas in the new materials of welded steel and plastics, in pieces from the scrap heap, or even through a combination of media – including telecommunications and photographic art. Colour, contrast, abstract expressionism, diversity of style, and experimentation are the hallmarks of Canadian artists, whose works show that they are an integral part of the modern world trend towards the avant-garde. Nor is the output of art restricted to any one section of the population: from Indians and Eskimos come the imaginative yet contemporary representations of folklore that keep Canada's earliest heritage alive. Summer schools and workshops (for instance, the Banff School of Fine Arts, run by the University of Calgary) provide instruction and incentive for students of all ages and professions. Another aspect of the visual arts, architecture, can be called a constant element of the daily scene in that it has kept pace with both technological and artistic development. Such commercial urban developments as Montreal's Place Ville Marie and Toronto's unique "clam shell" City Hall are the artistic equal of similar structures anywhere in the world; modern educational structures such as Simon Fraser University and Scarborough College (University of Toronto) have attracted world-wide attention.

"3 + 4 + 1" by Paul-Emile Borduas (1905-60), painted in 1956. [Oil on canvas, 78" x 98"]

"Tiger Lily" by Douglas Morton (b.1926). [Oil on canvas, 49½" x 49½"]

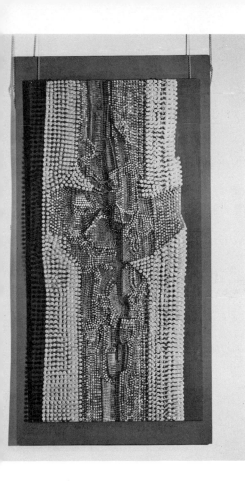

Top left: "Channelled Configuration" by David Partridge (b.1919). [Nails in wood, 84" high]
Top right: "Bronze Sculpture, 1965" by Charles Daudelin (b.1920). [Bronze, 9¼" high] Bottom: "Clothed Woman (In Memory of my Father)" by Michael Snow (b.1929), painted in 1963. [Oil and lucite on canvas, 60¼" x 152¼"]

SOME CANADIAN
ARTISTS OF THE
TWENTIETH CENTURY

The Festival Theatre at Stratford, Ontario. In 1957 this permanent theatre, mainly of concrete and glass, was built to replace the tent in which the Festival began its life in 1953. The present apron stage (see photograph below) is an adaptation of the original.

In the performing arts the modern addition to traditional forms is the element of experiment and the willingness to attempt new and independent forms. Succeeding to the talent and ability of the older generation in music of Sir Ernest MacMillan and Dr. Healey Willan is the new generation of Canadian composers, who cannot be labelled by any style or method. At the same time there has been growing public awareness of Canada's rich heritage of folk music, not only in French and English but in the languages of the many nations whose people have come to Canada in recent years. Amateur theatre, so popular in previous generations, continues to enjoy an expanding public audience and professional theatre has come into its own since the Second World War through the establishment of the Stratford Shakespearean Festival, summer stock companies, and year-round repertory groups in major Canadian cities. The amateur little theatre groups and the annual Dominion Drama Festival have created a generation of enthusiastic theatre-goers throughout Canada as well as giving an opportunity for a large number of aspiring young actors, many of whom have gone on to achieve international fame outside Canada. Suitable modern theatre buildings such as Montreal's Place des Arts, Toronto's O'Keefe Centre, the Confederation Centre in Charlottetown, and the National Art Centre in Ottawa provide further encouragement for theatre development. Two highly specialized forms of the performing arts, opera and ballet, have similarly shared in this great post-war expansion of

On stage at Stratford. Left: A scene from "The Three Musketeers" with (from left to right) Christopher Newton as Aramis, Douglas Rain as D'Artagnan, James Blendick as Porthos. Below: A scene from "Romeo and Juliet" with Amelia Hall as the Nurse, Louise Marleau as Juliet.

*Montreal – the old and the new. Left: Place Ville Marie.
Right: The city from Mount Royal.*

Canadian culture. The Royal Winnipeg Ballet and the National Ballet
Company have received international acclaim as has the Montreal Folk-
Dance Company and Les Feux Follets. Individual Canadian performers
such as the operatic tenor Jon Vickers, the pianists Glenn Gould and Ray
Dudley, and singers Lois Marshall and Maureen Forrester have achieved
international fame. To both the visual and the performing arts as well as
in the fields of literature, history, and social studies, the financial support
of the Canada Council has been instrumental in promoting both breadth
and depth of appreciation.

Since the Second World War the Canadian movie industry has acquired
a reputation, better known outside Canada than within, for its excellent
documentary and short theatrical films that have won top awards at many
international film festivals. In the production of feature-length films, however, Canada has never been able to compete with Hollywood, and as an
incentive for Canadian development of this film form parliament established in 1966 a corporation with a fund of $10 million for investment in
feature-film production and for awards for outstanding Canadian movie
accomplishments.

The greatest rival of the movie industry is television, the newest form
of mass entertainment and education. Canadian television along with
radio, the mass medium of earlier decades, has been called the cement of
Canada's cultural identity. Educational television, either in the classrooms
or by network broadcasting, has barely begun to make its influence felt in
Canada, but commercial television has developed so rapidly since 1950
that it now reaches over 94 per cent of Canadian households, broadcasting in English, French, Italian, German, Eskimo, and Indian. The proximity and predominance of American television (available directly in border
areas or through American programmes carried over Canadian stations)
has – as in the other mass media – presented the threat of cultural Ameri-
canization of Canada, and to meet this challenge the regulations of the
Board of Broadcast Governors require at least half "Canadian content" in
all Canadian television broadcasting.

The Canadian performing arts – theatre, movies, music, and television – have provided one of the most obvious examples of Canada's post-war "brain drain" (the migration of talented and trained individuals) to the United States, although the "brain drain" in science and engineering has been just as serious if less obvious. Numerous Canadian actors, writers, directors, and producers have found their way to fame and fortune in New York and Hollywood because Canada offers such limited opportunities for experience and advancement. This problem is compounded for English-speaking Canada which, unlike French Canada, lacks the language barrier to shield it from American influences. For English Canada the basic problem is how to create and maintain a distinctive culture while living next door to the attractions and influences of the United States – for French Canada the problem is that of preserving French culture in the midst of an English-speaking continent. Twentieth-century mass communications have made Canada part of the global village where Canadians are acutely aware of and responsive to events and trends such as the human rights movement and the student revolt in Europe as well as in the United States. It remains to be seen whether or not a Canadian identity – economic, political, cultural – can be permanently established under such diverse and forceful pressures and circumstances.

The Giant Yellowknife Mine, Northwest Territories, the larger of the two gold mines that support the economy of the Yellowknife area.

HISTORY FROM THE SOURCES

Canada – Colony of the United States?

Canadians have always been acutely aware that they have a very large, indeed almost overwhelming, neighbour sharing the North American continent with them. A great many are concerned about the effects this neighbour has on their own nation. The first reading is a summary of the Watkins Report, produced by a special task force set up to study the influence of American investment on the Canadian economy. The second is a group of selections from the Massey Commission Report on the state of Canadian culture. Are the two a fair evaluation of the extent to which the United States affects Canada?

Now we know.

For the first time since the torrent of American dollars began pouring across the border to buy up Canada, a detailed study has been made of the economic and political price we are paying for the good life that U.S. dollars helped to earn.

The report warns that our sovereign existence is already threatened as a direct result of American control of our manufacturing economy and our key industries.

• The most serious cost for Canada resulting from foreign ownership is the intrusion of American law and policy into Canada.

• Decision-making power, essential to any government, is being shifted across the border.

• If our standard of living is to improve, we require a continuing stream of American capital. But we must try to "maximize its benefits and decrease its costs."

• The way to do this is for the federal government to set up a "countervailing power" in laws, regulations and state agencies that will be able to resist unacceptable pressures and policies from U.S. corporations and from Washington itself.

The economists concentrate on the behavior of U.S. investment when it gets here and starts working. Their focus is on the "multinational corporation" – giant business firms with the parent company in the United States and wholly owned subsidiaries in various host countries.

Such corporations, the report says, are "confronted with two peaks of sovereignty" – its host and its parent – but are "likely to defer to the higher peak on which the foreign owners reside."

The implications for Canadians of this "uncomfortable" position is that in export policy U.S. subsidiaries follow American law rather than Canadian policy in regard to trade with China and Cuba.

They are required to do so by the U.S. Trading with the Enemy Act which forbids U.S. firms – or their foreign subsidiaries – from trading with the "enemy". The report regards this "extraterritorial" law as a prime intrusion on Canadian sovereignty.

It cites other instances where U.S. anti-trust law, patent law and balance-of-payment "guidelines" have invaded Canada.

The report says that "the essential feature of the problem (of foreign ownership) is not the economic cost but the loss of control over an important segment of Canadian economic life."

In effect, decisions affecting the wages, jobs, purchasing power and future of Canadians are being made in the boardrooms of American parent companies.

The depth of the penetration of U.S. ownership and control is carefully documented. It has made Canada the most heavily foreign-controlled industrial state in the developed world.

The report is particularly critical of the role tariff policy has played in the Canadian economy.

"Protected (by the tariff) from the stiff winds of international competition, both domestic and foreign firms have performed less well than their counterparts in the United States," the report says.

"The Canadian tariff created job opportunities in Canada and thereby probably increased the size of the Canadian population and total national income, and the share of manufacturing in it.

"It would appear to have done so, however, at the cost of a less efficient industrial structure than would have existed had tariffs been lower.

"This means, in turn, that the Canadian standard of living, or real per capita income, is lower than it would otherwise be."

The first requirement, the economists say, is for the government to have more information about the operations of U.S. subsidiaries. It recommends a special agency be created to collect information, exercise surveillance, examine licensing and taxation arrangements and generally keep an eye on the way branch plants are behaving.

It would require larger American corporations as a matter of law to reveal almost as much statistical information about their operations as is required by the U.S. government.

The report suggests that anti-combines legislation be beefed up and applied more vigorously, that tariff policy be re-examined and revised and that when too many firms are competing for the same product market, they be merged – perhaps with the Canada Development Corporation (a publicly-financed holding company), holding some shares.

One of the more radical proposals is for a state trading agency. This organization would try to find Canadian producers for overseas orders.

If an American subsidiary refused to sell to a Communist country – because it would break American law – the state agency would buy the products on its own account and thus presumably neutralize them for resale.

A network of new laws and regulations is recommended to prevent American courts from extending their decisions on anti-trust or patent cases into Canada.

The report suggests mandatory Canadian "guidelines" be placed upon U.S. subsidiaries to require them to behave as good corporate citizens of Canada and countervail U.S. guidelines.

There are proposals for the sale of equity in U.S. subsidiaries to Canadians – a course that is rarely followed now. This would be done through tax incentives.

The report makes clear these recommendations can be accepted singly or as a package.

Val Sears, "Now Canada really knows price of foreign capital" *Toronto Daily Star,* 16 February 1968, p. 24.

13.   Canada has, moreover, paid a heavy price for this easy dependence on charity and especially on American charity. First, many of our best students, on completing their studies at American institutions, accept positions there and do not return. The United States wisely relaxes its rigid immigration laws for all members of "learned professions" and profits accordingly. Our neighbours, able to take their choice of the foreign students attracted to their universities by far-seeing generosity, naturally choose many Canadians, partly because they are there in such numbers, partly because they fit in more readily with American ways than do others.

17.   In this general picture of American influence on our cultural life it is perhaps permissible to mention that it extends to an extraordinary degree into an area beyond the limits of our inquiry, but closely related to it. Teachers from English-speaking Canada who wish to improve their talents or raise their professional status almost automatically make their pilgrimage to Teachers' College at Columbia University or to one of half a dozen similar institutions. They return to occupy senior positions in elementary and high schools and to staff our normal schools and colleges of education. How many Canadians realize that over a large part of Canada the schools are accepting tacit direction from New York that they would not think of taking from Ottawa?

21.   Although in French-speaking Canada the difference in language offers some measure of protection, elsewhere in Canada the uncritical use of American training institutions, and therefore of American educational philosophy and what are referred to as teaching aids, has certainly tended to make our educational systems less Canadian, less suited to our traditions, less appreciative of the resources of our two cultures. It has also meant – and this is a matter with which we have a direct concern – that a large number of our leading teachers who are not only teachers but community leaders have received the final and often the most influential part of their training in the United States. This training may be excellent in itself, but it is surely permissible to wish that men and women who are go-

ing to exercise such a powerful influence on Canadian life should
meet and work in some institution which, however international its
staff may be, could put Canadian interests and problems in the first
place.
23.   Every intelligent Canadian acknowledges his debt to the
United States for excellent films, radio programmes and periodicals.
But the price may be excessive. Of films and radio we shall speak in
more detail later, but it may be noted in passing that our national
radio which carries the Sunday symphony from New York also carries the soap-opera. In the periodical press we receive indeed many
admirable American journals but also a flood of others much less
admirable which, as we have been clearly told, is threatening to sub-
merge completely our national product:

> "A Canadian culture with an English-French background," so runs
> the brief of the *Société des Ecrivains Canadiens,* "will never reach
> the level which we desire so long as suitable measures are not taken
> against the invasion of the Canadian press by one of the most
> detestable products of the American press, so long as thousands of
> pages *Made in United States* are slavishly reproduced by English
> language papers or translated for French-speaking readers, so long
> as pulp magazines and other works of the same nature enter or are
> distributed in Canada without any restriction, as is now the case."

24.   The Canadian Periodical Press Association tells the same
tale. Although during the last generation our periodicals have maintained and greatly strengthened their position, the competition they
face has been almost overwhelming. Canadian magazines with much
difficulty have achieved a circulation of nearly forty-two millions a
year as against an American circulation in Canada of over eighty-six
millions. "Canada . . . . is the only country of any size in the world,"
one of their members has observed, "whose people read more foreign
periodicals than they do periodicals published in their own land,
local newspapers excluded." The Canadian periodical cannot in its
turn invade the American market; for Americans, it seems, simply
do not know enough about Canada to appreciate Canadian material.
Our periodicals cannot hold their own except in their limited and un-
protected market, nine million English-speaking readers. These must
be set against the one hundred and sixty millions served by their
competitors in the whole North American continent.
25.   The American invasion by film, radio and periodical is formidable. Much of what comes to us is good and of this we shall be
speaking presently. It has, however, been represented to us that
many of the radio programmes have in fact no particular application
to Canada or to Canadian conditions and that some of them, including certain children's programmes of the "crime" and "horror" type,
are positively harmful. News commentaries too, and even live
broadcasts from American sources, are designed for American ears
and are almost certain to have an American slant and emphasis by

reason of what they include or omit, as well as because of the opinions expressed. We think it permissible to record these comments on American radio since we observe that in the United States many radio programmes and American broadcasting in general have recently been severely criticized. It will, we think, be readily agreed that we in Canada should take measures to avoid in our radio, and in our television, at least those aspects of American broadcasting which have provoked in the United States the most out-spoken and the sharpest opposition.

26.   American influences on Canadian life to say the least are impressive. There should be no thought of interfering with the liberty of all Canadians to enjoy them. Cultural exchanges are excellent in themselves. They widen the choice of the consumer and provide stimulating competition for the producer. It cannot be denied, however, that a vast and disproportionate amount of material coming from a single alien source may stifle rather than stimulate our own creative effort; and, passively accepted without any standard of comparison, this may weaken critical faculties. We are now spending millions to maintain a national independence which would be nothing but an empty shell without a vigorous and distinctive cultural life. We have seen that we have its elements in our traditions and in our history; we have made important progress, often aided by American generosity. We must not be blind, however, to the very present danger of permanent dependence.

Royal Commission on the Arts, Letters and Sciences (Ottawa, 1951), pp. 14-18.

At school in Sarnia, Ontario, the seven-year-old daughter of a Chippewa Indian family shows a classmate some of the capitals of the world during a Geography lesson.

Integration or Apartheid – The Problem of Canada's Native Population

Perhaps the most complex social problem facing Canada is that of her 250,000 native peoples – Eskimos and North American Indians. The

*problem was neatly summed up a couple of years ago by an older lady
from a northern Ontario community who said, "What problem? The
Indians I know are all good people. They live in their part of the town
and don't bother anyone else." The most serious aspect of the situation
is presented in the first selection, written by E. R. McEwen, Executive
Director of the Indian-Eskimo Association of Canada.*

Over 40 per cent of the Indian population is unemployed and living on relief. The situation does not appear to be improving. In
1964, 37.4 per cent were receiving relief; in 1966 the figure was 40
per cent.

About 47 per cent of Indian families earn less than $1,000 a year.
About three-quarters of all Indian families earn less than $2,000.
The unemployment rate is about ten times the national average. Statistics about the income and employment of Canada's Eskimo population are not available.

About 57 per cent of the Indian families live in houses of three
rooms or less compared to the national average of 11 per cent. Only
9 per cent have indoor toilets. Only 44 per cent have electricity (the
national average is 92 per cent). The standard of housing available
to Indians has been seriously below the Canadian standard and the
building program has been falling short of new family formations by
about 20 per cent.

Early in 1966, the Federal Government initiated a new housing
program for Indian reserve communities. This program provides for
about 12,000 new units in the next five years. New legislation has
been enacted (1967) to provide assistance in building a home off the
reserve near the place of employment. It is too early to estimate the
impact these new programs will make on the Indian housing program.

A new housing program was initiated for Eskimos in 1966.

The depth of poverty among Indians and Eskimos has health implications. While there are no available statistics to show the full
measure of the problem, it is estimated that they require or receive
hospital care at twice the rate of other Canadians. Medical statistics
show that the mortality rate of Indians is:

8   times the national rate for pre-school children;
3   times the national rate for school children;
2½   times the national rate for teenagers;
3½   times the national rate for adults.

The number of Indians being educated in Canada has increased.
High school enrolment has increased since 1948 – from 611 to
4,761 in 1965; university enrolment from 9 to 88 in the same period.

Yet, despite these gains, about 24 per cent of Canada's Indian
population remains functionally illiterate, which is to say they are

either completely illiterate or lack the elementary reading and writing skills required for even the most basic types of jobs. The children still in the educational system are often handicapped by the "cultural deprivation" characteristic of poor environment; no books or place to study undistracted, parents who may not place much value on education or if they do are unable to help their children with it.

In the Northwest Territories, a quarter of the school age Eskimo children are not enrolled in any educational institution (1966). In many cases Eskimo children do not attend school because they live in camps far from established schools or because of the nomadic life of their parents.

> E. R. McEwen, *Community Development Services for Canadian Indian and Métis Communities* (Toronto, 1968), pp. 24-5.

The following two selections suggest reasons why Canada's native peoples have had difficulty in fitting into the dominant culture of North America. Chief John Albany is a member of the Coast Salish tribe on Vancouver Island.

CHIEF JOHN ALBANY . . . The Indians never had any use for the ideas of time, or work, or saving. Time was a matter of days, and seasons. Work was a matter of building a house or catching fish, not working regular hours for regular wages. And why save for the future when there was always enough to eat? Sure, these old ideas have got to change, but it takes time to catch up with several centuries of White Man's progress.

> *The Way of the Indian* (Toronto, 1963). This volume is a transcript of a series of radio programmes.

. . . Indians and Eskimos have never had a sense of private property. It appears that they always felt that the land, and in fact the continent, belonged to the people and everyone had equal rights to the necessities of life. In the pre-Columbus period, about one million people occupied what is now Canada and the United States. There was no shortage of the necessities of life, food from game and fish was always plentiful and there was no scarcity of lands for the tribes which practised agriculture. There was, however, some understanding about boundaries establishing regions used by the various tribes, and tribal wars from time to time did result in some adjustments, but in all of this, private ownership was not a part of the cultural pattern.

The most honoured persons in Indian and Eskimo communities were those who had the most to share with the less fortunate. The good hunter and fisherman was held in the highest esteem since he had the most to share. This ability to contribute gave the individual the right to leadership, etc. Chiefs and councillors were usually those persons who were exceptionally good providers for the community. The accumulation of goods by an individual or families has always been, and continues to be, socially unacceptable in native cultures.

The Europeans brought to the continent a very different set of values. The white man's status was built on how well he was able to meet his family's needs and the greater his wealth, the greater his prestige. In this system, acquisitiveness is an admirable quality. While charity is also recognized as a significant quality, it must be exercised with caution . . . the notion being that the poor should be kept alive but they must always be given a measure of punishment. His plight is usually judged to be due to shiftlessness or laziness. The Europeans migrating to this continent brought with them a firm belief that work was a virtue to be cherished and, conversely, the idea that to be idle is to be sinful. This philosophy has been, and continues to be, a central theme in our schools and has unfailing support from our Chambers of Commerce. Under these circumstances, it has been rather difficult for Canada to understand the outlook of Indians and Eskimos.

E. R. McEwen, "Rights of Canada's First Citizens –
The Indian and Eskimo", Indian-Eskimo Association
of Canada (Toronto, n.d.), pp. 4-5.

Another aspect of the problem has been the willingness or unwillingness of white North American society to accept the Indian as he is. What reasons for these attitudes are suggested in the following readings? Mrs. Crowchild lives on the Sarcee Reserve near Calgary.

CHIEF JOHN ALBANY   The way of the Indian leads him more and more away from the reserves, more and more into the cities. The Indian finds it more difficult every year to lead his old sheltered life. He's learning the White Man's way of life and the White Man's standard of living, so he's got to get out to work at the White Man's jobs. We have told you about life on the reserves. Now we want to tell you some of the problems we meet when we leave the reserve to try to make our way in the world outside. It's an unfriendly world to most of us – we call it "Street Full of Strangers".

MRS. DAVE CROWCHILD   My daughter, after she finished school, she went to the employment office in Calgary and tried to get a job. I don't know how many times she went there. She started in the fall about August or September, starting to find a job, and when she went there they told her they had no scrubbing jobs for her. Just because she was an Indian they thought she was looking for some scrubbing job or some housework job. And she finally told them, she said: "I'm not looking for a housework job. I'm looking for something better than that because I've just finished my grade twelve and I'd like to get a job that's better than scrubbing." Because, I think the White Man always looks down on an Indian. When one Indian makes a mistake, they think every Indian is the same.

The Way of the Indian, pp. 39, 41.

Many who espouse his cause are merely sentimentalists whose knowledge of Indian affairs stems from having paid an occasional visit to a reserve or who have seen him dressed to the hilt in native costume – buckskin, beads, lipstick, feathers and dyed underwear – holding forth at the Ohsweken Indian fair, the Calgary Stampede or Banff's Indian Days. They do not realize that nine times out of ten to be present at these affairs, the Indians will have gone off and left crops and livestock unattended.

At a recent meeting of the Calgary Friends of Indians Society, a district agriculturalist cited instance after instance of local bands' poor records as farmers. When the urge comes upon them they up and leave their homes to spend a week or two with relatives. Dozens of times he has seen bright Indian 4H Club members raise top calves only to be dragged off by their parents to leave the calves to shift for themselves.

Because the Indian has a built-in sense of irresponsibility, many employers who demand good, steady, sober personnel, are adverse to Indian labor. I know one large farm employer who hires twice as many Indians as he needs on the assumption that half will have taken off by mid-season.

The Indian never worries. What tomorrow will bring is of no concern today. He won't put in a sustained effort at anything. He can do it, really, but just hasn't the inclination.

John T. Schmidt, "Lo, The Poor Irresponsible, Lazy Indian", *Saturday Night,* 21 November 1959.

What are the difficulties of assimilating the native population into the dominant European culture? Most Indians and Eskimos, like Negroes, are distinguishable by their physical appearance and, as the previous readings suggested, are rejected by many whites. The author of the second selection in the following group, Abraham Okpik, is the first Eskimo member of the Council of the Northwest Territories.

What are the changes that must take place in the Eskimo way of life before the gulf can be bridged? For the most part, changes in the primitive Eskimo habits of thought and behaviour which impede improvement of his material circumstances. He must learn to want all the things which signify higher living standards, not only because his non-Eskimo neighbours have them, but also because of the improvements in health, comfort, and convenience which they bring. He must learn to value such things more than he values the primitive leisure of carrying out traditional actions in traditional ways within traditional time concepts. He must learn to dislike being without the things he sees his white associates enjoying, but he must learn also that to acquire them he must work as hard and as long as they do. He must learn to want better food, clothing and housing more than he wants the freedom of being able to sleep, eat and hunt as the spirit moves him. He must learn to dislike being without all the white man has, more than he dislikes the forty to fifty hour work-week. He must learn also to judge, assess, and place appropriate value on a host of new enticements offered to him. He must learn to want better household and sanitary facilities more than records and record players; better food and cooking facilities more than the easy laxity of allowing the children unlimited sweets, toys and useless trade goods. He must learn to value better health, better clothing, and more comfort, more than he values the primitive pleasure of purchasing every useless gadget he sees. If these changes in the Eskimo's approach to living do not take place, twenty years from now we will have, with the exception of the fortunate few, a race of oil-barrel movers – half-life Canadians, to whom the white man's world is still a distant utopia. To speed these changes, the whole gamut of southern Canadian culture – jobs, physical comforts, possessions, entertainment, social contacts – should be available to the Eskimo in as full measure as practical and in proportion to his desire to improve himself.

A. F. Flucke, "Whither the Eskimo?",
North, January-February 1963.

To live happily, people need to feel they belong to something – a family, a group, a tribe, a nation, a race. The one thing which keeps people together is a common language.

When you learn to work and live the white man's way – you lose the Eskimo way. This can't be helped. We want progress and comfort and education and security. We can have these things – and still keep our language. We need our language to keep us happy together. If we lose our language, we lose our personality – we don't belong either to the Eskimo people or to the whites. An Eskimo who has lost his language is completely lost. He doesn't belong anywhere.

Keep our language alive, and keep the Eskimo people alive. Tell the old stories, sing the songs, dance the old dances, make jokes, enjoy this great power for thought developed from long ago by our ancestors.

The survival of the Eskimo people depends on the survival of the language. When people meet Eskimos, they are disappointed if they cannot show their knowledge of Eskimo ways. The Eskimo language is big. It could be used to give many great thoughts to the world. If the Eskimos themselves don't use their language more, it will be forgotten, and very soon the Eskimos too will be a forgotten people.

It is up to the Eskimos of today to use their Eskimo strength of word and thought. It is up to the young people. If they don't learn and use the language and the stories and songs, they will have nothing special to give to their children.

It's no good looking like an Eskimo if you can't speak like one.

Abraham Okpik, "What does it mean to be an Eskimo?"
North, March-April 1962.

FURTHER READING

The monthly newsletters of the Bank of Nova Scotia and of the Canadian Imperial Bank of Commerce are excellent sources of information on economic development.

Royal Commission on Canada's Economic Prospects: Final Report (Ottawa: Queen's Printer, 1957).

Foreign Ownership and the Structure of Canadian History. Report of the Task Force on the Structure of Canadian Industry (Ottawa: Privy Council Office, 1968). Controversial examination of American investment in Canada.

Laskin, D., ed. *Social Problems in Canada* (Toronto: McGraw Hill, 1964).

Reid, T. E., *Contemporary Canada: Readings in Economics* (Toronto: Holt, Rinehart, 1969)★.

25

The Canadian Political Scene

Completing Canada's Nationhood

After the war a self-confident Canada set out to complete her nationhood. The first step was the rounding out of the country to make it a nation truly "a mari usque ad mare". Newfoundland at last joined Confederation. The island had enjoyed responsible government from 1855 until 1934 and dominion status from 1919 until 1934. After 1900 the exploitation of Newfoundland's mineral and forest resources had lessened the economy's dependence on fishing and given a small measure of prosperity to the people, but the collapse of prices for newsprint, pulp, fish, and other primary commodities in the Great Depression ruined the island's economy and bankrupted its government. In 1934, the island surrendered its self-government and accepted British administration headed by an appointed commission. The Second World War created a demand for Newfoundland's traditional products, and increased sales made life easier once again for the people. After 1945, however, they were confronted with three choices: Newfoundland could continue under commission government; it might once again become a self-governing member of the Commonwealth; it could join Canada as a province.

In the discussion of these options, Joseph Smallwood, a former union organizer and a radio personality, emerged as the leading spokesman for union with Canada. "Joey" Smallwood campaigned hard to persuade the islanders to vote for union in the referendum held in June 1948, but when no option received a majority a second vote was taken in July. This time,

Joseph R. Smallwood is seated at the extreme left of this photograph showing the initial meeting to discuss the terms of Newfoundland's 1949 union with Canada.

The Confederation Building, St. John's, Newfoundland, the executive offices of the government of Newfoundland and Labrador since 1960.

52 per cent of the electorate voted to join Canada. Negotiations on the terms by which Newfoundland would enter Confederation followed. The Canadian government agreed to assume the island's debts and the Canadian National Railways took over the operation of the Newfoundland Railway. Besides the basic provincial subsidies, the new provincial government was to receive special financial assistance to bring its public services up to the level of other provinces and to compensate for its low revenues. On 31 March 1949 Newfoundland entered Confederation as Canada's tenth province, and the following day "Joey" Smallwood was asked to form its first provincial government.

The second step in completing Canadian nationhood was a series of acts and proclamations to complete the process of defining Canada's sovereignty. The Canadian Citizenship Act of 1946 established a citizenship distinctive to Canada, separate from the status of British subject, and provided for the naturalization of those wishing to acquire Canadian citizenship. In the following year, new Letters Patent were issued to the governor general, giving him authority to exercise all the Crown's prerogative powers in Canada on behalf of the sovereign. This authority meant that formal approval of the monarch was no longer needed for such acts of state as the ratification of treaties. In 1949 appeals in civil and constitutional matters to the Judicial Committee of the Privy Council were abolished by an amendment to the British North America Act, a measure which made the Supreme Court of Canada the final court of appeal and the interpreter of Canada's constitution.

In 1952 the first Canadian-born governor general, Vincent Massey, was appointed. Meanwhile, changes in nomenclature were taking place. The use of the adjective "British" in connection with the Commonwealth was quietly dropped, and in Canada the use of the word "Dominion" was eliminated as no longer appropriate for a sovereign state. Then in 1952 the Canadian government arranged that when Elizabeth II was crowned

W. L. Mackenzie King, Canada's prime minister from 1921-30, except for the 1926 interlude, and from 1935 until 1948. King held the office of chief minister of the Crown longer than any other person in the history of Britain or the Commonwealth. His political longevity was due in large part to his uncanny sense of what was politically acceptable or necessary to the average Canadian.

in the following year, she be proclaimed Queen of Canada as well as of Great Britain. Henceforth the nation was to be the Kingdom of Canada.

Only one limit on Canada's complete autonomy remains: amendment of the British North America Act still has to be carried out by the British parliament. Nowadays this limitation is no more than a legality – for the British parliament would be extremely unlikely to make any alteration to the Act unless it were specifically requested to do so by the Canadian parliament – but most Canadians feel that the machinery of altering the Act should be exercised in Canada. The problem has been that Canadians cannot agree on a way to amend their own constitution. Any method of amendment will have to provide safeguards for language and religious rights and for provincial rights. As might be expected, Quebec has been the province most concerned with establishing safeguards, and no procedure suggested so far has met general acceptance. Only one small breakthrough has been made: in 1949 the British North America Act was amended to permit the Canadian parliament to change the Act in purely federal matters. This power has been used to redistribute representation of seats in the House of Commons.

William Lyon Mackenzie King presided over the post-war government which had planned most of these changes. The aging leader, no longer

Louis St. Laurent in his role as "Uncle Louie" with a young Canadian at Dresden, Ontario, in April 1950. Image makers of the Liberal party worked hard to portray St. Laurent as a senior statesman, a father figure for Canadians, and a person somehow above politics. The opposition caricatured this image as "Uncle Louie", but the caricature was not unwelcome.

able to provide firm leadership in the cabinet, allowed his ministers increasing authority in the management of the transition from war to peace. In 1947 he announced his intention to retire and arranged for a leadership convention to choose his successor. Even after the convention he hesitated to hand over the reins of power and kept the new Liberal leader, Louis St. Laurent, waiting for months before finally resigning. King then set about arranging his personal papers and diary for posterity and retired from politics until his death on 22 July 1950.

Any judgement on King's place in Canadian history is bound to create controversy. Few people, it would seem, had loved him and many had hated him bitterly. Yet most Canadians had voted for him. His kind of leadership had inspired these mixed reactions; he was a master of discovering Canadian opinion on problems and equally a master in knowing what was politically possible, but personally he inspired little admiration or affection. His concern for national unity was good for the Liberal party but it did not make the country more genuinely united. He avoided any real French-English confrontation which would have destroyed that precarious unity. Cautious, essentially a conservative hiding under a Liberal cloak, he provided the kind of leadership which most Canadians wanted in the trials of depression and war. In the words of one Canadian historian, "King divided Canadians least." His retirement and death, after more years' service as prime minister than any other man in Commonwealth history, marked the end of a thirty-year era in Canadian politics.

The Decline of the Liberal Party

King's successor, Louis St. Laurent, was Canada's second French-Canadian prime minister. Completely bilingual, courtly, warm-hearted and dignified, St. Laurent seemed to represent the Canadian personality to a unique degree. As he grew older, people began referring to him as "Uncle Louie", a title partly poking fun, but partly reflecting the genuine esteem in which he was held by most Canadians. A successful corporation lawyer, St. Laurent had been persuaded by King to enter politics and become Minister of Justice following the death of Ernest Lapointe. His shrewd political sense – he appeared to be only an amateur who had wandered into politics late in life – and his ability showed very quickly in the cabinet, and in 1946 King made him the senior minister in the government, the Secretary of State for External Affairs. As prime minister, St. Laurent did not provide dynamic leadership, but he did bring to that office the personal qualities which had been so lacking in King.

St. Laurent remained prime minister through eight years of prosperity and growth. Heavy American investment in resource development primed the pump and covered the deficit between the amount Canadians paid in interest and dividends and spent on American goods, and what they received for selling their products in the United States. It was said that St. Laurent presided over a ministry of talents. The Liberal cabinet contained extraordinarily able administrators, men like C. D. Howe, the Minister of Trade and Commerce. Howe, an American-born engineer and self-made millionaire, had become a minister in 1935 before ever taking his seat in parliament. He had proved himself again and again to be efficient, particularly in his organization of the Ministry of Defence Production. Much of the credit for promoting the economic growth of the nineteen-fifties has to be given to Howe. Lester Pearson, Secretary of State for External Affairs since 1948, former history professor and civil servant, brought great prestige to himself and to Canada with his effective diplomacy and leadership in the department.

The government continued secure in office through elections in 1949 and 1953 in which the Liberals won 190 seats and 170 seats respectively, majorities which nearly annihilated the Opposition parties. But suspicion grew that these huge majorities had made the Liberals arrogant and indifferent to public wishes. Liberal complacency was revealed when the government raised the old-age pension, universally given since 1952 to all over seventy years of age, from $40 to $46 – an inadequate amount in view of the rapidly rising cost of living to which the government seemed indifferent. Symptomatic of Liberal arrogance was the famous "pipeline debate" in the summer of 1956. The government had authorized the building of a natural gas pipeline from Alberta to eastern Canada, a construction feat compared at the time to the building of the CPR. Trans-Canada Pipe Lines, an American-controlled company, was given the franchise to build the line across the prairies. Unable to raise the necessary capital to

*The trans-Canada natural gas pipeline from Alberta to Montreal was
laid mainly through forested and rocky terrain. This photograph, taken
in Northern Ontario in 1958, shows a gang welding thirty-inch-diameter
pipes beside the rock ditch through a heavy stand of timber.*

In the Senate Chamber Queen Elizabeth II reads the Speech from the Throne, outlining the government's legislative plans, at the opening of Canada's twenty-third parliament at Ottawa, in October 1957. John G. Diefenbaker, the prime minister, sits on the Queen's right, the Duke of Edinburgh on her left.

complete the work, the company asked the government to lend it $80 million and the government agreed. The Opposition in parliament immediately claimed that the government was "bailing out" an American company in trouble. The government, in order to get the money to the company by mid-summer, moved closure in the same speech in which the measure to provide the money was introduced. Debate in the House of Commons became increasingly acrimonious as closure was imposed four times, and fifty-three votes were taken to get the measure through in fifteen sitting days. One Opposition member was expelled from the House by the Speaker, another collapsed from exhaustion and had to be hospitalized. The Speaker's reputation was ruined when his impartiality was called into question. The whole pipeline affair seemed to demonstrate to most Canadians that the government was unwilling to permit free discussion, but would abuse its majority position by ramming its measures through parliament. The pipeline issue also bothered many Canadians who were worried about the extent of American investment in Canada. Few politicians seemed aware that Canadians had lost confidence in the Liberal government.

The new leader of the Conservative party, John G. Diefenbaker, seized on all the failings of the government to bring about its defeat. A successful trial lawyer who was passionately concerned about civil rights, Diefenbaker prosecuted the government for all its mistakes – its small increase in the old age pension, its arrogance in the pipeline debate, its failure to sell western wheat – and won his case. In the general election of June 1957 the Conservatives took 112 seats, the Liberals were reduced to 105. The country – and the Liberal party – was stunned by Diefenbaker's success.

St. Laurent, too old to continue after such a defeat and ineffective in opposition, retired, and the Liberals chose Lester B. Pearson to lead them. To Pearson fell the impossible task of leading a paralysed Liberal party into the election which Diefenbaker called for March 1958. Diefenbaker asked for a majority to make his government secure and promised measures to lessen Canadian economic dependence on the United States. The result was an overwhelming victory for the Conservatives, who won 208 seats and carried every province except Newfoundland. For the first time since 1887, the Conservatives won Quebec, gaining 50 of its 75 seats thanks to the support of Duplessis and his Union Nationale. The Liberals elected only 49 members, none west of Ontario. The CCF carried 8 seats but the Social Credit party was eliminated from the federal parliament.

The Diefenbaker Years

In the next four years, the Conservatives carried through an extensive and impressive legislative programme. The South Saskatchewan River power and irrigation project was begun; an independent broadcasting authority, the Board of Broadcast Governors, was set up to supervise and regulate both public and private radio and television broadcasting; old age pensions were increased; the franchise was extended to Indians; co-operation between labour and management to further economic growth was promoted by the creation of the National Productivity Council. The plans for Expo 67, the world's fair held at Montreal to coincide with Canada's centennial, were laid. The government also attempted to deal with the problems created by the technological changes that were reducing employment opportunities for unskilled workers. Under the Technical and Vocational Training Assistance Act of 1960 grants were made to assist provinces in the training and retraining of adults who lacked job skills. In addition, grants were provided to pay for the construction of technical and vocational training facilities in high schools, grants which, when provincial funds were added, meant that between 1960 and 1963 local education authorities could build these facilities at virtually no capital cost to themselves. The problem of regional economic disparity was tackled with the Agricultural and Rural Development Act (ARDA) which made funds available for research into better land use in marginal farm land areas, conservation, encouraging new industry to establish itself in rural areas, and manpower training. By 1965, some 729 projects had been undertaken under ARDA. But Diefenbaker's proudest achievement was the Canadian Bill of Rights passed in 1960. Unfortunately this measure to protect the basic freedoms of Canadians is not built into the British North America Act and has only the status of an ordinary statute. Besides all this legislation, the Conservatives brought new energy to the marketing of the enormous wheat sur-

pluses and virtually eliminated the stockpiles by selling enormous amounts to the USSR and Communist China.

Despite these achievements, the Diefenbaker government began to lose its popularity after 1960. A number of factors were responsible, but one reason was the Conservative government's inability to pull the country out of the recession which had begun during the winter of 1956-7. Perhaps the major factor in declining Conservative fortunes was the unsettled condition of Quebec politics. In 1960 the Liberals, led by Jean Lesage, defeated the Union Nationale government in Quebec. The death of Maurice Duplessis in 1959 had loosed a torrent of demands for change and reform in Quebec. Duplessis' successor, Paul Sauvé, promised change, but his death within months of taking office destroyed the Union Nationale's claim to be the party of the new Quebec. Lesage and the Liberals became the party of the "Quiet Revolution". Another political element in the Conservative decline was the formation in 1962 of the New Democratic party as a result of an agreement between the CCF and the Canadian Labour Congress. The old CCF had not been able to make much impression on the industrial areas of central Canada and the new party hoped to capitalize on labour support. T. C. Douglas, the premier of Saskatchewan since 1944, took on the leadership of the NDP. The emergence of a Social Credit party group in Quebec led by the colourful and vocal Real Caouette, was yet another force that Diefenbaker's government had to contend with.

In the general election of 1962 the Liberals made heavy inroads into the Conservative majorities in Ontario and Quebec. The Conservatives emerged with only 116 seats, having held on to only 14 seats in Quebec and lost their dominance in Ontario. The Liberals won 100 seats, 35 of them in Quebec, 44 in Ontario, but only 2 in the three prairie provinces. The NDP won 19 seats, its strength drawn from the industrial and urban areas of Ontario and British Columbia. The great surprise was the Social Credit party, which won 30 seats – mostly in the poorer rural areas of Quebec. Supported by the Social Credit group, the Conservative government clung to office briefly, only to be overwhelmed in 1963 by the problem of foreign policy and defence. Shortly after coming to power in 1957, the Diefenbaker government had agreed to accept American-made Bomarc missiles and build two bases in central Canada, at Mont Laurier (La

Expo 67, showing (from left to right) the pavilions of Quebec, Ontario, Canada, The Western Provinces (with the trees), The Atlantic Provinces (with flat roof), and the tepee-like pavilion of The Canadian Indians.

Macaza) and North Bay, to complete the United States' missile defence system against air attack. But the government had not accepted nuclear warheads for these missiles largely because some of the cabinet argued that this would contradict Canada's declared policy of promoting nuclear disarmament. Moreover, the Conservatives had hesitated in giving immediate support to the United States during the Cuban Missile crisis in 1962. In January 1963 an American general sharply criticized Canada for not living up to her treaty obligations in the joint air defence of North America. This statement threw the Conservative cabinet into a crisis. The Minister of National Defence, Douglas Harkness, resigned over the government's failure to accept nuclear warheads for the Bomarc missiles. Taking advantage of this confusion the Opposition, united for once, defeated the government in the Commons, and Diefenbaker was forced to call an election. A few days later, two more ministers resigned over the warhead issue and a number of others announced that they would not stand for re-election. In the election in April the Liberals swept central Canada and won 129 seats, the NDP took 17 seats, Social Credit 24 seats, and the Conservatives were reduced to 95 seats.

The Liberal Revival

Lester Pearson, since January 1963 a lukewarm convert to the necessity of Canada's accepting nuclear warheads, formed the new government. Liberal leaders had promised "Sixty Days of Decision" after they won office; it was a promise they soon regretted. The new government accepted the warheads quietly while proclaiming that it was honouring Canadian treaty obligations. In June the new Liberal government presented its budget, containing measures to discourage further takeovers of Canadian companies by Americans and to encourage American-controlled companies to sell shares to Canadians. The sales tax was extended to a number of items including construction materials. The budget created such a storm of protest that the discriminatory measures were all withdrawn, and on day sixty the finance minister offered his resignation to Prime Minister Pearson.

Despite the new government's poor start, some major achievements were accomplished in the next two years. The government's new Canadian flag caused bitter debate in parliament because many English-speaking Canadians saw the new flag as a repudiation of the ties with Britain. The automotive trade agreement providing for free entry of parts and automobiles from the United States, a major aid to the expansion of the Canadian industry, was negotiated and was signed in 1965. The agreement was so successful in achieving its purpose that in 1969 automobiles and automobile parts were Canada's most valuable export. The Canada Pension Plan, a universal contributory old age pension scheme, was also introduced and went into effect in 1966. Unification of the three branches of the armed forces was begun.

The major concern of the Pearson government was the resurgence of French-Canadian nationalism in Quebec. This movement was not merely the politics of survival for a cultural minority, rather it was the assertion by French-speaking Canadians that they should share totally in the life of the nation. The nationalists' demands ranged from simply asking that more money be transferred to the province from the federal government to the extreme position of the Front de Libération Québecoise, which was committed to the use of terrorist methods to attain independence for their province. The eruption of this discontent shocked English-speaking Canada.

The development of industry and with it urbanization had created a large and educated French-Canadian middle class. This new generation had discovered again that Quebec's economy was controlled by the English speaking, and that Quebec was backward and under-developed in comparison with the other large provinces. This explosion of resentment had been postponed during the 1950's by the presence of Louis St. Laurent in Ottawa and Maurice Duplessis in Quebec; although there had been a small coterie of intellectuals, among them Pierre Elliott Trudeau, who were critical both of the federal government's infringements on provincial rights and of the conservatism of the Quebec government. Then in 1958 the Conservative victory in federal politics loosened the demands for change as the whole country seemed to turn its back on the past decade. The death of Duplessis in 1959 and of Paul Sauvé, his successor, after only a few months in office, created within the Union Nationale confusion which allowed the initiative to pass to the resurgent provincial Liberal party. After the Liberal victory in 1960, the revolution began as Quebec's institutions and ideals came under question by the radical nationalists. Jean Lesage's new government vigorously demanded more money from Ottawa to expand educational opportunity, to develop welfare programmes, and to invest in industrial development. In 1963 Quebec nationalized the private hydro-electricity companies. The government appointed a Royal Commission to study education, the most extensive such study ever done in Canada.

After twenty-five years of strong leadership by the federal government, not merely Quebec but all the provinces were demanding more control of their own social and economic development. The Pearson government tried to be conciliatory, allowing Quebec to participate in federal welfare programmes on special terms. Federal ministers spoke of co-operative

"Perhaps we should have brought it out during Book Week instead of Brotherhood Week."

The late André Laurendeau, co-chairman with Davidson Dunton of the Royal Commission on Bilingualism and Biculturalism, is depicted in this cartoon from the "Vancouver Sun" making this disillusioned remark on the lack of public interest shown in the publication of the Preliminary Report in 1965.

federalism and of Canada as a country containing two nations. In English-speaking Canada, especially the west, the reaction to these policies was anger and the feeling that Pearson was allowing Quebec to weaken Confederation. The victory of the Union Nationale under Daniel Johnson, in 1966, made possible by the belief of many Québecois that the pace of change was too fast, enabled the federal government to take a stronger line in dealing with Quebec. The enthusiastic nationalism of centennial year papered over the cracks for a time, despite the visit of President de Gaulle from France and his encouragement of separatism. A Royal Commission was established to investigate how well French-speaking and English-speaking people were living together. The Bilingualism and Biculturalism (Bi and Bi) Commission produced a preliminary report that the situation was serious, that French-speaking Canadians were resentful of their status in Canada. The first part of its report, released in 1968, recommended that bilingualism be legally established in any area where there was an English or French minority constituting at least 10 per cent of the population. A second part recommended increased opportunity for education in their own language for French-speaking citizens in all parts of Canada. Meanwhile, the Ontario government was taking the initiative by calling a Provincial Premiers' Conference on the future of Confederation and by expanding French-language education in that province.

Nevertheless, the initial disillusionment with the Pearson government did not wear off. Its image was further tarnished in the winter of 1964-5 by the revelation that some members of Pearson's own staff – also mem-

"I don't know if we are winning or losing, Mon Général. We have requests from all ten provincial education ministers to attend our next conference."

General de Gaulle's visit to Quebec in 1967, accompanied by his rallying cry "Vive le Québec Libre" and his encouragement of closer ties between France and Quebec, brought censure from the federal government and disapproval from other provinces. The cartoonist is perhaps commenting on the fact that all the provinces, not only Quebec, may cherish hidden aspirations to constitutional independence from Ottawa.

bers of some other ministers' staffs – were involved with criminals. Pearson got rid of these officials, but the affair harmed the Liberals considerably. Many English-speaking Canadians were concerned that the government was gradually allowing Quebec to opt out of Confederation with the special formulae devised by the government in financial grants to that province. In 1965 Pearson called a new election, hoping to obtain a majority in the Commons. Diefenbaker appeared on the hustings as the defender of Canadian unity. Once more English-speaking Canada outside Ontario rebuffed the Liberals. They won only 131 seats out of 265, the Conservatives returned with 97 and the NDP with 21. The divided Social Credit group returned only 14 members, 9 of them dissident Creditistes from Quebec.

The next two years of parliament were frustrating ones for the country. After introducing a universal medical care plan to start operating on 1 July 1967, the federal government decided it could not afford to operate the plan and postponed its introduction for one year. Even then only two provinces entered the scheme, mainly because the costs could not be definitely determined. The unification plan for the armed forces was carried through only after a number of senior officers had been forced to resign. A major reform of the criminal code was proposed in 1968, but not passed. Through all this, the climate of debate in parliament became more bitter as the personal duel between Diefenbaker and Pearson, begun in 1958, became an obsession with the two leaders that damaged the prestige of parliament throughout the country.

Centennial year brought a pause in the partisanship and also marked the end of the Pearson-Diefenbaker duel. A number of Conservatives, fearful that Diefenbaker was a liability to their party in central and eastern Canada, engineered a leadership convention in the autumn of 1967 at which Diefenbaker was forced out of office and replaced by Robert Stanfield, the successful premier of Nova Scotia. This internal party fight weakened the Conservative party because many Conservatives disliked the treatment given "the Chief" and offered only lukewarm support to Stanfield. In November 1967 Pearson announced his intention to retire

Pierre Elliott Trudeau, the leader of the Liberal party, with some young autograph seekers. During the election campaign in 1968 Trudeau's public image was a great asset to the Liberals. He spoke briefly to huge meetings in arenas and shopping centres, then plunged into the crowds to greet the people.

after a convention had chosen his successor. In the spring of 1968 the Liberals chose Pierre Elliott Trudeau, a wealthy, brilliant, and attractive lawyer who had entered parliament only in 1965 to serve as Minister of Justice in the Pearson government.

In 1968 the country seemed unready for an election, but Trudeau decided to gamble on his popularity and on the public opinion polls which said that the Liberals had a majority of popular support. The Conservatives were anxious to meet the demands of French-Canadian nationalism in their election programme but found themselves outflanked by Trudeau, a French Canadian who attacked separatism and urged Canadian unity with special status for no province. By dropping the Liberal association with the concept of two nations, Trudeau was able to win the support in English-speaking Canada which had eluded Pearson. Sensing the more conservative mood of the electorate, the Liberals appropriated Stanfield's demands for cuts in government expenditures and caution in undertaking new programmes. The result was a Liberal sweep in Quebec and Ontario and considerable gains on the prairies and in British Columbia. The Conservatives held on only to the Maritimes and a few rural seats in Ontario and the prairies. The result – 155 seats for the Liberals, 72 for the Conservatives, 22 NDP, and 14 Creditistes – gave Canadians a majority government for the first time in six years.

The Trudeau government moved slowly to solve the problems it saw, too slowly for at least one minister, Paul Hellyer, who resigned in frustration over the failure of the government to deal dynamically with housing and other social problems. Nevertheless, in 1969, the Criminal Code was at last amended with the intention of bringing it more into line with contemporary views on morality and crime. The Official Languages Act implemented the recommendation of the first report of the Bi and Bi Commission by creating official bilingual districts. Arrangements for a federally sponsored medicare plan were finally worked out with all the provinces except Quebec. The government also moved to change Canada's role in NATO and reduce her military commitment in Europe. Foreseeing controversial legislation in the future, the government undertook to alter the procedural rules of the House of Commons to limit debate, a move which led to fierce Opposition objections.

Meanwhile, world wheat prices slipped and surpluses piled up, the rate of inflation and unemployment increased, and interest rates for home mortgages and other borrowing reached their highest levels since the 1920's. The continuing uneasiness of the electorate was shown by the voters' rejection of the Conservative government of Manitoba and the narrow victory of the NDP, and was underlined by warnings from economists of an approaching slowdown in the economy. Since 1958 a sense of

uncertainty and a demand for change, together with an awareness of innumerable problems – many of them apparently insoluble – have infil-
trated all aspects of Canadian life.

This condition was of course not peculiar to Canada – the whole world
seemed to be in ferment during the 1960's. But to Canadians, their own
problems – both the question of Quebec's future and the larger economic
issues – naturally seemed at least as important as the military and financial
crises that repeatedly disturbed the globe. Out of this mood of uncertainty
arose the Canadian desire for dynamic and personal leadership which
catapulted Pierre Elliott Trudeau into the office of prime minister. Only in
future years, from the vantage point of hindsight, will historians be able to
judge whether Canada's attraction since 1957 towards a cult of personality
did in fact give the nation the kind of government it needed, or deserved.

"It's a Mr. Johnson in Quebec
congratulating you on your
speech advocating two Chinas
and two Viet Nams in the UN,
sir . . . . but he's asking why you
didn't mention two Canadas . . ."

*The secretary to Paul Martin, Minister for
External Affairs in the Pearson government, is referring to Daniel Johnson, who
at that time (1966) was the premier of
Quebec. An angry monarch glares from
her framed portrait.*

HISTORY FROM THE SOURCES

What Does Quebec Want?

*This question fascinates English Canadians concerned with the future
of their country. But the problem is complicated by another question:
who speaks for Quebec? The three selections below – from a statement*

by Daniel Johnson, prime minister of Quebec from 1966-8, from the
Bi and Bi Report, and from an interview with René Lévesque – represent
three points of view. From each it is clear that the negative politics of
"operation survival" (a rough translation of "la survivance") are dead;
Quebec is now in its age of épanouissement (flowering) – of making
urgent demands for change.

A nation can be defined in two ways according to the degree of
evolution it has reached. It can be a sociological phenomenon before
being a political one, and its definition can spring just as much from
the sociological content as from the political reality.

The confusion between the English definition and ours arises
from the fact that the English relies more on the political content of
the word while the French puts more importance on the sociological
content. To make myself clear: Let's start with the "nation" definition which the Larousse dictionary gives us: "Human community,
most often installed on the same territory, and which, owing to a
certain historic, linguistic, religious or even economic unity, is
moved towards a common way of life (vouloir vivre)." . . . .

. . . There is not one, but two human communities which are
distinct by language, religion, culture, traditions, historic evolution,
and lastly, by a common "way of life" as, even in the provinces where
they are in minority, they tend to group themselves on the regional
or local plane, to give themselves on the regional or local plane, to
give themselves a favorable milieu for their accomplishments.

One must note that the fundamental element of a nation is not
its race, but its culture. No matter its name, its ethnic origin, a person
is from one nation or another according to his roots, his upbringing,
his choice, his style of life, his way of thinking and expression; he
belongs, he identifies himself with one or other cultural community. . . .

It will nevertheless happen, and this is a normal outcome, that
the cultural community, having once reached a certain stage of development, especially if it possesses undeniable historic rights, will
try to identify itself with a state. For to flourish in the sense of its own
genius, this cultural community needs cadres, institutions and channels of command that only a state can give. . . .

What we want is more than the powers granted to us in the 1867
constitution.

What we want, in fact, is the right to decide for ourselves, or to
have an equal share in deciding all matters concerning our national
life.

For are we masters in our own house when Ottawa alone rules
on all that concerns radio and television, media which may be the
most effective tools to our culture?

Are we masters in our own house when Ottawa refuses to protect with appropriate tariffs the products of some vital industries of French Canada?

Are we masters in our own house when a decision of the Bank of Canada can affect the credit of our enterprises, of our financial institutions and of the Quebec State itself?

Are we masters in our house when the federal revenue collector comes skimming our profits, proceeding from the exploitation of natural resources which belong to the Quebec community and, by the bias of the corporate tax structure, prevents us from fully planning our economy, a function of our particular needs?

Are we masters in our house when the Supreme Court, to which all judges are sworn by Ottawa, is the ultimate interpreter of our French law and the only tribunal to which we can submit our grievances against the federal government?

Federation, associated states, special status, a republic, whatever it may be, the new constitutional regime will have to give the French-Canadian nation all powers necessary to find her own destiny.

After three centuries of labour, our nation truly deserves to live freely. So much the better if she can feel herself at home from sea to sea. Which implies the recognition of her complete equality. If not, then Quebec independence will have to come.

Canada or Quebec? Where the French-Canadian nation will find freedom, there will be her country!

> "What Daniel Johnson Really Believes about Quebec",
> *The Financial Post,* 11 June 1966. Trans. by *FP.*

31. Among French-speaking Canadians, the expression "two founding peoples" was quite frequently used. "Our rights and privileges in the Canadian Federation are not completely honoured, and we feel our group should have priority precisely because it is one of the founding races," stated a Franco-Ontarian in Windsor.

Typically enough, he was linking the concept of founding peoples to the idea of a contract between them, which established French Canada's rights at the time of Confederation. In the past, two major versions of the compact theory have been elaborated: a compact among provinces and a treaty between "races". Quebec's rights (and those of the other provinces) have been based on the first version; the rights of French Canadians throughout Canada on the second. . . .

A number of people who were speaking to us raised the questions summarized in the preceding chapter, but this time from a political point of view: French minorities, bilingualism within the federal Civil Service, the armed forces, and the transportation system, more complete coverage by French radio and television networks, the role of the French language and of French-speaking Canadians in the Quebec economy, and so on. They sometimes asked that the equality of the two official languages be put into practice and formally written into the constitution. To some, this bilingualism meant even the recognition of unilingual geographical regions.

Others made the same demands but at the same time they were concerned about another aspect of the problem. According to them, it is necessary that the division of responsibilities between the federal government and the provinces be redefined and truly respected. . . .

84. The clearest and most radical political attitude expressed before the Commission, of course, was that of the separatists or militant "indépendantistes". It was also the attitude which English-speaking participants appeared to be most familiar with and which they attacked most vigorously, although they did not always fully understand it.

The "indépendantiste" position was clearly expressed in Quebec. At the evening meeting, a lawyer told us: "We do not blame the English Canadians for anything; they have behaved as all majorities do. What we want is much simpler than that. We want complete fiscal powers in order to put into effect these political powers, so that we may organize our institutions and finally attain the full development of the French Canadian nation." . . .

French-speaking Canadians in general insisted on the need for institutions which could safeguard and promote the French language and culture and give it full expression. . . .

According to many French-speaking people who spoke to us, the principal institutions in the country are frustrating their desire to live their lives fully as French Canadians. This situation, they said, prevails even in Quebec itself inside the economic institutions of the province: such and such a plant in the locality, managed by English-speaking people, was carrying on its business as though it were in "colonial territory", and was preventing the majority of its employees from working in their mother tongue once they reached a certain level. The English-speaking managerial group – often a tiny proportion of the population – felt no need to speak French and, as a result, rarely bothered to learn it. These people freely admitted that this sort of situation was not new and that, on the contrary, it has always existed in Quebec. But they added *that they could no longer allow it to continue.* . . .

The separatists drew their arguments from the old nationalist arsenal – except for their principal proposition: 'A well-treated minority, the French Canadians are nonetheless a minority. In order to regain control of their destiny they must decide in favour of the sovereign State of Quebec in which they will at last be a majority.' In the eyes of a separatist the double equation "majority=imperial rule" and "minority=colony" is no metaphor but a strict statement of fact. It means that in Canada the great political and economic decisions are taken outside "the French Canadian nation", which has to go along with them. The minority must therefore be "decolonized" so that it may be freed from its status as a "slave nation".

> *Royal Commission on Bilingualism and Biculturalism,* Preliminary
> Report (Ottawa, 1965), pp. 45-6, 63, 91-2, 109, 116-17.

Q Mr. Lévesque, is a separate Quebec a real possibility in the foreseeable future?

A If you look at "separate" in the sense that, politically, it's going to be a different country, I think it's not just a possibility – it's inevitable. We feel a growing need – modestly akin to the Jewish one – for our own "homeland."

Q How soon could that happen?

A The way things are moving, it should take between one and three elections inside the Province of Quebec – about five or six years at the most, perhaps less – to bring to power a majority government in Quebec with a mandate to make Quebec a sovereign state.

Q Why do you want sovereignty?

A To try to make it simple, in terms that people in the United States can understand, is a tough proposition. To be frank, there's a vast ignorance in the U.S. about Canada, and especially about Quebec.

Take it from this angle:

You've got about 5 million French Canadians who make up just about 80 per cent of the population of Quebec. In other words, you have a very well-knit, well-defined population whose common personality is tied to the fact that they speak French. And everything else more or less radiates around that.

Now, for a long time we were largely an uneducated population with a very small elite. But in the last 15 or 20 years we've been widening our educated population by leaps and bounds. Quebec's "revolution" is basically an educational revolution.

Quebec used to be a sort of inner colony of Canada – patient people without much education, with small jobs and limited horizons. Education has changed that, with results that are felt especially in politics.

We suddenly found out that, once you have available competent people in your own society, you can do your own job better than anybody else can do it.

Now, Quebec is like an individual who has arrived at maturity, with the right – and the capacity – to make his own decisions, make his own mistakes, achieve his own successes.

We have reached a point where we feel we can do an honest job for ourselves better than it can be done for us. To do that, we need the political tools – our own tax money, our own policy, our own place in the sun.

Q Would you settle for anything less than complete sovereignty?

A Necessarily, there is still some confusion among various groups.

Some say: "We want total independence and we want to break off all ties with the rest of Canada and start practically from scratch."

At the other extreme, there are so-called special-status people who would like to keep Quebec inside the federal structure and still have a semiseparate state – which would be quite impractical, politically; it couldn't help being permanent, built-in instability.

The group of which I am a part is trying to find a mainstream between the two extremes. We are convinced that politically we need sovereignty. But there is no reason why we could not negotiate a sort of common-market arrangement – an economic alliance – with the rest of Canada.

Q Is there anything that English-speaking Canada could do to take the steam out of the Quebec-sovereignty drive?

A I don't think so. It is something which is like a vital force. You have a population which was sort of patient, rather undereducated for too long, shielded by ignorance from any pressures for change, and living in a setup which was like being a colony inside a country. Now this is changing through education, and you can't go on.

Canada was based on two cultures, French and English. If we had become assimilated as French Canadians in a melting-pot setup, the kind that made the U.S. grow and last and keep on growing, there would be no problem. But Quebec, instead of assimilating, is developing in its own way.

You might stop it in a crazy way with guns and things like that. But this is a political situation that must run its course. And the course is, as in all maturing societies that have the tools for it, to have your own self-government.

So I don't see anything that the rest of Canada could do. If they try to block it, the effect will be just to accelerate it. If they try to buy it off by saying: "All right, what does Quebec want? We'll do this, we'll do that," the answer will be: "Quebec wants more."

You know, appeasement just breeds an appetite for more.

"The Case for a 'Free Quebec': Interview with a Leader in the Separatist Movement", *U.S. News and World Report*, 15 January 1968, pp. 44-6. From a copyrighted interview.

FURTHER READING

Students may gain considerable knowledge of the political scene in contemporary Canada simply by reading newspapers and magazines and listening to radio and TV programmes.

Fraser, Blair, *The Search for Identity* (Toronto: Doubleday, 1967). A popular anecdotal history.

Newman, Peter C., *Renegade in Power: The Diefenbaker Years* (Toronto: McClelland & Stewart, 1963)★.

Newman, Peter C., *The Distemper of Our Times* (Toronto: McClelland & Stewart, 1968)★.

Thomson, Dale C., *Louis St. Laurent* (Toronto: Macmillan, 1967).

Corbett, E. M., *Quebec Confronts Canada* (Baltimore: Johns Hopkins, 1967).

Oliver, M. K. and Scott, F. R., *Quebec States Her Case* (Toronto: Macmillan, 1964)★.

Desbarats, Peter, *The State of Quebec* (Toronto: McClelland & Stewart, 1964)★.

Cook, Ramsay, *Canada and the French-Canadian Question* (Toronto: Macmillan, 1966)★.

Macquarrie, Heath, *The Conservative Party* (Toronto: McClelland & Stewart, 1965)★.

Pickersgill, J. W., *The Liberal Party* (Toronto: McClelland & Stewart, 1962)★.

Trudeau, Pierre Elliott, *Federalism and the French Canadians* (Toronto: Macmillan, 1968)★.

26

Canada and the Wider World

Towards a New Foreign Policy

Four weeks after the Second World War ended, a Russian cipher clerk, Igor Gouzenko, quietly left the Soviet Embassy building at Ottawa, carrying documents that revealed the operations of a spy ring in Canada. Following months of investigation based on the documents and on Gouzenko's revelations, eighteen people were tried for security violations. Eight, including a Communist member of the Canadian parliament, were convicted. While Canada's spies proved to be rather pathetic people who had never had access to really vital information, the experience shook her confidence in the good faith of her wartime ally, the USSR, and forced Canada to reassess her own foreign policies.

In the following four years Canadians saw Russian troops remain in eastern Europe, where they established Communist governments at the end of the war in Poland, Hungary, Rumania, and Bulgaria. Albania and Yugoslavia also had pro-Communist governments. Western newspapers were not allowed into these countries, western radio broadcasts were jammed, the people were forbidden to leave their countries, and secret police organizations were set up to maintain the Communist governments in power. As Winston Churchill said in 1946, an "Iron Curtain" had dropped across Europe. Then in 1947 Communism appeared to be marching westward: through free elections the Communist parties of Italy and France became the largest parties in their respective parliaments and began to sabotage the recovery programmes of the governments in order to improve their own popular standings. The only reverses to Communism came in the success of the American Marshall Plan, which invested $12 billion in European industry to aid its recovery, and the defection of Tito's Yugoslavia from the Stalinist camp.

Despite the Gouzenko affair the reality of the cold war dawned slowly on Canadians. Then in 1948 the Communists seized Czechoslovakia and dismantled its democratic institutions. At the same time the Soviet Union broke its agreement with the western powers guaranteeing free access to Berlin, by imposing a blockade on the city to starve out the western allied

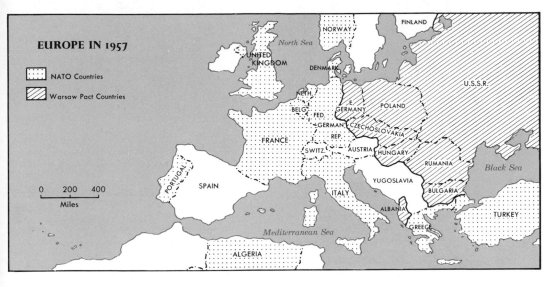

EUROPE IN 1957

NATO Countries

Warsaw Pact Countries

NORWAY
FINLAND
North Sea
UNITED KINGDOM
DENMARK
NETH.
U.S.S.R.
BELG.
E. GERMANY
POLAND
FED. GERMAN REP.
CZECHOSLOVAKIA
FRANCE
SWITZ.
AUSTRIA
HUNGARY
RUMANIA
Black Sea
YUGOSLAVIA
BULGARIA
SPAIN
PORTUGAL
ITALY
ALBANIA
TURKEY
GREECE
Mediterranean Sea

0   200   400
Miles

ALGERIA

garrisons. For nearly a year the city had to be supplied by aircraft. These two events, following the others, persuaded Canadians and Americans to join together with Britain, France, Italy, Iceland, Norway, Denmark, the Benelux countries, and Portugal to form the North Atlantic Treaty Organization (NATO) in 1949. These countries, joined later by Turkey, Greece, and West Germany, entered into a defensive alliance for twenty years by which members agreed to contribute military forces to their common defence. Canada had made her first definite peacetime military commitment to involve herself in other countries' problems.

In 1948 the Gallup public opinion poll claimed that 51 per cent of Canadians thought that a third world war was inevitable. This poll may have reflected the changing attitudes within Canada, which now favoured the country's entry into defensive alliances that she had so studiously avoided in the 1920's and 30's. Because of the post-war international tensions, the Canadian and United States' governments had already agreed in 1947 to carry on their continental defence co-operation through the Permanent Joint Board on Defence. The announcement of this agreement emphasized that collaboration would be limited and that special care would be taken to protect the principle of national sovereignty. But with the Soviet Union lying just across the North Pole from Canada, the Canadian Arctic was becoming strategically important to continental air defence, and beginning in 1948 a system of weather stations and radar warning posts was built in the Canadian north. The armed forces of the two countries also carried out joint manoeuvres. As the cold war intensified in the early 1950's, co-operation between the two North American nations became closer and joint procurement plans for war materials were devised.

The Canadian patrol ship H.M.C.S. "Labrador" in Arctic waters.

In this cold war era the Canadian government has regarded the United Nations as the essential institution in maintaining world peace. Canada served as a temporary member of the Security Council in 1948-9; in her opinion the United Nations was the only world forum in which opinion could be presented to influence the great powers. Defensive alliances were, therefore, from Canada's point of view, secondary to the work of the UN. By eliminating human and economic problems in the world, Canada believed that the United Nations could also bring peace and order. Thus in agencies and associated organizations of the UN, Canadians played a leading role. Dr. Brock Chisholm was the first director of the World Health Organization, Dr. Hugh Keenleyside the first director-general of the UN Technical Assistance Administration. Others served in senior positions in the United Nations Children's Fund (UNICEF), the Food and Agriculture Organization, and in similar international organizations.

In the immediate post-war years Mackenzie King was still as concerned as he had been before 1939 that membership in international bodies might mean unwelcome responsibilities for Canada. The government was glad to supply technical aid and expertise to aid other countries, but possible military commitments were unwelcome. When in 1947 Canada was asked to serve on the UN commission to supervise elections in Korea, King was unwilling to see Canadians involved because he feared trouble in the area. His opinion was based on a conversation, through a medium in London,

Troops of Canada's Mobile Command deploy on defence of Canada exercises in the North Bay area of Ontario. Mobile Command, created in the 1960's, is a highly flexible, integrated air-land-sea force intended for use on short notice wherever needed to cope with minor or "brush-fire" wars, or to carry out peace-keeping operations.

England, with his dead friend Franklin Roosevelt, who had warned him of impending trouble in Asia. Only after Louis St. Laurent, Secretary of State for External Affairs, had threatened to resign over the issue did King give way and permit Canada to serve. In June 1950 war did break out in Korea and the United States asked the UN Security Council to declare North Korea an aggressor and to authorize member states to send forces to defend South Korea. The Security Council was able to approve this action only because the Soviet Union could not exercise its veto since it was boycotting the Security Council for its refusal to seat Communist China in place of Nationalist China. The Canadian cabinet, now headed by St. Laurent as prime minister, delayed its decision to send Canadian troops until August, and then the government authorized the use of volunteers only. Twelve months later Canadian soldiers arrived in Korea, although three destroyers had been serving in Korean waters for a year. Until the cease fire, two years later, the Canadian brigade in Korea was the largest UN contingent except for the American, and it sustained more casualties in proportion to its size than any other UN unit. The Canadian government had had reservations about sending troops to remote Korea, but two imperatives compelled the cabinet to act. One was the need to contain Communist expansion, the other the need to support collective security through the United Nations. The unwelcome responsibility had to be met if the UN was not to fail as the League had failed.

Nor was the Canadian government prepared to watch the disintegration of such a useful institution as the Commonwealth when non-white former colonies gained their independence. At the Prime Ministers' Conference of 1948 India's Prime Minister Nehru explained to King that having served eight years in prison while fighting for Indian independence he did not want to hold office as prime minister under the British Crown. He

A Company of the Princess Patricia's Canadian Light Infantry advancing through a rice paddy on an enemy position in Korea, March 1951.

believed that India (non-white, and autonomous only after years of struggle) could never fully participate as a member. Even though King was gravely ill, he talked to Nehru all one night, telling him about the rebellions of 1837 and of one of his most prized possessions – a printed proclamation offering a reward for the capture of his grandfather, dead or alive. Nehru was converted to King's ideal of a multi-racial Commonwealth, and King later described the results of this conversation as one of the great achievements of his career. This ideal was furthered by Lester Pearson, appointed Canada's Secretary of State for External Affairs in 1948, who devised in 1950 the constitutional formula whereby India could remain a member of the Commonwealth as a republic and who persuaded the other members to accept this formula. Canada had become the constitutional architect of the post-war Commonwealth.

These developments during the first five years after the Second World War created the framework of Canadian foreign policy for the future. Replacing the pre-war reluctance to take an active role in world affairs came the slow realization that Canada can never be an "island unto herself". The gradual and almost reluctant emergence from isolation in these five years was in part a response to new world conditions of international tension, to the terrible threat of nuclear war, and to the emergence to full nationhood of many former colonies. It was also the result of greater national self-confidence growing out of Canada's wealth and her successful role in the recent war, which combined briefly in the immediate post-war period to make Canada a middle power. In addition, the quality of Canada's diplomatic corps was second to no other nation's; the prestige of Lester Pearson and of the officers of the Department of External Affairs enabled Canada to play an important part in the United Nations until the late 1950's, when the granting of independence to former European colonies brought many new members into that organization and altered its internal balance of power through the formation of the so-called Afro-Asian bloc.

The Eighteenth General Assembly of the United Nations met in New York in September 1963. To open its general debate statements were made by representatives from Brazil, Canada, and the Soviet Union. Here, addressing the Assembly, is Lester B. Pearson. Pearson was a strong supporter of the United Nations which, he believed, gave the best hope of preserving world peace.

Canada's Place in the North Atlantic and World Communities

Since the late 1940's Canadian foreign policy has been developed around four principles: that the United Nations is the best hope for world peace and international understanding; that the Commonwealth is a special kind of international organization with a fraternal relationship; that the North Atlantic Treaty Organization is a supplementary force guaranteeing national security; and that the United States is Canada's partner both in continental defence and in economic relations.

In the polarization of world powers caused by the cold war, Canada has drawn even closer to the United States, both politically and economically. Since the outbreak of the Korean War, joint defence production arrangements have been made which give Canadian manufacturers contracts for American requirements, and in return the Canadian government buys material from the United States for her armed forces. In 1957 the North American Air Defence (NORAD) agreement was signed, an agreement that provided for a joint command and for collaboration in defence. The Diefenbaker government entered into this arrangement uneasily, feeling it had been committed through prior negotiations by the St. Laurent government, and reservations about Canada's role in NORAD have been felt by every Canadian government since. But in certain matters Canada has pursued foreign policies independent of and even in opposition to American wishes. Canadian governments have continued to permit trade with Cuba despite American objections and have promoted wheat sales to the Communist world. In the Cuban missile crisis of 1962, the Diefenbaker government took nearly two days to decide to support the United States, a tardiness which brought an icy chill to relations between the two governments. After the Liberals took power in 1963, the situation improved somewhat, but Canadian disapproval of the Vietnam War and Canadian plans to recognize Red China continued to irritate many Americans and to influence Canadian-American relations.

The basic problem in the relations between the two nations is that Canadians do not always agree with the United States' interpretation of world events. Canadians are more cautious – more hesitant for example to leap to conclusions about the intentions of the USSR. They are also more sympathetic to nationalism in the Asian and African world. The Canadian government co-operates with the United States because Canada's security depends on American actions and because Canada hopes to moderate those American policies that differ from Canadian ones. Some groups in Canada criticize this involvement, however, because they distrust American world policy. Relations with the United States are the basic concern of Canadian foreign policy, but while Canada places the United States'

Left: United Nations observers sent to report on the Kashmir conflict find shelter in the foothills of the Himalayas. Above: A UN jeep, driven by a Canadian UN observer, in Tripoli (Lebanon).

policies at the top of its list of interests the United States places Canadian problems far down its scale of priorities.

Canada's second priority in world affairs is her relationship with the Commonwealth. There are no real political ties among the Commonwealth members, and few economic advantages to Canada, because most member nations have rival rather than complementary economies. Yet Canada supports the Commonwealth because it is a kind of small-scale United Nations where members share a peculiar relationship based on common traditions. To reinforce this attitude a Commonwealth Secretariat was established in 1965 with headquarters in London, to be a clearing house of information within the organization and to increase contacts between the older members and the emerging nations who belong to the Commonwealth. As the senior dominion and the architect of independence within the Commonwealth, Canada had consistently sympathized with and offered aid to the many British colonies which have advanced to nationhood since 1945. Through the Colombo Plan alone, Canada has given over half a billion dollars in aid to the South Asian members of the Commonwealth.

This concern for the future of the Commonwealth and for the newly independent members prompted the Canadian government to act forcefully in trying to solve the Suez crisis of 1956. When Britain and France occupied the north end of the Suez Canal area to protect the canal from damage in the Israeli-Egyptian War, their action looked like a revival of old-fashioned gunboat diplomacy as a means of forcing Egypt to return the canal to its former owners, themselves. Many Conservatives in Canada wanted to support Britain in the United Nations, but such action would have driven the non-white members of the Commonwealth out of the organization. Instead Canada sponsored a United Nations' resolution to send an emergency force into the area to maintain peace and to take over from the Anglo-French force. For his work in creating this face-saving compromise Lester Pearson was awarded the

A camel train passing a United Nations jeep with its Canadian forces personnel outside the walled city of Sanaa in the Yemen.

Nobel Peace Prize. In 1960, as South African racial policies made the working of a multi-racial Commonwealth increasingly difficult, the Conservative government of John Diefenbaker held the Commonwealth together at the Prime Ministers' Conference by sponsoring a resolution favouring racial equality – a resolution that forced South Africa out of the Commonwealth.

Just as the Commonwealth is regarded by many Canadians as a worldwide grouping based on common interests, the North Atlantic Treaty is seen as a similar but regional grouping. Canada was one of the founding members of NATO, and the fact that it became a trans-Atlantic alliance involving North America as well as western European states owes much to the vision of Louis St. Laurent. From NATO's inception Canada maintained a brigade group in Germany, also several squadrons of fighter aircraft in Germany and, until 1967, in France. In 1969, however, the government decided to reduce its military forces in Europe. Much of Canada's Atlantic fleet is also available for NATO duties. The cost to Canada of these defence commitments has been so heavy that it amounts to a very substantial part of the government's total defence bill. But although Canada was a strong supporter of the alliance, she always regretted its purely military character. Article 2 of the treaty, part of which advocates the promotion of world co-operation as a means to world stability, was included in the treaty largely at Canada's insistence, but the alliance has not developed as an economic bloc. Perhaps because of their proximity to the United States, Canadians have had reservations about American predominance within the alliance. The apparent thawing of the cold war in the mid-1960's,

Four CF-104 Starfighter planes from No. 1 Canadian Air Division based in West Germany flying over H.M.C.S. "Bonaventure", an aircraft carrier of Maritime Command, during NATO exercises in the eastern Atlantic.

which in a way reflected the very success of NATO in limiting Communist expansion, seemed to make the alliance less necessary. In the 1968 Canadian election, spokesmen of all the major parties suggested that the Canadian role in NATO should be re-examined with a view to the possibility of reducing the commitment and thereby saving money. But any reduction in the NATO commitment will probably lead to increased dependence on the United States.

The fact that Canada's foreign policy has been preoccupied above all with the maintenance of world peace explains why Canadians continue to be so involved in the work of the United Nations. The government has seen its role in the world organization as a "middle power", a term which in the post-war world describes nations that are technologically well developed but lack military strength. Canada played, at least during the first fifteen years after the war, the role of successful mediator or middleman between the conflicting interests of the great powers. Because of Canada's status as a former colony, as an industrialized state willing and able to share her technical knowledge, and as a nation without ambition except to live at peace, she has been able to play a much bigger part in world affairs than her military strength would suggest. In 1951 Canada made her first grant ($400,000) for external aid to developing countries; by 1964 her annual appropriation had reached $226 million for assisting sixty-three nations. Canadian assistance has been used in the development of power and transport facilities, in the exploitation of natural resources, in the establishment of educational institutions, and for the supply of food. In addition, hundreds of technical advisers and teachers have annually served abroad under the auspices of various Canadian aid programmes.

Whenever armed conflict has broken out or even threatened in the post-war world, Canada has been among the leaders in the United Nations in asking that body to act to preserve peace, and she has participated in every UN peace-keeping operation undertaken since 1948. In the clash between India and Pakistan over Kashmir, Canada acted as mediator in 1949 at the request of the UN Security Council. Canadians played a part in the negotiations leading to the establishment of Israel. Canadians have been part of the truce teams in Kashmir, Israel, Lebanon, Laos, Vietnam, and

Some of the Canadian contingent serving with the United Nations peace-keeping force in Cyprus in 1964. Composed of groups from Canada, Finland, Ireland, Sweden, and the United Kingdom, the force in Cyprus was established by the Security Council after an outbreak of civil war on the island between Turkish and Greek Cypriots, to help prevent further hostilities in the republic.

PAUL REVERE – '63

A modern Paul Revere warns of growing American influence in Canadian affairs. During the election of 1963 the Liberals promised to stockpile United States' nuclear warheads in Canada and later possibly to negotiate a nuclear role for Canadian forces.

DIEF HANGS ON

Cambodia. Canadian troops have formed part of the UN emergency forces sent to Korea, Egypt, the civil war in the Congo in 1960, and Cyprus in 1964. Indeed, the United Nations Emergency Force (UNEF) was largely a Canadian invention devised to meet the Suez crisis in 1956.

This active participation in peace-keeping operations has required extensive changes in Canada's own defence arrangements. Involvement in NATO meant creating and equipping a force to be sent to Europe, and membership in NORAD meant a further commitment to air defence and the acceptance, reluctantly, of Bomarc missiles and their nuclear warheads at Canadian bases. The cost of all these changes was high. As cold war tensions eased and the need for peace-keeping forces arose, the Canadian armed forces assumed a new role which required forces that would be more mobile and more flexible. This change in function led in 1963 to the decision to integrate the naval, air, and land forces. The first step was the unification of the command structure under a single Chief of Defence Staff, and in 1967 the government began the introduction of a common rank structure and uniform in the Canadian forces.

The problems of the present-day world – war, overpopulation, poverty, and famine – are likely to continue in the foreseeable future. Canadians frequently question whether Canada is doing enough to help solve these problems. It is estimated that by 2000 A.D. the present world population of approximately 3.5 billion people will have doubled, but sufficient food supplies and the development of resources may not be realized in time to avoid a major catastrophe. While North Americans continue to grow richer, produce more goods per person, and enjoy full employment, the rest of the world's population grows relatively poorer and faces the spectre of famine. At present Canada spends only half as much per capita on foreign aid as does the United States, and less than one-third as much per capita as France. In all these areas of world concern – famine relief, economic development, and peace-keeping – Canada and individual Canadians must determine their responsibilities and priorities.

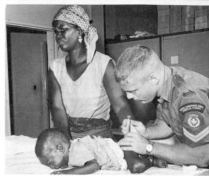

Canadians in their world.
Above: A United Nations master driller from Canada
operates a drilling rig in Upper Volta. Top right: members
of a UN-*assisted survey in Ecuador. Bottom right: A*
Congolese baby is given penicillin by a corporal of the
Canadian Medical Corps.

HISTORY FROM THE SOURCES

Canada and the World – What Is Canada's Role?

The hon. Mitchell Sharp, Secretary of State for External Affairs, gave
an outline of Canada's foreign policy to the United Nations General
Assembly on 9 October 1968.

> . . . My country . . . has made special efforts since 1945 to imple-
> ment the principles of the Charter and to nurture the growth of this
> organization. . . . I wish to re-affirm Canada's determination to do
> all it can to support these principles. . . .
> . . . no international order can be founded or can exist on the self-
> appointed right of any government or group of governments to im-
> pose their policies on other sovereign states by force. The invasion
> of Czechoslovakia by the Soviet Union and some of its allies was
> nothing less than the assertion of a proprietary right of a great power
> to exercise domination over Eastern Europe under the guise of a
> "fraternal" ideological relation. . . .
> While condemning the Soviet Union and its allies for what they
> have done, we must be ready to seize every opportunity for serious
> and constructive discussion of the issues that divide East and West.
> . . . the progress of such discussions will of necessity be slow and
> cautious. But there is one area in which we must press on: negotia-
> tions to end the arms race should be pursued vigorously. Progress
> on this front will benefit all nations, including Czechoslovakia.

Canada . . . was heartened by the announcement of the United States and the Soviet Union on July 1 of their agreement to begin negotiations on the limitation of strategic nuclear weapons, including anti-ballistic missiles. I urge the United States and the Soviet Union to begin these talks without delay and to support the early resumption of negotiations. . . .

My Government is interested, too, in the possibility of limiting supplies of armaments in regions of acute political and military confrontation and has noted with approval the recent indication that, under certain conditions, the USSR favors "the implementation of measures for regional disarmament and reduction of armaments in various parts of the world, including the Middle East".

We are often reminded that the United Nations is a centre for harmonizing the actions of nations. One of the main threats to such harmony is racial discrimination and the effects it has on international stability. The divisions amongst the membership which these questions provoke must not be allowed to lead to a breakdown in the communication between us. The object is clear: it is to ensure that the majority of the peoples of the countries of Southern Africa will no longer be deprived of their rightful place in the political, economic and social development of their countries. . . .

Violations of human rights are not restricted to Southern Africa. All member states are under an obligation to look to their own records of achievement in protecting human rights. My Government supports the initiatives which have been taken in the United Nations in the formulation of the various international covenants and declarations in the field of human rights. Canadian legislation reflects this concern in various enactments prohibiting discrimination based on sex, race, color, creed or national origin, in living practices, conditions of employment, public accommodation and trade union membership. . . .

This organization is dedicated to the elimination of poverty, ignorance and disease. At the end of the first development decade, this goal is still far off. . . .

Nevertheless, there is no hiding the fact that the level of international assistance to developing countries is inadequate. The needs grow faster than the resources are made available, partly because population increases so rapidly. So far as Canada is concerned, our aid program will continue to grow year by year to reach the goal of one per cent of the gross national product as quickly as possible. We are pursuing a set of economic policies which will free resources for high priority purposes. . . .

. . . the sad fact is that governments are all too often forced to give military expenditures priority over the requirements of peaceful development. . . . It may be utopian to believe that we can banish the use of force in relations amongst states. But we must strengthen the capacity of the United Nations to act as an agency for the control of conflict and the mediation of disputes. . . .

We shall not be able to improve very much the capacity of the United Nations to realize its full potential in promoting peace and security unless the institution itself reflects the world as it is. The question of universality of membership remains pressing. We regret the absence from this Assembly of states that play an important part in world affairs.

As we endeavor to meet new challenges, we should not lose sight of the fact that the effectiveness of the United Nations is bound to be measured in the eyes of world opinion against the practical results which follow from our resolutions. It is not by the number of resolutions we pass that posterity will judge us but rather by the determination we show in dealing with the pressing issues of our times and in carrying out the decisions that we make. In this spirit, on behalf of Canada, I pledge sustained and vigorous support of the United Nations.

Department of External Affairs,
Statements and Speeches, No. 68/15.

In January 1969 two ministers in the federal cabinet — Eric Kierans and Léo Cadieux — took opposing positions on the question of Canada's future role in NATO. The following speeches, one from each of the two men, clearly state the issues.

Our political attitudes and institutions have to be examined and criticized in the glare of naked nuclear power. NATO is one such institution.

Our membership in NATO determines our defence policy and this in turn decides our foreign aid policy because there is only so much we can spend on the two combined, it determines our policy toward Eastern Europe as much as to Western Europe and our policy at the United Nations where we are among a congerie of allies, and it determines the scale of resources and energy we can direct toward the rest of the world — Asia, Africa, South America — and it shapes their attitude toward us. This is the domino effect of membership in NATO. At the same time our hands are far from being entirely tied; we recognize Cuba and trade with mainland China and the United States does neither; we are the only member of NATO consistently involved in UN peacekeeping operations. . . .

NATO justifies itself on the premise that it has protected Western Europe from aggression, and it bases its international mandate upon

Article 51 of the United Nations Charter. I remind you that the same UN Article is cited in the treaty of the Warsaw Pact, and remind you also that Finland, which is not a member of NATO and is not protected by its charter, has enjoyed the same freedom from aggression, and for just as long.

NATO may or may not have been the appropriate answer to a particular threat in 1948. As a continuing institution, it is something else again. Instead of a genuine deterrent against a genuine threat, it has become a self-justifying deterrent against a non-existent military threat. NATO's existence guarantees that of the Warsaw Pact. . . . Russia can maintain its own political grip on Eastern Europe, using NATO as the excuse for its use of force. . . .

Canada's withdrawal from its military commitments would hasten this day of reckoning, – the realization by people on both sides of the Berlin wall that these billions are being spent each year, not as a deterrent against the other sides but to impose order on themselves. . . .

. . . The real battle I suggest is not the waning ideology of imperial Communism versus consumer capitalism; it is the waxing tensions of the world which, in a mirror-image of our own society, is increasingly divided into haves and have-nots. This real battle is not going to be decided by swords, or tanks or planes, but by schoolhouses and scholarships. . . .

We are also going to be held accountable by future generations. They will give us, I believe, few marks for perpetuating a sterile military bureaucracy. They will give us high marks, I am certain, if, even at the cost of withdrawing from a cosy and familiar club, we reallocate our limited resources to those people who most need them and to those problems of poverty, famine and illiteracy where solutions are the most needed. . . .

The Hon. Eric Kierans, Address to the
Nanaimo-Cowichan-The Islands Liberal
Association, 25 January 1969.

Let me now turn to Europe and NATO. You may recall that last December, in speaking to the Standing Committee of Parliament on External Affairs and Defence, I indicated that, in my view, there is only one major military threat to Canada. This is the threat associated with the catastrophe which would befall us if the superpowers were to become engaged, from whatever source or reason, in an exchange of nuclear weapons.

Where does Europe fit into this proposition? The Soviet Union has stated over and over again that it considers Eastern Europe as vital to its security. Similarly, the United States has taken great pains to convince both sides that it considers Western Europe vital to its security.

The Soviet Union gave ample illustration of its position when it invaded Czechoslovakia last August. . . .

We must assume that if any East European aggression towards Western Europe is not successfully contained at a low level of warfare, it can only result in escalation to a general nuclear exchange between the two superpowers. This obviously affects Canada's security. Furthermore, there is no other area in the world where the United States and the Soviet Union are both committed to the ultimate limit. Thus, aside from any considerations of history and tradition, Europe is of unique concern with respect to Canada's security.

Fortunately, machinery exists through which Canada can contribute to deterring aggression and maintaining stability in Europe – indeed this machinery exists in part because of the efforts of the Canadian government and parliament, fully supported by the Canadian people, in the uneasy years immediately following World War II. NATO, including its integrated command structure, provides, I believe, an effective means of ensuring that conflicts of interest or of ideology in Europe are contained and resolved without resort to cataclysmic violence. NATO represents today the only existing institutional arrangement for furthering Canada's security interests in Europe. . . .

At the same time, NATO gives us an opportunity to take part in the efforts toward détente between the nations of East and West Europe, which hopefully will, in time, create the climate of confidence in which an accommodation on the issues which now unsettle Europe can be reached. Only in the event of a large measure of success in the endeavours toward détente would withdrawal from the military aspects of the European Alliance be in Canada's interest. . . .

These two factors: the relation to Canada's security, and the alliance or collective nature of our major defence activities, suggest two questions . . . .

* First, with regard to security, what proportion of Canada's national resources should Canadians devote to their own security?

* Second, with regard to alliances, to what extent does Canada want to participate effectively in the decisions which affect its security?

The answers to the two questions must come ultimately from the people of Canada themselves. . . . security must ultimately rest on the national will to do what is necessary.

The Hon. Léo Cadieux, Address to the
Rotary Club of Ottawa, 27 January 1969.

FURTHER READING

Lyon, Peyton V., *The Policy Question: A Critical Appraisal of Canada's Role in World Affairs* (Toronto: McClelland & Stewart, 1963).

Minifee, James M., *Peacemaker or Powder-Monkey: Canada's Role in a Revolutionary World* (Toronto: McClelland & Stewart, 1960)★.

Craig, G. M. *The United States and Canada* (Cambridge, Mass.: Harvard University Press, 1968).

Dickey, J. S., ed. *The United States and Canada* (Englewood Cliffs, N.J.: Prentice-Hall, 1964)★.

Clarkson, Stephen, ed. *An Independent Foreign Policy for Canada* (Toronto: McClelland & Stewart, 1968)★. A collection of essays, essentially a printed debate, on Canadian foreign policy.

Spicer, Keith, *A Samaritan State? External Aid in Canada's Foreign Policy* (Toronto: University of Toronto Press, 1966).

Aitken, Hugh G. J. *et al., The American Economic Impact on Canada* (Durham, N.C.: Duke University Press, 1959).

Clark, Gerald, *Canada: The Uneasy Neighbour* (Toronto: McKay, 1965).

For a historical survey of external policy and relations since the Second World War, students should consult the various volumes of the series *Canada in World Affairs,* published by Oxford University Press under the auspices of the Canadian Institute for International Affairs.

Index

St. Maurice forges, 76, 104
Saint-Vallier, Jean Baptiste de, 68, 70
San Juan boundary, 311
Saskatchewan, province of, 155, 329, 355, 356, 415, 433-4
Sault Ste. Marie, 85, 86, 127, 156
Sauvé, Paul, 507, 509
Schultz, Dr. Christian, 307
Scots, 130, 131, 133, 166, 169, 188, 198
Scott, Thomas, 307, 308, 328, 330, 346
Sea otters, 159-60, 161
Secord, Laura, 178
Seigneurial System, 65-8, 142, 215, 262
Selkirk, Earl of, 166, 169, 188, 189, 199
Separate schools, Ontario, 260, 263, 264
Sept Iles, 472
Settlement, 38-41, 188-9, 199, 206-12
Seventh Report on Grievances, 223
Seven Oaks massacre, 189
H.M.S. Shannon, 175
Shaughnessy, Thomas G., 320, 321
Sherwood, Henry, 248, 249
Shipbuilding, 75, 104, 168, 387
Shirley, William, 108, 109
Sicotte, L.V., 284
Signay, Joseph, 232
Simcoe, John Graves, 164, 169, 170
Sirois, Joseph, 430
Smallwood, Joseph, 500-1
Smith, A. J., 292, 294
Smith, Donald (Lord Strathcona), 319, 321
Smoky River, 152, 153
Social Credit, 422, 424-5, 465
South West Fur Company, 188
Sovereign Council of New France, 54, 61, 62, 73, 84, 90
Spain, 28, 31, 34, 36, 38, 136, 160, 161
Stanfield, Robert, 511, 512
Stanley, Lord, 241-2, 252-3
Statute of Westminster (*1931*), 442
Stephen, George, 319, 321
Stirling, William Alexander, Earl of, 64
Strachan, John, 220, 221, 222, 258
Sudbury, 359, 473
Sullivan, Robert Baldwin, 184, 231-2
Sulpicians, 53, 85, 86
Superior, Lake, 45, 85, 88, 105, 148
Supreme Court of Canada, 316, 338, 442
Sydenham, Charles Edward Poulett Thomson, Lord, 238-41, 244, 245

T

Taché, Alexandre, 307, 328
Taché, Sir E. P., 263, 265, 285, 288, 299-300

Tadoussac, 39, 45, 54, 57
Talon, Jean, 75, 85, 86, 88
Tariff (*see also* National Policy, Reciprocity), 191, 301, 314, 317-8, 323-5, 343, 419; imperial preferences, 362, 420, 446; and Liberal party, 315-16, 339, 352, 356; Commission, 373
Tarte, Israël, 339, 351, 352
Taschereau, L. A., 426, 427
Tecumseh, 173, 178
Thames River, 170, 178
Thompson, David, 154, 155
Thompson, John Sparrow, 337, 338, 339
Tilley, Samuel Leonard, 287, 291, 292, 294, 295, 304, 323-5
Toronto (*see also* York), 7, 111, 170, 202, 223, 239
Toronto and Hamilton Railway, 277
Tory, Dr. Henry Marshall, 410
Tracy, Alexandre de Prouville de, 82-3
Trade, 104, 166-8, 377
Trade Unions, 343-4, 356-7
Trades and Labour Congress, 344, 396, 423
Trans-Canada Air Lines, 429
Treaties: Aix-la-Chapelle (*1748*), 108, 110; Anglo-Russian (*1825*), 364; Breda (*1667*), 64, 65; Ghent (*1814*), 180; Halibut Fisheries (*1923*), 440, 441; Jay's (*1794*), 152, 153, 167, 173; Locarno (*1925*), 441; Paris (*1783*), 137, 141; Reciprocity (*1854*), 251, 271, 273, 274, 287, 293, 310, 324, 367; Rush-Bagot (*1818*), 180; Ryswick (*1697*), 94, 95, 97; Tordesillas (*1494*), 28; Utrecht (*1713*), 96, 97, 103, 104, 106, 118, 149; Versailles (*1919*), 450; Washington (*1871*), 310-12
Trent, 283, 284, 286
Trois-Rivières, 52, 57, 58, 61, 63, 69, 74, 76, 99, 143, 156, 358
Troyes, Pierre de, 90, 93
Trudeau, Pierre Elliott, 509, 512, 513
Tupper, Sir Charles, 287, 291, 294, 295, 304, 325, 339, 351
Turnor, Philip, 155
Twelve Resolutions, 229

U

Ultramontanism, 62, 314
Unemployment, 421, 463
Uniacke, James B., 245, 247, 249
Union Act (*1840*), 261
Union Bill (*1822*), 214
Union Government (*1917*), 386, 399